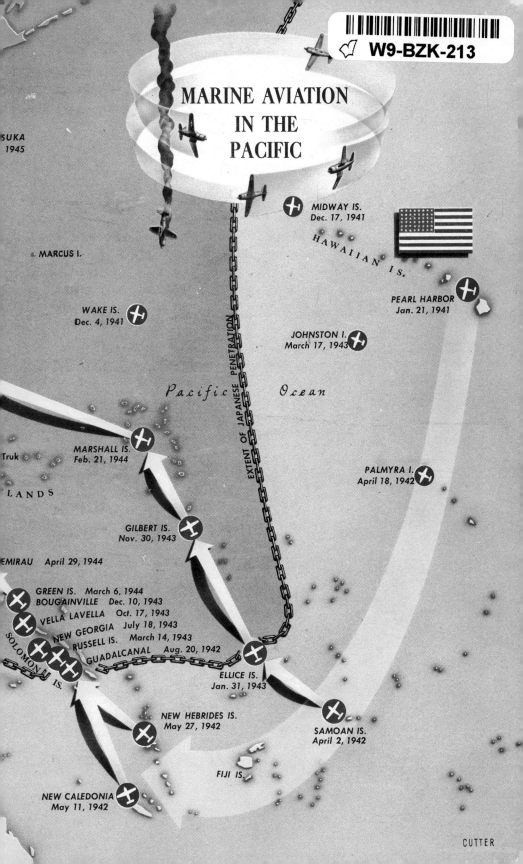

MARINE AVIATION IN THE PACIFIC

SUKA 1945

MARCUS I.

HAWAIIAN IS.

MIDWAY IS.
Dec. 17, 1941

PEARL HARBOR
Jan. 21, 1941

WAKE IS.
Dec. 4, 1941

JOHNSTON I.
March 17, 1943

Pacific *Ocean*

EXTENT OF JAPANESE PENETRATION

Truk

MARSHALL IS.
Feb. 21, 1944

PALMYRA I.
April 18, 1942

LANDS

GILBERT IS.
Nov. 30, 1943

EMIRAU   April 29, 1944

GREEN IS.   March 6, 1944
BOUGAINVILLE   Dec. 10, 1943
VELLA LAVELLA   Oct. 17, 1943
NEW GEORGIA   July 18, 1943
RUSSELL IS.   March 14, 1943
GUADALCANAL   Aug. 20, 1942

SOLOMON IS.

ELLICE IS.
Jan. 31, 1943

NEW HEBRIDES IS.
May 27, 1942

SAMOAN IS.
April 2, 1942

FIJI IS.

NEW CALEDONIA
May 11, 1942

CUTTER

History of Marine Corps
Aviation in World War II

WINGATE COLLEGE LIBRARY

5119

BY THE SAME AUTHOR

Tarawa: The Story of the Battle

On to Westward: War in the Central Pacific

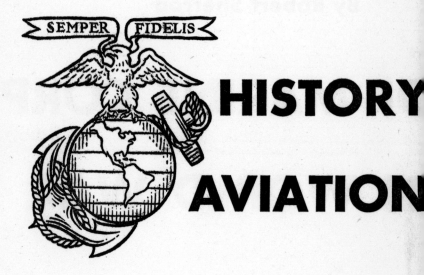

SEMPER FIDELIS

HISTORY

AVIATION

By Robert Sherrod

OF MARINE CORPS

N WORLD WAR II

Combat Forces Press · Washington

Copyright 1952

By Association of the United States Army

All rights reserved. No portion of this book may be reproduced in any form without permission. For information address Combat Forces Press, 1115 17th Street NW, Washington 6, D.C.

Library of Congress Catalogue Number: 52-6344

FIRST EDITION

All photographs from U.S. Marine Corps
or U.S. Navy unless otherwise credited.

MANUFACTURED IN THE UNITED STATES OF AMERICA

Contents

Author's Preface

This is a book written for the one per cent of the U.S. Armed Forces who served in Marine Corps aviation in World War II. One per cent equals about 150,000, including 8,000 women (who get less attention in this operational history than they deserve).

Thus far, the New York Public Library tells us, about 1,600 books and brochures classified as "unit histories" have been written since the end of World War II. This one is more extensive than most because Marine aviation operations were spread wide throughout the Pacific. The general reader may find some of the details too meticulous for his preference, but I have tried at all times to tell what the participants in an operation would like to know about it.

At the same time, I have written at some length about high-level decisions—American and Japanese—which concerned the member of any squadron only indirectly. A case in point is the debate in Chapter Eighteen on the decision to recapture the Philippines. I wrote about it on the assumption that the men of the 17 Marine squadrons which went to the Philippines would want to know why they happened to be sent there rather than to Formosa.

I undertook the writing of this history in 1948, soon after I cabled an acceptance from Shanghai, where I was then performing my journalistic assignment. I assumed that a six months' leave of absence would suffice to do the job, but it has taken more than three years, counting many interruptions, including a long assignment to Europe and the writing of the text for *Life's Picture History of World War II*. I have never had any directive except the one given orally by Colonel Clayton C. Jerome, president of the Marine Corps Aviation History Board: "Just tell what happened." The Commandant of the Marine Corps, General Clifton B. Cates, gave his assurance that I would be free to write as I saw fit. His successor, General Lemuel C. Shepherd Jr., who took office shortly before this volume went to press, subscribed to the same policy. There has been no censorship of the book, beyond routine security checks of material taken from classified documents. I am solely responsible for the opinions expressed herein. This is not an official history.

Like others who spent some of the most exciting years of their lives in the Pacific, I had a vast curiosity about what *really* happened out there. We all knew that the communiqué could be only an approximation—and sometimes not a very good one—until we got the enemy's records. Wherever possible I have cited these Japanese records in this book, but there are many still untranslated (about 5,160 cubic feet in the National Archives alone). Many others, including Japanese Army aircraft records, were burned at the end of the war.

Some of the claims made during the war were ridiculous, like the U.S. Navy's at the Battle of Tassafaronga and the Fifth Air Force's during the bombing of Rabaul. The Japanese nearly always managed to outdo us; they thought they had "positive proof" of sinking 468 American submarines, whereas they managed to get only 41.

Consistent over-claiming was done by the aviators. I do not agree with the Army Air Forces historian who says that the statistics of air warfare are useful chiefly "to emphasize the magnitude of the effort put forth." The yonder is not that wild or blue, and facts are still facts. We have seen what terrible trouble Admiral Halsey almost got into because he put too much faith in his carrier pilots' claims at Leyte Gulf, and how much hard work remained for AirSols aviators after General Kenney allegedly had "taken out" Rabaul. The perpetuation of myths should not be encouraged.

Marine Corps aviators made honest claims about some ships that they did not sink, and some planes they did not shoot down, but their record of accuracy appears to compare very favorably with that of other services. They made many contributions to the Pacific war. Outstanding among these were a major role in the defeat of the Japanese naval air force in the Solomons (which made enemy carrier operations virtually impossible after 1943) and the development of close-support aviation to a high degree of effectiveness.

Basic material for this book is several hundred war diaries and historical reports of the squadrons, groups, wings and other units in Marine aviation. More than 50 operations reports and action reports have been consulted, and I have interviewed about 250 Marine aviators, including several among the 100 who have since lost their lives in Korea.

Information has been gleaned from the published memoirs of virtually everyone who has written about the Pacific war, including Mr. Henry L. Stimson, General Henry H. Arnold, Admiral William D. Leahy, General Holland M. Smith, Admiral Frederick C. Sherman, Lieut. General Robert L. Eichelberger, General George C. Kenney, Admiral William F. Halsey, Commander Eric A. Feldt of the Royal Australian Naval Reserve, Major General Claire L. Chennault, and many others.

The most fruitful single source of published material has been Rear Admiral Samuel Eliot Morison's series on U.S. Naval Operations in World War II, of which five volumes have been published concerning the Pacific war. I have drawn heavily on Admiral Morison's works. Two volumes in the U.S. Army's Historical Series, *Guadalcanal: The First Offensive,* and *Okinawa: The Last Battle,* have been helpful, and so have Volumes I and IV of

The Army Air Forces in World War II: Plans and Early Operations (I) and *The Pacific: Guadalcanal to Saipan* (IV). *The U.S. Marines and Amphibious War*, by Jeter A. Isely and Philip A. Crowl, is an excellent study of the Pacific campaigns. Captain Walter Karig USN and his various collaborators have recorded some colorful accounts by individuals in their five-volume *Battle Report* series. The only postwar book about Marine aviation up to now is Captain John A. DeChant's *Devilbirds,* published in 1947, which has been an excellent guide on many occasions. Most of the 108 Pacific War volumes of the U.S. Strategic Bombing Survey have been consulted.

Major Charles W. Boggs USMC used the first draft of my chapters on the Philippines in writing his detailed monograph, *Marine Aviation in the Philippines,* but I am more obligated to him than he to me. Other historians who have lent a helping hand include Dr. Louis Morton, chief of the Pacific Section in the office of the U.S. Army's Chief of Military History; Dr. Henry M. Dater, Mr. Adrian O. Van Wyen and Miss Harriette L. Baker of the Naval Aviation History and Research Section; Dr. Chauncey E. Sanders and Dr. Edith C. Rodgers of the U.S. Air Force Research Studies Institute at Maxwell Field, Ala.; Mr. Joel D. Thacker, U.S. Marine Corps archivist, and three successive chiefs of the Marine Corps Historical Division, Lieut. Colonels Robert D. Heinl Jr., Gordon D. Gayle, and Frank O. Hough. From Admiral Morison's office, Lieut. Roger Pineau USN, a Japanese language scholar, and Ensign Richard S. Pattee USN, an expert on Japanese shipping, have been good enough to check the proof. They were able to correct errors stemming from the Joint Army-Navy Assessment Committee's *Japanese Naval and Merchant Shipping Losses,* which, however, remains the basic documentary source on the subject.

To all these and many others this book is indebted. But the larger debt is owed to the members of my office staff who have toiled long, loyally and beyond reasonable working hours. For three long years Lieut. Colonel Russell R. Riley USMC has supervised the office administration, collection of manuscript comments, photographs and a thousand other details. Captain Edna Loftus Smith USMCR-W has been the heart and soul of Marine Corps aviation history since 1947, when this book was first conceived (and before I got into it) and when she was called back to active duty to do the research for it. Before that she served as the Marine specialist in Naval aviation history.

Vicissitudes of marriage, childbirth and transfer have changed the rest of the staff complement several times during the past three and one-half years. For the last year Master Sergeant Annette Parziale has been the efficient staff secretary. Her loyal predecessors have included Tech. Sergeant Mildred A. Novotny, Sergeant Dana Williams, Sergeant Valentine Lawson and Mrs. Jane S. Glenn. Lieut. Ann F. Vaupel USMCWR, Mrs. Leah C. Mason, Mrs. Elizabeth L. Tierney and Mrs. Constance T. Ives contributed digests of World War II historical documents and other research during various periods between 1947 and 1950.

The author's thanks and those of the Marine Corps Aviation History

Board are due Mrs. Jane F. Blakeney, head of the Decorations and Medals Branch of the Marine Corps and Miss Gertrude S. Friedman, who furnished statistics from Marine Corps personnel files; to various members of the Combat Forces Press, particularly to Colonel Joseph I. Greene, the editor, Colonel Arthur Symons and Mr. Nicholas J. Anthony; to Mr. H. Stahley Thompson and Mr. Albert Margolies of Rinehart & Company, who managed the production of the book, including the photographic layout.

The maps and charts are the work of Mr. James Cutter. Line drawings which are spotted throughout the book were the kind contribution of Colonel Donald L. Dickson USMC, a veteran of Guadalcanal and Okinawa.

The late Admiral Forrest P. Sherman, Chief of Naval Operations, contributed indirectly to the book. Returning from a meeting of the Joint Chiefs of Staff one day in 1950, he remarked wryly to the author that another member of that august body had said: "There wasn't any Marine Corps aviation until World War II." That is what brought on the first two chapters, which had not been contemplated up to that time.

The profits of Post Exchanges financed publication of the book. These funds enable the Marine Corps Aviation History Board to present a copy of the book to all Marine aviation personnel who won a battle star in World War II (about 75,000 men) or to their survivors.

Throughout the text the designations "USMC" and "USMCR" have been omitted as a general rule. Officers and men of other services have been designated "USA" and "USN" regardless of their regular or reserve status.

ROBERT SHERROD

Washington
28 January 1952

Glossary

Abbreviations used in narrative

AA	Antiaircraft
AAF	Army Air Forces
ACIO	Air Combat Intelligence Office(r)
Acorn	Construction unit (amphibious)
ADC	Air Defense Command
ADCC	Air Defense Control Center
AGC	Amphibious force flagship
AI	Airborne Intercept (radar)
AK	Cargo vessel
AO	Oiler
AP, APA	Troop transport
APD	Troop transport (high speed)
Argus	Navy air-warning squadron
ASP	Antisubmarine patrol
ATC	Air Transport Command (Army)
ATIS	Allied Translation and Interrogation Service
AWS	Air-warning squadron
BB	Battleship
Blip	Echo on radar screen (also "pip")
Bogey	Unidentified plane
CA	Heavy cruiser
CL	Light cruiser
CAP	Combat air patrol
CASD	Carrier aircraft service detachment
CG	Commanding General
CO	Commanding Officer
CV	Aircraft carrier
CVE	Aircraft carrier, escort
CVL	Aircraft carrier, small
DD	Destroyer
DE	Destroyer escort
Dumbo	Air-sea rescue plane
ETO	European Theater of Operations
FM	Field manual (Army)
GCI	Ground Control Intercept (radar)
Hedron	Headquarters squadron
HqSq	Headquarters squadron
IFF	Identification, friend or foe (radar)
IJA	Imperial Japanese Army
IJN	Imperial Japanese Navy
JANAC	Joint Army-Navy Assessment Committe
JCS	Joint Chiefs of Staff
KIA	Killed in action
LCI	Landing craft, infantry
LCM	Landing craft, mechanized
LCP(R)	Landing craft, personnel (ramp)
LCS	Landing craft, support
LCT	Landing craft, tank
LCVP	Landing craft, vehicle and personnel
Loran	Long-range radio aid to navigation
LST	Landing ship, tank
LVT	Landing vehicle, tracked
MAG	Marine aircraft group
MAHA	Marine Aircraft, Hawaiian Area

MASG	Marine air support group	**VMBF, VMFB**	Marine fighter-bomber squadron
MASP	Marine Aircraft, South Pacific	**VMD**	Marine photographic squadron
MAW	Marine aircraft wing	**VMF**	Marine fighter squadron
MAWPac	Marine Aircraft Wings, Pacific	**VMF(CVS)**	Marine fighter squadron, carrier-based
MBDAG	Marine base defense air group	**VMF(N)**	Marine night-fighter squadron
MBDAW	Marine base defense air wing	**VMJ**	Marine utility squadron (see **VMR**)
MCAS	Marine Corps air station	**VMO**	Marine observation squadron
MCVG	Marine carrier group	**VMR**	Marine transport squadron (formerly **VMJ** which became designation for Marine towing detachments)
MIA	Missing in action		
NAP	Naval aviation pilot (enlisted)		
NATS	Naval Air Transport Service		
PAM-3	Field-lighting set		
POA	Pacific Ocean Areas		
POW	Prisoner of war	**VMS**	Marine scouting squadron
PT	Motor torpedo boat	**VMSB**	Marine scout- or dive-bomber squadron
RAF	Royal Air Force	**VMTB**	Marine torpedo-bombing squadron
RAAF	Royal Australian Air Force		
RNZAF	Royal New Zealand Air Force	**VMTB(CVS)**	Marine torpedo-bombing squadron (carrier-based)
SCAT	South Pacific Combat Air Transport Command	**VO**	Navy observation squadron
SCR	Signal Corps radio	**VP**	Navy patrol squadron
Seron	Service squadron	**VR**	Navy transport squadron
SG	Naval radar	**VS**	Navy scouting squadron
SMS	Marine service squadron		
TAG	Transport Air Group	**VS-1-D-14**	Inshore Navy patrol unit (14th Naval District)
TCAP	Target combat air patrol		
USSBS	United States Strategic Bombing Survey	**VSB**	Navy scout-bombing plane
VB	Navy bombing squadron	**VT**	Navy torpedo squadron
VC	Navy composite squadron	**VTB**	Navy torpedo-bomber
VF	Navy fighter squadron	**YP**	District patrol vessel
VF(N)	Navy night-fighter squadron	**ZB**	Air-navigation and landing aid
VHF	Very high frequency (radio)	**ZK-1M**	Marine Barrage Balloon Squadron 1
VMB	Marine bomber squadron		

Navy and Marine Corps Aircraft

The first letter tells the type of plane, as follows: B-bomber; F-fighter; J-utility; N-trainer; O-observation; R-transport; T-torpedo; S-scout. The digit after the first letter indicates the model number. The next letter is the manufacturer's key (A-Brewster; F-Grumman; Y-Consolidated). The final figure after the dash signifies mutation. Thus, the F4U is the Chance-Vought Corsair, but the F4U-4B has 20 mm. cannon instead of .50-caliber machine guns. In the following tables the digit (in parentheses) after the plane's nickname indicates the number of engines.

BG-1	——— (1), Great Lakes	OY	Sentinel (1), Stinson
F2A	Buffalo (1), Brewster	PBY	Catalina (2), Consolidated
F4B	——— (1), Boeing	PB4Y	Liberator (4), Consolidated
F6C	——— (1), Curtiss		
F4F	Wildcat (1), Grumman	PBJ	Mitchell (2), North American
FM	Wildcat (1), Martin		
F4U	Corsair (1), Chance-Vought	PV	Ventura (2), Vega
		R3D	——— (2), Douglas
FG	Corsair (1), Goodyear	R4D	Skytrain (2), Douglas
F6F	Hellcat (1), Grumman	R5C	Commando (2), Curtiss
F7F	Tigercat (2), Grumma·	R5D	Skymaster (4), Douglas
HS-2	——— (1), Curtiss	SB2U	Vindicator (1), Chance-Vought
J2F	Duck (1), Grummar		
JN	Jenny (1), Curtiss	SB2C	Helldiver (1), Curtiss
JO-2	——— (2), Lockheed	SBD	Dauntless (1), Douglas
JRB	Voyager (2), Beech	SNJ	Texan (1), North American
N9	(Trainer) (1), Curtiss		
O2B	——— (1), Boeing	SOC	Sea Gull (1), Curtiss
OD-1	——— (1), Douglas	TBF	Avenger (1), Grumman
O2U	Corsair (1), Vought	TBM	Avenger (1), General Motors
OS2U	Kingfisher (1), Vought-Sikorsky		

Army Aircraft

A is for attack plane (light bomber); B for bomber; C for cargo or transport plane; P for pursuit (fighter) plane.

A-20	Havoc (2), Douglas	P-38	Lightning (2), Lockheed
A-26	Invader (2), Douglas		
B-17	Flying Fortress (4), Boeing	P-39	Airacobra (1), Bell
		P-40	Warhawk (1), Curtiss
B-24	Liberator (4), Martin	P-47	Thunderbolt (1), Republic
B-25	Mitchell (2), North American		
		P-51	Mustang (1), North American
B-26	Marauder (2), Martin		
B-29	Superfortress (4), Boeing	P-61	Black Widow (2), Northrop
C-47	Skytrain (2), Douglas	P-70	Havoc (2), Douglas
C-54	Skymaster (4), Douglas	P-400	Airacobra (export) (1), Bell

Japanese Aircraft

Betty	Bomber (2), Mitsubishi	**Myrt**	Reconnaissance (1), Nakajima
Dinah	Reconnaissance (2), Mitsubishi	**Nate**	Fighter (1), Nakajima
Emily	Flying boat (4), Kawanishi	**Nell**	Bomber (2), Mitsubishi
		Nick	Fighter (1), Kawasaki
Frances	Bomber (2), Yokosuka	**Oscar**	Fighter (1), Nakajima
Frank	Fighter (1), Nakajima	**Pete**	Observation (1), Sasebo
Hamp	(Same as **Zeke**)		
Hap	(See **Hamp**)	**Rex**	Fighter (1), Kawanishi
Helen	Bomber (2), Nakajima	**Rufe**	Fighter (1)
Jack	Fighter (1), Mitsubishi	**Sally**	Bomber (2), Mitsubishi
Jake	Reconnaissance seaplane (1), Aichi	**Tabby**	Transport (2), Showa
		Tojo	Fighter (1), Nakajima
Judy	Bomber (1), Aichi	**Tony**	Fighter (1), Kawasaki
Kate	Attack (1), Hiro	**Val**	Bomber (1), Aichi
Lily	Bomber (2), Kawasaki	**Willow**	Trainer (1)
Mavis	Flying boat (4), Kawasaki	**Zeke**	Fighter (1), Mitsubishi
		Zero	(Same as **Zeke**)

History of Marine Corps Aviation in World War II

CHAPTER ONE

The Beginning

FOR THE AVIATORS who wear the Marine uniform World War II began at 0755 of that fair and fateful day, 7 December 1941, when a formation of Japanese Zero fighters swooped upon the Marine Corps Air Station at Ewa (pronounced "Evva")—ten miles west of Pearl Harbor—and destroyed or severely damaged 47 of the 48 planes which Marine Aircraft Group 21 (MAG-21) had in the Hawaiian Islands. Six hours later Japanese bombers flying from Kwajalein hit Wake Island, 1,994 nautical miles to the west, where there were 12 Grumman Wildcats constituting the forward echelon of Marine Fighter Squadron 211 (VMF-211), one of MAG-21's elements. Seven of the dozen planes were destroyed; the rest of them fought on until the last went down on 22 December. At the end VMF-211's pilots were fighting as infantrymen, as all had been trained to do.[1]

Thus the beginning. At this time Marine Corps aviation had already expanded under the pressure of the national emergency; since 31 August 1939 the number of pilots had increased from 232 to 641. Instead of 9 squadrons, there were now 13.

When the war ended in September 1945 there were 128 aircraft squadrons and 10,049 pilots; 5,389 ground officers and 101,086 enlisted men and women. Plans had been laid for the Marine flyers to render close support from escort carriers, and later from land bases, during the invasion of Japan.

This book primarily concerns the operations of Marine Corps aviation between 7 December 1941 and 2 September 1945; those operations embrace a fair proportion of the war against Japan. But first it is necessary to glance backward, far behind the beginning of World War II, and sketch the origins of this organization.

The first question which might quite properly be asked is this: Why should the United States Marine Corps have its own aviation? The marines of no other nation have planes.

The question was asked frequently in the early days of Marine aviation, and it was asked more pointedly after the end of World War II. From the beginning to the present the aviators, like the Marine Corps itself, have been

---

[1] See Chapter Three.

called upon continually to render an accounting. Such conditions entail a certain amount of aggravation—it is a terrible thing to have to hit a home run, or at least a triple, every time at bat—but in the case of the Marine Corps (including its aviation), some desirable results have been achieved.

The Army got into aviation first: the Aeronautical Division of the Signal Corps was set up 1 August 1907; its first plane was acquired from the Wright Brothers in 1909. The Navy constructed a platform on the cruiser *Birmingham* from which a civilian pilot flew 14 November 1910; the Navy's first three planes were delivered in July 1911.[2]

It was in 1911 that the first marine tried to fly. Alfred Austell Cunningham (born Atlanta, 8 March 1882) had served at age 16 as a corporal in the 2d and 3d Georgia Infantry Volunteers during the Spanish-American War. Returning from Cuba, he went to school, then into the real estate business. Ten years after he had been mustered out of the Army he applied for and received a commission in the Marine Corps. At the Marine Officers' School, at Port Royal, S.C., he stood fourth in a class of 55.

In 1911 Lieut. Cunningham was stationed at the Marine Barracks, Philadelphia. He had been obsessed with the idea of flying ever since he had taken a flight in a balloon in 1903, the year the Wrights first flew. In Philadelphia he squandered $25 of his $166.67 monthly pay to rent a contraption from a civilian aviator who had never been able to get it to fly. With some difficulty Cunningham talked the commandant of the Philadelphia Navy Yard into letting him test the "plane" on the half-mile field inside the Yard.

Despite Cunningham's strenuous efforts, the machine never flew, not even after he built a ramp at the end of the field to bounce it into the air. His enthusiasm for aviation was dimmed not a whit, however, and he joined the pioneering Aero Club of Philadelphia. Cunningham's enthusiasm was rewarded with orders to the Navy's new aviation camp at Annapolis. He reported for duty 22 May 1912, which date may fairly be considered the birth of Marine Corps aviation.

Naval aviation had by this time made some progress: a year and a half earlier Eugene Ely had flown on and off platforms built on the decks of warships. Lieut. John Rodgers USN flew from Annapolis to Washington and back, with stops at Baltimore and Havre de Grace; on 11 October 1911 Lieut. John H. Towers USN and Lieut. T. G. (Spuds) Ellyson USN, in Glenn Curtiss's first "convertible landplane-seaplane," had flown from Annapolis to Smith's Point, Va., 79 miles, in 85 minutes, though they had to make two landings for repairs and finished with four burnt-out bearings; Towers had even made night landings on the Severn River in Wright's first hydroaeroplane.

Congress gave the Navy $10,000 for aviation in its second year and authorized a total of $55,000 more from amounts originally appropriated for

---

[2] W. F. Craven and J. L. Cate, editors, *The Army Air Forces in World War II* (hereinafter cited as *The AAF in WW II*), Vol I, pp 6–7; Archibald D. Turnbull and Clifford L. Lord, *History of United States Naval Aviation*, pp 10–18.

other purposes. The skeptical admirals did not divert all the money, however. In the same year $100,000 was appropriated for Army aviation.[3]

Cunningham was ordered from Annapolis for flight training at the Burgess plant at Marblehead, Mass., and soloed 1 August 1912 after 2 hours and 40 minutes of instruction. He was made a member of the Chambers Board along with six naval officers, assuring the Marines of a representative in naval aviation almost from the beginning. A year later he asked to be detached from flying duty because his fiancée declined to marry a flyer; he was detached and married, but in 1915 he returned to flying duty.

Lieut. Bernard L. Smith, of Richmond, Va., was ordered to the Annapolis camp on aviation duty 12 September 1912. He became naval aviator No. 6 and Marine aviator No. 2.[4] (The first enlisted man was Sergeant James Maguire.) In January 1914 Smith was assigned to Guantánamo, Cuba, for maneuvers, where he and the third Marine flyer, Lieut. W. M. McIlvain— Smith in one of the Navy's two flying boats, McIlvain in a Curtiss amphibian —"gathered valuable data on spotting possibilities and on the ease with which a force attempting to land in small boats might be bombed from the air."[5] On the same exercises Lieut. S. W. Bogan, an observer (nonaviator) suggested camouflaging mines after the waters in which they were to be laid had been reconnoitered from the air.

In 1914 B. L. Smith was sent to Paris as assistant naval attaché. His superior reported that he considered "Captain Smith had as much knowledge of the theory and practice of aviation as any officer in the world." When war broke out in 1917 he returned to the U.S. for duty with Naval Operations, then established the Navy's school for aerial gunnery and bomb-dropping at Miami before leaving again for Paris. In 1919 he helped build the NC's which flew the Atlantic, but the Navy kept him from making the flight. He resigned from the Marine Corps in 1920 but returned to service as a lieutenant commander in the Naval Reserve in 1931 (at which time the Marine Corps was accepting no reserve officers). In 1937 B. L. Smith returned to the Marine Corps. In World War II as a lieutenant colonel he set up the Marine Corps barrage-balloon program. He was killed in an automobile accident at Coral Gables, Fla., 2 December 1946.

It was just prior to Smith's service in Cuba that the first designation of Marine aviation as a separate unit from naval aviation was made. Curiously, the name of the sender does not appear on this ancient document which was turned up in the National Archives:

---

[3] In the same year other nations spent larger sums on military aviation: France $6,400,000, Russia $5,000,000, Britain $2,100,000, Italy $2,000,000, Germany $1,500,000. (*History of United States Naval Aviation*, p 21.)

[4] Cunningham's hiatus caused his name to be omitted from the first list of pilots winning certificates, and B. L. Smith was listed as the first Marine flyer. In 1915 Cunningham's name was inserted as naval aviator No. 5 (Marine No. 1) as it should have been.

[5] Turnbull and Lord, *History of United States Naval Aviation*, p 38.

Op-MLB
January 6, 1914

TO: Lieutenant J. H. Towers USN
             (Thru Superintendent, Naval Academy)
SUBJECT: Marine Section of Navy Aviation Camp
REFERENCE: (a) Dept's letter N-13Z, 12/27/13

1. Reference (a) is hereby cancelled.

2. 1st Lieut. B. L. Smith USMC and 2d Lieut. W. M. McIlvain USMC will go by USS *Hancock* from Philadelphia, Pa. direct to Culebra with the Advance Base outfit, including Navy Flying Boat C-3, Navy OWL Boat E-1, two hangar tents, spare parts, and other equipment as requested by 1st Lieut. Smith.

3. This outfit is to be regarded as a Marine Section of the Navy Flying School to be established at the aeronautic station under your charge.

Although this memorandum indicates that the separation of naval and Marine aviation was in the back of someone's mind—and the Commandant's report for 1912 mentions possible benefits which trained aviators might bring to the Advance Base Force—the Marine aviators were in fact only Navy aviators in a different uniform. When Smith went to Paris as assistant naval attaché, Towers went to London in the same capacity and V. D. Herbster, naval aviator No. 4, to Berlin. In July 1915, when the first class of naval aviators was assembled at the new Pensacola school, the Marines were allotted two of the ten officers and four of the twenty enlisted men. To stimulate the training of enlisted mechanics, eight Navy petty officers and two Marine Corps sergeants were appointed together. The Naval Appropriations Act of 1915, which gave the Navy its first million dollars, provided that qualified pilots should receive 50 per cent extra pay for hazardous duty (35 per cent for students), and the limit of eligible personnel left the division at the standard four-to-one Navy-Marine Corps ratio: 48 officers and 96 enlisted men of the Navy; 12 officers and 24 enlisted men of the Marine Corps.[6]

Likewise, naval aviation's early development owed much to its Marine members. B. L. Smith shared with Herbster some of the first attempts at bombing from a naval plane; the bombardier's left arm was strapped to the side of the plane so he could lean over the side, release the wind-wheel and pitch the bomb. Cunningham was one of the first pilots to make a take-off attempt—on 10 November 1915—by catapult from a battleship (*North Carolina*) which was under way.[7] The mechanism failed and his back was injured when the Curtiss crashed into the sea.

Perhaps the most daring feat by any naval aviator in the days when every

[6] *Ibid.*

[7] But not, as legend has it, the first. Five days earlier Commander Henry C. Mustin had been catapulted from *North Carolina*.

flight was a deed of valor was performed by Captain Francis T. Evans, the fourth Marine flyer (and twenty-sixth naval aviator). At Pensacola on 13 February 1917, defying the experts who believed it was probably impossible to loop a seaplane, Evans looped an N-9 (floatplane Jenny) from 3,000 feet, not once but twice. Then he forced it into a spin and pulled it out safely—the experts also had serious doubts that a seaplane could be brought out of a spin. For this contribution to the science of aviation and the security of flight, Evans was finally awarded the Distinguished Flying Cross on 10 June 1936 (nine years after the decoration was created).

World War I Begins

B. L. Smith first proposed to the commanding officer of the Flying School, Pensacola, that Marine aviation be organized as a definite separate entity. His 1914 recommendation foresaw an aviation unit operating with Marine ground troops as a part of an advanced base force. This recommendation was later accepted by the General Board, and the Major General Commandant in his report covering the year 1915 stated that "by direction of the department a Marine Corps aviation company consisting of 10 officers and 40 enlisted men" was to be organized.[8]

But in June 1916 only five Marine officers were classed as naval aviators. Enlisted men numbered 18. At the outbreak of war on 6 April 1917 the increase was only 1 officer, 1 warrant officer, 25 enlisted men.

Marine aviator No. 5—after Cunningham, Smith, McIlvain and Evans—was Lieut. Roy Stanley Geiger,[9] whose naval aviator number was 49. The sixth Marine pilot was David L. S. Brewster. Both were selected by Cunningham in a letter submitted to the Major General Commandant. The first warrant officer pilot was Walter E. McCaughtry.

This strength of 7 pilots and 43 men compared with 131 officers and 1,087

---

[8] Captain Edna Loftus Smith USMCWR, *Aviation Organization in the United States Marine Corps, 1912–45,* monograph prepared for DCNO (Air), p 2.

[9] Roy Stanley Geiger was born in Florida 25 January 1885. LL.B. John B. Stetson University. First lieutenant 1915, captain 1916. Became an aviator (No. 5) 1917. Major (temporary) 1918. Won Navy Cross as commander Squadron 7 in France 1918. Major (permanent) 1920. Graduate of Army Command and General Staff School 1925, Army War College 1929. Commanded squadrons in Haiti, Santo Domingo and Nicaragua; flew relief planes for victims of Santo Domingo hurricane 1930, and Nicaragua earthquake 1931. Lieutenant colonel 1934, colonel 1936. Graduate of Naval War College 1940. Brigadier general 1941. Commanded 1st MAW August 1942 to April 1943, plus all aviation units on Guadalcanal September to November 1942. Awarded Gold Star in lieu of second Navy Cross for Guadalcanal service. Major general 1942. Director, Marine Aviation, May to October, 1943. CG I Amphibious Corps 1943 (Bougainville) becoming first aviator to command a corps. CG III Amphibious Corps 1944–45 (Guam, Peleliu, Okinawa; awarded DSM for each of the four operations). CG Tenth Army on Okinawa 18–21 June 1945, becoming first marine ever to command an army. Lieutenant general, CG FMFPac 1945. Died 23 January 1947. Promoted posthumously to rank of general by act of Congress.

men in the Army's air establishment and 43 officers and just over 200 men in the Navy's.[10]

The line of demarcation between Army and Navy had not been settled in aviation's early days to the satisfaction of all concerned—as indeed it had not been settled in 1951. At first it was assumed that the Navy would fly seaplanes, the Army landplanes. But it soon became obvious that such an arrangement would not work best at the Navy's advanced bases, where taking off from the land might be a lot more convenient than rising from the water.

Secretary of the Navy Josephus Daniels wrote the Secretary of War on 17 August 1915 requesting that officers of the Navy and Marine Corps be allowed to take instruction in landplane flying, in order to provide for advanced base work and, in the case of the Marines, so that "they will be available when acting with the Army." He offered at the same time to train Army aviators in "water flying" at Pensacola.

The Army's Chief Signal Officer (Brig. General George P. Scriven) answered three days later, extending the facilities of the Signal Corps Aviation School at San Diego to whatever officers the Navy might designate. Lieut. McIlvain of the Marine Corps and Lieut. (jg) G. de C. Chevalier of the Navy were chosen; they spent seven weeks at San Diego learning to fly planes that had wheels.

On 9 January 1915 the "Marine Section, Navy Flying School" was ordered organized. On 5 April 1917, on the eve of war against Germany, the designation was changed to "Marine Aviation Section, U.S. Naval Aeronautic Station" at Pensacola. It was here that the strength of 5 officers, 1 warrant officer, 43 enlisted men was reached, not counting Cunningham, who was absent on additional duty selecting sites for tentative "coastal air stations" on the East and Gulf Coasts.

Wartime expansion was pell-mell in Marine aviation, as in all U.S. military organizations. Twenty-one days after the declaration of war the Aviation Section was split to form the "Marine Aeronautic Company, Advance Base Force" at Philadelphia; four members came in from the Marine Corps Reserve Flying Corps, which had been set up under the Naval Appropriations Act of 29 August 1916 along with the Naval Reserve Flying Corps.[11]

This company in turn was divided on 12 October 1917 into the 1st Marine Aeronautic Company (seaplane)—with 10 officers (of whom only two were qualified pilots) and 93 men transferred on the 14th to Cape May, N.J., and the 1st Aviation Squadron (24 officers, 237 men) which was transferred on the 17th to Hazlehurst Field, Mineola, L.I.

---

[10] Craven and Cate *The AAF in WW II*, Vol I, p 7; Turnbull and Lord, *History of United States Naval Aviation*, p 96; H. H. Arnold, *Global Mission*, p 50, gave the Army aviation establishment's total officers at 52, enlisted men at 1,100. Of 130 pilots, General Arnold said, only 26 were "really qualified."

[11] The first USMCR aviator was Lieut. Allen H. Boynton, 21 September 1917. The other three referred to were Brock Davey, W. H. Batts and Edmund G. Chamberlain.

In the Azores

Shunted out of Philadelphia to make room for the Naval Aircraft Factory, the 1st Marine Aeronautic Company was destined to make its contribution to history as the first American flying unit of any service to go overseas completely equipped and trained. The Navy, in order to deny the further reaches of the Atlantic to the U-boats and to forestall any attempt by Germans to establish a submarine refueling base in the Azores, sought to acquire an additional base there. The State Department completed the arrangements with the Portuguese Government within a few days, and plans were made to send the 1st Marine Aeronautic Company to operate seaplanes out of the Islands.

Under the command of Captain Francis T. Evans the Company of 12 officers and 133 enlisted men sailed from Philadelphia on 9 January 1918 and arrived 13 days later at Ponta Delgada on the island of São Miguel. Its planes included 10 R-6's (Curtiss twin-float seaplanes), 2 N-9's (single-engined, single-float), plus 6 HS-2 flying boats which arrived late in the summer.[12]

For the next year the Aeronautic Company maintained a full schedule over the convoy lanes around the Azores, flying 70 miles out with only two hours' gasoline capacity. The American consul gave them a fine send-off when they departed in January 1919:

> The loyalty, harmony and good fellowship prevailing among the men under you speak well for your leadership. . . . The utter absence of any complaint on the part of the local authorities against your men testifies to the high standard of citizenship in your command.[13]

One pilot, Lieut. Walter S. Poague, was drowned when his plane crashed on 5 November 1918. Along with Captain David L. S. Brewster and Lieut. William P. T. Hill he was commended in a letter from the CO to the Commandant for frequent flights in inclement weather without "radio, pigeons or Very pistols." Or, it might have been added, reliable compasses.

The monotonous routine which is the lot of the patrol pilot palled on one young flyer who rashly wrote the Major General Commandant after three months of Azores duty:

> 1. It is requested that I be detached from this company and transferred to some aeronautic station as near the scene of operations in Europe as possible.
>
> 2. This request is a result of the continued inactivity at this station and the remotest chance that an attack will be delivered against this place.
>
> 3. In addition to the foregoing, the service at this base is most unpleasant and the undersigned does not consider it consistent with the demands of aviation duty.

---

[12] Turnbull and Lord, *History of United States Naval Aviation*, p 126, errs in stating the 90 Marine pilots went to the Azores. There were only 11.

[13] Letter John S. Wood to CO, 6 January 1919.

This poor fellow should have known better. The Commandant (Major General George Barnett) sent back a sizzling letter of reprimand, including the pointed statement:

> You are informed that the paramount duty of an officer is to accept the assignment to duty given him and to carry out said duty to the best of his ability, regardless of the fact that this particular duty might be unpleasant.

The Commandant rubbed a touch of salt into the officer's wounds by informing him that a cable had in fact been dispatched detaching him to the United States, but that order now stood revoked.

Others, however, did escape the Azores monotony. On 24 July 1918 half the Company was pulled out and sent home to train new pilots. Among them was Captain Evans, who was succeeded as CO by Brewster. The submarine menace turned out to be far less awesome in 1918 than it had been in 1917.[14]

World War I Organization

Marine aviators remember Mineola, L.I., and its Hazlehurst (now Roosevelt) Field chiefly because the 1st Aviation Squadron spent several very cold weeks there. The month of December was said to be the coldest ever recorded by the Weather Bureau in New York—17° below zero on the night of the 27th. An epidemic of pneumonia swept nearby Camp Mills, where the Rainbow Division was quartered.[15]

On New Year's Day, 1918, the Squadron left Mineola for a landplane base farther south. The destination turned out to be the Army's Gerstner Field, Lake Charles, La., although the marines had to spend three days aboard train coaches before quarters could be found for them in one of the Army's cadet schoolhouses.[16]

At Gerstner the Marine flyers settled quickly. They also learned about flying with stick control—although most aviators remember the JN (Jenny) as a stick-controlled JN-4-D, the 1st Squadron pilots at Mineola had learned to fly with wheel-controlled JN-4-B's, a very primitive plane indeed. At Gerstner there were also Canuck Jennys and old Thomas-Morse Scouts, single-seaters with a rotary Gnome engine.[17]

While Captain McIlvain trained his squadron at Lake Charles another unit was being formed at the Naval Air Station (NAS), Coconut Grove, Fla., which reported to Lieut. Marc Mitscher USN, CO of the station. Originally

---

[14] The author's thanks for much of the foregoing material—and for other information on the early days of Marine Corps aviation—are due Major General W. P. T. Hill, currently (1952) Quartermaster General of the Marine Corps.

[15] First Marine Aviation Force veterans' pamphlet, *Then and Now* (1945).

[16] *Ibid.*

[17] Letter Brig. General Karl S. Day USMCR 20 November 1950.

this detachment consisted of Captain Geiger, whose stamp on Marine aviation was beginning to make an imprint which would last 30 years, Lieut. Douglas Roben and Lieut. Arthur H. Page. McIlvain had the main increment in Louisiana but Geiger's Florida force was augmented in February and March by six newly commissioned permanent second lieutenants and about a dozen lieutenant reservists. The Marines were also represented by B. L. Smith, who was teaching Mitscher's men gunnery.

Geiger's crowd qualified in seaplanes and were duly designated naval aviators and awarded wings. As the pioneer, Geiger took his earliest qualifiers over to the edge of the Everglades to a small, sandy field which was being used by the old Curtiss Flying School, breaking away from the strictly water flyers under "Pete" Mitscher.

His original equipment consisted solely of three OX-5 Jennys until he acquired—through an exchange of reserve commissions for the Curtiss instructors—some even more ancient "Dep"-controlled Jennys. In Washington Captain Cunningham, who was serving as the first Officer in Charge (OinC) of Marine aviation (without being thus formally designated), got his hands on 20 Jennys with Hispano-Suiza engines.

On 1 April McIlvain arrived in Miami with his 1st Squadron. The new arrivals bulged all facilities at Curtiss Field, which was renamed the Marine Flying Field, the first in the history of the Corps.

It was also the last field the Marines got during the war despite various efforts to acquire a new base at Selma, Ala., or Charleston, S.C. Lest the reader envision the 1918 Miami in terms of luxurious hotels on the waterfront, let him ponder a contemporary report:

> Marines are still operating at the temporary field at Miami, living in tents, housing the machines in canvas hangars, which are about to fall down, using a landing field which is made of sand so soft that no grass can be made to grow in it and which is so near sea level that there is a possibility at any moment of having the whole field flooded and making it useless for several days. The surrounding country is almost entirely wild and uncultivated, making it impossible [sic] to land machines in only a very few places except right near the present field at Miami.[18]

Fortunately, the citizens of the young Miami were hospitable and "not so anxious to take a dollar away from you," as one aviator recalled 32 years later.

With the move to Miami there was a split (15 April) into a headquarters detachment and four landplane squadrons. The Navy allowed a flock of transfers. This was the organization—the "1st Marine Aviation Force"—which was ordered almost immediately to get ready to sail for France, to the concern of Cunningham, who feared they wouldn't be prepared for combat. As the senior at Miami, Geiger commanded Squadron A and was acting CO of the

---

[18] Memo Lieut. H. B. Mims to Commandant, 8 July 1918.

whole works. The other squadron commands went to McIlvain, Roben and Russell A. Presley.

At this time the Marines were trained mostly in Jennys. Four British-designed, American-manufactured DH-4's were expected, and they were awaited eagerly, but "positively not to be flown except by the most expert flyers you have and they are not to joy ride in them," Cunningham wrote Geiger 28 May.

The DH-4 was the British DeHavilland which became the standard American combat plane, not only for World War I, but for many years afterward. A two-seater, the DH-4 could stay in the air about four hours, had a ceiling of 19,000 feet and a speed of about 124 miles an hour. It could climb to 10,000 feet in 14 minutes and could carry a load of about 1,200 pounds. One of the drawbacks which caused it to be labeled the "Flying Coffin" was its design: the observer and pilot sitting in tandem, with the large gas tank between them.[19] This fault was corrected later in the DH-4B. Even worse was the overhead gravity feed, a 30-gallon tank whose contents a mild crack-up would spill onto the hot manifold pipes.

But not until May did the Marines get even Flying Coffins. Meanwhile, the pressure to send the squadrons overseas was increased, and the Navy didn't want two squadrons now and two later—the Navy wanted four right now.

In the summer of 1918 the Marines began drawing their flying students from the school the Navy had set up in April at Massachusetts Institute of Technology. Promising volunteers were sent there and given the rank of chief petty officer or gunnery sergeant during their preliminary training. "Marine flying candidates are all enlisted men of superior physique, weighing from 135 to 165 pounds, and with at least two years' college or university study to their credit. The age limits are 19 to 39 years."[20]

The course at MIT lasted ten weeks, following which graduates were sent on to Miami to learn to fly. Mechanics, riggers and armorers were drawn from the Marine section of the naval school for mechanics at Great Lakes Training Station, Chicago (eight-weeks course), and a similar school at San Diego.

About 100 Navy flying cadets were sent to Miami for transfer to the Marine Corps. On 1 June the 1st Marine Aviation Force could report that it had on hand 124 "satisfactory" pilots:

Regular Marines	23
Reserve 2d Lieuts.	17
2d Lieuts. (Ex-Navy)	20
Ensigns awaiting enroll.	10
Navy cadets awaiting enroll.	47
Enlisted Marine pilots	7

[19] H. H. Arnold, Global Mission, p 66.

[20] Report of Major General Commandant 10 October 1918 in "Report of the Secretary of the Navy for 1918," pp 1599–1600.

Seventeen of the Navy pilots were found unsatisfactory, which upset the Navy Department, but Marine Corps headquarters stood fast in its long-established insistence on selectivity, even though "they have practically stated they are not going to send us any more."[21]

The Balloon Company

As part of its Advanced Base Force—originally conceived for the defense of the Panama Canal from a base in the Caribbean—the Marine Corps planned a light-artillery battalion, four batteries of 5-inch naval guns and a battery of medium artillery. Headquarters of the organization were to contain an aerial company.

As the German Fleet's threat to the Western Atlantic diminished, other uses for the Marine Corps artillery were sought. The War Department advised that an additional brigade of Marine infantry would be welcome in the American Expeditionary Forces but "no artillery regiment could be accepted."

Early in 1918, however, the War Department approved a naval project to send some heavy artillery to the AEF and 14-inch railway guns and 7-inch converted naval guns on caterpillar mounts were selected. The 10th Marines was organized as the heavy-artillery unit, and continued training at Quantico with 3-inch guns until the 7-inch guns became available the following July.[22]

For artillery spotting with the 10th Marines a Balloon Detachment was organized 28 June 1918 under the command of Captain Arthur H. Page, the first Naval Academy graduate to go into Marine aviation. The Balloon Detachment, whose personnel had been trained by the Army at St. Louis and Omaha, was equipped with two Caquot balloons and two RC-6 seaplanes; the roster included 3 officers and 110 men.[23] Its chief function was to train nonflying observers.

But on 23 August the War Department made plain that it wanted no Marine artillery in France, and requested that the Marines' 7-inch naval guns be turned over to the Army. The Commandant protested, and managed to keep the guns (only two were delivered to the Marines before the Armistice, anyway). But no Marine heavy artillery ever got to France. The Balloon Detachment continued training with the artillerists, for whom bigger things were planned within a Marine division in 1919. These bigger things never came off, of course, and the Detachment was disbanded 7 April 1919.

A balloon observation unit (ZK-1M) was part of the Marine aviation organization from 1924 until December 1929.

Assignment to France

The devastating losses to U-boats in 1917 pointed up the role which naval aviation logically should play; 875,000 tons of shipping were sunk the

---

[21] Letter Cunningham to Geiger 8 June 1918.

[22] Clyde H. Metcalf, *A History of the U.S. Marine Corps*, p 459.

[23] Letters Mims to Cunningham 24 September and 30 October 1918.

month the United States entered the war. As a first installment on antisubmarine warfare 7 naval aviators and 122 mechanics were sent to France in June, with no planes and little training, mostly for morale purposes.[24] The commanding officer, Lieut. Kenneth Whiting USN, early recommended that American naval aviation be employed from Dunkerque in bombing the German submarine pens at Zeebrugge, Ostend and Bruges. It was believed that seaplanes, though they lacked the distance necessary to go out and find submarines, could catch the U-boats in their pens.

Eventually naval aviators were stationed at bases in England, Ireland, Italy and France, but these operations are beyond the purview of this volume.

The difficulties facing American aviators of all services seemed almost insurmountable—few planes, few trained pilots, and far less know-how than should have accrued to the nation which invented the airplane (invariably called "aeroplane" until after World War I). Following the recommendation of the Bolling Commission of June 1917, the Army decided to build only trainers and the DH-4 and the Liberty engine. The Navy's seaplane program was in better shape, and U.S. seaplanes were acknowledged the equal of any nation's, so no foreign-designed seaplanes were built in the U.S. But the seaplane was never intended to operate except on and near the water, where there seemed to be plenty of work for it if the German submarine was to be defeated. Until the U.S. factories could turn out more seaplanes, the French agreed to furnish them if the Americans would send over the raw materials. Of 138 planes promised by the French, only one third had been delivered by May 1918, and nearly all of these, it developed, were too slow to cope with German fighters.

It soon became evident that seaplanes were too short-ranged, too slow and were unable to carry the necessary bomb load. What ensued was a jurisdictional dispute with the Army Air Service. Major General Benjamin D. Foulois, head of the Army's overseas aviation units, insisted that the Navy had no business flying landplanes and attacking land targets: "Airplanes and engines now being built in the United States must be distributed to the Allied air services, including our own."[25]

The British, who had already consolidated their air services into a separate air force, put some pressure on the United States to do the same, and the U.S. Army air people were ready to jump at a chance to escape from control by their ground officers. Not so with the U.S. Navy, which was already witnessing the retrogression in the Royal Navy following the loss of most of its aviation to a separate service—a factor which was to prove disastrous to the Royal Navy in World War II.

The Navy's requests finally were set at 75 bombers and 40 single-seat

---

[24] Lieut. Commander Clifford L. Lord, *History of United States Naval Aviation, 1899–1939*, Vol IV, part II, p 302 (hereinafter cited as Lord manuscript). This is the original four-volume manuscript from which the Turnbull and Lord single-volume *History of United States Naval Aviation* (Yale University Press, 1949) was condensed.

[25] Lord manuscript, Vol IV, part II, p 462.

fighters to escort them. The Army, following General Pershing's decision that the Navy should bomb the submarine pens, agreed to furnish the fighters, but demurred at supplying the bombers. The Navy was stuck with its own seaplanes, plus whatever else it could pick up from foreign governments—Capronis from Italy, Handley-Pages from Britain, DD flying boats from France.

It was Cunningham himself who came up with the suggestion which eventually put the Navy and Marine Corps aviators solidly—if belatedly—into the war. Following a trip to Europe late in 1917, he appeared before the General Board on 24 January 1918 and said that at least four Marine fighter squadrons were necessary to help wrest control of the air in the Dunkerque–Calais area from the Germans. Lieut. Towers added that seaplane bombers were useless there without fighter escort.[26] Admiral Sims and his staff later decided that fast, around-the-clock bombers were more important than fighter escort, so the Marines never flew fighters.[27] But Cunningham had got the project rolling.

This was the genesis of the Northern Bombing Project and of the rushing of Marine squadrons to France despite Cunningham's fears that they were not ready for combat.

Geiger, McIlvain and Roben, commanding officers of Squadrons A, B and C, were sent ahead in June 1918 to join Chamberlain, the advance agent, for training with the British and French. Two weeks later Cunningham sailed in USS *DeKalb* with 1 captain, 16 first lieutenants, 79 second lieutenants, 657 enlisted men—the personnel of the three squadrons.

Cunningham and his 1st Marine Aviation Force reached Brest on 30 July. Sorrowfully he reported to Lieut. Harvey B. Mims, whom he had left behind in Washington as a very junior OinC: "We arrived day before yesterday and found that no one here knew what we were, where we were to go or what we were to do here. . . . The trouble is that no one in Washington took interest enough in us to cable when we would arrive and what we were for." The debut of the Marine flyers in France was not auspicious.

But Cunningham, confronted with wall-eyed stares from Army and Navy officers, once again proved his resourcefulness. He secured from the French ("God knows whom") a train manned by Frenchmen, loaded it with the three squadrons plus their equipment and some food, and took off for Calais. After three days and 400 miles the Marine entourage reached Calais. Squadrons A and B made their camp near Oye, a town between Calais and Dunkerque. Squadron C was assigned to La Frêne, a small village about ten miles northeast of Calais.[28]

Without planes, the Navy and Marine—and Army—aviators could only sit and wait. Despite elaborate production plans which called for 4,500 planes

---

[26] *Ibid*, Vol IV, part II, p 441.

[27] *Ibid*, Vol IV, part II, pp 456–457.

[28] Letter in Marine aviation history file from Major General Ford O. Rogers USMC (Ret), 3 November 1950; manuscript history of Squadron C by Lieut. Charles B. Todd Jr. USMCR, undated but probably written immediately after World War I (courtesy of Captain Robert S. Lytle USMCR).

at the front by 30 June 1918, the American effort fell far short and caused Congressional and Presidential investigations. The Germans were spurred by the well-advertised threat from the West to greater efforts of their own which they sarcastically called *Amerikaprogramm*.[29] It was 17 May 1918 before the the first American-built DH-4 was delivered (to the Army) in France. When they did arrive the American-built planes required a major overhaul; their spruce wings were usually warped; 40 per cent of the control wires were too short; the Liberty engines were carelessly or improperly assembled. Insofar as their own later allotment of planes was concerned, the Navy and Marine mechanics performed miracles of reconstruction and repair—the total number of changes was put at 118—but the agonizing delay put a crimp into the whole World War I effort. Assistant Secretary of the Navy F. D. Roosevelt after a brief investigation noted on 18 August that no naval plane could operate offensively, and only eight could take to the air. The "scandalous" situation he laid to Washington and to improper factory inspection.[30]

While they waited the American pilots were assigned to British squadrons, the Marines to Nos. 217 and 218, where they got their first taste of combat in DH's. The plan was to give each pilot three missions.

The Combat Record

Upon their arrival in France the Marine squadrons became the Day Wing of the Northern Bombing Group.[31] Their designations were officially changed from A, B and C to 7, 8 and 9. Personnel of the squadrons usually called them "First," "Second," or "Third." Major Cunningham set up his wing headquarters at Bois-en-Ardres. Supply bases were at Paulliac and at Eastleigh, England, where the first attempts at reconditioning and assembling the American-built DH-4's were made.

Captain McIlvain was sent to England to find the planes which after a month seemed to be no more than phantoms. In order that the reader may understand that SNAFU, under whatever name, was not limited to World War II, the following letter of McIlvain to Cunningham, under date of 2 September, is quoted:

> Found eight complete DH-4's at Eastleigh and parts of 24 more machines. Went over all the changes with Chevy and Howard and got them straightened out. Found they had no bomb sights nor any air speed indicators in the planes. Got Chevy to wire Hanrahan[32] so bomb sights, Pridot links for Martin guns, and Liberty or Oleo spark plugs are on their way now. An officer is following them up. Heard a rumor that 42 boxes

[29] Craven and Cate, *The AAF in WW II*, Vol I, p 9.

[30] Lord manuscript, Vol IV, part II, pp 529a–530.

[31] At this time all U.S. aviation followed the British system which reverses the modern American organization and makes wings subordinate units of groups.

[32] Captain D. C. Hanrahan USN, CO Northern Bombing Group.

of DH-4's were at Glasgow and had been since August 20. Chased that down here in London and found it true. . . . Went to Air Ministry armed with an order from Supply Dept. and secured air speed indicators, or rather promise of them. . . . Hold-up on planes will be due entirely to overhaul of motors. Absolute orders that all motors must be overhauled before leaving Eastleigh. Darned good plan, too, from what I can see or we would have pilots down all over France with motors in present condition. First machines can't be gotten before September 20. . . . If necessary will go after the 42 boxes myself.

Actually, it was 23 September before the first DeHavilland was received by the Marines in France. By 16 October there were still only 17 in the Day Wing (eight of them in commission).

The first raid in force by the Northern Bombing Group was carried out 14 October by Roben's Squadron 9.[33] Eight planes attacked Thielt railway junction at 15,000 feet and dropped 2,218 pounds of bombs.[34]

Operating with the 5th Group, Royal Air Force, the Northern Bombing Group raided canals, railroads, supply dumps, and airfields. Nearly all operations were carried out by Squadron 9, with pilots from other units attached at various times. All day squadrons moved forward as the Germans retreated, Squadron 8 reaching an abandoned enemy station at Knessalare, Belgium, on 1 November.

With the arrival on 8 October of Squadron D (relabeled "10") at La Frêne, the roster of the Day Wing was complete. Captain R. A. Presley, who had preceded his squadron, resumed command and was assigned repair and maintenance for the Day Wing, which was "drab and colorless" duty, its skipper recalled 32 years later. Presley himself was the only member on the sick list (influenza). He was also the only member to receive disciplinary action.

Pursuant to an approved request to visit the front lines after the Armistice, on or about November 15th, the CO accompanied by four of his officers went south along the old Front line to Chateau Therry [sic] and then, being within 20 miles, spent the night in Paris. The party had dinner that evening in the Continental Hotel. Coincidently, the NBG Commander, Captain Hanrahan, USN, was dining at the Continental. The captain stopped and warmly greeted this party of marines. Upon the return to La Frêne the CO received the following communication from the Wing Commander: "You will explain by endorsement hereon why, when given permission to visit the Front lines, you went into the City of Paris, when, by no stretch of the imagination, could Paris be con-

[33] Turnbull and Lord, *History of United States Naval Aviation*, p 140, gives the Marines credit for the raid but has the date wrong (13 October).

[34] Day Wing log's figures. Brig. General Karl S. Day USMCR, who as a captain flew on the mission, recalls the altitude as 3,000 or 4,000 feet.

sidered a part of the Front lines." For which the CO "10th" Squadron received ten days' arrest and confined to quarters. On the third day the CO was released from arrest and given orders to prepare his squadron for immediate transport to St. Nazaire and home. It is further worthy of note that Squadron 10 was the first intact unit to be returned to the U.S.A. after the Armistice.[35]

Before sailing from St. Nazaire on USS *Susquehanna* Captain Presley was called to the captain's cabin and told:

Captain, we have 700 Army casuals and 800 navy passengers aboard this ship in addition to your squadron. This Army Colonel here [*indicating*] states he cannot command Navy. This Navy commander states that he cannot command Army. A Marine officer can command both. You are herewith designated as CO troops for this voyage and responsible to me.[36]

Thus ended the wartime career of Squadron 10.

Altogether the Marines dropped about 14 tons of bombs on the enemy, as can be seen from the following table for the Bombing Group as a whole:

POUNDS OF BOMBS DROPPED

Naval pilots flying with Allied units	54,332	
Naval observers or gunners with Allied units	21,984	
Naval personnel, Northern Bombing Group (night)	22,670	98,986
Marine Corps pilots flying with Allied units	15,077	
Marine Corps observers or gunners with Allied units	625	
Marine Corps personnel, NBG (day)	11,614	27,316[37]
TOTAL		126,302

Actually, the Day Wing flew more missions in dropping 11,614 pounds than the Navy did with 22,670 poundage, since the Marines' bombs weighed only 50 to 100 pounds, as compared to the Navy's bombs weighing 500 to 1,500.

Some of the earliest recorded food-dropping missions were flown 1–2 October by Captain Francis P. Mulcahy,[38] Captain Robert S. Lytle, and Lieut.

---

[35] Letter Captain R. A. Presley, 26 November 1950.

[36] *Ibid.*

[37] These figures from *History of United States Naval Aviation*, p 141, are probably too low for Marine aviation. W. P. T. Hill's own accountants' accounting gives the Marines 52,000 pounds. By comparison, the Army flyers dropped 275,000 pounds, but they concentrated on pursuit flying, claiming 781 enemy planes against a loss of 289 (Craven and Cate, *The AAF in WW II*, Vol I, pp 11, 15).

[38] Francis Patrick Mulcahy was born in Rochester, N.Y. 9 March 1894. Graduate of Notre Dame University 1914. First lieutenant 1917. Designated naval aviator 1918. Captain (temporary) 1918. Served with Northern Bombing Group in France (Navy DSM). Major 1934, lieutenant colonel 1936, colonel 1941, brigadier general (tem-

Frank Nelms. A French regiment in an isolated salient had been without food for several days when the three DH-4's were loaded with canned goods and bread and flown over four times at an altitude of 100 feet in the face of German heavy machine-gun, rifle and artillery fire. The three pilots were awarded the Distinguished Service Medal;[39] the Navy Cross went to their observers, Gunnery Sergeants Archie Paschal, Amil Wiman, and Thomas L. McCullough.

Just how many planes the Marines shot down in World War I will never be known. Several earlier accounts mention 12, but that is obviously high. Official records as listed in the Day Wing log show only four: one by Mulcahy and his observer, McCullough, on 29 September; the other three by Lieut. Ralph Talbot and Corporal Robert Guy Robinson (see below). This is low. Captain Lytle and Gunnery Sergeant Wiman received the DSM for knocking down a plane on 14 October—the records disagree on whether this one was in addition to Talbot's two on that date, or whether one of Talbot's should have been credited to them. A certificate signed by Major B. S. Wemp RAF, commanding Squadron 218, credits Lieut. Everett Brewer and Sergeant Harry Wershiner with one Fokker and probably another on 28 September. Major Wemp credited the Americans with only these two planes while serving with his squadron during this period, but he added:

> Lieuts. Mulcahy, Brewer, Lytle, Talbot and Nelms and the late Lieut. Barr, with N.C.O. observers, have done wonderful work in this push during the past week, and when the time comes for those now here to leave the Squadron, I can assure you I will hate to part with their services.[40]

---

porary) 1942, major general (temporary) 1944. Between World Wars I and II served in Haiti, Santo Domingo, Nicaragua, Puerto Rico and Virgin Islands. In Second Nicaraguan Campaign commanded Marine Air from July 1931 to end of occupation in 1933. Graduate of Air Corps Tactical School, Command and General Staff School, Naval War College. When the Japanese attacked Pearl Harbor he was observer with British Western Desert Air Force in North Africa. CG 2d MAW August 1942. Arrived Guadalcanal in December with part of 2d MAW and assumed command of Allied land-based aircraft at Guadalcanal until February 1943. Commanded land-based aircraft in New Georgia Campaign, June–September 1943. CG Marine Fleet Air, West Coast (MarFAir West), May–September 1944. CG Aircraft, FMFPac, September 1944–February 1945. CG 2d MAW and Tactical Air Force (TAF) Tenth Army, February–July 1945. Gold Star in lieu of second DSM and Legion of Merit for World War II. Retired for physical disability 1 April 1946 with rank of lieutenant general.

[39] For World War I the DSM was awarded for heroism in combat and was superior to the Navy Cross; both were created in 1919. A revision in 1942 gave the Navy Cross precedence over the DSM.

[40] Wemp to Cunningham 6 October 1918. Major Wemp might have been considered reluctant to overpraise the Marines, and they certainly had become reluctant to overstate their own case. Earlier, a Marine pilot, who shall be nameless here, had forged RAF documents attesting that he had shot down five enemy planes in a single engagement. The pilot was court-martialed and dismissed from the service.

But shooting down enemy planes was not the mission of the DH bombers the Marines flew, either on their own or with Squadrons 217 and 218—and they flew no other planes excepting a few missions with RAF Squadron 213 in "hot," single-seater Sopwith Camel "scouts." The Marines were supposed to do the day bombing for the Northern Bombing Group and, when they eventually got their planes, that is what they did, although their original targets, the submarine pens, had by then lost their value.

Talbot and Robinson were awarded the Medal of Honor. On 8 October while flying with Squadron 218 their plane was attacked by nine enemy, and they shot down one of them. Six days later on the Thielt raid they were attacked by 12 German planes. They shot down one of those as Robinson was drilled through the elbow. They returned to the fight until Robinson was shot twice more in the stomach and once in the hip. Nevertheless, Talbot continued the attack, knocking down the nearest enemy scout with his forward guns, then flew across the enemy lines at 50 feet.

Robinson survived his "probably fatal" wounds; Talbot was killed 25 October in a crash. His observer on this occasion, Lieut. Colgate W. Darden, Jr., was thrown clear and survived, to become Governor of Virginia (1942–46) and president of the University of Virginia (in June 1947).

The first Marine aviator to lose his life as a result of enemy action was Lieut. Chapin C. Barr, who died 29 September of a severe leg wound that severed an artery. On 22 October Lieut. Harvey C. Norman and Lieut. Caleb W. Taylor, flying a DH-9, were shot down and killed on the Bruges–Ghent Canal. Three officers and 13 enlisted men died of influenza, including the highly esteemed CO of Squadron 9, Major Roben. Three flyers were wounded: Lieut. Everett Brewer and Gunnery Sergeants Harry Wershiner and Robinson.

Although the Marines were just beginning to get into the fight when the Armistice was declared, their record was one to be proud of. The tradition of combat readiness was an old one; when they called on the Marines they packed up and went. Whatever the shortcomings, these were shared by all American aviation, and were not the making of the men who flew the planes at the front.

In World War I a total of 282 officers and 2,180 enlisted men served in Marine aviation. Of these, about one half got overseas.[41]

---

[41] Edwin N. McClellan, *The United States Marine Corps in the World War*, p 73.

CHAPTER TWO

Between Wars

THOMAS C. TURNER was in many respects the most spectacular—and the most ambitious—officer in the history of Marine Corps aviation. Born in California, he had enlisted in the Marine Corps in 1901 at the age of 19. He was commissioned second lieutenant the next year and served five years in the Philippines and at Vera Cruz, where he commanded a machine-gun company.

The outbreak of war found him a major commanding the Marine Barracks at San Diego. In his spare time he learned to fly with the Army pilots, whose admiration of Turner seems to have amounted almost to adulation. In August 1917 Turner requested that he be detailed, not to naval aviation but to the Army, and the Aviation Section of the Signal Corps welcomed him. The following month, by special permission of the Secretary of the Navy and the Secretary of War he was designated a "junior military aviator."[1]

Turner's Army designation was revoked by the Judge Advocate General 17 December 1917, but two months later he was designated a naval aviator instead. He continued on duty with the Army, however. As early as 6 November 1917 Colonel H. H. Arnold, viewing Turner's "excellent record" and noting that Turner was already instructing Army flyers at San Diego, recommended that he be attached to the Signal Corps for aviation. Turner wanted to continue flying, but could not do so in the Marine Corps which had only one squadron. That one already had "full complement of personnel," said "Hap" Arnold, and "there is no possibility of another squadron being formed in the near future."[2] Turner reported to the Chief Signal Officer 17 days later. From there Turner went on to become OinC of flying at the Army's Ellington Field at Houston— a lone marine in the midst of thousands of soldiers.

In February 1918 Turner visited the Marines' 1st Squadron in training at Gerstner Field, La. From the eminence of his rank (major) and age (36), he entertained the young pilots with accounts of his experiences in the Philippines and of night-flying activities at Houston. When they asked him what was going to become of them he said he didn't know; he had heard that some planes were to be sent to the Mexican border, but whether it would be the Marine squadron—which he described as the only one in the U.S. with its full complement of officers and men—he knew not.

---

[1] A title also held by Cunningham and perhaps a few other naval aviators.
[2] Memo Arnold to The Adjutant General USA.

The upshot of this visit was a rumor reaching Washington that Turner had told the pilots Marine aviation was dead; there was no future in it. The Major General Commandant ordered a report made, but only one officer could be found (Lieut. Edmund G. Chamberlain) who would say in writing that Turner had made such a remark—and he got it second hand.

This incident illustrated (1) the nervousness this single squadron of Marine aviators felt about their position and (2) Turner's uncanny knack for showing up on the firing line. Even while he was at San Diego he stood down the Commander, Patrol Force, Pacific Fleet, who wanted to use the Marines' rifle range without due notice.

At Quantico several years later Turner, a colonel by then, took offense at the attitude of a lieutenant commander (Medical Corps) and asked why he didn't salute. The doctor said he had never in his 18 years in the Navy heard of saluting at 0615 in the morning when both officers were in civilian clothes. "You'll see," said Turner, and walked away. The result was a letter from the commanding general at Quantico to the doctor, ordering him to apologize to Colonel Turner and to read the regulations.[3]

The letter of commendation issued him by his Army superior when he relinquished command of Barron Field, Everman, Texas, and returned to the Marine Corps appears to characterize Turner as he was found throughout most of his career:

> Major Turner is, in my opinion, an officer of the very highest type. He is a strict disciplinarian, is tactful and earnest and possesses the respect of every man under his command. Their loyalty and admiration for him, in spite of the fact that he is not of the Army, is quite remarkable.[4]

The rising star of this absentee naval aviator was viewed with some alarm back in Washington. To Cunningham in France his assistant, Mims, wrote that a certain officer

> does not seem to want to do the right thing by you, and it has just been brought to my attention that he wrote B. L. Smith endeavoring to lock arms with him and get Lieutenant Colonel Turner transferred from the Army Aviation to assume command of Marine Aviation. . . . You can rest assured that I killed the entire matter.[5]

Turner was, of course, senior to Cunningham. He was appointed temporary lieutenant colonel the same day (28 August 1918) Cunningham was appointed major. His advent into naval aviation would prove embarrassing to the No. 1 Marine aviator.

---

[3] 10th endorsement CG Quantico to Major General Commandant, 10 September 1926.

[4] Colonel D. L. Roscoe, CO Taliaferro Field to Chief of the Air Division, 7 May 1919.

[5] Letter Mims to Cunningham, 7 October 1918.

This advent was delayed. Upon being detached from the Army Turner was immediately assigned to a four-year tour as adjutant of the 1st Brigade in Haiti. But after nine months in Haiti Turner requested aviation duty: "My ability in aviation is sufficiently well known. . . . I am already an expert aviator both practical and theoretical."

Turner Takes Over

Upon arrival in Washington Tommy Turner relieved Major Cunningham 13 December 1920 as OinC of Marine aviation. Cunningham had nursed Marine aviation through its first decade, but now he was through. He was given command of the 1st Squadron in Santo Domingo for the next year and a half. Following Marine Corps postwar policy,[6] which required all aviators to return to ground duty at certain intervals, Cunningham was relieved of flying orders. Although most aviators were able to get these orders revoked, or to return to aviation before their allotted time, Cunningham was never permitted to resume flying.[7] (It was explained that flying officers were needed, not administrative officers.) Cunningham padded out his career with sea service, quartermaster duty, and a tour in Nicaragua. In 1935 he was retired physically as a major,[8] aged 57. He died four years later at Sarasota, Fla., of coronary thrombosis. His memory is perpetuated in Cunningham Field, Cherry Point, N.C., which was dedicated 4 September 1941, and in the destroyer *Alfred A. Cunningham*, commissioned 23 November 1944.

The Scanty, Golden Twenties

The Cunningham decade gave way to the Turner decade. Impressive was the word for Turner; he was only slightly bigger (5 feet 10 inches, 180 pounds) than most of the officers serving under him, but to them he seemed eight feet tall. From the time he took over as OinC Turner ruled his pilots with an iron hand, even during the era when pilots were supposed to be (and were) brave young men constantly flirting with death.[9] For Marine aviation Turner's stern measures were undoubtedly beneficial; he never let the Marines get the idea that the best flyers are those without discipline.

---

[6] MarCorps Order No. 8, Series 1921.

[7] Geiger spent nearly a year away from aviation, but at his own request (at the Army's Command and General Staff School, Fort Leavenworth, Kansas, in 1924–25).

[8] He was promoted lieutenant colonel on the retired list 16 January 1936 by an act of Congress which provided that physically retired officers commended in combat be retired in the next higher grade.

[9] In 1922 Marine aviation acquired 17 new officer pilots and had 9 killed in crashes. Between June 1923 and June 1924, 11 new pilots were added, 4 pilots were killed. One young officer signing up for aviation in 1924 was asked whether he wanted a three-, four- or five-year term. "What's the casualty rate?" he asked. "Oh, about 25 per cent a year," he was told. "Put me down for five years," the second lieutenant said, "and I'll be 125 per cent dead when I return to the line." (Conversation Brig. General Clayton C. Jerome, 11 September 1950.)

One of Turner's first acts was to lead a two-plane flight of wartime DH-4's on 22 April 1921 from Washington to Santo Domingo, the longest unguarded flight of its kind ever flown over land and water up to that time.[10] For this the four participants were awarded the Distinguished Flying Cross 13 December 1927.

Regularly Turner was given a waiver for a hearing defect in each ear, and just as regularly he drew from his superiors an unending string of commendations. (Rear Admiral W. A. Moffett, Chief of the Bureau of Aeronautics, invariably marked him 4.0 in all categories.)

Certainly Marine Corps aviation was a bargain for the U.S. taxpayer during the 1920's. Efficiency was the slogan and economy was the watchword. The number of aviators on the payroll is an index:

1918	282[11]	1924	49
1919	127	1925	56
1920	67	1926	65
1921	43	1927	73
1922	46[12]	1928	85
1923	48	1929	100
		1930	132

Santo Domingo and Haiti

During these years the handful of Marine aviators managed to spread themselves across half the world, wherever Leathernecks were sent. The flyers' first overseas assignment was Santo Domingo, where Captain Walter E. McCaughtry arrived with a six-Jenny squadron at San Pedro de Marcorís on 27 February 1919 (a regiment of marines had been there since 1914). Attached to the 15th Regiment until February 1920, the 1st Air Squadron was transferred to the 2d Marine Brigade at Santo Domingo City and assisted the ground troops by strafing bandit positions, performing reconnaissance missions, evacuating wounded in two-seat planes.[13] The Squadron remained in Santo

---

[10] Turner flew in the rear cockpit; his pilot was Lieut. Basil G. Bradley. In the second plane were Lieut. Lawson H. M. Sanderson and Gunnery Sergeant Charles W. Rucker.

[11] This is the figure for officers, as given in SecNav report; it is not certain that these were all pilots.

[12] Figures 1922–28 in "Statistics–A9–10" folder No. 143. Earlier and later figures were taken from operational statistics and Commandant's reports.

[13] Captain Francis T. Evans designed an ambulance plane in 1922 by modifying a DH with a turtle-back fuselage and equipping it with a Stokes stretcher. The planes —two were built at the Naval Aircraft Factory, Philadelphia—could accommodate one reclining and one sitting patient. They were used frequently in Santo Domingo and Haiti, and could cut evacuation time from three days by muleback, cart and truck to two hours' round trip. (Information from Colonel F. T. Evans USMC (Ret), 20 November 1950.)

Domingo until 24 July 1924, when peace and a constitutional government had been restored. These lasted until the Dominican Army commander, General Rafael Trujillo, staged a bloodless coup in 1930 and set himself up as dictator. The military force which the Marines organized was thus turned to a purpose for which it was not intended, but this was a failure of U.S. foreign policy, not of the troops assigned to carry it out.

During the early 1920's the Marine Corps began accepting increasing numbers of enlisted men as pilots (NAP's—naval aviation pilots). After the war NAP's were trained at Pensacola, where all officer pilots had to be checked out. But during the Santo Domingo service the first three NAP's were trained and given their wings without previous training at Pensacola—Sergeants Belcher, Paschal and Abbot.[14] NAP's were usually skilled mechanics who became adept flyers, but who did not have the educational qualifications required for a commission. Designating enlisted men as pilots also was a device for giving the Marine Corps (and the Navy) additional flyers without pushing beyond authorized strength in the officer category.

Marines had been landed in Haiti as early as 1915 in an attempt to restore a semblance of order amid the financial and political chaos on which the State Department frowned. The 4th Air Squadron of marines, by then designated 1st Division, Squadron E, commanded by Captain Harvey B. Mims, with seven HS-2 seaplanes and six Jenny landplanes, disembarked on 31 March 1919 at Port-au-Prince.[15] There Marine aviators operated for 15 years, against the *caco* rebel leaders such as Charlemagne Peralte and his successor, Benoit Batraville. The Marine brigade consisted of about 80 officers and 1,200 enlisted men; it was assisted by an American-trained native gendarmerie of about 2,700.

It was the task of the Marines from time to time to isolate and run down numerous bandit groups. For reconnaissance the newly arrived planes were invaluable. Regular air-mail service was maintained between scattered detachments. The pilots also delivered messages and supplies, took aerial photographs, and employed a new type of bomb release to insure greater accuracy.

In 1919 Lieut. L. H. M. Sanderson found that he could hit a target more often by pointing his plane toward the target and releasing his bomb from a makeshift rack after diving to a low level (about 250 feet) at an angle of about 45°—the angle which came to be known as glide bombing in World War II. Pilots of VO-9M (as the 4th Squadron was eventually redesignated) adopted the technique as a regular maneuver. VO-9M, its personnel rotated about every two years, remained in Haiti until the marines were finally withdrawn. The Squadron took off from Port-au-Prince 12 August 1934 and landed in Quantico two days later. From there it went to the Virgin Islands, became VMS-3 and stayed until decommissioned in May 1944.

---

[14] Information from Major Edwin H. Brainard USMC (Ret), 30 October 1950.
[15] Major Roy Geiger, who took over from Mims, made a favorable impression on economy-minded Congressmen inspecting his command. Because he had no funds, for an office, Geiger had built one out of airplane crates and shingled it with flattened gasoline cans. (Information from Colonel Evans.)

Fighting in Nicaragua

As an instrument of American foreign policy, the Marine Corps had a long history of intervention in Nicaragua, but it was not until the most violent revolution, in the mid-twenties, that Marine aviators became involved. Following the landing of the 5th Marines in January 1927, the 8 officers and 81 enlisted men of VO-1M, commanded by Major Ross E. Rowell,[16] arrived at Corinto on 25 February and proceeded by train to Managua, hauling their six DH's on flat cars.

Anarchy was soon rampant. The Marines held 14 points along the railroad separating the U.S.-supported Diaz forces and the Moncada rebels.[17]

The addition of the 11th Marines on 23 May brought the U.S. ground forces up to brigade strength (despite the fact that 4,000 marines were in China, and others in Haiti). A second squadron, VO-4M, arrived from Quantico with the regiment, and Aircraft Squadrons, 2d Brigade, was formed under Rowell as the top aviation echelon three days later. Both Diaz and Moncada had agreed to disarmament when one of Moncada's leaders, Augusto Sandino, pulled out with 150 followers who were soon joined by others. Some dissidents soon clashed with marines along the railroad and an extensive occupation of outposts became necessary. But conditions looked so much brighter that all but 1,377 marines were withdrawn by the end of June, including most of the personnel of VO-1M (the remnants joined VO-4M, which was redesignated VO-7M on 1 July).

The peace was quickly shattered when a strong force of several hundred Sandinistas attacked the 37-man Marine garrison at Ocotal on the evening of 15 July. The night attack was beaten off, but when the beleaguered marines refused to surrender after daylight, Sandino's men struck harder than ever.

Ocotal is 125 miles from Managua, at least ten days' travel by the crude mountain trails, and the nearest Marine reinforcement was no nearer than halfway between the two points. The 37 marines in Ocotal and the 47 or 48 Nicaraguan guards (led by a marine) were in a desperate plight.

---

[16] Ross Erastus Rowell was born in Iowa 24 September 1884. Graduate of Iowa State College, then studied electrical engineering two years at University of Idaho. First lieutenant 1908, captain 1916, major (temporary) 1917. Served in Cuba 1906–09. Major (permanent) 1920. Learned to fly by paying for lessons. While serving as a quartermaster in 1921 Rowell requested duty as a student naval aviator but his superior recommended disapproval of his request and "that orders be issued directing him to devote his time to his required duties and that flying be incidental thereto rather than paramount." He finally succeeded in transferring to aviation in 1923 and got his wings at 39. Highest bombing score, 1924–25. His air command won Schiff Trophy (safety) 1926, 1932, 1933. Awarded first DFC ever received by a Marine aviator (November 1927) for Ocotal performance (see page 25). Lieutenant colonel 1932, colonel 1935, brigadier general 1939. CG 2d MAW September 1941 to August 1942. CG Marine Air Wings, Pacific, August 1942 to September 1944. Head of U.S. Aviation Mission to Peru 1944–46. Retired 1 November 1946. Died 6 September 1947.

[17] Metcalf, *A History of the U.S. Marine Corps*, p 421.

About 1010 two patrolling pilots, Lieut. Hayne D. Boyden and Marine Gunner Michael Wodarczyk,[18] appeared over Ocotal, and discovered the plight of the defenders. While Wodarczyk fired his ammunition at Sandino's men, Boyden landed to obtain a firsthand report in conversation (in Spanish) with a native. Then Boyden joined the other pilot, spent 20 minutes expending his own ammunition and returned to report to Major Rowell. Boyden and Wo- darczyk reached Managua at 1230.

Major Rowell led a five-plane flight of DH's, all that were available, from the little 400-yard runway. All pilots had been trained in dive bombing by Rowell, who had noticed pilots at Kelly Field practicing the technique in 1923 (the Army pilots credited its invention to the British in World War I). The five planes formed up in a bombing column, received fire from 1,500 feet as they circled the town. Major Rowell reported long afterward:

> I led off the attack and dived out of column from 1,500 feet, pulling out at about 600. Later we ended up by diving in from 1,000 and pulling out at about 300. Since the enemy had not been subjected to any form of bombing attack, other than the dynamite charges thrown from the Laird-Swallows by the Nicaraguan Air Force, they had no fear of us. They exposed themselves in such a manner that we were able to inflict damage which was out of proportion to what they might have suffered had they taken cover.[19]

Thus the first organized dive-bombing[20] attack and possibly the first low- altitude attack ever launched in support of ground troops. Ground officers estimated Sandino's casualties at 50 to 200; of these 40 to 80 were killed, Major Rowell reported.

---

[18] Known as the "Polish Warhorse," Wodarczyk had come to the U.S. from Poland when he was 14. A gunnery sergeant in France, he applied for aviation duty after the war. He flew for five years and compiled a total of over 1,000 hours' fly- ing time before he went through the formality of being designated a naval aviator— they gave him his wings and the DFC at the same ceremony. He retired as a colonel after service in the South Pacific in World War II.

[19] Interview Major General Rowell, Naval Aviation History Unit, Navy Depart- ment, 24 October 1946. The Nicaraguan Air Force was two planes, two pilots.

[20] After they returned from Nicaragua the Marine flyers put on many dive- bombing exhibitions in Montreal, New York, Chicago, and Miami. At one of the Cleveland Air Races a famous German ace, Ernst Udet, had been invited to partici- pate. He was intensely interested in the dive-bombing exhibition, and remarked that he could visualize some remarkable developments. This was the same Udet who, as a general, designed the Stukas which terrorized most of Europe early in World War II. "This was an aftermath of our dive-bombing shows wholly unanticipated," said "Rusty" Rowell. The publicity man's legend has the Marine Corps "inventing" dive bombing, with either Rowell or Sanderson or Chief Marine Gunner Elmo Reagan as the pioneer. Most senior Marine aviators doubt that any individual can claim credit for trying to hit his target by aiming his plane at it. But the Marines were first to adopt it as standing operating procedure and they worked hardest at it.

Rowell's planes flew a total of nearly 50 bombing missions against the Nicaraguan guerrillas.[21] On 28 February 1928 Wodarczyk had part of the tail of his plane shot away by rifle fire, but nonetheless dropped his bombs from very low altitude, killing Sandino's right-hand man, Espinosa. On 19 March Wodarczyk flew seven hours, led his patrol in three hard-fought engagements, had one of his observers, Captain Francis E. Pierce, wounded, received a bullet hole in his own parachute pack, had a wire shot away and got several holes in his plane. It was his twenty-fifth engagement, tops for the Squadron.

Several hundred of Sandino's followers ambushed two Marine columns on 30 December 1927, near Quílali. Four marines were killed, the commanders of both columns were wounded, along with 16 others. Although medicine was dropped twice by planes, to save the wounded men's lives it was necessary that they be flown out. To make a landing strip it was necessary to burn and level part of Quílali. This was done and Lieut. Christian F. Schilt—who had volunteered for the assignment—nuzzled in his O2U Corsair biplane (just received as replacement for the DH's), which had no brakes and had to be slowed down by waiting marines who hung on the wings. Time after time, from 6–8 January, Schilt made the precarious trip from Ocotal to Quílali, landing under fire on the home-made airfield and evacuating the wounded, until 18 were safely removed in ten hair-raising flights. For what the citation called "almost superhuman skill" Schilt received the Medal of Honor.

Although the aviators suffered no fatalities as a result of the enemy fire they so frequently encountered, a pilot and his gunner, Lieut. E. A. Thomas and Sergeant F. E. Dowdell, were captured by bandits when they crashed on Sapotillal Ridge on 8 October 1927. Ground patrols were sent out to rescue them but the nearest one, led by Lieut. Chappell, was besieged by 175 enemy troops. When planes spotted them the ground troops laid out panels indicating the direction and range of the enemy, and asked for an air attack. The subsequent bombing and strafing attack—the first known instance of an air attack being directed by ground troops—relieved the patrol's hazardous situation. Its mission was in vain. Thomas and Dowdell were never seen again. Mexican and Honduran newspapers later published pictures which indicated they had been tortured and hanged.

Among six others killed in Nicaragua, Captain William C. Byrd and Sergeant Rudolph A. Frankforter met a one-in-a-million fate. As they came in for a landing at Estelí on 8 March 1928, a buzzard flew into their O2B-1,[22] knocking off the outboard port strut. Byrd parachuted too late; Sergeant Frankforter stayed with the plane and was killed when it crashed.

The cargo transport record compiled by the two 2d Brigade squadrons was remarkable for the time, and foreshadowed the magnificent performances of South Pacific Combat Air Transport (SCAT) and Transport Air Group (TAG) over the islands of the Pacific. Only a few hundred pounds of cargo

---

[21] The total number of missions was higher, many pilots believe, but the records show no more.

[22] The O2B-1 was the old DH with a metal fuselage.

could be carried at a time in the O2U's and DH's, yet the squadrons managed to haul 30 tons or more per week over the formidable mountains of Nicaragua; the same pilot who hauled a load of gasoline might find himself engaged in dropping 17-pound bombs on the return trip.

Major E. H. Brainard, who had transferred to aviation in 1921, succeeded Turner as OinC of Marine aviation on 3 March 1925. He managed to obtain the first plane the Marines ever had which was built to transport cargo. It was like pulling a tooth, but "Chief" Brainard got a three-engined Fokker transport in 1927—mainly because he had an "in" with Secretary of the Navy Curtis D. Wilbur (whose aide Brainard was).

Brainard himself delivered the plane in Nicaragua on 4 December 1927 after a long and hazardous overwater flight. It was the first flight over the Caribbean and it marked a path for the initial Pan American Airways operation to Central and South America the following year. Brainard's copilot, Sergeant M. T. Shepard, stayed in Nicaragua and flew the plane over 1,000 hours in the following year.

Two more Fokkers were acquired and sent to Nicaragua. Marine cargo operations made military history. Three Fokkers, making six flights in one day, carried 9,654 pounds of freight on 10 February 1928. As larger Ford three-engined transports were also received, the figures shot even higher. During the week ending 11 August 1928 the squadrons hauled 68,614 pounds. In the week ending 20 October 1928 the Nicaragua marines made 209 flights, mostly freight hauls, using 20 planes (3 Fokkers, 6 OC's, 7 OL-8's, 4 O2U-1's). Even with the two Fords under repair in Panama, 63,252 pounds of cargo were carried.

In the Pacific

The first Marine aviators ever to serve west of San Francisco were 10 pilots and 90 enlisted men of Flight L, 4th Squadron, who reached Guam 17 March 1921 under the command of Lieut. Donald E. Keyhoe, who was relieved by Captain George W. Martin upon arrival. Flying N-9's, HS2L's, and F5L's (all seaplanes), Marine aviators did outpost duty on Guam for ten years. They were withdrawn 24 February 1931 and did not return until F4U's of MAG-21 arrived slightly over 13 years later.

Most of the Squadron had its outpost service interrupted for duty still farther west. In early 1927 a Chinese civil war threatened foreigners in Shanghai, Peking and other cities, as the Nationalist troops of Chiang Kai-shek began moving against the Northern war lords. Four regiments of marines were rushed to China, where they were organized as the 3d Brigade under command of Brig. General Smedley D. Butler. As aviation components a headquarters detachment and a fighter squadron were dispatched from San Diego under Major Francis T. Evans.

Meanwhile, on 11 April 4 officers and 94 men of the Guam squadron were shipped to Shanghai. The Guam and Stateside squadrons arrived 3 May only

to find that arrangements had not been completed with any Chinese government for use of a landing field. All sailed away in *Chaumont* the next day
and languished for six weeks at the naval station at Olongapo, P.I. (As Major
Brainard pointed out in hearing on the 1929 Naval Appropriations Bill, the
Marines wouldn't have needed a landing field or anybody's permission if they
had had a carrier.) [23]

During the next year and a half the three reorganized squadrons[24]—
usually a total of 15 pilots and about 150 other personnel—flew 3,818 sorties,
mostly reconnaissance around Tientsin, to keep an eye on the Chinese adver-
saries. This time there was no Boxer Rebellion.

The Marine flyers never fired a shot in anger, although they had seven
planes holed, but their state of readiness was the subject of a commendation
which Brig. General Butler sent to Lieut. Colonel Turner:[25]

> Our aircraft squadrons . . . have not been surpassed in their efficiency.
> Not only did they never fail immediately and successfully to respond to
> all calls, but they maintained themselves in the open for nearly eighteen
> months and at all times in readiness. . . . their performance at all times
> was brilliant. . . . there has not been one fatality or serious injury.[26]

Aviation's age of exploration found some marines participating. One of
the pilots in the 1926 Byrd North Pole Expedition was Captain Alton N.
Parker USMCR, a World War I naval aviator who transferred to the Marine
Corps Reserve. When Commander Byrd went to the south in 1929 Parker was
with him again, and on 5 December the marine became the first pilot to fly
over the Antarctic continent—the unexplored regions to the east of King Edward VII Land—showing, said Byrd, "a high degree of courage in flying far
from base over water and ice." He was awarded the DFC.

Three marines, Master Tech. Sergeant Victor H. Czegka, Gunnery Sergeant Kennard F. Bubier and Mess Sergeant Alphonse Carbone accompanied
the Antarctic Expedition and were awarded Navy Crosses. Sergeant Czegka
received another Navy Cross for the Second Byrd Antarctic Expedition (1933–
35).

Death of Turner

Turner took over again as OinC on 10 May 1929. He served until 28
October 1931, when he died of injuries suffered two days earlier. Landing at

---

[23] Hearings in the House and Senate, Naval Appropriations Bill 1929, pp 697–
705.

[24] Eventually redesignated VF-6M, VO-10M, VS-1M.

[25] Turner had assumed command of the "Asiatic" aviators in August 1927.

[26] One story concerning the legendary General Butler was born at Tientsin
during an exhibition of stunting. Captain James T. Moore zoomed over the crowds,
went into a spectacular climbing roll, lost both the wings off his plane and parachuted
into a moat in front of the stands. "Trust Smedley," a lady spectator commented.
"He always puts on a wonderful show."

Gonaives, Haiti, in a new Sikorsky amphibian, Turner impetuously shoved aside a sergeant and jumped out to inspect the damage caused by the plane's left wheel sinking two feet in the soft sand. He forgot to allow for the list as he walked under the propeller, which cleanly severed the right side of his face. Despite his appalling wound, Turner was somehow able to walk unassisted into the dispensary. Doctors said it was a miracle he lived two days.

Turner at 49 had been about to be promoted to brigadier general, a rank no other aviator attained until eight years later. He was the one-hundred-fourth Marine aviator to meet a violent death.

The middle decade served to give the Marine flyers "a sense of the ground" and to breed the mutual confidence between air and ground which is indispensable to effective tactical aviation. The combat experiences of the twenties came in handy in the forties—the young pilots who fought in Nicaragua turned up in World War II as group and wing commanders.

Marine aviators made their last flights on 22 December 1932, and were withdrawn from Nicaragua along with the remnants of the 2d Brigade the following month, leaving the policing of the country to the Marine-trained Guardia Nacional. The period 1930–32 witnessed the further development of aerial transport and the emergence of short-wave radio—a Ford transport arrived with the first set in early 1931.

The Thirties

Roy Geiger succeeded Turner as OinC and held the office for the four-year term 6 November 1931 to 29 May 1935. He in turn was succeeded by Ross Rowell, who served from 30 May 1935 to 10 March 1939. Rowell was followed by Ralph J. Mitchell,[27] who had entered aviation in 1921, six years after his graduation from the Naval Academy, and had commanded the Nicaragua squadrons in 1931. Mitchell's four-year term carried him through the first 15 months of World War II.

These were the three senior officers[28] of Marine aviation during the war

---

[27] Ralph Johnson Mitchell was born in Connecticut 25 September 1891. Naval Academy 1915. First lieutenant 1916, captain 1917, major (temporary) 1918. Served at MB, Guam, in World War I. Graduate of Air Corps Tactical School 1927, Army Command and General Staff School 1928. Major (permanent) 1928. Awarded DFC for service in Nicaragua 1929–31. Graduate of Naval War College 1933. Lieutenant colonel 1934, colonel 1939, brigadier general 1942, major general 1942. Upon vacating office of Director of Aviation, Mitchell assumed command of 1st MAW, which he held April 1943 to June 1945. Commander, Aircraft, Solomons, November 1943 to March 1944 (awarded Navy DSM). Additional duty as Commander Marine Aircraft, South Pacific, April 1943 to June 1944, and Commander Aircraft, Northern Solomons, 15 June 1944 to 4 June 1945. Awarded Army DSM, Army Legion of Merit, Navy Legion of Merit. Retired 1 May 1948.

[28] In Marine Corps seniority (commissioning as second lieutenant): Rowell 1906, Geiger 1909, Mitchell 1915. As aviator: Geiger 1917, Mitchell 1921, Rowell 1923. Geiger served two years as an enlisted man (1907–1909).

against Japan, and we shall meet them again and again in the pages of this book.

Throughout the Depression of the early thirties and the gradual recovery of the last half of the decade Marine aviation, like all the arms of all the services, operated on a starvation budget. The arrival of even half a dozen new planes—such as Boeing's F4B-4 fighter (1934), Chance Vought's SB2U-1 dive bomber (1934), or Brewster's F2A-1 fighter (1936)—was something to marvel at. The Marine aviators were the last to get the new planes (a condition that obtained until the closing months of World War II).

An idea of how hard was the core of Marine aviation, particularly before Munich (September 1938), may be gathered from the roster of pilots:

1931	129	1936	145
1932	132	1937	176
1933	133	1938	217
1934	138	1939	227
1935	138	1940	245[29]

Fleet Marine Force

For the Marine Corps the most notable event of the 1930's was the establishment on 8 December 1933 of the Fleet Marine Force (FMF). This took the Marines out of the "expeditionary forces" category and committed them to an overriding wartime mission: the seizure of bases for naval operations. The peacetime mission was just as important: the preparation and education for the wartime job, which entailed a general overhauling of the Marine Corps Schools.[30]

In other words, the Marine Corps shifted from a simple, rough-and-ready gang, which could fight banana wars or serve the Army as infantry, to a specialized organization with a primary mission. The Marines seized their new assignment with gusto, and if they were not the only service dealing in amphibious warfare, they were its most sincere practitioners. The skeptics could (and did) say, after reading the gloomy details of Gallipoli's failure, that it was impossible to land and stay landed in the face of heavy enemy opposition, but the Marines had their assignment and they worked on it.

The result was what the British military historian, Major General J. F. C. Fuller, calls "In all probability . . . the most far-reaching tactical innovation of the war."

. . . It is as well to outline the tactics now generally applied to these many island assaults. . . . First, the objective to be assaulted was bombed and bombarded, and under this protective fire the assaulting forces moved

---

[29] As of 30 June. By the end of 1940 there were 425.

[30] Jeter A. Isely and Philip A. Crowl, *The U.S. Marines and Amphibious War* (Princeton University Press, 1951), p 45.

across the water in three waves or echelons. First came a line of rocket-firing landing craft. . . . Next . . . "alligators"—cannon-armed amphibious tanks—moved forward to seize the beaches. Lastly came the troop-carrying landing craft, bearing infantry, artillery, and engineers, to give weight to the assault and to occupy, clean up and consolidate the ground gained.[31]

The establishment of the Fleet Marine Force placed the Marine Corps in the fleet organization "as an integral part thereof, subject to the orders, for tactical employment, of the Commander-in-Chief U.S. Fleet." When not assigned to the fleet the Marine Corps command was to be exercised by the Commandant, who remained responsible directly to the Secretary of the Navy. Finally, the Corps had outflanked the ever-present danger that it might be relegated to nothing except guard duty and other secondary tasks.

Aviation in the Fleet Marine Force

The development of the Fleet Marine Force brought about many changes in the organization of Marine Corps aviation. Aircraft Squadrons, East Coast Expeditionary Forces, was redesignated Aircraft One, Fleet Marine Force, and Aircraft Squadrons, West Coast Expeditionary Forces, became Aircraft Two, Fleet Marine Force. (The designation of the Forces on each coast as wings did not occur until 1941.) When detached for expeditions, the Forces took the name of the organization with which they operated; e.g., Aircraft, 2d Marine Brigade.[32]

In June 1935 aviation was taken from the Division of Operations and Training at Headquarters Marine Corps and established as an independent section under the Major General Commandant.[33] On 1 April 1936 the OinC (Rowell) became the Director of Marine Corps Aviation, which acquired division status.

The Director served as an adviser to the Commandant on all aviation matters, and as a liaison officer between the Marine Corps and the Navy's Bureau of Aeronautics. Unlike the Marine Corps infantry and artillery, which drew their supplies from both Army and Navy (in addition to furnishing much of their own), Marine aviation depended on the Navy for its planes and all other aviation equipment.

In January 1939 the Navy's General Board drafted Marine aviation's mission:

Marine Aviation is to be equipped, organized and trained primarily for the support of the Fleet Marine Force in landing operations and in

---

[31] *The Second World War*, p 207.

[32] MarCorps Order No. 67, 20 December 1933, quoted from Captain Smith's *Aviation Organization in the U.S. Marine Corps, 1912–1945*, p 12.

[33] Hq memo 1165 AD-37-kk, 5 June 1935—Status of Aviation Section.

support of troop activities in the field; and secondarily as replacement squadrons for carrier-based naval aircraft.[34]

The secondary mission which had been long advocated[35]—replacements for carrier aircraft—was a development of the first carrier-basing of Marine squadrons. Captain William J. Wallace's VS-14M went on board *Saratoga* 2 November 1931, and on the same day VS-15M (Lieut. William O. Brice as commanding officer) was stationed in *Lexington*.[36] These two squadrons stayed on board three years, until 14 November 1934, during which time about 60 of the 100 Marine aviators had carrier duty.[37]

Unfortunately, the U.S. had only the two carriers, plus the old converted collier *Langley*. The Marines never had carriers of their own (as Major Brainard advocated in 1928) until the last year of the war when they were assigned escort carriers (CVE's) for operational use. Thus, during most of World War II, the Marines were restricted in their support of amphibious operations, as we shall see, to those landings which were within fighter range of bases already won. Otherwise, aviation operations chiefly concerned base defense, to which the Marine Corps devoted only about one third of its efforts. It should be added, hastily, that the defense of Guadalcanal and Okinawa was just about the most important cause anyone could undertake in these first and last offensives of World War II.

In June 1940 Congress authorized the Navy's 10,000-plane program, with Marine aviation's allotment 1,167. Plans were drawn for the establishment of four groups of 11 squadrons each. After the landing exercises in 1941, the Commanding General, Atlantic Amphibious Force, decided that a single division making an amphibious landing required 12 fighter, 8 dive-bomber, 2 observation and 4 utility squadrons. But so many squadrons were a long time in accruing.

The 1st and 2d Marine Aircraft Wings (MAW) were commissioned in July 1941, but when war came five months later there was still only one group in each wing—MAG-11 at Quantico and MAG-21 mostly at Ewa on the island of Oahu, where it had been since January. The entire aviation organization consisted of 13 squadrons and 251 planes of all types, including 15 of the 1st MAW that were "combat worthy" in the estimation of a 1944 historian.

In the following table V equals aircraft (heavier-than-air); M equals Marine; F equals fighter; SB equals scout bomber; J equals utility; R equals

---

[34] Memo Major General Field Harris to SecNav 8 April 1946, serial AA-213 dek/DA-044949. Original 1939 document not found.

[35] Cunningham told the General Board 7 January 1919 marines should be trained so as to be able to fly off carriers "if required."

[36] Captain Walter G. Farrell, CO VS-14M, 3 July 1934 to November 1934. Captain Field Harris, CO VS-15M, 3 January 1933 to November 1934.

[37] Memo Captain Field Harris USMC to Lieut. Commander Schoeffel USN 30 March 1936.

transport; O equals observation. For a more complete glossary, see the foreword on abbreviations.

MARINE CORPS AVIATION, 6 DECEMBER 1941
Director: Colonel Ralph J. Mitchell

1st Marine Aircraft Wing, Brig. Gen. Roy S. Geiger, Quantico
Wing Hq   1 JRB-2, 1 SBC-4

MAG-11, Lieut. Colonel Harold D. Campbell. Group Hq   2 SBD-1

VMF-111[38]	15 F4F-3A,	2 SNJ-3	Major Thomas J. Walker Jr.
VMF-121[38]	20 F4F-3,	2 SNJ-3	Major Samuel S. Jack
VMO-151[38]	12 SBC-4		Major Thomas C. Green
VMSB-131	18 SB2U-3,	5 spares	Captain Paul Moret
VMSB-132	19 SBD		Major Albert D. Cooley
VMJ-152	1 JO-2,	3 J2F-4	Major Thomas J. McQuade
	2 R3D,	1 J2F-1	

2d Marine Aircraft Wing, Brig. Gen. Ross E. Rowell, San Diego
Wing Hq[39]

MAG-21, Lieut. Colonel Claude A. Larkin, Ewa, T.H.

VMF-211	12 F4F-3	at Wake	Major Paul A. Putnam
	10 F4F-3,	1 SNJ at Ewa	
VMF-221	14 F2A-3	in *Saratoga*	Major Verne J. McCaul
VMO-251[40]			Captain Elliott E. Bard
VMSB-231	18-SB2U-3	in *Lexington*	Major C. J. Chappell Jr.
	7 SB2U-3	at Ewa	
VMSB-232	19 SBD-1,	3 SBD-2 at Ewa	Major Ira L. Kimes
VMJ-252	2 R3D-2,	1 JO-2 at Ewa	Major Perry K. Smith
	2 J2F-4,	1 SB2U-3	
	1 JRS-1,	1 SBD-1	

Virgin Islands, Base Air Detachment-3

VMS-3	7 J2F-4,	1 JRF	Major Roger T. Carleson

Total planes, 204[41]

---

[38] On maneuvers at New Bern, N.C. Returned to Quantico 9 December.

[39] No record has been found which indicates how many planes were at San Diego in wing headquarters, if any. The same is true of group headquarters at Ewa.

[40] Commissioned 1 December at Naval Air Station, San Diego. No record of any planes received by 6 December.

[41] Available records show only 204 planes in the Marine organization as of 6 December 1941, as compared to 251 compiled in Hq USMC Historical Division in 1944.

CHAPTER THREE

Wake Island's Sixteen Days

WHEN WORLD WAR II flared across the broad, blue expanse of the Pacific, some 8,000 U.S. marines were serving in that area where more than 400,000 would meet the enemy before the embers died out nearly four years later. About 3,500 were trapped in the Philippines, where they had been recently evacuated from China; the rest were on Oahu, in the Hawaiian Islands, on board ships, at Midway, Samoa, Wake and Guam, in numbers that varied from inadequate to pitiful.

As noted in the previous chapter, the Marine Corps air arm, as a functional part of naval aviation, had had some limited experience in the farther reaches of the Pacific. From their carrier experience in the thirties Marine aviators also knew the Pacific from the air.

But the coming of World War II found only one Marine air group in the Pacific: MAG-21, which had reached Oahu 11 months earlier as 2d MAG. Its commanding officer, Lieut. Colonel C. A. (Sheriff) Larkin,[1] was the highest-ranking Marine flyer west of San Diego, with headquarters at the Ewa mooring mast. At Ewa Colonel Larkin's 48 planes consisted of: 10 F4F-3's and 1 SNJ of the rear echelon of VMF-211; 8 assorted utility planes of VMJ-252 (Major P. K. Smith); 22 SBD dive bombers of VMSB-232 (Major I. L. Kimes); and 7 SB2U-3 spares which had been part of the equipment left behind by VMSB-231. The lone plane to escape was an R3D-2 transport under repair at Ford Island.

---

[1] Claude Arthur Larkin was born in Garfield, Washington, 21 June 1891. Attended University of Washington and Trinity College, Dublin, Ireland. Enlisted December 1915, commissioned July 1917. First lieutenant 1917, captain (temporary) 1918. Served in Cuba with "Horse Marines." Designated naval aviator 1930. Major 1934, lieutenant colonel 1938. Served in Haiti, China, Virgin Islands. For a short time prior to World War II was assistant naval attaché and assistant naval attaché for air in London and Cairo in course of around-the-world inspection tour of Allied facilities. Senior Marine aviator in Pacific for first eight months of World War II. CO MAG-21 (awarded Legion of Merit). Colonel 1942. CO 4th MBDAW August to November 1942. Brigadier general 1943. CG 3d MAW December 1943 to April 1944 and August to December 1944. CG MASP May–June 1944. CG Marine Fleet Air, West Coast, March to July 1945. Major general 1945. CG 1st MAW August to November 1945. Awarded Bronze Star and Gold Star in lieu of second award of Legion of Merit. Retired March 1946.

More than half of Larkin's combat strength had just been dispatched westward when war broke out. Eighteen dive bombers of VMSB-231 (Major C. J. Chappell Jr.) were on board *Lexington,* being ferried to garrison Midway with its first combat planes. The only squadron with new planes was VMF-211 (Major Paul A. Putnam), whose advance echelon of 12 pilots flew Grumman F4F-3's on board *Enterprise* 28 November for transfer to the new airstrip at Wake Island.

Wake Island—which is actually a wishbone-shaped atoll of three islands named Wake, Wilkes and Peale—was named for the master of a British trading schooner who "discovered" the lonely mid-Pacific atoll in 1796. In fact, it had already had many names, the first of which was San Francisco, given it by a Spanish explorer named Alvaro de Mendaña who landed there in 1586. The first American survey was made in 1840 by Commodore Charles Wilkes, but it was not claimed in the name of the United States until 1898, when a Philippine Expeditionary transport paused to hoist a flag. Jurisdiction of the long-neglected atoll passed to the Navy Department in 1934, and the following year Pan American Airways first brought Wake to wide public notice by choosing it as a stop on its course to the Orient. A hotel was built to accommodate Wake's overnight flying-boat passengers.

In 1938 the Navy's Hepburn Board recommended that $7,500,000 be spent on Wake to develop it as an airbase for long-range patrol-plane reconnaissance. Work did not begin until 1941. By that time Admiral Husband E. Kimmel, Commander in Chief, Pacific (CinCPac), was worried about the defense of this outpost located 2,000 miles west of Honolulu, 1,300 east of Guam. On 18 April he wrote prophetically to Admiral Harold R. Stark, Chief of Naval Operations (CNO):

> To deny Wake to the enemy, without occupying it ourselves, would be difficult; to recapture it if the Japanese should seize it in the early period of hostilities, would require operations of some magnitude. Since the Japanese Fourth Fleet (based in the mandated islands) includes transports and troops with equipment especially suited for landing operations, it appears not unlikely that one of the initial operations of the Japanese may be directed against Wake.
>
> If Wake be defended, then for the Japanese to reduce it would require extended operations of their naval force in an area where we might be able to get at them; thus affording us opportunity to get at naval forces with naval forces. We should try, by every possible means, to get the Japanese to expose naval units. In order to do this, we must provide objectives that require such exposure.

The first military force to arrive on Wake was the advance detail of the 1st Marine Defense Battalion (5 officers, 173 marines and sailors) which came off USS *Regulus* 19 August 1941. They found the islands of Wake, Peale and

Wilkes not the bare, sandy coral which characterizes most atolls of the Central Pacific, but an area interlaced with big boulders, stubby trees and thick underbrush. Out of this growth the 1,200 civilian workmen had hacked a narrow airstrip, 5,000 by 200 feet, and had almost completed a road net.

Major James P. S. Devereux arrived at Wake 15 October to assume command of the Marine detachment. Besides shoveling out the gun emplacements for three 3-inch AA batteries and three 5-inch seacoast batteries, the marines refueled by hand the Army B-17's which were beginning to be flown across the Pacific to the Philippines in a frantic effort to prepare that westernmost American area against the threat of oncoming war. It was not until 2 November that USS *Castor* arrived, bringing 9 more officers and 200 men to fill out the 1st Defense Battalion's thin ranks. On 29 November the marines on Wake got their first evidence that combat aircraft were on the way: the aircraft tender *Wright* arrived with Major Walter L. J. Bayler, a communications expert from MAG-21's staff, and Lieut. Robert J. Conderman with a provisional service detachment of 47 marines drawn from MAG-21. Also on board *Wright* were the new island commander, Commander Winfield S. Cunningham, nine Navy officers and enough bluejackets to bring to 58 the initial detachment for establishment of the naval air base. These were unarmed, as were Captain Henry S. Wilson of the Army Signal Corps and five soldiers, who had arrived with him to man an Army communications radio van for assisting B-17's en route to the Philippines.[2]

Major Putnam and his 11 pilots of VMF-211 flew their Grumman F4F-3's off *Enterprise* on the morning of 4 December and reached the Wake airstrip about two hours later. They found the strip long enough but too narrow to permit more than one plane to take off at a time. Fueling had to be done by hand pumps. No shelter or aircraft revetments had been built. Parking areas were rough and unfinished; a plane could be damaged when it was simply being taxied or pushed off the airstrip to permit another plane to land.

Worst of all, the pilots, who had been used to the antiquated F3F biplanes hitherto consigned to Marine aviators, knew little about their Wildcat planes, engines or propellers, and their instruction manuals were to be destroyed the first day. Neither were there experienced airplane or engine mechanics among Conderman's men; all except two master sergeants were ordnancemen—an unhappy circumstance that was to plague not only the Wake defenders but also the Hawaiian remainder of MAG-21's service-squadron personnel, who were all engineers and no ordnancemen.[3]

The day before the war began Wake had 38 officers and 486 enlisted personnel, as follows:

---

[2] Figures from Brig. General J. P. S. Devereux USMC (Ret). They differ slightly from those given in other sources.

[3] It was expected that the mechanics would be flown in with a two-seater squadron.

	Officers	Enlisted
VMF-211 and attachments	12	49[4]
1st Defense Battalion detachment	15	373
Naval Air Station	10	58
Army Signal Corps	1	5
USS Triton (landed for medical attention)		1

The status of the Defense Battalion detachment on the eve of war is best described by the Marine Corps historian, Lieut. Colonel Robert D. Heinl Jr., in *The Defense of Wake,* a carefully detailed monograph published in 1947 by Marine Corps Headquarters:

> The ground defenses, embodying the complete artillery of a defense battalion, had by dint of unceasing 12-hour working days been emplaced, and some protective sandbagging and camouflage accomplished. To man these weapons, which even by the economical 1941 tables of organization required 43 officers and 939 enlisted, the First Defense Battalion detachment had but 15 officers and 373 enlisted. In terms of effect this meant that one three-inch antiaircraft battery was entirely without personnel, and that the other two batteries could each man but three of their four guns—therefore, that of twelve three-inch guns on the island, only six were active weapons. Only one three-inch battery (D), had its full allowance of fire-control equipment; Battery E had a director but no height-finder, and was thereby forced to rely for target-altitude data upon telephoned information from Battery D. Less than half the minimum personnel were on Wake to man the machine guns, both ground and anti-aircraft. Despite existing plans for its eventual provision, no radar, either fire-control or early-warning, had reached Wake, and the searchlight battery did not have its sound-locators to pick up the noise of approaching aircraft. Only the five-inch seacoast batteries were at or near authorized strengths, and even these, like all other units, were devilled by unending minor shortages of tools, spare parts and miscellaneous ordnance items.

There was no radar on Wake Island. According to one story, two radar sets were left on the dock at Pearl Harbor because of a clerical error. Another version has it that the radars were left in favor of a steamroller, and "Jimmy" Devereux, running for Congress in 1950, said, "They sent us garbage trucks when we needed radar!"

But after thorough investigation the writer is convinced no radar was left on the docks when *Wright* sailed for Wake. If radar had been taken along it would have been useless without trained operators to man it, and such operators were virtually nonexistent in those antediluvian days of radar.[5]

---

[4] Two of the enlisted men, Tech. Sergeant William J. Hamilton and Staff Sergeant Robert O. Arthur, were pilots.

[5] The writer first heard the radar story from the late Commodore Dixie Kiefer on board his carrier *Ticonderoga* on 18 December 1944. Kiefer was executive officer

Obviously, Major Putnam could not keep all his planes and pilots in the air all the time. Only with radar could Wake, isolated as it was, anticipate a raid in time to throw its full strength into the air to meet that raid. Even before word of the attack on Pearl Harbor came early in the morning of 8 December,[6] Major Putnam had four planes in the air on morning patrol. When the first patrol landed and heard of the attack, a second patrol consisting of Captain Henry Talmage Elrod, Lieuts. Carl R. Davidson and John F. Kinney, and Tech. Sergeant William Hamilton, took to the air. It seemed most likely that an attack might come from the south, where the Japanese-held Marshall Islands lay only about 600 nautical miles away.

It was while this patrol was out that the first Japanese attack came, at 1158.

But Elrod's patrol was at 12,000 feet on the north side of the island when the first Japanese bombers—36 twin-engined planes of the type later labeled Betty—came in undetected from the south through a rain squall at about 1,500 feet.[7] It was Air Attack Force No. 1 of the 24th Flotilla, based at Roi, one of the islands of Kwajalein Atoll, 620 miles southward in the Marshalls, and it met no air opposition when it struck. When the bombing and strafing had ended seven of Wake's eight planes on the ground were burned or blasted into uselessness, including the only two with self-sealing gasoline tanks. The eighth plane could be repaired. Tharin smashed his prop into some debris while taxiing a few minutes later. After one raid Wake was reduced to four planes and some pieces.

In this first, devastating raid, VMF-211 suffered the heaviest casualties. Twenty were killed or would die of wounds before morning, including pilots Graves, Holden, and Conderman; 11 others were wounded, including 4 pilots. Three of the latter could still fly, but Lieut. Webb was gravely hurt.

That was not all. The malfunctioning air-ground radio set was badly damaged; the two 12,500-gallon aviation gasoline tanks were afire and flooding the whole VMF-211 area with flames; numerous gasoline drums were afire; most of the oxygen was destroyed; the aviation spares and tools had been riddled and partially burned.

The First Invasion Attempt

The defenders of Wake prepared for more raids they knew would come. The aircraft revetments, which would have been completed if the enemy had delayed his raid until 1400, were finished. Burnt-out planes were scavenged for

---

of *Wright* during its last trip to Wake. The following have been kind enough to write letters contributing to the writer's conclusions: Captain Leonard Frisco USN, navigator of *Wright;* Captain W. S. Cunningham USN; Chief Boatswain Charles B. Parr USN (Ret), *Wright's* assistant First Lieutenant supervising loading; Commander P. S. Lucas USNR, her communications officer; and others.

[6] East longitude time. Wake is 22 hours ahead of Hawaii.

[7] Altitude estimate by Colonel Frank C. Tharin. Other estimates: Putnam 1,000; Devereux 2,500; Heinl 7,000.

spare parts. Battery positions were further camouflaged and sandbagged; more foxholes were dug. The most important trunk lines were dug underground.

In the early morning of the second day the four F4F's began scouting again, with particular attention to the sectors to the south.[8] They returned to report that no enemy task force was yet in sight. At 1145 the day's raid began, but this time planes were in the air. Lieut. David D. Kliewer and Sergeant Hamilton cut down one of them, which flamed into the sea from 13,000 feet.[9] Antiaircraft shot down another, and several others were hit—14, according to one Japanese document. But damage was again heavy: the contractor's hospital was burned out; the radio station was wrecked along with most of the Navy's equipment there; 4 marines and 55 civilians were killed. On the 10th, 26 bombers came over at 1045. This time Captain Elrod shot down two of them, but the bombers hit a cache of 125 tons of dynamite on Wilkes Island, which in turn set off all the 3-inch and 5-inch ready ammunition on the island, seriously crippling an AA battery and a seacoast battery.[10]

During the early days of Wake's travail plans deeply affecting the outpost were going forward: (1) at Pearl Harbor, where Admiral Kimmel's staff proposed its relief; (2) at Truk, where Admiral Inouye's Fourth Fleet officers plotted the atoll's capture.

When the Japanese struck Pearl Harbor the aircraft carrier *Saratoga* was at San Diego with the 18-plane (F2A) flight echelon of Major Verne J. McCaul's VMF-221 on board. Within 24 hours "*Sara*" was plowing toward Pearl Harbor, where Kimmel's staff was arranging a task force to accompany the carrier to Wake Island. Three heavy cruisers (*Astoria, Minneapolis, San Francisco*) were designated to supply heavy-ship fire power for Task Force 14, which would also include nine destroyers, the seaplane tender-transport *Tangier,* and a fleet oiler, *Neches. Tangier* was loaded at Pearl Harbor with about 300 marines of the 4th Defense Battalion, including two batteries and detachments of two other batteries, plus ground elements of VMF-221. Radar sets were taken on board, along with 21,000 rounds of 3-inch and 5-inch ammunition and 3,000,000 rounds of machine-gun bullets. Due to the delays and confusion and indecisiveness consequent to the Pearl Harbor attack, the task force did not get under way until 1600 of 15 December (on Wake: 16 December).

The Japanese expected to find 1,000 troops and 600 laborers at Wake Island.[11] They figured almost correctly that five American fighter planes were left after the first two days' bombing. Only 450 assault troops were allotted, so it was anticipated that destroyer crews might be needed also to storm the beaches. Rear Admiral Kajioka would command the landing, flying his flag

---

[8] Colonel Putnam denies that these planes flew out 60 to 80 miles, as Heinl says in *The Defense of Wake,* p 17.

[9] Several Wake Island survivors insist that Elrod shot down the first enemy plane. "I'm past arguing," says Putnam.

[10] Heinl, *The Defense of Wake,* p 19.

[11] United States Strategic Bombing Survey (Pacific), Naval Analysis Division, *Interrogations of Japanese Officials,* Vol II, p 371 (Hereinafter cited as USSBS, *Interrogations*); testimony of Captain Tadashi Koyama.

from the light cruiser *Yubari*. His force included also two other light cruisers (*Tatsuta, Tenryu*), six destroyers of Divisions 29 and 30, *Patrol Boats 32* and *33* (old destroyers converted to troop transports, carrying 225 troops each), two medium transports and two submarines.

This force arrived off the southernmost point of Wake Island before daylight of 11 December.[12] Despite heavy surf, boating operations were begun. Shortly after 0500 the three cruisers opened fire, hitting Diesel-oil tanks on Wake near Wilkes Channel; Wake's seacoast guns withheld their fire. When the flagship *Yubari* arrived 4,500 yards offshore, the nearest battery (A) turned loose its guns, after which the cruiser turned heel. But after several misses, *Yubari* caught two shells at 5,500 to 6,000 yards which slowed her down as she started belching smoke and steam. Two more shells hit her at 7,000 yards, slightly aft of the first hits, and *Yubari* was smoking heavily as she disappeared over the horizon.

Meanwhile, Battery L was active on Wilkes Island, where three destroyers, two cruisers and two transports appeared offshore. The leading destroyer, *Hayate*, hit by the third salvo at 0650, exploded violently and broke in two. Within two minutes she sank—the first Japanese surface warship sunk by U.S. naval forces in World War II. The destroyer *Oite* was seen to take a hit before smoke cloaked her whereabouts. Then Lieut. McAlister trained his guns on one of the medium transports, which appeared to be hit before it, too, retired behind the smoke screen. Nine thousand yards offshore, one of the light cruisers, which had swung around to the northwest from its original position, seemed to take a hit from Battery L's 5-inch guns before it retired. Battery B, on the tip of Peale Island, scored one hit on the northernmost destroyer, *Yayoi*, before it joined the retreating cripples.

During this shore-battery action, which lasted about 45 minutes, VMF-211's four senior pilots (Major Putnam, Captains Elrod, Freuler and Tharin) had been airborne, each carrying 100-pound bombs slung under the wings with homemade lugs. Their purpose during the exchange of surface fire had been to intercept whatever aircraft might come to Admiral Kajioka's support.

Then the four Grummans pounced upon the retreating force, bombing and strafing relentlessly. Both the light cruisers were hit, probably by Elrod and Tharin. Freuler dropped one of his small bombs on the stern of *Kongo Maru*, one of the medium transports. One of the converted destroyers (probably *Patrol Boat 33*) appeared also to have been hit, but information is lacking about the extent of the damage. The biggest prize was destroyer *Kisaragi*, which blew up about 0815 in a mighty explosion as one of the relief pilots, Lieut. John Kinney, prepared to attack it, 20 to 30 miles offshore.[13]

---

[12] Causing some hopeful civilians to go down to the beach, baggage in hand. (Information from Lieut. Colonel Kinney, 1948.)

[13] The sinking of *Kisaragi* provides a controversy which may never be settled. At war's end The Joint Army-Navy Assessment Committee (JANAC), which had been set up in 1943 to determine the cause of enemy shipping losses, credited the sinking of the destroyer to Wake's shore batteries. But Japanese sources, including Captain Koyama, say its loss was due to "bombing attacks." In any case,

VMF-211's pilots flew a total of ten sorties, dropped 20 bombs and expended about 20,000 rounds of .50-caliber ammunition. But ships' AA fire cut Elrod's main fuel line, and his plane was totally wrecked as he made the beach just short of the airstrip. Freuler's engine was badly damaged by bullets which pierced his oil cooler and one cylinder.

During this peak of their glory, the defenders of Wake sank two destroyers,[14] damaged seven other ships, and killed several hundred Japanese.[15]

The aviators were heartened by their demonstrable prowess, and would have been even prouder if they had known how much credit Admiral Kajioka gave them in his war diary: "Dec. 11—Wake Island landing after sunset [sic] unsuccessful because of fighter plane opposition. Two destroyers sunk."[16]

About 1600 on 11 December, Lieut. Kliewer claimed sinking a submarine. This is not substantiated by any official enemy records which have come to light, but some of Wake's survivors were led to believe that the claim was correct: after surrender the Americans were questioned at length about a submarine which had evidently failed to turn up from the Wake area.[17]

It was following the successful defense of 11 December that the American public was electrified by the message from Wake: "Send us more Japs!" After the war, Jimmy Devereux denied that any such message had ever been sent, and most historians have accepted the Marine commander's version. Actually, such a message was sent, but it was intended only as code padding and "no intelligent decoder would have considered it" as official, Cunningham's exec stated later.[18]

The raids on Wake left no doubt that the atoll was being softened for another landing. Within four hours of the landing attempt 30 Bettys were over again. Lieuts. Davidson and Kinney sailed into them with the two remaining

---

the explosion which sank the destroyer was delayed, and probably was due to the ship's own depth charges, of which it carried an extra supply. Most sources (*The Defense of Wake*; Samuel Eliot Morison, *The Rising Sun in the Pacific*, p 234) credit her sinking to a bomb planted by Elrod, but Wake's survivors simply don't know.

While JANAC made a notable effort to determine how each Japanese ship was sunk, errors inevitably crept into its analyses which were not corrected before its books were closed in February 1947, and more will be found as records come to light. For an analysis of some of JANAC's demonstrable errors, see Walton L. Robinson, "Who Sank What?", *Infantry Journal*, April 1948, p 48.

[14] The Navy communiqué (No. 2) classed one of the destroyers as a cruiser, as was often the case in ships' identification early in the war.

[15] Heinl's estimate in *The Defense of Wake*, p 28, is 700 killed in this abortive attempt but Captain Tashikazu Ohmae, foremost Japanese naval student of World War II, puts total Japanese losses during Wake Island's 16 days at "nearly 500." (Ohmae letter, 22 November 1951.)

[16] Allied Translation and Interrogation Service (hereinafter cited as ATIS) Document No. 16268, *Japanese Naval War Diary: Naval Directives of Grand Imperial Headquarters*.

[17] Interviews Tharin and Kinney.

[18] Letter Captain Campbell Keene USN to Lieut. Edna Loftus Smith USMCWR, 25 October 1945.

serviceable planes; the former shot down two, and Kinney smoked another. The AA batteries on Peale and Wake, despite their World War I ammunition, sent one more down in flames and left three trailing smoke. The first early morning raid occurred on the 12th, when two four-engined Kawanishi flying boats, flying up from Majuro, 840 nautical miles distant, dropped bombs around the airstrip. Captain Tharin, on morning patrol, shot down one of them. During the morning Lieut. Kinney, who performed engineering marvels throughout the defense of Wake, managed to patch a third plane into a state of serviceability. No noon raid hit Wake on the 12th, and there was no raid at all on the 13th. The breathing spell brought the first hot rations for the embattled defenders— a contribution by Mr. Nathan Dan Teters, boss of the civilian construction workers. One more fighter cracked up while taking off on patrol. Now there were two.

On the 14th there was an early morning raid by the flying boats, and at 1100 the 30 land-based Bettys arrived from Roi. They killed two marines of VMF-211 and wounded another. They also made a direct bomb hit on one of the two remaining planes. Lieut. Kinney, Sergeant Hamilton, and Aviation Machinist's Mate First Class James F. Hesson salvaged its engine two days later to bring another plane from the brink of the graveyard, and by 17 December they had managed to patch up two more: "Engines have been traded from plane to plane, have been junked, stripped, rebuilt and all but created."[19] The actions of Kinney, Hamilton and Hesson epitomized the American flair for improvisation which was such a notable contribution in the early days of the war in many theaters. In Major Putnam's words:

> These three, with the assistance of volunteers among the civilian workmen, did a truly remarkable and almost magical job. With almost no tools and a complete lack of normal equipment, they performed all types of repair and replacement work. They changed engines and propellers from one airplane to another, and even completely built new engines and propellers salvaged from wrecks. They replaced minor parts and assemblies, and repaired damage to fuselages and wings and landing gear; all this in spite of the fact that they were working with new types with which they had had no previous experience and were without instruction manuals of any kind. In the opinion of the squadron commander their performance was the outstanding event of the whole campaign.

On 17 December Commander Cunningham rendered to Pearl Harbor a report on his matériel status: half his trucks and engineering equipment had been destroyed; so had most of his commercial explosives and Diesel oil; machine and blacksmith shops, the building-supplies warehouse and Navy garage were burnt out. Civilian morale was low. Clearly, the relief expedition could arrive none too soon.

On 20 December a Navy PBY landed in the Wake lagoon, the first friendly contact with the outside world, bringing plans for the relief expedition which

---

[19] VMF-211 engineering report.

was now en route to Wake. Among its crew members was an ensign who stepped ashore with his baggage and asked for the Pan American Airways hotel (which bombs had destroyed), thereby affording the defenders a small measure of humor. On its return the PBY carried Major Bayler of MAG-21, later to become famed as "the last man off Wake Island," with reports from Wake's unit commanders. The plane turned its nose toward Pearl Harbor at 0700; at 0850 Wake suffered the heaviest raid to date: 29 bombers covered by 18 fighters. These were not planes from Roi; the carriers *Soryu* and *Hiryu* had been sent in to help soften Wake for the next landing attempt. But the raid was one of the least successful of the major attacks. Three hours later the land-based bombers from Roi arrived—33 of them—and when they departed, Wake's AA defense against enemy air action was reduced to four 3-inch guns of the 12 existing on 8 December. The number of serviceable F4F's was still two.

Such luxury was not long to be enjoyed. On the morning of 22 December Captain Freuler and Lieut. Davidson had the morning patrol when 33 bombers from the two Japanese carriers arrived, escorted by six fighters. Freuler managed to shoot down one of the Zeros, but it was so close that flames from the enemy proved his plane's undoing; flying fragments damaged his controls. As he tried desperately to maneuver his own plane toward the airstrip, Freuler looked around for Davidson and saw a Zero on his tail—Davidson was not seen again. Freuler was shot through the shoulder by another Zero. He crashed his scorched, shattered plane on the field and Wake was without aircraft. The surviving members of VMF-211—by now less than 20 were alive and unwounded—prepared to take their place as infantrymen. So long as they had planes, the aviators had fought well.[20] Now they would continue the fight on foot.

Wake's Fall

For the next landing attempt the Japanese Fourth Fleet commander took few chances. This time Admiral Kajioka was given the Maizuru 2d Special Naval Landing Force of about 1,000 men, sent over from Saipan, plus a reserve of 500 more in ships' landing parties. It was determined, if necessary, to sacrifice the converted destroyers, *Patrol Boats 32* and *33*, by running them aground. The carriers *Soryu* and *Hiryu* (which had been prevented by weather from delivering a scheduled strike against Midway) would provide the softening up, as we have seen, and would be ready in case an American task force contested the capture of Wake. Instead of three cruisers, this time there were nine in command of Rear Admiral Hiroaki Abe, including the new heavies, *Tone* and *Chikuma*, which supported the carriers. Two sister ships replaced the sunken destroyers *Kisaragi* and *Hayate*.

At 2000 on 21 December, the relief expedition from Pearl Harbor was only 627 miles east of Wake. But Rear Admiral Frank Jack Fletcher slowed

---

[20] Koyama: "The American fighter pilots were admired for their skill and bravery." (USSBS, *Interrogations*, Vol II, p 372.)

down to refuel on the 22d, though his destroyers' supply was sufficient.[21] Back at Pearl it was difficult for Admiral Pye (who had relieved Kimmel pending the arrival of Nimitz) to make up his mind to risk what was left of the Pacific Fleet.

On the night of 22 December (21 at Pearl) a compromise was effected: the F2A's of VMF-221 would be flown off at maximum range; *Tangier* would make a speed run into Wake with the marines and their supplies (including radar) while the rest of Task Force 14 retired with Task Force 11, built around *Lexington,* which had been ordered in support of 14. But these orders (which would probably have meant destruction of *Tangier*) were countermanded, and all ships turned to the north or east, leaving Wake to fend for itself. Admiral Halsey, who was covering the northern flank in the vicinity of Midway with *Enterprise* and the rest of Task Force 8, wrote later that he never knew why the force was diverted. "TF 14 could have been at Wake by then, of course, raising hell with the Jap occupation."[22] Many of the pilots on board *Saratoga* sat down and cried when they learned they were not allowed to succor the beleaguered forces on Wake. Heinl, who was on board *Tangier,* reported:

> Reactions varied from astonishment to shame and anger. There were even some staff officers who counselled Admiral Fletcher to disregard orders and make a dash into Wake. They did not know that at this very moment, some four enemy heavy criusers (Cruiser Division 6) were patrolling east of Wake, separated from any Japanese carrier air support by hundreds of miles, a sitting target for the airmen of the *Saratoga;* nor did they know that the Japanese attack force was disposed about Wake with no apparent measures for security against surface attack. Had all this been known, the story of Wake might have been very different.[23]

Again the surf was high. But *Patrol Boats 32* and *33* crashed through the darkness and climbed the reef on the south shore of Wake Island. A few minutes later, at about 0245, on 23 December, two barges reached the beach on Wilkes Island. Lieut. Hanna turned his 3-inch AA gun—now serving as antiboat—against *Patrol Boat 33,* killing 7 and wounding 25 while hitting it at least 14 times and breaking its back. Then he turned to *Patrol Boat 32,* nearby, and obtained several hits on it. But the Special Naval Landing Force on board had already jumped ashore without significant casualties. Excepting some men from Hanna's .50-caliber battery, the nearest group of marines to the beached *Patrol Boat 33* were the remnants of VMF-211, who took up positions to cover the single 3-inch antiboat gun against infiltrating attack. Marines of the Uchida Unit began creeping toward the position. Before daylight the VMF-211 area was surrounded, and every man of the one-time squadron was killed or

---

[21] Morison, *The Rising Sun in the Pacific,* p 243, gives fuel tables and average daily consumption.

[22] *Admiral Halsey's Story,* p 84.

[23] Heinl, *The Defense of Wake,* p 39.

wounded except six. Just before dawn Captain Elrod[24] was killed by a Japanese who played dead under a pile of casualties. Also among the dead were ten civilians who had joined the fight, and four marines. The Uchida Unit's casualties during the advance on the deadly 3-inch gun were at least 62,[25] including Lieut. Uchida himself.

The fight spread to Wilkes where the marines resisted bitterly. Japanese dive bombers and cruisers joined the battle during the daylight hours. By their desperate efforts the marines this day killed at least 125 Japanese and wounded as many more. But the fight was hopeless. Commander Cunningham determined at about 0700 that further resistance was useless and ordered the surrender. Major Devereux required more than six hours to make contact with all the pockets which were still fighting—Putnam felt his own handful of survivors "was still going strong."[26] It was 1330 before Devereux reached Wilkes Island. Only then did he learn that the dirty, grubby marines who came out of the bush to meet him had finally managed to exterminate or take prisoner all the Japanese who had landed on their island: 4 officers and 90 men.[27]

In his report which the PBY took away two days before the end, Major Putnam wrote perhaps the best farewell for the defeated on Wake Island—their legacy until they were again heard from nearly four years later: "All hands have behaved splendidly and held up in a manner of which the Marine Corps may well tell."

American prisoners of war were evacuated to the Empire about three weeks after the surrender, excepting about 100 civilian workmen who were retained to maintain the island's facilities. Following heavy carrier strikes and naval bombardment on 6–7 October 1943, Rear Admiral Sakaibara IJN, the island commander, ordered these civilians executed. The Admiral was tried as a war criminal and executed 19 June 1947.

Picking Up the Pieces

Pearl and Wake had cost Marine aviation the forward echelon of one squadron (which was immediately reconstituted at Ewa), 59 planes (nearly one third of the total), and some morale. When he arrived to take command of the Pacific Fleet on Christmas Day, Admiral Nimitz found Pearl Harbor steeped in gloom; among the staff he took over there were "too many people and too much pessimism," as he put it to an interviewer three years later.[28]

From the available records, it appears that "Sheriff" Larkin had little time for pessimism in the frantic days of December. On the 8th he became host to an Army pursuit squadron of 12 planes and 183 officers and men, who

---

[24] Whose performance on Wake was the first to gain for a Marine airman the Medal of Honor—though the facts to substantiate the award were not available until after the war, and it was not made until 1946.

[25] Heinl, *The Defense of Wake*, p 50.

[26] Interview, 1948.

[27] Heinl, *The Defense of Wake*, p 59.

[28] Robert Sherrod, *On to Westward* (1945), p 229.

stayed with him at Ewa until Wheeler Field could be fixed up. On the 10th, VMSB-231 returned from *Lexington,* stayed a week, then took off over-water for Midway.[29] VMF-221 arrived in *Saratoga* and had to be based at Ford Island overnight before returning to "*Sara*" for the abortive relief expedition to Wake.[30]

Larkin was cheered by news that the 1st MAW was on the way from the East Coast, and he started enlarging Ewa to take care of it. By 19 December construction had begun on an east-west runway of 3,200 feet and a north-south runway of 3,000 feet. The single, old 3,000-foot strip was lengthened to 4,200. New buildings went up which effectively dispersed the station's activities.[31]

Back in San Diego, Rowell could view events with a philosophical calm: "It may sound insane, but I am grateful for every plane destroyed on the ground. It will help us to build up a fine fighting outfit in the long run. The house is not on fire yet." He told Larkin to split his squadrons four ways, not to risk more than three or four experienced officers in a single squadron, lest the Marines make "the RAF error of washing out the major portion of our talent in the first battle. If we fail to prepare for a long war now, we shall never win it.[32]

Larkin still had only five planes at Ewa a month after Pearl Harbor. Whatever he had left had been sent to Midway, where Lieut. Colonel William J. Wallace on 1 March 1942 reorganized VMF-221 and VMSB-231 into MAG-22. On the same date MAG-23 was formed at Ewa by Major Raymond C. Scollin with two squadrons, and MAG-24 (Major I. L. Kimes) with two others. In April Wallace came back to Ewa and took over 23, and Kimes, after a brief jaunt to the South Pacific with a small advance echelon of MAG-24, went to Midway to assume command of 22. Actually, all of these groups and their squadrons struggled along almost without aircraft for several months; whatever could be spared was sent to Midway or elsewhere.

Larkin even lost his salvaged F4F's to the Navy, which left him only a few overhauled SBD-1's and SBD-2's which were "no good but gave us something to fly." When some new Buffaloes arrived Larkin sent Captain John L. Smith (VMF-223) and Captain Robert E. Galer (VMF-224) with ten of them, along with a dozen pilots and about 25 enlisted men, up to Barking Sands on the island of Kauai to practice night-fighter interception. They were the U.S. insurance against a raid on the Hawaiian Islands, of which there had been one (by a couple of four-engined flying boats on the night of 3–4 March). The raid was harmless, but Smith and Galer kept their bits of squadrons at the northern outpost of the Hawaiians until after Midway had decided the fate of the Pacific. Then they left for Guadalcanal.

---

29 See p 51.
30 See p 39.
31 Letter Larkin to Rowell, 19 December 1941.
32 Letter Rowell to Larkin, 16 December 1941.

Spreading Out

Geiger's 1st Wing had moved—lock, stock and aircraft—to the West Coast by 24 December. But the new Commander in Chief (CominCh) canceled the orders which had it proceeding to Ewa in January. Under the big reorganization of 1 March the Wing's MAG-11 underwent a quadruple amputation to create MAG's 12, 13, 14 and 15.

In Washington, Admiral Stark feared immediately after Pearl Harbor that Midway might have to be written off, but hoped to save Samoa, Johnston and Palmyra.[33] Admiral E. J. King, who relieved Stark 31 December, ordered Admiral Nimitz, the new CinCPac, to hold the Midway–Samoa–Fiji–Brisbane line "at all costs."

On Christmas Day, King, preparatory to taking over from Stark, asked the Chief of Naval Operations War Plans Division to make a study of the matter of a fueling base for ships passing through the Panama Canal from the Atlantic Coast to Australia. Borabora, an island of the Tuamotu group, 140 miles northwest of Tahiti, thus became the first selection among the new islands on which advanced bases were to be built—and also the farthest to the rear of any likely combat, being considerably closer to Lima than to Tokyo. A construction detachment sailed from Charleston 27 January, accompanied by 4,376 Army garrison personnel, and reached Borabora 17 February. An agreement with the French regarding use of the island was signed six days later.

Along the route to Australia there were other islands to be occupied and defended. Johnston, Palmyra, Christmas, Canton, Aitutakai, Samoa, Tongatabu and Fiji were already in American or British hands, but that was about all that could be said for them. The Navy had started the development of Johnston, Palmyra, Canton and Samoa before the war, and the Marines' 7th Defense Battalion had been on Samoa since 18 March 1941, the first unit of the Fleet Marine Force to serve in the Southern Hemisphere. None of the islands had air defenses except Fiji, where 22 British planes were stationed. The immediate problem was to build up the defenses along the island string before the rampaging Japanese cut the lifeline to the Southwest Pacific. Airfields were built on most of these islands as rapidly as possible; Army and Navy planes flew from them as soon as aircraft and fields were available.

The Japanese were doing very well. At a cost of only 29 planes they had knocked out the battle line of the U.S. Fleet at Pearl Harbor. Sinking Britain's *Repulse* and *Prince of Wales* cost only four planes. The capture of Burma, with its annual rice surplus amounting to 4,000,000 tons, was achieved with the loss of only 102 planes and 7,000 Japanese soldiers. At the time of greatest disaster elsewhere the Philippines were hopelessly beset, and their capture was finally achieved at a cost of only 4,100 Japanese soldiers' lives.[34]

---

[33] Morison, *The Rising Sun in the Pacific*, p 219.

[34] Information from Office of Military History, Department of the Army, July 1950.

The Japanese carrier striking force roamed from Hawaii to Ceylon, sinking or damaging 8 battleships, 4 cruisers, 8 destroyers and literally dozens of merchant ships—including 15 off the coast of India during one week of April. Hundreds of American, British and Dutch planes were destroyed (half of them on the ground). Docks, hangars and bases blazed or blew up submissively whenever Japanese flyers released their bombs. This cataclysm across one third of the globe was accomplished without a single ship of the carrier striking force being sunk or damaged by Allied action.

"Indeed," comments the U.S. Strategic Bombing Survey, "the force was seldom sighted and never effectively attacked."[35]

Could the Allies—principally the Americans—catch their breath in time?

Besides Midway, which in Japanese hands could control Pearl Harbor, the Marines were assigned certain other island bases to defend. Most urgent was the need at Samoa, where the 7th Defense Battalion was reinforced 23 January by the 2d Marine Brigade (8th Marines, 10th Marines, 2d Defense Battalion) loaded in four transports and one fleet cargo ship, with an ammunition ship and a fleet oiler. So vital was the movement that Nimitz sent two carriers as escort: Halsey's *Enterprise* force and Fletcher's force formed around *Yorktown*. Even while the Marine reinforcements were en route a Japanese submarine (on 11 January) shelled the Samoa naval station at Pago-Pago, wounding a naval officer and a member of the colorful native Fita Fita Guard.[36]

Except for a few light OS2U seaplanes of the Navy detachment, VS-1-D14, which came out with the reinforcements that reached Samoa 23 January, there was no air defense and none was immediately available. And the airstrip was barely started.

Colonel Thomas J. Walker's MAG-13 had been organized only one week when its first echelon embarked 8 March in *President Garfield* at San Diego. Two days later the second echelon, bringing 19 F4F-3's of VMF-111 (Major Daniel W. Torrey Jr.), left San Diego on board *Procyon*. The Group's dive-bomber squadron, VMO-151, embarked at Norfolk in four ships on 6 April with its ancient SBC-4 biplanes. Upon arrival at Samoa, Major Thomas Green, who brought VMO-151 out, became the Group executive officer, and Major Raymond B. Hurst took command of the Squadron.

The Navy detachment, VS-1-D14, was incorporated into MAG-13 on 22 April, hiking the Group's strength by seven OS2U's, two Grumman Ducks, 8 officers and 68 enlisted men, and marking the first time a naval aviation unit had been attached to a Marine group. A month later, after VMO-151 arrived at Tutuila, the detachment was sent 100 miles northwest to Satapaula on the British Samoa island of Upolu, to join the 7th Defense Battalion, which had been shifted there shortly after the arrival of the 2d Brigade.

North of Samoa, over halfway to Oahu, the island of Palmyra lay athwart the lifeline. Since March 1941 a detachment of the 1st Marine Defense Battal-

---

[35] USSBS, *The Campaigns of the Pacific War*, p 31. (Hereinafter cited as USSBS, *Campaigns*).

[36] *Marine Corps Gazette*, January 1944, p 18.

1. Lieut. Alfred A. Cunningham, about 1913

2. N-9 training plane, 1919

3. Kite balloon, 1918

4. DH-4B, 1920

5. JN-6, 1923

6. Flying field, Nicaragua

7. OD-1, 1929

8. F6C-3, 1930

9. F4B-4, 1933

10. BG-1, 1935

From an officer's album

11. Hsin Ho, China, 1928: A Japanese visitor calls on Captain Moore, Lieut. Colonel Turner and Lieut. Wallace

12. Lieut. Schilt receives Medal of Honor from President Coolidge at the White House, 5 April 1928

13.   Cutting sisal for Ewa's expansion, 1941

14.   The Ewa Mooring Mast, February 1941

15. 19 June 1941

16. 2 December 1941

GROWTH OF EWA

17. 5 April 1944. NAS Barber's Point at top

VISITORS TO EWA

18.   1941 — Vice Admiral
Halsey, Lieut. Col. Merritt

19.   Gen. Rowell, Col. James, Gen. Holcomb, Gen. Mitchell, Gen. Pickett

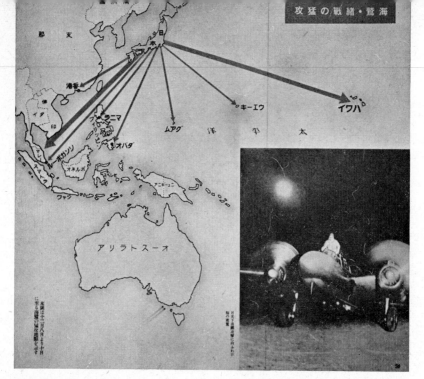

20. "Naval Eagles' Horrendous Attack" 8-10 December 1941

PHOTOGRAPHS FROM A JAPANESE BOOK 1943

21. "This is the way I knocked him down"

22. SB2U-3

EWA UNDER ATTACK

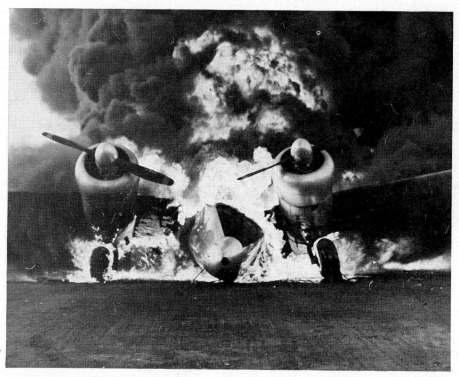

23. JO-2

24.   Waiting for the second blow

EWA UNDER ATTACK

25.   More indignity of 7 December 1941

26.   Remnants of planes litter the field

EWA AFTER THE ATTACK

27. Wake Island is actually an atoll of three islands

Japanese Picture Bo

28. The end of the line for VMF-211's F4F-3's

Japanese Picture Book (1943)

29. Memorial to Lieut. Uchida, whose company attacked the VMF-211 area on Wake, 23 December 1941

30. Flag raising 1941

33. Victors 1945

32.   Flag raising 1945

31.   Vanquished 1945

34. SB2U-3's (top)
    F2A-2 (center)

35. *Mikuma* devastated. Wreckage atop turret may be Captain Fleming's plane

MARINES AT MIDWAY

ion, similar to the Wake detachment, had been garrisoning Palmyra, and on 18 April 1942, VMF-211, reorganized after Wake by Major Luther S. Moore, flew its 14 F2A-3's off *Lexington*. It was just 20 days before that tragedy-haunted ship sank to the bottom of the Coral Sea.[37] Thus Palmyra became a sort of younger brother to Wake, without ever having to share Wake's fate.

Sam Moore and his 14 pilots found Palmyra appalling: the alternate runway had not been completed (despite assurances to the contrary); the civilian dredge crew had pulled out and left their duties to inexperienced naval personnel; there was only one bulldozer, all dump trucks were disintegrating; there was a shortage of both water and lumber. But the marines fell to, and morale never flagged. Above their dugout ready-room they wrote: Thru These Portals Pass the Best Damn Fighter Pilots in the World.[38]

---

[37] VMF-211 never paid its *Lexington* mess bill. "We'll mail you the bill," said the mess treasurer, but his records went down with the ship. (Conversation Colonel L. S. Moore, 18 December 1950.)

[38] Seven of whom became squadron commanders during the war.

CHAPTER FOUR

Midway

THE JAPANESE ATTACK which started the war contemplated no invasion of Midway, which is more than 1,000 miles nearer Pearl Harbor than Wake Island. What was contemplated was a bombardment of Midway by the destroyers *Sazanami* and *Ushio,* plus an air strike by the carriers on the return trip to Japan.[1]

For Americans, Midway had a broader historical façade than Wake, though the atoll apparently remained undiscovered, or at any rate unclaimed, until Captain N. C. Brooks of the Hawaiian bark *Gambia* took possession of the twin islands (eventually named Sand and Eastern) 5 July 1859 in the name of the United States. On 28 May 1867 Secretary of the Navy Gideon Welles ordered the North Pacific Squadron to take over Midway (first called Middlebrooks, then Brooks, Island), and Congress in 1869 appropriated $50,000 to dredge a channel into the lagoon. Lieut. Commander Montgomery Sicard USN in *Saginaw* directed the operation, which was abandoned after seven months; *Saginaw* was shipwrecked on Kure Island on the return voyage.[2]

The first Japanese poachers turned up at Midway in 1900, where they were found killing the islands' terns, goonies and black gannets for their feathers. These squatters became so numerous that President Theodore Roosevelt feared the Emperor might lay claim to Midway; on 20 January 1903 he placed the islands again under the active jurisdiction of the Navy Department. Lieut. Commander Hugh Rodman in *Iroquois* arrived 3 June and ordered the Japanese to leave. Meantime, the Pacific Commercial Cable Company had acquired the franchise to lay a cable from Honolulu to Luzon via Midway. This cable was completed 4 July 1903, following which Roosevelt sent the first message around the world. By May 1904, when a garrison force of 20 marines under Lieut. Owens arrived, Midway had a population of about 100, including contractors' employees and cable-station personnel. Soil was imported from

---

[1] USSBS, *Campaigns,* p 20, wherein *Sazanami* is erroneously called *Akebono* (correction by Captain Ohmae).

[2] Naval Air Station, Midway Island, history, 1941–45, contains a colorful summation of the nineteenth-century affairs at Midway, which include smuggling, shipwreck and murder. The ubiquitous Robert Louis Stevenson, foremost chronicler of the nineteenth-century Pacific, wrote *The Wrecker* around the experience of the crew of the British bark *Wandering Minstrel,* which sank in the Midway lagoon during a storm.

Honolulu to grow gardens; chickens, ducks, turkeys and cattle were brought in. The Marine detachment was withdrawn in 1908; except for its commercial tenants, Midway fell into three decades of neglect.

Pan American Airways established one of its trans-Pacific seaplane bases at Midway in 1935, and the Navy held fleet maneuvers around the islands the same year which included simulated attacks by airplanes and the landing of 750 marines. But the Hepburn Report of January 1939 gave Midway its clue for World War II, describing it as "second in importance only to Pearl Harbor. Needs facilities for two patrol plane squadrons, plus channel piers." The Navy dock was completed 1 September 1940; a reconnaissance party of marines which arrived in May was followed 29 September by 9 officers and 168 enlisted men with about one third of the 3d Defense Battalion's matériel, including one 5-inch gun battery (two guns). An Army engineer unit had been working on the channel between Sand and Eastern Islands since 1939. The remainder of the 3d Defense Battalion arrived in early 1941, and was relieved 11 September by the 6th Defense Battalion (Colonel Raphael Griffin) consisting of 34 officers and 750 men. The NAS was commissioned on 18 August, Commander Cyril T. Simard commanding. By this time the decision had been made to build an airstrip on Eastern Island to supplement the seaplane facilities originally envisaged. Griffin was relieved in October by Lieut. Colonel Harold D. Shannon.

When the war began 12 PBY patrol planes of VP-21 were on and around the Sand Island seaplane ramps, and two Dutch PBY's which had just taken off for the East Indies were recalled and commandeered. No planes capable of real combat were present, but Lieut. Loren D. Everton, of VMSB-232, with 40 enlisted men from MAG-21's three squadrons had arrived in *Wright* three days earlier to prepare for receiving 18 SB2U-3 dive bombers which were to be led off *Lexington* by VMSB-231's squadron commander, Major C. J. Chappell Jr., on 7 December.[3]

But the *Lexington* task force turned back when word came of the Japanese attack. On 10 December the pilots of VMSB-231 landed at the dazed world that was Pearl Harbor. A week later, led by a PBY, 17 planes reached Midway after a spectacular flight of 9 hours and 45 minutes from Pearl—the longest mass overwater single-engined flight on the records up to that time.[4]

During the day of 7 December it seemed that the Japanese might leave Midway alone, but a lookout observed a flashing light southwest of Sand Island just before dark, and at 2135 the first shells from destroyers *Sazanami* and *Ushio* fell between the reef and the beach. Captain Koname Konishi led his destroyers closer, and within a few minutes the 3,000-odd inhabitants of Midway Island incurred their first casualties: two marines and two sailors

---

[3] The SB2U-3 (Vindicator = "Wind Indicator") was partly fabric-covered, had one leakproof tank and three vulnerable, metal tanks.

[4] Vern Haugland, *The AAF Against Japan,* claims the record for a squadron of P-40's which made a similar flight to Midway 23 January 1943, but he was unaware that marines had done the trick 13 months earlier.

killed. During the shelling, which lasted 23 minutes, the roof of the seaplane hangar was burned, one plane was demolished, and most of the hangar's stores destroyed. Minor damage was incurred by the torpedo-and-bombsight building, power house, parachute loft, and unfinished radio-transmitter building. Shannon's 6th Defense Battalion guns started returning fire soon after the Japanese destroyers[5] closed range and a 3-inch battery claimed three hits on the destroyer while a 5-inch battery claimed two hits on the "cruiser" near the water-line forward.

Without much doubt, at least one of the Japanese ships was hit. Captain J. H. Hamilton of Pan American Airways' *Philippine Clipper* which had left Wake at 1250,[6] reached a point 35 miles west by south of Midway about an hour after the Japanese force retired, when he noted from 10,000 feet the wake of two ships bearing southwest, one of them burning intensely.

Commander Simard had a policy concerning non-co-operative civilians. At least five contract workmen and one Pan American Airways employee were confined and put on bread and water for "suspicious or demoralizing attitudes, statements or actions," or for "refusal to work because his year's contract had expired this date." On 26 and 27 December civilians numbering 864 (including prisoners) were evacuated on board *Wright* and *Tangier*.[7] Some civilians stayed on to render valuable service for several weeks longer.

The important thing was that Midway had escaped invasion or even serious damage. The air strike by carriers returning from the Pearl Harbor raid never came off because of weather. Instead, two carriers (*Soryu, Hiryu*), two cruisers (*Tone, Chikuma*), and two destroyers (*Tanikaze, Urakaze*) were diverted from the return trip to Japan in order that they might support the 23 December invasion of Wake, which had proved an unexpectedly tough nut.[8] So, Midway was granted six months' grace.

On Christmas Day, Midway received via *Saratoga* its first fighter planes, 14 F2A-3 Brewster Buffaloes of VMF-221, fresh from the frustration of trying to relieve Wake. Thus Midway was equipped with slow PBY patrol planes and a squadron each of obsolete fighters and dive bombers—hardly a formidable force to pit against the crack pilots flying the faster, more maneuverable Japanese Zeros, but the best the United States Navy would or could furnish without depleting its own flight decks. As it was, the 1st Marine Air Wing and MAG-21 were forced to surrender their few comparatively modern F4F-3's to the carriers before the end of December.[9]

In January Lieut. Colonel W. J. Wallace, who had arrived to command Midway's Marine aviation detachment, reported that operators were being inducted into the mysteries of radar calibration, personnel shelters were being

---

[5] Inevitably, one of the ships was called a cruiser, and the enemy force was estimated to include four ships.

[6] Wake time. It was 7 December on Midway, 8 December on Wake.

[7] Naval Air Station, Midway Island, history, 1941–45.

[8] USSBS, *Campaigns*, p 20.

[9] Letters Larkin to Rowell, 27 December 1941 and 8 January 1942.

constructed and portable fueling expedients devised for emergency use. A complete propeller shop was set up and a machine shop was nearing completion.[10]

On 25 January the Japanese came back: a submarine surfaced and threw 10 or 15 shells into the lagoon before a 3-inch salvo drove it away. The 1,785-ton *I-173*, probably this same submarine, was sunk two days later by a destroyer 240 miles to the northeast. On 8 February another submarine appeared and two days later, still another (or perhaps the same one), but both were routed by shore-battery fire or bombs.

One of the more exciting episodes of Midway in midpassage occurred on 10 March—an episode whose significance became clear only after the war. At 0950 that morning two four-engined Japanese flying boats took off from Wotje in the Marshalls, one headed for Midway, the other for Johnston. These planes were conducting an experiment which might have had far-reaching consequences throughout the Pacific: reconnoitering U.S. bases, then refueling from submarines, in this case from a large submarine near the reef at French Frigate Shoal (halfway between Midway and Pearl Harbor).[11] The Midway radar picked up a plane 45 miles to the southwest. A four-plane division of VMF-221, Captain James L. Neefus leading, caught it at 10,000 feet. Neefus made the first pass, brought smoke from one engine before the Japanese pilot dove for a cloud bank at 3,000 feet. While it was diving, Lieuts. McCarthy and Somers made one pass each. Marine Gunner Robert L. Dickey, in the fourth plane, made a tail approach but was wounded in the left shoulder and got seven holes in his plane. Then Neefus returned and made his second pass, whereupon the enemy aircraft dropped into the sea, burning debris scattering on the surface. The pilots received a bottle of bourbon and Colonel Wallace's congratulations.[12] A similar plan to refuel from big submarines just before the Midway battle was likewise frustrated—the subs got there all right, but they found seaplane tenders *Thornton* and *Ballard* already present, so the flying boats were never sent.[13]

MAG-22, under command of Lieut. Colonel Wallace, organized 1 March with four squadrons on paper: VMF-221, VMF-222, VMSB-241, VMSB-242. (VMSB-231, in name only, was transferred to MAG-23 being formed in Hawaii, but its personnel remained to take the new number VMSB-241.) This simply meant that the two Midway squadrons were divided: some experienced pilots went back to Hawaii as nuclei of the newly designated squadrons; some new pilots arrived on Midway as their replacements. Actually, Midway was left with the same planes and VMF-221 and VMSB-241, despite the changing of numbers and shifting of personnel which was typical in Marine aviation during its hand-over-fist expansion.

---

[10] Letters Wallace to Larkin, 18 and 20 January 1942.
[11] War Document Center, No. 161142, Group No. 23, Item No. B23D, p 3.
[12] VMF-221 history, p 17.
[13] Samuel Eliot Morison, *Coral Sea, Midway, and Submarine Actions*, p 94; USSBS, *Interrogations*, Vol II, p 465.

As might be expected, many pilots sent overseas early in 1942 were not fully trained. This caused concern among many senior officers, including Brig. General Ross E. Rowell, commander of the 2d Wing, the Midway Marine flyers' parent organization, who wrote from San Diego a month after the war began: "I have now accumulated 35 second lieutenants in various stages of advanced training. . . . If ComAirBatFor [Commander, Aircraft, Battle Force] approves and you want some half-baked flyers, send me a dispatch to that effect."[14] Admiral Halsey wanted Marine pilots, half-baked or well-done, so he approved. As a result, both Ewa and Midway became training bases as well as defense outposts.

Late in April the Navy high command began to suspect, through decoding Japanese dispatches, that an attack was brewing. In Washington, Admiral King believed that the objective would be the Hawaiian Islands, but Admiral Nimitz thought Midway the likelier target.[15] On 2 May Nimitz turned up at Midway. Following his visit preparations for an attack, then expected late in May, were intensified. Five more AA batteries, varying in size from 20-mm. to 3-inch, were detached from the 3d Defense Battalion at Pearl Harbor, and sent to Midway, along with two rifle companies of the 2d Marine Raider Battalion and a platoon of five light tanks for use as mobile reserve. Plane shelters were built, two new 4,000-gallon water tanks installed partly underground, a command post completed, camouflage and sandbagging of key installations were increased. On 24 May emergency rations were distributed to various locations, stored in dugouts or buried.[16]

On 20 April, Wallace was relieved as MAG-22 commander by Lieut. Colonel Ira L. Kimes. Both his squadrons were brought to overstrength by the arrival on 26 May of 22 fresh Marine pilots (mostly brand-new), 7 F4F-3's and 19 SBD-2's on board USS *Kitty Hawk*. Through subsequent radio intercepts the estimated date of the attack fortunately could be revised to the first week in June, which not only gave the defenders a little more time to prepare but, more important (it later developed), allowed *Yorktown* time to arrive in the vicinity, recovered from wounds received in the Coral Sea battle.

At May's end the airfield on Eastern Island was choked with airplanes: 4 B-26's and 17 B-17's of the Army Air Forces had been hastily flown in from Oahu to augment the defenses, and so had 6 torpedo-carrying Navy TBF's. There were now 16 Navy PBY-5A's for reconnaissance. The total of Marine planes was no less than 64: 19 SBD-2's, 17 SB2U-3's, 21 F2A-3's and 7 F4F-3's. The 28 fighters were commanded by Major Floyd B. Parks, the 36 dive bombers by Major Lofton R. Henderson. Fuel consumption of 65,000 gallons per day became a strain after 22 May when a sailor pulled the wrong switch during a demolition drill and set fire to 400,000 gallons of aviation fuel. Thereafter no planes could be refueled except from 55-gallon drums, by hand.

---

[14] Letter Rowell to Larkin, 8 January 1942

[15] Lieut. Colonel Robert D. Heinl Jr. USMC, *Marines at Midway* (Historical Division monograph), p 22.

[16] MAG-22 history, p 29; Heinl, *Marines at Midway*, p 22.

Admiral Nimitz stressed that the role of the land-based planes should be offensive rather than defensive:

> BALSA's air force must be employed to inflict prompt and early damage to the Jap carrier flight decks if recurring attacks are to be stopped. Our objectives will be, first, their flight decks rather than attempting to fight off the initial attacks on BALSA. . . . If this is correct, BALSA air force . . . should go all out for the carriers . . . leaving to BALSA's guns the first defense of the field.[17]

On board the 63,700-ton battleship *Yamato*, hovering between Midway and the Aleutians, Admiral Yamamoto himself commanded the attack on both, having sold the idea to a somewhat reluctant Imperial General Staff and Army.[18] The four carriers around which Admiral Nagumo's Midway striking force was built included Japan's largest, *Akagi* (36,500 tons) and *Kaga* (36,000 tons), and *Hiryu* and *Soryu* (18,000 tons each). Following three days of softening up by the carrier planes, plus two battleships, three cruisers, and accompanying destroyers, the occupation force, which had proceeded by a slower, more southerly route, would land its 2,500 troops: 1,500 men of the Special Naval Landing Force and 1,000 soldiers of the Ichiki Detachment.[19]

Marine planes were destined to play a minor, though valiant, role in the great Battle of Midway. First report of enemy forces came from a PBY which spotted 11 ships of the transport force 700 miles to the westward about 0900 on 3 June. The B-17's went out, found the same force, reported hitting two battleships or heavy cruisers and two transports, but actually touched nothing but the Pacific. The first hit was one by a PBY on an oiler at 0143 on 4 June. At 0525 the same morning a PBY patrol plane sent back the news everyone had been expecting—that the enemy fleet had been sighted, and at 0555 the Navy radar picked up "many" planes bearing 310°, 89 miles distant. The four Army B-26's and six Navy TBF's set off with torpedoes to attack the carrier, which had been placed at 180 miles, bearing 320°.

Both squadrons of the Marines' warmed-up planes were airborne within ten minutes of the first warning. Major Parks's fighters divided into two loose units of 12 and 13 planes: 7 F2A's and 5 F4F's under Parks went

---

[17] Memo to Captain Arthur C. Davis USN, undated. At this time Midway's code name was BALSA.

[18] Vice Admiral Shigeru Fukudome in USSBS, *Interrogations*, Vol II, p 525: "The Chief of the Naval General Staff, Admiral Nagano . . . appeared to have the feeling that if Admiral Yamamoto said that a certain plan promised success he would be willing to let Admiral Yamamoto proceed with its execution."

[19] The question became academic, but in the light of our own subsequent experiences at "well-softened" Tarawa and Iwo Jima, it is interesting to speculate whether a force of such size could have seized Midway from its more than 2,000 well-trained defenders behind their wire barriers, antiboat mines in the water, antipersonnel mines and antitank mines under the sand.

directly for the attacking planes, while Captain Kirk Armistead's 12 F2A's and 1 F4F were vectored ten miles out to await a possible attack from another direction.

The dive bombers were divided 16 SBD's under Henderson and 11 SB2U's under his executive officer, Major Ben Norris. Beginning at 0605 Colonel Kimes broadcast repeatedly: "Attack enemy carriers bearing 320° distance 180 miles course 135° speed 20 knots." Although this broadcast was received clearly, the acknowledgment did not get back to Midway, and the message was repeated for an hour.

The fighter pilots with Parks were 30 miles out at 14,000 feet when they sighted 2,000 feet below them many enemy dive bombers, with their screening fighters *beneath* them—the Japanese apparently were so confident of finding Midway asleep that they planned to use the Zero fighters only for strafing, catching whatever planes were present on the ground or as they were taking the air. This was fortunate, MAG-22's commanding officer reported later:

> This gave our people one pretty free pass at their bombers. Their score was quite good. After that the Zeros began to come through and they were busy with them as they tried to get more shots at the bombers.[20]

What the Marine fighters ran into were elements of a 108-plane striking force, divided into equal waves of attack planes, bombers and fighters, and commanded by the air officer of *Hiryu*.[21] Armistead's 13 planes joined the melee a few minutes later. The 25 did not succeed in breaking up such a formidable force, which pressed on toward Midway. But they materially lightened the blow; by the time it reached Midway the first wave consisted of only 20 horizontal-attack bombers instead of 36, according to the 6th Defense Battalion; and the second wave of 36 dive bombers had been cut down to 18 by the count of a VMSB-241 pilot (Captain Marshall A. Tyler) whose plane had been grounded. The Japanese succeeded in destroying the Eastern Island power-house; on Sand Island the seaplane hangars and fuel-oil tanks were burned. Thirteen were killed, including four MAG-22 ground crewmen, and 18 wounded in the attack on Midway.

In their "Detailed Battle Report" the Japanese admitted losing nine planes (six to interceptors, three to AA), and admitted that 34 others were damaged. The Marines' resolute attack with inferior planes left them with the heaviest losses they would sustain in World War II. Fifteen of the 25 fighter pilots, including Major Parks, did not survive the brief encounter. Of Parks's own dozen, only Captains John Carey and Marion Carl and Lieut. Clayton Canfield lived. Thirteen F2A's and two F4F's were missing, and of the remainder only

---

[20] Interview Lieut. Colonel Ira L. Kimes, Bureau of Aeronautics, 31 August 1942. Captain John F. Carey, who was one of Parks's division leaders and gave the original "Tally-ho," disagrees. He says the Zeros were above but behind the bombers. (Lieut. Colonel Carey's comment on first draft of this book, 1948.)

[21] *ONI Review*, p 7.

two planes were in condition to fly. Those whose fate it was to live were able to land only because "there was a very deliberate attempt on the part of the Japs not to damage the runways,"[22] an opinion borne out by the Japanese own report: "We are of the opinion that it is impractical to attempt to render such airfields inoperational through bombings."[23]

Quite naturally, the fighter pilots who lived were acrimonious. Captain Philip R. White registered his protest:

> It is my belief that any commander who orders pilots out for combat in an F2A should consider the pilot as lost before leaving the ground.

One pilot suggested that the F2A, or Brewster trainer, should be left Stateside as a training plane. Another said two Brewsters seemed tied to a string while he watched a Zero make passes at them. Even the pilots in the comparatively modern F4F's were surprised at the Zero's speed and versatility. Captain Carl, having shot down one Zero, headed his Grumman for home when

> I saw three Zero fighters at a low altitude that were making a wide circle, so I came down in a 45° dive with almost full throttle and had barely enough speed to drop in astern and to the inside of the circle made by one of the Zero fighters. I gave him a long burst, until he fell off on one wing and when last seen was out of control headed almost straight down with smoke streaming from the plane. The other two fighters had cut across and were closing on me so I headed for a cloud. One fighter gave up the pursuit, but the other came on and started firing. He fired steadily for several seconds, but was shooting low, for I could see the tracers going by on both sides and slightly below me. Finally, I felt the impact of the bullets striking the plane. He was gaining fast and had followed me through one cloud so I cut the throttle, threw the plane into a skid, and he overran me.[24]

VMF-221 had been wiped out as a fighting unit at Midway. Its personnel turned to as helpers of the raiders and other marines in fueling the gluttonous B-17's, which had to be serviced from cans and drums because the power house had been knocked out. The Marine fighter pilots who survived could take some consolation in the knowledge that the Japanese, though victorious in the first round, entered the ring weaker in the second.[25]

Because of the slaughter of the fighters—and because tactics were primitive anyway—the bombers which went after the Japanese task force were unprotected. For the torpedo planes (which first attacked at 0710) it was

---

[22] Interview Kimes, p 7.

[23] ONI, *The Japanese Story of the Battle of Midway*, prepared for top-echelon Japanese officers 15 June 1942, translated after the war.

[24] Statement in preliminary report of MAG-22, 8 June 1942.

[25] Morison, *Coral Sea, Midway, and Submarine Actions*, p 105.

simple massacre: five of six Navy TBF's and two of four Army B-26's were shot down by Japanese fighters or AA without scoring a hit,[26] although the Army intelligence officers enthusiastically claimed three torpedo hits on two carriers—and got back to Pearl to tell their story first. Nor, in fact, did any aerial torpedo reach a target during the battle, except the one already launched after midnight of 4 June from a PBY at the oiler of the transport force. Of the 41 torpedo bombers launched from the three U.S. carriers, only 6 returned.

But the sacrifice of the Marines' antiquated fighters was not in vain. At 0700, after the Japanese planes had finished their strike on Midway, the strike commander, Lieut. Tomonaga, confessed failure: "There is need for a second attack wave."[27]

Admiral Nagumo, commanding the carriers, was persuaded, and the persuasion was fatal. At 0715 Nagumo (who was not yet conscious of any American surface forces in the area) broke his state of readiness against air attack and ordered the flight decks of his four carriers cleared and his torpedo planes prepared for another attack against Midway instead of enemy shipping. It was half an hour before he accepted the word of a cruiser search plane which reported vaguely that there were American ships in that part of the Pacific. It was 0820 before he learned that at least one of the ships was a carrier. By then he was in even worse shape because his flight decks must be kept clear for the planes expected any minute from Midway.

Marine Dive Bombers Attack

Meantime, the 16 SBD's of Henderson and the 11 SB2U's led by Norris were winging their fateful way toward the Japanese carrier force. Henderson split his force into two divisions of four boxes, designating as commander of the second division Captain Elmer G. Glidden Jr.

Henderson's SBD's reached the enemy ships before the slower SB2U's. At least two carriers, clearly identified by red meatballs, were sighted. He began a wide let-down circle at 8,500 feet preparatory to launching a glide-bombing attack at 0800 from 4,000 feet (rather than a dive-bombing attack, since the pilots were barely acquainted with the SBD). At about 8,000 the first enemy fighters attacked. Henderson's plane was one of the first to begin burning.[28]

Just what damage the Marine dive bombers inflicted on the Japanese carriers is open to some question—but not much. Lieut. Colonel Heinl in

---

[26] USSBS, *Campaigns,* pp 59–60.

[27] Morison, *Coral Sea, Midway, and Submarine Actions,* p 107.

[28] Major Henderson did not crash his plane against an enemy carrier, and no one claimed that he did except a corporal gunner in another plane whose report was widely circulated. It is interesting to note that the damage report of *Hiryu* lists one American plane "self-exploded" (*The Japanese Story of the Battle of Midway,* p 54), but no other evidence, contemporaneous or later, corroborates or even mentions such an event, including the testimony of the flight officer and the navigator of *Hiryu.*

Marines at Midway, published in 1948, accepts the report of Captain Glidden, who took command when Henderson was shot down and led the Squadron in their dives which were made at five-second intervals:

> Immediately after coming out from the protection of the clouds the squadron was attacked again by fighter planes and heavy AA. After making my run I kept heading on for the water, and I headed on an approximate bearing home. Looking back I saw two hits and one miss that was right alongside the bow. The carrier was starting to smoke.

But most of the evidence says not.

It had been 45 minutes since the Midway-based torpedo bombers attacked. Fifteen B-17's from Midway attacked the carriers at 0810, ten minutes after the marines began their dives, but AAF historians admit that they hit nothing from their 20,000-foot altitude.[29] The torpedo bombers from the American carriers did not arrive until 0940 (whereupon for 34 minutes they were slaughtered, 35 out of 41), and the *Enterprise* and *Yorktown* dive bombers failed to find targets until 1014.[30]

So, whatever damage was done to the Japanese carriers at about 0800 in the morning was done by the Marine dive bombers. Wading through the labyrinth of enemy reports, the historian can find evidence that some hurt was inflicted: Admiral Nagumo's log carries two entries at 0810: "Enemy plane dives on *Soryu*" and "Bomb hits on *Akagi* and *Soryu* were noted."[31]

Captain Aoki, of *Akagi* (Nagumo's flagship), testified 9 October 1945 that

> ... two bombs by dive bombing, about two hours after sunrise (one started fire at after elevator). Planes were loaded up with bombs inside the hangar and caught afire.[32]

It seems a reasonable assumption that a professional sailor could remember how long after sunrise the most important event in his life happened, even if more than three years had elapsed between the event and the interrogation by the Americans.

Captain Aoki was questioned again on 23 December 1945 by Major General Orville Anderson USA, senior Army member of the U.S. Strategic Bombing Survey (Pacific), who made a determined but futile effort to prove that the Army planes had actually scored some hits on the Japanese carriers at Midway.[33]

---

[29] Craven and Cate, *The AAF in WW II*, Vol I, pp 457–458.

[30] Morison, *Coral Sea, Midway, and Submarine Actions*, chart pp 118–119.

[31] *The Japanese Story of the Battle of Midway*, p 15.

[32] USSBS, *Interrogations*, Vol I, p 13.

[33] This interrogation is No. 530, and is one of the most comprehensive covering the Battle of Midway (77 single-spaced, legal-sized pages in mimeograph). Japanese participants in the battle were questioned by AAF officers at intervals from 23 December 1945 to 14 January 1946. The results of this interrogation and of others

In this interview Captain Aoki makes it clear that it could not have been Marine bombers which hit *Akagi* (as presumed in *Marines at Midway*). The first attack, he says, came at "7 o'clock in the morning" (1000 of 4 June by American reckoning), just following the torpedo bombers (i.e., the carriers' 41 torpedo bombers, not the Midway TBF's).

Otherwise, the evidence is also overwhelming against hits by the Marine dive bombers. Most reliable source on the Battle of Midway is *The Japanese Story of the Battle of Midway*, Nagumo's story written only ten days after the battle. The damage charts (pp 52–58) leave no doubt that all hits on the four carriers were made by dive bombers from the carriers *Yorktown* and *Enterprise*. (*Hornet's* planes made a wrong turn and missed the battle.)

This authentic document also indicates that three of Henderson's planes probably made three near misses (within 20 meters) on *Kaga* at 0830, and four misses on *Hiryu* at 0850 (two at 50 meters, one at 80, another at 150). In this same attack one of the dive bombers (mislabeled a "fighter") strafed *Hiryu* and killed four men. This was all the damage accomplished by the marines. The other two carriers were not hit at all until the carrier planes came over about two hours later.

The Nagumo account of 0810, indicating that "bomb hits on *Akagi* and *Soryu* were noted," can only mean that these were noted, erroneously, from other ships.[34]

The Strategic Bombing Survey prepared charts of bomb hits on carriers in the Battle of Midway, in addition to a summary of attacks.[35] These also indicate that Henderson's SBD's scored no hits or, at best, inflicted very minor damage.

Eight of the 16 SBD's, including Henderson's, were shot down. Lieut. Daniel Iverson returned with his throat mike shot away and with 259 holes in his plane. (Later he was wounded at Guadalcanal, but he failed to survive a plane crash in the U.S.)

Major Norris's ancient SB2U's reached the enemy fleet about 15 minutes later than the SBD's, about 165 miles from Midway. They were attacked immediately by three Zeros—they came to be called Zekes later—one of which was shot down by rear-seat gunners. In the confusion the SB2U's found themselves at the opposite end of the fleet axis from the carriers. To try to traverse the axis would mean feckless suicide, so Norris's bombers selected an enemy battleship (*Haruna* or *Kirishima*) as their target. Their efforts, however heroic, were not successful. Despite some claimed hits, only minor damage was done by a near miss on *Kirishima* or *Haruna*,[36] probably the latter.

---

conducted by the AAF have never been published; the Navy published its interrogations in two volumes in 1946.

[34] This is the conclusion of Morison in *Coral Sea, Midway, and Submarine Actions,* pp 110–111*ff,* and is the only reasonable one.

[35] USSBS, *Campaigns,* pp 63–73.

[36] USSBS, *Interrogations,* Nos. 6, 11, 503. In interrogations the Japanese officers'

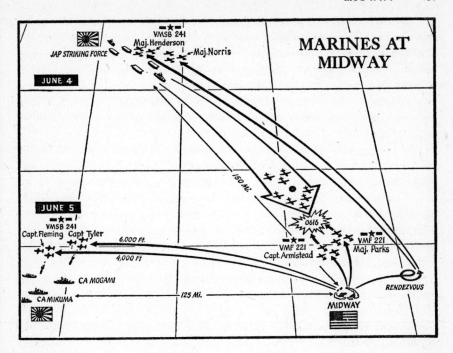

Two of Norris's planes were shot down and the crews killed. A third pilot crash-landed five miles at sea and was picked up by a PT boat, but his gunner was dead from Zero machine-gun fire. The gunner, Private Henry I. Starks, had never fired a machine gun when he took off from Midway that morning.[37]

At 1900 the six operational SBD's and five SB2U's took off to locate a "burning enemy carrier" 200 miles northwest of Midway. The carrier was not located. Forty miles from Midway on the return leg, Major Norris, who had succeeded to the Squadron command upon the death of Major Henderson, went into a steep right turn as he attempted to let down. He was not seen again.

On the morning of 5 June all hands were alerted at 0300, and at 0630 the remaining dive bombers of MAG-22 were ordered to attack "two enemy battleships (one crippled)" bearing 268°, distance 170 miles.[38] The six SBD's and six SB2U's which could be flown off had no difficulty in finding the cripple and its companion[39]—an oil slick 50 miles long provided an unerring guide.

---

answers were frequently tailored to fit the desires of his interrogator, Army or Navy. On this minor point of damage to *Haruna,* which was important only in determining whether the B-17's hit anything at all at Midway, the editors of *The AAF in WW II* say (p 461): "It is possible that this damage may have come from heavy bombers, but the survivors of that ship are positive that dive bombers hurt them."

[37] Statement Lieut. Daniel L. Cummings in MAG-22 preliminary report.

[38] MAG-22 history, p 57.

[39] The ships were the heavy cruisers *Mikuma* and *Mogami,* which had ap-

This time, Captain Marshall Tyler, who had become VMSB-241's third commanding officer within little more than 24 hours, determined to lead the SBD's in an orthodox dive from 10,000 feet, while the SB2U's under Captain Richard E. Fleming could glide in from 4,000 feet. The SBD's struck for *Mogami* and bracketed it with six near misses, one of them only ten meters away. About the same time, B-17's came over at 4,000–5,000 meters but their bombs fell 200–300 meters astern of both ships, according to Admiral Soji's postwar testimony.

What happened next was Captain Fleming's unit's surprising glide-bombing attack. As Fleming headed for the target his SB2U was hit forward and smoke began pouring from his engine. He dropped his bomb, and as he pulled out his plane burst into flames. Although none of the pilots accompanying him reported the action that way, Fleming's plane apparently dived into *Mikuma*. Admiral Soji regarded the act as a suicide attack, which it was hardly intended to be, and commented: "I saw a dive bomber dive into the last turret and start fires. He was very brave."

Captain Fleming was posthumously awarded the Medal of Honor. He had participated in all three of his squadron's attacks since the historic morning of 4 June.

On the 6th, as on the 4th, it remained for the carrier planes to finish the job started by the Marine airmen. Dive bombers from *Hornet* and *Enterprise* caught the two crippled ships, sank *Mikuma* and seriously damaged *Mogami* and the destroyer *Arashio* which was picking up survivors. The top honors at Midway belonged to the carrier pilots, who sank the four carriers and the cruiser.[40] The marines, badly outclassed in all equipment except courage, had nevertheless, in the words of Admiral Nimitz, "written a new and shining page in the annals of the Marine Corps."

One of the consequences of the Midway battle was a conflict between naval aviation and Army Air Forces which was to endure, with considerable bitterness, throughout the war. The first pilots to return to Oahu following the great battle were AAF personnel, some of whom left for Honolulu in four B-17's at 0140 on 5 June. The interviews they gave the press were completely one-sided and erroneous, indicating that the battle had been won by the B-17's. Brig. General Willis Hale USA "expressed the belief that the battle of Midway was primarily won by the blasting by the Flying Fortresses of the Japanese Naval Task Force, including carriers."[41]

---

proached Midway during the night intending to bombard the islands. Midway was saved this ordeal by a collision between the two, caused when *Mogami* was late in receiving an order for an emergency turn to the left to avoid an American submarine attack. *Mogami's* bow was partially sheared off. (Rear Admiral Akira Soji's testimony in USSBS, *Interrogations*, Vol II, p 363. Soji was *Mogami's* captain at Midway.)

[40] JANAC gives the marines joint credit for sinking *Mikuma*.

[41] *New York Times*, 12 June 1942. The usually cautious *Times* had already editorialized on 9 June: "So far as we can now learn the main damage to the Japanese fleet off Midway was inflicted by our land-based planes."

The Navy men knew enough to feel that their theory had been vindicated: maneuvering ships could not be hit successfully by bombers which did not come down low to insure their aim. The Air Forces continued to insist for almost a year that high-level bombing was still the answer. The AAF even "reaffirmed" their claims of 22 hits on ships during the Midway battle as late as January 1947.[42] It was only when their official history was published, in July 1948, that the AAF historians finally admitted

Japanese ships at sea would not be sunk or hit with any degree of success until the attacking planes were brought down to minimum levels.[43]

This conflict between Army and Navy (which centered around the use of air power) reached the highest levels in Washington. Secretary Stimson explained the basis of the conflict long after he had retired from office:

The Air Forces considered the Navy a backward service with no proper understanding of air power; the Navy considered the Air Forces a loud-mouthed and ignorant branch which had not even mastered its own element.... What too often came to Army and Navy headquarters in Washington were emotionally embroidered reports of the incompetence of the other service.[44]

This conflict had direct effect on Marine aviators, who were firmly committed to the naval aviation thesis. In practice Marine and Army aviators worked generally in harmony throughout the war.

The Midway battle went to the heart of the Marine Corps aviation organization. As in the case of Wake (on a smaller scale), the 24 dead included several potential group and squadron commanders. Major Henderson and Major Parks, the squadron commanders, were gone. So were Major Norris and five captains. Some of the younger officers would certainly have displayed command ability in the three years to follow. Among the 18 enlisted men killed were several veterans who would be sorely missed before many more months had passed.

Midway had been won but among the personnel of MAG-22 there was a feeling of dismay. The planes flown by the marines simply were inadequate for fighting a modern war against a well-equipped enemy. The protest against the old SB2U's and the F2A's was on the lips of every marine who had fought at Midway or had become acquainted with the facts of the battle. Back at Ewa, Lieut. Colonel Larkin took the matter of protesting into his own hands:

For your information I gave Jim Roosevelt a folder of the action

---

[42] Haugland, *The AAF Against Japan*, p 86.
[43] Craven and Cate, *The AAF in WW II*, Vol I, p 461.
[44] Henry L. Stimson and McGeorge Bundy, *On Active Service*, pp 516–517.

on Midway to take to his Dad. In about two weeks if you are ordered as president of a general court martial to try one fellow named Larkin— soften your heart.[45]

[45] Letter Larkin to Rowell, 15 June 1942. Major Roosevelt handed the folder to the President upon arriving at the White House. "I believe that it resulted in considerable improvement in the situation shortly thereafter," James Roosevelt recalled in a letter to the author, 26 July 1948.

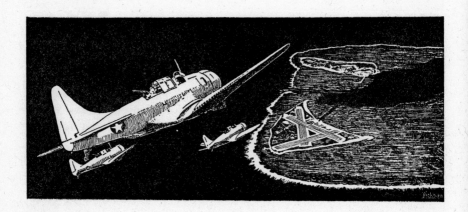

CHAPTER FIVE

Guadalcanal: Plans and Preparations

JAPAN'S TIDE WASHED southward over and around the Philippines, westward to the Netherlands East Indies and eastward toward New Guinea and the Bismarck Archipelago. Capital and principal settlement of the Bismarcks—160 miles to the northwest of the Solomons—was Rabaul, home of about 1,000 whites (mostly Australians) and several thousand Melanesians and Chinese traders.

Rabaul was overwhelmed on 23 January 1942. The little men from the north set to building up a great bastion from which they might dominate New Guinea and Australia on their right, while to the left they could look upon the Solomons, New Caledonia, Fiji and—if all went well—even New Zealand. The great port of Rabaul became the center of the Japanese effort in the Southwest Pacific; eventually it was headquarters for a fleet and fleet area, and an army with a total Japanese military force of 100,000 based thereabouts.

The recapture of Fortress Rabaul or its neutralization occupied the Allied South Pacific forces for the better part of two years before a series of hard-fought battles finally rendered the base ineffective. Insofar as Marine aviation is concerned, Rabaul was the focal point for a longer period than any other target in World War II. It is Rabaul—and the battles that were fought in its behalf—to which the next nine chapters are devoted. Each battle was simply another step toward Rabaul. And the closer the Allies got, the tougher Rabaul looked. It finally became evident that direct assault was madness.

Two months after the Japanese forces landed at Rabaul they pushed on to Bougainville, largest island in the Solomons and the most northerly. From Bougainville the tentacle on 4 May reached down 300 miles to Tulagi, capital of the Solomons, next door to Guadalcanal, a big jungle island discovered in 1568 by Pedro de Ortega and named for his home in Spain.

On the very day of their landing the forces of Rear Admiral Kiyohide Shima were caught at their Tulagi moorings by Rear Admiral Frank Jack Fletcher's Task Force 17, on its way up to intercept the Japanese landing force headed through the Coral Sea toward Port Moresby. The U.S. pilots (from *Yorktown*) expended 22 torpedoes, 76 half-ton bombs, and 83,000 rounds of machine-gun bullets. They reported a handsome victory in which were sunk two destroyers, a cargo ship and four gunboats, plus damage to another destroyer and the forcing ashore of a light cruiser. Unfortunately, the only actual destruction was the destroyer *Kikutsuki,* two small minesweepers and a few seaplanes.

The Tulagi occupation was intended to support the Port Moresby invasion, for which Vice Admiral Shigeyoshi Inouye, Commander in Chief of the Fourth Fleet, moved from Truk down to Rabaul.[1]

This operation was also a part of the greatly expanded Japanese strategy. The successes of the first three months came to the Emperor's subjects with bewildering ease. Greater East Asia was within their grasp in half the time any of them dared hope, and at a cheaper price.

The Tokyo planners were emboldened to enlarge their perimeter before the GEA areas and resources were consolidated. Step 1 was the occupation of Tulagi and Port Moresby, with which we are presently concerned. Step 2 was the occupation of Midway and the western Aleutians, whose frustration was described in Chapter Four. Step 3 was the conquest of New Caledonia, Fiji and Samoa—Admiral King had been properly concerned about Samoa, and if things had turned out as the Japanese intended, several thousands of marines would not have been left feeling for a long time that the war was passing them by.[2]

Holding the Line

The Guadalcanal operation had its origins as early as 18 February 1942, when Admiral King proposed to make a base out of the island of Efate in the New Hebrides, 690 miles southeast of Tulagi and 300 miles northeast of New Caledonia, to which base 14,789 men of the Army's Task Force 6814 (later reconstituted as the Americal Division) were already en route from New York.[3] On 2 March the Admiral elaborated: let Efate be the first rung in a ladder "from which a step-by-step general advance could be made through

---

[1] *Southeast Area Operations,* Part One (Navy), prepared by Japanese officers after the war for G-2, Far East Command, Department of the Army. Much of the enemy material on the Solomons chapters of this book is taken from these records.

[2] USSBS, *Summary Report (Pacific War),* p 3, indicates that the three-way expansion was planned only after the initial conquests, and the AAF historians in *The AAF in WW II,* Vol I, p 444, accept this premise. But Samuel Eliot Morison in *Coral Sea, Midway, and Submarine Actions,* p 6, points out that all three moves were in the Japanese basic war plan which dates from 1938. He says the only new elements were: (1) the shortening of the time table; and (2) Admiral Yamamoto's plan for a big fleet action (to smash the U.S. Pacific Fleet in 1942). Both say that the Doolittle raid of 18 April 1942 on Tokyo speeded up the expansion, and Winston Churchill in *The Hinge of Fate,* p 242, says the same thing. But Captain E. T. Layton, Admiral Nimitz's intelligence officer, who has studied the subject longer than anyone else, believes that the Doolittle raid made no difference in the timing. (Interview at Pearl Harbor, 15 October 1950.)

[3] Craven and Cate, *The AAF in WW II,* Vol I, p 433.

the New Hebrides, Solomons and Bismarcks"—which is exactly what happened in the ensuing 24 months.[4]

By the time the soldiers arrived in Nouméa on 12 March, things were popping all over the Pacific. Singapore had fallen, Bataan was doomed, and General MacArthur was already on his way out to take the Southwest Pacific command in Australia. Darwin had been bombed, Java would soon fall, and the Japanese had moved on to occupy Lae and Salamaua in New Guinea.

The Allies had done well to get started in Borabora, Tongatabu, Samoa, the Fijis and New Caledonia, but time had not permitted them to do very much in the base-building line. Nevertheless, Admiral King persevered, and about 25 March some 500 men of the Americal Division were sent up to Efate.[5] Along with the 4th Defense Battalion (reinforced), a forward echelon of MAG-24, which had been activated at Ewa only 28 days previously, arrived on 29 March at Efate's principal town, Vila, which is the capital of the Anglo-French condominium (that's what the joint government of the New Hebrides is called). The soldiers' and marines' mission was to build an airfield, under the command of Captain John K. Little USMCR, CO of MAG-24's headquarters squadron.

This proved an assignment "in the face of tremendous odds"[6] because the fine engineering equipment which the South Pacific came to know later was not available. Meanwhile, VMF-212, slated to occupy Efate, was being transferred from MAG-24 to MAG-21,[7] and from Oahu to the South Pacific in whatever transportation was available: on 29 April 11 officers were en route in *Hornet*, 10 officers and 2 enlisted men in *Enterprise;* three days later 3 officers and 55 men departed Pearl in *Pensacola*. On 11 May, 21 pilots in 21 F4F-3's flew off the carriers and landed at the new air base at Tontouta, 30 miles northwest of the New Caledonia capital, Nouméa. They were held there by order of Commander, Carriers, Pacific (ComCarPac), although Vila field had been operational since 30 April. Major Harold W. Bauer, the Squadron commander, went up with three planes on 27 May. By 9 June all the Squadron's planes had arrived at the Vila field.[8]

---

[4] Morison, *Coral Sea, Midway, and Submarine Actions,* p 246.

[5] Bureau of Yards and Docks, *Building the Navy's Bases in World War II* (1947), Vol II, p 204. The Navy had prepared to detach bluejackets from a carrier to be used temporarily to garrison Efate, but Major General Dwight D. Eisenhower in Washington offered to supply some soldiers so the carrier sailors could perform their regular duties. (Eisenhower, *Crusade in Europe,* p 26.)

[6] Letter of commendation to Little from Brig. General Neal C. Johnson USA, 24 November 1942.

[7] Later in the war the Squadron was shifted successively as follows, to MAG's 23, 41, 22, 24, 11, 12, 24, 12, 14, 21, 11, 14, 24, 14. Marine Corps aviation's mobility entails the frequent transferring of squadrons and of personnel within squadrons, and no attempt will be made in this history to record all such shifts.

[8] Which was later named for Bauer. Eventually three other fields on Efate were named for Marine aviators: Lieuts. Lawrence C. Taylor, Arthur E. Finucane, Richard D. Haring.

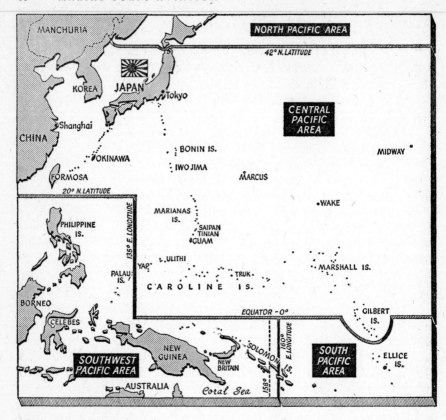

Starting an Offensive

On 4 April the Pacific had been divided by the Joint Chiefs of Staff between Admiral Nimitz and General MacArthur at 160° east longitude[9]— which gave MacArthur the southwest, including Australia, New Guinea, the Bismarck and Solomon Islands, and the Philippines. To Nimitz went the rest of the ocean.

The Battle of the Coral Sea (4–8 May) cost the Allies *Lexington,* but compelled the Japanese invasion force to turn back from Port Moresby. At Midway a month later Admiral Yamamoto lost whatever chance he had of winning the Pacific war and, among other things, this left him "no choice but to suspend the scheduled invasions of Fiji, Samoa and New Caledonia, and concentrate on immediate restoration of fighting strength."[10]

The question in Washington, Pearl and Melbourne now became: What operations could be undertaken in the Pacific within the limitations set by the

---

[9] On 1 August the line was shifted westward a degree so that the whole island of Guadalcanal came in Nimitz's area.

[10] *Southeast Area Operations,* Part One (Navy), p 7.

British and U.S. staffs long before Pearl Harbor ("If Japan does enter the war, the military strategy in the Far East will be defensive"), and confirmed by Roosevelt and Churchill ("Beat Hitler First") in January 1942?[11]

After Midway, General MacArthur proposed that Rabaul be captured; just give him a division trained in amphibious warfare, 12 transports, a couple of carriers and some big bombers, and he would undertake it in July. His Intelligence told him only one Japanese division was then stationed on New Britain and eastern New Guinea.

The Navy protested that MacArthur was making it sound too easy. Swarms of fighter planes would be needed to accomplish such a daring feat, and neither planes nor bases were available. The Navy had only four carriers (*Enterprise, Saratoga, Hornet, Wasp*—the latter had recently arrived in the Pacific from Atlantic ferry duty). These four, which must spearhead Allied offensive power for many months to come, the Navy did not choose to risk in poorly charted, submarine-infested waters north of the Solomons which were surrounded by Japanese land bases on three sides. The war in the Atlantic was going badly: May and June, when 235 merchant vessels were sunk, marked the worst of the German submarine war; this crisis threatened the entire prosecution of the war and engaged Navy transport and escort vessels which would be needed for such an assault as the General on the west side of the 160th meridian proposed.

The Navy's own plan, as vigorously projected by Admiral King, was for a limited offensive against the Guadalcanal–Tulagi area. For such an operation Army B-17's and Navy PBY's could furnish reconnaissance from the island of Espíritu Santo in the New Hebrides, 555 miles south of Guadalcanal, which was the nearest likely base beneath the Solomons. There was enough water surrounding the Solomons for the Navy's sparse carrier force to maneuver. Supply ships could make the run from Nouméa with a good chance of impunity from enemy submarines.

Admiral Nimitz came up with a plan on 28 May to seize Tulagi with a single raider battalion, but King, Marshall and MacArthur agreed that these troops would be insufficient. Less than two weeks later MacArthur offered his daring proposal to capture Rabaul itself.

Back in Washington, General Marshall supported the MacArthur plan (in it the 1st Marine Division would make the beachhead landing at Rabaul, and would be relieved by the two U.S. and one Australian divisions MacArthur had). King's plan favored an attack on the Santa Cruz Islands (which never came off) and on the Solomons (which, of course, did)—under Admiral Nimitz's command—while MacArthur conducted a diversion against the East Indies (which never happened, either).

Despite strenuous objections from Marshall, MacArthur and Vice Admiral Robert L. Ghormley, recently arrived from London as the Navy's South Pacific

---

[11] Morison, *The Rising Sun in the Pacific*, p 51; *Coral Sea, Midway, and Submarine Actions*, p 245.

commander, Ernie King had his way. A week before the Joint Chiefs of Staff ordered the operation on 2 July, Admiral King had alerted Admiral Nimitz, who in turn alerted Admiral Ghormley.

In Auckland next day Ghormley broke the shocking news to Major General A. A. Vandegrift, that he had five weeks before making an amphibious assault. Vandegrift had arrived in New Zealand only 12 days earlier with less than half of his 1st Marine Division. He had not expected to commit his division before early 1943. Vandegrift's 1st Regiment was only four days out of San Francisco, en route to New Zealand in eight cargo ships, auxiliary (AK's) that weren't even combat-loaded. His 7th Marines was dug in on Samoa as part of the big defense force there, so on 27 June Admiral King proposed that Vandegrift be allotted the 2d Marines of the 2d Marine Division. That outfit (reinforced) sailed, combat-loaded, from San Diego on 1 July.

Tulagi, as the chief port and capital of the Solomons, loomed larger in the Allied planners' eyes, but on 6 July word reached Washington that the Japanese had begun building an airfield on nearby Guadalcanal, the 25-by-90-mile island of high mountains and steaming jungles which lies 20 miles to the south across Sealark Channel.[12]

Intelligence about Guadalcanal and Tulagi was sparse and untrustworthy. Vandegrift's staff had around-the-clock huddles at his headquarters in the Cecil Hotel in Wellington, trying to plan an attack on beaches which hadn't even been photographed. He sent his intelligence officer to Australia to learn what he could from missionaries, planters and government officials who had left the Solomons in the face of the Japanese invasion. Two Marine officers learned a lot about Southwest Pacific geography in the pursuit of intelligence: they flew 1,500 miles to Sydney, 3,000 more to Port Moresby, then rode a B-17 reconnaissance plane 800 miles to take a look at this place called Guadalcanal. But they saw very little because their plane was attacked by float planes which rose from Tulagi.

D-day for Operation PESTILENCE was postponed on 10 July, from 1 August to 7 August. On 18 July the commander of the amphibious force, Rear Admiral Richmond Kelly Turner, arrived from Washington to take charge. The command set-up was now complete, with target date only three weeks away. As Commander, South Pacific (ComSoPac), Admiral Ghormley was over-all strategic commander, reporting to Nimitz at Pearl Harbor. But Ghormley would stay in Nouméa, 845 miles south of Guadalcanal, while Vice Admiral Fletcher commanded the expeditionary force on the spot. Turner commanded the amphibious force, which included Vandegrift, his 959 officers, 18,156 enlisted men, and, in effect, almost everything else, since Fletcher in practice stuck to providing air cover from *Enterprise, Saratoga* and *Hornet,* which were coming down from Pearl.

Second in command to Turner was Rear Admiral V. A. C. Crutchley RN,

---

[12] One Japanese officer, Captain Yasuji Watanabe IJN, testified after the war that the airfield was the idea of an officer who simply went over to Guadalcanal sightseeing. (USSBS *Interrogations,* Vol I, p 68.)

whose covering force would include 8 cruisers (3 Australian, 5 U.S.) and 15 destroyers (all U.S.). These would furnish naval gunfire and AA protection.

Land-Based Aviation

General MacArthur's contribution to the Guadalcanal landings consisted of about 16 B-17 bombers which flew reconnaissance over the area west of the 158° line[13] and attempted to interdict Japanese flights out of Rabaul.

In Ghormley's theater all land-based aviation—Army, Navy, Marine Corps, Royal New Zealand Air Force—was commanded by Vice Admiral John S. McCain, Commander, Aircraft, South Pacific (ComAirSoPac). His first task was to secure an airfield nearer to Guadalcanal than Efate (707 miles). On 12 July orders went out to construct a field on Espíritu Santo,[14] 150 miles closer, where a detachment of the 4th Defense Battalion, Seabees and Army engineers and soldiers had landed.

Within 16 days a strip had been cut out of jungle and coconut grove, and it was reported ready for fighters on 28 July. Espíritu Santo became one of the great bases of the Pacific, on which the Navy eventually spent $36,369,925 —an amount exceeded only at Guam, Leyte–Samar, Manus, Okinawa and Saipan, and it was to provide a temporary home for thousands of Marine aviators within the next two years.

On 2 August the first Marine squadron in the South Pacific since Bauer's VMF-212 reached Efate began arriving at Espíritu. Lieut. Colonel John N. Hart's VMO-251 within nine days was installed with 16 F4F-3P "long-range photographic planes"—but without the wing tanks for long-range flying until they were flown out from Pearl Harbor. The tanks arrived 20 August.

VMO-251 had arrived at Nouméa 12 July on board USS *Heywood* with its planes in crates and had set up camp at Tontouta. Hardly had this been done before the Squadron had been ordered up to Espíritu Santo to backstop the Guadalcanal invasion.

Several of VMO-251's 17 photographers participated in flights over Guadalcanal before the landings, using Navy cameras while flying in Army B-17's of the 11th Group. The first of these missions, on 23 July, was intercepted by five float Zeros.

Thus, at the time of the landings, 7 August, there were two Marine squadrons in the South Pacific. These two squadrons, VMF-212 and VMO-251, provided the fighters from the bases nearest the target, although they were too far away to provide direct support for the Guadalcanal landing. The 16 B-17's of Colonel L. G. Saunders were also based at Efate. At the next nearest base, New Caledonia, Admiral McCain had 22 Navy PBY's, 9 B-17's, 10 B-26's, 38 P-39's, 6 RNZAF Hudsons and 3 scout observation planes. Beyond that his nearest planes were a few oddments at Fiji and Tongatabu. That was all, though many

---

[13] For air search purposes the dividing line between South and Southwest Pacific was shifted one degree farther west.

[14] Frequently misspelled "Santos" in Marine Corps records.

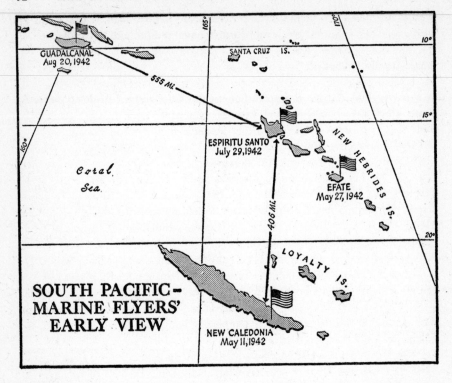

GUADALCANAL
Aug 20, 1942

SANTA CRUZ IS.

555 ML

ESPIRITU SANTO
July 29, 1942

NEW HEBRIDES IS.

Coral
Sea

EFATE
May 27, 1942

406 Mi.

LOYALTY IS.

SOUTH PACIFIC—
MARINE FLYERS'
EARLY VIEW

NEW CALEDONIA
May 11, 1942

more planes would find their way to the South Pacific before the bitter days of the next four months had ended, and Marine aviation would find itself committed to approximately the ultimate.

On paper the air alignment for Guadalcanal was skimpy if there was going to be a real fight. ComAirSoPac actually could count on 291 planes scattered from Samoa to Espíritu Santo, including 35 B-17's just arrived from Hawaii, and such lame birds as RNZAF Vincents and Singapores.[15]

The trouble with the 291 figure was (1) not all the planes could be used in the target area without leaving the back door of the Pacific wide open to Japanese attack; (2) a high percentage of them were obsolescent or obsolete; (3) most of the rest were ill-adapted for the kind of defense Guadalcanal needed; i.e., dive bombers and high-altitude fighters.

These factors were only too well known to the task force commanders. General Vandegrift had been promised land-based planes by D plus 3, when

[15] The 291: at *Efate:* 6 scouts, 18 fighters; in *New Caledonia:* 22 PBY's, 3 scouts, 38 P-39's and P-400's, 6 Hudson bombers of RNZAF, 27 B-17's, 10 B-26's, 16 F4F-3P's; at *Tongatabu:* 6 scouts, 24 fighters; in *Fijis:* 9 PBY's, 3 RNZAF Singapore patrol planes, 12 RNZAF Hudson bombers, 9 RNZAF Vincent bombers, 17 fighters, 12 B-26's, 8 B-17's; in *Samoa:* 10 scouts, 17 scout bombers, 18 fighters. (ONI Combat Narratives, *Solomon Islands Campaign,* I: *The Landing in the Solomons,* 7–8 August 1942, p 15, hereinafter cited as *Solomon Islands Campaign,* I).

the carriers would be withdrawn, provided the airfield was ready, as it was anticipated it would be. Not until the rehearsal at Koro Island 28–30 July in the Fijis did Vandegrift extract a promise that the carriers would stay even three days; Admiral Fletcher, conditioned to carrier raids, had anticipated keeping his three carriers in the Guadalcanal–Tulagi area only one day. The disillusioned marines began to realize that the Midway battle had not necessarily given Allied forces command of the seas.

MAG-23 Gets Ready

In the late June planning Admiral Nimitz promised McCain the four squadrons of Bill Wallace's MAG-23, which was then in training at Ewa. The Group at this time consisted of two fighter squadrons and two dive-bomber squadrons, a lot of very new pilots and very old planes. It took a lot of confidence to assign these young men to the defense of a beachhead whose ownership was bound to be hotly contested.

The forward echelon—one fighter squadron (VMF-223, Captain John L. Smith) and one dive-bomber squadron (VMSB-232, Major Richard C. Mangrum)—would have to be flown to the Guadalcanal airstrip from a carrier. And the pilots had not yet been taught to land on and take off from a flight deck. But Admiral Nimitz, a well-nigh imperturbable man, philosophically messaged SoPac 33 days before 1 August that, anyway, "their employment must be delayed until airfields in objective area have been completed."

VMF-223 and VMSB-232 not only were squadrons without carrier experience, but nearly all their pilots were fresh from flight school where they had piled up about 275 hours apiece, mostly in SNJ trainers. (The veteran Japanese Navy pilots they had to face averaged 800 hours' flying time even before Pearl Harbor.) Five of Mangrum's 15 pilots had had some practice bombing the target ship *Utah;* his ten newest dive-bomber pilots had done no dive bombing when the Group's orders were being issued at Pearl Harbor (the radio-gunners were slightly more experienced). Smith's fighter pilots, excepting the two captains (Rivers Morrell and Marion Carl) and a veteran enlisted pilot (Tech. Sergeant John D. Lindley), were second lieutenants ranging in age from 19 to 21, who had been in the Marine Corps a few months.

For their intensive last month's training, described by Mangrum as "flying the pants off them," both squadrons had to do with their old planes. Just before sailing on board the escort carrier *Long Island* on 2 August for Guadalcanal, Smith's squadron received brand-new F4F-4's with two-stage superchargers. They wished later they had had more time on oxygen. Mangrum's squadron turned in its old SBD-2's, which had been reconditioned after seeing their best days in the Coral Sea battle, and was furnished with SBD-3's which had self-sealing tanks and armor plate.[16]

The other two squadrons of the Group, VMF-224 (Captain Robert E.

---

[16] Interviews Lieut. Colonel John L. Smith, 11 February 1948, and Lieut. Colonel Richard C. Mangrum, 20 February 1948.

Galer) and VMSB-231 (Major Leo R. Smith), with 19 and 14 planes and pilots, respectively, were in a state of preparation approximating John Smith's and Mangrum's. This rear echelon of the Group would sail from Pearl Harbor 15 August on board the airplane transports *Kitty Hawk* and *Hammondsport.* Seven VMF-224 pilots qualified on *Hornet* the last day of July. Detachments of the ground crews preceded the rear echelon on board the high-speed seaplane tender (AVD) *McFarland* and the Navy transport (AP) *William Ward Burrows.*

Almost everything happened to impede land-based aviation's preparation for the onrushing D-day. When Admiral Turner arrived in Wellington he still faced the necessity of shaping up some kind of over-all plan and holding a pre-landing rehearsal of his amphibious forces.

His original plan was to fly VMO-251 and VMF-212 to the new Guadalcanal airfield from New Caledonia and Efate, respectively. They would furnish initial land-based fighter defense; the two MAG-23 dive-bomber squadrons would base at Guadalcanal also, VMF-223 to be at Espíritu Santo (whose airfield would be ready by the time it got to the South Pacific) and VMF-224 at Efate.[17]

The VMO-251 pilots could not be sent up by carrier because they weren't qualified in carrier landings. They also needed gunnery and tactical training, as did VMF-212. On the same day that Turner made his proposal for the first land-based squadrons, McCain replied by recommending that Bauer's outfit be left at Efate and Hart's at Espíritu.[18] This is what was done. Nimitz went ahead and ordered MAG-23's forward echelon to leave Pearl about 1 August, the rear echelon two weeks later.[19]

Four squadrons of Army B-17's from the 11th Bombardment Group were being rushed to the South Pacific from Hawaii, but the first ten planes arrived to find there were no gas tanks to fit into the radio compartments for long-range reconnaissance missions—which were the high-flying bombers' chief useful function. As if there weren't enough troubles, General DeGaulle (whose partisans had recently ousted the Vichy French as top men in the New Caledonia government) objected to closing the radio station at Nouméa. But in the interests of security it had to be done.

---

[17] Commander, Amphibious Force, Pacific (ComAmphForPac), to ComSoPac, 21 July 1942.

[18] ComAirSoPac to ComSoPac, 21 July.

[19] CinCPac to ComSoPac, 23 July.

CHAPTER SIX

Operation Shoestring

AN OVERCAST BLESSED the forces proceeding up to the Solomons, and no patrol bombers from Rabaul were overhead on 5–6 August. No submarine reported the movement of the Turner transports. The first beachhead landing U.S. forces had made since 1898 achieved remarkable surprise. Carrier planes destroyed 22 Japanese float planes at their Tulagi moorings.[1]

The Guadalcanal landing "proceeded with the precision of a peacetime drill," as the island's 600 Japanese soldiers (not 5,000 as Intelligence had estimated) fled with the 1,400 laborers into the jungle. On the islands of Tulagi–Gavutu–Tanambogo, 20 miles north, there was bitter resistance which was not ended until the 1,500 defenders were slain, almost to the last man, after they had killed 108 marines, wounded 140 others. The next question was one of unloading the supplies—a drill that proved much more difficult than unloading the marines. It was not long before the Guadalcanal beaches were stacked high with supplies which could not be moved farther inland unless marines on patrol were called to carry them by hand.

Rabaul's reaction to the Guadalcanal–Tulagi landing was not long in coming. Rear Admiral Sadayoshi Yamada, commanding the 25th Air Flotilla, had 93 planes up there[2]—soon he would have many more—and he dispatched 24 of them within a few hours after he got the radio flash announcing the surprise landings. At 1045 the ships off the beachhead received a radio message from Pearl Harbor that 24 enemy planes were on the way to attack Guadalcanal. Just how did Pearl Harbor know? Coastwatcher Paul Mason, a short, blond Australian ex-planter, perched in a jungle hide-out on a hill near Buin on Bougainville, 300 miles to the north, counted the planes and flashed the message —via Brisbane—which was relayed within 25 minutes. With more than two hours' warning, the bos'n's mate on the Canberra (one of the two cruisers MacArthur had loaned for the invasion) piped over the bullhorn: "The ship

---

[1] Buchanan, The Navy's Air War, p 156.

[2] As follows: 32 medium bombers, 16 carrier bombers, 39 fighters, 2 land-based reconnaissance planes, 4 flying boats. His table of organization called for 148 planes, but he was under strength. (Answers to questions by Lieut. Roger Pineau USNR of the staff of Captain Samuel Eliot Morison, asked in Tokyo in June 1949 of Captain T. Ohmae, who was in Rabaul in 1942 as chief of staff to Vice Admiral Mikawa, commanding Eighth Fleet. Lieut. Pineau, an expert in the Japanese language, was kind enough to get answers to several questions in behalf of this history.)

will be attacked at noon by 24 bombers. All hands will pipe to dinner at eleven o'clock."[3] Defending carrier planes shot down several of the attackers. Although the first bombers hit no ships, a second (surprise) attack by dive bombers at 1500 hit the destroyer *Mugford,* the first of many, many ship casualties off Guadalcanal. Twenty-two men were killed. *Saratoga's* fighters reported they shot down 10 of the 11 in this flight, and two more from another flight were destroyed after they had made unsuccessful attacks on ships off Guadalcanal and were on their way back north.

During this aerial mix-up unloading of the transports had to be discontinued, a loss as important as the planes shot down from Admiral Fletcher's carrier force. The carrier pilots had put in a dawn-to-dark day, what with almost constant calls for air support, particularly on the smaller islands in the Tulagi area. It became evident early that the Solomons invasion would require a lot of airplanes.

The next morning, 8 August, did nothing to dispel this feeling. This time it was Coastwatcher Jack Read, at Buka on the northern tip of the Solomons, who reported that Guadalcanal could expect a visit from 45 bombers en route from Kavieng (Rabaul's subsidiary base on New Ireland). The warning reached Admiral Turner at 1038. By the time the planes arrived 79 minutes later Turner had the transport groups and screens maneuvering evasively, but one Japanese plane flew into the deck of the transport *George F. Elliott* and another put a torpedo into the destroyer *Jarvis. Elliott's* fire got out of control and she had to be sunk; crippled *Jarvis* limped away toward Nouméa and was sunk with all hands next day by enemy torpedo bombers.[4] Japanese plane losses were counted as 6 to the carrier planes and 14 to the ships' AA fire.[5]

Admiral Fletcher lost no planes on 8 August, but he wanted to get his carriers away from Guadalcanal, and he sent a message at 1807 saying so to Admiral Ghormley in Nouméa. His stated reason: he had lost 21 of his 99 fighters, fuel was running low, and there were too many Japanese planes in the vicinity. It was to break this news of the withdrawal of his air support and the balance of his supplies that General Vandegrift was summoned that night to *McCawley,* Admiral Turner's flagship. While he was on board a minesweeper, returning from this painful conference, the roof seemed to fall in on the whole Solomons operation: a Japanese task force slipped in behind nearby Savo Island and all but wiped out the screening force, sinking the cruisers *Astoria, Quincy, Vincennes* and *Canberra,* and heavily damaging *Chicago.* If Admiral Mikawa had ventured six miles farther he could have destroyed Turner's transports like shooting deer with a machine gun, but the Admiral thought he'd better get out of there before daylight found him within range of U.S. carrier planes. It was only the first of several occasions when Japanese stupidity conspired to save the Americans in the Solomons.

---

[3] Commander Eric A. Feldt RAN, *The Coastwatchers,* pp 88–89. The coastwatchers began direct communication with Guadalcanal on 15 August.

[4] Samuel Eliot Morison, *The Struggle for Guadalcanal,* p 52.

[5] Actually a total of 17 (USSBS, *Interrogations,* Vol II, p 419).

There was the matter of Vandegrift's supplies, which were heaped on the beaches for three days in spite of Herculean efforts to disperse them. Why didn't the Japanese drop a string of bombs on the dumps?[6] The marines, now that they were on their own, were short enough already—no barbed wire or sandbags, insufficient food, practically no motor transportation, insufficient artillery and aviation ammunition, almost no gasoline for the shore-based planes if and when they arrived.

General Vandegrift turned his 1st Engineer Battalion to work on the airfield which was his No. 1 prize on Guadalcanal. The Japanese had almost finished it before taking to the jungle as the marines landed; they had expected by mid-August to bring in the first of 60 planes they were to base there. (They had already made trial landings.) Their lighter planes did not require a hard surface or long runway, so a graded and rolled dirt field was sufficient for their operations. The chief trouble was the way the field had been built: started at each end, so that the incomplete portion was a big hole about two thirds of the way down the length. The hole had to be filled in with about 5,000 cubic yards of soil, and the only way to do it, in the absence of the proper equipment (still on Turner's transports), was with hand shovels (of which there was a shortage) and captured Japanese dump trucks. Then there were three or four acres of banyan trees at the end of the runway which made a plane's approach twice as steep as it should be. These were dynamited.

Before the hole was filled General Vandegrift reported (8 August) that some retouching also would be needed and a 2,600-foot runway would be ready for operations in about two days. Within a week the field would be 3,800 feet long. But he had no aviation personnel on Guadalcanal except Major Kenneth H. Weir, Division air officer. On 12 August the Marine general sent his message: "Airfield Guadalcanal ready for fighters and dive bombers." He had 400 drums of 100-octane gasoline and was trying to put into operation a captured Japanese radio (his own radio had not been landed).

On 12 August the first U.S. plane, a PBY flown by Admiral McCain's aide, Lieut. William S. Sampson USN, made the first landing on the strip, which a few days later was to be named Henderson Field.[7] The field was announced to be in excellent condition. But the matter of getting some planes for Guadalcanal was still far from solved. The naval officer commanding Task Group 2.6 radioed on the 13th that the pilots in *Long Island* required additional carrier and combat training before they could be considered efficient fighting units. Furthermore, *Long Island* and the transport *William Ward Burrows* would have to be unloaded together, since the plane crews and spare equipment were on the latter. CTG 2.6 was writing a letter to ComAirSoPac about it.

Admiral McCain replied, "I need fighter planes at Guadalcanal now. . . ." On the 14th a solution was projected whereby Smith, Mangrum and some of

---

[6] That they didn't General Vandegrift considered his biggest streak of luck (Interview, June 1948).

[7] After Major Lofton R. Henderson, who led the Marine dive bombers at Midway.

their pilots would eventually get to Guadalcanal: *Long Island* would proceed from Suva (where it had stopped after news of the Savo Island disaster came through) to Vila, one of the Efate harbors. There Smith would trade some of his less-experienced pilots for the better-trained of Major Bauer's VMF-212 flyers. ComAirSoPac strongly recommended that any planes going into Guadalcanal carry spare plugs, tool kits, starter cartridges, tires, and whatever else could be taken in a single-engined plane. Oxygen-transfer equipment was particularly important.

The matter of supplies was going to be tough until air superiority could be regained. And that couldn't happen until some planes could be brought in. Admiral Ghormley found a partial answer in destroyer transports, which could make a run in at high speed, unload their cargo, and get out before the planes from Rabaul sent them all to the bottom.

On 15 August *Colhoun, Gregory, Little* and *McKean* made the first of these fast runs, bringing 400 drums of aviation gasoline, 32 drums of aviation lubricant, 282 bombs, belted ammunition, hand fuel pumps, tools, critical parts, and chamois skin for straining gasoline.[8] Admiral McCain sent along a specialist to see about getting Henderson Field operating: Major Charles H. (Fog) Hayes, executive officer of VMO-251, and a small group to whom the Marine aviators became devoted: 3 officers and 118 men of Cub 1 under the command of Ensign George W. Polk.[9]

Happily, the Japanese had not taken full advantage of their success at Savo Island. Having lost about half their Rabaul-based air strength in the first two days, they slackened their attacks. Anyway, there were no ships to bomb; only jungles containing marines, plus an airfield easily repaired. There were many minor raids: a few planes sweeping lazily over Henderson Field at will, dropping a bomb here, another there, tearing up the runway so that the engineers required all of a couple of hours to fix it. Submarines stood offshore of a day or evening to pump a few shells in the vicinity of the field, destroyers did their shelling at night. "Washing Machine Charlie" droned through much of the night, dropping small bombs at well-spaced intervals, "just to keep the forces there disturbed," said Captain Takashi Miyazaki, who sent Charlie down from Rabaul.

Japanese Intelligence estimated the U.S. landing force at 800 to 1,000 men. It was a simple matter to bring more planes down to Rabaul from the Marianas or even from Japan.[10] Since there was no U.S. air on Guadalcanal, and the Navy had been sunk or frightened away, and the ground forces were small in number and Americans were known to be inferior in combat, 900

---

[8] Major John L. Zimmerman, *The Guadalcanal Campaign* (USMC Historical Monograph, 1949), p 65.

[9] Of Cub-1 Mangrum said: "The Cub Unit people did a magnificent job. . . . they really delivered gasoline from drums to each plane as fast as they could." (Interview BuAer, 11 November 1942). Polk was killed in Greece in 1948, where he was a correspondent for the Columbia Broadcasting System.

[10] On 7 August, 9 medium bombers were flown in from Tinian; next day 17 more, one containing Rear Admiral N. Tsukahara, CO 11th Air Fleet.

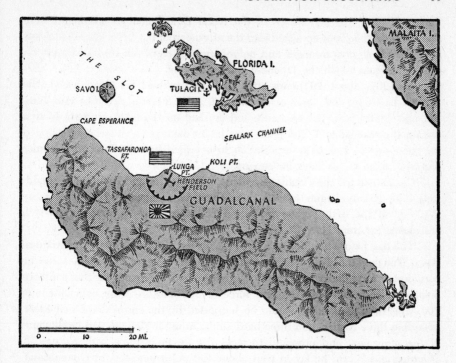

troops were deemed sufficient to reinforce Guadalcanal. They sailed from Guam, reached Truk 12 August and got to Guadalcanal six nights later in six destroyers of what came to be known to thousands of marines as the "Tokyo Express." These troops were the detachment of Colonel Kiyono Ichiki, originally scheduled to take Midway.[11]

Planes Arrive, Fireworks Begin

On the afternoon of 20 August *Long Island*, escorted by the cruiser *Helena* and destroyer *Dale*, turned into the wind 200 miles southeast of Guadalcanal and launched her planes, 19 F4F's and 12 SBD's—Smith had finally acquired eight of VMF-212's pilots in exchange for eight of his own greener men. Despite all the worry by the carrier people, the catapulting went off smoothly. At 1700 these 31 pioneers, commanded by Lieut. Colonel Charles L. Fike, executive officer of MAG-23, began landing on Henderson Field. Marine aviation was finally on Guadalcanal. "A shout of relief and welcome went up from every marine on the island," reported Lieut. Herbert L. Merillat.[12]

The arrival of the aviators coincided with the first blood-curdling battle the 1st MarDiv fought on Guadalcanal. After midnight of the 20th–21st there was continuous firing 3,000 yards east of the field. This was the Battle of the

---

[11] Morison, *The Struggle for Guadalcanal*, p 70.
[12] *The Island*, p 67.

Tenaru River;[13] the 900 troops of the Ichiki Detachment attacked and were slaughtered. The clean-up lasted into the afternoon of the 21st; VMF-223 pilots fired their first shots in anger and unlimbered their guns in strafing attacks on the beach from which the Japanese were attacking.

At 1207, about 19 hours after they had arrived on Guadalcanal, the fighters had their first taste of air combat. John Smith shot down one Zero. But one fighter was shot up badly and crashed on the field. An SBD blew a tire on the take-off and "the plane was badly damaged and is being stripped for parts due to lack of transportation to overhaul base."[14] Two other planes required eight to ten days for repairs.

On 22 August the Cactus Air Force,[15] as Smith's and Mangrum's squadrons had already begun to call themselves, was augmented by five Army P-400's[16] of the 67th Fighter Squadron (Captain Dale D. Brannon), which had flown up from New Caledonia.

The day before the Marine flyers had arrived at Guadalcanal Rear Admiral Raizo Tanaka, the Tokyo expressman, was gathering at Rabaul a force he considered formidable enough to dislodge the Americans in the southern Solomons: a special naval landing force of 800 and an Army detachment of 700. This time the landing would be supported by the entire Combined Fleet, including three carriers and three battleships. Admiral Fletcher had intelligence of the movement and prepared to meet the Japanese force with *Enterprise*, *Saratoga* and *Wasp;* he lay in wait about 100 miles southeast of Guadalcanal.

The Battle of the Eastern Solomons marked the Marine flyers' participation in the first of four major naval battles which would be fought around Guadalcanal in the next three months. It also marked the first major aerial combat for Smith's and Mangrum's pilots. At 1420 on 24 August VMF-223 intercepted a raid by 15 bombers and 12 fighters from the carrier *Ryujo*. The enemy aircraft never reached the field; the Marines shot down 16, including half the Zeros. Two bombers and a Zero were knocked off by Captain Marion Carl; and two planes apiece by Lieuts. Zennith A. Pond and Kenneth D. Frazier, and Marine Gunner Henry B. Hamilton.

Three of Smith's pilots did not return; another was shot down and spent a day at Tulagi. But Cactus Air Force gained 11 SBD's, unscheduled, together with their sterling crews. After *Enterprise* had received three bomb hits, Lieut.

---

[13] It was actually at Alligator Creek—such were our maps and advance intelligence—but the name has stuck.

[14] MAG-23 war diary, from which most accounts of the next few weeks are taken.

[15] Cactus was Guadalcanal's code name; the operation was called Watchtower —but the participants preferred "Shoestring."

[16] Unloved version of the early P-39's, manufactured for export to the British and equipped with the British high-pressure oxygen system for which no equipment was available. Armed with a 20-mm. cannon, two .50-caliber and four .30-caliber machine guns and capable of carrying one bomb. (*67th Fighter Squadron History*, pp 10, 25, 28.)

Turner Caldwell USN, low on gas and daylight, led his dive bombers ("Flight 300") to Guadalcanal. There they stayed and rendered golden service until 27 September.

This was a good day's work by the fighter pilots of VMF-223. It is necessary to remember that the Japanese Zero at this stage of the war was regarded with some of the awe in which the atomic bomb came to be held later. U.S. fighter pilots were apt to go into combat with a distinct inferiority complex. Tales from the Pacific had filtered back to the U.S. after the Bataan and early New Guinea fighting which attributed to the Zero (and the Japanese pilots) a sort of malevolent perfection that was beyond Occidental comprehension. The Japanese fighter plane had not been mastered at Coral Sea nor Midway—where the only fighter-vs.-fighter combat was between the land-based planes and the carrier-based Zeros—and the Zero certainly lost none of its prowess there. The Cactus fighters made a great contribution to the war by exploding the theory that the Zero was invincible; the Marines started the explosion on 24 August.

In spite of the loss of the light carrier *Ryujo* to *Saratoga's* bombers and some 90 aircraft to Navy and Marine fighters, Admiral Tanaka with the transport group continued toward Guadalcanal. At 0830 on the 25th the dive bombers from Henderson Field found his ships: the flagship cruiser *Jintsu* with eight destroyers and destroyer transports. Lieut. Lawrence Baldinus of VMSB-232 dropped his bomb on the cruiser, just forward of the bridge, and seriously damaged her. Tanaka transferred his flag to a DD. Ensign Christian Fink of the *Enterprise* flight dropped his 1,000-pound bomb amidships of the big transport *Kinryu Maru*, which burned furiously and finally had to be sunk by a destroyer, *Mutsuki*, which stopped to pick up survivors and in turn became one of the first Japanese warships to be hit by a B-17 since the war began. *Mutsuki* sank immediately. Another DD, *Uzuki*, was lightly damaged.

Next day the Japanese came back at noon with 16 twin-engined bombers escorted by fighters, and dropped about 50 bombs. Two thousand gallons of precious aviation gasoline were set on fire, which in turn exploded two 1,000-pound bombs. Fragmentation bombs riddled several parked aircraft and tore up the field radio station. But the dozen Marine fighters which had missed the raiders coming in caught them on the way out and shot down 13; Smith and Marion Carl of the home team accounted for two apiece and the volunteer pilots Smith had picked up from VMF-212 at Efate, performed handsomely as guest stars. Captain Loren D. Everton knocked down three of the bombers, Marine Gunner Hamilton got two, and Lieut. John H. King, Jr. another.

On the 28th Lieut. General Harukichi Hyakutake, commanding the 17th Army with headquarters at Rabaul, sent down another 3,500 troops to reinforce the garrison. It was not necessary for the 1st MarDiv to kill off these. Two scouting SBD's found the four destroyer transports coming down The Slot late in the afternoon, bombed but missed. Eleven more of Mangrum's and Caldwell's SBD's heard the contact reports and rushed up to do something about it. Destroyer *Asagiri* blew up with a terrific explosion, *Yugiri's* superstructure was set afire. *Shirakumo* was stopped but left afloat. The one undamaged destroyer took her in tow for the trip back to the Shortlands.[17] The survivors of Hyakutake's landing force had to wait another day to set foot on Guadalcanal. A smaller detachment of 450 soldiers managed to get in during the darkness of 29 August, however.

The VMF-223 pilots were clawing down the midday raiders very well. On the 29th they destroyed 4 bombers and 4 fighters; on the 30th the haul was 14 enemy aircraft (4 shot down by John Smith, 3 by Marion Carl). The Army's 67th Fighter Squadron, which had been augmented on the 27th by 9 more P-400's, also managed to bring down 4 of the Emperor's "eagles," but lost 4 of their own (2 of the pilots walked back) and six were damaged.

That left only three Army P-400's, and when the Japanese came back on the afternoon of the 30th (they sank the Marines' old friend *Colhoun*), the P-400's were ordered to fly around the island on reconnaissance rather than try to intercept. "No good at altitude and disheartening to the brave men who fly them," was ComAirSoPac's evaluation of this plane.

The Squadron historian recalled the 67th's plight:

> We can't maneuver and dogfight with the Zero—what good are we? Our enlisted men are risking their lives every day trying to get the planes patched up—for what? We're just eating up food—and there's not enough to go around anyway, and using up valuable gasoline—and the gas supply is getting lower every day. Hell, we can't fight. When the Japs come we're told to "go on reconnaissance." What good are we?

Nonetheless, the Army pilots proved valuable in support of ground troops, with their P-400's and P-39's received in October. The Airacobras could strafe Japanese troops and landing barges; they could tote a 500-pound bomb over the lines and drop it on enemy concentrations. Eventually, they were loaded with depth charges which caused havoc among enemy troops hidden in ravines—the depth charge's concussion could literally blast the Japanese out of their clothes and shoes, leaving their bodies intact but very dead.[18]

The Way It Was

The first pilots operated under a score of handicaps which would not be substantially eased until hundreds of pilots had struggled through the same handicaps for nearly half a year. Henderson Field was a bowl of black dust which fouled airplane engines or it was a quagmire of black mud which made the take-off resemble nothing more than a fly trying to rise from a runway of molasses. The heavier SBD's operational difficulties had it the worst: for a

---

[17] Morison, *The Struggle for Guadalcanal*, p 109.

[18] The depth charge was also used against land targets in North Africa, on 9 November by cruiser planes of *Savannah*. (Samuel Eliot Morison, *Operations in North African Waters*, p 127.)

couple of weeks there were no bomb hoists, and 500-pound bombs had to be lugged over and loaded by hand. Besides, the first SBD's were equipped, not with pneumatic tires on the tail wheels but with hard rubber intended for carrier landings. These chewed up the runway like a plowshare. Down in Nouméa AirSoPac made some wooden wheels; these, too, were unsuccessful.

The simple act of refueling a handful of planes often required several hours. Whatever gasoline was available was in 55-gallon drums. For a few days gassing had to be done out of the drums themselves, with hand pumps through chamois or from drums that were strung up in the rafters of the inherited Japanese hangars. Later, when there were gas trucks, the fuel had to be pumped from drums to trucks.

Radio communications were a nightmare. When the planes took off they could count on receiving the makeshift Guadalcanal radio only 20 miles out; fortunately, the plane radios were slightly better and Guadalcanal could usually pick up their scouting reports 100 miles from the base. The assigned frequency (6970) was all right for overwater carrier work; for working around a land mass it was awful.

Guadalcanal's first pilots (who had done very little high flying before) learned early that they had to wipe their six .50-caliber guns clean of oil before they took off; otherwise, the guns froze before they struggled up to the necessary 25,000 or 30,000 feet. They learned above all not to try to dogfight the more maneuverable Zero. Their primary targets were the bombers, which usually came over 26 at a time in a V-of-V's formation. Usually it was possible to dive on the bombers at least once and flame a few of them before the Zeros jumped the Grummans. The marines evolved their tactics which remained basic throughout the war: a direct overhead or high-side pass on the bombers (to avoid their tail stingers); one quick burst at an attacking Zero (they flamed easily) then dive for home. It didn't always work out that way, of course. Sometimes a pilot got tangled in a dogfight with the faster, better-climbing Zero. In that case he had best pray that somebody would shoot the Zero off his tail, because that is where the Zero usually would be found. The two-plane mutually protecting flight section was evolved very quickly. As one pilot put it: "The Zero could outmaneuver, outclimb, outspeed us. One Zero against one Grumman is not an even fight, but with mutual support two Grummans are worth four or five Zeros."

Despite their many disadvantages, the Guadalcanal fighter pilots found they had a sturdy plane with great fire power ("a Zero can't take two seconds' fire from a Grumman," said Major Joe Renner, "and a Grumman can sometimes take as high as fifteen minutes' fire from a Zero.") Under Secretary of the Navy Forrestal declared after a visit that "Grumman saved Guadalcanal," which may have been on the side of poetic license, since many things saved Guadalcanal, including half a dozen miracles, but it was true that the Marine pilots, skeptical since Midway, learned to place great confidence in their planes.

Living conditions were appalling. Pilots had to fight and fly all day on a diet of dehydrated potatoes, Spam or cold hash—and sometimes Japanese rice. The cigarettes they smoked—when there was anything to smoke—were frequently Japanese brands, too. Sleeping in a mud-floored tent was constantly interrupted by Japanese cruiser planes ("Louie the Louse" or Washing Machine Charlie) which flew around murdering sleep and dropping occasional bombs, or by destroyers or submarines which stood offshore and lobbed shells at Henderson Field. When a man could get away for a bath in the Lunga River, the only time he could take his clothes off, he frequently found there wasn't any soap. If he didn't catch malaria from the Anopheles mosquitoes which swarmed into his foxhole, he was almost certain to get dysentery that tormented his bowels, and many acquired both diseases.

On 29 August *William Ward Burrows* slipped into Sealark Channel with MAG-23's forward-echelon equipment and ground personnel. Word came of a cruiser task force's approach that night, and she sought refuge at Tulagi, where she promptly went aground. Some of the equipment was hauled over to Guadalcanal by Higgins boat, tank lighter and YP (Yippee) boat, but tons of matériel were thrown overboard to get the ship off the reef.

To share their misery, the Cactus pilots received welcome company at 1430 on 30 August when their first sizable reinforcements arrived, appropriately enough, in the middle of an air raid (the one which sank *Colhoun* five minutes later). Colonel Wallace, the Group commander, led in 19 F4F-4's of VMF-224 (Major Robert E. Galer) and 12 SBD-3's of VMSB-231 (Major Leo R. Smith). After maintenance crews worked over the day's damaged aircraft Guadalcanal could count 86 pilots and 64 planes (including 3 Army, 10 Navy). Two days later 5 officers, 387 men, and two bulldozers of the 6th Seabees came in to help make an airfield out of Henderson and to clear a short grassy strip a mile to the east called Fighter 1.

Welcome as these reinforcements were, the high command was understandably in a state of tremor. Manifestly, the Japanese intended to make Guadalcanal a major battleground. There was no reason to the contrary: the enemy could count on naval supremacy. With the ground reinforcements that were being poured into Guadalcanal by the precisely timed Tokyo Express destroyers which came in each night under cover of darkness, he would soon be able to attack Vandegrift's underfed, malarial, dysentery-wracked troops in strength. Despite the wretched condition of Guadalcanal's small air force, the Japanese were having great trouble gaining aerial supremacy. Already Rabaul had lost most of its original allotment of planes to the carrier-based and Henderson-based fighters and to the AA of ships and the 3d Defense Battalion. The one big factor in the Americans' favor was distance: they operated in and around their own airfield (and saved most of their pilots whose planes went down) whereas the Japanese were flying their bombers 560 miles from Rabaul and their fighters 300 miles from Buin. The Japanese couldn't stay around long, and they had to fight heavy with gas for the return trip.

But they began to throw greater strength into the air—as against 31 new planes for Henderson, Rabaul was reinforced on 1 September by twice as many —36 fighters and 27 medium bombers.[19]

What was needed more than anything else on Guadalcanal was air defense against the daily bombings and against the ever-present threat of an all-out naval siege. Apparently there was not much that airplanes could do about the nightly reinforcements the enemy destroyers were bringing in, nor about the ships which came on nocturnal prowls to lob shells into Henderson Field; the SBD's and occasionally PBY's tried glide bombing at night but they never hit anything. In the absence of U.S. surface craft to intercept these bombardments some PT boats would have helped, but it was October before the PT's arrived. It would have been splendid, of course, if the task forces could have been caught on the way down The Slot, but that would have required long-range planes to intercept them in daylight, far to the northwest. The B-17's were long-ranged but they couldn't use Henderson Field except in emergencies because there wasn't enough gasoline there to fuel them, nor a runway to accommodate them safely. Besides, the B-17's weren't very good at hitting ships.

The *sine qua non* was to get more suitable fighters into Guadalcanal immediately to deny the Japanese the air supremacy they were seeking. Admiral McCain recommended two more squadrons of F4F's or P-38's, the high-flying, twin-engined Army fighters which were just beginning to arrive in the Southwest Pacific. "Guadalcanal can be consolidated, expanded and exploited to the enemy's mortal hurt," he radioed Nimitz and Ghormley, "the reverse is true if we lose Guadalcanal and if reinforcement required is not available Guadalcanal cannot be supplied and hence cannot be held."

Ghormley asked MacArthur to spare as many P-38's as he could, but the General had only 18 and he was himself threatened with an invasion of Port Moresby, by land and by sea. Couldn't Ghormley lend *him* some carriers?

It was obvious everybody thought the strength lay with the other fellow; actually, weaknesses were prevalent, chronic and contagious. MacArthur kept his P-38's. Ghormley retained his four carriers and Guadalcanal was left where it was when the exchange of SOS messages started.

On 3 September the first transport plane landed on Guadalcanal, bearing no less than the commander of the 1st MAW, Brig. General Roy S. Geiger, and his chief of staff, Colonel Louis E. Woods,[20] and intelligence officer, Lieut.

---

[19] Information furnished Lieut. Pineau by Captain Ohmae in June 1949.

[20] Louis Earnest Woods was born in Fredonia, N.Y., 7 October 1895. Attended Syracuse University. First lieutenant (temporary) 1917, captain (temporary) 1917, major (temporary) 1919, lieutenant colonel 1936, colonel 1941, brigadier general (temporary) 1942, major general 1944. In World War I he served in *Georgia* and later commanded the Marine detachment in *Pittsburgh*. He was designated naval aviator in 1922, and served in Haiti with squadron of 1st Marine Brigade. Instructed at Marine Corps Schools, Quantico; was attached to the Division of Aviation and was Chief of Staff of the 1st MAW when the Wing was ordered into combat. CG advance echelon 1st MAW 4 November 1942 commanding Allied

Colonel John C. Munn. With them they brought good news: MAG-14 (Lieut. Colonel Albert D. Cooley) with two combat squadrons and an excellent service squadron—a total of 111 officers and 1,116 enlisted men—was already on the way to the South Pacific from the West Coast.[21]

Having operated in the early days as Indian fighters, Guadalcanal's airmen began now to get some system into their operations. Under Geiger something resembling staff work began to take shape. The Old Man himself had a knack of holding together an outfit of kids; he had been a Marine aviator since 1917, when most of Guadalcanal's flyers hadn't been born.

Geiger sent some of his officers to Espíritu to set up wing headquarters. He stayed on as ComAirCactus, his headquarters audaciously established in a wooden shack ("the Pagoda") only 200 yards from the runway ("the Bullseye").

There was a radar now, which helped a lot: the Japs had learned the coastwatchers were spotting them and they frequently flew off course far enough to avoid detection.

Otherwise, there wasn't much improvement in conditions as of early September. The 1st MarDiv and its reinforcements had a reasonably firm grip on the perimeter surrounding the airfield, but Vandegrift dared not extend his lines any farther. At night the Japanese had complete control of the seas. U.S. Navy managed to slip through a submarine or a destroyer occasionally with meager supplies, but these were expendable too—on the night of 4–5 September Japanese surface forces sank *Colhoun's* sister ships, *Little* and *Gregory*, just off Lunga Point. And Japanese submarines were gathering in increasing numbers (September was their best month of the war).

On 5 September Lieut. Colonel Wyman F. Marshall, a 49-year-old former airlines pilot, executive officer of MAG-25, flew in (under enemy fire) an R4D which contained a ton and a half of candy and cigarettes. On the return trip he carried wounded. Thus began MAG-25 operations, which were another factor in the saving of Guadalcanal.

The transport pilots of MAG-25 owed much to some friends outside the Marine Corps. Until World War II began Marine pilots had had little training in aerial navigation. In February 1942 Captain Philip V. Weems USN (Ret) offered to train six marines without charge at his famous navigation school at

---

Air on Guadalcanal until December. Awarded DSM for service in the Solomons. As Director of Aviation in 1943 he received the Legion of Merit, and served in Washington until ordered to command the 4th Marine Base Defense Air Wing (MBDAW) in the Central Pacific in August 1944, for which service he won a second award of the Legion of Merit. CG 2d MAW on Okinawa 11 June 1945 until after the surrender. Third award of Legion of Merit for the Okinawa campaign. In lieu of a fourth award of the Legion of Merit, he received the Army's Oak Leaf Cluster as CG of the 1st MAW in China from November 1945 to March 1946. Retired 1951.

[21] It was a time of movement in the rear areas, too. Marine Air Wings, Pacific (MAWPac), organized in San Diego 15 August with Major General Rowell as CG moved its headquarters to Ewa in late September. The 4th MBDAW was organized in Ewa by Colonel Larkin on 22 August.

Annapolis. Mr. Edwin A. Link, of Binghamton, N.Y., inventor of the Link Trainer, loaned them his private plane to conduct celestial navigation problems. When these six—Captains Warren E. Sweetser Jr., Henry C. Lane, Wilfrid H. Stiles, Elmore W. Seeds, Lieut. Russell L. Young and Sergeant M. Garner —graduated they were sent, three to each wing, as instructors. The first class they taught finished in August 1942, and the graduates promptly navigated the 5,200 miles from San Diego to New Caledonia. All 13 planes of VMJ-253 had arrived at Tontouta by 3 September.

Hammer and Tongs

The new pilots of VMF-224 had their first enemy contact when they went along with some of the "older" VMF-223 crowd to intercept a 40-plane raid at 1130 on 2 September. The Japanese lost seven planes, two of them to the newly arrived Squadron CO, Bob Galer. Next day Mangrum and Leo Smith took some SBD's to bomb and strafe a group of 34 landing boats—bad omens —which were sighted off Santa Isabel Island, north of Tulagi. On 4 September both squadrons of SBD's attacked more of these targets: a third of them were 70 feet long, the rest about 40 feet.

The task of these boats became plain a day later when six F4F's and two P-400's located 15 of them landing a total of more than 1,000 troops in broad daylight between Visale and Lever's Pass on the west coast of Guadalcanal. Fourteen boats reached shore, but the pilots thought their strafing might have caused 50 per cent casualties. One F4F crashed into the sea, having flown through heavy ground fire from small-caliber machine guns. We know now that 5,200 enemy troops were landed by 7 September; Major General Kawaguchi arrived 31 August to command them.[22]

On 6 September two SBD's were lost when they ran into heavy weather after attacking ships in Gizo Harbor, 200 miles to the northwest, but one pilot whom nobody had ever expected to see again returned to camp. He was Lieut. Richard R. Amerine of VMF-224, who had been shot down six days earlier. He had bailed out 30 miles to the west but had made his way back through enemy patrols, after being forced to kill four Japanese soldiers in the process. His was the first of many survival escapades: Marion Carl was missing for five days after being shot down—he owed his life to friendly natives who helped him get back.

The Cactus Air Force was doing fine—in daylight. Its count was probably overoptimistic but indicative: about five enemy aircraft for every plane CAF lost in combat, and the Japanese ships and barges learned not to venture near until after sundown. But its assets dribbled away also in operational losses, caused chiefly by inexperienced pilots and by the wretched condition of Henderson Field. Hardly a day passed but a pilot or two failed to get off the muddy strip and crashed at the end of the runway. On the afternoon of 8 September, 16 F4F's took off during an alert in the rain and fog. As the weather worsened

---

[22] *Southeast Area Operations*, Part One (Navy), p 19.

and darkness fell Munn persuaded Geiger to recall the planes, and they came in between 1900 and 1930 trying to land on the deeply rutted strip. One pilot crashed into a bulldozer. Four others cracked up, and the rest probably would have, had not Captain Darrell D. Irwin and Lieut. Pond signalled them on board with flashlights, carrier fashion. Next day one plane crashed on the take-off, four more were shot down as the two fighter squadrons downed only seven Zeros and B-26-type Japanese bombers (Bettys). Despite four new planes escorted up from Espíritu on the 7th, the fighter pilots could see their machine strength ebbing away. On 10 September Guadalcanal's effective air strength was 11 F4F's, 22 SBD's, 3 P-400's.

For the pilots on Guadalcanal 11 September seemed like many another day. There was an air-raid alarm at 0930 but the nine intercepting planes from the two fighter squadrons found it was false. At the same time nine SBD's took off on the four-hour round trip to Gizo—there wasn't much to bomb there except a few buildings but the high command had ordered it as the proper area for reconnaissance. At 1210 ("Tokyo time") there was an alarm that wasn't false; this time 26 bombers came over with eight Zeros and some of them got through to the field, killing 11 marines and wounding 17 others, destroying one P-400 on the ground and shooting down Bob Galer after he had knocked down a bomber and a Zero (Galer landed in the water and swam ashore). John Smith shot down two Japanese bombers, Lieuts. Kenneth Frazier, Eugene Trowbridge and Noyes McLennan one apiece. At 1515, 13 SBD's took off and looked for a heavy cruiser and two destroyers 100 miles to the northwest. Four of the planes found the ships, despite poor visibility, but got no hits.[23]

At 1620 that afternoon 24 F4F's of VF-5, which had been grounded at Espíritu since 31 August after their home base, *Saratoga*, was torpedoed by a submarine, were led into Henderson Field by Lieut. Commander Leroy C. Simpler. Admiral Ghormley had consistently refused to allow carrier aircraft to operate from Guadalcanal (except Caldwell's handful of SBD's), and only 14 hours earlier he had assured Admiral Fletcher he had "no intention directing planes now on carriers to base Guadalcanal or issuing any directive unduly restricting your freedom of movement." Something must be up.

And something was up. Intelligence reported that a superior naval and military force was lurking in the Truk-Palau area, and they expected a heavy attack which, co-ordinated with the attacks of Rabaul-based planes and a push against Vandegrift's troops by newly landed Japanese soldiers, might well cook the Guadalcanal goose. Ghormley began his message to Nimitz bluntly: "The situation as I view it is very critical . . . food situation at Guadalcanal not good. Our transportation problem increases steadily as Japs perfect their

---

[23] September 1942 was a poor month for sinking Japanese ships; the South Pacific forces sank none whatsoever. One destroyer was sunk in the Southwest. Only 14 Japanese cargo ships went down; 12 of them were victims of U.S. submarines, one was sunk by a British plane off Burma, another by an American Army plane in the Aleutians.

blockade methods." He only hoped that "hostile attacks will find us with a dry field."[24]

Simpler's squadron got there just in time. Forty-two planes came down from the north at 1100 of the 12th, to be met by 21 of Simpler's planes, 5 of John Smith's and 6 of Galer's. The Japanese lost 12 bombers and 3 fighters—10 planes to marines and 5 to the Navy pilots. The only fatality was an ensign killed in a dead-stick landing crash.

That was only one blow in a three-way attack that was supposed to capture Henderson Field. During the afternoon seven destroyers were spotted on the way to Guadalcanal, and at 2100 they made their presence felt: the field, bivouac area and beach were shelled by four ships—a light cruiser and three destroyers—on at least three different occasions. Three Marine dive-bomber pilots were killed (including Baldinus, who had hit *Jintsu*), one other and a radio-gunner were wounded.

Almost at the moment of the first shelling from the sea, the soldiers of General Kawaguchi fell on the Americans just south of Henderson Field. Three battalions probed into the thinly held line of Colonel Merritt Edson's 1st Raider Battalion and two companies of attached parachutists. The sporadic fighting lasted all night, into the 13th. On that day there were three air attacks: one at 0950 and another at 1300, and a float-plane attack at 1730 which picked off an SBD as it was landing. The Japanese lost a total of 11 planes, but knocked down 5 Marine and Navy planes, killing 5 flyers and wounding 2 others. That night (the 13th–14th) Bloody Ridge reached its full fury; the battered marines in front of the airfield wavered but they held. A few enemy did manage to filter through far enough to be killed by General Vandergrift's headquarters staff between the Ridge and Henderson Field. Marine machine-gun, rifle and artillery fire killed more than 600 Japanese before the attack petered out.[25] The greatest single threat to Henderson Field was over.

Toward the end of the attack on Bloody Ridge three P-400's—"klunkers" their pilots called them—pounced into it with a strafing attack that all but annihilated the last of the enemy concentration. Before he signed off one Japanese officer paid his respects to the Army klunkers; the last entry in the

---

[24] Among other things, the critical situation prevented the 7th Marines being sent to General MacArthur, who had been pleading for some amphibious-trained troops, even a regiment. Admiral King had ordered such a regiment to the Southwest Pacific on 8 September, and the 7th Marines seemed to be elected. But Rear Admiral Kelly Turner, who though absent was still in charge of the Guadalcanal assault, protested: "Adequate air and naval strength have not been made available to insure Guadalcanal and Tulagi's security, and in the absence of these forces much greater dependence must be placed on troop defense." He won his point. The 7th Marines was hurriedly loaded at Samoa and headed toward Guadalcanal. Then the Navy high command came up with a plan to send the 8th Marines of the 2d MarDiv to MacArthur, but by the time they could be made ready they, too, were needed at Guadalcanal.

[25] 1st MarDiv final report, Phase IV, p 11.

diary found on his body glumly noted, "Intensive bombing and strafing followed our unsuccessful attack at dawn and our efforts to take the field are doomed to failure."

The high command threw everything it could spare into Henderson Field on the 13th: Navy pilots off *Hornet* and *Wasp* ferried in 18 additional F4F's which were fed into VMF-223 and VMF-224,[26] augmenting those squadrons' fighter strength by 200 per cent. In the afternoon more *Saratoga* pilots and planes arrived from Espíritu to help save what had begun to look like a very risky investment: Lieut. Commander Louis J. Kirn brought in 12 SBD's of VS-3 and Henderson Field got its first torpedo planes when Lieut. Harold H. Larsen USN brought in six TBF's of VT-8. During the day Cactus lost 6 planes while shooting down 11 of the enemy.

Again Admiral Mikawa was able to beat Ghormley at the game of reinforcing. Whereas Henderson Field was furnished 60 additional planes 11–13 September, Rabaul received 140 on the 12th. These were 60 fighters, 72 medium bombers and 8 reconnaissance planes of the 26th Air Flotilla, Vice Admiral Masasato Yamagata commanding. The new flotilla had been intended as relief for the 25th, but the failure of Kawaguchi's detachment to take Henderson Field changed their mission to one of reinforcement.[27]

The crisis of mid-September ended in another disaster. *Hornet* and *Wasp*, only carriers operating in the Pacific while *Saratoga* and *Enterprise* were in for repairs, moved into waters southeast of Guadalcanal to escort six transports carrying the 7th Marines. It happened that the Japanese had just sowed this area with another division of submarines. Two or three 21-inch torpedoes tore into *Wasp* which became a sinking inferno. By 2100 there was one CV left operational in the Pacific. For good measure the battleship *North Carolina* was holed by another torpedo, and the destroyer *O'Brien* caught a fish which opened a hole in her bow. After temporary repairs had been made and *O'Brien* was on her way to the West Coast she broke in two and sank. The naval balance in the Pacific, already precarious, tipped ominously as September started over the hill and fateful October appeared on the horizon.

The loss or temporary inactivation of the Navy's carriers had one salutary effect: Navy planes and pilots who otherwise would have been unemployed were pouring into Henderson Field.[28] On 17 September there were 63 planes operational (29 F4F's, 26 SBD's, 5 TBF's, 3 P-400's), of which 36 were recent arrivals. Six Navy TBF's arrived 18 September, ten more SBD's and TBF's came in ten days later. During the last half of September a plane or two or three were lost daily, more often to the weather or the muddy runway than to combat (enemy air raids slackened noticeably), but constant reinforcements and continuous repair enabled General Geiger to hang on with 50 to 70

---

[26] With the exception of four of them which were shot down or cracked up before they could be assigned to squadrons.

[27] Information furnished Lieut. Pineau by Captain Ohmae.

[28] This caused General Rowell to observe wryly, "What saved Guadalcanal was the loss of so many carriers."

planes operational at all times. Despite steady attrition, he had 58 planes when 1 October dawned over the Guadalcanal jungle.

Aviation personnel on Guadalcanal during this period (as of 22 September) totalled 1,014, including 33 Army and 64 Navy.[29] Next day there were a few more—MAG-14's skipper, Lieut. Colonel Cooley, and five pilots of his dive-bomber squadron, VMSB-141, flew in.[30] Geiger put Cooley in charge of all the bombers; Wallace became fighter commander.

A few more filtered in from time to time. On 25 September the first five pilots of Cooley's VMF-121 arrived to begin that squadron's illustrious record. Like most new arrivals they came in by VMJ-253's taxi service. But on the same day the enemy could report an operational air strength of 100 fighters and 80 bombers at Rabaul.[31]

On the 27th the remainder (5 pilots and 11 gunners) of Caldwell's "Flight 300" left Guadalcanal to return to their ship.

But on 28 September six new SBD's of Lieut. Commander John Eldridge's VS-71 arrived, along with four more torpedo planes from VT-8, to begin as valiant service as was performed in the dark, desperate days ahead.

Thirty-one Japanese planes were intercepted over Henderson Field on the 27th, following warning from a coastwatcher. Eleven of them were shot down— 6 bombers and 5 fighters—by the 16 Marine and 18 Navy Wildcats which took after them. On the 28th the Emperor's Rabaul "eagles" came down 55 strong, and what followed was the hottest performance to date: 23 bombers and a fighter sent flaming to earth. Scores were credited as follows: VMF-223 7, VMF-224 8, VF-5 9.

One of the planes was destroyed by Lieut. Colonel Bauer, up from Efate on one of his periodic visits. It was that way at Cactus—a few new men being fed in to take the places of those who didn't come back; sick and wounded being flown out; a handful of planes ferried up from "Santo." VMSB-141 got there in driblets, five pilots on one occasion, six on another, five more on another. Who could tell? Those three pilots on temporary duty from Efate or Espíritu might make the difference between victory and defeat. The six SBD's just arrived in Nouméa might turn the tide—rush them up to Cactus right away!

Keeping records was one of the last things they thought about on Cactus in the fall of 1942. It was not possible to say who was flying on Guadalcanal at any given time. Most of the pilots of VMO-251 might be flying off Henderson Field while the Squadron was officially stationed on Espíritu—where its

---

[29] 1st MarDiv personnel report.

[30] Cooley tells this story of how he was notified that his group was going to Guadalcanal: At San Diego late in August General Geiger encountered Cooley. "Al," he said, "got your Group ready to go to war?" Cooley's dive-bomber squadron had just been split four ways to form new squadrons, and he had just received a new, untrained fighter squadron. So, he said, "Not ready, sir, but willing." Said Geiger, "Well, you're goin' next Saturday." They did—over 1,200 officers and men sailing for Nouméa.

[31] Information furnished Lieut. Pineau by Captain Ohmae.

ground echelon was doing a fine job running an air base, arming and gassing transient planes and quartering and feeding transient airmen. Said one VMO-251 pilot,[32] who was on "temporary duty" at Guadalcanal from October to January, "We never knew what squadron we were in; we were never carried as an administrative unit."

"Units" became inextricably mixed, and a pilot frequently had no idea what outfit his wingman belonged to. On 3 October Lieut. Commander Eldridge led a flight of five dive bombers drawn from four different squadrons: VS-71, VS-3, VMSB-141, VMSB-231. And on the same day a Japanese air attack was met by 29 fighters: 15 from VF-5, 5 from VMF-223, 9 from VMF-224 (including two pilots on temporary duty from VMF-212, one of whom, Bauer, shot down four planes).

Throughout Geiger's command there was always a sense of desperation, but never defeatism. Sink that ship! Knock down those bombers! That was the idea. The Old Man himself, aged 57, entered into the spirit of the thing. One day (22 September) when some pilots were grousing about having to take off from the pocked runway, he crawled into an SBD, weaved his way down the strip, took off and dropped a 1,000-pound bomb in the Visale area, where Japanese troops had been reported.

---

[32] Major William R. Campbell.

CHAPTER SEVEN

Crisis in October

LIEUT. GENERAL HYAKUTAKE went ahead with his plans to recapture Guadalcanal in October before moving on to Port Moresby in November. He had lost the Ichiki Detachment of about 900 men, in his first attempt to retake Henderson Field. Then a reinforced brigade (Kawaguchi Force), five times greater, had been cut to ribbons at the Ridge, leaving barely half its numbers wandering around the jungles of Guadalcanal. The Americans, estimated by the General's Intelligence on 19 September to number about 7,500,[1] were being stubbornly annoying in holding their 10-square-mile plot on the shores of the Lunga River. This in spite of Japan's demonstrable advantages: (1) naval supremacy, (2) shorter supply lines, (3) the *Bushido* spirit, that ennobling and all-pervading force which had swept the Emperor's subjects to one success after another.

In September Hyakutake went from Rabaul to Truk for a conference to deal with this problem of dislodging the U.S. Marines. At this meeting with the C-in-C Combined Fleet and C-in-C Southeastern Fleet, plans were laid to crush the Americans and recapture Guadalcanal on 21 October, after which 17th Army reserves would wipe out the Americans and Australians at Port Moresby, which had been Hyakutake's original assignment. He had drawn up the plans for capturing Port Moresby while he was in Tokyo, but the Solomons invasion intervened just as he was leaving for the South Seas in August, so his task was broadened. Now he put first things first.

Hyakutake's forces, including tanks and heavy artillery which had been in conspicuous shortage when Ichiki and Kawaguchi attempted to eliminate this southern threat, were built around two infantry divisions: the 2d (also called the *Sendai* Division because it had been originally recruited in Sendai, a city of a quarter million not far from Tokyo) and the 38th (a veteran division which had helped capture Hong Kong and Java). The *Sendai,* commanded by Lieut. General Masao Maruyama, had arrived at Rabaul and the Shortland Islands in August from the Philippines and Java; the 38th was reassembled in late September from the easy pickings at Java, Amboina, Timor and Sumatra in the Netherlands East Indies.[2]

---

[1] Actually there were more than 19,000 on that date.

[2] John Miller Jr., *Guadalcanal: The First Offensive* (a volume in the official history of the Army in World War II), p 138.

More naval aircraft were flown down to Rabaul to keep operational strength at about 180—three times as many planes as Geiger could count on. The base at Buka in the northern Solomons could also accommodate bombers, which shortened their run to Guadalcanal by 160 miles. The new fighter strip at Buin in southern Bougainville was ready, and 30 fighters were sent down 20 October. General Hyakutake would be able to count on additional naval support. Battleships had not yet been used in the Solomons, but for the October show *Kongo, Haruna, Hiei* and *Kirishima* were readied. More submarines were added to bring the total to an even dozen.

General Hyakutake sounded a note of grandeur in his message to the 17th Army: "The operation to surround and recapture Guadalcanal will truly decide the fate of the control of the entire Pacific."

The Unstoppable Express

There simply wasn't much that could be done about the Hyakutake forces which streamed into Guadalcanal, using the cover of darkness with diabolical skill. The Tokyo Express left the Shortlands–Faisi area each afternoon, its destroyers bearing up to a thousand troops. By 1800, about half an hour before darkness settles over the tropics, the Express arrived within 200-mile range of the Guadalcanal-based SBD's and TBF's. That meant the dive bombers and torpedo bombers could take one crack at the destroyers before they had to hurry for home. But a maneuvering destroyer is difficult to hit under the best of circumstances. Pilots sometimes claimed "possibly damaging near misses," and on 5 October the flyers led by Lieut. Commander Lou Kirn of VS-3 thought they saw one of the Express's six destroyers sink. But postwar records indicate that not one of the destroyers was sunk.

Each night the destroyers, having evaded these twilight efforts to stop them, shifted into high gear and hauled up to Guadalcanal about midnight to unload Hyakutake's troops, just across the Matanikau River, only eight or ten miles west of Henderson Field. The unloading was usually synchronized with nuisance bombing by Japanese planes and/or by shelling of the field by a cruiser or a destroyer.

To say the least, it was difficult to get planes off the field under these conditions. The Guadalcanal flyers tried. While one SBD dropped flares over the discharging destroyers, others strove to hit the ships by glide bombing. They were eminently unsuccessful and they lost several planes and pilots trying it. A couple of PBY's came up from Espíritu Santo which were equipped with a primitive aircraft radar, but they were too close to the land mass for the radar to function properly and their bombing was no more accurate than that of the SBD's.

Within two or three hours the destroyers had emptied their decks of Hyakutake's soldiers and scooted northward. By daylight they were again out of range. By destroyer and by barge the Japanese forces on Guadalcanal had been built up to about 20,000 before the great October crisis.[3]

---

[3] *Ibid,* p 139. Other estimates run as high as 28,000.

An entry of 3 October in the MAG-23 war diary is typical of the unsuccessful efforts to stop the Tokyo Express:

1615. On receipt of Lt. Milner's radio contact 8 SBD's and 3 TBF's led by Lt. (j.g.) F. L. Frank, VS-3, directed to attack enemy ships. 1 SBD returned immediately due to engine trouble. At 1725 contact was made resulting in 3 near misses on CA by SBD's and 1 claimed hit with 500# bomb by a TBF. Several near misses on DD. All ships maneuvered violently in circles during attack and laid up heavy AA barrage. 6 Zeros attacked our planes after attack, one of which was shot down by Gunter, Henry's radioman, and one by TBF. Later report by Ens. Russell indicated no visible damage and ships continued on original course. . . .

2220. Second attack group of 5 SBD's led by Lt. Cmdr. J. Eldridge, Jr., VS-71. . . . Lt. Hanna returned immediately due to poor visibility and lack of radio communication. Radio control was established by use of receiver and transmitter in plane near operations tent as planes used in mission had just arrived and frequency not adjusted to our control. Only Lt. Cmdr. Eldridge and Ens. Purdun contacted objective and ineffectively dropped bombs. The 4 or 5 DD's were moving rapidly in vicinity of Pt. Cruz.

5 more SBD's followed, loaded with flares and again attack was without results. 2nd Lt. Glen B. Loeffel sighted and attacked CA on course 330°, 20 miles North of Cape Esperance and believed to have scored hit. Later verified by morning striking force. DD's were unloading at Gaughlan Harbor. Lieut. Hull did not return from flight. Pilot and gunner recovered safely October 5th.

Operations during this night were extremely difficult as two enemy planes were constantly cruising over Henderson Field, and 4 bombs were dropped.

Only on one day was blood drawn from the highly successful Tokyo Express. Late in the afternoon of 5 October nine SBD's under Lieut. Commander Kirn contacted six destroyers 150 miles distant. Kirn and Ensign Weary attacked one ship; Lieut. (jg) Frank, Ensign Murphy and Lieut. Joseph M. Waterman of VMSB-141 attacked another. The claim: one sunk, the other possibly sunk. The reality: major damage to both destroyers (*Minegumo, Murasame*) from near misses.[4] Some time after midnight three destroyers—presumably uninjured—were located ten miles west of Lunga Point. Attempts to bomb them were unsuccessful and they were gone before daylight.

General Hyakutake himself arrived on the Tokyo Express on the night of the 9th to take personal charge of the recapture of Guadalcanal. He chose the spot where General Vandegrift, accompanied by staff officers and interpreters, carrying a white flag and an American flag, would surrender.

---

[4] MAG-23 war diary, p 68; USSBS, *Campaigns,* p 164.

Geiger's Team

During early October the shoestring operations at Henderson Field were tangled and knotted. Six of John Smith's VMF-223 pilots had been killed, six wounded, but the rest stayed on until the Squadron was relieved 12 October. Galer's VMF-224 was in slightly better shape, and so was VF-5.[5] The Army's 67th Fighter Squadron received occasional replacements and managed to keep six to eight P-400's strafing and bombing barges and Japanese troops; on 7 October the Squadron was augmented by the arrival of 11 P-39's, which could operate very well in medium altitudes, and could even climb to 27,000, but still found their best use in ground support. On 9 October MAG-14's squadron of fighters, VMF-121, led by its CO, Major Leonard K. (Duke) Davis and his executive officer, Captain Joseph J. Foss, arrived to raise the F4F-4 strength at Guadalcanal from 26 to 46. In addition, two or three pilots at a time were fed in for temporary duty from VMF-212 at Efate and VMO-251 at Espíritu.

The situation regarding the Henderson-based bombers was also inextricably involved. By 1 October Mangrum's original VMSB-232 was finished,[6] and so was Lieut. Commander Caldwell's Flight 300. Besides the remnants of VMSB-231 and VS-3, there were available a handful of planes brought in by Eldridge of VS-71 in late September, and some torpedo planes of VT-8. Replacement pilots were fed in a few at a time, sometimes by the Douglases operated by MAG-25's VMJ-253 between New Caledonia and Guadalcanal, sometimes in General Geiger's own PBY, sometimes by a quick APD run, and sometimes in B-17's which had begun making occasional landings at Henderson. By 6 October Major Gordon A. Bell's VMSB-141 pilots, who had been arriving on the installment plan, numbered 21.

In spite of the apparent range of talent based on the Guadalcanal airfields, there was a shortage of planes that was never overcome until after the Guadalcanal crisis ended in mid-November. General Geiger could count 58 serviceable planes on 1 October (34 F4F-4's, 16 SBD's, 5 TBF's, 3 P-400's). This had dropped to 49 two days later, but was back to 61 by 7 October and to 81 with the arrival of VMF-121 two days after that.

The Battle of Cape Esperance

For eight days following 3 October no Japanese planes bothered Guadalcanal in daylight. But at 1220 on the 11th the radar on the ridge southeast of Henderson picked up two flights of unidentified planes at 138 miles. Colonel Wallace scrambled 8 planes of VF-5, 15 of VMF-121, 16 of VMF-223 and VMF-224, 3 P-400's and 9 P-39's. VMF-121 failed to join up and VF-5 made

---

[5] Both Galer and Smith were shot down 2 October, after Galer had got his tenth and eleventh planes, Smith his eighteenth. Both parachuted successfully. Their Guadalcanal feats won for them the Medal of Honor.

[6] Mangrum (evacuated 12 October) was the only pilot in his squadron able to walk away from Henderson Field. Seven of them were killed, four wounded, the others flown out for hospitalization. Four rear-seat gunners were killed, one wounded.

no contact. The new P-39's failed to struggle higher than 19,000 feet: oxygen trouble again. But planes of the two remaining Marine squadrons found plenty of targets at 25,000 feet: 34 bombers accompanied by 29 Zeros. The bombers never found Henderson Field, which had a propitious movement of clouds to conceal it by the time they arrived, and dropped their bombs far to the east. Seven bombers and four Zeros were shot down, Lieuts. Charles M. Kunz, Thomas H. Mann Jr., George L. Hollowell and Matthew H. Kennedy scoring two apiece. Captain Sharpsteen of the 67th Fighter finished off a crippled bomber.

This raid was calculated as a preliminary for bigger things that night. Within two hours two SBD reconnaissance pilots, Staff Sergeant Henry K. Bruce of VMSB-141 and Ensign Harold N. Murphy of VS-71, reported they had sighted "two cruisers and six destroyers" 200 miles to the northwest, bearing on Guadalcanal. At 1730 Lieut. F. L. Frank of VS-3 and Lieut. Walter R. Bartosh of VMSB-141 found the force again, now only 110 miles away.

As cover for a convoy bringing the first Army reinforcements to Guadalcanal (164th Infantry) ComSoPac had ordered a surface force to take up station near Rennell Island, 100 miles south of Guadalcanal, to "search for and destroy enemy ships and landing craft." Rear Admiral Norman Scott cleared the decks of his four cruisers (*San Francisco, Salt Lake City, Boise, Helena*) and five destroyers to prepare for night action.

What the Japs had planned was the landing of troops from six destroyers and the landing of heavy artillery and tanks from two seaplane tenders, while four cruisers blasted the Guadalcanal planes and airfields. Rear Admiral Goto, on board the heavy cruiser *Aoba*, was so confident he did not become suspicious when bright flares lit up the black waters off Guadalcanal; he assumed the three ships of the supply force were signaling him and he turned on his searchlights. (Actually, what he saw was flares contained in a *Salt Lake City* plane which crashed and burned after being catapulted.) The greatest surprise of his career awaited him.

Helena opened fire at 2346, followed immediately by *Salt Lake City, Boise,* and the destroyer *Farenholt. Aoba* was hit and damaged badly, with many on the bridge killed, including Admiral Goto (who died as his chief of staff assured him two U.S. cruisers had already gone down). The destroyer *Fubuki,* following *Aoba* in a right turn, was also hit and sank before it could complete the turn. The heavy cruiser *Furutaka,* next in line, caught the whole load of gunfire from the U.S. ships and sank 22 miles northwest of Savo Island. The heavy cruiser *Kinugasa* had made a lucky "wrong" turn to the left and thus had freedom of action to batter *Boise* severely and *Salt Lake City* slightly. The U.S. destroyer *Duncan* was sunk in this battle; *Farenholt* was heavily damaged.

The Battle of Cape Esperance was a victory of sorts for the U.S. surface forces (the first such since the war began), but nothing like what was believed at the time (four cruisers, four destroyers sunk). Admiral Scott retired with his damaged ships. The heavy artillery had been landed to the west of the

Matanikau just the same. And for the Americans on Guadalcanal the mid-October emergency was only beginning.

The destroyer *Murakumo* had escaped damage during the furious 34-minute naval engagement, having been obscured by smoke from *Aoba*.[7] *Murakumo* started to retire with the cripples but was ordered back to pick up survivors, in which task she was joined by the relief destroyer *Natsugumo*. At 0515 on the morning of the 12th two divisions of SBD's started for these ships; 5 planes led by Lieut. Commander Eldridge, 11 others by Lieut. Colonel Cooley. They were escorted by 16 F4F's and half as many P-39's.

The SBD's reported sighting a single destroyer plus a pair nearby, north of the Russells. Eldridge's division attacked the single ship, but reported no hits. Cooley's bombers struck at the pair of destroyers and left one of them smoking. "Ships continued on course at 25 knots but later observed to have slowed down to 10 knots, trailing an oil slick," the returning pilots reported.[8]

By 0806 the Guadalcanal planes were ready for another go at the retreating Japanese remnants. Lieut. Commander Kirn took out 4 Navy and 2 Marine dive bombers, Lieut. Larsen 6 torpedo planes, while Major John Dobbin of VMF-224 led 14 F4F's from three Marine squadrons. This time two destroyers were located 170 miles out. Three of the SBD's dropped their bombs close aboard, then while the fighters strafed the AA guns the TBF's made their runs. One torpedo found its target and the destroyer was left dead in the water.

Six hours later Eldridge led 11 SBD's, 1 TBF, 8 F4F's and 4 P-39's and found four ships in the same spot, including the one which was still dead in the water and two others which presumably had joined up in the retreat. This time Eldridge dropped his bomb on one of the destroyers, just aft of amidship, causing an explosion so violent the pilots believed it sinking. A close look convinced them also that the destroyer dead in the water was abandoning ship. What is known is that Japan lost the destroyers *Murakumo* and *Natsugumo*.[9]

The Big Bombardment

The 13th was a day when everything went wrong. Both the coastwatchers and the radar failed to give warning in time, and at 1202 Wallace's 42 F4F's, 7 P-39's and 6 P-400's were still climbing to altitude when bombs from 24 Japanese planes began raining on Henderson Field and Fighter 1. Big gashes were torn in both runways, some planes were damaged, and 5,000 gallons of aviation fuel were set afire. The only Japanese losses were one bomber which was caught going away and one of the 15 accompanying Zeros, shot down by Lieuts. Mann and William B. Freeman of VMF-121. Freeman's plane was hit, and he had to land in the water east of Henderson but was rescued.

---

[7] USSBS, *Interrogations*, Vol II, p 456.

[8] MAG-23 war diary, p 79.

[9] USSBS, *Campaigns*, properly credits Guadalcanal-based planes with sinking both destroyers. JANAC says *Natsugumo* was sunk by surface fire during the Battle of Cape Esperance, but USSBS testimony indicates clearly that *Natsugumo* was not present during the battle.

At 1350 the raiders were over again: 15 bombers with 7 to 10 Zeros. Again Henderson Field was damaged, and again interception was tardy (the fighters were refueling). Captain Foss shot down one Zero, but the rest of the enemy planes got away.

During the morning the first Army reinforcements—who had been delayed by the night cruiser battle—began landing. After going through the two worst air raids the island had known, they might well have asked what kind of a place this was. But they hadn't seen anything yet. Guadalcanal's aviation was almost written off during the ensuing 24 hours, as the next step in Hyakutake's recapture of the place.

General MacArthur made plans to withstand an all-out effort against Australia in case the Solomons fell, and urged the entire resources of the U.S. be diverted temporarily to the Southwest Pacific.[10]

"Purple nights" were what Lieut. Merillat called those times when

an impersonal danger filled the air and brooded over every one of the defenders huddled together within the defense perimeter around Henderson Field. The night of October 13–14 was splashed with deeper color than any of the others. We had been through "purple nights" before, but they faded to dainty lavender compared to the events of this and succeeding nights.[11]

The preliminaries began at 1830 when Japanese shells began falling on the western end of Henderson Field—a surprise to its defenders comparable to the attack on Pearl Harbor; nothing like this had happened before—being shelled when no ships were offshore. It was, of course, Hyakutake's 150-mm. guns which had been landed from the tenders two nights earlier—of heavy artillery he had landed a regiment plus three batteries. Not all of the big guns were firing at once, of course—the optimistic Americans concluded from the sporadic shelling that only one gun was involved, and it was promptly named "Pistol Pete." They also learned that Pistol Pete was not easily silenced; General Vandegrift had no sound-and-flash units, no effective counterbattery artillery (his biggest guns were 5-inch seacoast guns manned by the 3d Defense Battalion and the 105-mm. guns of the 11th Marines).

An hour later a Japanese plane circled Henderson Field, then scooted away when the searchlights focused on him. Around the perimeter flares were fired intermittently during the early evening. Other planes came over, singly or in pairs. Hyakutake's big guns fired an occasional burst. Plainly, there would be no sleep around Henderson Field this night. At 0138 Louie the Louse—or perhaps it was several Lice—flew over from Rekata Bay and dropped flares over the field: a red one over the west end, a white one in the middle, a green for the east end. Then all hell broke loose. A Japanese task force stood offshore for 97 minutes, throwing shells on the strip, into the taxiways and revetments.

[10] USSBS, *Employment of Forces Under the Southwest Pacific Command*, p 15.
[11] *The Island*, p 140.

The earth shook. Palm trees splintered. Buildings crashed and crumpled. Burning gasoline made the entire airfield look like "a sea of flame" to one Japanese observer. This was the first time battleships' guns had been trained on the field, and *Haruna* and *Kongo* made the most of it, firing 918 rounds of 14-inch (36-cm.) shells—625 armor-piercing, 293 high-explosive. There was nothing to put in opposition except four PT boats which had arrived at Tulagi the day before, and the 5-inch coast artillery guns which could only range the accompanying destroyers.

Occasional enemy bombers kept the Henderson Field defenders awake the rest of the night. At 0530 Pistol Pete opened up again, but this time his rounds fell short of the field. When the bleary-eyed marines and soldiers at last climbed out of their foxholes they surveyed a wreckage exceeding anything they had imagined: Henderson Field was a shambles, its Marston mat twisted into grotesque shapes of tangled steel. Of the 39 SBD's, only 4 could be flown, and everyone knew there would be more enemy ships on the way. The Pagoda was damaged and by orders from General Geiger it was bulldozed out of existence next day (it provided an excellent aiming point for the Japanese). The command post had to be moved to the eastern end of Henderson Field.

Among 41 Americans killed in the bombardment were Major Bell, CO of the newly arrived VMSB-141, and four of his pilots: Captains Edward F. Miller and Robert A. Abbott and Lieuts. Henry F. Chaney Jr. and George L. Haley.

Three enlisted men of HqSq-23 were also killed: Sergeant Frank E. Winterling, Corporal George W. Terwilliger and Private Robert D. Burke, when a direct hit demolished a dugout in which six men had sought shelter. One of them, Corporal Otto L. Yeater, crawled out of the debris and dug desperately with his bare hands to uncover his trapped comrades. His shouts for help were heard by twelve marines who answered his call. All were without tools but dug frantically, exposed to the rain of shell fire and a bombing attack. They succeeded in extricating two men alive and recovered the bodies of the other three. A flight surgeon, Lieut. Henry R. Ringness USN, continued to administer morphine and blood plasma to wounded marines in his foxhole, though he had been paralyzed. He died of his wounds three days later.

Although a few planes had dropped bombs on "the cow pasture" (Fighter 1), the battleships' guns had left it alone. It was suitable only for fighters in dry weather, but most operations were transferred from Henderson until Pistol Pete could be knocked out (despite great damage it was still possible for planes to take off from Henderson if they carefully avoided holes in the strip). An SBD which got off early in the morning of the 14th found 8 destroyers and 6 transports 140 miles northwest of Guadalcanal—this time Hyakutake was bringing real shiploads of troops and supplies. In the afternoon a sector search reported another force 180 miles away composed of 1 battleship, 3 cruisers and 4 destroyers; this meant another night bombardment.

Twenty-five unchallenged Japanese bombers hit Henderson Field at 1206 —again the warning had come too late, so 24 fighters scrambled tardily. An hour later 15 bombers and 10 Zeros came over, and this time the fighters were

WINGATE COLLEGE LIBRARY

ready: 9 bombers and 3 Zeros were shot down at a cost of 2 VMF-121 pilots and 1 from the 67th.

Lieut. William L. Woodruff, an engineering officer responsible for keeping the planes at Henderson Field in commission, with daring initiative and outstanding technical skill directed the ground crews who worked feverishly all day under intermittent shell fire repairing those SBD's which had not been totally destroyed.

By late afternoon two flights totaling 13 dive bombers and 7 Army fighters with bombs took off to intercept the Japanese destroyers and transports, which had been located near the southeast tip of Santa Isabel Island, about 70 miles north of Guadalcanal. Several possible hits were claimed, and a coastwatcher reported seeing one of the transports sink.[12] But the force was not deterred from its objective, which was the Japanese side of the Matanikau River.

Among the planes based at Henderson Field on the night of 13–14 October were eight B-17's. Two of them were wrecked by the naval bombardment; the other six took off (some on three engines) for Espíritu, carrying their personal effects and such of their ground personnel as had been sent to Henderson.[13] There were good reasons for sending the B-17's home: they were not likely to be able to interfere with enemy landing operations, and they drank too much gasoline, which had suddenly become critically short on Guadalcanal. Before the day was over the two damaged B-17's were drained of what fuel they contained. Not even the arrival of eight SBD's of VB-6 (Lieut. Commander Ray Davis) raised spirits at Henderson Field very much when the inhabitants of the field realized there might not be any gasoline to get them off the ground.

Actually, the fuel supply was better than it seemed at first (it couldn't have been worse than that). About 400 drums of 100-octane gasoline had been carefully hidden in holes and revetments several hundred yards from Henderson Field and had been all but forgotten.[14] When these drums were enthusiastically recovered Geiger could breathe easier—they would constitute about two days' supply. The agitation to get gasoline to Guadalcanal shook the whole South Pacific. Transport planes of VMJ-253 dropped all other duties to fly in ten drums at a time. YP boats brought 200 drums over from Tulagi. The destroyer-seaplane tender *McFarland* was rushed up from the south with 300 drums.

The night of 14–15 October brought another shelling by the cruisers *Chokai* and *Kinugasa*, which threw 752 8-inch shells into Henderson Field and environs.[15] Dawn of 15 October brought a sight that was insulting— so cocky were the Japanese about the elimination of air opposition that they

---

[12] A sinking not borne out by JANAC, but which in the light of other testimony and subsequent events may have occurred.

[13] *67th Fighter Squadron History*, pp 42–43.

[14] They hadn't been forgotten by Brig. General Louis Woods, who was on Espíritu Santo setting up 1st MAW headquarters. Earlier in October Woods had written General Geiger about the hidden fuel, but when he returned to Guadalcanal after the October crisis he found his letter in Geiger's pocket—still unopened.

[15] Morison, *The Struggle for Guadalcanal*, p 176.

stood off Tassafaronga, ten miles away, unloading troops, supplies and ammunition from five transports, in naked daylight. This time there were only three SBD's able to fly. One fell into a crater en route to the runway. Another was wrecked as it hit a crater taking off. Its pilot, Lieut. Robert M. Patterson of VMSB-141, tried again with the last bomber. He got away this time. Meanwhile, expert mechanics went into their third day of constant repairing without sleep. One by one the disabled SBD's were patched up again.

Four single-plane attacks were delivered on the transports before 0700, and hits were scored by Lieuts. Waterman and Ashcroft. The F4F's couldn't sink ships, but they could strafe troops being discharged. Major Davis of VMF-121 led a six-plane attack in which Lieut. (jg) E. T. Stover of VF-5 shot down a floatplane and collided with it on the way down, but managed to return. Tech. Sergeant Alexander Thomson was shot down.

Three planes of VMSB-141 were lost during the day, their pilots and gunners killed. Among the dead was the Squadron's first arrival, Lieut. Anthony J. Turtora Jr. Sometime after his last mission Lieut. Turtora's parents in the Bronx received an eloquent postscript to his life: "Always pray, not that I shall come back, but that I will have the courage to do my duty."[16]

Geiger stopped the single-plane attacks until he could muster something bigger. Then he threw everything he had at the transports, despite the constant overhead patrol of 30 Zeros. Twelve SBD's were ready by 1000. They were loaded with 500- and 1,000-pound bombs which they dropped on the brazen enemy ships; after they dropped their bombs they strafed the decks. P-39's and P-400's made three missions and claimed three hits which set fire to the ships. B-17's up from Espíritu Santo joined in the pounding and helped to sink one more. Geiger's own pilot, Major Jack Cram, who arrived the previous night from Espíritu with two torpedoes slung under the wings of his slow, ponderous PBY-5A, now contributed his share. Since all the torpedo planes had been destroyed by naval shelling, Cram asked to be allowed to make a twin-torpedo run with his old *Blue Goose*. This unorthodox maneuver exemplified that day's desperation on Guadalcanal; Cram made his run, released his torpedoes, one after the other, toward one of the transports. Then a gang of Zeros descended upon him. They perforated his plane constantly as he waddled home, and the last was eliminated only when he reached Fighter 1— Lieut. Roger Haberman of VMF-121 shot it down as he was approaching to land his own smoking plane.

At the end of the day the Guadalcanal defenders had burnt up the *Kyushu Maru, Sasako Maru* and *Azumasan Maru*, all good-sized passenger-cargo ships of 7,000 to 9,000 tons, together with most of their supplies, including much of General Hyakutake's artillery ammunition. These ships were beached. The other three were pulled out at 1550. But 4,500 troops of the 230th Infantry (38th Division) and 16th Infantry (*Sendai* Division) had been landed, somewhat the worse for wear.

There was another shelling from 0025 to 0125 on the morning of the 16th

---

[16] *Time,* 30 November 1942.

—1,500 shells from the heavy cruisers *Myoko* and *Maya*—and more U.S. planes were knocked out. General Geiger counted his three-day losses to the Japanese naval bombardment: 23 SBD's destroyed or requiring major overhaul; 6 F4F's; 8 TBF's; 4 P-39's. Thirteen SBD's and 3 F4F's had been damaged but put in flyable condition again. Altogether, there were now 34 planes—only 9 of them F4F's—to stop whatever the Japanese sent down against Guadalcanal.

A hurry-up call brought Lieut. Colonel Bauer's VMF-212, 19 F4F's, up from Efate, he also brought 7 SBD replacements (planes and crews). The planes circled to land late in the afternoon, and ran smack into a nine-plane dive-bombing attack. Although his fuel tanks were almost empty, Bauer set out after the Vals and shot down four of them before making his landing. In the opinion of the Henderson Field denizens, this was the most remarkable individual achievement by any airman in the annals of Guadalcanal. For it, Joe Bauer was awarded the Medal of Honor, though he didn't live to receive it.

One of the dive bombers got through and planted a bomb on the depth-charge racks of *McFarland,* which had come in that morning with 40,000 gallons of precious aviation fuel and after unloading had taken on board 160 hospital patients and war neurotics for evacuation. Twenty-seven men on board *McFarland* were killed, including four enlisted men of VMF-223, whose ground crew was in the process of evacuation by that ship and by the transport *Zeilin.*

MAG-23 Relieved

The arrival of new pilots permitted the evacuation of others whose relief from constant flying (including as much as seven hours a day of high-altitude combat duty) was long overdue. Besides VMF-223 and VMSB-232 flyers, the last of whom left 12 October, the last six pilots of Simpler's VF-5 were relieved; so were Major Dobbin and eleven other pilots of VMF-224, and two pilots and their gunners of VMSB-231.

Wallace turned over tactical command to MAG-14. Between 20 August and 16 October, MAG-23 and attached units' total claims showed 244 Japanese planes shot down (111½ by Smith's VMF-223, 60½ by Galer's VMF-224, 38 by Simpler's VF-5, and 8 by Brannon's 67th Fighter, the rest by the newly arrived VMF-121 and VMF-212, and by gunners on dive bombers and torpedo bombers). The attached bombers claimed to have hit 28 ships, including 6 of which were "seen to sink" and 4 others believed to have sunk.[17] MAG-23 lost 22 of its own pilots (3 to naval gunfire), plus 33 pilots of attached Marine, Army and Navy squadrons (5 of them to naval gunfire). For pilots green to combat, operating under conditions which often seemed hopeless against a skillful enemy whose aircraft were superior in many respects, Wallace's men had done very well.

An Australian officer with an intimate acquaintance with jungle warfare,

---

[17] Actually, 7 were sunk: *Natsugumo,* plus 6 credited to the Henderson flyers by JANAC: 2 destroyers, 3 transports, 1 auxiliary cruiser converted to transport duty (*Kinryu Maru*).

Commander Eric Feldt, paid the following tribute to the Cactus pilots:

> This is not the place to tell the heroic story of the Henderson Field
> flyers, who fought on day after day, while their friends were killed around
> them. Compared to the enemy's, the Wildcat pilots' losses were light, but
> they were severe against their own unaugmented numbers. It was their
> unabated aggressiveness, taking to the air at every alarm, that began the
> decline of the Japanese Air Force.
>
> The beating which the Japanese were taking in the air had its effect
> on the Marines on the ground. Only those who have watched the enemy
> do what he willed in the air can know the relief felt by Guadalcanal
> groundlings when they saw the Japanese aircraft defeated with heavy
> losses at each visit.[18]

One reason for the Group's low rate of fatalities was the diligent rescue
work shared by Americans, Australians, and the natives whose good will was
as valuable in saving lives as it was in spying on the enemy. More than half
the pilots shot down over or around Guadalcanal lived to fight another day.
One of the more valuable machines on Guadalcanal was the Grumman Duck
(small amphibian plane) which Lieut. Colonel Fike and other pilots flew out to
pick up pilots in the water. On 20 September Ensign Fink and his gunner,
Aviation Machinist's Mate Third Class M. L. Kimberlin, who sank the *Kinryu
Maru*, were picked out of the water between Savo Island and Cape Esperance.
Next day Major Joe Renner used the same aircraft to drop supplies to Ensign
Ralph M. Taurman, who had gone down on Santa Isabel; the day after that
he rescued a pilot and gunner of VMSB-231 from the same island. On 7 October
two more Ducks arrived for duty at Henderson; 24 hours later one of them
had rescued the resolute Lieut. Commander Eldridge from Tunnibuli on Santa
Isabel, and Eldridge was leading another strike before another 24 hours had
passed.

No less famous than the Ducks was "Horton's Schooner," a dilapidated
coastwise boat which coastwatcher Horton operated in and out of enemy-
patrolled coves to pick up downed pilots, evacuate missionaries, and distribute
supplies. Once he brought in five airmen whom coastwatchers had been hiding
and caring for. The gratitude of the Americans to the Solomons natives was
expressed in a letter in October from the Wing intelligence officer, Colonel
Munn, to General Woods:

> A native chief on Rennell Island saved three of our boys lately and
> they feel they should send him something. If you can get a bolt or two of
> calico or some other cloth, it will be a big help. Since the war it is impos-
> sible for the natives to get such stuff, as all the traders have gone to other
> places.

---

[18] *The Coastwatchers*, p 96.

The officers and men who had been relieved were sent back to the U.S. to impart their experience to new pilots and crews. Mangrum, Smith and Carl reached the West Coast on 21 October, and were given the "hero treatment" by press and public—War Bond rallies, magazine stories, public receptions.

After a few weeks of this most of the pilots were willing and eager to return to combat. But sensible Marine Corps policy dictated that they do their Stateside stint.[19] There had been too much emphasis, anyway, on individual "scores," which were intensely interesting to the public but not conducive to the best teamwork.[20]

Squaring Away

On 16 October Admiral Ghormley received word at his Nouméa headquarters of big Japanese naval concentrations off the Santa Cruz Islands, including a carrier. "This appears to be all-out enemy effort against Guadalcanal," he radioed Admiral Nimitz. "My forces totally inadequate to meet situation. Urgently request all aviation reinforcements possible."[21] Next day he sent his recommendations for a back-to-the-wall stand: send him all submarines in MacArthur's area, transfer cruisers and destroyers from Alaska, send all PT boats in the Pacific except those at Midway, review the entire destroyer assignment in the Atlantic as well as the Pacific. Of Army planes he wanted 90 heavy bombers, 80 medium bombers, 60 dive bombers, plus two groups of fighters (including those P-38's he had been requesting so long).

Back in Washington Secretary of the Navy Frank Knox held a press conference on 16 October. Asked whether Guadalcanal could be held, he answered: "I certainly hope so. I expect so. I don't want to make any predictions, but every man out there, ashore or afloat, will give a good account of himself."

The dismal outlook in Nouméa and Washington was fully justified by events in the Solomons. On 11 October a big segment of the Combined Fleet sailed from Truk; altogether Admiral Yamamoto had available 5 carriers, 5 battleships, 14 cruisers, 44 destroyers (although he never committed them all at once). Henderson Field, the plum in this vast pudding, got its share of stepped-up bombings.

The fresh fighter squadrons (VMF-121 and VMF-212) sailed into the

---

[19] When Smith applied for more combat duty he was told, "Not until you have trained 150 John Smiths." (Interview Brig. General Clayton C. Jerome, who was then Assistant Director of the Division of Aviation.) Smith didn't get overseas again for nearly two years.

[20] This opinion about individual scores came to be held generally by Marine Corps commanders after the first flushes of publicity had worn off. But some airmen of the AAF deliberately fostered competition between flyers under their command, and General Kenney radioed his score card to Washington (*General Kenney Reports*, pp 440, 470).

[21] ComSoPac war diary, 16 October 1942.

Japanese bombers and accompanying Zeros with great effect: on the 17th Duke Davis led a flight of 8 in an interception which accounted for 9 planes; next day 5 pilots from 121, 6 from 212, and 2 Navy pilots from VF-5 participated in a fight which cost the Japanese a total of 7 bombers and 13 Zeros. On the 19th 2 of 6 attacking Zeros were shot out of the Guadalcanal skies, and on the 20th Foss and Everton led an intercept that accounted for 7 Zeros and 3 bombers. The aerial softening up that was part of Hyakutake's preparation for his big attack was being rather well nullified by a group of determined Grumman Wildcat pilots. The Americans didn't have very many planes, but they could maintain local air superiority against the Japanese who had to come such a long way before reaching their target.

Meantime, Ghormley was relieved on 18 October by Vice Admiral William F. Halsey, who received his surprise orders as he stepped on board a whaleboat from a four-engined PB2Y at Nouméa. Admiral Nimitz had decided that "the critical situation requires a more aggressive commander,"[22] and that is just what the flamboyant, fun-loving "Bull" Halsey proved to be—a shot in the arm when the patient seemed in danger of passing away.

Two days after he took over, Admiral Halsey called a conference on board USS *Argonne* at Nouméa, to decide what could be done about the impending attack on the Guadalcanal perimeter. General Vandegrift flew down for it. Also present were Major General Millard F. Harmon, Commanding General, South Pacific (ComGenSoPac), Major General Alexander M. Patch, who would relieve Vandegrift's marines with Army troops when and if that became feasible, and even the Marines' Commandant, Lieut. General Thomas Holcomb, who happened to be in the South Pacific on an inspection tour.

Admiral Halsey recounts the story of the conference:

> Archie Vandegrift and Miff Harmon told their bitter stories. It was quite late when they finished. I asked, "Are we going to evacuate or hold?"
>
> Archie answered, "I can hold, but I've got to have more active support than I've been getting."
>
> Rear Adm. Kelly Turner, commanding the Amphibious Forces Pacific, protested that the Navy was already doing its utmost. He correctly pointed out that the few bottoms we had were becoming fewer almost daily; we did not have the warships to protect them; there were no bases at Guadalcanal where they could shelter, no open water permitting evasive tactics; and enemy submarines were thick and active.
>
> When Kelly had finished, Archie looked at me, waiting. What Kelly had said was of course true. It was also true that Guadalcanal had to be held.
>
> I told Archie, "All right. Go on back. I'll promise you everything I've got.[23]

---

[22] Morison, *The Struggle for Guadalcanal*, p 183.

[23] William F. Halsey and J. Bryan III, *Admiral Halsey's Story*, p 117.

Hyakutake's plan entailed an eastward attack along the coast by Major General Sumiyoshi, across the mouth of the Matanikau; another right hook on the Matanikau position from the south, under Colonel Oka; with the main effort (nine infantry battalions, plus artillery, engineer and medical troops) under the *Sendai* CG, Lieut. General Maruyama, being directed against Henderson Field from the south. This latter push meant a prodigious amount of hand labor: toting supplies across the Matanikau and Lunga Rivers, through the jungles where they are thickest, to a position directly south of Henderson Field. Before the supplies, artillery and ammunition (each soldier was directed to lug one shell) could be hauled into position, the Japanese engineers had to whack a path through some of the world's thickest undergrowth. But it was done: the Japanese never shunned back-breaking labor. Hyakutake issued his tactical plans 15 October, and on the 17th Maruyama's forces set out on their wide enveloping march along the path the engineers had cut through the jungle. Heavy rains delayed the main force trying to cross the upper Lunga; the date of attack, which had been set forward to the 18th, then the 19th, was postponed until 22 October. The troops got hungrier with each delay, having been put on half rations. The slippery trails grew slimier. All Maruyama's artillery pieces had to be left along the oozing route.

End of October Fighting

General Hyakutake's big attack was a complete failure. Even under favorable circumstances, it was a most complicated plan extremely difficult of execution. Communications between his outfits, widely scattered as they were around the perimeter, failed badly. The various units never co-ordinated their attacks properly. Repeated postponements confused Hyakutake's own commanders more than Vandegrift. Sumiyoshi's artillery began a heavy concentrated fire at 1800 on 23 October, followed by a tank attack across the sand bar of the Matanikau. Del Valle's artillery fired a series of murderous barrages, which prevented the Japanese infantry from moving and, incidentally, killed about 600 of them and knocked out three tanks (one which got to the Marine lines was disposed of by a hand grenade which crippled it and a half-track 75 which finished it). Until dark the Henderson SBD's furnished continuous air support with 100- and 500-pound bombs on the enemy concentrations.

Lieut. General Maruyama had got his dates mixed, as well as his line of departure, and failed to deliver the simultaneous attack against the southern perimeter. He was not ready until 0030 on 25 October to deliver his attack on the left wing of the southern flank. When he did attack, General Kawaguchi, who commanded the right wing of the southern flank, had lost his directions, ended up behind Maruyama, and failed to co-ordinate the push against Henderson Field which was supposed to be delivered from his direction. A few of Maruyama's men managed to break through the U.S. lines after heavy fighting, but the 1st Battalion, 7th Marines, and soldiers of the 3d Battalion, 164th Infantry, who were fed into the Marine lines, beat back the screaming Japanese all night long. Reorganized lines and a stiffened defense threw back with terrific loss an even stronger attack the next night. Weak attacks continued for the next two nights, and by 28 October it was evident that the enemy had been finally defeated at every point of contact. Conservative estimates indicate 3,400 Japanese had been killed and hundreds of wounded died in the retreat.

Meanwhile, the Japanese had sent down another heavy air attack on 23 October to soften up the U.S. perimeter in preparation for Hyakutake's big effort. Twenty-four F4F's from the two Marine and one Navy fighter squadrons rose to meet them and claimed the heaviest toll since Guadalcanal was invaded: 20 Zeros and 4 bombers. Captain Foss shot down four Zeros.

There was no air raid on the torrential 24th, but 25 October was the big day, forever memorialized in Marine annals as "Dugout Sunday." It was also the day most planes were immobilized by mud on Fighter 1 until afternoon. Maruyama's postmidnight attack was only the beginning of what was supposed to be a co-ordinated land, sea and air attack to recapture Guadalcanal. Geiger's headquarters lost count of the air raids, and the war diary (assembled some time later) simply notes that: "Enemy fighter planes were over Cactus at irregular intervals throughout the daylight hours. Our Grummans were almost continuously in the air, landing, refueling, reloading and taking off again time after time."[24]

Escorted by Zeros, 16 heavy bombers came over at 1430, by which time the field had dried enough to permit take-offs. Nine dive bombers arrived half an hour later and fortunately wasted their cargo on Geiger's "boneyard" of wrecked planes. Lieut. Jack E. Conger of VMF-212 shot down a Zero and rammed the tail of another. Conger parachuted but the Japanese pilot crashed with his plane.

While Conger was in the water waiting to be rescued the pilot of another enemy plane drifted down and landed within half a mile of him. After the boat picked up Conger the crew went on to rescue the Japanese who had determined not to be rescued. He swam away but the boat overtook him. When he was being hauled on board he whipped out his pistol to shoot Conger, but it did not go off. Then the Jap tried to shoot himself but the pistol again failed to fire. By then Conger's patience was exhausted so he and an enlisted man knocked the Japanese unconscious and pulled him into the boat.

Duke Davis shot down a Zero and a bomber, and Lieut. Joseph L. Narr two Zeros and a bomber. For the second time in three days Joe Foss picked off four Zeros. Altogether, despite the late start, 22 planes were again knocked down by the fighter planes, and the shore-based antiaircraft, which had been improving steadily, got four others while they were attempting to strafe the field.

A predawn search had revealed "much small boat traffic between Russell Island and Guadalcanal," and at 0700 a search plane and a coastwatcher noted

---

[24] Final Report on Guadalcanal, phase V, pp 25–26.

a force of three destroyers only 35 miles away. By 1000 they were off Lunga Point, where they audaciously shelled the beach, sank *Seminole* and a YP boat. Four fighters finally managed to get out of the mud for an attack, but their strafing was deemed ineffective.

At 1300, when the field had dried off, Eldridge of VS-71 led five planes in an attack on another Japanese naval force which was lurking in the background only 30 miles northeast of Florida Island: light cruiser *Yura* and five DD's. Eldridge dropped a half-ton bomb on the cruiser and left it dead in the water. Three P-39's followed up an hour and a half later with 500-pound bombs, and Lieut. Commander Ray Davis of VB-6 led four more dive bombers in an attack at 1500. At 1629 a fourth striking force (Eldridge), consisting of 4 SBD's and 4 P-39's, attacked, and by 1700 flaming *Yura* was a goner. Two destroyers, *Harusame* and *Yudachi,* administered the *coup de grâce* with torpedoes.[25] Besides disposing of *Yura,* the Guadalcanal-based planes also hit the destroyer *Akizuki.*

Admiral Kondo of the Second Fleet and Nagumo of the Third Fleet had been hovering in the northeast since the 22d with much more terrifying plans. With them was the biggest Japanese task force in many months: 4 carriers, 4 battleships, 8 cruisers and 28 destroyers, 4 oilers and 3 cargo ships. The cargo ships were awaiting the signal to put in at Guadalcanal as soon as General Vandegrift surrendered to General Hyakutake.

On the 25th Nagumo radioed Hyakutake that he'd better get on with the surrender; the supporting fleet would be forced to retire due to lack of fuel if the attack weren't carried out immediately.[26]

The constant delays which had been forced on Hyakutake by the Vandegrift and Geiger forces "bought time with blood," in Admiral Halsey's words. Down at Halsey's South Pacific headquarters they had been expecting the attack, of course, and they knew the big task forces were standing off near the Santa Cruz Islands. If the attack had come 23 October (as SoPac expected), there would have been only one carrier, *Hornet,* to interfere. But *Enterprise,* with the battleship *South Dakota,* two cruisers and eight destroyers, was hurrying back to the South Pacific from Pearl Harbor repairs. The *Hornet* force and the *Enterprise* force joined up on the 24th.

The *Enterprise* search groups failed to find the Nagumo forces on the 25th, but U.S. and Japanese carrier striking forces passed each other next morning. On paper the results of the Battle of Santa Cruz look like a defeat for the U.S. forces: *Hornet* sunk, the destroyer *Porter* sunk, *Enterprise* damaged by two bomb hits, the battleship *South Dakota* and the cruiser *San Juan* hit by a bomb apiece, while the destroyer *Smith* was struck by an early *kamikaze.* The Japanese lost only *Yura,* which was not involved in the carrier battle.

But this is another case where the box score is deceptive. *Hornet's* pilots hit

---

[25] Morison, *The Struggle for Guadalcanal,* p 197.
[26] USSBS, *Campaigns,* p 120.

big *Shokaku*[27] with four 1,000-pound bombs on the port side and two more near the after elevator. The small carrier *Zuiho* was slightly damaged. The Japanese admirals were unable to furnish carrier air support for the next big effort to recapture Guadalcanal, in November, and, in fact, did not venture forth again with their carriers until the Battle of the Philippine Sea, 19 months later. Plane losses were about equal: U.S. 74, Japanese 69.

The strenuous air battles of the 23d and 25th, plus operational accidents attendant upon the wretched condition of the airstrips, had left General Geiger quite desperate in so far as sound airplanes were concerned. For 26 October he had only 30 planes available: 12 F4F-4's, 11 SBD's, 3 P-400's, 3 P-39's, and a lone F4F-7 photographic plane. Fortunately, Guadalcanal had four straight raidless days after the 25th, and Geiger's pilots had nothing more strenuous to do than to bomb and strafe Hyakutake's retreating forces while the mechs patched up what was left of Cactus Air Force.

---

[27] *Shokaku's* record after the Pearl Harbor attack was one frustration after another. This time she went out of the war for nine months. In June 1944 she was sunk by the submarine USS *Cavalla.*

CHAPTER EIGHT

Guadalcanal Secured

ANOTHER GROUP OF four squadrons, Lieut. Colonel William O. Brice's MAG-11, arrived on New Caledonia 30 October and began feeding pilots and planes into Guadalcanal: Major Joe Sailer with his SBD's from VMSB-132 began operations from Henderson on 1 November; Major Paul Fontana flew up with nine of his VMF-112 pilots in a transport plane 2 November. The Group completed its move up to Espíritu Santo 11 November where a camp was established at Turtle Bay. From there most of the flight personnel of VMSB-142 (Major Robert Richard) followed in its own planes on 12 November with three VMF-122 pilots, in time for the big doings of mid-November, and so did VMSB-131[1] (Lieut. Colonel Paul Moret), the Marines' first torpedo bomber squadron, which had just been converted from a dive-bombing outfit and trained 22 days at Ewa in TBF's. In mid-November there were 1,748 men in Guadalcanal's aviation units, 1,557 of them marines.

There were other signs of progress during the comparative lull of late October and early November. To supplement Henderson Field a new fighter strip was completed in three days by cutting the brush, filling in old foxholes, leveling and rolling the turf. The veteran airline pilots of VMJ-253 were joined by another squadron (VMJ-152) and by the Army's 13th Troop Carrier Squadron from the 403d Transport Command. The whole was organized on 24 November at New Caledonia into South Pacific Combat Air Transport Command (SCAT) under Lieut. Colonel Perry K. Smith, who maintained the only consistent transport between Guadalcanal and the outside world.[2] Besides hauling every wanted necessity from mail to torpedoes, MAG-25 made history with its evacuation of the wounded and the sick—the first time such evacuation had been attempted wholesale.[3]

Although candy and cigarettes had comprised the first cargo landed on

---

[1] VMSB-131, attached to MAG-14, was equipped with TBF's in September 1942 but was not redesignated VMTB until June 1943.

[2] MAG-25 was the basic ingredient of what became famous as SCAT. Throughout the 27 months of its existence SCAT was commanded by Marine officers: Colonels P. K. Smith, W. F. Marshall, W. A. Willis, and A. C. Koonce.

[3] The Army Air Transport Command made its first air evacuation flight 17 January 1943, seven patients from Karachi to Accra. (Oliver LaFarge, *The Eagle in the Egg*, ATC history, p 230.)

5 September, the very next day planes of VMJ-253 had hastened to Guadalcanal with much more strategic supplies. Drums of gasoline, ammunition, machine guns and mortar shells were rushed to the beleaguered island. Relief pilots and an entire AA unit were flown in later. Before SCAT was dissolved in February 1945, its flying boxcars had flown enough miles in the South Pacific to engirdle the earth 340 times, and in its first 18 months of operations nearly a quarter of a million passengers were carried. Neither darkness nor bad weather deterred the unarmed, unarmored planes which shuttled over vast expanses of water to deliver critically needed supplies and personnel. Only one plane was lost in the first seven months' operations.

Before the 1st Marine Division left Guadalcanal in December, Smith's planes had flown out 2,879 casualties, nearly three times as many as were evacuated by ships.[4]

The Commanding General of AAF took note of MAG-25's proficiency during a late 1942 visit to Guadalcanal—and "Hap" Arnold was no man to pass around idle compliments about other services:

> The Marine transport planes, like their other units, were doing an excellent job. A grand job! They made the 800-mile [sic] trip into Guadalcanal, carried enough gas for the return trip, and still lugged 3,000 pounds of cargo. And they carried out as many of the wounded as their planes would hold.[5]

By November, Army bomber strength in the South Pacific grew to 50 B-17's and 20 B-26's; 23 more heavies were ordered from Hawaii to meet the new emergency. The Marine Corps' first four-engined planes, Liberators of VMD-154 (Lieut. Colonel Elliott E. Bard) began operating from Espíritu Santo, helping the Army B-17's in mapping and photographing the whole South Pacific—a chore that normally would have been undertaken before the invasion of Guadalcanal, of course, but one which had to await the equipment. When Bard's planes weren't taking pictures they were hauling gasoline and other supplies, or bombing the Japs with empty, whistling Coca-Cola or beer bottles. For photographic reconnaissance of Japanese front lines and installations on Guadalcanal there were now a couple of F4F-7's, from which guns had been removed and replaced with unprotected internal wing tanks bringing the fuel capacity to 685 gallons. Two officers from Geiger's intelligence staff (Major Michael Sampas and Captain Herman A. Hansen) flew daily from 19 October to 1 November 1942 in what amounted to the first close-up photographic reconnaissance ever made of Guadalcanal.

During early November the Japanese succeeded in landing many additional destroyer-borne troops in spite of heroic efforts to stop them.[6] Total

---

[4] 1st MarDiv Report, Phase V, Annex T, p 9. Ships evacuated 1,040.

[5] Arnold, Global Mission, p 343.

[6] One such effort on 2 November cost the life of the tenacious Lieut. Commander Eldridge of VS-71, two Marine lieutenants (Melvin R. Nawman and Wayne R.

between 2 and 10 November: 65 destroyer loads, 2 cruiser loads.[7] Sometimes the Tokyo Express could be turned back by the brave little PT boats. The SBD's heckled enemy ships into reversing their course once. On 7 November Major Sailer with 7 SBD's and Lieut. Larsen with 3 TBF's of VT-8, led an interception of a cruiser and nine destroyers 100 miles north of Guadalcanal. Lieut. Sandretto of VMSB-141 dropped his bomb on the cruiser, and two of the Navy pilots got their torpedoes into the cruiser and a destroyer. En route to the target 8 covering P-39's found 5 float fighter planes about to attack two Grummans and knocked them all down. Twenty-three Marine fighters which also made an attack against the ships shot down 9 more, 3 each by Marontate and Foss, who was himself shot down but recovered later. Three of our planes were lost, and one pilot. Anyone could see that the Japanese had now landed fresh troops to the east, at Koli Point, and despite their battering on the 7th, they were back again on the three following nights. To the defenders of Guadalcanal it looked like another big attack brewing, and the U.S. Navy wasn't likely to be as strong as the attacking Japanese warships. Of the 8th, Lieut. Merillat recorded:

> It was a glum night in the Marine encampment. Despite everything that had been done to meet the Japanese as soon as they landed, it looked as if there was no way to stop their ships from coming in almost any night they chose to come.[8]

Louis Woods, now a brigadier general, came up from 1st MAW headquarters at Espíritu Santo on 7 November to relieve General Geiger who, for the first time, went back to see what his headquarters looked like. Admiral Halsey arrived from Nouméa on the 8th "to familiarize himself with the spot situation." An enemy destroyer provided him with the proper atmosphere by lobbing a few shells during the night.

When Halsey returned to Nouméa next day he was met with Intelligence estimates of the new Japanese attack—one which made Nagumo's October effort look puny indeed. To meet the attack it appeared that Halsey would have less than he had for the Battle of Santa Cruz: *Hornet* had been sunk and *Enterprise* and *South Dakota* were still being repaired at Nouméa.

Enemy Plans

On 26 October Captain Toshikazu Ohmae, Chief of Staff of the Southeastern Fleet at Rabaul, went to Guadalcanal by destroyer. There was bitterness

---

Gentry) from VMSB-132 and their three gunners. In spite of hazardous weather, the SBD airmen had volunteered for a night flight after B-17's reported 4 cruisers and 17 destroyers approaching Guadalcanal. The bodies of Eldridge and Nawman were found later on Santa Isabel Island. In 35 days on Guadalcanal Eldridge had led 14 missions against Japanese ships. His last flight was undertaken against orders of General Geiger who had grounded Eldridge "because he had already done so much."

[7] *Southeast Area Operations,* Part One (Navy), p 41.

[8] *The Island,* p 202.

in his heart. The failure of Hyakutake's attack, he felt, could be blamed only on the Army, which had failed to carry out its schedule. "The Navy lost ships, airplanes and pilots while trying to give support to the land assault which was continually delayed," he testified five years later. "The Army did not understand the position of the Navy in that it could not stay in one area indefinitely without being attacked. We were also consuming valuable fuel."[9]

When he sat down with General Hyakutake this time, Ohmae had a new proposal from his naval bosses. The main trouble in October had been trying to take the U.S. airfields by land; too much emphasis had been placed on the land assault. Now, in November, the airfield would simply be knocked out by bombardment: not enough attention had been paid to bombardment last time. Thus, the troops would land without being harassed by those Guadalcanal planes. What Ohmae wanted from Hyakutake was the 38th (*Hiroshima*) Division, only three battalions of which had been sent to Guadalcanal for the October attack. This meant postponing the Port Moresby attack, which had been the 38th's assignment, but Hyakutake was willing. Guadalcanal had assumed an importance considerably transcending Port Moresby's. The plan called for landing the 38th at Koli Point, to the east of the American perimeter, causing the Americans to divide their land forces into two weak halves. (This plan was later changed to a westward landing between Cape Esperance and Tassafaronga; the forces already landed at Koli Point by destroyer were withdrawn by mountain trails behind the perimeter.) In addition to the 38th, the Southeastern Fleet sent along 3,500 special naval landing force troops.

The Battle of Guadalcanal

The Japanese struck the first blow on 11 November, in the first air raids in more than a week. In two attacks the Japanese lost 11 bombers and Zeros, without accomplishing more than slight damage to the transport *Zeilin* in the harbor, but the Henderson flyers paid 7 planes and 5 pilots, an unusually high relative loss.

On the 12th two battalions of the Army's 182d Infantry Regiment were unloading off Kukum Point when the Japanese sent over 25 torpedo planes with 8 escorting Zeros. One crashed into the after control station of the cruiser *San Francisco,* killing 30 men including the executive officer, Commander Mark H. Crouter USN. Three transports took only minor casualties. The destroyer *Buchanan* was hit by friendly AA and had to go south that night. But only one Japanese bomber survived the attack; the F4F's and P-39's shot down 16 bombers and 5 Zeros. AA accounted for 5 more bombers. Three Marine planes and one P-39 were lost in return. Admiral Turner had his transports 90 per cent unloaded when they were withdrawn.

During the afternoon 11 Japanese transports, escorted by 12 destroyers, headed south to finish off the soldiers and marines after the battlewagons had finished off Henderson Field.

---

[9] USSBS, *Interrogations,* Vol II, p 468.

The Battle of Guadalcanal—"the fiercest naval battle ever fought," Admiral King called it—began at 0124 on 13 November when the cruiser *Helena's* SG radar picked up the Japanese bombardment force moving in at 27,000 yards: the battleships *Hiei* and *Kirishima,* one light cruiser (*Nagara*) and 14 destroyers. Admiral Callaghan, on board *San Francisco,* was handicapped by having his best radar on another ship than his own, and he was heavily outgunned. Against the 2 battleships, 1 light cruiser and 14 destroyers he had only 5 cruisers and 8 destroyers. It was a dark night, the intership communication was poor, and the land mass confused the radar readings. Admiral Callaghan steamed between two columns of Japanese ships, and the action began at 3,000 yards. In the general melee it was almost impossible to distinguish friend from foe. In 24 minutes the furious battleship-cruiser duel was over, *San Francisco* had been heavily damaged and Admiral Callaghan and most of his staff killed, and *Portland* had been crippled. *Atlanta,* flying Rear Admiral Norman Scott's flag, was hit and he was killed. *Atlanta* limped away but succumbed to her ghastly wounds early that evening. Of the 8 U.S. destroyers, 4 were sunk, 3 damaged. Callaghan had put himself alongside the enemy at heavy cost; it would have been worse if the Japanese battleships had had armor-piercing shells, but they had come only prepared to shell the airfields and knock out General Woods's planes. Next morning a submarine torpedo from *I-26* blew up the cruiser *Juneau;* 700 of her crew—all but 10 men—died, including 5 Sullivan brothers.

The Japanese had only two destroyers sunk, but the battleship *Hiei* had not only been frustrated in her bombardment mission, but also had been hit 85 times and had lost control of her steering gear. When daylight came the Guadalcanal-based pilots jumped on the first battleship they had ever been able to corner—there it was, just ten miles north of Savo Island. First, *Hiei* was attacked by 6 SBD's, which got one direct hit. Then 4 TBF's led by Captain George E. Dooley of VMSB-131 put a torpedo into the frantic monster. Seven SBD's came in next, then 9 TBF's from *Enterprise,* which had been flown to Guadalcanal with 6 fighters to ease operations on the damaged north-bound carrier and to augment the strength of the besieged island, got three torpedo hits. According to MAG-14's records, there were at least five other attacks on *Hiei* with torpedoes and 1,000-pound bombs during the day. That night the Japanese gave up and scuttled her. Eight Zero fighter planes sent down from Buin to protect *Hiei* were shot down.

During the night of 13–14 November the Japanese sent in their cruiser bombardment force—3 cruisers and 4 destroyers—and Henderson Field and the two fighter strips went through another hell of a shelling—about 1,000 8-inch shells. But it lasted only 45 minutes, and apparently was ended abruptly, possibly because two little PT boats began making runs on the cruisers. The bombardment caused less damage than had been suffered in the purple nights of October; 2 F4F's were destroyed, 1 SBD and 15 F4F's were holed by fragments but most were in commission by the end of the day. None of eight P-38's which had arrived from MacArthur's theater the day before was hit. The holes in Fighter No. 1 were quickly repaired. By dawn the regular searches were on their way. They found the 3 cruisers and 4 destroyers and put two torpedoes into the CA *Kinugasa* which *Enterprise* flyers sank later in the morning. Two other cruisers and a destroyer were damaged.

Although their cruisers had been singularly unsuccessful in knocking out the airfields, the Japanese on board the big transport force bearing on Guadalcanal knew nothing of the kind. Commander Tadashi Yamamoto, on board destroyer *Hoyashio* escorting the 11 transports, recalled later: "We were very happy because we thought that the bombardment groups had succeeded in destroying your planes the night before." But at 1215, and thereafter for the rest of the 14th, the transports bearing the 38th Division and the naval landing troops underwent a nightmare past endurance. All afternoon every plane on Guadalcanal that could fly loaded up with bombs and torpedoes and tore into the transports unmercifully. Major Joe Sailer, Major Bob Richard and Lieut. Albert P. Coffin USN of VT-10 got their strikes in first; they scored hits with two 1,000-pound bombs on a 7,000-ton transport, and four more on another ship of the same size; a third transport was hit six times and its accompanying cruiser hit twice. Just after Sailer's and Richard's planes had struck from starboard, Coffin's pilots came in from port side and put torpedoes in two of the burning transports. The entire air group of *Enterprise* had been hurriedly flown into Guadalcanal. It joined in the slaughter. Lieut. Commander James R. Lee USN led a group of 16 VB-10 and VS-10 pilots who claimed ten hits on at least eight transports. By evening seven transports of 5,425 to 9,683 tons had been sunk; the other four, crippled, went on to Guadalcanal and beached themselves where they were gutted next day by the same pilots and by the destroyer *Meade* which potted them at leisure. Altogether, about 4,000 Japanese troops out of 10,000 managed to reach Guadalcanal; some were drowned but many were rescued by destroyers.[10] Out of the whole convoy only five tons of supplies—260 cases of ammunition and 1,500 bags of rice—were landed.

This was a great victory—as great as any Marine aviators would participate in. The CO of the 1st Battalion, 7th Marines, Lieut. Colonel Lewis B. Puller, who had been wounded a few days earlier, recalled more than three years later that he finally realized the tide had turned when he lay on his hospital cot near Lunga Point, listening to fragmentary returns from Cactus Air Force attacks. Everyone realized that Guadalcanal was over the hump when it became known that the great enemy convoy was being cut to pieces.[11]

The "buzzard patrol" of the 14th had lost 6 SBD's and 2 F4F's with their pilots. Among the missing was Joe Bauer, the Cactus Air Force's highly esteemed fighter commander. He was seen in the water in his Mae West after he was shot down, but four days of intense searching by planes and by Russell Islands natives failed to locate any further trace of him.

---

[10] Miller, *Guadalcanal: The First Offensive*, p 188. Another estimate says there were 7,700 of whom 3,000 drowned, 3,000 landed, and 1,700 were picked up.

[11] Zimmerman, *The Guadalcanal Campaign*, p 153.

Despite disaster after disaster, Vice Admiral Kondo was not through at Guadalcanal. With the remnants of the bombardment force he approached shortly after midnight of 14–15 November. By this time Vice Admiral Willis A. Lee had managed to rush up with the battleships *Washington* and *South Dakota*. The last act was a battleship duel: the two Americans versus *Hiei's* sister ship, *Kirishima*. The Japanese lost one destroyer and the battleship, which was hit by 9 16-inch shells and 40 5-inchers, and had to be scuttled. Admiral Lee lost three destroyers and had *South Dakota* and a destroyer damaged.

The threat to Guadalcanal was over. There would be some fighting later, mostly in the air, but the Japanese never made another real effort to contest American supremacy in the southern Solomons. Of the four-day Battle of Guadalcanal Admiral Halsey wrote:

> Now, nearly five years later, I can face the alternative frankly. If our ships and planes had been routed in this battle, if we had lost it, our troops on Guadalcanal would have been trapped as were our troops on Bataan. . . . Unobstructed, the enemy would have driven south, cut our supply lines to New Zealand and Australia and enveloped them.[12]

The Battle of Tassafaronga

The Japanese had no intention as yet of giving up Guadalcanal. But to carry on the fight it was necessary to get some supplies to the infelicitous remnants of General Hyakutake's forces on Guadalcanal. There was a new wrinkle now—to dump drums of supplies offshore and let them float into the beach on next morning's tide. For this purpose fast destroyer transports were concentrated in the Shortland Islands—a concentration that did nothing to alleviate the uneasiness felt among the Americans on Guadalcanal. Submarines were also utilized as supply ships. On 27 November Admiral Halsey sent up a task force of 5 cruisers and 4 destroyers to intercept the latest edition of the Tokyo Express, which he knew was due off Tassafaronga Point, 15 miles west of Henderson Field, during the night of 30 November.

The Japanese destroyers arrived all right—eight of them. One destroyer, *Takanami,* disobeyed Admiral Tanaka's orders and opened fire.[13] She was promptly sunk by the blanket of fire from the bigger guns of Rear Admiral Carleton Wright's force. But the other seven destroyers never fired a gun; they simply executed a maneuver they had been practicing at night for a year and a half: a fast torpedo run, a simultaneous, 24-knot turn to the left and away. Result: *Northampton* sunk, *New Orleans, Pensacola* and *Minneapolis* damaged so severely they were out of action nearly a year. About all that could be said for the U.S. Navy was that the Tokyo Express probably failed to land many of the 1,100 drums of supplies intended to be floated toward the shore.[14]

---

[12] *Admiral Halsey's Story,* p 131.
[13] USSBS, *Campaigns,* p 139.
[14] The Navy communiqué, however, said plenty: "The enemy suffered the fol-

The loss of four more cruisers at the Battle of Tassafaronga did nothing to dispel the anticipation of another all-out Japanese attack. But its over-all significance was pale compared to the great sea and air and land battles which had preceded it. South Pacific naval strength grew mightily between November and January. *Enterprise* and *Saratoga* were both back in commission. *Washington* and *North Carolina* were joined by three 16-inch-gun battleships, *Indiana, Colorado* and *Maryland,* and by two old 14-inchers, *New Mexico* and *Mississippi*. Several new cruisers, a flock of destroyers, and more PT boats were available to meet whatever the Japanese sent down into southern Solomons waters. As early as 22 November Admiral Nimitz, in ordering 17 submarines back to Empire waters from SoPac emergency, had informed Halsey that he considered Guadalcanal as "past the most critical period."[15] Bad as it was, Tassafaronga did nothing to alter this top-level conception. Nor did the Tokyo Express, which continued to make regular trips with a handful of troops or canfuls of supplies.

Guadalcanal Grows Up

There was at long last a turnover of ground troops. The haggard, malarial 1st MarDiv was relieved early in December; some of Vandegrift's marines were found too weak to climb the cargo nets to board the transports.[16] Vandegrift's command passed to the Army's Major General Alexander D. Patch, who brought up the rest of his Americal Division, plus Major General J. Lawton Collins's 25th Infantry Division, which was diverted while en route from Hawaii to Sydney. For it Halsey swapped MacArthur the marines he had long sought, though it would be a year before the battered 1st MarDiv could be sent into combat again.[17] General Patch also assembled a Marine division on Guadalcanal: the 2d. The 2d Marine Regiment had landed with the 1st MarDiv; it would stay more than a month yet to claim the honor of fighting the Guadalcanal battle longer than any other ground forces. The 8th Marine Regiment of the 2d MarDiv had landed 4 November; the 6th Marine Regiment arrived 4 January 1943 to complete the Division's infantry line-up. The 2d MarDiv—excepting its 2d Marines—saw comparatively little fighting on Guadalcanal but by the time it was pulled out and sent to New Zealand it was blooded enough to call itself "veteran." This was a good thing. A green division, even of shockproof marines, probably could not have taken Tarawa in November 1943, at what turned out to be the heaviest casualty rate any division suffered during the war (1,000 a day).

---

lowing losses during the engagement: (a) two large destroyers (or cruisers) sunk, (b) four destroyers sunk, (c) two troop transports sunk, (d) one cargo ship sunk." (Communiqué No. 211.)

[15] ComSoPac war diary, November 1942.

[16] Frank O. Hough, *The Island War,* p 86.

[17] When he made the swap Commander, Southwest Pacific (ComSoWesPac), had no idea the 1st was in such shape. (Information from Colonel Lloyd Lehrbas USA, aide to General MacArthur.)

Incisive as these changes on land and sea might be, they were equaled if not surpassed by the transformation of Guadalcanal's aerial facilities. Admiral Fitch, ComAirSoPac, designated Henderson Field a Marine Corps air base 15 November.[18] Fighter No. 1 was so vulnerable during rainy weather it had to be abandoned. Fighter No. 2 (Kukum) was used instead from the middle of December 1942 to March 1943.

The base commander, Colonel William J. Fox, began to build up the entire runway system of Henderson and Fighter No. 2 to get proper drainage. For this it was necessary to haul coral: the coral on Lunga Plain was too rotten and slushy. There still were not enough tools—the 2½-ton bundles of Marston mats sometimes had to be broken down before they could be unloaded, for lack of a hoist—and it was still necessary to use the four small Japanese road rollers which had been captured more than three months earlier, but Guadalcanal's air facilities soon took on the appearance of semipermanence. Even the barrage-balloon squadrons[19] were sent up from Nouméa, to fend off enemy dive bombers.

General Woods stayed on as Commander, Aircraft, Cactus Air Force (ComAirCactus) until 26 December, when he was relieved by Brig. General Francis P. Mulcahy, CG of 2d MAW. Colonel Oscar Brice succeeded Al Cooley as strike commander (the term itself didn't enter Marine aviation, however, until several months later). Following Bauer's disappearance on 15 November, Lieut. Colonel Samuel S. Jack took over the fighter command. More squadrons—Marine, Navy and Army—arrived and departed so rapidly that any neat group organization had to go by the board. MAG-14 was administrative in its function, feeding and housing the flyers, leaving the tactical employment in the hands of ComAirCactus. Likewise, MAG-11 was the training and supply command at Espíritu Santo, though its own squadrons were sent on to Guadalcanal, sometimes piecemeal, sometimes as entities.

The number of planes available showed a comfortable rise. By 20 November there were 101: 8 TBF's, 1 P-400, 16 P-39's, 17 P-38's, 35 F4F-4's, 24 SBD's. Nine days later there were 188, including 71 F4F's. So many squadrons flew into Guadalcanal the last two months of the year, some of them for only a few days at a time, that it is doubtful that any unimpeachable record exists of all transitions. Soon after the naval Battle of Guadalcanal eight B-17's of the AAF's merged 11th and 5th Bombardment Groups were based on Guadalcanal, in order to perform longer-range reconnaissance. During such a reconnaissance the B-17's claimed 12 enemy planes on 18 November. These B-17's were

---

[18] Major Thomas F. Riley's 1st Marine Aviation Engineers relieved the 6th CB's on 1 December, and Major Chester Clark's 2d Marine Aviation Engineers arrived 30 January 1943. They were the only outfits of their kind and with the CB's and Division engineers developed the air facilities on Guadalcanal.

[19] There were four of these squadrons, plus one at Samoa. All were trained by the pioneer Marine aviator, Lieut. Colonel Bernard L. Smith USMCR. They were more of a hazard to us than to the enemy and were ordered disbanded 1 July 1943, and their 60 officers and 1,200 men were absorbed into defense battalions.

rotated almost daily, from the eight squadrons of the two groups. The 339th Fighter Squadron provided P-38's in increasing numbers. On 23 November VS-4 landed with six OS2U's for antisubmarine patrol. Three days later the first Allied flyers came in: the 3d Reconnaissance Squadron (Lockheed Hudson planes) of the Royal New Zealand Air Force (RNZAF). Two PBY's of VP-12 arrived 15 December, the first night-prowling Black Cats, and the rest of the Squadron reached Guadalcanal by Christmas Day. The Army sent in three additional fighter squadrons, 12th, 68th and 70th, in December, and moved its 69th Bombardment Squadron (B-26's) up from Espíritu Santo the last day of that month. Daily gasoline consumption at Cactus went up to 45,000 gallons— 80,000 when the carrier planes were in.

This increased strength was thrown against the Tokyo Express every time it ventured down The Slot. On 3 December eight dive bombers, led by Lieut. Lionel N. Pool of VMSB-142, and seven TBF's, under Captain Jens C. Aggerbeck of VMSB-131, intercepted ten ships 160 miles northwest of Henderson. They claimed to sink two "cruisers" and damage two others, and got a commendation from ComSoPac for the deed; one TBF pilot, Lieut. Bruce C. Pelto, and his crew failed to return.[20] Postwar records indicate only that one destroyer, *Makinami*, was slightly damaged.[21]

On 7 December Major Joe Sailer took 13 SBD's nearly 200 miles up The Slot to try to knock out 11 destroyers. The Dauntlesses attacked at 1635, just after sunset, and scored a near miss which opened a big hole in destroyer *Nowaki's* starboard side which flooded the forward engine room and No. 2 fire room. Two other destroyers were slightly damaged.

But the attack cost the Marines their dive-bomber leader, Joe Sailer, who contributed as much to the great November victory as any individual. In five weeks Major Sailer flew 25 missions, made contact with the enemy 19 times, dropped his bombs 12 times, was credited with 6 hits and 3 near misses. "Joe was the best dive-bomber pilot in the Pacific," said his successor, Major Ben Robertshaw. "He hit every kind of ship the Japs sent down The Slot except a destroyer." His anxiety to get one of the wriggling cans proved Sailer's undoing. While trying for a destroyer he was hit, couldn't close his flaps, and a Zero shot him down as he straggled homeward. In Bauer and Sailer the Marines lost two of their young officers who had been marked for a group command; six months later they lost another when Pat Moret died in a transport-plane crash in New Caledonia.

Admiral Tanaka detached two destroyers to escort the cripples and sent the rest of the Express on to Guadalcanal. Four PT boats met the oncoming destroyers about midnight, fired 12 torpedoes and scared the Express away.

On 11 December Robertshaw led 14 SBD's to attack 11 destroyers off northern New Georgia. They claimed "four destroyers left burning and a fifth

[20] MAG-14 record of events, 16 October 1942 to 16 December 1942.
[21] USSBS, *Campaigns,* p 166. JANAC does not confirm sinkings.

damaged," but Japanese records fail to show any hits. The Express came on, but was jolted at 0100 December 12 when a PT boat fired two torpedoes into DD *Teruzuki,* which sank at 0440. Other units of the Express unloaded 1,200 drum cans offshore, but not more than 200 were retrieved.

Following the Battle of Guadalcanal General Woods began granting leave to the aviators, individually or as units. All of the original VMF-121 pilots had left by 25 November for a week's leave in Sydney and a rest at Espíritu Santo. The arrival of replacement pilots from Samoa in December enabled VMF-121 to continue functioning as a unit while its veterans were relieved.

The survivors of VMSB-141's flight echelon left Guadalcanal 19 November after losing 22 pilots and 15 gunners (50 per cent) during its seven weeks' tour; the Squadron's ground echelon stayed on until 19 January before returning Stateside.

VMO-251, which had been sending pilots from Espíritu to Guadalcanal since the earliest days, officially moved up to The Island 1 December. During the month its ranks also were braced by replacements sent over from Samoa. VMF-112 left Guadalcanal in December for a blessed week in Sydney. VMSB-142 remained until 1 February before going down to Australia via Espíritu.

VMSB-131, which had arrived just before the Battle of Guadalcanal, stayed on until 18 February in its first tour, under the command of Captain Aggerbeck (its first CO, Pat Moret, became Cooley's operations officer). The Squadron, which had been limited to carrying torpedoes, finally was allowed to tote bombs. "Torpedoes might have been fun," said Aggerbeck, "but our torpedoes in those days weren't much good."[22]

VMSB-132, relieved by VMSB-233 (Major Clyde T. Mattison), departed for Espíritu Christmas Eve and arrived in Sydney just in time to celebrate New Year's Eve.

Having rested, reorganized and retrained, the various squadrons went back up to Guadalcanal for another tour. The VMF-121 pilots who went to Sydney got back early in January and remained on Guadalcanal until the 29th of that month, when the whole Squadron was relieved.

This brief second tour enabled Joe Foss to break a notable record: since 1918 Captain Eddie Rickenbacker's score of 25 enemy planes[23] had made him the American "ace of aces." On 15 January Foss knocked down three planes to bring his own score to 26.[24]

On the same day that Foss broke the record, Lieut. William Marontate of

---

[22] For a discussion of faulty American torpedoes see Morison, *Coral Sea, Midway, and Submarine Actions,* p 230.

[23] Including four balloons, two of which were grounded. (*Air Corps News,* 14 November 1930, which itemizes Rickenbacker's World War I kills.)

[24] Foss's score was exceeded in World War II by five AAF pilots (20 if grounded planes are counted, as they were in Europe but not in the Southwest Pacific), one Navy pilot and one marine.

the same squadron failed to return after scoring his thirteenth plane. Altogether VMF-121 was credited with 164 planes in 122 days of combat, while losing 20 of its own pilots.

The Enemy Changes Signals

On 2 December a warrior of great renown arrived at Rabaul to command the recapture of Guadalcanal. General Hitoshi Imamura had his orders from Tokyo when he left Java, and he brought 50,000 troops from his 8th Area Army to reinforce Hyakutake's 17th Army before recapturing Guadalcanal.[25] But on 4 January the Imperial War Council changed his orders again: evacuate the troops on Guadalcanal and establish a final defensive position to the north, around the Kolombangara–Munda area. It seems that Tokyo was worried about the course of events in New Guinea. A small force of Japanese soldiers had attempted to cross the Owen Stanley mountain range and capture Port Moresby, a feat manifestly improbable with the supplies and troops on hand. General Imamura was told to relieve the forces on New Guinea while pinning down the Americans on Guadalcanal.

After the war Captain Ohmae offered a plausible reason for abandoning the plan to recapture Guadalcanal:

> The Army, particularly, desired to [retake Guadalcanal], but the transportation was too difficult, mainly due to your dive-bombers and strafing planes, which were able to locate and destroy the transports and landing barges which were hidden during the day time. Following the battle [of Guadalcanal], it was decided to do as much as we could by reinforcing the Guadalcanal garrison by destroyers, while a sufficient supporting force of aircraft was being built up at Rabaul. This plan was not too successful.[26]

This was stated in simple terms by Japanese soldiers in their diaries, which were captured later:

> *December 23.* Haven't seen one of our planes for ages, but every day enemy planes dance in the sky, fly low, strafe, bomb and numerous officers and men fall and there is no medicine for them.
>
> *December 26.* We are about to welcome the New Year with no provisions; the sick are moaning within the dismal tents and men are dying daily. . . . O friendly planes! I beg that you come over soon and cheer us up![27]

Imperial Headquarters didn't intend that Guadalcanal should have life easy after the evacuation. On 24 November a convoy pulled up at Munda Point,

---

[25] USSBS, *The Allied Campaign Against Rabaul*, p 9.
[26] USSBS, *Interrogations*, Vol II, p 471.
[27] Morison, *The Struggle for Guadalcanal*, pp 316–317.

on New Georgia Island, 175 miles north of Henderson Field, and a construction crew immediately began building an airfield. At last the Zeros would have a field that wouldn't strain their gasoline capacity!

ComSoPac had suspected that the Japanese were paying more and more attention to the New Georgia area; now considerable photographic evidence was brought in by reconnaissance planes. VMD-154's cameras showed 5 December that the airstrip at Munda was almost complete. A clever bit of camouflage had almost worked; the Japanese had stretched wires over their construction work, and on the net thus formed they had left the tops of palm trees, giving the appearance that nothing unusual was going on underneath.[28]

But once the deception was discovered, the Guadalcanal-based pilots went to work. On 12 December nine VMSB-142 planes dived on Munda's gun emplacements, runway and oil dumps, which gave off big fires. Thereafter, the Munda field was struck almost daily—by everything from fighter bullets to B-17 bombloads—but since runways don't stay knocked out very long after a bombing, the Japanese soon had fighters staging through there.

On the day before Christmas 9 SBD's, escorted by 9 P-39's, 4 P-38's and 4 F4F's hit a jackpot which had been there less than 24 hours. Four Zeros were already airborne and 20 more lined up to take off. The 4 in the air were popped, and 10 more which got off were also shot down (4 by Major Donald Yost of VMF-121, 3 by his wingman, Lieut. Kenneth J. Kirk Jr. of VMO-251), while the other 10 were caught and crumpled at the end of the runway by the dive bombers. That afternoon 9 SBD's covered by 4 F4F's and 4 P-39's caught 13 troop-carrying barges near Munda and smashed to bits 9 of them, including their passengers.

Conditions were better on Guadalcanal at the end of the year, and the Americans on Guadalcanal may be forgiven for hoping there would never be another like 1942. The perimeter was being constantly expanded; Pistol Pete had finally been eliminated; there were more planes and more room to operate them; air raids on Guadalcanal were fewer; even Washing Machine Charlie was relatively quiescent. The Tokyo Express was still running but now to Munda rather than Guadalcanal. Munda was able to operate part of the time, at least. And there were reports of 100 ships concentrated at Rabaul, which caused Admiral Halsey again to request supporting strikes from General Mac-Arthur's B-17's against that area. To the men on Guadalcanal it looked like a long war against an inexhaustible supply of Japanese Navy.

Admiral Halsey considered the South Pacific spirit so low that he felt moved to make the most startling prediction of the war: the end of 1943 would see the Allied forces in Tokyo. He explained his peculiar reasoning five years later:

> The severest criticism was centered on my prophecy about Tokyo. The production leaders at home put up a bellow that I could hear in

---

[28] Feldt, *The Coastwatchers*, p 117, says native scouts detected and reported the deception.

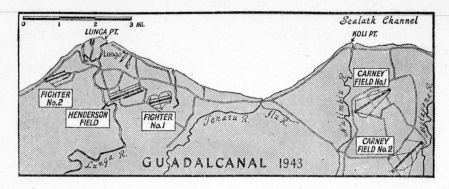

Nouméa. They were terrified that labor would take my word as gospel and quit their war jobs. The draft authorities also complained, as did a lot of other officials. They accused me of everything from recklessness to drunkenness. God Almighty, I knew we wouldn't be in Toyko that soon! I knew we wouldn't be there even by the end of 1944. I may be tactless, but I'm not a damned fool!

What the civilian bigwigs didn't consider is this: my forces were tired; their morale was low; they were beginning to think that they were abused and forgotten, that they had been fighting too much and too long. Moreover, the myth of Japanese invincibility had not yet been entirely discredited.[29]

Halsey didn't want to be remembered as "Bull,"[30] but this famed admiral's propensity for such chest-thumping prophecy marked him as fair game for the men who were still shaking their heads, wondering how they had held on at Guadalcanal and whether it might not yet be lost. Like other leaders before and after him, Admiral Halsey learned that the man in the front line is hard to fool. To them "Bull" he was and "Bull" he remained.

During December nearly all aerial combat in the Solomons took place a long way from Guadalcanal—usually during escort missions against or near Munda. After 11 December the Express gave up until after New Year's. About the middle of January this course of events changed, and for a good reason which goes back to Japanese Army-Navy friction. The Army had a lot of starving, malarial troops on Guadalcanal, and wanted to push the recapture of the island. The Navy, having been burned severely, was no longer so enthusiastic about Guadalcanal, said in effect: "Why don't you send some of your own pilots over here to get shot down? We've had to shoulder this load a long time, and we've lost a lot of our best pilots."[31] Result: in December 100 Japanese Army planes, with pilot veterans of the Malaya campaign, were shifted by carrier from Soerabaja to Truk, whence they were flown down to Rabaul. Their

---

[29] *Admiral Halsey's Story*, p 142.
[30] *Ibid*, p 1.
[31] Including 21st, 24th, 25th and 26th Air Groups, according to Captain Ohmae.

mission was changed to one of supporting the evacuation. The presence of those first Army planes was noted 5 January over Rabaul, where they intercepted some B-17's. The Japanese lost eight Army Zeros which were covering the Tokyo Express, on 15 January, but shot down five U.S. fighters and a dive bomber.

On 25 January there was a raid on Henderson Field by 30 of these planes. Three of them were shot down by marines, two others by Army pilots. Next day Captain Hunter Reinburg of VMF-121 knocked down two enemy planes while on an escort mission. On the 27th, when the Japanese came again, 3 U.S. planes were lost, 2 of them in a mid-air collision, but the enemy lost 10.

The Japanese tried to manifest this increased aerial strength in other ways. On the night of 21 January a bomber or two flew from Rekata Bay all the way down to Espíritu in one of the rare bombing missions against this rear-area base. Since Secretary of the Navy Knox and Admiral Nimitz had arrived that day, many SoPac officers believed the Japanese might have known they were there by breaking the American code. When the same notables arrived at Guadalcanal next day and drew a very heavy nocturnal bombing with planes overhead for eight hours, everyone in the area was convinced. Actually, it was just a coincidence.

An even bigger surprise than the "bombing of the brass" occurred on 29 January. Admiral Halsey had ordered one of his cruiser task forces (GEORGE) up from Efate to cover four transports which were bringing more Army units into Guadalcanal; GEORGE (Rear Admiral Robert C. Giffen) was under way when Halsey received a message indicating that the Japanese were assembling another powerful force, perhaps to attempt the recapture of Guadalcanal (he knew nothing about the decision to evacuate the island). Halsey immediately ordered his other five task forces (two centered around carriers, two around battleships, one around cruisers) to the area south of Guadalcanal.

The surprise came to the GEORGE force when it was 48 miles southwest of Guadalcanal, shortly after sunset. Unidentified planes began appearing on the SG radar screen of the destroyer *Edwards,* and shortly thereafter on the screens of other ships in the task force. As darkness settled yellow and white flares exploded and hung over the force. At 2023 the destroyer *Waller* was strafed; the cruiser *Chicago* shot down one plane; the flagship *Wichita* received a strafing attack. Several ships noted torpedo wakes. At 2038 a torpedo plane crashed on the starboard quarter of *Waller,* another exploded close aboard *Chicago's* bow, brilliantly silhouetting that unlucky ship. Two minutes later— at 2040—she was struck by a torpedo whose wake was not seen, and after a few minutes, by another. A torpedo also bumped *Wichita's* side but did not explode. This was something to confound every admiral in the Pacific: the Japanese had learned how, by the skillful use of flares, to put on a night torpedo attack, something we had been yearning to achieve ever since the Tokyo Express first began to chug down The Slot.

The estimate of 11 to 13 Japanese planes shot down was slight consolation. The Japanese, already feared as jungle night fighters, had added something new to the war at sea. At 1743 next afternoon, despite coverage from fighters of *Enterprise* and two auxiliary carriers, crippled *Chicago*, which was under tow by *Louisville* at four knots, was caught again and sunk by more Japanese torpedo bombers, which also put a fish into the destroyer *LaVallette*, causing that vessel to call for a tow to Espíritu.

The intensified Japanese air activity continued, and the intensified counter-activity by the Americans reminded veterans of the old October days. (On the 30th VMF-112's war diary noted: "Pilots are flying 5–6 hours per day and Wing Operations is still dreaming up more.") On 31 January Lieut. Jefferson J. DeBlanc of VMF-112 won the Medal of Honor while escorting SBD's and TBF's to bomb shipping in Vella Gulf.

DeBlanc's flight sailed into a superior enemy force, enabling the dive bombers and torpedo planes to complete their runs on the Japanese surface ships. In spite of a low fuel supply DeBlanc continued to engage the enemy against heavy odds and succeeded in shooting down three float planes and two Zeros before he was forced to abandon his own damaged plane at a very low altitude over enemy-held Kolombangara.

Staff Sergeant James A. Feliton, who was on the same mission, was also forced to parachute. Both DeBlanc and Feliton were taken under the protective wing of the coastwatcher on Kolombangara and returned by Duck to Guadalcanal 13 days later.

At about 1600 on 1 February 5 dive bombers with 30 Zeros got through and hit the destroyer *DeHaven* with three bombs. She sank in five minutes. The attackers, when discovered, lost 21 planes, of which Lieut. Gilbert Percy of VMF-112 shot down 4, Captain Robert B. Fraser 3.

These planes were down from Buin to cover 20 destroyers of the Express, which were attacked off the coast of New Georgia by SBD's and TBF's escorted by F4F's and P-40's. Three SBD's were lost. Lieut. Abram H. Moss (VMSB-234), pilot of one of the SBD's, was hit by AA and his rear-seat gunner, Sergeant Gilbert H. Henze, although he could not fly, took over the controls. Major Ray L. Vroome, flying escort, gave Henze flight instructions until they reached the Russells where the SBD ran out of gas on one tank and Vroome's radio went bad. Henze put the plane into a dive and bailed out, hitting the stabilizer which amputated one leg below the knee. He checked the flow of blood until he hit the water, then blacked out. He was picked up by natives and returned to Tulagi two days later in good mental and physical condition, in spite of his wound, but two months later he died.

The planes seriously damaged the flagship *Makinami*, which had to be towed back to Shortland. But the other 19 enemy DD's came on to Guadalcanal Island, where *Makigumo* struck a mine and sank.

Something was in the air, and Admiral Halsey knew it. Every day he sent planes, including the newly arrived VMSB-144 (Captain Roscoe M. Nelson), to attack the Tokyo Express or shipping concentrations off Vila, Kolombangara and Munda. He ordered his submarines (TF 42) to "tighten the Buka–Rabaul line." Again he asked that MacArthur's bombers hit the Shortlands, where the

Express made up, but Halsey also had his eye on a big Japanese force (2 carriers, 4 battleships, 6 heavy cruisers, 2 light cruisers, 12 destroyers) which B-17 reconnaissance planes reported south of Truk. Although he had six task forces he could have disposed to intercept the Express, Admiral Halsey refused to be lured by the minnows. His forces stood south of Guadalcanal, waiting for the whales. Minnows and whales alike got away.

On 4 February a cruiser and 22 destroyers set out from the Shortlands for a second evacuation trip, escorted by many Zeros. The force was met by 33 SBD's and TBF's, covered by 31 fighters. One destroyer was disabled, 3 others were less seriously damaged; 17 Japanese planes were lost, against 10 American. But the evacuation went through, and searching planes found no trace of the Express next morning.

Still the SoPac and Guadalcanal commands believed the Japanese were reinforcing the island.

The last run was 7 February. Only 15 SBD's got through a rain squall, and their only two hits failed to deter any ship. During the three nights the Japanese had evacuated 11,706 men in a most skillful performance.[32]

In his report Admiral Nimitz did not attempt to conceal a touch of admiration for the enemy's feat:

> The end was as abrupt as the beginning of the struggle for Guadalcanal. Until the last moment it appeared that the Japanese were attempting a major reinforcement effort. Only skill in keeping their plans disguised and bold celerity in carrying them out enabled the Japanese to withdraw the remnants of the Guadalcanal garrison. Not until all organized forces had been evacuated on 8 February did we realize the purpose of their air and naval dispositions. Otherwise, with the strong forces available to us ashore on Guadalcanal and our powerful fleet in the South Pacific we might have converted the withdrawal into a disastrous rout.

For the ground forces Guadalcanal was over. The cost to the Marines was 1,044 killed, 2,894 wounded; to the Army 550 killed, 1,289 wounded. For the Japanese ground troops the cost had been much greater—14,800 killed or missing, 9,000 dead of disease, 1,000 taken prisoner, out of a total force of more than 36,000.[33]

How many Japanese sailors were killed will never be known, nor has the U.S. Navy yet compiled its own losses—they certainly were greater than the number killed on the ground. Combat-vessel losses on both sides were about even—24 ships (including two aircraft carriers) of 126,240 tons for the Allies, 24 ships (including two battleships) of 134,839 tons for the Japanese.[34]

---

[32] Morison, *The Struggle for Guadalcanal*, p 370. Miller, *Guadalcanal: The First Offensive*, p 349, puts the number at 13,000–12,000 from the 17th Army, 1,000 Navy personnel.

[33] Miller, *Guadalcanal: The First Offensive*, p 350.

[34] Morison, *The Struggle for Guadalcanal*, p 372.

The results in the air are much more difficult to calculate. During the six months of Guadalcanal the total pilots employed in 15 Marine operative combat squadrons was 464. Of this total 271 pilots were lost or became noneffective; 94 were killed or missing in action, and the remaining 177 were evacuated as casualties, for rehabilitation, or for noncombat flying.[35]

In 2,117 sorties made by Marine aviation against enemy aircraft through January 1943 we lost 118 planes to the enemy and 30 operationally, but the Marines alone claimed to destroy 427 Japanese planes.[36]

In 1949 a Japanese officer stated that the Japanese naval air forces lost only 136 planes (53 bombers, 83 fighters) between the U.S. landing on 7 August 1942 and the Japanese evacuation of Guadalcanal 7 February 1943.[37] (This is almost exactly ten per cent of the daylight sorties flown—562 bombers, 869 fighters—there were no losses from Rabaul-based night attacks.) In addition, about two thirds as many planes were lost operationally and in U.S. attacks on Japanese bases. Incredibly low as this figure appears, it must be respected. It does not include carrier-plane losses nor Japanese Army losses.

In any event, the losses had been more than the Japanese could stand. The warlords of Tokyo, still confident of their omniscience and infallibility, had been stopped in their reach farther into the South Seas. From now on they would be on the defensive, and the Allies would roll inexorably toward Tokyo. Much long and desperate fighting lay ahead, but there would never again be any doubt on our side about the outcome.

The Stateside Picture

The lessons of Guadalcanal were welded into standard doctrine for Marine aviators. Dozens of returning pilots took over fledglings and taught them "how it was on the 'Canal." The great new West Coast bases, El Toro, Santa Barbara, El Centro, Mojave, welded into a command that was a wing in all but name—Marine Fleet Air, West Coast (MarFAirWest), Colonel Lewie G. Merritt commanding, was activated in January 1943. The 3d MAW, activated in November 1942, Lieut. Colonel Calvin R. Freeman commanding, took care of a similar expansion on the East Coast with the addition of 11 training fields in North and South Carolina. By 1 July 1943 there were 4,989 Marine pilots, and the cry always was "More!"

In February 1943 a Women's Reserve was established for the first time in the Marine Corps, in order to relieve male personnel for combat duty. Before the war ended 23,145 women served in the Corps, nearly one-third of them in aviation—not only as stenographers and switchboard operators, but as control-tower operators, parachute riggers, Link-trainer instructors, radio operators and mechanics. Not so fortunate in the choice of a Congressional committee as their

---

[35] Report prepared by Medical Department, 1st MAW (20 August 1942 to 20 February 1943).

[36] *An Evaluation of Air Operations Affecting the U.S. Marine Corps in World War II*, pp 2–21.

[37] Captain Ohmae's answers to questions for this history, Tokyo, June 1949.

sisters in the Women's Army Corps (WAC), the women marines (and Waves), were forbidden to serve overseas until late 1944 (and then they were permitted no farther west than Pearl Harbor). Nevertheless, the WR's served their country valiantly and well, and better marines than they were not found in any front-line battalion or in the cockpit of a Corsair.

Some Things That Didn't Come Off

In the spring of 1943 the Marine Corps finally abandoned a glider program to which a great deal of time and effort had been devoted for two years. Like many other Americans, the Secretary of the Navy, Mr. Frank Knox, had been impressed by the Germans' use of gliders and paratroopers in the capture of Crete in May 1941, and the Marines were ordered to look into gliders right away.

At first the concept was modest: 75 gliders and 150 Marine pilots (enough to transport two battalions). By June 1942 the program looked toward 1,371 gliders and 3,436 pilots and co-pilots flying 10,800 men—despite the evidence that gliders would be about as useful on the Pacific islands as pogo sticks. Eventually sounder counsel prevailed, and after reaching a maximum strength of 36 officers and 246 men (with 21 gliders) the Marine Corps program was liquidated 29 May 1943. After the war it was learned that Hitler considered gliders so unprofitable at Crete he never used them again.

More fantastic was Operation X-ray, which was conceived by a Pennsylvania surgeon, tried out and abandoned by the Army, given to the Navy, then handed to the Marine Corps. The doctor's idea was to set the paper cities of Japan afire by releasing bats from airplanes flying over those cities. To each bat would be clipped a small incendiary capsule. After the bat sought refuge in a building his bomb would explode and set the building afire.

When the Army was experimenting, one of the bats set fire to a hangar at an auxiliary airfield at Carlsbad, New Mexico, and to a general's automobile.

The first Marine Corps experiments were carried out 13 December 1943. Thirty fires were started. Twenty-two went out but four of them would have required the services of professional fire-fighters. A new and more powerful incendiary was ordered.

Operation X-ray had many complications. The bats had to be frozen (i.e., hibernated) in ice-cube trays, then armed and packaged in containers which would be dropped from high altitudes. The idea was that they would awaken when they descended into warm air, then start raising hell all over Japan. But in a test of 25 bats, 15 spun in, 5 flew away, 1 dropped his capsule, 3 were able to fly for only one minute, and a lone, hardy individual glided to a safe landing. Besides, it was found, the female bats got pregnant—during which time the males didn't eat properly—and their usefulness was narrowed to the last five months of the year. Full-scale tests were planned for August 1944, but when CNO learned that it would be 15 more months before the bats could be used, he canceled the project (March 1944).

CHAPTER NINE

South Pacific Interlude

NOW THAT GUADALCANAL was ours, the planners of the Pacific war turned their attention to further steps in what Admiral King called the offensive-defensive.[1] The offensive, it turned out, would have to wait for the opening of the Central Pacific late in 1943, but this was not anticipated by many planners early in that year.

Truk was still considered an inevitable target; so it remained in Allied planning until after U.S. carriers rendered it strategically useless in February 1944.[2] But for Nimitz to get at Truk or for MacArthur to advance westward along the New Guinea coast it was necessary to proceed first to Fortress Rabaul which, so long as it remained effective, was a threat to Allied operations in the Central, Southwest and South Pacific. The movement toward Rabaul would not be easy with the means at hand which, although they were steadily augmented and would never again reach the low ebb of Guadalcanal, were necessarily subordinated to the strength allotted the European Theater.

From Guadalcanal northwest to Rabaul is 560 miles; from Port Moresby northeastward it is 445 miles. While MacArthur waited to advance up the coast of New Guinea, Halsey started up the Solomons ladder. Admiral Halsey's attempt to break the Bismarcks barrier was fiercely contested by the enemy on nearly every usable island along the way. And Japanese Imperial Headquarters officers, though Guadalcanal had lost them the strategic initiative, had no intention of retiring from other Solomons positions. It had become apparent even before the Guadalcanal evacuation that the Japanese were reinforcing the other rungs of the ladder. "Conversely," said Admiral King, "having pushed them out of the southern Solomons area, our next undertaking was to push them out of the northern Solomons."[3] Until late 1943 Rabaul headquarters of the Japanese Naval Air Force maintained about 250 planes to counter all pushes—more than that came forth angrily to dispute the final offense.

The advance up the Solomons was a job suited to the employment of

---

[1] Official Reports by Fleet Admiral Ernest J. King, *The U.S. Navy at War*, pp 49–70.

[2] Intelligence "largely overrated" Truk's strength and facilities. Though the Japanese Combined Fleet operated out of its harbor from July 1942 to February 1944, Truk was never strongly fortified until after the Fleet had ceased using it. (USSBS, *The Reduction of Truk*, pp 2–4.)

[3] *The U.S. Navy at War*, p 63.

land-based aviation. U.S. carrier strength was low—only *Enterprise* and oft-crippled *Saratoga* remained of the big carriers—and new *Essex*-class ships, on which the Navy came later to rely so heavily, would not see combat until August 1943. In contrast to the Central Pacific, whose chief reliance was on carriers, the South Pacific's air strength in 1943 lay in land-based planes. And it was there that Marine aviation performed a major part of its function throughout the war. Without anyone intending it quite that way, Marine aviation became an air force for the South Pacific. On the other hand, the Marine Corps' ground troops found their main employment after Guadalcanal in the great sweep across the Central Pacific: in the Gilberts, Marshalls, Marianas, Palaus, and Iwo Jima. Finally at Okinawa Marine aviation and Marine divisions were linked in a major operation.

The South Pacific aerial load was borne by all services. Although Marine aviators were the original settlers in the Solomons war, Army, land-based Navy, and New Zealand units were employed throughout.[4] U.S. Army planes were organized on 13 February 1943 into the Thirteenth Air Force, which furnished about a quarter of the fighters and most of the heavy bombardment flown from Solomons fields. The Thirteenth was shifted to the Southwest Pacific 15 June 1944.

The conglomeration of many types of planes and pilots using different tactics, supply and techniques obviously required organization beyond the time when General Geiger's Cactus pilots fought off the Japanese as best they could. Brig. General Mulcahy controlled not only his 2d MAW, but also all Guadalcanal land-based aviation until 15 February 1943, when Rear Admiral Charles P. Mason was appointed Commander, Aircraft, Solomons (ComAirSols), responsible to ComAirSoPac, and commander of all land-based aviation except sea-search, which remained the province of ComAirSoPac.

AirSols was a unique and singularly effective organization. Its staff was a mixture of Navy, Army, Marine and New Zealand air officers and the top job itself was rotated fairly regularly among the services. Admiral Mason was succeeded after six weeks by Rear Admiral Marc A. Mitscher, who was followed five months later (on 25 July 1943) by the AAF's Major General Nathan F. Twining. The Marines' Major General Ralph J. Mitchell, who arrived in April 1943 to succeed Geiger as CG 1st MAW, assumed command of AirSols 20 November 1943. On 15 March 1944, after Rabaul was bare of planes, Mitchell turned over the job to Major General Hubert R. Harmon of the AAF, and became ComAirSoPac. Harmon was in turn succeeded by two more marines: Brig. General Field Harris[5] (20 April 1944) and Brig. General James T. Moore[6] (29 May 1944).

---

[4] All four organizations flew fighters; Strike Command (SBD's, TBF's) was the province of Navy and Marines; the Army had most of the medium and heavy bombers but the Navy, Marines and New Zealanders used a few for search and patrol.

[5] Field Harris was born in Kentucky 18 September 1895. Graduate of U.S. Naval Academy, 1917; LL.B., George Washington University 1925; Chemical Warfare School 1927; Air Corps Tactical School 1931; Naval War College 1939. First lieutenant

On 15 June 1944, D-day for the U.S. invasion of the Marianas, SoPac was recognized for what it had been in fact for several months: a secondary rear area. Admiral Halsey relinquished command and went to sea as Commander, Third Fleet, which title he had assumed 15 March. AirSoPac became a logistical command and its tactical and operational functions were taken over by General Mitchell as Commander, Aircraft, Northern Solomons (ComAirNorSols), under the Southwest Pacific's Seventh Fleet, with seven subordinate units: Commander, Aircraft, Green Island, Piva, Emirau, Munda, Treasury, Torokina, and Admiralties.[7]

For 13 months following the mid-1944 reorganization Marine aviation continued to pour a high percentage of its total effort into Rabaul, even though it had by then become just another by-passed base.

This outline of the complicated aviation set-up in the Solomons is presented to the reader at this point in the hope that he may follow the events in the Solomons and Bismarcks from the beginning of 1943. It was in the Solomons, starting with Guadalcanal, that Marine aviation made one of its most important contributions to the winning of the war against Japan: the major role in the destruction of the best elements of the enemy's Naval Air Force, which was superior in quality to his Army Air Force.[8]

In opposing the Allied threat to the anchor of their perimeter at Rabaul

. . . the Japanese committed in piecemeal fashion and lost all of their fully trained naval air units, including those rescued at Midway, and a

---

(temporary) 1917, captain (temporary) 1917. Designated naval aviator 1929. Major 1934, lieutenant colonel 1937, colonel (temporary) 1942, brigadier general (temporary) 1942, major general 1944. Served in USS *Wyoming;* staff of Marine Corps Schools, Quantico; in Haiti; CO of VS-15-M in USS *Lexington;* London as Assistant Naval Attaché for Air; ComAirNorSols in Bougainville Campaign; CG, Forward Echelon, 1st MAW and ComAirGreen February-April 1944; ComAirSols April-May 1944; Director of Marine Aviation July 1944 to February 1948. Awarded Legion of Merit four times, Bronze Star, Navy Commendation Ribbon.

[6] James Tillinghast Moore was born in South Carolina 5 September 1895. Graduate of The Citadel 1916. Mustered into service 8 July 1916. Resigned 26 September as second lieutenant, 2d Infantry, South Carolina National Guard. First lieutenant (temporary) 1917, captain (temporary) 1917. During World War I served with 4th Marine Regiment in Santo Domingo. Major (temporary) 1919. Designated naval aviator 1921. Graduate Air Corps Tactical School 1930. Lieutenant colonel 1935. Graduate Naval War College 1938. Colonel 1940. Foreign duty at Haiti, Guam, Philippines, North and South China, Virgin Islands and Peru. Brigadier general 1942. CG 4th MBDAW December 1942 to May 1943. Major general 1944. CG 1st MAW February-June 1944; CG Emirau April-May 1944; CG 2d MAW and Commander, Garrison Air Force, Western Caroline Islands June 1944 to February 1945 (awarded DSM); CG AirFMFPac February 1945 to end of war. Legion of Merit for services in Solomons. Retired November 1946.

[7] Operations Plan 1–44, paragraph 1 (b), 6 June 1944, ComAirNorSols war diary October 1944.

[8] *Admiral Halsey's Story,* p 181; *General Kenney Reports,* p 437. USSBS, *Japanese Air Power,* Exhibit K, p 40, indicates that enemy Navy pilots during the first two years of the war were considerably better trained than Army pilots.

portion of their best Army air units. The Japanese never fully recovered from this disaster, the effects of which influenced all subsequent campaigns.[9]

Just how serious was the Japanese loss of well-trained pilots in the Solomons was nowhere better illustrated than in the "Marianas turkey shoot" during the Battle of the Philippine Sea more than a year later, when U.S. Navy pilots shot down 383 planes because enemy pilots' training "was not sufficient to meet the demand of an actual battle,"[10] although 19 months had elapsed since the last previous carrier battle. Having lost their better pilots early in the war, the Japanese were thereafter unable to train replacements who could offer serious aerial opposition in any orthodox fashion. Ten months before the war ended they developed the *kamikaze* technique, which required little training beyond inculcating their pilots to seek certain death. This suicidal disposition restored to the Japanese an effective air weapon which had been lacking since it was lost in the Solomons.[11]

The number of planes and pilots lost by the Japanese in the South Pacific probably will never be known.[12] SoPac claims amounted to 2,520; this does not count the number claimed in raids on Rabaul from the Southwest Pacific. Of this SoPac figure, Marine claims in aerial combat alone were 1,520⅓;[13] the Marines didn't knock over many enemy aircraft on the ground. These figures indicate the Marines' proportionate role in disposing of the Emperor's finest "eagles."

From the beginning of the advance up the Solomons the JCS laid out the whole plan which would lead up to the mouth of Rabaul, though it would be altered in some details by by-passing and alternate landings. On 28 February 1943, eight months before the invasion of Bougainville, JCS declared:

> Airdromes in southeastern Bougainville are required by South Pacific forces for operations against Rabaul or Kavieng and to support naval striking force. Such bases exist in the Buin–Faisi area. Enemy airdromes in New Georgia are interspersed between the Guadalcanal bases and the bases in the Buin–Faisi area. Those must be captured or neutralized prior to the assault on the Bougainville bases. With the enemy in possession with a line of supporting airdromes at Kavieng, Rabaul, Buka and Buin–Faisi it is improbable that amphibious forces can operate successfully in the New Georgia area prior to neutralization of rearward bases. Airdromes in the

---

[9] USSBS, *Summary Report (Pacific War)*, p 6.

[10] Translation of top secret Japanese document quoted in USSBS, *Campaigns*, p 264.

[11] USSBS, *Summary Report (Pacific War)*, p 10; USSBS, *Japanese Air Power*, p 27.

[12] A reference to Japanese losses may be found in the author's preface to this volume.

[13] OpNav, *Marine Air Intelligence Bulletin*, August–September 1945. This is 64 per cent of all Marine claims in World War II.

Vitiaz Strait area are required to effect this neutralization. Therefore, the operations against New Georgia are visualized as following the operations to secure airdromes in the Vitiaz Strait area.[14]

Development of plans for the capture of bases on New Georgia were left to ComSoPac and, under the anomalous geographical and top-command set-up existing, the time of initiation of the operations was left to the control of General MacArthur. Fortunately, Admiral Halsey found that he could get along well with MacArthur;[15] the General left the Admiral to his own tactical devices.

Advent of the Corsair

On 12 February the South Pacific acquired something new indeed: the first squadron equipped with F4U Vought Corsair fighters. Twelve of these gull-winged planes of VMF-124 (Major William E. Gise) were flown up in the morning from Espíritu Santo, then took off to escort a rescue mission before lunch.[16] Altogether these pilots logged nine hours in their F4U's the first day —a fair indication of the extent to which marines would employ their new plane. On the second day the F4U's escorted Navy PB4Y's all the way to Bougainville—a 300-mile hop which theretofore had been out of the question

[14] JCS ELKTON I: Plan of Operations in the Pacific, pp 1–3.
[15] Admiral Halsey's Story, p 155.
[16] Interview Lieut. Kenneth Walsh, Bureau of Aeronautics, 23 November 1943.

for Marine fighters. A Zero[17] came down and looked over the new planes with what amounted to undisguised curiosity. The F4U not only could fly faster than any plane the Japanese possessed, but it could also climb nearly 3,000 feet a minute and it could go twice as far as the F4F. Some Navy flyers complained that the F4U was still full of bugs and at least one air officer declined to have it on board his carrier.[18] It was just what the Marines had been looking for. Admiral King had sought and failed to obtain Army fighter planes for his land-based Marine flyers following the disastrous casualties among the F2A's and the F4F's at Midway,[19] but in the F4U the Marine flyers acquired a plane that was to become as closely identified with them as the F6F with the Navy carriers, or the B-29 with the AAF. Many Japanese officers, interrogated after the war, said they considered it the premier U.S. fighter plane in any service.

On 14 February, their third day in the combat area, the F4U pilots learned that Japanese flyers had not lost their skill or aggressiveness. About 50 well-alerted Zeros were waiting for the raid on Kahili Field in southern Bougainville. The Japanese shot down two F4U's, two Navy PB4Y's, two P-40's and the entire top cover of four P-38's, with a loss to themselves of only three Zeros, one of which collided with an F4U. This "Saint Valentine's Day massacre" was a painful blow to the Guadalcanal-based flyers of all services.

Thereafter the F4U's gained aerial superiority over the Japanese fighters which they never relinquished. In combat in the Solomons VMF-124 claimed 68 enemy planes against a loss of 11 planes and 3 pilots.[20] Within six months all Marine fighter squadrons in the South Pacific, eight in number, were equipped with F4U's.[21]

Once the higher-altitude P-38's and F4U's came into common usage, the formula for the air offensive to the north was established: the bombers usually flew at 20,000 feet and the P-40's furnished low protective cover. At 30,000 to

---

[17] In December 1942 the South Pacific forces adopted male (fighter) and female (bomber) nomenclature to identify various types of Japanese planes. This system of identification had been devised in the middle of 1942 in the Southwest Pacific by an Army officer, Captain Frank T. McCoy Jr. Thus the Zero, or Mitsubishi 1940-type low-winged monoplane fighter, came to be called Zeke (but not by Marine flyers until about June 1943), and other fighters became Nate, Oscar, Rufe, Pete, Tony, Frank and late in the war, one of the best Japanese fighters was called Jack. The basic twin-engined bomber was known as Betty, the Aichi dive bomber Val, the four-engined Kawanishi patrol plane Emily, and other bombers Lily, Sally, and Nell. One Japanese fighter, a Mark II Zeke, was at first called Hap as a gesture complimenting General Henry H. (Hap) Arnold, Commanding General AAF, but the General somewhat explosively declined the honor. A radio message to the Southwest Pacific caused the fighter's name to be altered to Hamp. (Haugland, *The AAF Against Japan*, pp 367–371.)

[18] Fletcher Pratt, *The Marines' War*, p 121.

[19] Craven and Cate, *The AAF in WW II*, Vol I, p 462.

[20] But operational losses ran the total to 28 planes, 7 pilots.

[21] As follows: VMF-213 on 11 March; VMF-121 on 15 April; VMF-112 and VMF-221 by 19 May; VMF-122 on 16 June; VMF-214 on 19 June; VMF-123 on 2 July.

34,000 feet the Army P-38's flew high cover. Between 20,000 and 30,000 feet layers of F4U's were staggered, with four to eight fighters per layer weaving over an area two to four miles wide. Sometimes the Japanese fighters flew alongside the American fighter planes, as close at 1,500 feet, but usually did not attack unless formation was broken. Once an American fighter broke off, he was likely to be pounced upon by several enemy planes, and if he straggled on the way back from Bougainville he might expect a Zero lurking as far south as New Georgia.

Halsey's first move up the Solomons chain was modest enough: to the Russell Islands, 55 miles northwest of Henderson Field and about halfway to the New Georgia group. The unopposed landing was made 21 February by the 3d Marine Raider Battalion and elements of the Army's 43d Infantry Division.

Before the 33d CB's had finished an airfield on Banika (one of the Russells) the advance echelon of MAG-21 (Lieut. Colonel Raymond E. Hopper) arrived from Ewa on board USS *Wright* on 14 March. The remainder of the Group was there by 4 April.

This group was originally composed of a headquarters and service squadron, plus three F4F-equipped fighter squadrons. MAG-21's primary mission was to intercept Japanese planes and ships coming down The Slot and to escort bombers flying up from Guadalcanal to attack airfields, principally Munda on New Georgia and Vila–Stanmore on the southern tip of Kolombangara. A fighter strip on the Russells afforded more effective fighter escort to Kahili airdrome on Bougainville, which became AirSols's prime target for the ensuing months.

Mines

Admiral Halsey could now give some attention to mine-laying up and down harbors of the Solomons chain. U.S. destroyers had begun such operations on 1 February during the evacuation of Guadalcanal, and the first mine field laid in the Pacific claimed *Makigumo* six miles from Cape Esperance before the night was over.[22] Cheered by this success, Halsey requested CinCPac's permission on 28 February to lay aerial mines farther north in the Buin–Tonolei–Shortland area.[23]

The Navy now had a 1,600-pound aerial magnetic mine which had been developed originally by the Germans and dropped off the English coast, where one of them was recovered in 1939.[24] These mines were exceptionally difficult to sweep. They could be set to detonate in different ways. One ship or two or three might pass over the mine with an impunity not granted to a fourth or fifth which set off the explosion.

The first aerial mine-laying mission in the South Pacific was a 300-mile flight of 42 TBF's to Kahili 20 March, led by Major John W. Sapp of VMTB-

---

[22] CinCPac Special Action Report for February 1943.
[23] ComSoPac war diary, 28 February.
[24] Winston Churchill, *The Gathering Storm*, p 706.

143, which also included planes of three different Navy squadrons. The effectiveness of this and other early experiments was difficult to assess, but it is known now that one destroyer was damaged by this plant, as was a cargo ship, and it sank a 6,400-ton merchantman on 18 April.[25]

The charts we had of Kahili and other ports in the Bougainville–Shortlands area were inaccurate, when accuracy was essential for mines which were self-anchoring on the harbor bottom. Japanese searchlights could easily pick up the TBF's as they parachuted the mines from altitudes of 800 to 1,300 feet, and casualties were too heavy to warrant the continuation.[26]

Aerial mining was resumed in May, and nearly a hundred mines were sown in the northern Solomons harbors, with uncertain results. It always seemed to the TBF pilots that casualties were outrageously high.

On the night of 14 February 1944 16 TBF's of VMTB-233 sortied to Simpson Harbor to lay mines. Only 10 came back. Two were observed to crash —one went down into Blanche Bay east of Vulcan, another was shot down north of Lakunai field. The fate of the other three was never learned. An attempt to lay 16 mines had cost 18 officers and men and six TBF's.

The Biggest Blow

In March, Imperial Headquarters decided that revenge—crushing, humiliating revenge—for the loss of Guadalcanal was in order. Admiral Yamamoto himself went down to Rabaul to take personal charge of this vengeance, and he ordered his carrier pilots off their ships (*Zuikaku, Zuiho, Junyo, Hiyo*) into Rabaul to make a go of it—96 fighters, 65 dive bombers and a few torpedo planes to join up with the land-based force of the 11th Air Fleet (86 fighters, 27 dive bombers, 72 twin-engined bombers, some torpedo planes).[27] Altogether an impressive array of aircraft.

This was known as the "I Operation." It was divided into two phases: Guadalcanal and New Guinea. As a warm-up, 58 Zeros swept down the Solomons on 1 April in an attempt to knock out American fighters based on Banika and Guadalcanal. They shot down 6 of the defenders, but lost 18 in the process: 8 to Navy squadrons, 10 to the Marines (Walsh of VMF-124 got 3, as did Lieut. William N. Snider of VMF-221).

On 6 April P-38 photographic planes noted a vast increase in the number of planes on northern Solomons fields—114 at Kahili against 40 the day before, 95 at Ballale which had had none the day before.[28] Shortly after noon of 7 April the coastwatchers began reporting the planes on their way; soon the radar screens showed flutterings like autumn leaves. En route were 67 Val dive bombers covered by no less than 110 Zeros (the AirSols count of 160 was

---

[25] Samuel Eliot Morison, *Breaking the Bismarcks Barrier,* p 112.
[26] Interview Lieut. Colonel John W. Sapp, 12 February 1948.
[27] Morison, *Breaking the Bismarcks Barrier,* p 118.
[28] *Ibid,* pp 120–123.

unusually accurate). "Condition *Very* Red," Guadalcanal Base broadcast to ships and troops.

Up to meet them rose 76 Army, Navy and Marine fighter planes. While they were engaged by the Japanese fighters the Vals made for the ships in Tulagi Harbor and off Guadalcanal. The 14,500-ton tanker *Kanawha* was hit by five planes and finally sank that night; the New Zealand corvette *Moa* took only four minutes to go down; the destroyer *Aaron Ward* had her engine room wrecked and sank while under tow to Tulagi. It was a costly day.

But the clouds of Japanese did not get away unscathed. A four-plane division of F4F's led by Lieut. James E. Swett "intercepted the dive bombers over Tulagi and pretty well messed up the raid there."[29] Swett ignored a hail of friendly AA and shot down 3 of the Vals in their dives, then chased 4 more across Florida Island and shot them down—7 planes in 15 minutes, a performance which won for the 22-year-old pilot the Medal of Honor and created an ambition among hundreds of young marines to "do a Jimmy Swett." His cooling system destroyed and his face scratched by flying windshield glass, Swett was forced to make a water landing in the harbor, but he was rescued.

Pilots and AA gunners initially claimed about 100 planes, but Air Intelligence scaled them down to 12 Vals and 27 Zeros—28 of the 39 credited to: VMF-213 (1), 214 (10), 221 (17). Japanese records seen after the war admitted losing the 12 dive bombers but showed a loss of only 9 Zeros.[30] The three Marine squadrons lost 7 F4F's, but all pilots were rescued.

The "I Operation" continued with two massive raids on New Guinea bases, but only sank a Netherlands transport and damaged a couple of other ships; plane losses were 12 Japanese and 5 American. But Yamamoto was deceived by his pilots' claims into terminating "I" and sending the carrier pilots back to their ships.

Death of Yamamoto[31]

Two days after he called off the "I Operation" Yamamoto and his staff took off from Rabaul in two Bettys for an inspection trip to Kahili, his main air base south of Rabaul. Word of this proposed tour got to Pearl Harbor and orders went out to ComAirSols to see that Yamamoto did not return to Tokyo alive. It was known that Yamamoto would arrive over Kahili about 1135 on Sunday, 18 April 1943.

Admiral Mitscher called in the exec of his ComAirSols Fighter Command, Lieut. Colonel L. S. Moore. "Sam," he said, "work me up a plan to get this bird." Some officers wanted to nail Yamamoto in his launch as he motored to Ballale after the arrival at Kahili; but this was discarded in favor of an aerial kill. Moore assigned to the job 18 P-38's—the longest-legged fighters in the Command, the 6 best shots in the "trigger section," 12 more as cover—com-

[29] VMF-221 war diary April 1943.
[30] Morison, *Breaking the Bismarcks Barrier*, p 124.
[31] *Ibid*, pp 128–129; interview Colonel L. S. Moore USMC.

manded by Major John W. Mitchell, USA. The job of plotting a course from Henderson Field to southern Bougainville was handed to Fighter Command's operations officer, Major John P. Condon.

Condon's course sent the Army flyers outside The Slot, along the coast of New Georgia. Moore instructed the pilots to fly at 50 feet, off the coast of New Georgia, to try to avoid radar detection. The instructions read: "Destroy the target at any cost." That, said Moore, meant ramming Yamamoto's Betty if necessary. "And," he said seven years later, "I believe they would have done it if necessary." Major Mitchell was given a Navy compass, the better to navigate.

On the take-off two of the triggermen were scratched because one blew a tire and the other had a belly-tank fueling failure. That left 4 shooters and 12 cover planes.

As Yamamoto's two planes circled to land at Kahili at 1135 the Lightnings arrived also. Captain Thomas G. Lanphier USA shot down one, and Fleet Admiral Isoroku Yamamoto crashed to his death in the jungle. Lieut. Rex T. Barber USA shot the other aircraft into the sea with Yamamoto's Chief of Staff, Vice Admiral Ugaki, in it—he was badly hurt but he lived. In the dogfight overhead 9 Zeros which had been flying cover for Yamamoto tangled with the 12 covering P-38's. Three Japanese fighters were shot down, as was Lieut. Raymond K. Hine USA.

The greatest Japanese admiral was dead, a cause for much rejoicing. "Sounds as though one of the ducks in their bag was a peacock," Admiral Halsey messaged to Mitscher. "April 18th is your lucky day." (It was the anniversary of the Doolittle raid on Tokyo, flown off Mitscher's carrier *Hornet*.)

For several Sundays thereafter the P-38's were sent up to Bougainville so that the Yamamoto affair wouldn't look like the result of very special intelligence. It may have worked. It was 33 days before the Japanese could bring themselves to announce the "unbearable blow."

Yamamoto was succeeded by Admiral Mineichi Koga, who met his death 11 months later while flying through a storm between the Palaus and the Philippines.

Other Raids

The Japanese hit Guadalcanal and the Russells more rarely, but they didn't leave the Allies altogether free to build their air and naval bases for the inevitable move northward. On 25 April four F4U's of VMF-213 returning from an escort mission ran into a force of 16 bombers and 20 to 30 Zeros. Despite the odds of 9 to 1 or more, the marines shot down 5 of the fighters and drove off the bombers. Two Corsairs and a pilot were lost, and Major Monfurd K. Peyton, the flight leader, landed with 78 bullet holes in his plane.

On 10 May Admiral Koga sent 58 fighters and 49 Bettys from Truk to Rabaul, and the first effects were felt three days later between the Russells and Florida Island, when Army and Marine fighters ran into 25 Zeros escorting a reconnaissance plane that was apparently anxious to know how many airfields were on Guadalcanal now (there were four). Against a loss of 3 F4U's (including VMF-124's squadron commander, Major Gise), the Americans shot down 16 of the Zeros. Captain Archie Donahue of VMF-112 accounted for 4, Lieut. Ken Walsh for 3, and other marines for 8 more. The sixteenth was shot down by a Lightning equipped for night fighting.

But the northern Solomons were still well stocked with planes. Intelligence showed on the same day (13 May) 98 fighters and 32 bombers at Kahili, 96 and 1 at Ballale, 36 and 6 at Buka, plus 10 float planes in the Shortlands area—total 279.

Koga sent down 112 aircraft on 7 June and lost 23 of them (7 to VMF-112, 8 to P-40's, the others to Navy and New Zealand pilots). Four Corsairs and a P-40 were lost, but all personnel except the Army pilot were rescued. On 16 June the raid brought an estimated 120 planes, and Admiral Halsey's figures showed no less than 107 of them shot down—80 by planes, the rest by AA.[32] Most of the enemy aircraft were credited to Army and Navy squadrons—VF-11 got 31. The three Marine squadrons participating chalked up a total of eight. Six U.S. planes and five pilots (one a marine) were lost.[33]

In this melee the cargo ship *Celano* and one of the first LST's in the South Pacific were damaged. But this disaster was enough for Koga. Never again was Guadalcanal raided in daylight.

Survival Against Odds

Now that more missions were being flown greater distances from the Solomons bases, many sensational rescues of American pilots took place deep in enemy territory.

Men whose chances of survival seemed almost nil were rescued day after day by friendly natives, heroic actions of patrol or amphibian planes,[34] simply by magnificent luck, or a combination of all three. Two of these incidents took place during the big dogfight of 7 June near the Russell Islands. Twenty-two-year-old Lieut. Samuel S. Logan of VMF-112 was hit as he went to the rescue of a New Zealand P-40 and bailed out of his burning plane at 20,000 feet, whereupon a Japanese fighter pilot began making repeated runs on him. He was unsuccessful in shooting Logan so he finally tried to cut him up with his propeller. He did succeed in chopping off part of Logan's right foot and left heel but Flight Leader Herrich of the RNZAF drove off the would-be butcher. The marine completed his descent and was rescued at sea by a Grumman Duck piloted by Lieut. Colonel Nathaniel S. Clifford of MAG-21.

The other incident of 7 June involved a million-to-one chance. Lieut.

---

[32] Curiously, *Southeast Area Operations,* Navy, Part One, which is the principal source for enemy air records in the Solomons, makes no mention of this raid.

[33] ComAirSols daily intelligence summaries for 16 and 18 June 1943; VF-11, VMF-121, VMF-122 and VMF-124 war diaries; VMTB-144 history, p 10.

[34] During a three-and-a-half-month period Major Michael Sampas rescued 39 pilots, 61 crewmen, and evacuated 237 others. (ComSoPac commendation.)

Gilbert Percy had his elevator control and wing tanks shot out, causing him to decide to bail out at 2,000 feet while he was flying about 350 knots. With some difficulty he got out of the plane and pulled the rip cord. His chute trailed but did not open and he fell more than a quarter of a mile, landing feet first. He was able to swim for about three hours before reaching a reef. Next morning four natives picked him up and summoned a captain who was fishing from a nearby whaleboat. Percy sustained a fractured pelvis and two sprained ankles and 20-mm. wounds in an arm and both legs, but lived to tell the story of a fall nearly twice as high as the Empire State Building. After a year in the hospital he returned to active duty on 3 June 1944.

At other times there were other spectacular incidents of survival against odds. On 13 April Staff Sergeant William I. Coffeen (VMF-213) took off with 15 other F4U pilots to escort 12 TBF's on a bombing mission against Munda. When his oil pressure dropped to zero and the engine began to smoke he turned around and headed back to the Russells. But his plane's condition caused him to parachute when he had lowered to 3,000 feet. His Mae West had a hole in it, so he inflated his rubber boat and fortunately found it intact. He was in a well-traveled lane somewhere between Choiseul and Kolombangara, and planes passed over him, but he was unable to attract their attention. Rain, wind and waves tossed his rubber boat in all directions. Finally he capsized and lost almost all his possessions, including his shoes and paddles. Next day he paddled with his hands continuously toward land and finally reached the shore badly sunburned and bruised. He stayed on the island two days without finding any life on it. Then he started out again. This time he reached Wagini Island and spent one night.

Next day Coffeen started paddling again toward Choiseul. Restlessly, he kept moving, hoping for assistance, spending the nights on small islands, eating coconuts and nothing else. After what he imagined was about 15 days he found a coconut island with a small house on it. There he found and ate some limes and rotten eggs which caused him no harm. Again he paddled away, though his hands were infected and he was growing weak from his coconut diet. At last, after he had become delirious, a native discovered him on a small island and carried him to a hut. There he had his first hot food in 32 days. Finally a PBY came for Coffeen on 25 June. When he arrived back at Guadalcanal he found his squadron had been to its allotted rest in Sydney and had already returned for its second combat tour.

One of many Marine pilots who owed his life to a coastwatcher was Lieut. Sheldon O. Hall of VMF-213. Hall was on a flight 18 July with some F4U's, P-40's and P-38's which were escorting B-24's to Kahili. On the way home, about 40 miles down The Slot, Hall shot down two Zeros but another came out of a cloud layer and put a 20-mm. high-explosive shell into his throttle quadrant. Hall didn't bail out but chose to fly his wrecked plane into a water landing. The Zero continued to strafe him after he got his rubber boat inflated, but the Japanese pilot went away and Hall went to sleep in his boat. He paddled all next day and reached a sandy beach at 2000 that night. On the morning of 20 July he walked along a native trail, crossed a log bridge and stopped next to a camouflaged sandbagged outpost when he heard conversation in Japanese. He could have reached out and touched the two enemy soldiers he saw there. Hall dropped to his hands and knees and managed to get away. After four days of walking around the island he reached a native village. One of the natives—name of Harry—did not run away, but promised to help Hall. That evening all the natives gathered around Hall and held church services (Methodist) for him. On 28 July the natives accompanied him across the island to the coastwatcher who was already taking care of a TBF crew. On 3 August they went to a smaller island and waited for the PBY which came in answer to a signal and picked them up.

Another pilot, Captain Jack R. Moore of VMO-251, was shot down between Santa Isabel and New Georgia Islands. He took to his rubber boat and headed for Santa Isabel but could get no farther than a bay just above Farona Island. When he went ashore there he was rescued by natives who bathed and fed him, then put him on board a canoe and took him to another village. After that they walked over the mountains with him and gave him over to the coastwatcher. The coastwatcher, who had already taken care of 15 pilots, had no facilities for evacuating him, so a native canoe with a crew of 15 took him back to Tulagi where he arrived 13 days after he had been shot down.[35]

Neither fate nor the natives were as kind to Lieut. Alexander R. Berry of VMTB-143 a few weeks later. On the first strike TBF's ever made against Bougainville, the night of 28 February, to bomb Kahili airfield and enemy shipping, Berry was shot down. Piloting *Peggy,* named for his wife, and with Sergeant Donnelly C. Cameron and Pfc. Cephas Kelly as his crew, Ray Berry dived so low on a ship that the concussion of his bombs "made the plane bounce like a tennis ball."[36] A huge hole was torn in its belly and when Berry hit the water the plane flipped over on its back. Kelly got out without any trouble, the Lieutenant floated up, bleeding from his mouth and nose, but Cameron was never seen again. The pilot was almost unconscious and Kelly helped take off his chute and inflate his Mae West—then *Peggy* slid out of sight. They waited ten minutes for Cameron to appear, then struck out for Bougainville. After daybreak they reached an islet a mile off the Bougainville coast and spent the day there; that night they swam the mile-wide channel to the big island.

They slept and hid all day and at night worked their way north. Although they had no food Berry collected rain water by an ingenious arrangement of broad leaves and hollow reeds which served as conduits. On the morning of the fifth day they came to a native village where they were generously fed, but in the midst of their feast a boy rushed in and warned that the Japanese were coming. The marines hid in the bush and fell asleep, only to be kicked awake by "a caricaturist's dream, short and fat with huge buck teeth and thick-lensed

---

[35] These incidents are taken from ATAD, CNO, *Air Battle Notes from the South Pacific* (February 1944).

[36] Letter Pfc. Cephas Kelly to Captain Edna Loftus Smith USMCR-W, 8 November 1949.

glasses." They were returned to the treacherous village—the chief received five kilos of rice for reporting them—and thence to a stockade where they spent 30 days, during which Berry was hanged by the heels while water was poured down his nose. The Japanese also beat him mercilessly and several times they laid his head on a chopping block to wrest information from him.

In April Berry and Kelly were shipped to Rabaul—their only comfort was seeing the beached hulk of the vessel they had hit the night they were shot down. They were incarcerated together until November 1943, when Kelly was chosen with eight others to go to a prison in Tokyo. Berry after ten months of questioning, floggings, filth, vermin, malaria, dysentery, tropical ulcers and starvation weighed less than a hundred pounds "but he was as game as they come."[37]

Kelly left and the rest of the story was told by Lieut. Jose L. Holquin USA, who was imprisoned with Berry. On 2 March 1944 Rabaul was virtually razed by fires caused by Allied bombers, and the prisoners were moved into the hills. On two succeeding nights a group of blindfolded, handcuffed prisoners was removed from the 30- by 5-foot cave in which they were kept, tied together, and moved to unknown destinations. Berry was among those moved the night of the 4th. Two days later Holquin and the remaining prisoners heard that Berry and 39 other POW's had been killed by our own bombers while waiting for a boat to transport them to Watom Island. Of Berry's death Holquin is certain. Of the manner in which death came to Berry he is still in doubt for ". . . we heard rifle shots both nights after the prisoners had been taken out into the darkness."[38]

No finer epitaph could be written than what Pfc. Cephas Kelly wrote of Lieut. Berry:

> His precision bombing, magnificent flying ability and heroic conduct under the most difficult circumstances imaginable were truly in keeping, I'm sure, with the highest and finest tradition of the Marine Corps.

Admiral Halsey's plans envisaged "major operations" in the New Georgia group in early April, or even sooner "if preliminary reconnaissance showed practicability."[39] On 4 March he told General MacArthur the only SoWesPac aid needed would be limited air action against the Shortlands–Faisi area.[40] But when Halsey flew over to Brisbane early in April to get acquainted with MacArthur, L-day was set for 15 May, to coincide with the General's advances in New Guinea and his occupation of Woodlark and Trobriand Islands. Said Admiral Halsey:

---

[37] *Ibid.*

[38] Letter Lieut. Jose L. Holquin to Major General Harris, undated, received some time in 1945.

[39] ComSoPac war diary, 25 February 1943, p 45.

[40] *Ibid,* 4 March 1943.

This made little difference to us. Our plans, and even our preliminary attacks, had been under way since December, when we began bombing Munda's newly discovered airfield.[41]

After Christmas Eve of 1942, when all 24 of their grounded fighters were destroyed or damaged, the Japanese attempted to base no more planes at Munda, and used the field only to service planes returning to Rabaul from raiding Guadalcanal.[42] Runways were frequently damaged by bombing and by the shelling from cruiser and destroyer task forces, but this damage could be repaired in two or three days; ammunition dumps were constantly destroyed until Munda's 10,000 defenders had little left; about 200 gunners were lost in strafing attacks between February and May, and "it was difficult to maintain antiaircraft gun crew discipline."[43]

---

[41] *Admiral Halsey's Story*, p 157.

[42] USSBS, *Interrogations*, Vol I, pp 192–193, testimony of Lieut. Commander S. Yunoki.

[43] *Ibid.* Native scouts reported to coastwatchers new gun emplacements which "were pinpointed for dive bombers to attack. Indiscriminate bombing of jungle positions is generally harmless, but this precise delivery of high explosives on selected targets was something else again." (Feldt, *The Coastwatchers*, p 118.)

36. Tontouta, New Caledonia   37. Bauer Field, Efate

38. Control tower, Espíritu Santo   39. Barrage balloon

EARLY SOUTH PACIFIC BASES

GUADALCANAL: ATTACKERS

40. Japanese Bettys attacking transports

AND DEFENDERS

41. F4F-4 fighter

42. SBD dive bombers

43. VMF-223: *Standing:* Howard K. Marvin, Kenneth D. Frazier, John L. Smith, Marion E. Carl, Charles S. Hughes, Charles Kendrick*. *Front row:* Robert R. Read, Fred E. Gutt, Willis S. Lees*, Conrad G. Winter, Cloyd R. Jeans, Clayton M. Canfield

44. VMF-121: Roger A. Haberman, Cecil J. Doyle*, Joseph J. Foss, William P. Marontate*, Roy M. A. Ruddell*

SOME GUADALCANAL FIGHTER PILOTS

lled in action

45. Henderson Field
(1943)

THE VITAL, MISERABLE ISLAND

46. This was Guadalcanal

By LIFE photographer Ralph Morse
© TIME, INC.

47.   QM storage tent

48.   Fire after bombing

49.   F4F broken

50.   Hangar demolished

Courtesy Lieut. Colonel Michael Sampas

51. Major Gen. Geiger,
    Lieut. Colonel Bauer

52. One less enemy in the Guadalcanal sky

53.   Taps on Guadalcanal

By LIFE photographer Ralph Morse Ⓒ TIME, INC.

54-55-56.   Three views of enemy ships
beached and burned 15 November 1942

By LIFE photographer Frank Scherschel © TIME, INC.

By LIFE photographer Frank Scherschel © TIME, INC.

57.   Before the invasion

58.   As Seabees started rebuilding

59.   Twenty-one days after capture

THREE VIEWS OF MUNDA AIRFIELD

60. Russell Islands
scramble

SOUTHERN
SOLOMONS
AIRFIELDS

61. Control tower, Segi
U.S. Army Photo

62. Twin strip, Ondong

63. Torokina

NORTHERN SOLOMONS AIRFIELDS

64. Piva bomber strip

65. Stirling

66. Major Boyington
briefs pilots

TARGET
RABAUL

67. Bombs ready for load-
ing on Bougainville

68. "Hottest target south
of Tokyo"

69. *Lyons Maru,* sunk
    24 January 1944

**TARGET
RABAUL**

70. SBD explodes dump

71. Simpson Harbor,
    October 1945

Courtesy LIFE © TIME, INC.

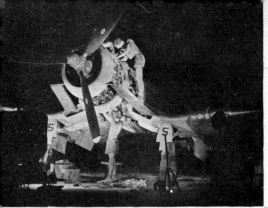

72. Mechs working at night

73. Boresighting Corsair guns

74. TBF's en route to Rabaul

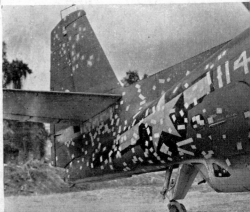

75. This TBF survived over 400 enemy bullets

76. Marine PB4Y photographic plane

77. Truk's picture, taken by Marine PB4Y, 4 February 1944

78. PV-1 of VMF(N)-531

TWIN-ENGINED MARINE PLANES

79. First PBJ raid on Rabaul, 17 March 1944

CHAPTER TEN

The Central Solomons

FOR THE NEW GEORGIA operation three principal task forces had been designated. From his headquarters in Nouméa Admiral Halsey himself retained command of the covering force, with Rear Admiral Walden L. Ainsworth and Rear Admiral Aaron S. Merrill commanding his principal groups of cruisers and destroyers which would provide surface protection and fire support. The amphibious landing organization, Task Force 31, was again commanded by Rear Admiral Richmond Kelly Turner, who was relieved by Rear Admiral Theodore S. Wilkinson after the first two weeks. Commander of the ground forces was Major General John H. Hester USA, CG 43d Infantry Division.

The third task force was 33, under Vice Admiral Aubrey W. Fitch, ComAirSoPac. His principal deputy, Rear Admiral Marc A. Mitscher, ComAir-Sols, had tactical command of the land-based planes, which would fly from Guadalcanal and Russells fields.

The number of planes in TF 33 seemed fantastic contrasted to the lean days on Guadalcanal: of the 533 total, 455 were available on L-day (213 fighters, 170 light bombers, 72 four-engined bombers and search planes).[1]

Due to the difficulty of approaching Munda over a reef barrier and to the possibility of flank attack, the landing operation plan was complicated. The first landing occurred 21 June, nine days before L-day, when Companies O and P of the 4th Marine Raider Battalion went ashore at Segi Point on the southern tip of New Georgia. Next day Companies A and D, 103d Infantry (43d Division) and a survey party of Acorn 7 followed. Construction of an emergency fighter strip was begun at Segi 30 June, by which time an air liaison party had arrived. The emergency strip was completed 11 July and Lieut. Colonel Perry O. Parmelee was nominated Commander, Aircraft, Segi (ComAirSegi), one of the subordinate commanders of Commander, Aircraft, New Georgia (ComAir-NewGeorgia), Brig. General Francis P. Mulcahy.

The Raiders began a gruesome overland march through the New Georgia jungle, toward Viru Harbor. After four days of fighting the sucking mud they had reached their destination and completed the encirclement of the harbor. Planes from VMSB-132 and VB-11 were sent over to see what help they could

---

[1] *Combat Narratives; Solomon Islands Campaign, Vol X: Operations in the New Georgia Area,* p 62. Hereinafter cited as *Combat Narratives X.*

provide for the "lost" Raiders, with whom headquarters had no communication. They bombed for about 20 minutes, surprising the Raiders no less than the Japanese. But the bombing was a lucky stroke:

> Timing probably couldn't have been more perfect if planned. Walker's firing in Tombi drew the Japs of Tetemara out into the open and then our dive bombers started on Tetemara, driving the Japs to the west away from their prepared positions into the jungle—toward us. Then within 15 minutes after the bombing had ceased the point made the first contact.[2]

After a vicious five-hour battle, during which 8 Raiders and at least 100 Japanese were killed and 79 drowned attempting to cross a river, the battle for Viru Harbor was over. Three Navy vessels entered the harbor to attempt to make a PT base there.

On 30 June a landing took place at Wickham Anchorage to the south in the Vangunu Island area. Units of the 169th Infantry (43d Division) landed at Onaiavisi entrance to Roviana Lagoon, a mile off the coast of New Georgia, to secure entrance to the lagoon which would lead to Zanana on New Georgia, six miles east of Munda Point. The most important supplemental landing was made 5 July at Rice Anchorage by two battalions of the 37th Infantry Division and the 1st Raider Battalion—the intended effect of this northern force was to prevent the Japanese at Munda from receiving reinforcements either from other parts of New Georgia or from the neighboring island of Kolombangara, where there were over 9,000 enemy, including units which had made good the escape from Guadalcanal.[3]

All these landings were insurance for the capture of Munda airfield and the extermination of the Japanese defending it. And even landing on the Munda area of New Georgia proper had to wait on major preliminary landings on Rendova Island, seven miles south of Munda. The Rendova landings would be made by the 9th Marine Defense Battalion and the 43d Division troops whose assignment it was to capture Munda. Having landed at Rendova, they would move through the entrance in the reef barrier, across Roviana Lagoon "to capture the airfield in a quick stroke." Transportation provided for the shore-to-shore movement was assault boats—LCM's, LCVP's, LCP(R)'s—from the Rendova boat pool.

Headquarters, New Georgia Air Force (forward echelon of 2d MAW), under General Mulcahy, embarked 29 June in the transports *McCawley* (Admiral Turner's flagship) and *Adams* at Koli Point, Guadalcanal. On the ground only a few Japanese were encountered by the landing force[4] and Com-

---

[2] Major Roy J. Batterton Jr., "You Fight by the Book," *Marine Corps Gazette* (July 1949), pp 14–21.

[3] *Combat Narratives* X, pp 4 and 19; Air Command, Solomons Islands intelligence summary 2 July 1943.

[4] Feldt, *The Coastwatchers*, pp 118–119, estimates the number of enemy on Rendova at 100. Enemy sources [*Southeast Area Naval Operations*, Part Two, p 29] put it at 150.

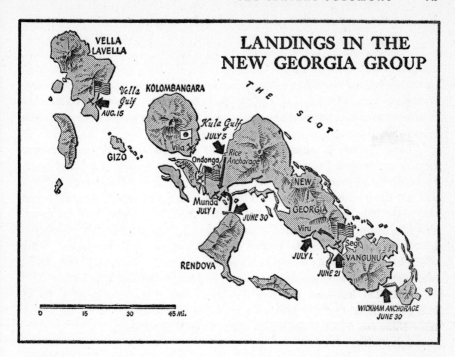

LANDINGS IN THE NEW GEORGIA GROUP

AirNewGeorgia was ashore at Rendova by 0830 on the morning of 30 June. The Japanese batteries on Munda Point were more troublesome—*Gwin,* only destroyer survivor of the night action of 14–15 November, caught a shell in her engine room. But *Buchanan* and *Farenholt* undertook to silence the batteries and succeeded in knocking out seven of them, leaving only sporadic fire during the rest of the day.[5]

A constant 32-plane fighter patrol was maintained over the landings during daylight by Allied squadrons stationed on Guadalcanal and the Russells. This cover was directed by the task force during what turned out to be one of the busiest days since the war began. In the morning two Japanese attempts at bombing the ships off Rendova were turned back with heavy losses. During the afternoon there was another raid of 28 torpedo bombers covered by an undetermined number of fighters. All except two of the bombers were shot down by fighters or ships' AA, but one of them managed to put a torpedo into the guts of *McCawley,* stopping her dead in the water and causing the force commander to shift his flag to destroyer *Farenholt.* Three more torpedoes hit the "*Wacky Mac*" at 2023 and she sank in 30 seconds. Later it was determined that the final blow was administered by US Navy PT boats which hadn't got the word and expected only enemy vessels in Blanche Channel.

The Allies claimed 101 planes during the day. Marine squadrons reported shooting down 58 of them (VMF-121 18, VMF-122 4, VMF-213 20, VMF-221

---

[5] *Combat Narratives* X, p 11.

16), but the Navy squadron, VF-21, put in the biggest claim, 30 planes. The P-40's accounted for 11 float planes, and the TBF's picked off a fighter and a dive bomber. Radio Tokyo reported the fight somewhat differently: 32 American planes shot down against no Japanese losses. At that, the enemy propaganda report concerning our losses was more accurate than usual: 14 American planes were shot down with a loss of 7 pilots. Despite the 5-to-1 claim, MAG-21's historian reported the "general impression was that enemy pilots were more proficient than those met in earlier engagements."[6]

Lieut. Wilbur J. Thomas of VMF-213 was credited with four Japanese fighters and reported that "my plane performed wonderfully." Lieuts. Morgan, Shaw, Hall and Jones, also of VMF-213, ran into a flight of nine float biplanes and left them without a survivor. Their CO, Major Gregory J. Weissenberger, was in the fight only 60 seconds, but he shot down three Zekes before a fourth shot him down. He parachuted from less than a thousand feet; his plane's tail hit him in the chest, but he landed only 500 yards from the destroyer *Talbot* which hauled him in. As he was being pulled on board "some wonderful son of a bitch got a Betty head-on that was about to get my destroyer," he said.

VMF-121 lost four planes to the Japs, recovering only one pilot. Its 18 kills over and around Rendova were scored in two different flights; three captains (Shuman, Ford, Baker) shot down three Zekes apiece.

The Rendova Rangers

Throughout the first half of July the fighter planes had to ward off one Japanese attack after another. Occasionally the Japanese managed to get through the fighter patrol. On 2 July—as landing craft began ferrying 43d Division troops to Zanana Point for the landing on New Georgia proper—a flight of Bettys, variously estimated at 18 or 25, came in under cover of 13 Zekes. They dropped an estimated 50 bombs in the Rendova landing area, causing the heaviest casualties of any single raid on American positions in the South Pacific: 59 killed, 77 wounded.[7] About three fourths of the casualties were among 43d Division headquarters personnel, the rest sailors and marines.

The odd thing about this raid was its timing. At 1201 Admiral Mitscher directed the Allied fighter patrol to return to Guadalcanal; a storm was reported brewing. These orders were thrice confirmed in the clear. The air was also full of complaints from the amphibious force ships, and of pilots reporting to Fighter Control that they were leaving station.[8] Whether these radio signals were intercepted by the Japanese or not was never learned, but it would be

---

[6] Postwar Japanese records indicate that the margin was 3 to 2 instead of 5 to 1, and admit the loss of only 17 bombers and 13 fighters [*Southeast Area Naval Operations,* Part Two, p 29]. ComAirSols intelligence summary 1 July 1943 is the source of friendly losses.

[7] ComAirNewGeorgia daily intelligence summary 2 July 1943.

[8] ComAirNewGeorgia had assumed responsibility for fighter direction a few hours earlier.

difficult to convince many men who were in the South Pacific at the time that such an interception was not responsible for the successful raid—in those days the average soldier, sailor and marine credited the Japanese with extraordinary facilities for Intelligence. What the Japanese airmen could not have known was that the only radar on Rendova would not be functioning between 1325 and 1335 while its oil was being changed. The raid, at 1330, came as a complete surprise. Admiral Mitscher promised not to let it happen again, and thereafter the Munda operation never lacked for adequate fighter cover.[9]

Hardly a day passed without the patrol clashing with flights of Bettys escorted by Zekes—60 seems to have been a favorite number among the Japanese operations officers.

On 7 July 9 to 12 Bettys, covered by 60 Zekes, hit for the ships off Rendova but they never even came close; a passel of enemy planes was knocked down (including 10 by VMF-122, 3 by 121, 3 by 221). VMF-213 had the patrol over Rendova on 11 July and shot down 4 planes and 2 probables. On 14 July VMF-221 was credited with 6; Lieut. Harold Segal shot down half of them. Next day ComAirNewGeorgia planes were credited with 15 bombers and 29 fighters, of which VMF-122 claimed 14 and VMF-213 claimed 16.

During July, 28,748 personnel were unloaded at Rendova (25,556 of them soldiers), plus 4,806 tons of rations, 3,486 tons of fuel, 9,961 tons of ammunition, and more than 12,000 tons of other freight. The part played by the fighters in this successful amphibious operation was acknowledged by the Navy:

> The success of the Rendova patrol in warding off Japanese attacks is attested by the fact that during the entire operation only three hits were registered on our ships by bombing and torpedo plane attacks and only one horizontal bombing attack reached the objective during daylight hours.[10]

The South Pacific's aviation had not yet reached the stage of being very helpful at night. Harassing raids by enemy bombers continued spasmodically throughout most of every night, particularly during moonlight. These planes, mostly of the float variety, usually stayed outside AA range for several sleep-murdering hours before making a single pass at the beachhead. Their tactics, combined with the mud which was hip-deep in places, made Rendova a thoroughly uncomfortable island.

By 9 July the infantry on New Georgia was ready to make its jungle push toward Munda airfield on a front extending three fourths of a mile. The first day it advanced nearly half the distance to the airstrip, but there it was stopped cold by concealed coconut-log pillboxes which the Japanese hadn't had time to build on Guadalcanal, but which soldiers and marines would encounter on many

---

[9] Conversation General Mulcahy 9 April 1948. He was convinced the raid was purely coincidental.

[10] *Combat Narratives* X, p 14. *Southeast Area Naval Operations*, Part Two, pp 28–29, cites claims for 30 June by the Japanese: 8 transports were set afire or severely damaged, 2 destroyers and 1 cruiser sunk, 2 destroyers set afire.

another Pacific island. Behind these formidable emplacements the enemy troops dug in like so many chiggers. Heavy artillery, bombing and naval gunfire failed to dislodge them. One colonel sent back 360 men of his regiment as "war nerves" cases after one day's fighting (and got relieved for it). Admiral Halsey sent his senior Army commander, General Harmon, up to New Georgia to straighten out the infantry. Harmon's visit resulted in Major General Oscar W. Griswold USA, XIV Corps commander, going up to relieve the ground forces CG. The "quick stroke" at Munda airfield required five weeks and the combined efforts of the Army's 43d, 25th and 37th Infantry Divisions.

Admiral Halsey wrote four years later:

> Our original plan allotted 15,000 men to wipe out the 9,000 Japs on New Georgia; by the time the island was secured, we had sent in more than 50,000. When I look back on ELKTON, the smoke of charred reputations still makes me cough.[11]

An Attempt at Modern Close Support

One significant innovation in the New Georgia campaign was a system of rudimentary close air support for the ground troops ("close" meaning within 1,000 yards of the front). No aviation volunteer specialists for air-ground liaison had yet arrived in the South Pacific, so eight officers (six of them Marine aviators) and eight enlisted radiomen under Major Wilfred Stiles were designated as air liaison parties. Their equipment consisted of four command cars (ancestors of the radio jeeps which became ubiquitous in later infantry battles) each equipped with an SCR-193 radio, an Aldis lamp, pyrotechnic equipment, and Isenburg cloth for panels.

The air liaison parties were swapped from one assignment to another throughout the New Georgia campaign. Two pilots served at Segi with a battalion of the 103d Infantry (43d Division) from 30 June to 12 July; one pilot and one Air Combat Intelligence (ACI) officer with a battalion of the 103d on Vangunu from 30 June to 20 July; one pilot and one ACI officer with the 172d Regimental Combat Team at Rendova from 30 June to 6 July; one pilot with the 43d Division on the Munda front from 29 July to 4 August; one ACI officer with the 43d Division on the same front 4–9 August; one pilot with the 37th Division on the Munda front from 22 July to 8 August; and one pilot with the 25th Division on the same front from 4 August.[12]

Execution of air-support missions was primitive compared to the smooth operation which had been perfected by the time Marine planes undertook such work in the Philippines. Of 44 requests for such missions, 35 were made the day before the execution. Only 7 requests were made from the front lines and 3 of these were not executed; 24 came from the top ground command at Rendova or

---

[11] *Admiral Halsey's Story*, p 161.

[12] SoPac intelligence report 1 September 1943, "Employment of Air-Ground Liaison Officers in the New Georgia Campaign," p 3.

well back of the front. There was no request for air support from the Munda front until 12 July, when on the next day 12 SBD's delivered a bombing attack on the right flank, in front of the 169th Infantry. The target was well marked by mortar smoke, but such was the confusion in the Munda jungle that it proved to be 600 yards off the grid co-ordinates which had been supplied initially to the aviators.

The ground troops were afraid of the bombers—the close-in jungle fighting meant that in many cases the enemy might not be more than a few yards away; therefore, the small number of requests. (A TBF killed 3 soldiers, wounded 10 on 16 July.) Pillboxes and coral foxholes, the usual Japanese positions, were too small and only a direct hit would suffice. Generally speaking, artillery was more suitable. Unless the jungle was too heavy it could pinpoint positions within a hundred yards of friendly troops, while a 500-yard margin was required by the strike command for bombers (300 yards in an emergency).

All in all, ComAirNewGeorgia didn't think much of close support under combat conditions at Munda:

> The use of aircraft in close support of ground troops proved to be impractical. . . . The dense jungle encountered made the location of enemy positions suitable for air attack impossible until friendly troops were too close to the prospective target for safety. As 200 to 300 yards was a good day's advance, it was not practical to withdraw sufficiently to use air attacks. . . . The gridded aerial mosaic which was used as standard for the operation was very poor, as no detail was shown on it other than the coastline. Frequently troops could not locate their own position on the map, much less the position of the enemy. Target designation by the use of smoke shells was quite good but depended on close timing and good plane-to-ground communication, and the latter was unreliable. The method employed to utilize bombing in support of the ground forces was to attack enemy supply dumps, bivouac areas and artillery positions. The targets selected were always well clear of friendly troops and were selected a day ahead whenever practicable to allow time for the squadrons making the attack to be properly briefed.[13]

Yet even on New Georgia the airplane as an infantry-support weapon could not be called a complete failure. On 1 August a strike of 18 SBD's and 18 TBF's covered by 30 F4U's and P-40's hit Japanese guns in the northeast corner of Lambeti Plantation, enabling 43d Division troops, who were waiting at the east edge of the plantation, to advance. On 25 July heavy bombers were used for one of the few occasions in the Pacific war as close-support weapons when 56 B-24's and 10 B-17's hit a 500-yard shoreline area between Terere and Lambeti, after the eastern edge of the target had been carefully marked by smoke. Com-

---

[13] Headquarters New Georgia Air Force (Forward Echelon, 2d MAW) special action report covering first phase of the New Georgia campaign, 29 June 1943 to 13 August 1943.

AirNewGeorgia and ComAirSols considered the strike successful. Troops were able to push into the area immediately but sufficient supporting troops had not been made available to exploit the advantage and the advancing troops drew back. On the same day Bibilo Hill was hit by Marine and Navy planes—53 TBF's and 54 SBD's, followed by 37 and 24 on the 26th, when AA positions were reported "thoroughly silenced."

Altogether 1,833 sorties were flown in the 37 air-support missions which passed through ComAirNewGeorgia during the campaign, 1,649 of them by SBD's and TBF's. A total of 1,317 bombs was dropped; several million rounds of bullets were fired by pilots during strafing runs. One SBD from VMSB-132 was lost to Japanese AA fire on 26 July, one radioman killed the previous day.

The Rice Anchorage landing on 5 July, which had been expected to prevent Japanese reinforcement of Munda from the north by a subsequent overland attack against Enogai Inlet and Bairoko Harbor, succeeded in blocking the Bairoko–Munda trail but finally bogged down. After slogging their way through thick mud and a rain forest, Colonel Harry Liversedge's Raiders and the attached battalion of the 148th Infantry (37th Division) captured Enogai on 11 July but Bairoko was successfully defended by well-concealed Japanese troops using heavy mortars and machine guns, although the 4th Raider Battalion and a battalion of the 145th Infantry were also called in. Since he had no artillery, Liversedge repeatedly sent calls back to AirNewGeorgia for air support and received 35 TBF's and SBD's on 6 July, 18 SBD's on 9 July, 36 on the 15th, 18 SBD's, 19 TBF's and 8 B-25's on 19 July, 36 SBD's and 37 TBF's on the 24th, and 12 B-25's and 6 B-17's on 2 August. Although the planes reported many times that "good hits" had been secured on Bairoko's guns and targets had been "well covered,"[14] Liversedge finally had to withdraw his forces and retire with 243 casualties.[15] The Liversedge force and the soldiers on the Munda side were supplied during critical periods—and there were many—by SCAT, which made air drops of food, water, ammunition and medicine totalling 100,000 pounds; frequently the R4D transport pilots had to brave AA fire to see that the soldiers and marines got the supplies they had to have.

Encounters at Sea

Bairoko–Enogai was an important target, situated as it was on the south shore of Kula Gulf which separates New Georgia from Kolombangara. To deny the Gulf to the Japanese to keep them from (1) reinforcing New Georgia, and (2) escaping from New Georgia to Kolombangara, Admiral Ainsworth entered Kula Gulf on the night of 4–5 July with three cruisers and four destroyers to shell the gun emplacements at Bairoko–Enogai and at the airstrip at Vila-Stanmore on Kolombangara. The destroyer Strong caught a torpedo and sank

---

[14] *Ibid;* Annex D, Air Support Requests—New Georgia Campaign, 30 June–5 August 1943.

[15] Fletcher Pratt, *The Marines' War,* p 131.

soon after the bombardment had been completed; it was believed (wrongly) the victim of a Japanese two-man submarine.[16] Next afternoon as he was returning to Tulagi, Admiral Ainsworth was ordered to reverse his course and proceed into the Kula Gulf area again to intercept the Tokyo Express, which no longer ran all the way down the Solomons chain but still supplied and reinforced Japanese forces in the New Georgia–Kolombangara area. The result was the Battle of Kula Gulf, a melee which was divided into three phases lasting from 0157 on 6 July until daylight, during which the cruiser *Helena* was torpedoed and sunk.

The first dispatch from Admiral Ainsworth indicated that a minimum of six enemy ships had been sunk,[17] and one beached. One correspondent called the Battle of Kula Gulf "the most devastating, the most one-sidedly murderous night sea battle of the Pacific War,"[18] but later intelligence scaled down enemy losses and postwar reports brought the battle into proper perspective: in exchange for *Helena* the US Navy forces sank the destroyers *Nagatsuki* and *Niizuki* and slightly damaged four others.[19] *Helena* was the eighth US cruiser sunk in the Solomons, and the last the Japanese sank until *Indianapolis* went down at the war's end two years later.

There was another engagement shortly after midnight of 12–13 July at the entrance to Kula Gulf, when Admiral Ainsworth intercepted a Japanese force with 3 cruisers and 10 destroyers. Again it was US radar-controlled gunfire against Japanese torpedoes and again the Navy had to tip its hat to the enemy's long-range fish ("The speed and accuracy of the Japanese torpedo fire was impressive").[20] When it was over Ainsworth's guns had sunk the light cruiser *Jintsu,* which had been repaired since it was badly damaged 11 months earlier by the late Lieut. Baldinus of VMSB-232. But all three of Ainsworth's cruisers (*Honolulu, St. Louis* and the New Zealander *Leander*) were damaged by torpedoes and *Gwin* was crippled so badly she had to be sunk by *Ralph Talbot.*[21]

Serious as these losses were, the actions which caused them served the purpose: the Japanese ceased trying to reinforce Kolombangara via The Slot and were reduced to sending ships and barges the longer way around to the west of Vella Lavella.[22] Nor, as we shall see, did this expedient last long.

Strikes Up North

The reason the Japanese had given up all attempts at daylight reinforcement was the planes which flew in droves from the Russells and Guadalcanal, keeping the enemy ships and barges at arm's length. The first long-range day-

---

[16] *Combat Narratives* X, p 21.

[17] *Ibid,* p 30.

[18] Dispatch to *Chicago Daily News,* quoted in Duncan Norton-Taylor, *With My Heart in My Mouth,* p 155.

[19] USSBS, *Campaigns,* pp 142, 168–169.

[20] *Combat Narratives* X, p 44.

[21] *Ibid.*

[22] USSBS, *Campaigns,* p 142.

light raid by dive bombers accompanied by TBF's took place 5 June when 80 planes reached the target area—ships in the Kahili–Buin waters—a long 300-mile leap from Guadalcanal. A fighter sweep of 32 planes preceded by five minutes the striking group of 15 SBD's, 12 TBF's covered by 21 F4U's. Fifteen Japanese planes were shot down while four of our planes were lost. One enemy destroyer, an AK, a corvette, and a schooner loaded with supplies were destroyed.

Almost daily heavy bombers hit the Kahili area; TBF's regularly flew night prowling missions. In a very well-co-ordinated attack that took the Japanese by surprise, Strike Command sent 78 bombers (36 SBD's, 35 TBF's, 7 B-24's) covered by 114 fighters (23 P-40's, 12 P-38's, 35 F4F's, 44 F4U's) on the morning of 17 July against shipping off Kahili. Four squadrons of Marine fighters contributed to the attackers' escort, and claimed 41 Japanese planes[23] out of 52 shot down.

VMSB-132 furnished 18 of the 36 SBD's (Navy squadrons furnished 18 dive bombers plus 35 glide-bombing TBF's on the 300-mile mission). This squadron claimed 3 hits on a cruiser (or big destroyer), 2 on an oiler, 4 on a destroyer and 1 on each of 2 other destroyers out of a total of 8 ships spotted off the coast of Kahili.[24] The Navy dive bombers (VB-11) claimed 6 hits on 4 ships. Postwar records reveal that only one destroyer, the 1,950-ton *Hatsuyuki,* was sunk, and three other destroyers were damaged.[25]

The following day pilots of VMF-214 from Espíritu Santo were on the dusk patrol when directed to go to the aid of the seaplane tender *Chincoteague*. For nearly three days she had suffered intermittent attacks by Japanese bombers and lay dead in the water off Vanikoro Island when, on the third day, three Nells came in for the kill. Led by Major William H. Pace, CO of the Squadron, four Corsairs shot down the enemy bombers before they could deliver the *coup de grâce* to the valiant little ship.

On 22 July another big shipping strike caught a "three-stack cruiser with square fantail" off the east coast of Bougainville, escorted by two destroyers. The "cruiser" actually was the 9,000-ton seaplane tender *Nisshin,* under way for Buin with 22 medium tanks and 667 troops. It sank after 18 TBF's, 18 SBD's and 18 B-24's, escorted by 134 fighters, fell upon it. VMTB-143, its 18 "torpeckers" carrying bombs, aimed all of its missiles at the "cruiser," claimed 7 direct hits: 4 on or about the fantail, 1 amidships, 1 just aft of the bridge, 1 on the bow. Of its other 11 2,000-pound bombs, none missed by more than 90 feet, reported the pilots. Postwar Japanese records indicate only 6 hits on the ship in the half hour before she went under. At any rate, *Nisshin* sank with "bow and stern high, amidships under."[26]

---

[23] Seven by VMF-121, 14 by VMF-122, 14 by VMF-213, 6 by VMF-221 (Captain Albert Hacking got 4 of them). VMSB-132 is credited with 1 Zeke.

[24] SBD operations mission report, 17 July 1943; VMSB-132 war diary 1 June–31 August 1943.

[25] USSBS, *Campaigns,* p 169.

[26] VMTB-143 war diary, July 1943.

The longer-range Army bombers were working constantly on Japanese installations in the Bougainville and Shortlands area. On 26 July 10 B-24's dropped fragmentation clusters on Kahili airfield after 21 Marine Corsairs had swept the revetments and gun emplacements with their 126 .50-caliber machine guns. During the night 6 B-17's struck Kahili and the airstrip on Ballale Island a few miles south of Kahili. On 30 July 9 B-24's, escorted by 62 fighters, hit Ballale again. The Thirteenth Air Force's total for the month—delivered principally at Kahili—was 778 tons of bombs.

The Japanese could see plainly that the war was moving farther north, and plainly they intended to resist at every point along the road to Rabaul. With Munda teetering they stepped up reinforcement of Kolombangara, next up the ladder, by the Tokyo Express and by barge. The idea was to make a Guadalcanal or a Munda out of every island. This SoPac was just as determined to avoid. The pilots gleefully shot at every barge and every individual.

The Japanese were not the only sufferers. Many friendly natives were killed on various islands in bombing and strafing runs by American pilots, despite repeated pleas by coastwatchers and repeated orders from various headquarters. Attacking native canoes was forbidden, but a pilot flying at 300 knots had difficulty distinguishing a native canoe from a Japanese barge. Indiscriminate strafing of any shore line was also prohibited,[27] but to many pilots, especially new arrivals, "the country on our side of the line was friendly, and that on the other side hostile,"[28] whereas, in fact, the country on the other side was friendly, too, except in spots controlled by the enemy.

Natives on Kolombangara, which we knew harbored several thousand Japanese, suffered most. Coastwatcher Evans warned against strafing the coast and predicted that he would "probably find very few natives prepared to act as coastal sentries from now on. This is not the first time this has happened." Evans took every precaution to insure that his scout area would not be bombed. When it was bombed, he felt he could no longer ask the natives' co-operation, and requested that he be recalled.[29]

On the night of 6 August six U.S. destroyers under Commander Frederick Moosbrugger intercepted four Japanese destroyers carrying 950 troops and supplies to Vila. Three of the enemy destroyers sank almost before they knew what hit them (it was torpedoes and 5-inch shells, about equally divided).

Munda finally fell on 5 August and the Seabees started work even before the farther end of the airstrip was captured. Nine days later VMF-123 and VMF-124 were operating from Munda, and Mulcahy had set up headquarters there. During five weeks defending Munda the Japanese had expended, in our estimates at the time, 358 planes (259 fighters, 60 twin-engined bombers, 23 dive bombers, and 16 float planes).[30] Of these the Marines had accounted for 187, the Army, Navy, New Zealanders and AA for the rest. The cost was 94

---

[27] Strike Command war diary, 26 July to 19 November 1943.
[28] Feldt, The Coastwatchers, p 154.
[29] Feldt, loc. cit.
[30] Combat Narratives X, p 58.

planes,[31] 34 of them Marine. Probably the heaviest continuous bombardment in such a concentrated area was made during this period when 950 tons were dropped.

Vella Lavella Taken

Almost a month before Munda fell, Admiral Halsey proposed—and Nimitz approved—hopping over Kolombangara and its 10,000 Japanese troops, skipping up to Vella Lavella, next northwest and 35 miles nearer Bougainville. It was the first by-passing operation of the Pacific war, excepting only the North Pacific leap past Kiska when Attu was invaded 11 May 1943.

L-day at Barakoma Beach on Vella Lavella was 15 August (VMF-123 and VMF-124 operating from Munda provided CAP) and by sunset 4,600 troops (4th Marine Defense Battalion, 35th Regimental Combat Team, 58th Seabees) had been put ashore under command of Brig. General Robert B. McClure USA.[32] On the beaches it was no contest but, as might have been expected at a spot only 90 miles from the big Japanese base at Kahili, Japanese airplanes were overhead early and often.

An elaborate system of continuous fighter cover, in addition to repeated bombings of the Japanese field at Kahili, Ballale and Buin, had been worked out. Time after time raids on ships and beachhead were broken up—54 in the morning, 59 after noon, 8 in the late afternoon. Sometimes a Japanese bomber or strafing plane got through, and at least four near misses were scored on ships offshore. But not one was hit during daylight, and despite proficient night search and attack by the Japanese, the LST's and other ships survived the night with fragmentary sprays. L-day attacks on the beachhead killed 12 and wounded 40. The Japanese admitted losing 17 planes on 15 August. Lieut. Ken Walsh, who had recently returned to combat with VMF-124 after its recreation tour in Sydney, shot down his eleventh, twelfth and thirteenth planes while helping to fight off the Japanese attackers over the beach and over the ships offshore. Leading a division of five Corsairs, Walsh got into a melee after being jumped by five Zekes at 10,000 feet. Walsh chased an enemy fighter which he shot down five miles north of Vella Lavella.

"More bogeys on the way!" the fighter director said. Walsh turned alone into nine Vals, came up under them and splashed two. Sandwiched between Vals below and Zekes above, he got two 20-mm. holes in his right wing, his hydraulic line cut, his horizontal stabilizer punctured and his right tire popped. They cheered Walsh back at the Munda field—opened the day before—when

---

[31] Haugland, *The AAF Against Japan*, p 145; Marine squadron war diaries. No Japanese totals for the period are available.

[32] Barakoma had been selected as a likely spot for an airfield by a reconnaissance party of six Army, Navy and Marine officers landed by PT boat on the night of 21–22 July and taken in charge by Coastwatcher Josselyn. They met no enemy and were taken off six days later along with the rescued crew of a PBY. (*Combat Narratives; Solomon Islands Campaign*, Vol XI: *Kolombangara and Vella Lavella*, p 15. Hereinafter cited as *Combat Narratives XI.*)

he made a perfect landing with a plane so badly mauled it had to be junked forthwith.

Fifteen days later Walsh had engine trouble, landed his plane at Munda and got another. Then he rejoined his group 'way up at Kahili. There he shot down four enemy fighters during a lone battle with "approximately 50" of them. Again he was shot up, this time too badly to get back to dry land. But Walsh survived his dead-stick landing off Vella Lavella. For these exploits the ex-NAP was awarded the Medal of Honor.[33]

Another ex-NAP, Lieut. Alvin J. Jensen of VMF-214, performed one of the great single-handed feats of the Pacific war during a sweep of Kahili, on 28 August. Separated in a tropical storm from the rest of his flight, Jensen came out of it upside down, smack over the Japanese field. He flipped his plane over at the north end and started strafing the aircraft lined up along the runway. Flying only a few feet above the ground, he burned up 8 Zekes, 4 Vals and 12 Bettys before streaking for home. Photographs taken next day confirmed his claim of destroying 24 grounded planes, and Lieut. Jensen was awarded the Navy Cross.[34]

Kolombangara Evacuated

Having reinforced Kolombangara, the Japanese now faced the task of evacuating the by-passed island. This they did with destroyer transports and barges, principally *Daihatsu*, a metal-hulled, Diesel-powered craft, 41 to 49 feet long, capable of making 8 knots and carrying 100 to 120 men or 10 to 15 tons of cargo. At first these barges—of which 100 were dispatched from Bougainville—staged through Horaniu, on Vella Lavella's northeast coast, but when that was captured on 14 September Choiseul became the relay point.[35]

Whenever the planes could catch them by day, these barges were often sunk—F4U's of VMF-123 and VMF-222 sank nine on 9 September. At night destroyers and PT boats had a more difficult time; on the night of 28–29 September alone, 3,806 Japanese escaped from northern Kolombangara to Choiseul and to Rabaul, by barge and by destroyer. This was part of a big five-day movement that netted 9,400 evacuees.[36] Admiral Halsey thought his forces sank 56 barges in the first four days of October—and the Japanese admit losing 29—but his estimate of 3,000 to 4,000 enemy killed ("rich, rewarding, beautiful slaughter")[37] appears to be three or four times too high. As at Guadalcanal in February, the Japanese got away from Kolombangara in September and October. It was a hell of a way to win a war, though.

---

[33] Walsh's citation; *Conway's* action report; VMF-124 war diary; John A. DeChant, *Devilbirds*, p 111.

[34] On 20 May 1949 Jensen, by now a captain, was killed before 800 spectators at NAS, Patuxent, Md., when the wing of his F2H Banshee jet fighter fell off as he pulled out of a dive from 40,000 feet.

[35] Morison, *Breaking the Bismarcks Barrier*, pp 208, 241.

[36] *Ibid*, p 242.

[37] *Admiral Halsey's Story*, p 172.

CHAPTER ELEVEN

Enter the Night Fighters

THE POSSIBILITY OF intercepting enemy aircraft at night by means of radar had been brought into sharp military focus during the blitz of London. Here was a new, highly complex operation which involved not only the aircraft and its crew but also the controller on the ground whose task it was to direct the airmen by means of radar to an interception point where the plane's own radar could seek out the foe so its guns could shoot him down. Daytime control officers who vectored day fighters to the vicinity of the enemy were important, but the primary responsibility for interception lay with the pilots themselves. For night work a controller was required whose skill had to be as decisive as that of the man flying the plane.

Although the U.S. Navy had led in experiments with radar in the 1920's and early 1930's and had even christened it,[1] the British had made the great advances in the years prior to 1941, particularly in developing the Plan Position Indicator and the first microwave tube. It was to the British that the U.S. turned for guidance, particularly regarding the use of radar in aircraft. For more intensive microwave exploration the National Defense Research Council established, with the British scientists' assistance, the Radiation Laboratory early in 1941 at Massachusetts Institute of Technology.

To learn about RAF operations many U.S. Army, Navy and Marine officers were sent to Great Britain in 1941. Among the first Marine Corps observers were Brig. General Ross E. Rowell, Lieut. Colonels Claude A. Larkin and Walter G. Farrell, Captains Perry O. Parmelee and E. Colston Dyer, each of whom arrived in London to spend several weeks or several months. Two others, Colonel Lewie G. Merritt and Major Frank H. Schwable, were in the middle of an around-the-world observers' trip when the Japanese attacked Pearl Harbor. Schwable spent three and a half months in England working and living with the RAF and attending the fighter director school at Stanmore, as Dyer, a communications specialist, had done before him. When he returned to Washington Schwable brought with him operating information on the British Mark IV aircraft interception (AI) radar (although the British were by then using newer Mark VII sets in their planes).

Except for these necessarily limited courses of instruction, Marine Corps

---

[1] The term is short for *Radio Detection and Ranging*.

aviation soon after Pearl Harbor started its night-fighter program from scratch.[2] Was such a program necessary? Both Army and Navy had embarked somewhat gropingly on night fighting—the M.I.T. Radiation Laboratory in 1941 had built 15 experimental models of AI radar for experimental models of the P-61 (Black Widow) night fighters, and one of these sets had been installed in an A-20 as early as September 1941. The Navy was planning to install M.I.T.-developed AI in F4U's and F6F's, both single-seaters which were not yet ready for combat.

On 20 January 1942 Captain Ralph E. Davison committed the Bureau of Aeronautics: "The job of the Marines was to seize a beachhead and hold it until replaced by the Army. To do this successfully night fighters would be an absolute necessity."[3]

But when the authorization emerged in March from the office of the Marine Corps' Commandant, Lieut. General Thomas Holcomb, the night-fighter program seemed something for future generations: eight 12-plane squadrons had been authorized for 1 January to 30 June 1945! With its hands full of new projects and with knowledge of the difficulty of changing procurement plans for new planes, the Marine Corps viewed a new diversion in the gloomy days of early 1942 with skepticism, if not pessimism.

In a memorandum to the Director of Aviation, 4 May 1942, Major Dyer reported the Navy had planned a separate night-fighter training unit "but little has been done." British ground control interception equipment had been ordered for Marine aviation by the Navy's Bureau of Ships, and the British AI, Mark IV, equipment, now being manufactured in the U.S., would be available in August. Dyer recommended that "this office push the formation of a night fighter training unit."

This was done. The Commandant on 12 June wrote to the Chief of Naval Operations:

Air Operations in Europe indicate that as our day fighter superiority is established, the enemy will inevitably be forced to resort to bombing at night. In order to meet this [a similar] development [in the Pacific] it is recommended that the dates for the formation of Marine Corps night fighter squadrons be advanced to the period 1 January–30 June 1943.

On 25 July the first night-fighter squadron, of 12 planes, was authorized for 1 January 1943 (instead of two years later). Major Schwable was designated commanding officer of the Squadron, which was numbered VMF(N)-531. Cherry Point was selected as the location for forming the Squadron, a process begun on 1 October.

[2] The Marines' first experience with night interception was the hastily organized night fighter unit sent from Ewa to Kauai in May 1942 to work with a unit from the Navy's Fighter Director School; Army radar equipment was used in the Kauai pioneering (see p 46).

[3] Memo Lieut. Colonel Harold C. Major to Colonel Ralph J. Mitchell, Director of Aviation, 21 January 1942, following an interview with Captain Davison.

From the start the matter of selecting a night-fighter plane bedeviled the Marine Corps planners, who eventually ran the gamut of possibilities from Army P-61's (due for delivery in June 1943), A-20's, A-26's to British Beaufighters and Mosquitoes, to Navy SB2C's and F4U's (to be ready in January 1943). In a Bureau of Aeronautics conference on 2 July, Majors Dyer and Schwable learned that "a possibility does exist for obtaining a few Venturas, similar to the B-34 (Vega) for training purposes and combat (318 m.p.h.) in a pinch." Although later attempts were made to procure Army P-70's, A-26A's and P-61's, the first Marine night-fighter squadron eventually had to accept the "pinch" plane, the twin-engined Vega Ventura (PV-1 in Navy designation). For the armed services of a nation newly at war demands were too great and the supplies sternly limited—VMF(N)-531 took what it could get.

The Squadron was commissioned at U.S. Marine Corps Air Station, Cherry Point, 16 November 1942. Lieut. Colonel Schwable had as his executive officer Major John D. Harshberger, who had been bitten early by the night-fighter bug. Three other officers and 46 enlisted men were attached for duty. Initially, the Squadron borrowed engineering, clerical and radio personnel from other outfits. Its quarters were a corner of an unheated, unlighted hangar, and its only aircraft two SNJ trainers, later augmented by SB2A-4's, whose instrument panels were inscribed in Dutch—the planes had been ordered originally for the defense of the Netherlands East Indies.

By the end of America's first year at war night fighters' priority status was improving steadily. The enemy in the Pacific was indeed switching from day to night bombardment, which was a sleep-killing nuisance if not a direct threat. This was made clear in a dispatch from Admiral Halsey in Nouméa, 27 December 1942:

> Current night nuisance raids over CACTUS are lowering combat efficiency of our troops through loss of sleep and increased exposure to malaria during hours of darkness spent in foxholes and dugouts. Recommend that minimum of six night fighting aircraft with homing radars and personnel now undergoing night fighter training plus ground equipment be dispatched CACTUS earliest time. Best available altitude determining interceptor radars with night fighter directing personnel should accompany.

General Rowell at Pearl Harbor passed the message on to Washington, strongly requesting that a "small unit be made available immediately for overseas duty." This was roughly comparable to Admiral Dewey requesting radar at Manila Bay. The first night-fighter squadron had not yet even received its combat planes. Seven weeks later two PV-1's had been delivered, but one of them was at Quonset Point for the installation of IFF (Identification, Friend or Foe), VHF (Very High Frequency) radio and Mark IV radar; armament had not been installed. The second plane was at Naval Air Station, Norfolk, having a new nose built for the installation of four additional .50-caliber guns; within a few days it would be ready for radar installation.[4] While it awaited its combat planes, the Squadron was learning night flying in SNJ's and SB2A-4's. Following Halsey's dispatch CominCh (Admiral King) showed a lively and sometimes inflammatory interest in the Marines' night fighters—Halsey had sold him on the necessity.

But on 16 March Lieut. Colonel Schwable reported only "mediocre progress" had been achieved by his squadron and "results must be considered disappointing." No complete radar-controlled aerial interception had yet been practiced because (1) the VHF ground radio was not providing satisfactory two-way communication at operational distance, (2) calibration of the SCR-588 radar had not been completed, (3) the plane radar had not worked well because the PV-1 electrical system had failed consistently, and the Squadron had been able to fly the PV-1 only 25.7 hours in its first month. VMF(N)-531 was plagued by a shortage of spare parts in radars, test equipment, radios, and planes—one PV-1 had been grounded 11 days for lack of brushes for one electrical starter motor; the supply department at Naval Aircraft Factory reported that only one spare PV-1 battery existed on the East Coast.

Of his 26 pilots, Schwable reported that all except eight were new. They had to be taught not only night-fighter techniques, but also the use of oxygen, blind flying, and navigation. For the new men, soloing in the PV-1 was still far away; they got lost simply flying from Cherry Point to Raleigh. Plotters, navigators, tube readers and talkers were trained locally. And, of course, the 322 enlisted men were also starting from scratch.

In February 1943, following a futile attempt to have an RAF Beaufighter squadron sent to the Solomons, Lieut. Colonel Edward A. Montgomery and five other officers[5] were flown to England to learn all phases of night fighting. Three more officers and nine enlisted men followed them in March. Four officers and four enlisted men of VMF(N)-531 headed by Major Robert O. Bisson reported in March to the General Electric Company at Syracuse, New York, for instruction in the new, mobile SCR-527A radar, which was due to replace the SCR-588, which required concrete foundation and permanent installation.

Under constant pressure to deliver night fighters overseas, Dyer in Washington and Schwable in Cherry Point worked under maddening conditions. AI radar was installed in the planes at Quonset Point. More than once they had to be sent back a second time because of improper antenna matching or defective voltage-regulator system. Guns, oxygen equipment and sights were installed at Norfolk with delays up to two months. Sights were likely to vibrate so that accuracy was impossible. On one plane the factory-installed top guns produced blinding flashes, and the four Norfolk-installed guns practically never fired simultaneously. No PV had yet been taken above 15,000 feet because of improperly functioning oxygen systems—and the marines were warned to expect

---

[4] Memo Lieut. Colonel Dyer to Director of Aviation, 14 February 1943.

[5] Majors Guy M. Morrow, Marion M. Magruder; Captains Homer G. Hutchinson Jr., Peter D. Lambrecht, Thomas E. Hicks Jr.

"most interceptions to take place above 25,000 feet"[6]—though the PV-1 was anything but a high-altitude plane. Conditioning a plane for night-fighter work meant considerable rebuilding—and the Navy did not yet have the men who knew how.

Marine Night Fighter Group 53 was commissioned 1 April 1943—a date whose significance was not lost upon the participants—and Schwable was designated its commanding officer, while Harshberger took over VMF(N)-531. This necessitated splitting the original squadron into two combat squadrons— VMF(N)-532 became the second—a headquarters squadron and a service squadron. When VMF(N)-531 was sent overseas, however, Schwable reverted to his status as its CO.

Schwable made known his troubles in a memorandum to Dyer 28 May 1943. But, he added,

> If it is the desire of the Bureau to have this unit [MAG(N)-53] proceed to the combat zone in an airplane that is admittedly makeshift for the job, with guns that may or may not all fire and with instruments that are difficult to read and with radar that so far has an average of one out of three working, this unit will plan accordingly and accept, without comment, the experimental installations furnished.

Movement Overseas

On 15 May Lieut. Colonel Bisson and the small ground radar detachment were transferred to San Diego for further training with the SCR-527A equipment.[7] The Squadron's ground echelon left by train and arrived at San Diego 22 June. On 28 June Schwable took a flight echelon of 8 officers and 22 men in six PV-1's across the country; two of the planes were delayed due to minor accidents but by 3 July that part of the Squadron destined for assignment overseas was on the West Coast.

The ground echelon sailed for Nouméa 16 July under command of Captain Thompson S. Baker on *President Polk*. The GCI equipment, 5 officers and 50 enlisted men, sailed from San Diego for Espíritu Santo on 30 July. The six PV-1's were hoisted aboard the aircraft carrier *Long Island* 31 July, and with the flight echelon arrived at Pearl Harbor 8 August. The inadequacy of his planes still haunted Schwable, as he wrote from *Long Island:*

> It is only if the Japs are more stupid than anybody thinks they are, and come down to 15,000 ft. do we even stand a chance to knock them down—if we can go fast enough to catch them! If we lack speed expert vectoring may put us in a position to do some good, but if the Japs

---

[6] Memo DA-09871 General Geiger, 26 July 1943.

[7] The SCR-527A was obsolete with the RAF when 531 took delivery of its second set at San Diego in June 1943.

fly thousands of feet higher than our planes can physically be pushed up to, there's not one damned thing on God's green earth we can do about it.[8]

Schwable considered he had three alternatives: (1) to strip the PV-1 of turret and overhead guns to achieve altitude, (2) to "steal" a P-38, install a radar whose operator would ride piggy-back, or (3) write the Bureau, "OK, I give up, let me have single-engined airplanes quick." (The first Navy night-fighter squadrons and the second Marine squadron were being equipped with single-engined F4U's whose pilots had to do all the work—navigating, scanning and firing—that was done by three men in the PV-1, in spite of the fact that the British had proved and advocated twin-engined night fighters.)

The flight echelon flew from Hawaii to Espíritu Santo, then to the Russell Islands, arriving at Banika 11 September to begin night patrols immediately. One plane—that of Lieut. John E. Mason and his crew of two—was lost east of the Russells on a training flight 16 September without a trace. The Squadron's forward echelon was reunited by 23 September, but VMF(N)-531's controllers were not permitted to operate from Munda without further indoctrination, although the air crews continued to fly night patrols with whatever controllers were available. It was 18 October before the Squadron, located at Vella Lavella, worked together as a combat unit with its own GCI controllers.

At this time in the South Pacific the term "night fighter" was subject to various interpretations. Early in 1943 P-38 pilots without radar equipment had shot down several high-flying Japanese night bombers by closing in for the kill after searchlights on Guadalcanal or the Russells had spotted them. (They claimed seven on the night of 7 April.) This was all right when it worked, but the enemy could not be shot down outside limited searchlight range and usually not until he had dropped his bombs.[9] But a "true" night-fighter interception, wherein the ground-based controller vectored the night fighter to a point many miles away from the base, where he could pick up the enemy on his own radar, had never been made in the Pacific. Some well-worn Army P-70's which had been equipped with radar and sent to Guadalcanal in March—to be controlled by a New Zealand radar unit (under command of Major Ethridge C. Best)— were unable to reach the 25,000-foot altitude at which Japanese night bombers usually flew, and their pilots were shifted to searchlight-controlled P-38's.

VMF(N)-531's planes were not destined to make the first such interception, though its ground controller managed it. The first squadron[10] of Navy night-fighting F4U's arrived in the combat area 23 September, shortly after Schwable's outfit. One of its pilots shot down a Betty on the night of 31 October–1 November. This first successful night interception in the Pacific was

---

[8] Letter to Dyer 2 August 1943.

[9] The British had attempted to overcome this defect by installing a "turbinlight" (powerful searchlight) in the nose of a radar-directed plane, which guided accompanying normal day fighters to the target. (Schwable report, 5 June 1942.)

[10] VF(N)-75.

conducted by Major Hicks and Tech. Sergeant Gleason with VMF(N)-531's GCI equipment, by then located at Pakoi Bay on Vella Lavella.

Two weeks later Captain Duane Jenkins made VMF(N)-531's first score: a Betty shot down in the moonlight as it headed for a naval task force in the company of five other bombers. Conversely, this interception was directed not by the Squadron's own GCI, but by a fighter director in the task force south of Torokina Point.

The marines failed in their efforts to install their own radar on Bougainville —which they could have had in operation on D-day. As it was, the clumsier New Zealand radar which was chosen wasn't operational until more than a month after D-day (1 November 1943).[11]

When the Squadron's GCI unit was covering one spot, its planes always seemed to be ordered to cover another under shipboard control. This control by Army, Navy and New Zealand officers unfamiliar with the exactness required in night vectoring was considered inadequate, so Hicks inaugurated a series of instructions in night-time control for the task force fighter-director officers. Following this, considerable improvement was noted.[12]

How It Was Done

One of the Squadron's own controllers (Captain Owen M. Hines) vectored a VMF(N)-531 pilot to a kill for the first time on 6 December when Harshberger and his turret gunner, Staff Sergeant Walter E. Tiedeman, destroyed a single-engined, twin-boat plane off Motupina Point on Bougainville.

A typical night interception—not necessarily the first one—is described by Lieut. Colonel Harshberger:

> The inadequate characteristic of the PV-1 required us to be airborne for interception of a direct approaching Japanese aircraft. So on call airstrip lights are turned on long enough for us to become airborne. Immediately upon take-off the lights on the field and aircraft running lights are extinguished.
>
> A call to our fighter director center informs the defense command of our location, and we are directed or automatically shifted to the channel of the local GCI control officer who instructs, "Vector one eight zero Angels eight." In answering the pilot repeats, "Vector one eight zero Angels eight," and climbs to altitude on the heading given. When the controller sees the blip he reports, "I have you," but to assure a more positive identification usually gives a change in course, "Vector right two seven zero." The pilot acknowledges as before and continues following the instructions throughout interception. Whether by GCI controller or by his own radar

---

[11] Memo Major Owen Hines USMCR to Marine Corps Aviation History Board.
[12] Schwable report, 25 February 1944.

operator, instructions give (1) control, (2) information. Thus the controller says, "Vector 240°, gate, Angels ten." Acknowledgment of instructions requiring a change in speed, direction, or altitude are always repeated by the pilot.

The controller next proceeds to enlighten the airborne crews as to the situation; for instance, "Bogey bears two o'clock distance 20 miles." With the pilot on a heading of 240° he knows that the bogey is bearing about 60° off to his right and is 20 miles away from him. Any change in heading or altitude of the pilot changes the relative position of the bogey. Thus any new control instructions from the controller ground or airborne require a new description of the situation. If the bogey is moving from west to east, pilot on 240° eventually the target becomes dead ahead, assuming the controller has chosen correct headings for the night fighter. So, as the chase narrows down, controller continues to present a new picture even though he is not compelled to give added control instructions to the pilot. So as we approach, it becomes "Target one o'clock, distance ten miles, closing." "Target, dead ahead, closing." "Target—vector 150°, Buster." "Vector 090°, Judy." From the latter the pilot understands that the two blips—his own and the enemy's are merging.

The controller has done his best to put us astern of the bogey, on its course, has not made it a tail chase, and with both blips merging can no longer advise us. In the ideal situation, before the controller is forced to say "Judy," the radar operator has blocked out ground communications indicating a blip on his airborne radar scope by the word "Contact." "Vector hard left, speed up." Then when the pilot is in his turn and has a firm contact, "He is 40° left, slightly above us, climb 500 feet." "Ease your turn, ease your turn, steady." "Target is slightly above us and 5,000 feet range, closing slowly. Speed up." Thus by an ever-narrowing set of orders coupled, as the time between controller instructions permit, with a word picture of the situation the radar operator coaches pilot to target. All the above must be completely worked out using standard words and phrases as developed through experience plus an understanding, development of reactions, and faith between pilot and airborne radar operator. On the final interception, as the plane approaches its minimum radar range, the pilot may hear, "Closing slowly, target dead ahead and slightly up, look up, target moving slowly left, turn left, look up, closing to minimum range. No further indication, within minimum range."

By this time it is hoped that the pilot has made visual contact. As this is an ideal problem the pilot previously made a visual interception; but, to provide against the bogey attempting to lose the fighter by a violent movement or unforeseen condition he has not called the radar operator off his scopes. When the visual first seen as a moving light among the stars or a black shadow against an overcast, is firmly established pilot informs radar operator who immediately leaves his scopes and aids in visual identification

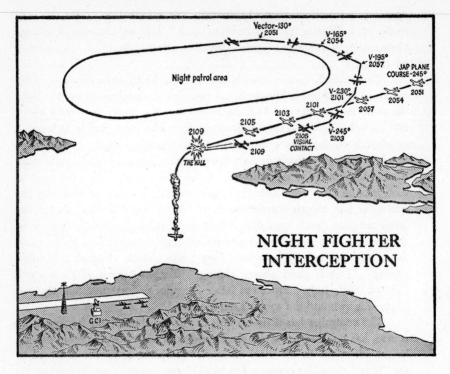

Vector-130°
↙ 2051

V-165°
↙ 2054

V-195°
2057

JAP PLANE
COURSE-245°

Night patrol area

V-230°
2101

2051

2054

2057

2103

2101

2105

2105
2109

2105
VISUAL
CONTACT

V-245°
2103

2109

2109

THE KILL

GCI

NIGHT FIGHTER INTERCEPTION

or watches the results of his coaching. In most cases it is necessary to close well within the minimum radar range before visual identification can be certain. This is accomplished by flying below and astern the other airplane and, dependent on cloud and light conditions, placing the target a little to the left or right. The shoot-down would start from a position below by pulling the plane up firmly until the bogey's shadow appears in the dimly lighted gun sight. Firing usually takes place as the pilot eases the plane forward to keep the target in the semiring of the gun sight. Destruction varies between an explosion enveloping the attacker, momentarily, in flames or a downward movement of the target trailing flames, oil, or smoke, the latter not usually visible at night except under most extreme light conditions.

A "splash" to the ground controller indicates success.[13]

Perhaps the greatest obstacle VMF(N)-531 had to contend with was aversion among officers of all services to the new idea. When the enemy came over at night the boom of AA was comforting to the men on the beaches and the ships, and officers were reluctant to silence this morale builder, regardless of the British experience that night fighters were more effective in knocking down the

[13] Memo to author, 14 January 1949.

night-flying bombers. Schwable found it agonizing to be sent circling eight miles away, as he was on the night of 7 October, while AA guns barked loudly but futilely at a Japanese intruder which dropped its bombs on Munda and headed for home. Despite frequent vectorings away from friendly forces during raids, Schwable figured he got shot at oftener by friends than by the enemy.[14]

The surprise of early night-fighter operations was the Japanese tactics. They flew low, after all—an unaccountable deviation from their practice at Guadalcanal. Despite this unexpected amelioration of one of the PV-1's shortcomings, Schwable was convinced the PV-1 "is not and never will be a good night fighter," though he firmly contended that a twin-engined, multiplace plane was the answer. He reported:

> Strangely enough, there has been a greater loss of contacts due to the PV's inability to slow down, to climb, or to turn sharply, than from a lack of speed sufficient to overtake the Jap. Regardless of how ineffective AIA radar presentations may be, this squadron is convinced that night fighting is best accomplished by a two-man team. Radar, like radio, must be continuously tuned to get the best results. To get the most out of the tubes during an interception, they *must be studied*—not glanced at. The pilot has his hands full with flying his plane, communications, searching for the bogey, planning his approach, etc. He definitely needs help. . . . The interception can be completed by single-engine planes. . . . The F4U's have demonstrated this,[15] but the F4U's would have shot down many more bogeys had they had a radar operator to help them, just as the PV's would have shot down many more bogeys if they had had the F4U's performance.

The Lessons of Combat

The first Marine night fighters also learned that they must often get "dangerously close" to the enemy plane before opening fire, in order to insure both definite identification and certain destruction.[16] Otherwise, the Squadron would have shot down friendly planes with faulty IFF to which it was vectored. Once the plane had been vectored close enough (the SCR-527A could read height within 1,500 feet) to pick up the enemy on the AI radar (which could pick up the bogey at one to two miles), it was still necessary to close within 150 to 700 feet to identify him visually (against a cloud bank, the moon or the stars). On 12 January 1944 Colonel Schwable, with Sergeant Robert I. Ward as radar operator, Sergeant William J. Fletcher as turret gunner, and Captain

---

[14] Conversation 8 April 1948.

[15] The F4U's of VF(N)-75 shot down six planes in its four months, 23 September 1943 to 31 January 1944.

[16] VMF(N)-531 history, p 7.

Baker as controller, shot down a Kate at such close range he could feel scorching heat as he swung hard left to avoid the exploding enemy aircraft.[17] Troops on Torokina who witnessed the Kate flame cheered loudly.

On the night of 9 February Harshberger was flying in the Empress Augusta Bay area after a disappointing hour-and-a-half chase of a bogey when the controller at Torokina vectored him to another bogey 25 miles away. Harshberger obtained an AI contact and a few minutes later made a visual of two Betty-type planes flying formation. Gunners in both planes saw him and opened up on Harshberger with their 20-mm. tail guns. Five of Harshberger's six nose guns were knocked out and a big hole left in the nose. One shell came through the cabin behind Harshberger's head knocking out his radio. Harshberger continued to fire at one with his only remaining nose gun while turret gunner Tiedeman fired bursts into the other which broke off the engagement and flew out of range. Both concentrated on the one plane and soon saw it descend in flames. Attempts to relocate the second bogey again failed. When he tried to land without radio contact the field turned the searchlights on him and the AA did a fine job of trying to shoot him down. The PV was finally recognized as a "friendly" and landed safely. Climbing out of the plane, Harshberger's only comment was, "Never had so much fun in my life."[18]

The night of 14 February 1944, Colonel Schwable, in shooting down a Jake, came so close to the enemy his windshield was covered with oil, and the turret gunner, Sergeant Fletcher, said the Japanese pilot seemed close enough to hit on the head with his gun butt.[19] On another night Harshberger brought back his victim's debris in his engine cowling.

The last of the Squadron's 15 PV's arrived on 19 February with more of the rear ground echelon; eight months after leaving Cherry Point VMF(N)-531 assembled as a complete unit, consisting of 19 pilots, 21 ground officers, and 352 men.

Among the scores of lessons in night fighting gained by VMF(N)-531— lessons which paid off in superior performance by other squadrons throughout the remainder of the Pacific war—none was more important than a method of calibrating the SCR-527A ground radar for overwater detection. The radar had been built by the Army (after an RAF model) for overland interception, and Lieut. Colonel Bisson had been informed that low overwater intercepts were impossible due to wave and tide movements. But the ideal GCI site, which required a location free of heavy vegetation, having regular sloping terrain on all azimuths for at least a mile and a half and no masking hills, simply did not exist in the South Pacific jungles. Even coconut groves offered so much ab-

---

[17] VMF(N)-531 ACA report No 6, 12 January 1944. Schwable shot down four planes in 72 night-combat missions before he relinquished command to Harshberger on 17 February 1944. Harshberger also accounted for four. When it was relieved in June 1944 the Squadron's total was 12, all at altitudes of 7,000 to 15,000 feet. Squadron controllers accounted for 10 shot down—Hines 5, Baker 4, Hicks 1.

[18] ACA report No 8; letter Major T. E. Hicks Jr. USMCR.

[19] ACA report No 9, 14 February 1944.

sorption to radar frequency radiation that little usable range could be obtained through them. Bisson located his radar near the water, worked out tables of calibrations to vary with tide conditions, and found that the SCR-527A worked well.

Lieut. Kenneth Mudie and Master Tech. Sergeant Burns had to learn a lot about the effect of Pacific moisture on the GCI equipment which was not in the handbook of instructions. They mastered the most difficult problem—namely, keeping the equipment operating. Never once was 531's equipment "off the air" when bogeys were in the vicinity. Major Eugene Flater, temporarily attached to VMF(N)-531 at the Russell Islands and Vella Lavella, made important contributions to the technical aspects of "how to get the most out of a radar."

From Espíritu to Guadalcanal, Vella Lavella, Bougainville to Green Island and Emirau, VMF(N)-531 learned its lessons in night interception, which were passed on to replacement pilots and to other squadrons being trained in the U.S.[20] Those lessons formed the basis for highly successful night interception later in the war. The made-to-order two-seater night fighter (F7F) eventually developed was never ready in time for use against Japan, but the F4U and F6F night fighters which marines flew later took their lessons from the persistent PV-1 pioneers who had to learn the hard way. In night fighting, Marine aviators were thrown into pioneering of the most daring sort, but despite tribulations that often seemed insurmountable they eventually delivered a record unique in World War II.

Probably the most important contribution that VMF(N)-531 made to the developments that led to later successful operations against the Japanese was to prove the desirability of landing GCI equipment on D-day, in order to provide efficient ground control for night fighters during the troops' first few critical nights ashore. At Green Island, in Rabaul's back yard, a GCI was landed for the first time on D-day. By the second night the ground control was on the air and the two Japanese raids that were initiated that night were staved off by the night-fighter–GCI team at a cost to the enemy of two of his scarce night-flying planes.[21]

---

[20] Whose experiences are recounted in subsequent chapters.

[21] VMF(N)-531 report of operations in the South Pacific, 25 November 1943–25 February 1944.

CHAPTER TWELVE

Bougainville

RABAUL WAS STILL the target, and one more island lay athwart the path that led to Rabaul. This was Bougainville, largest of the Solomons—bigger by a third than Guadalcanal—with the highest mountains and the wildest jungles.

There was one reason, and one only, for landing on Bougainville. Airfields were wanted for basing fighter planes that could escort the heavy bombers to Rabaul, and for basing the short-legged, sharpshooting SBD's and TBF's that were needed to sink Rabaul's ships and silence her guns. Until the Combined Chiefs of Staff conference at Quebec in August 1943, the invasion of Rabaul was still contemplated. After that, Rabaul was no target for the Army and Marine divisions; instead, it was marked for strangulation by the aviators. It was for this that airfields on Bougainville were required.

The original conception of the invasion of Bougainville underwent many changes. Admiral Halsey first planned to seize the heavily defended southern part of the island, including Kahili, biggest of Bougainville's five airfields, plus the nearby Shortland Islands and the Ballale field.[1] On 5 August, when it appeared that he didn't have enough ground forces to assault Bougainville proper,[2] Admiral Halsey limited the plan to seizure of the islands to the south. But direct assault on heavily defended areas was discarded as too expensive in lives and too time-consuming.

After intensive study, supplemented by reconnaissance landings at various points on Bougainville, the invasion boiled down to two possibilities: (1) a landing at Kieta on the east coast, or (2) a landing at Cape Torokina in Empress Augusta Bay, midway up the island on the western coast. It was not until 1 October that Admiral Halsey informed General MacArthur he had decided on the Torokina landing, with 1 November as Dog-day (later designated Love-day). In his capacity as over-all strategic commander west of 159°, General MacArthur concurred and promised all practicable air support from the Southwest Pacific.

---

[1] ComSoPac letter 11 July 1943, quoted in *Combat Narratives; Solomon Islands Campaign*, XII: *The Bougainville Landing and the Battle of Empress Augusta Bay, 27 October–2 November 1943* (hereinafter referred to as *Combat Narratives, XII*).

[2] The 2d MarDiv had been taken away from Halsey and assigned to the Central Pacific for the Gilberts operation—an operation which Halsey had initially opposed when it was broached in February, though conceding the desirability of "confusing" the Japanese throughout the Pacific. (ComSoPac war diary, 17 February 1943.)

Excepting Guadalcanal, no operation in the Pacific war was bolder in its planning than CHERRYBLOSSOM (as the Empress Augusta Bay landing was christened). Torokina faced the open sea, which would make landings from small boats risky. Its treacherous waters were poorly charted. The beachhead would be subjected to possible air attack not only from the Kahili, Ballale, Buka, Bonis and Kara airfields and the Kieta seaplane base, all within 65 miles, but also from Rabaul's five airfields, only 210 miles to the northwest. Clearly, AirSoPac planes faced a prodigious task if they were to keep all these fields quiescent while the ships stood off Bougainville's shore.

The plan envisaged not the capture of the whole of Bougainville, which is as forbidding and inhospitable as the Devil's furnace room, but only the seizure of a beachhead about six by eight miles; this beachhead would by-pass all but a couple of thousand of the 40,000 Japanese in the Bougainville area— nearly all of whom were concentrated far to the north and, more especially, to the south. This meant prolonged fighting by the troops guarding the perimeter while the airfields were being prepared from which Rabaul itself would be strangled.

South Pacific Aviation

AirSoPac consisted of four separate services integrated for tactical purposes: (1) the 1st and 2d MAW's, (2) the AAF's Thirteenth Air Force, (3) various USN units under ComFAirSoPac, and (4) units of the RNZAF. Tactical and operational aviation functions in the Solomons were under the cognizance of ComAirSols, a subordinate command of AirSoPac, set up on 15 February 1943. From 25 July to 20 November 1943, it was commanded by Major General N. F. Twining USA. On the latter date he was relieved by Major General Ralph J. Mitchell USMC, who had been Acting ComAirSoPac from 8 October to 16 November.

Under General Twining and, later, General Mitchell, were four type commands:

(1) *Fighter Command,* under a marine (Colonel W. O. Brice) from 24 October 1943 to 15 March 1944 and after that an Army officer (Brig. General Earle W. Barnes). It included fighter planes from all four services, and also had operational control over all information centers, fighter direction stations, radar nets and AA in vicinity of airfields in the forward area.

(2) *Strike Command,* controlling all Navy, Marine and RNZAF dive-bombing, torpedo-bombing and search planes, under Lieut. Colonel David F. O'Neill USMC.

(3) *Bomber Command,* under an Army officer (Brig. General William A. Matheny), controlling heavy and medium bombers (chiefly B-24's and B-25's). Mostly Army, the command also included Navy PB4Y bombing squadrons.

(4) *Photo Wing,* commanded by Colonel George W. Hansen USA, operating all photographic aircraft.

General Twining's operation plan for Bougainville showed that he could count on an estimated 728 AirSols planes totaling 52 squadrons, as follows:[3]

Service	Squadrons	Planes
NAVY	19	274
ARMY	16	216
MARINES	14	181
RNZAF	3	57
	52	728

These were to be based initially by types of planes, as follows:[4]

Number	Base	Type

FIGHTERS

Number	Base	Type
45	Guadalcanal	AAF P-38's, P-39's, P-40's
27	Russells	Marine F4U's and PV's, AAF P-38's
48	Segi	Navy F6F's
31	Munda	Navy F4U's, AAF P-39's
103	Ondonga	Navy F4U's, AAF P-39's, RNZAF P-40's
60	Barakoma	Marine F4U's
TOTAL 314		

BOMBERS

Number	Base	Type
52	Guadalcanal	AAF B-24's
27	Guadalcanal	Navy PB4Y's
15	Guadalcanal	RNZAF PV's
48	Russells	AAF B-25's
27	Russells	Navy PV's
100	Munda	Marine and Navy SBD's
48	Munda	Marine and Navy TBF's
TOTAL 317		

PATROL, PHOTO, TRANSPORT

Number	Base	Type
30	Guadalcanal	Navy SBD's and OS2U's
10	Guadalcanal	Navy PB4Y's, AAF F5A's
21	Guadalcanal	Marine R4D's, AAF C-47's
6	Guadalcanal	Navy PBY-5A "Black Cats"
27	Tulagi	Navy PBY-5A's
3	Munda	AAF F5A's
TOTAL 97		

GRAND TOTAL 728

---

[3] Compiled from ComAirSols operation plan T1-43, 21 October 1943, Annex A, and ComAirSoPac operation plan 9-43, 25 October 1943, Annex A.

[4] *Ibid.*

Marines in AirSols

All 14 Marine squadrons in AirSols were in action against the enemy from the beginning of the Bougainville operation. But the usual policy in Marine aviation at this stage of the war—and other services had similar policies—was to keep a squadron in the forward combat area four to six weeks, then give the pilots and combat crews a week's leave in Sydney or Auckland, which were admirably adapted for such purposes in that life was pleasant and civilized, the climate temperate and the people hospitable—in short, everything was as different from the forward area as day from night.

Following this brief vacation from war, the squadrons usually were eased into combat again via the SoPac "back area"—at Espíritu Santo or Efate, where two to four weeks were spent in training and absorbing replacements. Then back to AirSols—Guadalcanal, the Russells, New Georgia, or Vella Lavella.

New Marine squadrons and replacements for old squadrons were sent out from MarFAirWest, under command of Colonel Wallace since his return from Guadalcanal. MarFAirWest, which saw to equipping the units and to completion of the Marine aviator's training, was a subordinate command of Major General Rowell's MAWPac which by late 1943 included two administrative wings: Marine Aircraft, South Pacific (MASP) under Major General Ralph Mitchell and Marine Aircraft, Hawaiian Area (MAHA), under Brig. General Walter G. Farrell. (MAHA's duties were taken over by the 3d MAW when that Wing arrived in Hawaii 8 May 1944.)

MASP, prior to the Bougainville invasion, consisted of the 1st MAW (Major General Mitchell) at Espíritu Santo and the 2d MAW (Brig. General Mulcahy) at Munda. Under their administrative command were six groups:

MAG-11 (Lieut. Colonel Joe A. Smoak) at Espíritu; MAG-12 (Colonel Vernon M. Guymon) at Efate; MAG-14 (Colonel Brice) at Ondonga; MAG-21 (Colonel Raymond E. Hopper) at Russells until 18 November; MAG-24 (Colonel William L. McKittrick) at Russells after 17 November; and MAG-25 (Colonel Wyman F. Marshall) at New Caledonia.

MASP groups included 22 squadrons, of which 14 were available to AirSols, as we have noted, for the beginning of the Bougainville operation. These 14 were:

Five fighter squadrons: VMF-211 (Major Robert A. Harvey); VMF-212 (Major Hugh M. Elwood); VMF-215 (Lieut. Colonel Herbert H. Williamson); VMF-221 (Major Nathan T. Post Jr.); and VMF(N)-531 (Lieut. Colonel Frank H. Schwable).

Three dive-bomber squadrons: VMSB-144 (Major Frank E. Hollar); VMSB-234 (Major Harold B. Penne); VMSB-244 (Major Robert J. Johnson).

Three torpedo-bomber squadrons: VMTB-143 (Major Warren G. Mollenkamp); VMTB-232 (Major Rolland F. Smith); VMTB-233 (Major Royce W. Coln).

Three transport squadrons: VMJ-152 (Lieut. Colonel Elmore W. Seeds); VMJ-153 (Major Robert B. Bell); VMJ-253 (Major Freeman W. Williams).

Four of the eight non-AirSols squadrons were due for Stateside return,[5] and were not available for Bougainville planning. The other four moved up and came under AirSols later.[6]

Besides these combat units, ComGenMarAirSoPac had under his command a Marine air depot, a repair and salvage squadron, and a Marine air base squadron. The personnel rosters of aviation marines in the South Pacific totaled 15,000 officers and men.

During its early months the command of MASP devolved upon the commanding general of the 1st MAW but CominCh, who had opposed a separate command, relented on 3 December 1943, and approved the divided establishment with a separate headquarters for MASP.[7]

Invasion Preliminaries

Throughout September and early October, Japanese airfields in the Bougainville area were combed steadily by planes from the 12 AirSols strips.[8] But the intensified preinvasion air campaign may be said to have begun 15 October.

From that date the momentum of the strikes increased, as the following table indicates.

---

[5] VMF-123, VMF-213, VMSB-132, VMD-154.

[6] VMF-214, VMF-222, VMSB-235, VMSB-236.

[7] The Commandant ordered MASP set up in a dispatch dated 14 April 1943, but it was an irregular organization until Admiral King approved it. The foregoing material on administration is taken chiefly from *Aviation Organization in the United States Marine Corps, 1912–45,* by Captain Edna Loftus Smith USMCWR, Vol V, in a monograph entitled *Essays in the History of Naval Air Operations;* and from *The Role of Aviation in the Bougainville Operation* by Captain Warren H. Goodman USMCR, a monograph prepared for the Historical Division USMC.

[8] Guadalcanal 4, Russells 2, Segi 1, Munda 2, Ondonga 2, Barakoma 1. In mid-October Strike Command moved to Munda, and ComAirSols followed a few days later.

AIR STRIKES
ON ENEMY AIR INSTALLATIONS AND STRIPS
15–31 October 1943

Oct.	Planes	Target	Comments	Enemy	Allied
				Losses	
15	21 B-24's, 16 F4U's, and 12 P-38's	Kahili personnel and supply	4 explosions, several fires, good pattern, 10–15 Zekes intercepting	6	0
	6 B-25's	Buka	Large explosions and fires	0	0
	6 B-25's	Ballale	Good pattern on runway	0	0
	3 B-24's	Kara and Kahili airdromes	Unobserved results	0	0
17	21 F4U's	Ballale	Engaged 30–40 Zekes and Hamps	14	(1 op)
18	28 B-24's, 32 SBD's	Kahili	29 tons bombs—many hits	3	0
	19 F4U's	Kahili	Encountered 15–20 Zekes	8	0
19	4 PV's	Ballale	AA position—4 explosions	0	0
	4 PV's	Kara	Large explosion, one fire	0	1
	24 B-24's, 14 P-38's	Kahili	Large fires started, one AA position hit	6	(2 op)
	12 TBF's, 20 SBD's, and 20 VF	Kara	AA positions and buildings hit.	0	0
	2 F4U's	Kara	Many hits on runway Strafing attack on strip	5 (on ground)	0
20	4 PV's	Kakasa	8 tons dropped, large explosion, heavy smoke	0	0
	24 F4U's	Kahili	Encountered 20 Zekes	3	2

Oct.	Planes	Target	Comments	Losses Enemy	Losses Allied
	24 P-40's	Kahili	No enemy contacts	0	0
	2 PV's	Kakasa	Report village badly damaged from previous raid	0	0
	7 SBD's, plus VF	Kakasa	2 explosions, much smoke	0	0
21	2 B-25's, 36 VF	Kara	7 tons on airdrome, 15 hits on runway and buildings	0	0
	3 PV's	Kakasa	2 tons dropped, unobserved results	0	0
22	10 B-24's, 20 F6F's	Kahili	33 tons with unobserved results	0	0
	9 B-29's, 12 F6F's	Pora Pora, Choiseul	36 tons on beach	0	0
	9 B-24's, 8 F6F's	Choiseul coast	9 tons, unobserved results	1	2
	12 B-24's, 16 P-40's	Kahili	48 tons on Emberley's Lease. 9 Zekes intercepted	0	0
	24 TBF's, 48 SBD's, and 68 VF	Kahili	32 tons dropped; 15 hits destroyed 2 grounded Bettys and several AA guns	2	0
	24 VF	Kara	Runway strafed, 16 grounded planes destroyed	16 (on ground)	0
23	24 SBD's, 18 TBF's, and 60 VF	Kara	28 tons on runway and AA positions	0	(1 op)
	11 B-24's, 16 P-38's	Kahili	44 tons on runway	0	0
	6 B-24's, 16 VF	Kahili	24 tons on runway, many craters noted	0	0

Oct.	Planes	Target	Comments	Losses Enemy	Allied
	24 SBD's, 18 TBF's, and 36 VF		36 tons on gun positions, ammo dumps, runway and dispersal	0	1
24	9 B-24's, 13 VF	Kara	26 tons on runway and revetments	0	0
	47 SBD's, 22 TBF's, and 28 VF	Kahili	Many hits on runway, gun positions, operations tower	0	0
	19 B-24's, 14 VF	Kahili	26 tons on runway, dispersal and repair areas	0	0
	30 B-25's, 39 VF	Kahili	44 tons on runway, revetments and repair area. Fires started	0	0
25	31 SBD's, 30 VF, and 18 TBF's	Ballale	33 tons, 11 hits on runway, others on AA position	1 (on ground)	0
26	30 SBD's, 42 VF, and 18 TBF's	Kara	33 tons; many hits on runway, AA positions, buildings	0	0
	7 PB4Y's, 15 P-38's	Kahili	17 tons; many hits on runway	0	0
	36 TBF's, 49 SBD's, 22 B-25's, and 69 VF	Kahili	88 tons; runway and AA positions severely pounded	0	1
	20 B-24's, 16 VF	Kahili	Many hits on center of strip	0	0
	8 B-24's	Buka	Grounded planes and many personnel destroyed	6 (on ground)	0

Oct.	Planes	Target	Comments	Losses Enemy	Losses Allied
	6 B-25's, 15 P-38's	Buka	216 parafrag bombs dropped. Grounded planes and control tower hit	5 (on ground)	0
	5 PV's	Mono Island	7½ tons; started large fire and demolished huts at Falami	0	0
27	17 B-24's	Kara and Kahili	16½ tons; many hits on runways	0	0
	32 VF	Treasury Islands	Fighter cover for landing on Treasury Islands	12	0
28	39 SBD's, 46 VF, and 19 TBF's	Kara	33½ tons on runway	0	0
	19 B-24's	Kara	54 tons of which 70% hit runway and revetments	0	0
	38 SBD's, 32 VF, and 21 TBF's	Ballale	39 tons on runway and revetments	0	0
29	40 B-25's, 22 F4F's	Buka	Runway and revetments bombed and strafed	0	0
	9 B-25's	Buka	648 parafrags on Buka strip. Grounded planes hit	0	0
	21 B-24's	Buka	28 tons on runway and revetments	0	0
	11 B-24's, 24 VF	Buka	16½ tons on runway and dispersals	0	0
	12 PV's, 1 B-25	Bonis	3 tons and 48 parafrag bombs, 90% on runway and revetments	0	0

Oct.	Planes	Target	Comments	Losses Enemy	Losses Allied
30	12 TBF's, 26 VF	Choiseul	2 tons in support of ground troops	0	0
	16 B-24's	Kara	47½ tons; unobserved results	0	0
	68 SBD's, 27 TBF's, and 50 VF	Kara	61 tons dropped	0	0
	6 B-25's, 32 VF	Kieta	2½ tons on runway, installations strafed	0	3
	4 PV's, 12 P-39's	Kieta	Frag clusters dropped, runway strafed	0	0
31	14 VF, 12 P-39's	Tonolei Harbor	Strafed shipping	0	0
	19 B-24's	Kara	75 tons; 80% on runway	0	0
	34 SBD's, 54 VF, and 24 TBF's	Kara	39 tons; many hits on runways and AA guns	0	0
	23 B-25's, 16 VF	Kara	34 tons dropped	0	0

It seemed to the Allied pilots that these fields were taking a lot of knocking out. Each day they appeared operational again, despite yesterday's pasting. But Japanese postwar reports tell the story:

> . . . after the 17th the air strikes against Buin, Ballale, and Rabaul were intensified, with the Buin and Ballale airfields, in particular, being put out of operation by repeated raids over a period of several days. It appeared that the enemy was planning a new operation in the area. After the 18th it became impossible to use the Ballale airfield for hours at a time, and the same situation prevailed at Buin after the 21st; for all practical purposes, the airfields on Bougainville were useless as operational bases.[9]

Meantime, Southwest Pacific B-24's and B-25's, escorted by P-38's, were working over Rabaul. General George C. Kenney, MacArthur's air chief, had promised Rabaul would be "dead" about 20 October, but despite several big raids the Japanese still had some 200 planes operational on that date. Kenney sent over an average of more than 100 planes in each of three raids on 23, 24 and 25 October, and claimed 175 of Rabaul's planes destroyed, but Japanese records credit him only with shooting down 9, destroying 25 on the ground, and damaging 27. On 29 October General Kenney claimed 45 planes shot down and destroyed, but actually got only 10 if the Japanese records are accurate. Weather prevented Southwest Pacific attacks on Rabaul 30 October and 1 November, but on 2 November General Kenney sent over 75 B-25's covered by 80 P-38's. He lost 9 bombers and 10 fighters and claimed 85 planes definitely destroyed and 23 probables, plus the destruction or damaging of 114,000 tons of shipping. Actually, the Japanese say, he destroyed 20 planes and sank 3 small ships totaling 5,100 tons. However, in the words of Samuel Eliot Morison, the Japanese "out-Kenneyed Kenney" by claiming as "sure kills" 22 B-25's and 79 P-38's.[10]

The Landings

Prior to Cape Torokina two preliminary landings on L minus 5 succeeded in deceiving the Japanese. One of these was on Mono and Stirling in the Treasury Islands, halfway between Vella Lavella and Torokina, where the North Africa-seasoned 8th New Zealand Brigade Group under Brigadier R. A.

---

[9] *Southeast Area Naval Operations,* Part Three.

[10] The foregoing information is from Morison, *Breaking the Bismarcks Barrier,* pp 287–288, whose principal source was *Southeast Area Naval Operations* augmented by translations of Japanese documents. *General Kenney Reports,* published in 1949, repeats the wartime claims of destruction by Southwest Pacific planes and in some cases slightly amplifies them. USSBS No. 70A, *Air Campaigns of the Pacific War* (hereinafter referred to as *Air Campaigns*), pp 7, 9, 17, 27, which the Army aviators hastily printed in 1947, says of the 2 November raid: "So complete was the destruction of the enemy air force that the attacking flights ran out of air targets and attacked and burned the shore installations as an alternate."

Row landed on 27 October against minor Japanese opposition. Seventeen enemy planes got through the fighter patrol of 40 Army planes and seriously damaged the fighter-director destroyer *Cony* but lost a dozen of their aircraft.[11]

The other landing was purely diversionary: the 2d Parachute Battalion under Lieut. Colonel Victor H. Krulak went ashore at midnight, 27 October, on the west coast of Choiseul Island, where the marines made a big noise, raided several Japanese installations over a 25-mile area and killed 143 of the enemy before withdrawing nine days later. "Brute" Krulak's Choiseul diversion was aptly described by Major General Geiger, who took over command of I Marine Amphibious Corps (IMAC) from General Vandegrift on 9 November as "a series of short right jabs designed to throw the enemy off balance and conceal the real power of the left hook to his midriff at Empress Augusta Bay." AirSols planes rendered effective support during an attack by Krulak's men on 30 October, and during their re-embarkation 2 November.

For the landing on Bougainville Admiral Halsey provided not only the preliminary at the Treasury Islands (where the 87th Seabees started building a strip on Stirling Island immediately) and the Choiseul diversion, but also a carrier task force: big, old *Saratoga* and light carrier *Princeton* under Rear Admiral Frederick Sherman struck at the northernmost Bougainville airfields at Buka and Bonis on L-day, a few hours after Rear Admiral Aaron S. (Tip) Merrill's cruisers and destroyers had shelled the same targets. Meanwhile, Merrill's 12 ships raced the length of the island and threw another shelling into the Shortlands and Ballale 55 minutes before the marines started ashore at the Torokina midriff.

Five minutes before the marines of Major General Allen H. Turnage's 3d MarDiv and Lieut. Colonel Alan Shapley's 2d Raider Regiment began landing at Torokina, 31 TBF's and 8 SBD's bombed and strafed the beaches.[12] ComSoPac called the attacks "excellently timed and executed" in reducing resistance, but IMAC, while agreeing, found them "not considered to be in sufficient strength." The 270 Japanese in the area put up enough resistance to kill 78 marines, wound 104 more in the first three days. Most of the enemy were killed; the rest fled inland. The landing beaches were narrow and surf was heavy; 64 LCVP's and 22 LCM's broached and were stranded during landing operations. But the audacious attack at Cape Torokina caught the Rabaul admirals napping; the landing was in the best hit-'em-where-they-ain't tradition.

To ward off enemy raiders which were certain to come flying over from Rabaul's four airfields, ComAirSols had ordered a 32-plane constant patrol over the beaches. Sure enough, at 0718, just before the first landing craft began to hit the beach, the warning of approaching planes was given.

---

[11] *Southeast Area Naval Operations*, Part Three, p 10, says 39 fighters and 10 bombers made the attack, but lists no losses and claims they sank "two transports and two cruisers."

[12] From VMTB-143, VMTB-232, VMTB-233, VMSB-144 and VC-38 (a Navy composite squadron). They were covered by VMF-215, VMF-221, and Navy Fighter Squadron 17.

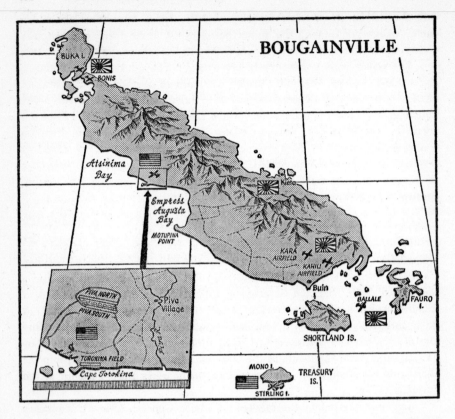

Ready to meet the first 30 Zekes were low-flying P-40's of the New Zealanders' No. 18 Squadron. They knocked down seven without a loss. Ten minutes later eight P-38's from AAF's 18th Fighter Group met Japanese fighters and bombers, shooting down eight of them.[13] Captain James E. Swett of VMF-221, who had lost contact with the other two F4U's of his flight, joined the P-38's and shot down two Vals. Then he went down to help a P-40 pilot who had several Tonys on his tail. He smoked one, whose fate he never ascertained, then headed home when tracer bullets began to zip past him.[14]

While patrolling over the task force at 1240 a flight of F4U's from VMF-215 encountered between 20 and 30 Zekes, Haps and Kates, and engaged eight of them. They shot down five, of which Lieut. Robert M. Hanson got three before he was shot down, probably by the rear gunner of a Kate. Hanson landed in the water safely, got into his rubber boat and stayed there the rest of the day. Late in the afternoon he spotted part of the Torokina screening force and began paddling frantically toward the destroyer Sigourney,

---

[13] Craven and Cate, *The AAF in WW II*, Vol IV, p 256, says these bombers were Bettys; Morison, *Breaking the Bismarcks Barrier*, p 303, and other Navy sources call them Val dive bombers.

[14] VMF-221 war diary, November 1943.

singing as he went, "You'd Be So Nice to Come Home To." He got home all right. The destroyer, on its way to Guadalcanal to pick up the second echelon, spotted him and took him south and Hanson was back at his Vella Lavella base only a few days after being reported missing.[15]

During the day the Japanese made four major attacks but managed to score only a near-miss on the destroyer *Wadsworth* which killed 2 sailors and wounded 5. In the air the Japanese admitted losing 22 planes, only 4 less than the Allies claimed (22 by fighters, 4 by AA). AirSols lost four planes, including that of Lieut. Robert L. Keister of VMF-215, who failed to return from one of the missions to Empress Augusta Bay.

Rabaul's Eagles

Obviously the Japanese were in great strength at Rabaul. A total of 120 planes—104 Zekes and 16 carrier bombers, we know now—had attacked the Bougainville beachhead on L-day, but their lack of success didn't mean that they wouldn't come back in coveys.

Rabaul was swarming with planes because Imperial Headquarters had issued a directive on 30 September, as follows:

> Make every effort to hold the important southeastern area extending eastward from the eastern part of New Guinea to the Solomon Islands by repulsing all enemy attacks in the area. To accomplish this purpose: (a) Consider Rabaul as the center and make every effort for a protracted defense of important positions in the Bismarck Archipelago and Bougainville Areas. (b) Endeavor to hold out in the northern New Guinea area by reinforcing important positions in this area. (c) Endeavor to destroy the attacking enemy before landings are made by using air and surface forces. (d) In case the enemy succeeds in landing operations endeavor to destroy him before he consolidates his position, thereby disrupting his plan for counterattack. (e) Endeavor to concentrate military supplies for high speed transport to the above-mentioned important positions, particularly to those in New Guinea.[16]

Admiral Koga, on board *Musashi* at Truk, suspected that something was about to happen in the northern Solomons—probably a move into the Shortlands or Kahili.[17] In April Yamamoto had set out to smash the Allies with his "I" Operation.[18] Now Koga ordered Operation "Ro," which meant taking his planes off carriers to land-base at Rabaul in order to smash the Allied offensive. He wavered during October, and actually took the entire Combined Fleet from

---

[15] VMF-215 war diary, November 1943; Hanson's personnel record, including his Medal of Honor citation which credits him with only one plane—probably erroneously, since the Japanese admitted losing almost as many planes on this day as we claimed.

[16] USSBS, *Campaigns,* p 186.

[17] Morison, *Breaking the Bismarcks Barrier,* p 284.

[18] See Chapter Nine.

Truk up to Eniwetok—he suspected an invasion of Wake Island was in the wind, and here now might be the opportunity for the big fleet engagement he was seeking. But no U.S. ships appeared after the big 5–6 October carrier strike, and Koga took his ships back to Truk.[19]

On 28 October Koga ordered the planes of the Third Air Fleet off the carriers onto Rabaul's airfields, just as Yamamoto had done in April. These 173 aircraft—82 Zekes, 45 Vals, 40 Kates and 6 reconnaissance planes—joined about 200 others of the Eleventh Air Fleet which were operational at the time.[20]

By 1 November all of the carrier planes had reached Rabaul, but they apparently were not used until the following day.[21] The 120 planes involved in the L-day attacks, including the 22 lost, were Eleventh Air Fleet aircraft.

At 1700 Vice Admiral Sentaro Omori with 4 cruisers and 6 destroyers was sent out from Rabaul with orders to destroy the invading transport force. When his ships had been discovered by U.S. search planes, Omori sent back some fast transports he brought along with a small counterlanding force, and steamed ahead toward Torokina to knock off the ships at the beachhead.

Rear Admiral "Tip" Merrill's hard-working task force of 4 light cruisers and 8 destroyers met Omori's 4 cruisers (2 of them heavies) and 6 destroyers at about 0230 on the morning of 2 November. The two forces chased and sniped at each other for three hours in what CinCPac described as an action "far more complicated than that of any surface engagement of the past year."[22] Japanese attempts at illuminating the U.S. force were spoiled by successful smoke-making; superior American radar therefore proved decisive. When the battle's last shell and torpedo had been fired the Japanese light cruiser *Sendai* and destroyer *Hatsukaze* were sunk, two heavy cruisers and a destroyer damaged. Merrill had the cruiser *Denver* and two destroyers damaged. Omori feared to stay in the area until daylight brought air attacks upon him. He broke off the action and retired to Rabaul where he was relieved of his command.[23]

After daylight, 89 Zekes and 18 dive bombers of the Third Air Fleet found Merrill's force, and sailed into it with great gusto. But they scored only two ineffective hits, and lost 25 planes—17 to ships' AA, 8 to AirSols fighters (none of them Marine)—according to our claims.[24]

---

[19] See Chapter Fifteen.

[20] USSBS, *Rabaul*, pp 11 and 24, puts the number at about 600, and Craven and Cate, *The AAF in WW II*, Vol IV, pp 259 and 738, accepts a similar figure, but *Southeast Area Naval Operations*, Part Three, says Eleventh Air Fleet, "as a result of heavy losses in successive air operations," had only 200 planes operating. According to USSBS, *Rabaul*, pp 50–51, losses between 1 June and 1 November were 341 planes—95 near Rabaul itself, 246 in the Solomons.

[21] *Southeast Area Naval Operations*, Part Three.

[22] *Combat Narratives, XII*, p 54.

[23] USSBS, *Campaigns*, p 152.

[24] Japanese records do not mention losses, but claim sinking a DD and damaging a cruiser and two transports.

Six hours later General Kenney's big 2 November raid was engaging the attention of the Japanese planes. Although it fell far short of what Kenney claimed for it, and came too late to interfere with the attempt to annihilate Merrill's force, this raid provided a helpful diversion during a critical period off the Torokina beachhead.

There is some evidence that Admiral Koga didn't mean to commit his carrier pilots so heavily at Bougainville. But the commander in the Rabaul area pleaded so hard for aviation that Koga finally decided to send a small number of carrier-based planes to be used for a short time at Rabaul. He might as well have tried to control a land mine after he stepped on it. "The actual strength that was sent to Rabaul was most of the planes of Ozawa's Air Fleet," said Vice Admiral Fukudome after the war, ". . . ; and in spite of the fact that they didn't intend to use these planes for such operations, they just couldn't stand by and not employ them."[25] Vice Admiral Jisaburo Ozawa himself went down to Rabaul to help commit his last carrier division. After helping the Southeast Area fleet commander, Vice Admiral Kusaka, lose them wholesale he returned to Truk 20 November.

Carriers Against Rabaul

With the Bougainville landing forces ComAirSols had sent a subordinate tactical command, ComAirNorSols,[26] in the person of Brig. General Field Harris USMC, who had been his chief of staff until 25 July. General Harris was set up and operating with his headquarters detachment, controlling all planes in the air over the Bougainville area, by L plus 1. The patrol under his control drove off an attack by 20-25 Zekes and 6 other Japanese planes on 3 November, but two pilots of VMF-211 and a crew of VMTB-143 were lost during the day. For the next few days Japanese interference at the beachhead consisted chiefly of occasional night raiders, because Sherman's carriers returned and struck a blow of historic proportions at Rabaul.

This was what happened: On 4 November a powerful force under the Second Fleet's Vice Admiral Takeo Kurita, 7 heavy cruisers, 1 light cruiser and 4 destroyers, was en route from Truk to join 2 heavy cruisers, 2 light cruisers and at least 4 destroyers already at Rabaul. The purpose obviously was to wreck the landing and to sink the ships at Cape Torokina. Merrill's force, far to the south, was not only exhausted and damaged, but inferior in strength. What he called "the most desperate emergency in my entire term as ComSoPac" confronted Admiral Halsey.

---

[25] USSBS, *Interrogations*, Vol II, pp 514–515. In Interrogation No. 524 (Military Analysis Division) Fukudome states: "Admiral Koga planned to lose no more than about one-fifth of the carrier planes thus committed."

[26] Not to be confused with AirNorSols which took over from AirSols in June 1944. The original AirNorSols was dissolved in January 1944, when AirSols moved forward, just as its counterpart for the New Georgia campaign, AirNewGeorgia, had been dissolved 20 October 1943.

The only solution was to stop the Japanese armada in daylight, and that meant a carrier attack on Rabaul itself—something that wasn't in the books at that stage of the war. From the decks of *Saratoga* and *Princeton* Admiral Sherman was able to put 97 planes over Rabaul because AirSols furnished a Barakoma-based combat air patrol of Navy fighters over the carriers—the first time such a co-ordinated effort had been made in SoPac area.

Sherman's carrier pilots bored through foul weather and intense AA in one of the most heroic carrier episodes of the war. They sank no ships but damaged 4 heavy cruisers, 2 light cruisers and 2 destroyers, and claimed 25 enemy planes[27] while losing 10 of their own. The heavy cruisers limped to Japan or Truk for repairs, to return to Rabaul no more.

The Bougainville beachhead was at least temporarily safe, not only in the clear daylight when land-based planes could protect it, but also safe from men-o'-war prowling in foul weather and at night.

The Japanese threat had the effect of scaring CinCPac into sending part of the Central Pacific carrier fleet to SoPac. Most of the capital ships of the U.S. Navy, including 11 fast carriers and 12 battleships, were en route to Tarawa and Makin for the invasions on 20 November, but three of the carriers (CV's *Essex, Bunker Hill,* CVL *Independence*) under Rear Admiral Alfred E. Montgomery were sidetracked to lend a hand to Halsey.

This was another attack on Rabaul's warships by the five carrier air groups on 11 November, Sherman's two operating from the east, Montgomery's three from the south. Weather and a scarcity of shipping in Simpson Harbor cut the carrier planes' pickings to one destroyer sunk, a light cruiser and another destroyer seriously damaged. Japanese planes which followed Montgomery's planes back to their carriers provided a field day for Navy pilots based at Ondonga and Segi, who, with the AA gunners and carrier pilots, claimed 74.[28]

Marine planes of VMF-221 and VMF-212, based at Vella Lavella, were part of the covering force, but they had been relieved on station when the Japanese aircraft were encountered.

After the strike Montgomery's ships raced to the Gilberts. The dependence of the Central and South Pacific, one upon the other, during November was not completely understood until postwar interrogations revealed that SoPac's Bougainville invasion had tied Ozawa's planes to Rabaul and most available units of the Combined Fleet to their Truk anchorage. The U.S. Navy was concentrating on the Gilberts, but the Japanese admirals regarded Bougainville as the more important, if not the only, impending action.[29]

Admiral Koga had one bit of supreme strategy: save up his full strength,

---

[27] The Japanese admitted losing only four planes (*Southeast Area Naval Operations,* Part Three, and *Japanese Naval War Diary,* ATIS 16568).

[28] *Admiral Halsey's Story,* pp 183–184. Actually, 41 were lost—6 in one attack, 35 in another—according to Japanese count in *Southeast Area Naval Operations,* Part Three. Japs claimed 77 of ours (*Japanese Naval War Diary,* ATIS 16568), but got only 14.

[29] USSBS, *Interrogations,* Vol II, p 514.

including carriers, for a single decisive engagement with the U.S. Navy but "the fact that the fleet's air strength had been so badly depleted enabled us to send only very small air support to Tarawa and Makin."[30] This had the effect of causing the Japanese strategists to give up the Marshalls–Gilberts defense line and make the Marianas–Carolines the "last line" of defense. Only behind that line now lay Koga's chance for the decisive engagement, and his forces with which that engagement could be fought were rapidly running out of airplanes.

Final Raids on the Beachhead

Early in the morning of the 7th, four Japanese destroyers from Rabaul arrived offshore in Empress Augusta Bay. A force of about 475 troops made a surprise landing just west of the U.S. perimeter and launched an attack on 3d MarDiv positions, but by the next day 377 Japanese bodies were counted on the field.[31] General Imamura had planned to land three echelons totaling about 3,000 men, but the Japanese had lost command of the air and sea, and only these ill-fated few got through.

The second part of the second echelon of the Allied landing force was unloading troops and supplies from six transports and AKA's at noon on 8 November when more than a hundred Zekes and bombers flashed over the busy waters of Empress Augusta Bay. A few enemy planes pierced the 28-plane screen; two bombs hit the transport *Fuller* and killed 5 and wounded 20. By 1837 the transports were unloaded and hightailing it away from Bougainville. Four P-40's, two F6F's, a P-38, and a Marine Corsair and pilot, Lieut. Edward T. Brown of VMF-212, were lost. Twenty-six Japanese planes were claimed, including 5 by VMF-212, but postwar records admit the loss of only 5 fighters and 10 carrier bombers in this raid.

At dusk the same day 21 torpedo bombers found Admiral DuBose's covering force 25 miles off Motupina Point and, in what the Japanese called "The Second Air Battle Off Bougainville," made three attacks on the force in two hours. Although the Third and Eleventh Air Fleets between them claimed the fantastic score of 4 battleships and 2 cruisers sunk and 6 cruisers and destroyers "set afire," actually only *Birmingham* took any punishment at all— three hits which failed even to slow her up in the formation. Ten of the bombers were lost to ships' AA fire.

November 8 marked the last big raid on the Bougainville beachhead. Thereafter, the Japanese came in smaller daytime raids or at night—and even the darkness, with night fighters threatening, was not as safe as it had been. Between 28 October and 25 November VMF(N)-531 flew 300 hours of night patrol covering task units, Treasury Island, or Empress Augusta Bay, and it

---

[30] *Ibid.*, p 516.

[31] Major John N. Rentz USMCR, *Bougainville and the Northern Solomons* (USMC Historical Division monograph), p 46. The Marines had 17 killed in this action.

was at 0420 on 13 November that Captain Duane Jenkins made the second successful interception by an AirSols night fighter.[32] The necessity of night fighters was stressed 35 minutes later, when the cruiser *Denver* was seriously damaged by another Betty.

Following the loss of 25 planes on the 8th and 41 more in the carrier chase of the 11th, Admiral Koga decided to pull out what he had left of his Third Air Fleet—"further combat would rob it of even a skeleton force around which to rebuild."[33] In less than two weeks of operating from land bases at Rabaul the carrier outfits had lost 121 of their 173 planes. Furthermore, 75 per cent of the dive-bomber crews and 40 per cent of the torpedo-bomber crews were dead.

Consequently, the remnants were withdrawn to Truk on 13 November and replaced on the 15th by 26 carrier bombers diverted from the Marshalls— just six days before they might have proved handy in the Gilberts operation.[34]

At 0350 of 17 November the fifth echelon of the invasion force, carrying marines in 8 LST's and 8 APD's, was attacked 22 miles from Torokina by a flight of torpedo bombers from Rabaul. Five of the bombers were shot down by antiaircraft fire, but the destroyer-transport *McKean* caught a fish in her after-magazine and depth-charge storage and sank with a loss of 64 sailors and 52 marines. It was the only ship lost in the Bougainville operation—and the fourth of the converted four-stackers sunk in Solomons waters (the others: *Little, Gregory, Colhoun*).[35]

But the Japanese called this night action "The Fifth Air Battle Off Bougainville," and glorified it as a large carrier "blown up and sunk," and the following simply "sunk": 2 medium carriers, 3 cruisers and 1 unidentified ship.

Later in the morning of the 17th, 55 Zekes and 10 carrier bombers were dispatched from Rabaul to attack "8 transports and 10 destroyers" in Empress Augusta Bay. A big patrol of Army, Navy and Marine Corps planes was waiting for them, and claimed to shoot down 16 of them, including 3 by Major Post and 3 by Lieut. Harold E. Segal of VMF-221.[36]

Again Rabaul claimed a great victory: 3 transports sunk, 1 transport run aground, 1 destroyer set afire. Nothing of the sort happened, but the Japanese did get the record straight on the number of planes they shot down: two fighters of VF-17.

By this time Operation "Ro" was a washout despite an Imperial Rescript praising it. It ended on the 17th, "for all practical purposes," although termination orders were never issued.[37] Admiral Kusaka was told he would have to get along with what he had, and a 37-plane medium-bomber unit which had

---

[32] See Chapter Eleven.

[33] *Southeast Area Naval Operations*, Part Three.

[34] *Ibid.*

[35] Morison, *Breaking the Bismarcks Barrier*, p 351.

[36] *Southeast Area Naval Operations*, Part Three, says 4 of the bombers and 6 fighters were lost.

[37] *Southeast Area Naval Operations*, Part Three.

been scheduled for Rabaul was withheld from him. In the 16 days since the Bougainville landing, the air-base force at Rabaul had lost 70 planes in addition to the 121 expended by the carrier forces. More planes would be sent in for the defense of Rabaul, but the contest around Bougainville simmered down to small-scale attacks, mostly at night.

The fantastic Japanese Intelligence interpreted Bougainville as a great victory, and the word was relayed on 10 December to Adolf Hitler:

> After some initial success this American thrust, executed with great tenacity and with reckless use of material, was temporarily checked on Bougainville. In four small-scale naval engagements and six great air operations, 5 battleships, 10 carriers, 19 cruisers, 7 destroyers and 9 transports were sunk there since 27 October.[38]

On 19 November Major Donald H. Sapp of VMF-222 popped a prowling bomber. Five men on the beachhead were killed in a small raid on the night of 18-19 November and six others on 20 November. Seven strafing Japanese fighters were lost to Navy and Marine pilots on 21 November. During the whole of November Bougainville invasion forces underwent 90 alerts and 22 bombings and strafings, which caused a total of 24 killed, 98 wounded.[39]

Close Support Improves

From the standpoint of Marine aviation, perhaps the most satisfactory aspect of the Bougainville campaign was the progress made in close air support. Bougainville, in fact, marked the beginning of such tactics in the "modern" sense of the term.

Preparations for close air support were begun more than three months before L-day when 3 officers (bomber pilots) and 6 enlisted men (radiomen) of the 1st MAW reported to the 3d MarDiv for air-liaison duty. The Division Air Officer, Lieut. Colonel John T. L. D. Gabbert, organized an air-liaison party school to teach the capabilities and limitations of close air support, procedure for requesting such support, and details of air-ground communication methods. An officer from the -3 section of each battalion and regiment was ordered to attend the school.

A thorough study was made of the employment of air power at Guadalcanal and New Georgia, and it was decided that the capabilities of air as a close-support weapon "had not been utilized to the fullest possible extent." Ground troops had often been bombed by the planes they had requested, and their faith in air power had been shaken. White

---

[38] *Führer Conferences on Matters Dealing with the German Navy,* 1943, pp 152–154.

[39] ComSoPac war diary, 2 December 1943.

smoke had been used to mark targets and the enemy had confused the airmen by placing smoke flares themselves. This had given rise to the practice of withdrawing friendly troops to create a margin of safety for the bombers. But when this was done, the enemy tended to advance and occupy the ground which our forces had vacated.[40]

To remedy the confusion caused by white smoke, colored-smoke hand grenades were employed at Bougainville. Constant practice with communications equipment brought its operators to a high state of proficiency. Extensive tests proved the reliability of the following safety margin at which bombs could be employed from the ground forces' own front lines:

Bomb (Pounds)	Normal Use[41] (Yards)	Closest Possible Use[41] (Yards)
100	100	75
500	500	300
1,000	1,000	500
2,000	1,000	700

One of the specific missions of Harris's AirNorSols, when it was activated 1 September at Espíritu Santo, was to co-ordinate requests for close air support with the commands which could deliver such support. Three air-liaison parties were attached to the 3d MarDiv for operations on Bougainville, two others to the New Zealanders' 8th Brigade Group on Treasury.[42]

No call for direct support by bombers was received until 9 November, when 3d MarDiv requested 18 TBF's to be on station over Piva Village at 0915 on 10 November, for an attack on the village preliminary to an assault scheduled for 1015. After the target area had been marked by colored smoke, AirSols sent 12 TBF's from VMTB-143 and VMTB-233, each loaded with twelve 100-pound bombs. These were dropped within 120 yards of friendly troops, who attacked in the wake of the bombs. The enemy scrambled out of the area, leaving behind considerable equipment and 30 to 40 dead.

A second call by 3d MarDiv on 13 November resulted in a strike the following day by 18 TBF's from VC-38 and VC-40, using 100-pound bombs only 100 yards in front of the troops. The Navy pilots were credited with 95 per cent hits in the target area, which caused it to be "hastily abandoned."

"Hellzapoppin' Ridge," where 300 enemy dug in and put up the final and fiercest resistance on the beachhead, was the target 13 December for 3 SBD's and 3 TBF's which happened to be at the recently completed Torokina airfield. One plane missed the target and dropped on friendly troops 600 yards away,

---

[40] Goodman, *The Role of Aviation in the Bougainville Operation,* p 8.

[41] *Normal:* in flat terrain when friendly troops are flat on the ground. *Closest possible:* when friendly troops are in holes or behind shelter.

[42] There was never enough opposition on Treasury to warrant the use of close air support.

killing 2 men and wounding 6 in the only such accident in the Bougainville campaign.[43]

Such accidents had been partially responsible for the Army aviators' denial of the efficiency of air support.[44] But the marines kept trying to smash the ridge called Hellzapoppin'. On 14 December after the friendly lines had been marked with violet smoke and the target with white smoke, 16 Marine TBF's, led by Major Rolland F. Smith at 700 feet, dropped 90 per cent of the 192 bombs within the target area (which was 50 by 150 yards). Neither this attack nor another by 18 TBF's on the following day dislodged the Japanese. Obviously the bombs, fuzed to go off one tenth of a second after impact, were not reaching the well-dug-in enemy. A strike was requested for 18 December with four fifths of a second delay fuzes.

Eleven TBF's of VMTB-134 struck at 1200 from treetop level, 75 yards in front of the men of the 1st Battalion, 21st Marines. All bombs hit in the target area, but the enemy had moved to the other side of the ridge. Five of the planes landed at Torokina for another try. After dropping their bombs they made dummy runs to cover the advance of the ground troops, who thereupon bayoneted and grenaded their way through the final resistance and took Hellzapoppin'.

This attack with delayed-fuze bombs was praised by the 3d MarDiv in a manner which probably deserves designation as historical: for perhaps the first time in World War II the aviators were credited with a support mission beyond the scope of artillery:

> It was the air attacks which proved to be the most effective factor in the taking of the ridge. Lt. Colonel Butler, Executive Officer of the Twenty-first Marines, was ordered to plot and direct the strikes. He flew with the flight leader[45] to spot the enemy positions, with which he was now thoroughly familiar.
>
> The two final strikes proved to be the most successful examples of close air support thus far in the Pacific war. The planes, flying at times only fifty feet above the ground, bombed and strafed the enemy as close as 75 yards from the Marines' positions. The Japanese, who held out so desperately against infantry and artillery attack, were almost completely destroyed. Following the second air strike the 1st Battalion, Twenty-

---

[43] Goodman, *The Role of Aviation in the Bougainville Campaign*, p 13.

[44] Army FM 100–20, *Command and Employment of Air Power*, published in July 1943 (but without the approval of Army Ground Forces) is a virtual diatribe against close air support. For an analysis of this unusual field manual see "Tactical Use of Air Power in World War II: the Army Experience," by James A. Huston, Professor of History at Purdue University (and a former infantry major) in *Military Affairs*, Headquarters Gazette (Continued), Winter 1950. FM 100–20, says Dr. Huston, "tended to confirm Ground Forces officers in their view that the Air Staff was indifferent to co-operation of air with ground troops."

[45] Actually with Lieut. Colonel William K. Pottinger, AirSols operations officer, who controlled the strikes from an SBD. (Strike Command TBF intelligence report.)

first Marines, smashed through the last resistance with bayonet and grenade. . . .[46]

There were other ground-support missions. On 25 December, TBF's of VMTB-232 and VC-40 participated in dislodging enemy troops when our own troops were 500 yards from the target. On 26 December, at 0945, VMTB-143 dropped 100-pound bombs to clear the Japanese still left in slit trenches and splinter-proof emplacements. Afternoon patrols on the 26th reported the area completely covered by bombs, few trees standing, 100 per cent hits and the area cleared of 800 Japanese.

Except for limited employment at Peleliu and Iwo, this was also the last time Marine aviation supported Marine ground troops until the final battle of the war, at Okinawa. The improvement in technique fashioned by AirSols marines paid big dividends, however, to General MacArthur's soldiers when the Marine aviators moved from Bougainville over to the Philippines.

---

[46] Robert A. Aurthur and Kenneth Cohlmia, *The Third Marine Division* (Robert T. Vance, ed.), p 78.

CHAPTER THIRTEEN

Rabaul Strangled

THE NORTHEASTERN TIP of New Britain contains one of the finest natural harbors in the South Pacific, almost landlocked, protected from low-level attack on the seaward side by five volcanic mountains rising up to 2,247 feet and on the opposite side by 760-foot-high Vulcan crater. From Rabaul the Japanese planned to dominate the Solomons on the south, New Guinea on the west and the coast of Australia beyond the Coral Sea to the southwest. Port Moresby is 433 miles southwest from Rabaul, Townsville 959. It is 210 miles to Empress Augusta Bay, 565 to Guadalcanal. The supply line from Japan to Rabaul ran through Truk, 695 miles to the north.

After Rabaul was taken from a handful of Australians on 23 January 1942, the Imperial Navy lost no time in developing this key base which was needed for the defense of the fleet anchorage at Truk, and for further offensives west and southeast. By June 1942, 21,570 men were on the base force station list at Rabaul; 19,500 others were in New Ireland, Bougainville, and at Lae, New Guinea. Between 153 and 173 planes were already at Rabaul, and some were expected to extend operations as far south as the new airfield on Guadalcanal (in mid-August). When the Americans landed in the southern Solomons Rabaul's importance increased. The Japanese were forced to concentrate on the southeast, however, rather than on New Guinea on the west, where the capture of Port Moresby had been the original cornerstone of future planning.

Guadalcanal refused to topple, though 50,000 additional Japanese troops were sent to Rabaul and the Solomons. After Guadalcanal was evacuated, the build-up of Rabaul and New Britain was continued.

In November 1943 troop strength in Rabaul and the rest of New Britain was 97,870 men, about three-fourths Army, one-fourth Navy. The number of planes at Rabaul as of 1 November was 373 (200 from the Eleventh Air Fleet, 173 from the 1st Air Squadron). These flew from Lakunai and Vunakanau airfields, which had been captured from the Australians, and from two others the Japanese themselves built, Rapopo and Tobera. A fifth was never finished.

Most of the few postwar histories which have treated the matter at all set the demise of Rabaul as an effective base at November 1943. USSBS Naval

Analysis Division's *The Campaigns of the Pacific War*[1] has only this to say about Rabaul's last days:

> By the end of November, a total of 4,481 sorties by United States aircraft from the South Pacific command with the loss of only 69 planes had reduced the Japanese air garrison to impotence and forced them to resort to sporadic night raids of limited effectiveness.

USSBS, *The Fifth Air Force in the War Against Japan*,[2] taking the General Kenney line, emphatically claims the victory for Southwest Pacific aircraft:

> Heavy raids in October and a final strike 2 November by B-25s and P-38s, completely surprised the enemy and resulted in such heavy destruction that it was obvious that Rabaul was no longer a satisfactory base for any kind of operations.

This conclusion wasn't obvious to the carrier pilots who made the raids of 5 and 11 November and the SoPac land-based pilots who continued finding Rabaul a tough nut for many weeks. *Japanese Naval War Diary* reports 270 operational planes (plus 83 damaged) in the Southeast Area on 10 November[3] —and there were more to come.

General Kenney attempted his last strike on Rabaul 11 November—it was "washed out by weather"—from now on AirSols would have the big base to itself.[4]

Boyington Sweeps Rabaul

The defense of Bougainville gave way to the AirSols offensive against Rabaul.

For this job Mitchell chose a twofold weapon: he continued the relentless bombing of Rabaul with his two- and four-engined Army bombers, but he also brought into play the fighter sweep, which means simply sending up fighter planes to pick off enemy planes. There is nothing devious about a fighter sweep: it is a head-on attack. It had worked well in eliminating Japanese aviation in the Solomons, particularly at the main Kahili base.

The fighters could start whittling at Rabaul's muscle as soon as the base was ready at Torokina. Ground crews of VMF-212 and VMF-215 arrived at Torokina on 9 December, the day before the 71st Seabees finished the airstrip;

---

[1] Page 155.

[2] Page 59.

[3] ATIS 16568.

[4] Southwest Pacific planes had been raiding Rabaul sporadically since 23 February 1942, when four B-17's made a high-altitude raid with unobserved results. The first skip-bombing by New Guinea-based planes was employed 23 October 1942. General Kenney's big effort against Rabaul began 12 October 1943.

on 10 December 17 F4U's of VMF-216 were the first to land, followed by 6 SBD's and 4 SCAT transports. To lead the Rabaul sweeps Mitchell chose Major Gregory Boyington, CO of VMF-214, a brash, swashbuckling pilot whose belligerent career had included a term with the Flying Tigers in China (where he was credited with shooting down six Japanese planes). Boyington was not only a natural pilot, but he was also a skillful leader of a squadron (the "Black Sheep") he put together at Espíritu Santo, largely from replacements and remnants of various units which had moved elsewhere.

Mitchell sent out the first sweep on 17 December (31 F4U's, 23 P-40's, 22 F6F's). Results were less than overwhelming, despite Boyington's radioed pleas (on 6050 kilocycles) to the Japanese to come on up and fight (to which an enemy voice replied: "Come on down, sucker!")[5] Not many defenders rose to meet the challenge. Most of what combat there was fell to the low-flying P-40's, piloted by the New Zealand 14th and 16th Squadrons, which shot down five enemy fighters (a Navy pilot and a marine were credited with two others). Three New Zealanders were lost, including Wing Commander Freeman, who was seen to go down over New Ireland.

Boyington argued that 76 planes were too many for efficient management —36 to 48 were plenty.[6] The next fighter sweep, on 23 December, employed 48 planes and came closer to fulfilling the mission of destroying the air power remaining at Rabaul. A heavy-bomber strike, accompanied by 48 fighters, had preceded Boyington's sweep, and some 40 Japanese fighters were still airborne. Thirty of them were claimed shot down, including an even dozen by Boyington's own squadron. Boyington's personal score rose from 20 to 24 (including the 6 credited to him in China). Three American planes were lost.

The VMF-214 pilots noted in the 23 December raid that Japanese fighters were dropping small aerial bombs with long tentacles, in their efforts to destroy American bombers. These tactics were repeated from time to time, and the Japanese thought they knocked down at least 29 bombers, but Allied flyers never regarded the aerial bombs as an effective weapon.[7] Another bomber-escort mission to Vunakanau and a fighter sweep on Christmas Eve claimed 26 additional Japanese planes.

On the morning of Christmas Day 1943 the enemy base at Kavieng, on the upper tip of New Ireland, was struck by Sherman's two-carrier task force, which sank a minesweeper and an AK. The lack of shipping targets was disappointing, but the threat to this No. 2 base of the Bismarcks caused 30 Zekes to be rushed to Kavieng.[8] At noon on the same day Rabaul Town was hit by 15 AirSols heavies and 63 escorting fighters which claimed 13 sure kills and had the effect of preventing a counterattack on Sherman's task force.

---

[5] ComAirSols Fighter Command war diary, December 1943.
[6] ONI, *The Combat Strategy and Tactics of Major Gregory Boyington, USMCR,* 15 February 1944.
[7] USSBS, *Rabaul,* pp 22, 58.
[8] *Southeast Area Naval Operations,* Part Three.

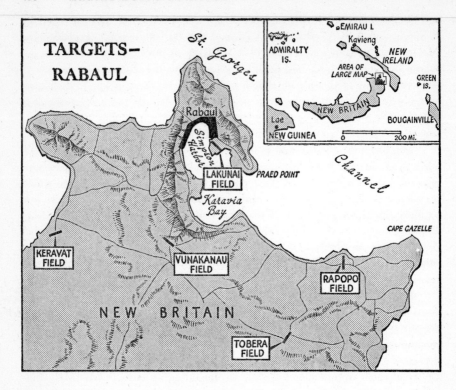

Grasshoppers at Cape Gloucester

On 26 December the 1st MarDiv, under MacArthur's command since Guadalcanal, landed at Cape Gloucester on the western end of New Britain, after the target had been hit by 3,926 tons of Fifth Air Force bombs in the preceding 38 days.[9]

Believing that the convoy sighted along eastern New Guinea was a reinforcement of Arawe on the south coast of New Britain, which had been invaded 15 December by MacArthur's forces, the Japanese had sent 63 fighters and 25 carrier bombers to the Arawe area where they made an attack. It wasn't until later in the day that enemy air interfered with the landing, sinking *Brownson* and damaging two other destroyers, but lost 17 planes.[10] Subsequent heavy raids on Rabaul obligated the enemy's air power so that counterattacks in the Cape Gloucester area were negligible.

Cape Gloucester put the first Marine artillery-spotting squadron into combat. This unorthodox outfit was the brain child of Major General William H. Rupertus, CG of the 1st MarDiv, who had acquired ten battered Piper Cubs from the Army. The next step was to find men to service them. Rupertus called on his aide, Captain Theodore A. Petras, who rounded up 22 officers

---

[9] USSBS, *The Fifth Air Force in the War Against Japan*, pp 64, 66–67.
[10] *General Kenney Reports*, ρ 335, claims 61 for his fighters, 5 for naval AA.

and men. An artillery captain, a tank officer, two Pfc's of the Special Weapons Battalion and one infantry Pfc. were among those with flight experience. Another Pfc. had been foreman in a Piper Cub plant. The hybrid unit flew 1,000 hours' spotting, reconnaissance, transport and general utility missions in the Cape Gloucester campaign, although none of the pilots had either flight orders or wings, nor received flight pay. Each won the Air Medal before the unit was disbanded six weeks before the Peleliu invasion. At that time VMO-3 took over the duties of its unconventional predecessor.

Some Marine air generals fought the chore of artillery spotting and one wrote sorrowfully, "MarCorps has licked us," but the OY's became indispensable, and it was only common sense for the Marine aviators to fly them.

Early January Raids

Between 17 December and New Year's Day a total of 147 planes had been claimed shot out of the air in sweeps over Rabaul.[11]

On 27 and 28 December the fighters claimed 52[12] of these, 33 of them by the four Marine squadrons then staging through Torokina.[13]

On the first day of 1944 a sweep accounted for 8 planes and an escort mission for 5 more. On 3 January at least 6 more were shot down, but a reconnaissance photograph showed 200 planes still on the Rabaul fields.

It was on 3 January that Major Boyington was shot down, together with his wingman, Captain George M. Ashmun. Pilots Chatham and Matheson reported that they had seen Boyington shoot down one plane before he went down. This brought his personal score to 26 planes, tieing Joe Foss's year-old record. Boyington parachuted into St. George's Channel when his flaming plane had only 200 or 300 feet of altitude left. Four Zekes strafed him for 15 or 20 minutes, but never hit him. Just before dark a Japanese submarine surfaced and took him prisoner. At Rabaul Boyington was allowed no medical treatment for ten days. After six weeks he was put on board a transport plane during the evacuation to Truk, where he landed in the midst of the great carrier strike of 17 February and crouched in a concrete slit trench as he watched an F6F blow up the transport plane. Eventually the Japanese carried their No. 1 aviator prisoner to Japan, where he was beaten regularly until rescued at the end of the war. On 12 April 1944 this "superb airman and determined fighter against overwhelming odds" was awarded the Medal of Honor—his first decoration (he later got the Navy Cross, too). After the war Boyington described how he had shot down two additional planes on his last flight, bringing his total score to 28.

The short-range bombers did not hit Rabaul until the airstrips at Piva

---

[11] The Japanese admitted losing 64 (USSBS, *Rabaul*, pp 50–51).

[12] ComAirSols intelligence summary claimed 43, then added: "late reports from Torokina F4U's for the 27th added 6 Zekes, 2 Hamps, 1 Tony for the day's scrap." (Day ending 0800 29 December 1943.)

[13] VMF's 214, 216, 223, 321.

were completed. They had waited a long time for such lively targets as hot airfields; bombing of jungle-hidden soldiers had been the lot of the light bombers for long weeks. By 5 January the north field, Piva Uncle, was usable as a staging point, and 150 SBD's and TBF's flew up from Munda for a big strike on Rabaul's shipping and AA emplacements. Towering cumulus clouds caused the strike to be canceled, and the 150 pilots to return to Munda. Two days later the TBF's and SBD's reached Rabaul, but the primary target, Tobera Field, was closed in, and faulty briefing at the last minute caused the bombers to pass up well-loaded Rapopo Field and the harbor. The first light-bomber mission to Rabaul was a bust.

On 9 January the weather finally permitted the dive bombers and torpedo bombers to strike a primary target, and Tobera airfield was knocked out, at least temporarily. It was estimated that 40 to 60 enemy fighters rose to meet the strike, of which 21 were claimed destroyed. Lakunai was next day's target, but again Rabaul's mid-day clouds foiled the bombers. And again the formidable lighthouse at Cape St. George on the southern end of New Ireland, was bombed as a secondary target (this lighthouse withstood all efforts to knock it out; pilots almost believed their own facile theory that every time the top of the lighthouse was knocked off the Japanese built a new section at the bottom of a shaft, then pushed it up).

On 12 January B-25's of the Thirteenth Air Force began operating from the new strip on Stirling Island (Treasury Group). Now heavy bombers (usually 4 squadrons at a time), medium bombers (3 squadrons in the forward area) and 7 squadrons of TBF's and SBD's began bombing Rabaul every day. About 200 AirSols fighters were available at all times. Primary targets were airfields, both before and after Japanese planes disappeared: by-passing an island obviates the necessity of landing on it, but also imposes the responsibility for keeping it knocked out. "The task of restricting to the minimum the possibility of the enemy using these fields always came first."[14] General Mitchell found his formula: the TBF's could be relied upon to put 75 per cent of their bombs on the strips; the SBD's meanwhile concentrated on AA installations surrounding the fields.

The Japanese Concede

Rabaul in January was still fat with shipping targets, from Blanche Bay to the innermost recesses of Simpson Harbor. The Marines' first shipping strike —on 14 January—by 36 dive bombers and 16 "turkeys" (torpedo bombers), claimed 9 hits on 7 ships. None was sunk; available postwar records do not include damage to merchant ships, but one of the ships hit was a DD, the *Matsukaze*, which only took some holes in her hull.[15] Twenty-nine planes were claimed in the ensuing dogfights, 19 of them by VMF-215.

---

[14] ComSoPac report on the reduction of Rabaul, 8 June 1944.
[15] USSBS, *Campaigns,* p 172.

One of the TBF crews which did not return from this mission was that of Lieut. Lester V. Swenson of VMTB-232 and his gunners, Staff Sergeant James A. Brooks and Corporal Frederick E. Betz. They were shot down by three fighters and landed in Simpson Harbor. The crew secured their equipment to the life raft and after weathering a storm, found themselves, 24 hours later, some 60 miles away from Rabaul.

Japanese planes continually flying overhead convinced them that they might be safer ashore on New Britain. There they rested and were fed by friendly natives until word was received that the Japanese were coming. They put out to sea again. The raft was sighted by Allied planes and the rescue plane also attracted the Japanese ashore, but the crew evaded the searching enemy, and again went ashore where natives cared for them and guided them to an Australian coastwatcher. He sent Swenson and Brooks to safety 74 days after going down. Betz, who suffered from an infected arm and from exhaustion, followed three weeks later.

Swenson was sent promptly to Washington where he was seen in a hotel lobby dressed in pants and polo shirt, having been unable to provide himself with proper uniform and insignia. He was declared a draft dodger and after relating his story to an FBI agent was told, "Tell that to the Marines!"[16]

On 17 January the strike consisted of 29 SBD's (13 Navy, 16 from VMSB-341) and 18 TBF's from VMTB-232, escorted by 70 fighters. Seventy-nine Japanese fighters intercepted, and 17 were shot down, 11 by marines (VMF-321, 3; VMF-212, 3; VMF-211, 4; and a single by a TBF tail gunner). Five Japanese ships were sunk.[17]

Of VMTB-232's 18 planes, 15 reported hits. For Marine pilots it was the most successful shipping strike since November 1942. For the AAF P-38 pilots, flying at 14,500 feet, the going was not so good—eight of their planes shot down, plus one each of TBF, SBD, F6F and F4U. Lieut. Harold J. Millar Jr. of VMTB-232 was flying the TBF that was lost—one of its wings struck a Japanese ship in the pull-out.

Seven days later Simpson Harbor again yielded notable returns. This time it was a strike by 18 TBF's against ships in Keravia Bay, at the south end of the harbor. The bombers (12 from VC-40, 6 from VMTB-143) were led by Navy Lieut. H. S. Jackson. Their loads: 2,000-pound bombs with four-fifths-second delay fuzes. Again 5 Japanese ships were sunk.[18] The 84 Army, Navy, Marine and New Zealand pilots claimed 23 planes (16 of them by marines).

Shortly thereafter Japanese Navy planes of the 2d Air Squadron—"the

---

[16] Morison, *Breaking the Bismarcks Barrier*, pp 404–405.

[17] *Hakkai Maru* 5,114 tons, *Kenshin Maru* 3,126, *Kosei Maru* 1,920, *Lyons Maru* 7,017, *Tenshin Maru* 1,500. JANAC credits the ships to "Navy land-based planes."

[18] *Koan Maru* 3,462 tons, *Ogashima Maru* 1,424 tons, *Naruto* (tanker) 6,500, *Taisho Maru* 4,815, *Yamayuri Maru* 5,028 tons. JANAC erroneously lists these ships as sunk by carrier-based aircraft (which were nowhere in the area). VMTB-143 claimed a 225-foot AK sunk, a 455-foot AO badly damaged.

very best of the carrier air force which constituted the backbone of our surface strength"—were flown down from Truk—62 fighters, 18 dive bombers, 18 torpedo planes—and once again Rabaul had about 300 planes.[19] This was the result of bad guessing: Koga thought the Central Pacific would remain quiet after the Gilberts. But the invasion of the Marshalls followed immediately.

After this strike concentrations of the larger Japanese ships stayed away from Rabaul. On 30 January a hastily assembled late-afternoon strike (18 TBF's again, from VMTB-233) sank the water tender *Iwate Maru* (2,984 tons). Against a loss of 2 Corsairs and 1 Avenger, the accompanying fighters shot down 21 of the newly arrived Japanese fighters. Lieut. Robert M. Hanson of VMF-215 shot down 4 planes to bring his total to 25 (all but five of them in a 17-day period). He was killed three days later when his Corsair failed to pull out of a strafing run on Cape St. George.[20] On 1 August he was posthumously awarded the Medal of Honor.

Most of the waterborne targets at Rabaul throughout the rest of its long siege were barges. At the end of February, 427 could be counted in photographs of Simpson Harbor, Keravia Bay and the Raluana Point area. Three months later only 86 could be found.[21] The more than 90,000 troops stranded on Rabaul and the rest of the Bismarcks didn't even receive any mail from Japan after February 1944.[22]

Meanwhile on 21 January the South Piva Field (Yoke) began operations. VMF-211 moved over from Torokina the same day. Three days later a Navy Corsair squadron (VF-17) arrived with 32 planes and 49 pilots. They were joined shortly by VMF-321 and a New Zealand P-40 squadron.

During January and February a total of 4,229 tons of bombs was dropped on Rabaul's installations. The airfields were becoming less and less tenable (although it was May before ComAirSols claimed that all five fields were rendered inoperable simultaneously). The last important air opposition was 19 February, when 50 fighter planes met a 145-plane formation of TBF's, SBD's, F4U's, P-40's and F6F's. Twenty-three of the Japanese planes were shot down, according to AirSols figures. Next day the remnants of the Rabaul planes were pulled back to Truk, where the carrier pilots of Pete Mitscher's Task Force 58 had just sunk over 200,000 tons of shipping and wrecked 325 planes which had been intended as reinforcements for Rabaul.[23]

---

[19] *Southeast Area Naval Operations*, Part Three. Morison, *Breaking the Bismarcks Barrier*, p 400, says 133 planes were flown in.

[20] Hanson had been scheduled to return Stateside a week after his last mission. The No. 2 and No. 3 men in high-scoring VMF-215, Captain Donald N. Aldrich with 20 planes and Captain Harold Spears with 15, were both killed in operational accidents following their return, Spears in 1944, Aldrich in 1947.

[21] ComSoPac report on the reduction of Rabaul, 8 June 1944.

[22] USSBS, *Rabaul*, p 80.

[23] See p 206.

The great air battles over Rabaul had ended—although there was no way of knowing it at the time, and there was the suspicion for a long time that the Japanese might come back in strength.

Just how many planes the Japanese lost in the period 17 December to 19 February probably will never be known accurately. They started with an estimated 292, were reinforced by 40 in late December by carriers, and by 98 more in late January.[24] These 430 were nearly all lost, excepting only those withdrawn to Truk.[25]

Japanese testimony on the number of planes evacuated from Rabaul (as on many other points) is conflicting. Admiral Kusaka listed 56 or 57; *Japanese Naval War Diary* (ATIS 16568) says 37 fighters, 4 bombers, 2 long-range bombers. Commander Hori said 70.[26] Captain Takashi Miyazaki, senior staff officer of 25th Air Flotilla at Rabaul until April 1944, says 120 planes were pulled back when Truk was attacked, leaving 10,[27] but this seems highly unlikely. It appears that the Japanese concede nearly 400 planes to AirSols between mid-December and mid-February.

AirSols claims were without doubt considerably higher than the number actually shot down. For the two-month period they total 730—147 in the last two weeks of December, 412 in January, 171 in the 19 days of February.[28] Of this two-month total, marines claimed 393, Navy 166, Army 131, New Zealand 40. Nothing is more difficult than an accurate count during an air battle in which several dozen planes are involved; it is very easy for two pilots to claim the same plane at which both are shooting. The smoking plane may get back to its base; it may not even have been actually smoking.

In World War II this overclaiming was universal. Official Air Force historians say that "the sampling has indicated that the Eighth Air Force claims were far more exaggerated than even their severest critics had assumed," and cite one instance where B-17's over Europe claimed 102 German fighters shot down, probably shot down or damaged—claims later reduced to 57—when the actual score was 1 or 2.[29] Even the conservative British, in what they thought was the "biggest" day in the Battle of Britain, shot down only 56 planes against 183 claimed, and during the 16-week battle got only 2 planes for every 3 claimed (1,733 against 2,698).[30]

---

[24] Morison, *Breaking the Bismarcks Barrier*, pp 395, 398, 400.

[25] In postwar interrogations at Rabaul Admiral Kusaka admitted losing only 41 in December, 120 in January, 58 in February. (USSBS, *Rabaul*, p 50.)

[26] USSBS, *Rabaul*, pp 47, 54.

[27] USSBS, *Interrogations*, Vol II, p 414.

[28] Compiled from ComAirSols intelligence summaries.

[29] Craven and Cate, *The AAF in WW II*, Vol II, pp xiii, 222. In Vol III, p 803, of the same work, published in 1951 (two years after Vol II), the authors state that subsequently discovered evidence indicates 11 planes actually shot down in this famous raid, and 11 more damaged. They also conclude (p xxix) that the AAF "shot down perhaps half as many German Air Force fighters as were claimed."

[30] Winston Churchill, *Their Finest Hour*, pp 337–340.

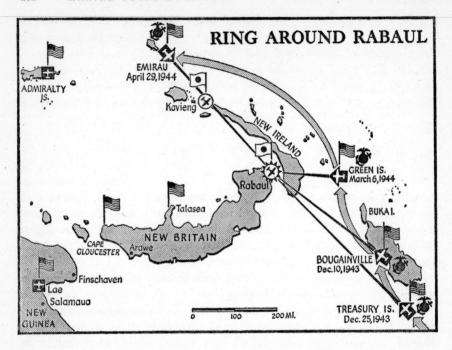

If, as seems likely, AirSols pilots shot down slightly more than one plane for every two they claimed over Rabaul, their record of high-altitude estimating is far more accurate than that of most pilots in other theaters of the great global conflict.

After 19 February no more than six planes ever rose to meet the attackers. Nearly always there was no opposition whatsoever. By mid-March the Navy communiqué could state: "Our bombers attacked Rabaul without fighter escort." The lack of suitable targets on the "milk run" made the following exchange a favorite gag among Solomons- and Bismarcks-based pilots: Q. "What did you do this morning?" A. "Oh, I bombed an outhouse on New Ireland."

Green Islands, 115 miles east of Rabaul, were occupied by the New Zealanders on 15 February, under cover of eight Marine squadrons; VMF-212 had the duty when 15 Vals attacked, and by flying through intense AA from friendly destroyers, shot down six planes at 200–300 feet—three by Captain Philip C. DeLong. Three fighter controllers and 11 experienced maintenance crewmen from VMF(N)-531 landed on D-day with the Navy's Argus 7[31] and its fighter-director radar and VHF. On the second night Captain Owen Hines directed Colonel Schwable and Lieut. Jack M. Plunkett to successful interceptions which resulted in killing off two snoopers. Three nights later he sent Harshberger in for a kill.

Emirau Island, 90 miles north of Kavieng, was taken by the 4th Marines

---

[31] Shore-based fighter director unit.

20 March as a substitute for Kavieng, whose invasion had been canceled in the notable JCS directive of 12 March 1944. Green and Emirau became bases which figured prominently in Marine aviation annals, for the further purpose of bombing Rabaul, which was the task of so many Marine flyers until the fall of Japan ended what seemed never would end. To complete the ring around Rabaul Southwest Pacific forces seized the Admiralty Islands after some stiff fighting in March, and Manus became a great naval base.

Arrival of the PBJ's

The most significant innovation in South Pacific aviation in 1944 was the arrival in March of what were, for the Marines, big planes with six-man crews. Although General Rowell recommended the acquisition of medium bombers for night heckling before Pearl Harbor, there seems to have been no special reason for the Marines to have PBJ's (B-25's)[32] except that the Army was overstocked by several hundred planes, and the Marines would try anything. They were used to being given whatever tools the Army or Navy were tired of, or had in surplus.

When VMB-413, the first PBJ squadron, was commissioned at Cherry Point 1 March 1943, Guadalcanal had just been rid of the Japanese; what direction the war would take was obscure; Marine pilots were being turned out in larger quantities.[33]

VMB-413 had a few prewar aviators, but mostly graduates fresh from flight school. Navigators, radiomen and gunners had to be trained after the first PBJ's were received. This meant the first squadron had to provide nuclei and training syllabi for all subsequent squadrons flying the same planes. Therefore, a full year elapsed between VMB-413's commissioning and its first mission against the enemy—a respectable record, however, when the training and pioneering factors are considered.

Meantime, VMB's 423, 433 and 443 had been commissioned 15 September 1943. VMB-611, VMB-612, VMB-613 and VMB-614 were activated 1 October.

When 413 and 423 were alerted at MCAS, Edenton, North Carolina, for overseas duty there was a scramble in "midnight requisitioning procedure." Lieut. Colonel Ronald D. Salmon, CO of the pioneer squadron, insisted later that when 413 opened its crates one of 423's guards was found inside. "Fortunately or unfortunately, both squadrons came out of the exchange with about the same amount of gear as when they started."[34]

VMB-413, commanded by Lieut. Colonel Andrew B. Galatian Jr., after

---

[32] Exhaustive checking of Navy Department files and interviewing of numerous Marine and Navy officers fail to reveal the precise reason for originating the PBJ program.

[33] In March 1942 there were 885 Marine aviators; in March 1943 there were 3,191.

[34] VMB-423 history.

Salmon went to MarAirSoPac staff, was ordered to the West Coast 3 December 1943. In January it flew down to Espíritu Santo for six weeks' further training. The Squadron then moved to Stirling Island in mid-March for the months of hazardous night heckling of Rabaul, Kavieng and Bougainville areas, beside daylight bombing of Rabaul every third day. Early losses were heavy: two planes and crews were lost 22 March; a water landing cost two men their lives 1 April; another plane crashed 21 April with total casualties; on 5 May, ten days before it was relieved by VMB-423, AA at Rabaul's Tobera airfield shot down Lieut. Glen W. Smith's plane. A second tour brought the Squadron back to Munda in July.

The Squadron's effectiveness was attested by a commendation from Brig. General William A. Matheny USA, AirSols Bomber Commander:

> . . . in day formation and bombing technique . . . you have, in the space of a few weeks matched similar units which have been operating under ComAirSols for nine months. You have, further, developed the dangerous, tiresome mission of night heckling against the enemy bases to the highest perfection it has attained in the fourteen months I have been working under ComAirSols.[35]

Under Lieut. Colonel John L. Winston, VMB-423 flew from Stirling and Green Islands and, later in the war, Emirau. On 9 June, four months after the last enemy plane had been seen, Lieut. William H. Hopper was flying his PBJ at 8,000 feet when he was jumped by two Oscars. He chose to fight it out, repeatedly turning into the Japanese planes, so he could bring his nose and turret guns to bear. Nobody on either side got hurt beyond the shock to Hopper's crew's sense of surprise. Had Rabaul finally been reinforced? No. But nobody could tell at the time. What had happened was this: the Japanese had succeeded in rebuilding 5 to 7 planes from salvaged parts.[36]

Thirty-five thousand Oklahoma City school children bought a PBJ and signed a scroll telling how U.S. small fry were helping the war effort. The scroll was dropped by an all-Oklahoma crew of VMB-423 on Rapopo airstrip, Rabaul, 27 May, and Tojo was booted out of office less than three weeks later. This result is usually ascribed to the Battle of Saipan, however.

In July 1944 Lieut. Colonel Norman J. Anderson, who was to fly a record 107 bombing missions, relieved Winston as CO of VMB-423. The Squadron remained in the Solomons–Bismarcks area until August 1945, as did VMB's 413, 433 and 443. Then they all went to Malabang in the Philippines with the rest of 1st MAW. Its relief from the Rabaul monotony consisted of leave in Sydney, five crews at a time. On 8 April 1945, the New Zealanders of No. 2 Squadron and Australians of No. 15 Squadron noted their gratitude

---

[35] VMB-413 history, 20 April 1944, p 5.
[36] Lieut. Commander Henry Salomon Jr. USNR, ATIS 16270.

to VMB-423, and on 16 May Lieut. General Stan E. Savage of II Australian Corps (which took over the Bougainville perimeter from the Americans) sent ComAirNorSols a thank-you note for the effective bombing of Buin and other Bougainville targets by 423 and by RNZAF squadrons at Green Island.[37]

Twelve PBJ squadrons, each with 15 planes and 30 crews, were commissioned, although only seven of them got far enough beyond the paper stage to be sent overseas—five served in the South and Southwest Pacific; VMB's 612 and 613 were assigned to the Central Pacific. Colonel Perry K. Smith's MAG-61, which operated in SoPac from July 1944, was the only all-PBJ group.

The Marines lost 45 PBJ's and 173 officers and men, as follows:

Squadron[38]	A/C Lost (Operational)	A/C Lost (Combat)	Officers	Men
VMB-413	2	5	13	19
VMB-423	7	3	12	23
VMB-433	1	2	4	6
VMB-443	2	2	6	9
VMB-611	2	6	11	23
VMB-612	4	7	14	25
VMB-613	1	1	2	6
	19	26	62	111

Truk Has Its Picture Taken

On the night of 3 February 1944, two PB4Y's of VMD-254 piloted by Major James R. Christensen and Captain James Q. Yawn took off from the five-week-old airstrip on Stirling Island on a mission of transcending importance. Their assignment: to fly their photographic planes over Truk,[39] 1,000 miles to the northwest, and make pictures of the fleet base in preparation for Admiral Mitscher's carrier raid and, possibly, for the invasion which was then still on the books. The very name of Truk was enough to send shivers down the spine of any man serving below the Equator: the most mysterious of Japan's many islands of mystery.

The two pilots and their ten-man crews arrived over the target at 20,000 feet on the morning of 4 February. Below their cameras lay much of the Japanese Combined Fleet, including the 63,000-ton battleship Musashi, 1 carrier, 9 or 10 cruisers, 20 destroyers, and 12 submarines, plus many cargo

---

[37] VMB-423 history.

[38] Five squadrons, which were commissioned too late for combat, lost no aircraft or personnel: VMB's 614, 453, 463, 473, 483.

[39] A similar mission had been approved by the War Department as early as 26 November 1941, and one of two B-24's which were to photograph Truk and Jaluit reached Hawaii just two days before the Pearl Harbor attack. (Craven and Cate, The AAF in WW II, Vol I, pp 189–190.)

ships.[40] Christensen and Yawn got in unobserved and were taking pictures before anybody detected them. Then a battleship opened up, and two or three Zekes plus two or three seaplane fighters (Rufes) went up to intercept.[41] After spending 20 to 30 throbbing minutes over Truk the two Marine pilots dived away and headed for the Solomons. Both planes were in the air for approximately 12 hours before they landed at Piva after one of the most daring photographic missions of the war. Complete coverage was not possible, due to cloudiness, but what the marines' cameras brought back did nothing to dispel the dread that Truk induced.

Unfortunately the B-24 that made a photographic reconnaissance of Truk on 4 February 1944 was seen by the Jap fleet. The commander of the Combined Fleet, which was then at anchor in Truk, considered it a harbinger of bad news. The fleet weighed anchor on 10 February 1944 and left Truk never to return.[42]

Admiral Koga had already been worried about his extended line: the Gilberts were gone and the Marshalls had just been invaded. The sight of a four-engined plane overhead was enough. He took off in his flagship *Musashi* for Yokosuka in the home islands with part of the fleet; the rest went to Singapore.[43] But about 50 merchant ships and auxiliaries had their departure delayed by rough weather. Three light cruisers and eight destroyers remained behind with them, and Truk's airfields were jammed with planes en route to Rabaul—these were delayed for want of ferry pilots.

Thirteen days after the photographic mission Mitscher's carrier planes struck; surface ships helped finish off the cripples. Three cruisers went down, and so did three destroyers, 2 submarine tenders, an aircraft ferry, 6 tankers, 3 auxiliary cruisers and 19 cargo vessels—a total tonnage of more than 200,000. About 325 airplanes were destroyed or damaged; so were storage facilities for food and fuel (which had not been put underground). Truk was left all but defenseless by this brilliant strike. Despite their staggering losses, the Japanese found in the escape of the fleet "a bright spot in the midst of our misfortune."[44]

---

[40] Samuel Eliot Morison, *Aleutians, Gilberts and Marshalls,* p 319.

[41] USSBS, *The Reduction of Truk,* p 4, indicates the Japanese spotted only one of the planes.

[42] USSBS Naval and Naval Air Field Team No. 3, Rear Admiral Calvin T. Durgin, "A Study of the Effects of Allied Warfare Against Truk" (2 December 1945).

[43] USSBS, *The Reduction of Truk,* p 4, with corrections according to Ensign Richard S. Pattee's study of Japanese naval documents.

[44] *Southeast Area Naval Operations,* Part Three. CominCh planners had feared something of the sort: "The longer we postpone a raid on Truk the less likely we are to find Japanese fleet units there." (Memo Rear Admiral C. T. Joy to CominCh, F-123, 24 December 1943.)

The Battle of the Bougainville Perimeter

We left General Hyakutake as he was evacuating his 17th Army from Guadalcanal via the Toyko Express.[45] In November 1943 we find him on Bougainville engaged in the business of making a very wrong guess, akin to that of Adolf Hitler, who wouldn't believe that the Allies' Normandy landing was anything more than a feint.

Hyakutake's 40,000 troops were concentrated mainly in the south at Buin and the Shortlands and at Buka on the northern tip of Bougainville. The naval supreme command wanted to launch an all-out attack against the Torokina beachhead, but the General argued stubbornly that the Americans would "at the first opportunity attempt to occupy the Buin sector with his main force and the Buka sector with other elements."[46]

Consequently, Hyakutake waited at Buin for the landing that never came, and he managed to get a few reinforcements through to Buka, where they, too, waited (and were subjected to frequent harassment by AirSols planes).

Meantime, General Geiger's IMAC (3d Marine Division, 2d Raider Regiment, 1st Parachute Regiment, 37th Infantry Division) fought off repeated counterattacks on the expanding perimeter by the 2,000 Japanese who had been in the Torokina area from the beginning. On 15 December 1943 IMAC was relieved by XIV Corps (Major General Oscar W. Griswold), and the Marines, to whom had fallen most of the fighting, were relieved by the Americal Division (Major General John R. Hodge). At this time the perimeter, which contained one completed airfield and two more fast a-building under the aegis of eight Seabee battalions and a New Zealand engineer brigade, was about four miles deep and five miles wide.[47]

The soldiers began to dig in for the assault that was bound to come. The perimeter was a dangerously small area in which to build three airfields, all of which must be exposed to enemy artillery when guns were brought up, but the total boundary line to be defended was over 13 miles around, and it was important no deep penetration be made at any point. This required determined, well-emplaced troops who had absolute air superiority.

The Japanese managed to send about 1,400 troops by barge up to Empress Augusta Bay from Buin. But the main attacking forces consisted of the entire 6th Division and other troops which added up to 15,000 men. Against these General Griswold had about 27,000 in the two infantry divisions, plus the 3d Marine Defense Battalion, the Army's 49th Coast Artillery Battalion, six destroyers, a PT squadron, Colonel O'Neill's Strike Command and MAG-24, which was operating at Piva Uncle (the north strip).

Early in February 1944 MAG-24 consisted of ten squadrons: VMF's 211, 212, 215, 218, 222, 223, VMSB's 235 and 244, and VMTB's 134 and 232.

---

[45] See pp 122–127 (Chapter Eight).
[46] *Southeast Area Naval Operations,* Part Three.
[47] Rentz, *Bougainville and the Northern Solomons,* p 85.

On the 19th its CO, Colonel William L. McKittrick, was detached to become Commander Air, Emirau, after that island's capture, and Lieut. Colonel Lewis H. Delano Jr. took over the Group.

About the end of December 1943 General Hyakutake was finally persuaded that there wouldn't be any other landing, and he began the grueling process of hauling his artillery along the jungle trails. His troops approached the perimeter in three columns, from the northwest, the north and the east. Their ultimate goal was the Torokina airstrip on the beach, but first they had to take the two adjoining strips nearest the periphery: Piva Uncle (bomber) and Piva Yoke (fighter). A document captured by General Griswold's soldiers told what the Japanese were fighting for: "Avenge the shame of our country's humiliation on Guadalcanal. . . . There can be no rest until our bastard foes are battered, and bowed in shame. . . . Strike fear in the hearts of the bold as we proudly attack Torokina Bay and crush our opponents forever."[48] A map captured at the end of February designated the point at which the American general would surrender—a formality which the Japanese planners always seemed to give first priority.

About the same time MAG-24 was organized into two infantry-type battalions of four companies each, for the defense of the north sector. Each battalion was reinforced by an Army heavy-weapons company. By 6 March gun emplacements and rifle pits had been completed for MAG-24's defense.

The attack was supported by the most field artillery the Japanese had managed to concentrate anywhere in the South Pacific.[49] Prisoners later said that bringing up each 100-pound shell required two men to make a four-day trip.[50]

This artillery was set up behind steep hills which the Americans designated by their foot-altitudes: Hill 501, Hill 600, etc. Defiladed as they were against counterbattery fire, these positions provided targets for SBD's and TBF's of Strike Command which could not be easily reached by any other means.

At 0600 on 8 March between 100 and 200 shells began falling in the Torokina perimeter for the first time in 1944, wrecking three F4U's on the Piva South (Yoke) strip. One B-24 was destroyed at Piva Uncle. Nineteen other planes were slightly damaged but quickly repaired. Among aviation personnel one was killed and a dozen were wounded. During the shelling after dark ten others were wounded, two seriously. TBF Operations and Intelligence found the shelling so hot that their quarters in the revetment area had to be abandoned.

During the day Strike Command flew 120 sorties, dropping 60 tons of bombs on the Japanese on the other side of the line. P-39 fighter bombers dropped 500-pound bombs on enemy guns spotted at Hanemo and Mom, and

---

[48] Morison, *Breaking the Bismarcks Barrier*, p 428.
[49] *Ibid*, p 429.
[50] *Admiral Halsey's Story*, p 191.

F4U's strafed the same targets. For the first time since the Torokina strip was finished AirSols B-25's and B-24's bombed Rabaul without fighter cover.

Next day Japanese infantry made their charge against the perimeter, and carved a slice out at Hill 700 which they held for three days. Strike Command flew 107 bombing missions, dropping 65 tons on Hills 1111, 1000 and 250. In the first of 14 spotting sorties Lieut. W. B. Gilbert's SBD from VMSB-244 exploded in midair, killing him and his observer, Lieut. Vernon H. Brooks USA; it was assumed that the plane had been hit by machine-gun fire or AA, although U.S. artillery was active in the area at the time.[51]

ComAirSoPac's Plan Able, providing for the evacuation of all planes at night to Barakoma, Munda or Green Island (whose airstrip began operating 6 March) was executed 9 March. This meant that the ground crews at each of these fields had to service 40 to 100 extra planes each night, and to care for their crews. In the morning the loaded planes would return to Bougainville for another turn at the attackers, dropping their bombs on an enemy position before landing the first time.[52]

On 10 March 160 Strike Command sorties were flown, and in the perimeter "where Pistol Pete has brought in all his relatives in the past two or three days" no shells fell. But on 12 March the shelling intensified again on both the Piva strips, worse on Yoke, only 2,000 yards from the front lines. One Cub plane was destroyed and the Marston mat on all three airstrips was holed. By now 114 SBD's and 45 TBF's were flying "almost continuously" and AirSols Intelligence noted that gun positions were being pinpointed more accurately. Aviation personnel casualties were 1 killed, 14 wounded.

On the 13th, 131 SBD and 95 TBF sorties dropped 123 tons of bombs and also spotted for the artillery and for destroyers firing their 5-inch guns offshore. On the 14th, 145 tons of bombs were unloaded by Strike Command on gun positions around Hills 111, 500, 501, 600 and 150—"one good reason why Pistol Pete was quiet for once."[53]

But Pistol Pete and his kin were good for several more shots before Hyakutake's attack finally failed. Ninety rounds of 75-mm. and 150-mm. fell in the Piva airstrip area during a big counterattack on 15 March, which captured some pillboxes before the infantry drove back the suicidal Japanese two days later. In the early morning of the 18th a night raider dropped the first bombs in the Torokina area in 34 days, killing 1 man in the MAG-24 camp and wounding 7 others.

Although many SBD's and TBF's were permitted to resume their bombing of Rabaul, Lieut. Colonel Schwable (who relieved "Peg" O'Neill on 15 March as Strike Commander) kept an average of 30 light bombers on perimeter duty. Army fighter bombers (P-39's and P-40's) stayed at the same task.

The last big effort was staged by Hyakutake's soldiers on the night of

---

[51] ComAirSols intelligence summary, 9 March 1944.

[52] ComAirSols Strike Command war diary, 15 March–1 June 1944.

[53] ComAirSols intelligence summary, 15 March 1944.

23-24 March. They made some penetration but were thrown back a few hours after they started. Pistol Pete showed that he was not dead by wounding 16 men, including 2 pilots in the MAG-24 camp. Prisoners reported that Griswold's artillery had scattered the attackers.

After 16 days the airfields in the Torokina perimeter were free to continue the bombing of Rabaul, and on Kavieng (which Strike Command began hitting on 16 March with 36 SBD's and 24 TBF's after staging through Green Islands).[54] General Hyakutake had lost 5,469 of his troops in the attack on the perimeter, against 263 of Griswold's soldiers. He planned another offensive for May, but he had to put his hungry soldiers to growing food after the rice ration fell from 700 grams daily (before the Torokina landing) to 250 grams in April to nothing in September.[55] Strike Command was ordered to help along this food shortage by "potato runs." Altogether 2,500 gallons of Diesel oil were dropped on the Japanese vegetable gardens, but the success of the experiment was doubted, even by the TBF pilots who sprayed the oil.[56]

The ground crews in the Bougainville perimeter proved as efficient under fire as they had at Guadalcanal. VMF-223's ground crew stayed at Torokina to service the planes of VMF-114 after its own pilots had gone to Sydney for leave. VMF-215 kept its plane availability at 95 per cent, despite a high rate of ulcers, dysentery, malaria and fatigue. Stray bullets frequently pierced VMF-215's tents; miraculously, only one man was killed. The ground echelon of VMSB-244 suffered ten per cent casualties, but still claimed the highest availability rate on the island; Master Tech. Sergeant Nick F. Graziani and Tech. Sergeant Mark J. Gaspers were awarded medals for rescuing wounded men.

The ground echelon of VMSB-235, which had six men wounded in the shelling of 18 March, was commended by ComAirSols for "untiring efforts, unselfish devotion to duty. . . . Their disregard of their own personal safety during the shelling of the Bougainville airfields, in order that the aircraft assigned to them could continue to operate, is worthy of the highest praise and admiration." A similar recommendation went to HqSq-24, SMS-24, VMF-218, VMF-223, VMTB-232, VMSB-244 and VMTB-134.

Well illustrated throughout the Solomons was the airman's adage that no outfit is better than its ground crews. The men who kept the planes flying to Rabaul were largely unsung, but to the pilots whose machines they tended they were heroes of the highest order. When the occasion demanded that their lives be risked, there were always men of the ground crews ready. When a Japanese bomb set afire a bomb-laden TBF on Bougainville, five men unhesitatingly rushed to the rescue—Master Tech. Sergeants Clair S. Dennis,

---

[54] Some Japanese planes were flown in to reinforce Kavieng after Rabaul was permanently barren.

[55] Morison, *Breaking the Bismarcks Barrier*, p 431.

[56] ComAirSols Strike Command war diary, Part V (Statistics).

Charles R. McClary, Robert E. Johnson and Howard T. Lindsay and Tech. Sergeant Charles Cadmus. Before the bombs could explode in the midst of other parked planes these five men calmly defuzed them. Dennis, who had previously removed a burning flare from another bomb-laden plane, was promoted to warrant officer after the award of his second Navy and Marine Corps Medal.

Rabaul Could Take It[57]

In the long air campaign against Rabaul, from February 1942 to August 1945—the entire span of the war excepting the first two months—98 U.S. combat squadrons and several Australian, New Zealand and Indian units took part. The U.S. squadrons:

Army (Fifth AF 18, Thirteenth AF 20)	38
Navy (Land-based 13, carrier 14)	27
Marine Corps	33

The figures are barely indicative, of course, in that some squadrons in the Army or Navy made only a few raids, one in some cases. The Marines and Navy planes dropped lighter bomb loads but, according to Japanese testimony, far more accurately than the higher-flying Army heavy bombers. The Marine squadrons were stuck with the Rabaul job much longer than the others, of course.

After Green Islands and Emirau were captured, most of the Rabaul strikes were flown from those bases[58] (where most of the Army's Truk raids also originated).

The Rabaul area, including Kavieng and the New Britain targets outside Rabaul, throughout 44 months was subjected to 20,584 tons of bombs[59] plus 383 tons of naval shells delivered during infrequent destroyer sorties in 1944 and 1945. What were the results?

About 10,000 Japanese died, of whom approximately 4,700 were killed in action—most of them during the October 1943–July 1944 period, 907 of them in November and December 1943. Thus, more than four tons of bombs

---

[57] Unless otherwise noted, this material is from USSBS, The Allied Campaign Against Rabaul.

[58] The most detailed history by any Marine group to come to this writer's attention is that of MAG-14 by Captain Robert C. Rothafel. Its 278 pages devoted to the Green Islands campaign contain such miscellaneous data as this: whereas 60 per cent of the Group's Catholics attended religious services (p 163), only 10 per cent of the men of other faiths attended; the parachute loft could dry over 200 'chutes simultaneously; from Green Island 7,000 sorties totalling 40,000 hours were flown; and the ground crews of MAG-14 worked so hard their aircraft availability record was slightly over 85 per cent. As many as 175 planes had Green as home base during its March–July 1944 peak; this doesn't count Army bombers staging through to Truk.

[59] 3,360 tons by the Fifth Air Force, the rest by SoPac units.

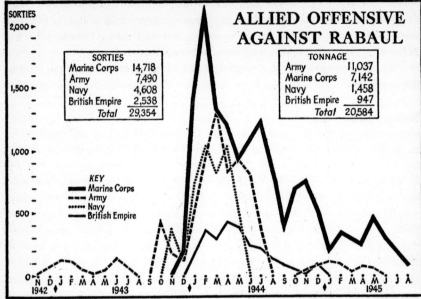

ALLIED OFFENSIVE AGAINST RABAUL

SORTIES	
Marine Corps	14,718
Army	7,490
Navy	4,608
British Empire	2,538
Total	29,354

TONNAGE	
Army	11,037
Marine Corps	7,142
Navy	1,458
British Empire	947
Total	20,584

KEY
Marine Corps
Army
Navy
British Empire

Source: U.S.S.B.S., The Allied Campaign Against Rabaul

were required to kill each enemy.[60] Reason: the Japanese went underground in February 1944, into 350 miles of tunnels and caves they built.

The Japanese preparation for invasion was almost fantastically complete. Possible landing beaches were fortified by underwater obstacles consisting of waterproof mines, concrete and log antiboat blocks, antipersonnel and anti-tank mines, concrete pillboxes and barbed-wire entanglements.

Rabaul had 367 AA guns, of which 93 were destroyed during the course of the war. Air defense consisted of seven air groups of the 11th Air Fleet, plus about 300 shore-based carrier planes.

Some other items:

Nearly 1,000 buildings with nearly 3,000,000 square feet. All these were destroyed by bombing.

Of 4,913 motor vehicles, 884 were destroyed and 1,697 others wore out.

Nineteen Type-1, Model-2 radar sets with 360-degree coverage and 90-mile range. Six of the 11 larger sets were destroyed. Twenty plane sets were removed for use on the ground, but only 11 were used (7 on New Ireland, 4 on New Britain). Through their telephone, radar and radio the Japanese had a "most satisfactory" air-warning system. When the Allies were flying direct from Bougainville fields the Buka radar gave Rabaul a 60-minute warning; from northeast the St. George radar set gave half-an-hour's warning if the planes swung around and came in from the northeast. The telephone

---

[60] In ETO it took 2.6 tons to kill each German civilian. (*Life's Picture History of World War II*, p 240, which compiled figures from USSBS reports.)

system included a submarine cable that crossed Simpson Harbor and extended along the coast in four lengths. The Japanese Army had about 1,000 radio sets, the Navy 315, including six 5-kw. receiver-transmitters that could reach Truk. This does not include well-dispersed stocks in reserve.

At the end of 1943 the Army had 30,000 tons of ammunition, so well dispersed that only 500 tons were destroyed by bombing. Navy ammunition included 1,547,449 rounds ranging from 20-mm. to 150-mm. There were 55,000 tons of food, of which 23,500 tons were destroyed. Extensive garden plots supplemented the stocks, and the Rabaul defenders never suffered the malnutrition and starvation that whittled down the Marshalls garrisons. Rationing was instituted in January 1944, in the expectation of a long war, but at the time of the surrender the daily ration had fallen only from 3,400 calories to 2,200. There was cannibalism at Rabaul but it was purely ceremonial.

Morale on Rabaul never suffered noticeably until the early months of 1945, when Luzon, Iwo and Okinawa made it appear even to some officers that the war might not be going so well. All hands were issued a monthly allotment of soap, toothpaste, shaving cream and razor blades. A schedule of sexual entertainment was provided by 500 to 600 Korean and Japanese prostitutes who arrived early in the war.

Of 4,500 horses on Rabaul, 250 were killed by bombings.

The weakest Japanese link was probably the most important: the Allied bombing destroyed water communications. Rabaul's water transport included 640 *Daihatsu*, fishing boats and barges; 20 destroyers, 10 submarines, 10 sea trucks. Of the 640 boats, 517 were destroyed. Also sunk: 30 naval vessels, 154 large cargo vessels, 70 small cargo ships. The larger ships remaining were withdrawn in February 1944, and the last cargo submarine left in April 1944. Thus, the blockade became complete.

Over Rabaul 100 marines were killed, 27 wounded; at Kavieng the count was 17 killed, 7 wounded.[61]

The Strategic Bombing Survey found that "attacks on Rabaul and other by-passed positions were continued longer and in greater volume than required."[62] It can be argued, however, that there were no other active areas where the short-range Marine planes could have been employed during this period, and Rabaul was still excellent training for the proposed invasion of Japan to which the 1st MAW had been assigned.

Fortunate it was indeed that the Joint Chiefs of Staff never ordered the capture of Rabaul and that the by-passing strategy was employed instead. Tarawa, Iwo Jima and Okinawa would have faded to pale pink in comparison with the blood that would have flowed if the Allies had attempted an assault on Fortress Rabaul.[63]

---

[61] Figures from Casualty Division USMC, 21 March 1949.

[62] USSBS, *Summary Report (Pacific War)*, p 29.

[63] Morison, *Breaking the Bismarcks Barrier*, pp 408–409.

On 15 July 1945, ComAirNorSols was finally terminated and the Bismarcks and Solomons were redesignated "Island Area," under the Air Officer Commanding, Headquarters, New Zealand Air Task Force (ComZeAirTAF), who was in turn responsible to the Royal Australian Air Force. During this last month of the war MAG-61 continued operations under this New Zealand command.

CHAPTER FOURTEEN

Northwest from Samoa[1]

THE CENTRAL PACIFIC was the biggest of all the theaters.[2] Its many millions of square miles of blue water contained but little land mass worthy of the designation. Because its islands were of the fly-speck variety, the Central Pacific never attained a prominence in Marine aviation operations to match the South Pacific's—once the Central Pacific offensive got under way the leaps forward were too great to be covered by any planes except long-range bombers and carrier-based aircraft. The Marine flyers could only maintain the rear guard until the fighting was over and new airfields ready.

Many times at Tarawa, Saipan and Iwo Jima the writer heard marines of various divisions wish for close support from their own flyers. But it would have been necessary to start the Marines' carrier program at least a year earlier, and Marine aviation was fully committed in that earlier period to whittling down Japanese air strength in the Solomons. The Marine Corps forgot to throw out an anchor to windward, and consequently was found high and dry in so far as Central Pacific aviation was concerned.

Until 1945 the Marine flyers' job in the Central Pacific could never, with minor exceptions, have been called front-line offensive in the same sense that the Marine divisions operated offensively.

---

[1] Principal sources: Commanding General, Defense Force, Samoa (ComGenDef-ForSamoa); 4th MBDAW, MCAS, Ewa; MAG-13; VMF-111; VMSB-151; VMO-155; VMSB-241; VMF-441; histories and war diaries; J. C. Furnas, *Anatomy of Paradise: Hawaii and the Islands of the South Seas* (1948); Morison, *The Rising Sun in the Pacific*; USSBS, *Campaigns*; Craven and Cate, *The AAF in WW II*, Vol I; Clive Howard and Joe Whitley, *One Damned Island after Another: The Saga of the Seventh* [*Air Force*]; *Admiral Halsey's Story*; Bureau of Yards and Docks, *Building the Navy's Bases in World War II*, Vol II; DeChant, *Devilbirds*; Hough, *The Island War*; CinCPac war diary; JCS minutes; Fairfield Osborn, ed., *The Pacific World* (1944); CinCPac reprints of *Early Reports of Operations in Pacific Areas*, February 1942–August 1943.

[2] Strictly speaking, there was no Central Pacific Area until Admiral Spruance was named ComCenPac on 5 August 1943. The Samoa–Ellice area remained part of ComSoPac's command. Geographically speaking, the Central Pacific was those parts of the Pacific Ocean Areas not embraced in the Southwest Pacific, South Pacific or North Pacific. For Marine aviators the Central Pacific trail was a 4,825-mile string of bases from the Samoa Group through the Ellices, Gilberts, Marshalls, Marianas, to Iwo Jima and Okinawa.

The United States had taken a strategic interest in Samoa since President Grant's time. Recurrent squabbles over the islands took place in the nineteenth century between the United States, Germany and Great Britain. This feuding reached a climax in 1889 with warships from all three nations in the harbor at Apia, on the island of Upolu in western Samoa. Despite weather warnings, the commanders of the six ships (three American, one British, two German) refused to budge from the harbor, though it was known as a trap in a storm. Finally, HMS *Calliope* steamed out to safety; the other five ships were wrecked. The German sloop *Adler* still lies on the reef "like a schoolboy's cap on a shelf."[3]

In 1899 by tripartite treaty Germany was awarded the two larger Samoan islands, Savaii and Upolu, and the United States got smaller Tutuila (76 square miles) with its fine harbor at Pago Pago. American Samoa was put under Navy administration, where it remained until the Interior Department took over in 1951.

Twenty years after its acquisition Pago Pago had only 350 tons of coal and three small barges. The Germans continued their commercial domination of the Southeast Pacific until World War I. After that war a Class C League-of-Nations mandate gave virtual sovereignty over western Samoa to New Zealand, but 30 years later native children playing soldier in remote villages could be heard shouting "*Achtung! Ein, zwei, drei, vier. . . .*"[4]

Contracts amounting to more than $10,000,000 had been authorized on Tutuila in 1940, and civilian workers were busy on oil-storage and station facilities when the Japanese struck at Pearl Harbor. But the airstrip was barely started. Except for a few light OS2U seaplanes of VS-1-D14 which came out with the 2d Marine Brigade in January 1942, Samoa's air defense would have to wait a while, not only for construction, but even for groups and squadrons to be organized.

Initially the air defense of Samoa was based on the 2,500-by-250-foot runway at Tafuna, five miles south of Pago Pago harbor. The completion of the strip to this usable length coincided with the arrival of MAG-13's first planes 2 April 1942;[5] after that the strip was quickly lengthened as hundreds of thousands of tons of coral and volcanic rock were filled into the shallow lagoon. It was completed several months later, and the contractors sailed for home, leaving the Seabees alone to complete the other defenses throughout the Samoan Islands.

The first problem confronting Colonel Thomas J. Walker was training his pilots. Like other outfits which had expanded hurriedly since Pearl Harbor, MAG-13 was mostly untrained—VMO-151, for example, had 3 experienced pilots out of 20; VMF-111 was better off with 10. Living conditions imposed another serious problem. The enervating heat, swarms of coconut bugs, mosqui-

---

[3] Robert Louis Stevenson, *A Footnote to History*, p. 284.

[4] Furnas, *Anatomy of Paradise*, p 241.

[5] See p 48.

toes, knee-deep mud, and five-inch rains made the construction of an adequate camp a headache.

The solution was the *fale* (pronounced "folly")—a light prefabricated building based on a 16-by-16-foot floor space with an 8-by-8-foot prefabricated wall section, which the civilians had constructed prior to arrival of the Group and VMF-111 personnel in March. VMO-151 arrived in May and lived in tents at first, with no decking and only mosquito nets for protection against the filariasis, malaria and dengue the insects brought around.

To defend Samoa against the attack which for a long time seemed highly probable, Colonel Walker ordered each squadron to mobilize as an infantry company containing two platoons plus one .30-caliber-machine-gun platoon. Supporting units for the Group consisted of a tank company, a heavy-weapons platoon, a 3-inch battery and one section of the island's barrage-balloon squadron.

Quite logically, considering their fantastic successes, the Japanese were still assessed supermen in these weeks before Midway. For purposes of defense it was estimated that the Japanese not only could bomb Samoa with patrol boats from the Gilbert Islands, about 1,400 miles away, but also could attack with carrier-based planes operating within 1,000 miles (!) though it was "doubtful if enemy aircraft would have attempted to make attacks from such maximum distances."[6]

For the pilots of MAG-13 life on Samoa has been described by one of their number as "constant patrol and alert, chasing bogeys that always turned out to be friendly."[7] Certainly there were enough alarms—on more than one occasion the pilots sat up all night, waiting for the enemy that existed only on primitive radar screens. But the defenders of Samoa were taking no chances. Wasn't the top brass always saying Samoa's time would come? If Guadalcanal were lost, as seemed likely until November, Samoa was an obvious plum. As late as March 1943 Canton Island was bombed three times, and on the 28th of that month Admiral King warned the JCS that, although New Caledonia and Fiji were now safer, "Samoa is definitely exposed . . . the enemy can seriously damage Samoa unless we are on guard."

Concern was also felt for tiny Johnston Island, 800 miles southwest of Pearl Harbor, and VMSB-243 at Ewa was split in half. Major William M. Hudson took 12 of its planes to Johnston in March 1943, where they stayed six uneventful months.

Upolu and Wallis

At one time or another four Marine regiments[8] served on Samoa, as many as three of them at a time, in addition to other units which made up the 2d and 3d Brigades. Like the air units, these ground forces were dis-

---

[6] MAG-13 history, p 32.

[7] Interview Major Joseph H. Reinburg, 7 April 1948.

[8] The 3d, 7th, 8th, 22d.

tributed throughout the Samoa–Wallis groups—in the two large islands of British Samoa, and on Uea Island in Wallis Archipelago, 300 miles west of Samoa, which had belonged to France since 1854. The Seabees started work on Upolu on 10 May and on Wallis 26 May (after waiting at Tutuila three weeks while diplomatic negotiations with the French were completed).[9]

The first detachment of Marine planes to be sent outside Tutuila was six F4F-3's of VMF-111 to Upolu on 10 August 1942. Six SBD's (which began to replace the SBC's in December) of VMSB-151 and nine F4F-4's of VMF-441 went to Wallis 27 January 1943, when the airfield there was ready.

Pilots preferred duty at Faleolo Field on Upolu, where the 4,000-foot runway was completed by July. The capital, Apia, 15 miles east of Faleolo, seemed to resemble civilization; there was a small British colony which extended its hospitality to the Americans. MAG-13 pilots liked temporary duty in British Samoa and everybody tried to get it. Flying the mail between the various islands (in a J2F) was another plum. Nobody cared for service on dirty, primitive Wallis, which finally had an airstrip sufficiently long to accommodate bombers but too late for the Army to use it. One squadron historian noted that "Wallis has gained the reputation as about the best spot on God's earth to keep away from."[10]

British Samoa was almost free of the blight of the other islands: filariasis (local name: *mumu*), which came to be dreaded more than any other disease in the Pacific. Makes a man impotent, they said. The incidence of filariasis was barely noticed during the first few months on Samoa—fungus infection was worse—and aviation personnel became convinced it was only a disease for natives.[11] But by early 1943 hospitals were full of *mumu* patients, who were evacuated by the shiploads. Marine Barracks at Klamath Falls, Oregon, was designated to study and treat men with filariasis. A report of the disease by the senior medical officer at Klamath Falls, issued after the war, showed that approximately 3,000 men underwent treatment for filariasis and were discharged as cured (and virile).

The increase in cases of filariasis convinced the Marine Corps Commandant that Samoa should be discontinued as a replacement training center; ComSoPac and Commanding General, I Marine Amphibious Corps (ComGen-IMAC) concurred, and in the spring of 1943 the military population of Samoa finally dropped.[12]

There was more work than merely chasing bogeys that turned out friendly. Squadrons engaged in antisubmarine patrol, convoy cover, photographic flights, fixed gunnery, instrument training, and night flying. The training was excellent, as Samoa-trained pilots proved when they were hurriedly

---

[9] Bureau of Yards and Docks, *Building the Navy's Bases in World War II*, Vol II, pp 212–215.

[10] VMBF-331 history, p 3.

[11] Information from Major John Hughes, VMO-151.

[12] ComSoPac war diaries, 28 April and 5 May 1943.

thrown into Guadalcanal as replacements for some of the first squadrons sent there.[13]

The purely defensive role of such organizations as MAG-13, MAG-21 (Ewa) and MAG-22 (Midway) was recognized on 22 August 1942 when they were taken from the 1st and 2d Wings and incorporated into the new 4th Marine Base Defense Aircraft Wing (MBDAW). Administration of this command was allotted to Colonel Larkin at Ewa (he was succeeded 17 November by Colonel Walker, who was relieved a month later by Brig. General James T. Moore). Operational control of the three groups was split between ComSoPac (MAG-13) and Hawaiian Sea Frontier (MAG's 21, 22). MAG-21, however, was transferred to the 1st MAW in February 1943, and MAG-24, fresh from the States, joined the Wing at Ewa on the 11th to remain until September 1943, when it went to the New Hebrides.

The Move to Funafuti and Guadalcanal

MAG-13's two squadrons were split into four on 1 October 1942, although no additional planes were available.[14] VMF-111 spawned VMF-441 (Major Daniel W. Torrey Jr.) and handed its offspring 21 officers, 98 enlisted men, 8 F4F-3's and 1 SNJ trainer. VMSB-151 (redesignated from VMO) gave birth to VMO-155 (Captain John P. Haines Jr.) comprised of 19 officers, 109 enlisted men, 10 SBC-4's and 1 J2F-5. However, 6 officers and 15 enlisted men returned to the States 5 December as a nucleus to form the new VMO-155.[15]

---

[13] See below and p 121.

[14] Commanding General, Defense Force, Samoa (ComGenDefForSamoa) report No 5, October 1942. At the time there were only 32 combat planes and 9 auxiliary planes, including the 4 Navy OS2U's and the first 2 PBY-5A's the Marine Corps had.

[15] VMO-155 furnished the first marines to fly combat missions from a carrier. When the Squadron returned to the U.S. from Samoa, photography was stressed in its training, and on 17 April 1943 a detachment of 6 pilots and 9 enlisted men went on board the CVE *Nassau* with three F4F-3P photographic planes. The marines helped Navy pilots cover the Attu invasion beginning 11 May, thus also becoming the only Marine aviation unit to serve in the North Pacific. On 15 May Lieut. Waldo P. Breeden, just commissioned from technical sergeant, was killed when his plane spun into the icy water off Attu. (VMO-155 history; Squadron muster roll for April 1943.)

Nassau was the first carrier in the Pacific assigned for close air support (Morison, *Aleutians, Gilberts and Marshalls,* p 38), chiefly upon the insistence of Colonel Frank H. Lamson-Scribner USMC, air officer on Admiral Rockwell's Amphibious Force staff in *Pennsylvania.* The Navy pilots on board *Nassau,* flying 26 F4F-4's, were trained in close air support by Lieut. Colonel Peter P. Schrider USMC, who sailed with them as air support operations officer. Four naval gunfire observation teams acted as air support directors controlling both Army and Navy aircraft from the ground—an innovation by these forefathers of the famous Air Liaison Parties—while Colonel William O. Eareckson USA acted as airborne coordinator in a B-24, the first man to stay over the target all day. Fog prohibited effective support of the ground troops, by planes of any service, but as a laboratory Attu was invaluable.

Making new squadrons was not the only symptom of ambition during the dismal fall of 1942. On 2 October, in order to "deny the Ellice Islands to the enemy and to prepare the position as an air base,"[16] a task force of 2 cruisers, 6 destroyers, 2 transports and a cargo ship sailed into the lagoon of Funafuti Atoll and landed the 5th Marine Defense Battalion, reinforced, and 2 officers and 120 men from the 2d Seabees. This bold move put U.S. forces within 700 miles of Japanese-held Tarawa.

Its audacity was shortly accented in the Solomons, where crisis piled upon crisis and drew all available material plus some personnel. Whatever could be spared from the U.S. and even from the Southwest Pacific was poured into Guadalcanal in the desperate effort to hold it.

The Seabees went to work immediately on Funafuti Island's 7-miles-by-100-yards sandspit, and within 30 days of the felling of the first palm, Major General Charles F. B. Price, Commanding General, Samoa, was able to report that his PBY-5A had made the first landing.[17]

Few other planes landed on Funafuti for a long time. Four Navy OS2U's from the thinly spread VS-1-D14 detachment were sent up early in December for close-in submarine patrol.[18] If the Japanese had gone after Funafuti at the turn of the year no combat planes could have challenged them. It was 31 January before ComSoPac ordered ComGenSamoa to send 6 SBD's (commanded by Lieut. Colonel George A. Sarles) and 9 F4F-4's (Captain Walter J. Meyer) to Funafuti from Wallis. Three more SBD's joined the others next day. But all 18 combat planes returned to Tutuila after three weeks, and the forwardmost base in the area was without protection.

The Japanese also were too heavily engaged during these lean months. Like Samoa, Funafuti seemed destined to remain in the backwash of war, unnoticed and unsung.

Despite its paper expansion MAG-13 (under the command of Colonel Pierson Conradt since 6 October 1942) was nearly depleted in December when Guadalcanal cried "More planes!" No less than 49 of its approximately 75 pilots were suddenly ordered to the Solomons as replacements—remember the Japanese were still expected to make another try at retaking Guadalcanal and, in fact, they planned it that way up to 4 January.[19]

On 10 December, 18 pilots and 21 rear-seat gunners of VMSB-151 were flown in three R4D's of MAG-25 to Nandi and Espíritu Santo; 12 of the pilots were immediately reassigned to fighter duty and later went up to Guadalcanal with VMO-251; the other 6 presumably stuck with the dive bombers (though records on this hectic phase of the war are incomplete).

---

[16] CominCh, *Battle Experience, Solomon Islands Actions*, Chapter XXII, 15 March 1943.

[17] ComSoPac war diary, 11 November 1942.

[18] On 14 November 1942 this squadron rescued Captain Eddie Rickenbacker and his companions, who had been adrift at sea for many days after their plane ran out of gas.

[19] See p 122.

Five days later Major Don Yost and 30 other fighter pilots of his VMF-111 left via the same route and joined up with VMF-121 on Guadalcanal 23 December, leaving behind them in Samoa only the squadron number and a nucleus.

Funafuti Under Fire

Funafuti was quiet until March 1943, neither a target for the enemy nor a base to be used against the enemy. On 22 March, VMF-441 rushed up 6 pilots, 6 enlisted men and 6 F4F's for detached duty. Five days later the radar picked up enemy planes approaching Funafuti, and two pilots, Captain William P. Boland and Lieut. Ralph H. Spanjer, were sent out to intercept. They made contact with four enemy bombers 20 miles out; Spanjer's guns jammed on the first run but Boland shot down one bomber and damaged another. At long last something had happened south of the Equator and east of meridian 180.

In April Major General Willis H. Hale USA, commanding the Seventh Air Force, brought 24 B-24's to Funafuti from Hickam Field to mount a raid against Nauru Island, 1,000 miles to the northwest, which had been occupied by the Japanese the previous August. During the night of 19 April, 22 of the big bombers took off with 28 1,000-pound and 45 500-pound bombs plus 45 fragmentation clusters. Their targets were runways, dispersal areas and the island's phosphate works. All targets were reported "battered viciously." Five B-24's were damaged by Nauru-based fighters and one man was killed.[20]

Following this mission, which had as one of its purposes the training of green crews, the B-24's prepared for a raid on Betio Island, Tarawa Atoll, 704 miles north of Funafuti. But at 0330 on 23 April, day of the scheduled raid, the Japanese struck back. Probably acting on intelligence supplied by submarines,[21] nine bombers (supposedly from Tarawa) came over in a full moonlight which caused the white-stone church of the London Missionary Society to stand out "like a radiant diamond."[22] The first run was relatively harmless, but on the second, 20 minutes later, the Japanese bombardment was remarkably accurate. The natives who had gathered in the church for safety were dispersed into the coconut groves by a marine at gun point before a bomb hit and blew up the church. Two B-24's were destroyed, several others damaged. Only twelve could be sent out on the Tarawa raid, which finally took off late that evening. The Japanese raid also destroyed one F4F and damaged eight others of VMF-441, which had arrived at Funafuti a month earlier on temporary duty. The Japanese killed 5, wounded 27—none of them from MAG-13.

---

[20] Howard and Whitley, One Damned Island After Another, p 138; CinCPac, Early Reports of Operations in Pacific Areas, April 1943.

[21] Twenty Japanese submarines were operating in the Central Pacific about this time. (USSBS, Interrogations, No 366, p 295.)

[22] Howard and Whitley, One Damned Island After Another, p 139.

On 26 April MAG-13 received a second dive-bomber squadron, VMSB-241 (Major Wayne M. Cargill) with its 22 SBD-4's. VS-65, with 13 pilots in OS2U's reached Funafuti 10 May. The rest of VMF-441 moved up to Funafuti on 27 May, and the arrival of the new SBD squadron made it possible for VMSB-151, which had already sent a detachment to base at Funafuti, to climb up to Wallis from Tutuila on 6 June. On 29 June MAG-13 was given a task-group designation (TG 33.6).

One reason for the consistent movement of the flank northward was, of course, the securing of the lower Solomons, coupled with an increasing flow of new aircraft and trained pilots. In October all land-based planes in the two-month-old Central Pacific Area were designated Task Force 57 and came under the command of Rear Admiral John H. Hoover, Commander Aircraft, Central Pacific (ComAirCenPac). Besides Marine planes these included the Army's Seventh Air Force (8 heavy and 4 medium-bomber squadrons, 10 fighter squadrons),[23] plus 6 Navy patrol squadrons.

During this gradual build-up of strength Pacific Ocean Areas (POA) operations reports monotonously record that the Central Pacific was "relatively quiet." In June, for example, "enemy activity in the Central Pacific was conspicuous by its absence." Occasionally—about once a month—there were minor raids against Funafuti. On 8 August Captain Boland shot down a second bomber headed for Funafuti. These raids served to give personnel on the base a sense of participation in the war which was being fought largely elsewhere.

Although a Central Pacific offensive had been broached as early as February 1943, several months were required to sell it to the JCS and CCS and to work out the plans. Finally, on 20 July, the JCS instructed Admiral Nimitz to prepare for operations in the Ellice and Gilbert Islands, having decided that an attempt to land in the Marshalls was unwise at this time. At the Quebec Conference in August the route of advance through the Central Pacific was delineated: Gilberts, Marshalls and Marianas or Carolines.[24]

Plans for further development of Marine aviation strength in the Samoa–Funafuti area were completed in midsummer. The 4th MBDAW, now commanded by Brig. General Harold D. Campbell, moved in August from Ewa to Tutuila. In October, when Brig. General Lewie G. Merritt assumed command, the Wing was augmented by the arrival of MAG-31, with four squadrons —VMF-321 (Major Edmund F. Overend) at Tutuila, VMSB-341 (Major George J. Waldie Jr.) at Upolu, VMF-311 (Major Harry B. Hooper) and VMSB-331 (Major Paul B. Byrum) at Wallis. MAG-13 received a new squadron, VMF-224 (Major Darrell D. Irwin), in October, which was sent to Funafuti.

Upon the departure of the 4th Wing a provisional command designated

---

[23] *Ibid,* p 148.
[24] General MacArthur's reaction against this "island hopping" is quoted on p 264.

Marine Air, Hawaiian Area (MAHA) was established 1 September 1943 to carry on its administrative functions at Ewa (operational control remained with the Hawaiian Sea Frontier). At this time MAG-22 at Midway was made a unit of the new command. However, MAHA was disbanded on 8 May 1944 upon the arrival at Ewa of the 3d MAW from Cherry Point, N.C. Preparatory to the move of the 3d MAW from Cherry Point the 9th MAW was organized (1 April 1944) to succeed it. Thus, Marine aviation reached its peak of five wings.

Getting Ready for the Gilberts

Two minor preliminary movements preceded the jump into the Gilberts. On 25 August, detachments of Seabees and 2d Marine Airdrome Battalion, reinforced, went into Nukufetau, a small rectangular atoll 75 miles northwest of Funafuti. VMF-111 landed on the fighter strip 20 October. Later the Seabees cut down 50,000 coconut trees, built a 2,000-foot fill and made a bomber strip. VB-108 was based there 7 November and VMSB-331 moved up to Nukufetau with 16 SBD's on the 15th.

The other landing was 250 miles northwest of Funafuti at Nanomea, where a detachment of the 16th Seabees went ashore with a detachment of the 7th Marine Defense Battalion, reinforced, on 28 August. On 7 September ten Japanese twin-engine bombers dropped approximately 20 bombs on Nanomea from 3,000 to 5,000 feet, causing little material damage, but killing 5 and wounding 7.

VMF-441 disembarked at Nanomea 28 September; in the process a weighted container with the Squadron records and intelligence material was dropped overboard and lost. The Squadron found life on Nanomea "fairly uneventful" during its three-month tour.[25] Two of VMF-441's planes were sent out to intercept bogeys the night of 10 November but without radar guidance the gesture was idle, and three Japanese planes got through the darkness, causing minor damage to equipment and killing one soldier. The Squadron was relieved by an Army fighter squadron 30 November and VMF-441 went back to Tafuna to swap its F4F's and FM's for new F4U-1's.

Two AAF heavy-bomber squadrons (27th, 38th) moved into Nanomea and one (98th) into Nukufetau in November.[26] With other squadrons of the Seventh Air Force based at Funafuti, Canton and Baker, they helped Rear Admiral Charles A. Pownall's four carrier groups of Task Force 50 to support the landings of 20 November on Makin and Tarawa.

---

[25] VMF-441 history, p 3.

[26] Howard and Whitley, *One Damned Island After Another,* pp 148, 152.

CHAPTER FIFTEEN

The Gilberts and Marshalls

WHEN TASK FORCE 57 was activated 9 November 1943, General Merritt's 4th MBDAW consisted of 2 groups[1] and 10 squadrons[2] with 40 F4F's, 60 F4U's, 72 SBD's, and 11 R4D's and 3 PBY's scattered from Samoa to Nanomea. Merritt's command, Task Group 57.4, was made responsible for providing "fighter protection for our bases . . . protective patrols over own bases or shipping as directed . . . air transportation."[3]

In preparation for the latter function Central Pacific Combat Air Transport Service (CenCATS) was established at Tutuila on 16 November to serve as the new theater's counterpart of SCAT, which had been operating with great success in the South Pacific for more than a year.[4] CenCATS way stations on the eve of the Gilberts invasion were located at Upolu, Wallis, and Funafuti.

Aerial preparation for the amphibious assaults on Tarawa and Makin was entirely in the hands of Army and Navy flyers. Between 13 November and 19 November (west longitude dates) the Seventh Air Force, with an average strength of 80 B-24's, staged through the new advanced bases at Nanomea and Baker Island and flew six missions against Tarawa, dropping a total of 50 tons of bombs. Other missions were flown against Nauru, Makin and the Marshalls.[5]

Rear Admiral Alfred E. Montgomery's Southern Carrier Group, up from the 11 November raid on Rabaul, dropped 115 tons of bombs on Tarawa 18 November and 69 tons the next day, while strikes from the three other fast-carrier groups were made on the various Marshall Islands, Makin, Nauru, Wake and Kusaie. Close support at Tarawa was furnished chiefly from five escort carriers of Rear Admiral Van H. Ragsdale's TG 53.6 and at Makin by three CVE's of Rear Admiral Henry M. Mullinix's northern counterpart. About 900 carrier aircraft—far more than the Navy previously had been able to put in the air for any operation—supported the Gilberts operation. They flew a total of 2,278 sorties. During the operation the Japanese lost a complete air

---

[1] MAG's 13, 31.

[2] VMF's 111, 224, 311, 321, 441; VMSB's 151, 241, 331, 341; VMJ-353.

[3] 4th MBDAW history, p 14.

[4] The Samoan Combat Air Transport Service (VMJ-353) operated as "SCAT" from 1 November 1943, but this plagiarism was abandoned when CenCATS was formed two weeks later.

[5] USSBS, *The Seventh and Eleventh Air Forces in the War Against Japan*, p 4.

Task Organization
CENTRAL PACIFIC FORCE
November 1943

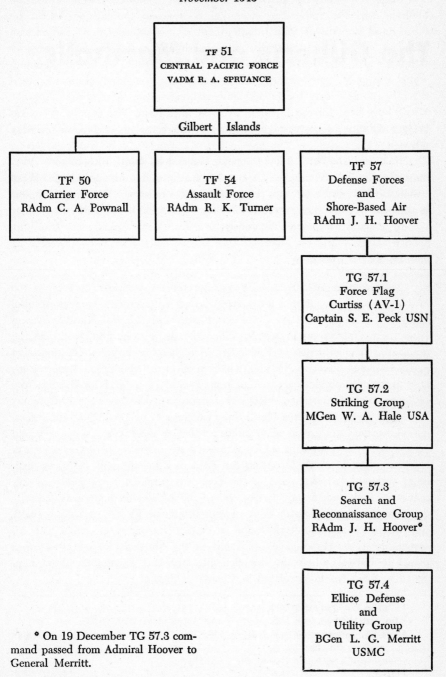

TF 51
CENTRAL PACIFIC FORCE
VADM R. A. SPRUANCE

Gilbert | Islands

TF 50
Carrier Force
RAdm C. A. Pownall

TF 54
Assault Force
RAdm R. K. Turner

TF 57
Defense Forces
and
Shore-Based Air
RAdm J. H. Hoover

TG 57.1
Force Flag
Curtiss (AV-1)
Captain S. E. Peck USN

TG 57.2
Striking Group
MGen W. A. Hale USA

TG 57.3
Search and
Reconnaissance Group
RAdm J. H. Hoover*

TG 57.4
Ellice Defense
and
Utility Group
BGen L. G. Merritt
USMC

* On 19 December TG 57.3 command passed from Admiral Hoover to General Merritt.

flotilla, about a hundred planes, in a half-hearted attempt to defend the Central Pacific.[6]

During the bitterly contested invasion of Tarawa by the 2d Marine Division and the somewhat more lightly opposed landing on Makin by elements of the Army's 27th Infantry Division, the Marine flyers served as a backstop in the rear areas, directing search and patrol, escorting friendly shipping (including the torpedoed carrier *Independence*). Under the planning, which relegated the Marines' short-legged, single-engined planes to base defense, the only way they could have got very deep into the Gilberts war would have been for the Japanese to strike back hard. This was by no means an impossibility, as postwar documents and interrogations of Japanese officers show.

Following the battle Lieut. General Holland M. Smith recommended that "consideration be given to the assignment of at least one Marine Aircraft Wing specifically for direct air support in landing operations."[7] But the Navy was in no mood yet to assign escort carriers for the Marine flyers, particularly since nobody pushed the project vigorously.

The Enemy's Dilemma

In September 1943 Admiral Koga expected an American invasion of the Marshalls so, in preparation for a decisive fleet engagement, he sent Admiral Ozawa's carrier planes (the Third Air Fleet) and Admiral Kurita's Second Fleet from Truk up to Eniwetok. When the Americans didn't come to the Marshalls, these returned to Truk.[8] On 30 September Imperial Headquarters in Tokyo issued directive No. 280, which in effect ordered Koga to shorten his lines and stiffen his defenses in the South Pacific, particularly at Rabaul, "the ultimate point of resistance."[9] Koga thereupon issued orders (in mid-October) sending Ozawa's 173 planes (from three carriers) to bolster Rabaul's defenses.

But radio intelligence again indicated that an American task force would raid Wake or the Marshalls, so Koga ordered submarine *I-36* to take a look at Hawaii before Ozawa's force left for Rabaul. The sub sent its plane over Pearl and reported that most of the fleet was gone, so Koga held Ozawa's planes at Truk and, flying his flag aboard the 63,700-ton battleship *Musashi*, departed for Eniwetok with most of the Combined Fleet.[10] A week passed, the Americans still didn't show up, so on 23 October Koga sailed with his armada to Truk. He canceled the alert in the Marshalls and sent Ozawa's planes to Rabaul, where the last elements arrived 1 November. What happened to them has been related in Chapter Thirteen.

---

[6] USSBS, *Campaigns*, p 193.

[7] Isely and Crowl, *The U.S. Marines and Amphibious War*, p 230.

[8] USSBS, *Interrogations*, Vol II, p 513. Vice Admiral Fukudome was Koga's chief of staff at the time.

[9] *Southeast Area Naval Operations*, Part Three.

[10] *Ibid.*

By the time the marines were in the transports headed for Bougainville, Koga was turning his head faster than a man watching a tennis match. Now he had no choice but to throw his strength into Rabaul. All he could spare to the Central Pacific was some garrison reinforcements (2,600 shifted from the Philippines in November and December) who were destined to spend an unhappy war in the Marshalls, and an extra 50 planes which lasted no longer than the 50 already in the Marshalls. Marine aviators back in Samoa and in the Ellices saw very little war during the Marine infantry's finest hour —the Gilberts invasion.[11]

Early Operations from the Gilberts

Seabees and Army aviation engineers set to work immediately on the newly captured islands, constructing two airfields on Tarawa Atoll, one on Makin and one on Abemama. The old Japanese field on Tarawa was reconditioned rapidly enough that CenCATS could bring in a transport plane on 26 November, three days after the capture.[12] Regularly scheduled passenger flights into Makin and Abemama began 16 December. On Christmas Day the forward echelon of 4th MBDAW began moving up to Tarawa from Funafuti, and on 2 January 1944 its rear echelon moved from Tutuila to Funafuti.

First Marine aviation unit to engage in combat from the new bases was VMSB-331,[13] which flew a detachment of six SBD's with ground maintenance men to Tarawa on 30 November to assist in patrol operations and possibly for strike purposes. The strike came off 21 December when 5 of the dive bombers, together with 12 Army B-24's and 15 Navy F6F's, attacked shipping at Jaluit. The Squadron claimed to sink a 6,000-7,000-ton AK in the Jaluit lagoon, but postwar records make it fairly clear that what they hit was the 1,912-ton *Goryu Maru,* a converted water tender which had already been bombed on 20 November by two TBF's from *Yorktown,* and beached.[14] This was the only offensive action by a 4th MBDAW unit until 4 March 1944.

The planes of VMSB-331 returned from Tarawa to Nukufetau, where the

---

[11] Exception: two air raids on Funafuti 13 and 17 November. In the first, two planes burned. In the second two Seabees were killed and one B-24 and a C-47 were destroyed. (CinCPac war diary, November 1943.)

[12] Major Edmund L. Zonne, executive officer of VMJ-353, and Lieut. Donald C. Popalisky landed the first transport on Tarawa.

[13] 4th MBDAW history, pp 6, 18.

[14] VT-5 action report, 20 November; VMBF-331 history, p 5; interrogation of Ensign Tasaki in USSBS, *The American Campaign Against Wotje, Maloelap, Mille and Jaluit* (hereinafter cited as *Wotje, Maloelap, Mille and Jaluit*), p 292. Warrant Officer Yanemoto says the *Soryu Maru* [sic] was sunk in October or November, but the last of five 70-ton interisland ships survived until February (p 291); Warrant Officer Tanaka agrees with Tasaki that the last large steamship arrived at Jaluit in November (p 283). Photographs of the beached *Goryu Maru* are on pp 342–343 of the last-cited work. JANAC (p 52) puts the date of the ship's "sinking" at 4 February 1944, and credits it to Navy land-based aircraft, but this appears to be erroneous also.

Squadron was transferred on 1 January from MAG-31 to MAG-13 in one of several shifts preparatory to operations in the Marshalls.

Plans for the invasion of the Marshalls again relegated Marine planes to rear-area (i.e., the Gilberts and Ellices) search and patrol, transport or garrison aircraft (which would be pushed up into the foremost areas as soon as there were new air bases where single-engined, land-based planes could be used).

MAG-13, now commanded by Colonel Lawrence Norman, became an all-dive-bomber group with the shift of VMSB-331 and the addition of VMSB-231 (Major Elmer Glidden) from Hawaii. MAG-13 had headquarters at Majuro, after that island was seized 31 January by the 2d Battalion of the 106th Infantry (27th Infantry Division).

Colonel Calvin R. Freeman's MAG-31 for purposes of Marshalls operations became a fighter group. It was destined for Roi Island, at the northern end of Kwajalein Atoll, when it was secured. Three fighter squadrons joined the group 1 January: VMF-111 (Major J. Frank Cole), VMF-224 (Major D. D. Irwin), VMF-441 (Major James B. Moore). Two weeks later VMF-113 (Major L. D. Everton) was added, and on the same day the first night-fighter squadron in the Central Pacific, VMF(N)-532 (Major Everette H. Vaughan) arrived at Tarawa, which had been pestered by some 30 minor night raids between the Gilberts and Marshalls landings.[15]

Many of these assignments lasted only a few weeks, since the mobility of Marine aviation required frequent shifts to suit rapidly changing situations.

A third group of the 4th MBDAW labeled for the Marshalls was MAG-22 (Colonel James M. Daly), which rejoined after having been relieved at long last from its monotonous duty on Midway.

A Squadron is Lost[16]

One of Daly's squadrons, VMF-422, was detached from the group at Midway 15 December and flown by transport planes to Ewa. There its 40 pilots (who averaged about 500 hours flying time, including 100 to 180 hours in F4U's) received 24 new Corsairs from MAHA. Twenty-seven of the pilots went on board the escort carrier *Kalinin Bay* 17 January with the new planes. The ship arrived off Tarawa 24 January, and the planes were catapulted that morning, landing at Hawkins Field, Tarawa, between 0900 and 1100.

Admiral Hoover, who had assumed direct operational command of garrison aircraft on 11 January, ordered the new squadron to Funafuti pending its disposition in the FLINTLOCK (Marshalls) operation. General Merritt had

---

[15] USSBS, *The Seventh and Eleventh Air Forces Against Japan*, p 6.

[16] Primary sources: VMF-422 history and war diary; record of Board of Investigation 15 February 1944; Com TF 57 serial 00296, 4 April 1944; memo CNO to Acting SecNav, serial 3256, 4 May 1944; CNO serial 3310, 8 May 1944; explanatory letter Merritt to CMC 13 August 1945, addenda to same 9 January 1946.

no operational control over the Squadron, but he directed his operations officer, Colonel Lawrence T. Burke, to inform Major John S. MacLaughlin Jr., the Squadron commander. Major MacLaughlin asked whether an escort plane would be provided for the 700-mile flight to Funafuti (with a stopover at Nanomea, 463 miles from Tarawa), but did not request one, as he was privileged to do.

The staff aerologist on board *Curtiss* reported that the weather was good from Tarawa to a few miles north of Nanomea. From there to Funafuti scattered showers and squalls could be expected, with flying conditions undesirable in the showers. MacLaughlin was furnished with charts, navigational aids and maps, and staff officers discussed general plans for the flight with him, which he passed along to his pilots.

After spending the night of 24 January on board the converted yacht *Southern Seas,* the pilots of VMF-422 went ashore and were briefed again by Major MacLaughlin. It was never known whether he saw a new weather report, posted on the bulletin board at 0830, which showed the weather in the islands slightly worse than it had been on the previous day (this news itself was 14 hours old by the time it was received and posted).

At about 0930, 23 pilots of VMF-422 took off for Nanomea, about two and a half hour's flying time from Tarawa, with a margin of 211 gallons, good an additional 3 hours and 50 minutes.[17] But the gasoline consumption situation was almost the only feature of the flight which could be called satisfactory, as the board of investigation report shows:

> It was planned to communicate with the operations towers on the various fields in the Gilbert and Ellice Islands on 6970 kilocycles, which according to the communication plan all of them guarded, and to communicate between [sic] on that frequency also. The ZB was not calibrated and could not be used. The radio aids data were incomplete. The voice calls for the bases were not listed. The range legs bearings for the Funafuti range were not given. It was not stated which quadrants of the Nanomea range were A and which were N quadrants. The flight was not cleared by anyone at Hawkins Field. After it departed, an enlisted man on watch in the tower called Lieutenant Sandlin at the Air Command Post, telling him of its departure and saying he understood its destination was Funafuti. Lieutenant Sandlin sent a departure report to Funafuti. . . . Nothing was sent to Nanomea telling of the flight until requested by Nanomea. At no time was the Island Commander officially advised of the proposed flight, although the Island Operations officer and his assistant at Hawkins Field were aware that it was to be made and of the approximate time of take-off. The Island Operations Officer would have provided an escort had he known about the flight and considered the flight to be under his orders.

---

[17] One pilot had starter trouble and did not get off.

The 23 F4U's flew about 400 miles through fair weather without incident, following the long row of the southern Gilberts on the left as check points. Then about 1210—15 minutes short of Nanomea—they ran into bad weather. The flight dropped down to 200 feet as it entered a heavy cloud. About 1225 Major MacLaughlin unaccountably made a sharp left turn and the Squadron followed him with some difficulty; after more turns in several directions everyone lost his way. Three of the pilots lost contact with the others, who managed to stay together.

Of these three, Captain John F. Rogers was not heard of again. Lieut. John E. Hansen managed to get the dial setting for Funafuti from one of the other pilots and flew on to that base, landing with 80 gallons of fuel. The third, Lieut. Walter A. Wilson, landed on the island of Niutao, where the natives took good care of him until he was rescued by a destroyer.

The 20 pilots who remained together came into a clear area after about an hour, passing over a Higgins boat and another small craft, and then circling over Nui Island—about halfway between Nanomea and Funafuti. One pilot, Lieut. Christian F. Lauesen, made a water landing after he reported engine trouble. Lieut. Robert C. Lehnert bailed out to help him, but never saw him between then and the time he himself was picked up 48 hours later. The 18 remaining planes orbited, then flew probably southeasterly until they entered another squall. Major MacLaughlin was lost after turning over the lead to Captain Cloyd R. Jeans. Into the tropical storm Lieut. Earl C. Thompson disappeared and was not seen again. That left 16. One of them, Lieut. Robert P. Moran, became separated but at 1420 managed to contact Nanomea (which had been plotting the flight by radar since 1225 at 10 to 70 miles distance). Nanomea—which had not been advised of the flight and assumed it consisted of bombers—said fly 260° magnetic. Lieut. Moran bailed out over Nui but became entangled in his shroud lines and drowned in the heavy surf. He was buried by the natives.

Now there were 15. Two pilots advised Captain Jeans they would have to land shortly. Captain Jeans decided that all should land and remain together. Thirteen planes hit the water together; the other two landed seven miles apart and some distance from the main group. One of the two, Lieut. William A. Aycrigg II, was never found; the other was picked up by a destroyer. The group of 13 stuck together for two days in 12 one-man rubber boats. They were finally sighted by a PBY-5A of VP-53 about 100 miles WSW of Funafuti, but the rescue plane was damaged in landing and the destroyer *Hobby* had to rescue the lot.

Total cost to VMF-422 of this series of errors: 6 pilots and 22 planes.

Invasion of the Marshalls

The Gilberts assault was followed immediately by heavier raids on the Marshalls. During December Army and Navy land-based bombers of TF 57 made 46 attacks on the Marshalls (550 tons) and Nauru (28 tons)—about 60 per cent of the tonnage being dropped by B-24's and PB4Y's. AA fire was frequently intense, especially over Maloelap, and 12 heavy bombers were lost.

Compared to the other main theaters, the new Central Pacific was as yet only an infant. In December, including carrier strikes, only 1,154 sorties were flown in the Central Pacific, as against 4,411 in SoPac and 6,113 in SoWesPac.[18]

The same was true in January, although the number of planes stationed on the new Gilberts airfields rose from 125 to 350 during the month. Comparative figures of sorties flown were: CenPac 1,161, SoPac 3,815, SoWesPac 4,550.[19]

Marine aviation units during January spent their time getting ready to move into the Marshalls as soon as those islands were seized. The only mention of Marine aviation in the January operations in POA survey concerns the loss of VMF-422, together with the comment that "planes in the Ellice Islands were used on few occasions."

At noon on 3 February the forward echelon of VMSB-231 arrived at Majuro in the heart of the enemy-held Marshalls. The Seabees completed the airfield 19 February, and on the 21st Major Glidden led in the Squadron's SBD's from CVE *Gambier Bay*. Five days later VMSB-331 arrived. For the next eight months these two MAG-13 squadrons alternated in trying to keep the Japanese battered and bewildered on the by-passed islands, 231 one day, 331 the next.

MAG-31 moved up to Roi about the same time, arriving 7 February, five days after the 4th Marine Division captured the twin islands of Roi–Namur, and only two days after the last Japanese were killed by the 7th Infantry Division on Kwajalein Island, 50 miles to the south. At 0230 on 12 February the Japanese, flying 12 to 14 seaplanes from Ponape, made a devastating raid on the embryonic base, hitting a bomb dump in an old crater and creating a tremendous blast. The resultant casualties were the greatest to any land target since December 1941: 26 killed, 130 wounded, including 5 enlisted men killed and 67 enlisted men and 6 officers wounded from MAG-31.[20] Eighty per cent of the supplies and 20 per cent of the construction equipment on Roi were destroyed or damaged. Approximately 100 officers and men of MAG-31 lost all their clothing, equipment and personal effects.[21] The Marine wounded were sent back to Pearl Harbor in the ship that brought them. No planes

---

[18] *Operations in POA*, December 1943, p 5.

[19] *Ibid*, January 1944, plate 4. In February, however, when the fast-carrier task force came into its own with the Marshalls invasions and the Truk and Marianas raids, emphasis shifted to the Central Pacific: Carriers 6,407 sorties, CenPac 1,110, SoPac 4,736, SoWesPac 4,110. (*Ibid*, February 1944, plate 1.)

[20] *Ibid*, February 1944, p 9; MAG-31 history, p 7; Bureau of Yards and Docks, *Building the Navy's Bases in World War II*, Vol II, p 322, says 157 casualties were incurred by its two Seabee battalions ashore, which, with the Marines added, would bring the total to 235 instead of 156.

[21] MAG-31 war diary, February 1944.

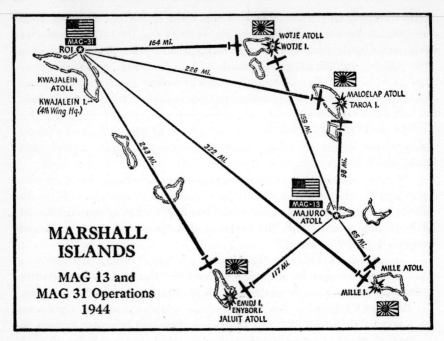

MARSHALL
ISLANDS

MAG 13 and
MAG 31 Operations
1944

were available to intercept the raiders, who fouled the radar scopes with large amounts of window.[22]

Seventeen planes of MAG-31 arrived at Roi 15 February and began day and night combat air patrol immediately. Ten pilots of VMF-224 arrived from Funafuti and started flying the next day. To intercept the night intruders seven planes of VMF(N)-532 were brought up from Tarawa, where the SCR-527 ground radar had been performing miserably during the frequent small raids (real or imaginary). Major Vaughan brought the seven F4U-2's via Makin to Roi, accompanied by two CenCATS R4D's of VMJ-353 which flew in with the fighter controllers and their crews and a skeleton ground crew. The seven remaining night fighters were led in by Captain Nathan Bedell on 23 February.[23]

The capture of Eniwetok (wanted as a fleet base) was scheduled for 10 May, but the quick success of the Kwajalein invasion inspired the high command to make the 340-mile westward hop immediately, using the 22d Marines and 106th Infantry which had been brought along as a Kwajalein reserve.[24] The invasion was timed to coincide with the great carrier task force raid on Truk 16–17 February.

---

[22] Window = metal strips cut into various lengths, depending on the wave lengths to be jammed. (See *Marine Corps Gazette*, April 1946, pp 46–48.)

[23] VMF(N)-532 history, pp 8, 9.

[24] General H. M. Smith, *Coral and Brass*, p 149, says he had the Eniwetok plans in his hip pocket and sprang them on Admirals Turner and Spruance as soon as Kwajalein came off quickly and successfully.

On 18 February Engebi Island at the north end of the Eniwetok Atoll was seized in less than eight hours by two battalions of the 22d Marines, who finally found a shooting war after 18 months on Upolu, Wallis and Savaii. Then soldiers and marines moved south to grab Eniwetok Island and a few days later the 22d Marines took the third important (and toughest) island of the atoll, Parry. Most of the 3,400 Japanese on the atoll had arrived within the past six weeks; the rapidity of the invasion had not allowed them time to build up the defenses after the fashion of Tarawa. Many guns and fortification materials had not yet been emplaced.[25] But the Japanese fought like fiends, killing 200 Americans and wounding 500 before they were slain.

The Marine aviation units were not far behind the assault troops. In fact, one squadron mechanic of VMF-422 was wounded aboard *LST 484* as his ship lay inside Eniwetok Lagoon on 17 February.[26] The ground echelon of VMF-113 went ashore on 19 February at Engebi while mopping-up operations were still in progress, and had a view of what was to be its new base:

> The unsuspecting initiates were confronted with a disturbing scene as they looked over the newly won island. Enemy dead were grotesquely strewn over the landscape. Duds varying from 14-inch shells to grenades littered the battleground. All types of enemy ordnance and material, as well as Marine, were scattered over the scarred surface of Engebi. . . . All hands set to work and before the sun reached its high point on February 20, temporary shelters had been erected with many a bomb crater serving as an expedient foxhole.[27]

Colonel Daly and MAG-22 headquarters arrived at Engebi 20 February. One flight echelon of VMSB-151 (Major Gordon H. Knott) flew up from Wallis Island, 2,000 miles to the southeast, arriving on 29 February after a five-day flight, to begin reef patrols and antisubmarine patrols. The other echelon remained at Roi to fly patrols and cover minor Marshall Islands landings. Everton's VMF-113 had arrived 27 February from Kwajalein.

On 27 February a detachment of eight planes of VMF(N)-532 was ordered from Roi to Engebi. The Squadron was split between the two bases until 11 June, its duty to protect all the Marshalls airfields. Air Warning Squadron One (AWS-1, Captain William D. Felder Jr.) with 9 officers and 218 enlisted men arrived from the West Coast on 20 February, unloaded its radars (1 SCR-270, 1 SCR-527) and on 1 March assumed primary control of all aircraft in the area, including the two day-fighter squadrons, the VMF(N)-532 detachment and VMSB-151. A similar function was performed by the Navy's Argus 22 at Eniwetok.

The first enemy strike on Engebi, eight planes, occurred 8 March. AWS-1

---

[25] *Operations in POA*, February 1944, annex B, p 4; USSBS, *Campaigns*, p 194.
[26] VMF-422 history, p 25.
[27] *Ibid.*

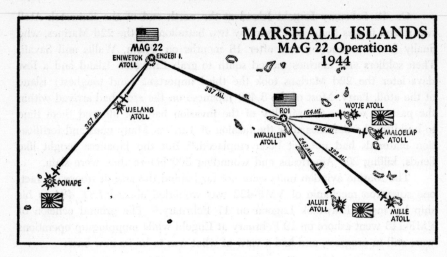

radars picked up the bogeys at 0332. One plane was on night patrol and another was sent up to intercept, but the fighter-direction altitude reading was erroneous, and neither plane made contact.[28] The Japanese employed several clever devices: they used window, and sent a decoy to lure the interceptors away from the main attack. The first bomb drop at 0407 knocked out the ground radar, and the next eliminated VHF communication. The intruders stayed an hour and a half and made three bombing runs. Total Marine casualties: 1 killed, 7 wounded.

On the night of 14 April VMF(N)-532 made the Marines' first successful interception by F4U night fighters. Lieut. Edward A. Sovik was able to reach 20,000 feet in ten minutes and explode an enemy plane four minutes after that; Captain Howard W. Bollman shot down another with which he almost collided. Both explosions were witnessed by ground observers. One pilot was lost: Lieut. Donald Spatz, whose plane the Argus unit at Eniwetok confused with another—he was given an erroneous vector which led him out of control range, and he did not return. Lieut. Joel E. Bonner Jr. got a "probable" on a Japanese bomber, but his own plane in turn was so damaged that he was forced to parachute. A destroyer rescued him.

All enemy bombs fell into the water. Three controllers of AWS-1, Captain Reinert M. Torgerson, and Lieuts. William W. Thames and Frank G. McClintock, received CinCPac commendations for directing the planes to successful interceptions.

March Operations

On 9 March General Merritt moved his Wing's forward echelon again: from Tarawa to Kwajalein. The Wing was augmented on 1 April by the addition of MAG-15 (Lieut. Colonel Ben Z. Redfield) which had expected

---

[28] MAG-22 history, p 77; VMF(N)-532 history, p 10; AWS-1 history, p 8.

to get overseas since its formation two years previously, but had served as a training group for transport, observation and photographic squadrons at Camp Kearney on the West Coast.[29] VMJ-252 and VMJ-353 were attached to the MAG upon its arrival at Abemama. The Group became one part of Transport Air Group (TAG), successor to CenCATS; the other part was the Army's 9th Troop Carrier Squadron. TAG took up where CenCATS left off, flying from Samoa to Engebi, with stops at Funafuti, Nanomea, Tarawa, Makin, Majuro, Kwajalein, Roi and Eniwetok. The Army, Navy and Marines all operated TAG stations; however, the planes and personnel during this period were approximately 70 per cent Marine and 30 per cent Army.

On 4 March the 10 fighter and 4 bomber squadrons of the 4th MBDAW began their long, unrelenting attacks on the by-passed Marshalls atolls of Wotje, Maloelap, Mille and Jaluit.[30] On that date VMSB-331 made the first bombing mission staged from Majuro, against Jaluit. Forty per cent of the participating planes were hit by intense and accurate AA fire, indicating to the surprised pilots that the 498 tons of bombs dropped on Jaluit since November by Army and Navy planes had not eliminated all resistance.[31]

Next day VMSB-231 struck back at the Jaluit AA battery. Thus began the schedule of alternating missions between the two Majuro-based SBD squadrons.

It should not be supposed that the 4th MBDAW squadrons were invading virgin territory when the mission of bombing the by-passed Marshalls was handed them. Army and Navy planes—principally Seventh Air Force bombers, of which 11 squadrons were on hand[32]—had been bombing the four islands for four months before marines started. The Army continued to hit the islands until the Seventh moved to Saipan in the summer of 1944, and land-based Navy planes flew intermittent strikes throughout 1944. Carrier planes had flown 1,671 sorties against the Marshalls before the Marines began. Postwar interrogations indicate that a high percentage of the damage to the four islands occurred before March. No more air opposition was encountered in the Marshalls after 30 January.[33]

The effects of the long bombing campaign against the battered atolls as disclosed in postwar surveys of the thorough USSBS volume, *The American Campaign Against Wotje, Maloelap, Mille and Jaluit*, are discussed in the next chapter. The job was tiresome and monotonous and without much glory, but the Marines were assigned to this rear-area task and they carried out their assignment, faithfully if not always cheerfully.

---

[29] MAG-15 history, p 1.

[30] During March and April all the rest of the 32 islands and atolls of the Marshalls were occupied by marines or soldiers, including one named Bikini which was outposted by five Japanese who committed suicide. Most of the islands held no enemy. (*Operations in POA,* March 1944, p 4.)

[31] VMSB-331 history, p 6. The bomb tonnage is from USSBS, *Wotje, Maloelap, Mille and Jaluit,* table 2, p 360.

[32] USSBS, *The Seventh and Eleventh Air Forces Against Japan,* p 5.

[33] *Ibid.*

One of the more interesting experiments conducted by the 4th MBDAW, with the by-passed islands as their laboratory, was the use of the fighter plane as a dive bomber—a technique which was subsequently adopted by the Navy's carriers with resultant additional fire power to protect the ships against *kamikaze* tactics.

The F4U was used as a fighter bomber for the first time in the Marshalls on 18 March when eight Makin-based Corsairs of VMF-111 dropped 1,000-pound bombs on Mille's AA installations.[34] Subsequent experiments revealed that the F4U could be safely and efficiently employed as a dive bomber in dives up to 85°. The plane's six .50-caliber guns were used for strafing in the latter stages of the dive.

The only wholesale kills made by 4th MBDAW planes came in the Marines' first strike against the Carolines. Ponape, 367 miles southwest of Eniwetok, was an enemy supply center for the Marshalls and the most important Carolines island except the Truk and Palau islands to the westward.[35] It was first attacked by 42 Seventh Air Force B-24's on 15 February in a supporting operation for the Eniwetok invasion.[36] The AAF planes hit the island several times again in February. On 28 March six F4U's of VMF-113 escorted four B-25's of the AAF's 48th Bomber Squadron to Ponape for the first time, flushed 12 Japanese planes, shot down 8 of them, and destroyed 1 on the ground. Two Zekes were credited to the Squadron CO, Major Everton, the others to Captain Frank C. Drury (1), Lieuts. Joe V. Schellack (2½), Emmett O. Anglin (1), Bernard A. Nelson (½), and Master Sergeant Peter Tunno (1). In addition Nelson destroyed one on the ground. The only other planes shot down in the Central Pacific during 1944 were those two by VMF(N)-532 on 14 April.

VMF's 113 and 422 and VMSB-151 made several other missions to Ponape during March and April, but enemy planes were not encountered again. The 4th MBDAW squadrons thereupon reverted to bombing the by-passed Marshalls.

---

[34] VMF-111 ACA report No 1. The Navy's VF-17 had begun similar experiments a month earlier, with Rabaul as the target. Both Navy and Marine pilots used home-made bomb racks.

[35] After the war many sailors judged Ponape as the prettiest ex-Japanese island in the Pacific.

[36] USSBS, *The Seventh and Eleventh Air Forces Against Japan*, p 5.

CHAPTER SIXTEEN

The Doldrums of 1944—I

Assignment to the Rear Areas

WHEN HE PULLED the Combined Fleet out of Truk on 10 February Admiral Koga had no intention of returning,[1] but the danger at Truk was apparent. In Allied hands it could become the advanced base where South Pacific and Central Pacific forces might join for the assault on Japan's inner ring of defenses. Therefore, during 1944 the Japanese built up Truk to something resembling what the Americans thought it was all along. The Army sent in troops; pillboxes and minefields were installed; coast defense and AA guns were emplaced; the Navy brought in torpedo boats and rocket launchers and built eight stations from which one-man torpedoes could set out for suicidal night attacks.[2]

On 12 March the JCS ordered the neutralization, rather than the capture, of Truk.[3] The belated build-up of Truk's defenses never exacted the toll of American invaders which the Japanese intended and, like the by-passed Marshalls and Rabaul, Truk was left to wither on the vine, forever harassed by long-range Army and Navy bombers based on the Admiralties and Marshalls.

Canceling Truk erased a job for the Marine aviators and relegated them to the by-passed islands. Following the seizure of Satawan, 160 miles south of Truk, Moen Island in Truk was due for attack (on D plus 2). The latter would have served as a base for 20 squadrons of Marine fighters and dive bombers to support the rest of the five-division (three Marine, two Army) show on Truk.[4]

The trouble with by-passed bases is that they don't simply wither without constant artificial scorching. Somebody has to keep them shriveled lest they bloom again.

There was not much glory in the monotonous bombing of something far to the rear; *homo sapiens* was constituted by his Maker to face forward. So far as credit back home was concerned—and, oh, how important is that credit to the man in uniform!—it was the front lines that made the front pages. The

---

[1] USSBS, *The Reduction of Truk*, p 4.
[2] *Ibid.*
[3] JCS No 71469. See p 265.
[4] JCS ROADMASTER study, 26 February 1944.

number of enemy planes shot down in the rear areas was negligible. The tonnage of ships sunk "is not as impressive as that of other forces," but "their daily sorties kept the stopper in the bottle, forcing the Japanese to use submarines for supply which might otherwise have been used to destroy Allied shipping."[5]

The Strategic Bombing Survey also concluded that "our air attacks on these by-passed positions were often continued longer and in greater weight than was reasonably required or profitable."[6] This does not take into account the invaluable training provided by the by-passed targets—for Okinawa in the case of the Marshalls, for the Philippines and Kyushu in the case of Rabaul. During the long, bitter fighting on Okinawa it required a rash intelligence officer to predict that the invasion of Kyushu would not be necessary come autumn of 1945.

The forces attacking the by-passed Japanese positions also had the duty to protect their own rear areas. Considering the Japanese impulse toward suicide, it is remarkable that more one-way sorties were not attempted. If a few planes or a few warships had been sneaked into the Marshalls or into Truk or Rabaul, the Japanese could not have changed the course of the war but they could have upset plans and time tables and socked the U.S. Fleet with heavy casualties.

A few such attempts were made, notably the suicide attack starting from Kyushu for the great Navy anchorage at Ulithi at 1900 on 11 March 1945, when two *kamikazes* of a flight of 24 committed suicide (one dived into a small island, the other into the carrier *Randolph*).[7] Besides this, the Japanese made a dozen attacks, suicidal and orthodox, on the B-29 bases at Saipan and Tinian in November and December 1944. Those were not exactly comparable to the Ulithi act, since the Marianas were not so far to the rear and since some of the attackers did return. But it was remarkable that the enemy waited four months after the Marianas invasion to make such attacks. A total of 12 U.S. planes was destroyed, 10 badly damaged and 45 slightly damaged.[8]

The most fantastic attack never came off. Postwar reports disclosed that a force of 150 to 200 Japanese Navy transport planes and bombers was being assembled in the Hokkaido–Northern Honshu area five days before the war ended. The plan: 1,500 to 2,000 airborne troops to make suicide attacks on the Marianas bases somewhat after the fashion of the Japanese Army's airborne landings on Yontan airfield, Okinawa. This was on the day the second atomic bomb was dropped, on Nagasaki, long after Iwo Jima and Okinawa had been captured. Considering that the Marianas were far to the rear, it is possible that the American defenders might have been caught unprepared and great havoc might have been spread among about 1,000 B-29's. Fortunately, the

---

[5] USSBS, *Campaigns*, p 380.

[6] USSBS, *Summary Report (Pacific War)*, p 13.

[7] WDC No 160575, Group 42, Item 42KK, p 1, filed in FDB Library. USSBS, *Japanese Air Power*, p 65, says the 24 planes were twin-engined bombers.

[8] *Operations in POA*, November 1944 (pp 25–26), December 1944 (pp 25–26). During the period the Japanese lost 19 planes to AA, 10 to U.S. fighters.

attack never happened because Halsey's fast-carrier task forces caught the assembled aircraft on the ground 9–10 August and destroyed them.[9]

But the threat of such attacks kept American commanders alert throughout the war. In January 1945 Rear Admiral Harold B. Sallada, commanding the Marshalls–Gilberts area, was ordered to slow down the bombing of those well-pulverized islands;[10] in February only 30 tons were dropped on Maloelap and Mille, none at all on Jaluit and Wotje. But under his successor, Rear Admiral William Keen Harrill, the bombing was resumed. In March the 4th MAW flew 214 sorties, dropped 140 tons on the four atolls.[11]

Also in March, a converted B-24 bomber carrying Lieut. General Millard F. Harmon USA from the Marianas to Honolulu mysteriously disappeared somewhere between the Marshalls and Wake Island. This caused many officers to believe the Japanese had sneaked a plane into one of the islands; some puzzling enemy radio transmissions that night enhanced the enigma. During April and May the bombing of the islands was stepped up again.[12]

The threat which haunted American commanders in the Marshalls was noted by the Strategic Bombing Survey:

> It was always theoretically possible for the enemy to fly in bombers and stage damaging raids upon our supply line; moreover he was able to defend the bases from which such attacks might come, since his AA fire, while diminishing in intensity, was still potent. Even when our capture of bases in the southern Marianas blocked off one of his supply routes, there were still two left by which he could fly planes to his by-passed positions. For this reason, continued neutralization was necessary.[13]

The bombing of the by-passed islands went on. Even Wake, one of the most isolated atolls in Japanese hands, was occasionally visited by Army or Navy planes and by warships—1,982 tons of bombs and several thousand rounds of naval gunfire fell on Wake between 23 December 1941 and the acceptance of the Japanese surrender. During this period 700 to 800 Japanese died under the American bombs or guns, and 1,500 others starved to death, too weak even to catch the rats which enabled survivors to live.[14]

---

[9] USSBS, *Campaigns*, p 339, and *Japanese Air Power*, p 60; *U.S. Navy at War*, p 189. General MacArthur suspected that a mass attack on Okinawa was in the making, and requested Halsey to shift from Kyushu to the northern Honshu–Hokkaido area. In this area on 9–10 August Admiral Halsey's total claims of planes destroyed or damaged were 720 (*Admiral Halsey's Story*, pp 266–267.

[10] CinCPOA to ComMarGils, 17 January 1945.

[11] Interview Major General Louis E. Woods, 11 January 1949: USSBS, *Wotje, Maloelap, Mille and Jaluit*, pp 28–31.

[12] *Ibid.* The Harmon mystery was never solved. It is the belief of General Woods (then CG 4th MAW) that the plane simply blew up, possibly from gasoline fumes igniting.

[13] USSBS, *The Seventh and Eleventh Air Forces in the War Against Japan*, p 10.

[14] USSBS, *The Reduction of Wake Island*, pp 14, 21.

Mountainous Nauru—once a target for invasion—was isolated even farther to the south than Wake to the north. On 28 November 1944 VMF-441 planes, staging through Tarawa, bombed Nauru—then 2,600 miles behind the front lines in the Philippines, 1,571 miles behind the Marianas.[15]

The Marshalls[16]

Until late 1943 the Japanese had in the Marshalls and Gilberts vicinity eight air strips (Mille, Maloelap, Wotje, Kwajalein, Eniwetok, Nauru, Tarawa, Wake) and two seaplane bases (Jaluit, Makin).

The seizure of Tarawa and Makin left them with seven air bases and one seaplane base. When Kwajalein and Eniwetok were taken, all the others had been leapfrogged. Wake and Nauru were kept subdued almost wholly by Army and Navy planes and guns. Until March 1944, so were the four main atolls of the Marshalls—Wotje, Maloelap, Mille, Jaluit—then the 4th MBDAW completed its move forward to take over most of the burden. By this time all Japanese aviation had been eliminated from the four islands; all the Marines had to do was keep the Marshalls quiet and despondent.

The Marshall Islands had been under Japanese domination since the Versailles Treaty gave them the mandate in 1920. Contrary to widely held wartime theories, the Japanese had not been fortifying the islands for twenty years in anticipation of waging war. In the 1930's an airstrip had been built at Roi, one of the northern islands of the big Kwajalein Atoll; on Kwajalein Island a potential supply center for the whole area existed. But the defenses of these "islands of mystery" were not started until 1941, and most of the building took place after the war began.

All four of the by-passed atolls reached their peak strength shortly after the American invasion of the Gilberts. Apparently the Japanese had intended to garrison each with 4,000 to 5,000 troops, but only Mille reached its proposed strength. Maximum strength (13,701) was divided as follows:

Mille	5,101	(Navy 2,500, Army 2,600, civilians 1)
Wotje	3,298	(Navy 2,103, Army 429, civilians 766)
Jaluit	2,205	(Navy 1,401, Army 719, civilians 85)
Maloelap	3,097	(Navy 1,772, Army 368, civilians 957)

The defenses for each atoll consisted mainly of AA and coast-defense guns of all calibers, with large stocks of ammunition. The number of pillboxes and beach mines varied, depending on the atoll commander's industry and ingenuity. Wotje, for example, was well prepared to resist a landing attempt; Mille's beach defenses were relatively weak, consisting of several widely dispersed minefields, few underwater obstructions and wire entanglements.

The coast defense system on Taroa Island (Maloelap), controlled by

---

[15] MAG-31 history, p 17.

[16] The principal source hereinafter is USSBS, *The American Campaign Against Wotje, Maloelap, Mille and Jaluit.*

seven observation posts and three fire-control stations, was average for the four atolls:

coast-defense guns, 15-cm.	8
coast-defense guns, 12-cm.	2
AA dual-purpose guns, 12.7-cm., twin-mount	5
AA guns, 25-mm., twin-mount	3
AA guns, 20-mm.	2
AA guns, 13.2-mm.	21
AA guns, 7.7-mm.	7
AA guns, 6.5-mm.	35
howitzers, 15-cm.	4
infantry guns, 7-cm.	2
naval infantry guns, 5-cm.	1

By the end of 1941 airstrips had been constructed on Wotje and Maloelap. Wotje was also a seaplane base, and similar facilities were started at Jaluit. The first pioneer detachment did not arrive at Mille to start building anything until April 1942.

Only Maloelap had any planes during the first few months of the war— 20 twin-engined bombers and 15 fighters operated from there. When the Mille strip was completed in November 1942, 12 twin-engined Nells came in. The total number of planes in the four atolls never exceeded 65 during 1942.

The Japanese fed small units into the Marshalls throughout 1943: 30 to 40 bombers and 50 fighters to Maloelap, 14 or 15 float planes to Jaluit, a dozen Zekes and twice as many Val dive bombers to Mille, a few flying boats to Wotje.

In November, when Admiral Koga was trying to decide whether to stop the Americans in the South or Central Pacific—he wasn't strong enough to shoot the works in both places—the dive bombers were pulled out of Mille and sent to Rabaul. Koga partially compensated for this shift by sending 20 Kates (torpedo bombers) to Wotje in December, but he changed his mind again in January and pulled the six survivors of this squadron, plus the Wotje flying boats, back to Truk. There they met their fate in Mitscher's February raid.

The Marines Start to Work

As has been noted, Army and Navy planes eliminated all Marshalls air opposition and sank what sizable ships were left.

The daily milk runs were shared by Army and Navy planes and marines of MAG's 13, 22 and 31. Insofar as the Marines are concerned, there is a monotonous consistency in the chronological reports:

24 March: 13 Marine SBD's of 231 and 12 Corsairs of VMF-224 and VMF-331 dropped six tons of bombs on the Wotje radio station.

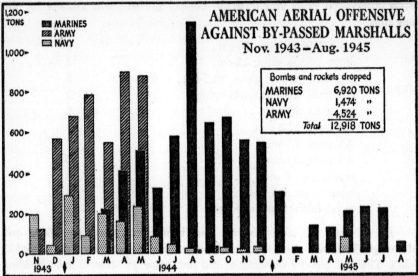

AMERICAN AERIAL OFFENSIVE AGAINST BY-PASSED MARSHALLS
Nov. 1943 – Aug. 1945

Bombs and rockets dropped

MARINES	6,920 TONS
NAVY	1,474 "
ARMY	4,524 "
Total	12,918 TONS

Source: U.S.S.B.S.- The American Campaign Against Wotje, Maloelap, Mille and Jaluit

27 March: VMSB-231, based at Majuro, and VMF-311, based at Roi, coordinated with VF-39 in an attack on Wotje. VMF-224 Corsairs dive-bombed Wotje.

30 March: Army, Navy and Marine planes joined in strikes on Wotje, Mille and Jaluit.

7 April: 13 U's of VMF-311 dive-bombed Wotje and two were slightly damaged by AA.

14 April: Wotje was strafed and bombed by Marine Corsairs and SBD's; Mille was hit by an Army B-25 and six Marine U's, while VF-39 dropped four tons of bombs on Taroa.

2 May: VMF-224 Corsairs hit the power plant at Wotje, blowing off the roof after direct hits by Major Jack W. Morrison, Lieuts. Edwin W. Nedbalek and Edward R. Agnew Jr.

4 May: Wotje was the target for 3,456 propaganda leaflets and 72 cans of salmon dropped by VMSB-331 and VF-39 while SBD's of the Ace of Spades Squadron (VMSB-231) bombed and strafed magazines, and the southeast coast-defense battery of Taroa and dropped propaganda leaflets and salmon there.

13 May: Jaluit was harassed during the night by SBD's dropping single bombs for an hour, while fighters of VMF-331 performed a similar mission on Mille.

15 June: (A day of momentous events on Saipan, 1,040 miles to the westward). Routine bombing of Wotje Island by VMF-224. The plane of Captain Edwin A. Tucker was hit by AA and pilot was forced to make a water landing in heavy swells. He was picked up by Dumbo but plane was lost.

In June the Seventh Air Force moved to the Marianas, leaving the Marshalls bombing in command of Brig. General Thomas J. Cushman, who had relieved General Merritt as CG 4th MBDAW 16 May. Cushman had besides his three Marine groups a Navy fighter squadron, VF-39.

Mid-1944 Moves

Until the thrust into the Marianas the 4th MBDAW had at least been as far forward as any other American units in the Central Pacific, although its pilots were facing most of the time toward the by-passed enemy. But, with exceptions noted below, notably VMO squadrons and MAG-21, Marine aviation was left far behind in both the South and Central Pacific.

It was with this in mind that Major General Rowell wrote to Brig. General Woods on 25 June: "At this writing I have one brigadier general and four or five colonels in MarAirSoPac who are out on a limb as to useful and active employment." General Woods might as well take his time about turning over the Director of Aviation job to Brig. General Field Harris, said the elder officer.

General Rowell himself was relieved on 16 September 1944.

Marine Aircraft Wings, Pacific (MAWPac), created 15 August 1942, was thereupon redesignated Aircraft, Fleet Marine Force, Pacific (AirFMFPac), and from this relatively late date in the war (September 1944) co-ordination between Admiral Nimitz's headquarters and Ewa steadily improved. It had long since become obvious that Marine flyers would stay in the background until they got on carriers. The escort-carrier program did not get under way until the fall, but in Washington Woods and Colonel A. D. Cooley were laying the keel despite opposition from some Navy and Marine quarters.

In the South Pacific 15 June was a notable date. SoPac commands had been absorbed by the Third Fleet, and administrative control of the area passed to ComSoWesPac. AirSoPac became a logistical command and Air-NorSols, activated the same day under General Mitchell, took command of tactical and operational functions of Solomons.

June 1944 to August 1945

The bombing of the Marshalls went on. A single pilot, Major Elmer Glidden, CO of VMSB-231, gained the nickname "Iron Man" after 104 dive-bombing missions. In August Louis Woods relieved General Cushman, and in September was promoted to major general. A month after that the 4th MBDAW became an honest-to-God Air Wing without the "Base Defense."[17]

---

[17] General Rowell had tried to have it thus designated in August 1942 in a letter to the Commandant. He said, "Such units may be employed defensively today and offensively tomorrow. . . . The use of the word 'defense' in designating a military unit tends to segregate it as a passive organization which is a term not conducive to the high morale that fosters the desirable offensive spirit of war."

At the end of 1944 the Navy withdrew its last Marshalls units excepting a few patrol bombers. For the rest of the war the Marines had the monotony largely to themselves,[18] though an occasional carrier unit took a swipe in passing.

On the four by-passed atolls 12,918 tons of bombs (including about 300 tons of napalm and rockets) were dropped between November 1943 and August 1945. Slightly more than half the total tonnage was the Marine effort. In addition, the same targets were shelled by 2,340 tons of naval gunfire.

What were the results of these most-harassed islands on earth?

Of 13,701 Japanese on the four atolls, 7,440 failed to survive.[19] Only 2,564 of these were killed in action—the rest starved or died of disease. On some of the islands the Japanese ate human flesh. On Mille 200 men were killed trying to dynamite fish, which provided oil to flavor boiled rats.

The high-level bombers of the Army burnt out a large proportion of the aviation facilities, barracks and storage areas on the four atolls. But after these were destroyed the effectiveness of pattern bombing from high levels was not great. The major installations, particularly gun emplacements, were targets for precision bombing. The postwar Strategic Bombing Survey party estimated that about 90 per cent of the installations on the four atolls were destroyed by Marine squadrons.[20]

None of Wotje's 14 heavy guns was operational at war's close, but 92 medium and light weapons survived to fight off low-level attacks to the bitter end. On Maloelap 50 of the 90 well-protected guns were destroyed; 8 of 11 command posts and fire-control points were obliterated. Twenty-two of Mille's 122 guns still fired at the end. On Jaluit only 26 of 66 guns were destroyed and only about half the vehicles and boats.

Against heavy reinforced concrete buildings—command posts, radio stations and communications centers—it was found necessary to use 1,000-pound semi-armor-piercing bombs or heavier general-purpose bombs, fuzed to allow maximum penetration. Targets suitable for napalm had already been burned out before its use became general. Rockets were not so effective as the American survey party hoped to find.

And Japanese morale? A few succumbed to the surrender leaflets and

---

[18] But in less strength. In April 1945 MAG's 22 and 31 went forward to Okinawa, leaving only two VMSB squadrons of MAG-13 (Lieut. Colonel Chauncey V. Burnett) and Colonel T. J. Walker's MAG-94 (which arrived in the Marshalls from Stateside in February) with two VMF's, one VMF(N), one VMSB, and one VMB. Until November 1944 MAG-94 had been designated MAG-34.

[19] Wotje 1,969; Maloelap 2,056; Mille 2,580; on Jaluit Rear Admiral Nisuke Masuda managed to keep his deaths down to 835. "No one starved," he said proudly, despite the fact that three F4U squadrons blanketed Jabor Town with napalm to kill all the pigs and chickens on 12 November 1944. Rather than face the Americans' questions about their prisoners of war, the Admiral declared, "It is now high time for me to choose death," and killed himself. It was indeed high time; he would have had to answer for American hobnails and one identification tag which were found in his crematorium. (USSBS, *Wotje, Maloelap, Mille and Jaluit*, pp 50, 295.)

[20] *Ibid.*

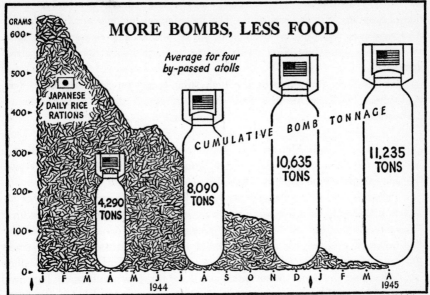

MORE BOMBS, LESS FOOD

Average for four by-passed atolls

JAPANESE DAILY RICE RATIONS

CUMULATIVE BOMB TONNAGE

4,290 TONS

8,090 TONS

10,635 TONS

11,235 TONS

GRAMS
600
500
400
300
200
100
0

J F M A M J J A S O N D J F M A
1944   1945

Source: U.S.S.B.S. – The American Campaign Against Wotje, Maloelap, Mille and Jaluit

swam out to American ships lying offshore. Some officers even admitted they had begun late in the war to disbelieve their own Domei broadcasts. But not on Jaluit, where the proud admiral kept up his men's morale—presumably he believed executing American flyers helped. Not until Okinawa, was serious consideration given to the possibility that Japan might lose the war. Such was the enemy's fanaticism.

The Price and the Yield

Marine losses in a year and a half of bombing the by-passed Marshalls were 16 officers and 6 enlisted men.[21] That is almost exactly 50 per cent of the total shot down over enemy territory: 16 officers and 5 men were rescued, chiefly through the skill and valor of standby destroyermen and Dumbo crews of VP-53, the same 4th MAW squadron which picked up 14 of ill-fated VMF-422's pilots. Nineteen officers and 7 men were wounded.

The exchange for a major share in killing or starving 7,440 enemy was cheap if such bookkeeping methods could be employed—which is impossible because all the other Pacific casualties would have to be added on both sides of the ledger, including even Bougainville and the rest of the Solomons which kept the enemy off the Central Pacific's neck. And the importance of killing the Marshalls Japanese enters the columns.

But the workout on the Marshalls contributed more than the deaths of

---

[21] At Wotje 9, Maloelap 7, Jaluit 4, Mille 2. (Information from Casualty Division, Hq USMC.)

the isolated little men on the unhappy atolls. The 4th MAW's perfection of the napalm fire jelly formula was a big contribution to the rest of the Pacific. Also important was the development of the fighter bomber, that trusty weapon so sorely needed when more planes had to be had to save the fleet from the *kamikaze*.

The indispensable role of the men "practicing" on Maloelap *et al* was made clear by Rear Admiral DeWitt C. Ramsey, Chief of the Bureau of Aeronautics:

> The Fourth Marine Air Wing in the Central Pacific has had opportunity to test fighter-bombing technique daily in large scale operations for the past nine months. Over 75 percent of the targets have been 50 feet or less in diameter whereas the normal dive bomber target is 200 feet in diameter. These targets in the main were Japanese gun positions which were eliminated one by one by fighter bombers. The Marine squadrons involved tried several techniques but the most effective for the Corsair seemed to be a 70–80 degree dive at a high speed. The Fourth Air Wing also developed low-altitude attacks at small targets, usually Japanese blockhouses 50 feet square and only 20 feet high, which have also been eliminated by bomb-carrying Marine fighters. A Marine fighter-bomber pilot just back from this work reported that he would like to have a try at some of the German targets, "and if they asked me to bomb a factory," he said, "my first question would be—what department?"[22]

Not all fighter-bombers were flown by marines. But all who manned fighter-bombers learned from textbooks written by the marines, chiefly over the atolls with the cacophonous names: Wotje, Maloelap, Mille and Jaluit.

The Other Ocean

No Marine aviation units were destined to serve in the European Theater of Operations; the only squadron based east of the United States after Pearl Harbor was VMS-3, which went to the Virgin Islands in 1934, and remained there until it was decommissioned in May 1944. During its wartime service it flew antisubmarine patrols and convoy escort missions, using successively J2F's, OS2U's and SBD's. The Squadron reported three submarine sightings but inflicted no damage on the Germans.[23]

---

[22] Statement to the press 27 December 1944. Op. 31, October 1944, "Data for Naval History of Second War," contains request of Chief BuAer to CG 4th MBDAW for testing the F4U-1D's ability to deliver three 1,000-pound bombs. The conclusion: ". . . easily carry and effectively deliver."

In October 1944 a 4th Wing directive changed VMSB's 231 and 331 to "VMBF" (bomber-fighter) upon exchanging their SBD's for F4U's. At this time the plane complement of all VF squadrons was increased to 24. The two squadrons reverted to "VMSB" on 30 December when they received SBD's again.

[23] VMS-3 war diaries.

In mid-1944, in the midst of the doldrums, a more exciting mission against the Germans was scheduled for MAG-51, then undergoing intensive training at Cherry Point. On 1 July the Group was assigned highest priority for rocket training (which was not then in the syllabus for Marine squadrons), and 27 pilots each were sent to Boca Chica, Fla., and Manteo, N.C., and 42 others to Quonset Point. The combat readiness of the group was already good, excepting that of VMF-514, the last squadron commissioned. An additional squadron, VMO-351, already in shape for combat, was assigned to MAG-51, joining VMF-514, VMF-511, VMF-512 and VMF-513.[24] This gave the Group a total of 125 F4U's.

Project CROSSBOW (known as DANNY to the Marines) was conceived after the German V-1 began battering England in June 1944, after the Allied landing on the Normandy beaches. The JCS picked the 11.75-inch aircraft rocket ("Tiny Tim"), which had been developed by scientists at California Institute of Technology as a weapon to knock out the buzz-bomb launching sites, and MAG-51 as an agent.

On 11 July MAG-51 was ordered to be ready six days later for transfer overseas with 60 planes. VMR-352[25] began immediately flying the Group's forward echelon matériel to Norfolk while the flight echelons completed their Tiny Tim training at Oak Grove, Inyokern, Boca Chica, Quonset and Manteo, meanwhile standing by for the signal to fly to Norfolk and be loaded on board a carrier.[26] The rear echelon, comprising the bulk of SMS-51, VMF-513 and VMF-514, continued rocket training.

But the reality lagged behind the hope. Tiny Tim was not yet in mass production. Only about two missiles per squadron could be assigned for training —most pilots had to sharpen their aim with dummies or 5-inch rockets. Cal Tech was still trying to lick the launching problem, even as the Group's gear piled up at Norfolk.[27] On 30 July the Group's two-day readiness status was canceled, the U.S. and British infantry had to capture the V-1 sites and Europe remained the Army, Navy and Air Force war.

The highly mobile Marine flyers had been told to get ready quickly for an emergency job with a new weapon. One day after the cancellation MAG-51's CO reported: "This group in performance of its mission completed rocket-projectile training and was prepared for movement overseas."[28]

---

[24] MAG-51 history; CominCh secret dispatch 302050 (June 1944); 9th MAW Special Order No 94A-1944; letter Colonel Edward L. Pugh, CO MAG-51 in 1944.

[25] In June and July 1944 all VMJ (utility) squadrons were redesignated VMR (transport); actually, these units had been transport, rather than simply utility, squadrons for nearly two years.

[26] Letter Colonel Edward L. Pugh to author, 22 February 1949.

[27] For Tiny Tim's troubles, see Baxter, *Scientists Against Time*, p 210.

[28] Pugh report, 31 July 1944. An interesting account of heavy bombers' troubles with the V-weapon sites may be found in Craven and Cate, *The AAF in WW II*, Vol III, pp 84–106, 525–546.

CHAPTER SEVENTEEN

The Doldrums of 1944—II

To the Marianas

BY JUNE THE Allies were strong enough to stage two amphibious landings half a world apart—Normandy one week, Saipan the next—each of which dwarfed all previous operations in either theater.

There was, of course, but little similarity between Eisenhower's OVER-LORD and Nimitz's FORAGER (as the capture of the Marianas was called). The one eventually involved over 2,000,000 troops, the latter only 165,672.[1] Whereas the European landing was only a jump across the English Channel, the Pacific operation was an extension of the front line over 1,000 miles—all the way from Eniwetok to Saipan, Tinian and Guam. No better illustration of the essential differences between the European and Pacific wars can be found.

For FORAGER Admiral Spruance as commander of the Fifth Fleet had more than 800 ships—93 of them in Mitscher's Fast Carrier Task Force, 535[2] in Kelly Turner's Joint Expeditionary Force. Mitscher had 15 fast carriers as the heart of his force which was "prepared for an aggressive, hard-hitting battle if the Japanese did venture to the eastward," although prevailing opinion had it that the Japanese Navy would not fight for the Marianas.[3] Turner had 11 escort carriers for offshore operations (air support, antisubmarine patrol). Lieut. General Holland M. Smith's Expeditionary Troops included the 2d, 3d, 4th Marine Divisions, 1st Provisional Marine Brigade, the Army's 27th and 77th Infantry Divisions.

Amphibious warfare had come a long way since Turner and Vandegrift ventured toward Guadalcanal 22 months earlier with 82 ships.[4]

Total shore-based aircraft assigned for the Marianas operation: 879 planes (Marines 352, Army 269, Navy 258). Of the Marines' planes 172 were day fighters, 36 night fighters, 72 dive bombers, 36 torpedo bombers, 36 transports.[5]

---

[1] Carl W. Proehl, ed., *The Fourth Marine Division in World War II*, p 58.

[2] CominCh, "Battle Experience: Secret Information Bulletin No 20," June–August 1944, p 74–1.

[3] *Ibid*, p 74–23.

[4] *Combat Narratives I*, pp 5–9.

[5] USSBS, *Campaigns*, p 235.

MARIANAS TASK ORGANIZATION ASHORE

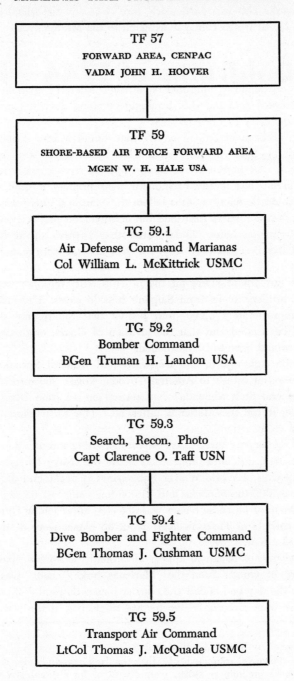

TF 57
FORWARD AREA, CENPAC
VADM JOHN H. HOOVER

TF 59
SHORE-BASED AIR FORCE FORWARD AREA
MGEN W. H. HALE USA

TG 59.1
Air Defense Command Marianas
Col William L. McKittrick USMC

TG 59.2
Bomber Command
BGen Truman H. Landon USA

TG 59.3
Search, Recon, Photo
Capt Clarence O. Taff USN

TG 59.4
Dive Bomber and Fighter Command
BGen Thomas J. Cushman USMC

TG 59.5
Transport Air Command
LtCol Thomas J. McQuade USMC

Despite these impressive figures—which include the backstops in the Marshalls and Gilberts—shore-based air played a relatively minor role in the Marianas assault. This was particularly true at Guam, the island most distant from enemy bases, which CinCPac assigned to the Marine flyers.

Saipan

"Almost unanimously, informed Japanese considered Saipan as the decisive battle of the war," said the U.S. Strategic Bombing Survey, "and its loss as ending all hope for a Japanese victory."[6]

But the invasion of Saipan on 15 June found Marine aviation left out in the lukewarm. Back in Washington CNO had not yet been tackled with the proposition that Marine flyers should operate from carriers if they were to perform in the rest of the Pacific war their primary mission of close air support; it would be many months before the Marine CVE's were ready.

Mitscher's fast carriers furnished the first aviation preparation on Saipan, claiming 150[7] planes before D-day; after that Turner's escort carriers took over most of the direct-support duty. All their aircraft were manned by Navy flyers.

The 2d and 4th MarDivs hit the beaches that were hot with Japanese mortars and artillery shells from Saipan's hillside caves. The first two days' casualties, approximately 4,200, told plainly that the reserve division, the 27th, would be needed and that the invasion of Guam, originally scheduled for 18 June, would have to be postponed.

Submarine sightings to the westward told Admiral Spruance that the Japanese Fleet (on orders to Admiral Toyoda, Koga's successor, from Chief of Naval General Staff Shimada) had sortied on 13 June from Tawi Tawi and would fight for the Marianas, after all.[8] The Fifth Fleet commander prepared for early action.

When large enemy forces were reported coming through San Bernardino Strait on the 15th, no doubt remained. For the U.S. Navy 19 June was one of the significant days of World War II. Submarines (*Cavalla* and *Albacore*) sank two carriers, 30,000-ton *Shokaku* and 31,000-ton *Taiho*. At 0800 in the morning a large group of Japanese planes was detected approaching Guam from the seven other carriers of Toyoda's fleet; about 35 planes were destroyed in the next hour and a half.

But more planes began to appear all around the horizon, particularly to the westward of Guam. Soon the "Marianas turkey shoot" was going full blast. Before the day had ended U.S. carrier planes downed 383 enemy planes (366 of these were airborne)—the biggest single bag of the war. Obviously,

---

[6] *Ibid*, p 220.

[7] Buchanan, *The Navy's Air War*, p 205.

[8] Toyoda, however, estimated (1) that the landings would be at Palau, (2) that the Marianas preliminary strikes were diversions for General MacArthur's Biak operation. (USSBS, *Campaigns*, p 213.)

the Japanese had used up the skilled pilots with which they started the war; now in the words of one analyst, "the degree of the training was not sufficient to meet the demand of an actual battle"[9]—again, the attrition of the Solomons was telling fatally on the Emperor's stock of Wild Eagles.

On 20 June Admiral Mitscher sent out his carrier planes, at extreme range, for the kill. The carrier *Hiyo* was sunk, as were 2 oilers, but the rest of the fleet, including 6 carriers and 5 battleships, got away to fight again at Leyte Gulf. Eighty planes of TF 58 were lost operationally while trying to find their way back to Mitscher's carriers.

Of this great sea battle the marines and soldiers on Saipan had scant knowledge. The fighting ashore on Saipan ran its bloody course, ending after 26 days in a desperate banzai attack by the last 2,000 organized defenders. U.S. dead numbered 3,471, the wounded 12,893.[10] Nearly 31,000 Japanese died on this fulcrum of the Pacific.

Seventy-three P-47's of the AAF's 318th Group were catapulted from the CVE's—a new experience for the Army pilots—between 22 and 24 June. During the latter stages of the Saipan battle and during the subsequent Tinian invasion they helped Navy planes furnish close support for the troops.

The nigh-universal complaint about the Navy and Army close air support was that "too much time was required getting strikes executed. . . . A large majority of the requested missions were cancelled by reason of the infantry advancing past targets before the planes appeared."[11] After the battle Lieut. General Holland Smith recommended again that Marine aviation provide air groups for CVE's, and Admiral Nimitz replied that four escort carriers had been assigned to them.

In late June the Navy brought in some napalm powder, which was used in fire bombs against Tinian on 22 July for the first time in the Pacific war. The first strike (to burn out heavy brush overlooking the landing beach) was arranged by Captain Holt McAloney after films of the new weapon had been shown troop officers. The Army pilots dropping the belly-tankfuls of fire found the early mixture with gasoline less than satisfactory, but a deadly and effective formula using engine oil, and gasoline along with the napalm powder was finally evolved which proved the scourge of cave-dwelling Japanese for the rest of the war.[12]

During the Saipan battle Marine aviation was represented by VMO-2 (Major Robert W. Edmondson) and VMO-4 (Captain Nathan D. Blaha) flying high-winged "grasshopper" monoplanes as artillery spotters for the

---

[9] WDC Translation 239992, "Impressions and Battle Lessons (Air) in the 'A' Operations," quoted in USSBS, *Campaigns*, p 264.

[10] Adjusted figures from 2d and 4th MarDiv and 27th InfDiv histories and Major Carl W. Hoffman, *Saipan: The Beginning of the End* (USMC official monograph series)—none of which has the correct overall data.

[11] Hoffman, *Saipan*, p 250.

[12] Howard and Whitley, *One Damned Island After Another*, pp 217–236; Haugland, *The AAF Against Japan*, p 191; *Operations in POA*, July 1944, p 66.

2d and 4th MarDivs. For the first time the grasshoppers flew off carriers (on D plus 2). They landed on Yellow Beach or on the dirt strip at Charan-Kanoa, and moved to Aslito when that field had been taken. VMO-4 had 1 pilot killed when he crash-landed after being hit by enemy fire, and an air raid on 26 June killed 3 enlisted men, wounded 3 officers and 6 enlisted men of the Squadron (another pilot was killed over Tinian in July). VMO-2 flew 243 missions and VMO-4 400 during the Saipan battle.

Air Warning Squadron 5 also operated with the ground troops at Saipan, one detachment serving with the Corps troops, the other two with the two MarDivs. One officer and an enlisted man were killed while serving with the 4th MarDiv.

Although Admiral Nimitz had two squadrons of well-trained Marine night fighters available in the Marshalls, he elected to send a flight of Army P-61 Black Widows to Saipan. Of some 150 Japanese raiders (between 15 June and 7 July), the night fighters shot down 8, AA 7.[13] The Saipan night fighters were augmented after the battle ended by 12 Marine night fighters of VMF(N)-532, flown from a carrier on 12 July, but by the time of the intensified Japanese attacks on the B-29's based there the marines and their F4U's had been withdrawn to Guam and in September returned to the U.S.

Guam

The long-delayed invasion of Guam caused much physical and mental discomfort to the men who literally had to sweat out the postponement. Men of the 3d Marine Division, 1st Provisional Marine Brigade and 77th Infantry Division spent long, boresome days at sea. Then they sailed back to Eniwetok to await the end of the Saipan battle and the beginning of Guam. Crowded, steaming quarters, indifferent food and long hours of nothingness made for the apex of anticlimax among men who were keyed up for combat.

MAG-21 was detached from the 2d MAW on 4 June and attached to the 4th MBDAW. That day the Group's forward echelon sailed from Efate in *Typhoon, Cetus* and *Young American*. After a stopover at Guadalcanal the ships sailed for Guam, but were sidetracked at Eniwetok from 19 June to 23 July. A squadron historian recorded the reaction:

> Thirty-odd days of boredom and heat in the blazing sun of the Central Pacific was no picnic for the aviation men. . . . The *Typhoon* was very crowded. The food was as good as could be expected. Cigarettes were plentiful most of the time, and candy could be purchased at the ship's store several times a week. But there were no movies, no entertainment of any kind, except a 30-minute show put on by the men over the ship's public address system. Boxing was organized but not many men took part. Most of them were tired—didn't feel like boxing. They only wanted to get on with the trip.

---

[13] USSBS, *Campaigns,* p 213.

But MAG-21's troubles were not over. Orote Peninsula had to be reasonably secure before the airfield could be rebuilt there, and Orote turned out to be the hottest spot on Guam. Six days after 21 July (D-day) the forward echelon was still waiting on board ship. On 29 July a 50-man working party went ashore to help clear the old airstrip of shell fragments and dead Japanese. They were followed by the others within the next few days. Snipers were still active around the strip. Other plagues: torrential rains, flies bearing dysentery, and dengue fever. It was a month and a half more before the sick list began to diminish.

On 31 July the Group commander, Colonel Peter P. Schrider, asked a Navy TBF to make a trial landing on the airstrip. The pilot stayed only three minutes because of intense sniper activity. On 4 August Marine aviation finally returned to Guam, after 13 years' absence. Major Ross Mickey, CO of VMF(N)-534, led in the F6F night fighters, followed by the flight echelons of VMF's 216, 217 and 225. All the planes were launched from CVE *Santee*.

MAG-21's torpedo-bomber squadrons not only were spared the boredom, the dysentery and the snipers, but also made what was, in 1944, an unprecedented mass flight of single-engined planes. On 11 August, VMTB-131 (Major George E. Dooley), followed two days later by VMTB-242 (Major William W. Dean), took off from Espíritu and flew to Funafuti, then Tarawa, Kwajalein and Engebi. From the latter base 131 flew to Guam to rejoin the rest of the Squadron; 242 flew to its new base at Tinian. Both squadrons were assigned to antisubmarine patrol.

MAG-21 became an outsized group. By mid-November 1944, two months after Colonel Edward B. Carney had replaced Schrider as CO, the Group had 12 squadrons (4 VMF, 1 VMF(N), 2 VMTB, 1 VMB, 1 VMR, 2 VMO, 1 AWS) with a total personnel count of 529 officers and 3,778 enlisted men. Aircraft: 204.

Although the Navy alone put $280,000,000 worth of installations into Guam,[14] the Japanese left the great base untouched. MAG-21, which had seen so much action at Pearl Harbor, Midway, and in the Solomons, was destined to see only one other enemy plane for the rest of the war. But this one caused a lot of excitement among the high command. These were the circumstances: an intercepted message indicated that a very important enemy would be a passenger in a seaplane, en route from Truk to Iwo. Four F6F night fighters of VMF(N)-534 were summoned up to Saipan from Guam, and a destroyer took on board controllers from AWS-2 who would act as fighter directors. When the Myrt showed up—in daylight instead of darkness—two of the F6F's intercepted, and Lieut. Brett E. Roueche made the kill 110 miles northeast of Saipan.[15] This writer has never been able to determine

---

[14] Bureau of Yards and Docks, *Building the Navy's Bases in WW II*, Vol II, p iii.
[15] Information from various officers serving in the Marianas at the time; VMF(N)-534 war diary, February 1945; ComForArea war diary, 28 January–3 February 1945, p 13.

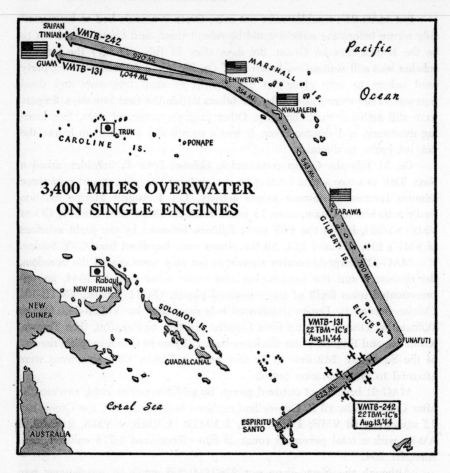

who the VIP was, or whether there was one, but suspects that the long-range, single-engined reconnaissance plane was only a courier.

Besides defending Guam, MAG-21 joined Army and Navy planes in periodic practice attacks on Pagan Island, 280 miles north of Guam, and Rota, half the 110-mile distance to Saipan. This short run prompted one MAG-21 pilot to toss off a parody: "Sighted Rota, sank same and got home in time for lunch."

But Rota—the poor man's Maloelap—was not always a picnic. The enemy gunners, defending the "practice range," improved also; their twin 25-mm. AA gun in a cave became a legend. Three Marine pilots lost their lives over Rota. One of these, Lieut. William J. Gill of VMF-225, parachuted on 25 November 1944 over the island after ack-ack knocked down his F4U. The chute was only 900 yards from a designated rescue spot. Six days after he was shot down a PBY crew spotted a mirror flashing in the sun, and later the crew of another PBY noticed a man near the beach. Three close friends of the downed pilot ventured almost to the beach in a small patrol craft, but detected no signals. After the war Japanese prisoners on Rota said Gill had died of wounds the day he was shot down.

2d MAW to Peleliu

On 10 May Admiral Nimitz designated Halsey (Third Fleet) the overall commander of STALEMATE (code name for the invasion of Peleliu and Angaur in the Palaus). The target date was set for 15 September and the Turner-Smith counterparts for the invasion were to be Vice Admiral Theodore S. Wilkinson (Commander, III Amphibious Force) as Commander, Joint Expeditionary Forces and Major General R. S. Geiger (Commanding General, III Amphibious Corps) to command Joint Expeditionary Troops.

On 29 May a warning order from CinCPOA envisioned the seizure of the entire Palau group in September—an operation more grandiose than either Saipan or Guam. Peleliu and Angaur would be the target for III PhibCorps while Babelthuap, second largest island in all Micronesia, would be assaulted by the Army's XXIV Corps. However, due to the difficulties and delays encountered in seizing Saipan and Guam, and to the shortage of shipping available, CinCPOA on 7 July issued a new order redesignating the operation as STALEMATE II consisting of two phases: Phase I, invasion of the southern Palaus on 15 September; Phase II, Yap and Ulithi rather than Babelthuap to be invaded on 5 October.

Major General Julian C. Smith USMC became Commander, Expeditionary Troops and Landing Force, and General Geiger became Commander, Western Landing Forces to carry out Phase I.

Once again the target was too remote for land-based aviation to provide cover, but the 2d MAW was designated Garrison Air Force, Western Carolines. This Wing, which had long languished in the lower Solomons, was brought up in June to two-group strength (MAG's 11 and 25). On 14 June it was ordered to become "an independent and self-sustaining unit" as soon as possible. On 7 July Major General James T. Moore relieved Brig. General Harold D. Campbell, who had served as the Wing's CG since March. Wing headquarters began to move from Vila to Turtle Bay (Espíritu Santo) on 30 June to join its squadrons there.

During a two-day raid in March 1944 fast carriers had pounded the defenses of Palau with 600 tons of bombs. In June General MacArthur's bombers made frequent neutralization attacks on enemy installations there, in support of the Marianas invasion. Preinvasion carrier strikes rendered enemy air opposition negligible.

Air support during the Peleliu landings was furnished by 4 CV's, 4 CVL's and 10 CVE's.[16]

In spite of the air attacks and bombardment by surface craft the 1st MarDiv under Major General William H. Rupertus found the Peleliu beach-

[16] *Operations in POA*, September 1944.

head on 15 September one to compare with Tarawa and Saipan. For eight hours "some of the fiercest and most confused fighting of the Pacific war"[17] took place on the left flank of the beachhead; the center was a little calmer; and so was the right flank. The Division casualties on D-day amounted to 1,111, including 210 killed.

Ground elements of the 2d MAW landed only an hour behind the assault waves, and soon found themselves serving as stretcher bearers, grave diggers, unloading details and doing various other jobs not usually associated with airplanes. During the September fighting for Peleliu, 4 aviation personnel were killed, 17 wounded.[18] During October 6 were killed and nearly 50 wounded by enemy ground action.

The airfield was the first objective, and it was captured on D plus 2, but no planes except Captain Wallace J. Slappey's VMO-3 artillery spotters could be brought in before 24 September. On that date General Moore landed in an R5C escorting the first eight F6F night fighters of VMF(N)-541, which had staged from Emirau through Owi Island, off New Guinea. Two days later the white-nosed Corsairs of Major Robert F. Stout's VMF-114 landed. Transports began taking out casualties 4 October. In five days VMR-952 alone evacuated 247 wounded from Peleliu to Momote in the Admiralties.

Angaur, five miles southwest of Peleliu, was invaded on the 17th by elements of the 81st Infantry Division. Opposition was light; the island was secured by the 20th and work begun on an airfield from which B-24's could bomb the Philippines.

On 28 September the Corsairs were assigned the job of supporting the landing of the 3d Battalion, 5th Marines, on Ngesebus, a small island 500 yards north of Peleliu. After the Peleliu artillery and the naval guns offshore had worked over the island for two hours, the job of reducing Ngesebus was turned over to the Marine aviators. They bombed and strafed for half an hour, then waited 20 minutes while the artillery took another crack. Beginning at 0840, 20 F4U's strafed the beach just ahead of the troops for 15 minutes with results that were described by one POW as both terrifying and effective.[19] Generals Smith, Geiger, Rupertus and Moore watched the Corsairs fly in at 50 feet. General Rupertus was so impressed that he later said to "Cowboy" Stout: "I hand out very few compliments and when I do they mean something. That was a very 'gutty' show you put on."[20] At a cost of 28 casualties, the marines (air and ground) killed 440 enemy and captured 23 more on Ngesebus.[21]

[17] Major Frank O. Hough USMCR, *The Assault on Peleliu* (USMC official monograph series), p 40.

[18] MAG-11 war diary, September 1944.

[19] Isely and Crowl, *The U.S. Marines and Amphibious War*, p 421.

[20] VMF-114 war diary, September 1944.

[21] Hough, *The Assault on Peleliu*, p 123, which pays tribute to the "magnificent performance" of the aviators but errs in stating that this was "the first instance of the war when air support for a Marine landing was furnished exclusively by Marine Corps planes." There had been previous samples on Wotho, Ujae and Lae in the Eniwetok Atoll 9–13 March 1944.

The remaining flight echelon of Colonel Caleb T. Bailey's MAG-11 remained at Emirau, awaiting call until airfield facilities on Peleliu were available. VMF-122 arrived 1 October, VMTB-134 five days later, and VMF-121 flew in 25 October—all escorted by planes of VMR-952.

During the rest of the Peleliu battle the Marine flyers provided close support for the ground troops, whose main remaining task was the reduction of the Umurbrogol mountain system of defense, whose chief prominence was "Bloody Nose Ridge." Here the Japanese defenders holed up in limestone caves and rifle pits and for over two months defied the best efforts of the Marines and of the 81st InfDiv soldiers to oust them. It took less than 15 seconds for a napalm-bearing Corsair to make its run from the airfield to Bloody Nose Ridge—frequently the planes never even bothered to raise their wheels. On 30 September VMF-114 dropped exactly 20 half-ton bombs within an area only about 100 yards square. As the fighting dragged into October the Marine aviators began dropping unfuzed napalm tanks, which were then set afire by the infantry using phosphorus shells.[22] The infantry used flame throwers so extensively that TAG planes had to fly in 4,500 pounds of hydrogen to replenish the supply.[23]

The close air support on Peleliu—most of which was furnished by VMF-114—the reticent General Rupertus found "executed in a manner leaving little to be desired."

After the bloody Peleliu battle had ended MAG-11 took up its garrison duties, which were considerable. The Marines flew routine antisubmarine and combat air patrols, and bombing and rocket missions over the other Palau islands (Koror, Babelthuap) and over Yap.

The only enemy aircraft destroyed in the air by a marine in the Palaus was a Jake intercepted and shot down the night of 31 October by Major Norman L. Mitchell of VMF(N)-541. Two other Jakes were claimed to have been destroyed on the deck by pilots of VMF-122 as late as December.

Colonel Karl Day, who became CO of Marine Air Base, Peleliu, found himself in the hotel business in a fairly big way. On the night of 11–12 January 1945, for example, 176 transient aircraft remained overnight; 1,240 officers and men were housed, and 1,430 fed in the transient camp. Approximately 96 per cent of all transient traffic was en route to or from the Philippines area.

On 18 January 64 Japanese from the northern Palaus managed counter-landings on the eastern shore and the western beach near MAG-11's new officers' camp. The landing was not repulsed, but the enemy soldiers were killed before much harm had been done except to the aviators' nerves.[24]

In the long and torturous process of fighting off Japanese who popped out

[22] Isely and Crowl, *The U.S. Marines and Amphibious War*, p 422.

[23] Sergeant James J. McElroy, "Victory Line," *The Leatherneck*, May 1945, p 41.

[24] One story says that these Japanese had been sent down from Koror because they disgraced themselves by fleeing from Peleliu in the first place. (Interview Lieut. Colonel Jens C. Aggerbeck, 30 March 1948.)

of caves or got in from other islands an occasional amusing note crept in. One enemy POW was highly incensed when captured. It seems that his cave-mates threw him out because he had dysentery. His revenge was to point out their hiding place, which was thereupon smothered by artillery.

"Another milk run" was the characterization generally given to the Peleliu bombing of the other Palaus and of Yap, but the pilots didn't get out unscathed. From October 1944 to June 1945 no fewer than 28 Marine planes were shot down, including the redoubtable Major Stout, who was killed by AA over Koror on 4 March. Altogether 16 pilots, 4 of whom were majors, and 2 crewmen were killed. In addition, 2 majors, 1 lieutenant and 1 crewman were wounded and evacuated.

MAG-45 at Ulithi

Phase II of STALEMATE II, the invasion of Yap and Ulithi, had been scheduled to follow the capture of Peleliu. But the success of Admiral Halsey's strikes on the Philippines—the Third Fleet estimated it destroyed 432 planes during the first two weeks of September—persuaded Halsey and, later, Nimitz and MacArthur, that some wholesale by-passing was in order. Not only could Mindanao be omitted; it was unnecessary to exterminate the estimated 10,000 Japanese on Yap. (Halsey had wanted to skip Palau also, but he was over-ruled on that one.) The XXIV Corps (7th and 96th InfDivs) and the 77th InfDiv, scheduled for Yap and Ulithi, were shunted to MacArthur for Leyte.

Troops of the 81st Division went ashore in the big Ulithi anchorage on 21 September 1944, against no opposition. There were no casualties except a few natives wounded and the daughter of King Ueg killed during preliminary bombardment. Plasma administered on the beach and treatment aboard a destroyer failed to save her.

To provide the land-based air defense for the biggest anchorage in the western Pacific MBDAG-45,[25] commanded by Colonel Frank M. June, was selected. The Group had been activated the previous February in Santa Barbara, and had been in a state of constant flux ever since. Three of its torpedo and dive-bomber squadrons were transferred on 3 August. One squadron, VMF(N)-542, was attached 22 August. By the time the Group sailed on 9 September all its 59 officers except 4 were brand-new to the organization.

MBDAG-45 landed on Falalop Island, at the east side of Ulithi, on 8 October and set up its own shore party (the assigned beachmaster and beach party never arrived from Pearl Harbor, so three Group officers and their crew assumed the duty). The Group found that Army engineers had started clearing Falalop of its coconut, pandanus, papaya and breadfruit. This unit was replaced by the 51st Seabees, who finished a 3,514-foot airstrip within three weeks. An Army C-47, en route from Peleliu to Guam, made the first landing 28 October.

---

[25] Redesignated MAG-45 in November.

Major William Kellum's night fighters arrived 29 October and began flying day and night CAP on the 30th. Four days later Major Menard Doswell's VMTB-232—the Group's other squadron, just arrived from Espíritu via Peleliu—flew the first mission against Yap, a hundred miles to the southwest.[26]

The Group's primary function was to furnish air defense for the fleet anchorage, which held at times as many as 500 ships, including nearly all the striking force of the U.S. Navy. In practice the Navy sent planes ashore to furnish daytime CAP, left night work to the Marine planes. A necessary adjunct was the neutralization of Yap, which was shared with the planes of MAG-11 at Peleliu. In addition, MAG-45 operated the air base. This island administrative duty wasn't in the tactical book, but lonely MAG-45 managed to do it, anyway.[27]

The Japanese never tried to capitalize on the most lucrative target area in the Pacific, beyond a solitary suicide attempt of 11 March 1945.[28] MAG-45 saw but little of the enemy at Ulithi; its function was to help maintain the vital aerial guard duty, and to be ready in case the guard was challenged.

A Tribute to TAG

Falalop, bare, broiling and only 10° north of the Equator, was anything but a luxury spot, and the understrength Marines had their hands full. Hardest worked of all was the small contingent at the Ulithi TAG terminal, which faced the awesome project of unloading the six Marine transport planes that brought 20,000 pounds of mail for the fleet from Guam every morning, then loading them again with outbound mail.[29]

On 1 December 1944, when the officer in charge received and dispatched a total of 62,708 pounds of mail and cargo, he sat down and wrote a memorandum about it. One of his men was suffering from spinal rheumatism, another had lost 40 pounds in the month since the airstrip was opened, and, said he, in a masterpiece of understatement: "The excessively heavy tonnage handled at this station, coupled with the lack of fresh food is apparently working undue hardships on our men."[30] The atoll commander loaned him nine marines to help out temporarily.

But TAG was doing a job that was appreciated by some of the thousands of sailors who received the mail, and occasionally by visitors. One of these visitors, Wayne Parrish, editor of *American Aviation Daily*, wrote:

> Far out in the Forward Area of the Central Pacific is a military airline system that for my money has done one of the outstanding aviation

---

[26] MAG-45 history, pp 8–10.

[27] Colonel Frank M. June, "Report of Operations MAG-45," to CG 4th MAW, 23 January 1945. Colonel Richard C. Mangrum relieved June on 28 January.

[28] See p 238.

[29] *All Hands,* (BuPers Information Bulletin), May 1949, p 3.

[30] Lieut. Patrick E. Wildman to CO Troop Carrier Group, 1 December 1944.

jobs of the war. This airline is called TAG, which stands for Transport Air Group. . . . After flying all over the Pacific on every air transport service in that area, I concluded that if I was to award a medal to the air transport unit doing the best single job under the toughest wartime conditions I would nominate TAG.[31]

Wizards in PBJ's

The most unusual Marine squadron to enter the Central Pacific war owed its characteristics to the chagrin suffered by all hands in early days of the Solomons, when Japanese ships made the run down The Slot with impunity. The Navy directed that three squadrons be trained to operate at night with radar-operated bomb sights and search gear. Two of these were Navy squadrons of Venturas and Liberators. The third was Lieut. Colonel Jack Cram's VMB-612, flying PBJ's.

Cram's squadron had been commissioned 1 October 1943 as an orthodox daylight outfit, but in February 1944 it was chosen for experimental work in night bombing and torpedo launching. After routine but intense training on the East Coast the Squadron started moving overseas, when CominCh informed CinCPac that it was "exceptionally well-trained for night work,"[32] and VMB-612 was in the rocket-launching business. At San Diego during August 1944, a prototype plane was equipped with zero-length rocket launchers, and the other 15 planes were similarly equipped when the Squadron reached Oahu.

The idea was this, as described by the Squadron commander:

> We figured that by flying at a definite altitude, say 300 feet, in level flight and knowing the ballistics of the rocket, we could predict where it would hit the water. . . . By making a temperature correction, a correction for the weight which affects the attitude of the rocket, using a constant altitude and figuring in the wind drift and the velocity, we had a correction that gave us a very accurate range.[33]

The Squadron moved even farther west before its theories were given tests. Finally at Eniwetok a suitable target was found: a small island, 200 feet long and 100 feet wide, similar in size to the many Japanese ships which traveled at night. The Squadron fired 250-odd rockets at this island, and scored 56 per cent hits. Clearly, here was something new and startling for the "wizard war."

VMB-612 had orders to Peleliu, but few targets were left there. Major General Willis H. Hale USA, CG of Shore-Based Air in the Forward Area, thought the Squadron should go to the Philippines, where there appeared to

---

[31] In *Liberty*, 20 January 1945.
[32] CominCh to CinCPac, 23 June 1944.
[33] Interview Lieut. Colonel Jack Cram, Air Intelligence Group, ONI, 13 March 1945.

be plenty of shipping, but General MacArthur declined the offer. VMB-612 stopped at Saipan, arriving there 6 November after a month's practice at Eniwetok.

One week later the Squadron began operations under Hale's shore-based command (administratively, VMB-612 was a unit of MAG-21). The nearest shipping targets to Saipan were at Iwo Jima, 630 miles to the north, and at Chichi, 120 miles farther. To achieve this range overhead turrets were removed, as were the package guns and everything else that wasn't necessary to flying, navigating and carrying radar equipment and eight rockets. Cram found that he could carry 1,520 gallons of gasoline, fly 10½ hours at 140 knots and still return to Saipan with 400 gallons of gas.

During the first two weeks at Saipan the 27 crews, all of whom were green, showed little proficiency. Some got lost, others couldn't find their targets and still others had trouble with such intricate equipment as the APS-3 search gear, the 729 interrogator-responder, IFF, and loran. It was found that more shipping targets were at Chichi than Iwo, which meant a longer flight—sometimes the PBJ's flew out 900 miles and back (12 hours). Three planes searched every night, one in the Iwo area, another up the west side of Haha and down the east side, and the third around Chichi. Three planes stood by at Saipan until midnight, in case a convoy were sighted.

But the crews improved with experience. On two straight nights all planes claimed to hit Japanese shipping—six straight hits in two nights. During the Saipan phase of the Squadron's operations two ships were claimed as probably sunk, 27 damaged[34] (the squadron moved up to Iwo Jima and began operating on 10 April 1945 against Japanese harbors). From Saipan 49 antishipping attacks were made, among 334 missions flown. Three planes were lost, along with 5 officers and 8 men.

---

[34] I have been unable to find any Japanese records to confirm or deny these claims.

CHAPTER EIGHTEEN

Return to the Philippines

WHEN GENERAL DOUGLAS MacARTHUR was ordered from Corregidor in 1942 to command the Allied Forces in the Southwest Pacific he fervently announced that he would return. So far as the public was concerned, the General said he was going to return and, two and a half years later, he did. But, as MacArthur's Eighth Army commander wrote five years later: "Few non-military people know the invasion of the Philippines almost didn't happen."[1]

Generally speaking, the Navy was against the return to the Philippines—though there were many variations of Navy viewpoint. Some admirals were in favor of going to Mindanao, but not to the principal island of Luzon. Others wanted to recapture Luzon, provided the approach were made via the Central Pacific forces under Navy command. After the Central Pacific offensive got rolling some didn't think any invasion whatsoever of the Philippines was necessary. It seemed to Admiral Halsey that he and Nimitz were almost alone among the senior admirals in supporting the return; Halsey's viewpoint was advocated by his chief of staff, Rear Admiral Robert B. Carney, who thought Luzon necessary for staging troops for the final invasion of Japan.[2]

General MacArthur was more consistent than the admirals. He wanted to go back and recapture all the Philippines, and that is what eventually happened. The Navy had its way, too, and fought its own, more spectacular path all the way across the Pacific, but the Navy plan to go to the China coast was successfully stalled by MacArthur. The roads which led eventually to Tokyo were (1) MacArthur's northward, Australia–New Guinea–Philippines, and (2) Nimitz's westward, Marianas–Iwo Jima–Okinawa.

Just what was or was not essential in the Pacific war will be argued for a long time to come. The enthusiastic Army aviators of the Military Analysis Division of the Strategic Bombing Survey were the most preposterous of the Monday-morning quarterbacks—they claimed in 1947 that the proper route to Japan's defeat, "had our strategy been oriented toward airpower and air weapons," was New Guinea–Solomons to Admiralties, Truk, Marianas, Iwo."[3]

---

[1] Lieut. General Robert L. Eichelberger, *Our Jungle Road to Tokyo.* p 165.

[2] *Admiral Halsey's Story,* p 195; the writer's conversation with Admiral Carney in 1949.

[3] USSBS, *Air Campaigns,* p 57.

Only that and nothing more: no Gilberts and Marshalls, no Okinawa, no Philippines, no flank protection.

Since the Philippines engaged a big segment of Marine aviation, readers of this history may be interested in some of the events that led up to their participation.

The first year of the war in the Pacific consisted of holding on, but the Casablanca conference between Roosevelt and Churchill in January 1943, set certain long-range Pacific missions: continuation up from New Guinea and Guadalcanal until Rabaul was captured and the Bismarcks barrier broken, plus an advance westward toward Truk and Guam. The TRIDENT conference of May 1943 envisioned a different role for MacArthur's forces after the Bismarcks breakthrough: an advance along the north coast of New Guinea, through the Celebes into the South China Sea, while the British were recapturing Singapore and the strategic bombing of Japan was increased from bases that would be built in China.[4] This latter depended on the recapture of Hong Kong. There was no mention of a return to the Philippines.[5]

It soon became evident that the British were not going to recapture Singapore—or even Burma—at any foreseeable date. Neither was Hong Kong going to be seized; nor would strategic bombing from China—a pet scheme of President Roosevelt's—ever amount to much.

In August of 1943 the Combined Chiefs of Staff met at Quebec for the QUADRANT conference. The South East Asia Command under Lord Louis Mountbatten was created, and plans were made for the strategic bombing of Japan by B-29's based in China (limited by the supply of gasoline that could be flown over The Hump). General MacArthur was ordered to continue his operations up the New Guinea coast to reach the Philippines by the fall of 1944. But the most important step of all (though few realized it at the time), the seizure of the Gilberts, Marshalls and Marianas, was agreed to.[6]

Actually, this Quebec conference merely approved a scheme which had been cooking in the admirals' minds for some time. As early as 15 February 1943, Admiral Nimitz had asked for Halsey's comments on "the proposed Ellice–Gilbert operations" (Halsey was against them).[7] A month after that Admiral King was grumbling at a JCS meeting about having to delay Solomons operations until MacArthur had occupied the Huon Peninsula, and was asking why naval forces couldn't be used meantime against the Gilberts or Marshalls.[8] On 15 June General Marshall informed General MacArthur of the decision to strike through the Central Pacific, and MacArthur replied that he still

---

[4] Morison, *Breaking the Bismarcks Barrier*, p 8.

[5] USSBS, *Employment of Forces Under the Southwest Pacific Command* (prepared in General MacArthur's headquarters, 1947), p 28.

[6] *The War Reports of General of the Army George C. Marshall, General of the Army H. H. Arnold, Fleet Admiral Ernest J. King* (hereinafter cited as *War Reports*), p 220.

[7] ComSoPac war diary, 15–17 February 1943.

[8] JCS, minutes of 67th meeting, 19 March 1943.

thought that the main effort should be directed through New Guinea to Mindanao, and that the Central Pacific attack should be regarded as diversionary.[9] Admiral King attempted to reclaim the 1st MarDiv from the Southwest Pacific for use in the Gilberts, but MacArthur successfully blocked the attempt.[10] The 2d MarDiv was released from the South Pacific to the Central Pacific, however.

On 20 July the JCS ordered Admiral Nimitz to plan and prepare for operations against the Ellice and Gilbert Islands. This was the alert which the Quebec conference put into a formal order. QUADRANT also directed the neutralization rather than the capture of Rabaul, and the JCS ordered MacArthur to plan the seizure of Kavieng and the Admiralties. He was also ordered to plan advances along the New Guinea coast as far as Vogelkop ("Duck's Head"). The Southwest Pacific general feared that the JCS, "from the nature of the messages," intended to pinch off his operations at this western tip of New Guinea.[11]

This was too much, and in September MacArthur took his case to the public in an extraordinary pronouncement from his Brisbane headquarters:

> My strategic concept for the Pacific contemplates massive strokes against only the main strategic objectives, utilizing surprise air and ground striking power, supported and assisted by the fleet. . . . Island hopping . . . is not my idea of how to end the war as soon and as cheaply as possible.[12]

Just what he hoped to gain by such a statement is not clear. Unlike the General, the public had no idea that a campaign against the islands was about to begin. The *New York Times* reporter attributed MacArthur's pique to the Mountbatten appointment. The invasion of Tarawa and Makin took place just the same, on 20 November.

At the Cairo conference in December 1943 the JCS and CCS added another strategic objective in the Pacific: an attack in the Formosa–Luzon–China coast area in the spring of 1945. Although the New Guinea–East Indies–Philippines advance was to be continued, the Central Pacific received higher priority because its rate of advance promised to be more rapid.[13] About this time Admiral King's plans officer, Vice Admiral Charles M. Cooke Jr., visited General MacArthur in company of General Marshall, and reported back to Navy headquarters: "General MacArthur apparently had the idea that the Navy was not disposed to help him get into the Philippines." Cooke assured the General that the Navy wanted to get him back to the Philippines

---

[9] USSBS, *Employment of Forces Under the Southwest Pacific Command*, p 29.
[10] *Ibid;* undated memos King to Marshall (probably 20 and 29 June 1943).
[11] *Ibid.*
[12] *The New York Times*, 22 September 1943, p 1.
[13] USSBS, *Employment of Forces Under the Southwest Pacific Command*, p 30.

as early as possible,[14] probably because Navy planners themselves had not yet grasped the overriding importance of the Central Pacific drive.

On 27–28 January 1944 a special conference took place at Pearl Harbor between representatives of MacArthur and Nimitz. "A regular love feast," it seemed to General Kenney:

> Admiral McMorris, Nimitz's Chief of Staff, argued for the importance of capturing the Carolines and the Marshalls, but everyone else was for pooling everything along the New Guinea–Philippines axis. Admiral Sherman and Sutherland were to go to Washington to present the case to the Joint Chiefs of Staff for approval. The meeting finished with everyone feeling good and ready to work together and get the war over.[15]

When the notes of this conference reached Washington Admiral King read them "with indignant dismay," he informed Nimitz.[16] The idea of certain Central Pacific officers agreeing to the by-passing of the Marianas and Carolines was too much for the bald eagle of Constitution Avenue. After singling out Admirals Towers and Calhoun for special castigation, King pointed out:

> In any event, it will be necessary for us to either seize the Marianas and dry up Truk or to seize Truk itself. Further, this process will speed up rather than delay the war. The idea of rolling up the Japanese along the New Guinea coast through the Halmaheras and Mindanao, and up through the Philippines to Luzon as our major strategic concept, to the exclusion of clearing our Central Pacific line of communications to the Philippines is to me absurd.[17]

After the conference which caused Admiral King so much distress, General MacArthur sent his chief of staff, Lieut. General Richard K. Sutherland, to see the JCS in Washington and firm up the plan to concentrate the Pacific advance into a single drive up the New Guinea coast to the Philippines.[18]

In the momentous directive of 12 March 1944 the JCS compromised; they canceled the assault on Kavieng which MacArthur had substituted for Rabaul —the big harbor at Manus in the newly won Admiralties would suffice—but ordered the Southwest Pacific commander to plan for the invasion of Mindanao. At the same time the Navy scheme to invade Truk was turned down, but the Southern Marianas became Nimitz's Central Pacific target. For purposes of planning, the JCS assigned Luzon to MacArthur, Formosa to Nimitz, target

---

[14] Letter Cooke to King, 21 December 1943, in CNO Planning Files.

[15] *General Kenney Reports*, p 348. The General probably meant "the Carolines and Marianas"—it was too late to argue about the Marshalls, which were invaded three days later.

[16] Memo King to Nimitz, FF-11A6613, 8 February 1944.

[17] *Ibid.*

[18] USSBS, *Employment of Forces Under the Southwest Pacific Command*, p 31.

date 15 February 1945—it was indicated that Formosa would certainly be seized, but Luzon might not be necessary.[19]

Thus the JCS compromise favored King and the Central Pacific over MacArthur and the Southwest Pacific. It seemed possible that General MacArthur might get a toehold on the Southern Philippines, but no triumphal ride into Manila.

MacArthur's air commander was dumbfounded: "The suggestion that we by-pass the main Philippine island of Luzon and go to Formosa before liberating the Filipinos was unthinkable to me."[20]

But General MacArthur went ahead and revised his plan again; RENO V was hopefully based on the assumption that Luzon would be seized before Formosa.

In the first half of 1944 the twin drives of MacArthur and Nimitz made progress along their respective roads to Japan, but the Central Pacific was indeed faster. While MacArthur was seizing the Admiralties and Hollandia and Biak Island, Nimitz's carriers and amphibious forces were on the blitz with a 1,500-mile leap from the Marshalls to the Marianas.

Shortly after RENO V was sent to Washington, the JCS planners drew up proposals that would by-pass the Philippines in favor of Formosa. General MacArthur, fearful that creating a Filipino famine would react against the Allies throughout the Far East, "strenuously objected."[21]

Soon after Saipan had been secured, the Commander in Chief himself took a hand in the dispute, which by this time entailed a great deal of bitterness. The Democratic Convention which was to renominate him was in progress at Chicago when President Roosevelt boarded cruiser *Baltimore* in San Diego for Pearl Harbor. General MacArthur flew up from Brisbane—the only trip he made outside his own theater during the war—and met on 27–28 July with Nimitz and the President at a Waikiki palace in Honolulu.

The records of this meeting are sketchy, and nearly everything that has been printed came second- or third-hand. General Eichelberger pictured MacArthur as believing he had lost the debate, and that his "was a lost cause." But as MacArthur bowed and started to leave the room, the President called him back and the Philippines invasion was on again.[22] Robert E. Sherwood reported that there were cynics, especially in the Navy, who remarked in undertones that perhaps the President's choice had been influenced by the thought that the Philippines would provide a more popular victory in an election year.[23] Samuel Eliot Morison has written that Roosevelt asked, upon being greeted by MacArthur on the deck of *Baltimore*, "Douglas, where do we go from here?" and that MacArthur replied: "Leyte, Mr. President; and then Luzon!"[24]

---

[19] JCS No. 71469, 12 March 1944.
[20] *General Kenney Reports*, p 371.
[21] USSBS, *Employment of Forces Under the Southwest Pacific Command*, p 36.
[22] Eichelberger, *Our Jungle Road to Tokyo*, p 166.
[23] Robert E. Sherwood, *Roosevelt and Hopkins*, p 809.
[24] Samuel Eliot Morison and Henry Steele Commager, *The Growth of the American Republic* (4th ed., revised, 1950), p 769.

Admiral Leahy, who was present, observed that the two days of meetings were pleasant and informative—"much more peaceful than I had expected after what I had been hearing in Washington." MacArthur told John Gunther in 1950 "with the most vivid relish" how Roosevelt had finally sided with him, saying, "But I am going to have a hell of a time over this with that old bear, Ernie King!"[25] One can only speculate about the effect—on Formosa, on China and on history—had King been the Navy's representative at this meeting, rather than the more pliable Nimitz.

Luzon went back on the books, target date March 1945. Formosa was not canceled, but it was left up in the air (where it stayed for the rest of the war). It became more familiar to the public in postwar headlines.

Halsey Gets in the Act

In contrast to Nimitz, whose far-ranging carriers gave him air superiority wherever there was water to float the big ships. MacArthur in his advances was limited to the range of his fighter planes. Consequently, MacArthur's plan for re-entering the Philippines—outlined 9 September—was ultraconservative.

After invading Morotai 15 September the General planned to hop on 15 October to the Talaud Islands, halfway to Sarangani Bay at the southern end of Mindanao. A month after that he expected to leap the other half of the distance to Sarangani Bay. Target date for Leyte was 20 December.

All this laborious plan was changed, thanks to the irrepressible "Bull" Halsey, who was back at sea for the first time in over two years. In support of the Palau and Morotai landings, Halsey's carrier planes struck the Central Philippines with 1,200 sorties on 12 September, and kept hammering for two more days. His air combat intelligence officers showed Halsey a box score that "made me whistle," he said. In three days the claims were 173 planes shot down, 305 more destroyed on the ground, 59 ships sunk, all at a cost of 9 U.S. planes, 10 men. The Central Philippines seemed a hollow shell.[26]

The Admiral dashed off a message to Nimitz: why not cancel the Palau and Yap landings (Yap was Phase II of the Palau operation), and send those troops to MacArthur for use against Leyte at the earliest possible date? Nimitz passed the message on to Admiral King, who was with the Combined Chiefs of Staff and Roosevelt and Churchill at the OCTAGON conference in Quebec. MacArthur's views were requested in a message which reminded him that the suggested operation would advance the war "by many months." MacArthur agreed,[27] Yap was canceled (but not Palau), XXIV Corps was loaned by Nimitz to MacArthur plus the 77th Infantry Division, garrison forces, and six old battleships. Mindanao was by-passed for the time being, and the invasion of Leyte was scheduled for 20 October.

[25] Fleet Admiral William D. Leahy, *I Was There*, pp 250–251; John Gunther, *The Riddle of MacArthur*, p 10.

[26] *Admiral Halsey's Story*, p 199.

[27] MacArthur himself was on a cruiser off Morotai and didn't learn until later that the plan had been accepted in his name. (*General Kenney Reports*, pp 432–434.)

Seeking a Mission

Meantime, Major General Mitchell's Marine flyers were looking for employment. To follow their job-seeking it is necessary to revert four months, to May 1944. At that time General Mitchell was ComAirSoPac and he knew that his forces, along with other remnants in the South Pacific, would come under direct command of SoWesPac in the 15 June change-over (Mitchell would become ComAirNorSols).

Mitchell flew over to Brisbane some time in May to see General MacArthur; Admiral Kinkaid, Seventh Fleet commander; and General Kenney, whose expanded command was about to be labeled Far East Air Forces. Mitchell's purpose: to tell his new bosses that he had a lot of hot outfits that were eager to get in on whatever operations that were being planned.

It was pointed out that the South Pacific air forces had been continously fighting since August 1942, and that these forces were completely equipped and ready by virtue of continuous combat for future operations. Meanwhile, it was emphasized that Jap air in the Northern Solomons –Rabaul area had been whipped and that we had run out of Jap air resistance.[28]

But when AirNorSols was set up shortly after this visit, General Kenney ordered it only to support XIV Corps, which meant more bombing of bypassed Japanese—General Kenney assured Mitchell that this was important work, and not simply "kicking a corpse around,"[29] but he didn't sound very convincing to the marine.

On 6 August, Mitchell, accompanied as before by his chief of staff, Colonel Clayton C. Jerome, paid a second visit to Brisbane to see Kenney "and further needled him about my desire for as much combat activity as possible."[30] General Kenney said he already had more planes than airfields to accommodate. "See how they are backed up for 2,000 miles," he told the two visitors, describing an arc from Biak to Brisbane.[31]

Nonetheless, General Kenney promised General Mitchell the shore-based air command during the Sarangani Bay operation, which was due in about ten weeks; the 1st MAW to be augmented by certain unspecified Army air units.

Mitchell's hopes were short-lived. On 26 August one of Kenney's staff officers told General Mitchell that the Solomons were too far away—shipping was too scarce for a "rapid turnaround" to bring up the second and third

[28] Memo Mitchell to Major General Field Harris, Director of Marine Corps Aviation, 26 March 1946.
[29] Kenney to Mitchell, 28 June 1944, quoted in Craven and Cate, *The AAF in WW II*, Vol IV, p 647.
[30] Mitchell to Harris, *op. cit.*
[31] Information from Colonel Jerome.

echelons. Halsey's proposition to skip Sarangani made it even less likely that the Marines were going to see any combat within the next few months.[32]

Colonel Jerome was permitted to attend the Morotai landings 15 September as an observer, and General Mitchell did the same thing at Leyte. But the rest of the AirNorSols marines stuck to the thumping of Rabaul and Kavieng.

Although the Marines lost their assault assignment, General Kenney did not rule out the possibility of using them later:

> The 5th Air Force was marked for the assault as usual; the 13th Air Force would be offered a significant part in forward operations. Even ComAirNorSols, long stuck in the Solomons, might be moved up to the P.I. in the course of time.[33]

Toyoda Shoots the Works

Following the loss of the Marianas, the Japanese outlined the *Sho* ("Conquer") plans: (1) for the defense of the Philippines; (2) for the Formosa–Nansei Shoto–Southern Kyushu area; (3) for the Kyushu–Shikoku–Honshu area; and (4) for Hokkaido.[34]

The Japanese had lost their trained carrier groups. Now they were willing, in the general strategic plan, to throw the remainder of the fleet—still formidable if weak in trained carrier pilots—against the American invaders, probably in the Philippines, which was considered the most likely objective. "There would be no sense in saving the fleet at the expense of the loss of the Philippines," said Admiral Toyoda, successor to Koga as CinC Combined Fleet.

Halsey was chewing up the land-based aviation strength of the Philippines. His late September strikes on Luzon were spectacularly successful—405 planes and 103 ships claimed in and around Manila on the 21st, 36 more planes and 34 ships on the 24th, to bring the three weeks' total to 1,005 planes destroyed and 153 ships sunk—not counting the "probables." Even allowing for Halsey's customary jubilance and tendency to overestimate, these carrier achievements far outweighed any previous mass destruction by U.S. forces.

After refueling at the great new anchorage in Ulithi, Halsey's Third Fleet sauntered north to hit the long arc of Nansei Shoto (including Okinawa Island) between Japan and Formosa on 10 October. This time the total

---

[32] Major Charles W. Boggs Jr., *Marine Aviation in the Philippines* (USMC historical monograph) p 9. General Mitchell's memo to General Harris leaves the impression that the cancellation of Sarangani was solely responsible for the Marines' loss of a job, but he clarifies this point in a notation on Boggs's chronology of events. General Kenney, in a letter to Boggs dated 27 October 1950, also seems to be under the impression that the Marines would have had the Sarangani operation if Leyte hadn't been substituted.

[33] General George C. Kenney, "Monograph on Leyte" (Early Planning), p 1.

[34] USSBS, *Campaigns*, p 281.

showed 93 planes and 87 ships.[35] Formosa itself was next, 12 and 13 October, and tougher resistance there cost 52 carrier planes, but Halsey claimed no less than 520 planes destroyed and 37 ships sunk.[36] Toyoda almost believed the claims of his naval pilots—now land-based—of sinking 13 U.S. carriers, but reconnaissance on the 16th showed him his enemy still had at least 7 carriers left.

The Battle for Leyte Gulf

On 17 October, when an advance party of Rangers began landing on small islands in the mouth of Leyte Gulf, Toyoda alerted his entire fleet for *Sho No. 1*, the defense of the Philippines. If he was ever going to strike, the time was now. Admiral Kurita's force, 5 battleships, 12 cruisers, 15 destroyers, began moving from Singapore toward Brunei Bay, on the way to the Philippines, intent upon striking at the beachhead through San Bernardino Strait just north of Samar. Admiral Nishimura's smaller Southern Force, containing 2 battleships, 1 cruiser, 4 destroyers, aimed for the beachhead through Surigao Strait just north of Mindanao. The remnants of Japan's once-mighty carrier aviation force—Admiral Ozawa's so-called "Main Body" of 4 carriers with partial air groups, 2 hermaphroditic battleship-carriers without planes, 3 light cruisers and 8 destroyers—sortied from the Inland Sea of Japan on 20 October as a decoy, hoping to engage Halsey's attention while Kurita's guns smashed Kinkaid's amphibious forces at Leyte. Only 116 planes had Ozawa.[37] But he had enough ships to lure the Americans' main strength northward if they took the bait.

On 20 October the main landings, by X and XXIV Corps, began on an 18-mile front between Dulag and Tacloban on the east coast of Leyte. On loan to the Army were 1,528 marines, mostly from V Amphibious Corps artillery.

Admiral Nishimura failed dismally in his attempt to come through Surigao Strait, and paid for it with his life. Admiral Oldendorf's old battleships crossed his T in a night action, and what they didn't sink the carrier planes did, next dawn, excepting a lone destroyer. At the last moment, the Japanese had ordered Admiral Shima, commanding a small force of 2 heavy cruisers, 1 light cruiser, and 4 destroyers, to support Nishimura's attack. Shima, however, entered Surigao Strait only to find that Nishimura's force had been all but annihilated ahead of him. He promptly turned tail and withdrew, but only after a torpedo had hit and disabled the light cruiser *Abukuma*, which was finished off the next day by Army B-24's.

Task Force 38 was ready when Kurita started to press through San Bernardino. The mighty, 63,700-ton *Musashi*, with her ultrasecret 18.1-inch guns, went to the bottom holed by at least ten aerial torpedo and 16 bomb hits.

---

[35] JANAC shows 12 ships (of more than 500 tons).
[36] *Admiral Halsey's Story*, p 205.
[37] James A. Field Jr., *The Japanese at Leyte Gulf: The Sho Operation*, p 36.

Kurita was already suffering cruiser losses—two had been sunk on 23 October by submarines *Darter* and *Dace,* and a third damaged. The pilots crippled two more cruisers and damaged two battleships—and claimed a lot more ("dangerously optimistic," Halsey termed their reports later).

But Halsey didn't wait around to evaluate his pilots' claims. His reconnaissance planes had spotted Admiral Ozawa coming down from the north, and the carriers were what Halsey was looking for—he had no way of knowing that they were only decoys. So, he took off for the north, and due to an egregious misunderstanding, he neglected to let Admiral Kinkaid know that he was taking all of TF 38 with him.

Meantime, Kurita proceeded on his suicide mission, damaged though his force was. He still had *Musashi's* sister ship, *Yamato,* 3 other battleships, 8 cruisers and 10 destroyers. And off the Leyte beachhead nothing opposed him except 6 CVE's, 3 DD's and 4 DE's. Kurita opened fire from 14 miles, but Admiral "Ziggy" Sprague's little CVE's were already launching planes—and his 3 DD's and 4 DE's also got ready for the attack.

What happened was an episode of gallantry rarely matched in naval annals. The small carriers' planes sank three heavy cruisers; a torpedo from d yer *Johnston* damaged another before *"Johnny"* went down. Kurita's big ans sank her, along with DD *Hoel,* DE *Roberts,* and CVE *Gambier Bay.* This s the most one-sided naval engagement of the war, and it was the most heroic.

So heroic that Admiral Kurita broke off the action, while within only five miles of the other carriers, and, just beyond, the transports at Leyte. When Admiral Kurita had a chance to pull off the most devastating attack of the war he turned around and went back through San Bernardino Strait.

This turnaround when in sight of victory he later ascribed to: (1) lack of intelligence regarding the U.S. forces; (2) fear that the Tacloban airstrip was operational; (3) false intelligence about a more lucrative target off Samar; (4) a preference for combat in the open sea rather than the confines of Leyte Gulf. In any case, he turned around and the transports were saved.

Meantime, Admiral Halsey, far to the north off Cape Engaño (in Spanish, "deceit"), sank 4 of the impotent carriers, 1 light cruiser, 2 destroyers, and damaged 2 battleships, 2 light cruisers and 4 destroyers.

The battle for Leyte Gulf was the greatest naval engagement of all time. When it was over the Japanese Navy "as a Navy, had ceased to exist,"[38] even though this battle, like the air battle off Formosa, was celebrated in Japan as a great victory and a special *sake* ration was issued to the populace.[39]

The Beachhead Problem

The Tacloban airstrip proved to be one of the worst headaches on any beachhead in the Pacific. Its rainy-season muck was churned into deeper mud.

---

[38] USSBS, *Campaigns,* p 286.
[39] Masuo Kato, *The Lost War,* p 113.

Four or five of the Navy planes from the suffering escort carriers cracked up trying to make emergency landings while Marine General Mitchell, present with three of his staff officers as observers, waved a pair of signal flags in an effort to land them safely, carrier-style. The remarkable thing was that Mitchell and other "acting" landing signal officers were able to bring in 40 to 50 planes without anybody getting killed. The planes were rearmed immediately and dispatched to chase Kurita's cripples. The field was so terrible, however, that 25 Navy planes cracked up during the day and night.[40]

The Japanese strategy became clear soon after the landing: Leyte was the spot where the Emperor's men would make their Philippines stand. Although the 16,000 Japanese troops already on Leyte were withdrawn from the eastern half of the island, heavy reinforcements began to pour into Ormoc on the west coast. Increments arrived from Mindanao and the Visayas. On 1 November a large convoy unloaded at Ormoc. A veteran Manchuria division en route to Luzon was diverted to Leyte. FEAF planes managed to sink some ships, but by early November at least 25,000 reinforcements had arrived. Barges began shuttling more troops and supplies from Cebu, by way of the Camotes Islands.[41]

Plagued by the mud and incessant rains which prohibited airfield development, General MacArthur, who dismissed the carriers and turned over air defense to his FEAF planes on 27 October, was forced to request the return of the carriers two days later. The Third Fleet provided air defense almost a month longer than had been planned.[42] This caused the first carrier strike on Japan to be postponed.

The fast-carrier planes could not also provide immediate defenses for the Leyte beachhead. That was up to the Army fighters which had flown in on 27 October. This task they found difficult. There simply was not enough runway, nor dispersal area for enough planes. Although they were credited with 130 Japanese planes from their arrival until 15 November, FEAF units lost 48 P-38's (13 in aerial combat, 14 destroyed on the ground, 1 to friendly AA, 20 operationally).[43]

Advent of the Kamikazes

Something else arose to plague General MacArthur and Admiral Halsey and the whole Pacific Fleet, too. This was the *kamikaze*,[44] the "body-crashing" Japanese pilot who dived his plane into the Allied ship and earned himself a ticket to the Japanese Valhalla at Yasukuni Shrine.

The *kamikaze* was the single most effective air weapon developed by the

---

[40] MS, *History of V Fighter Command*, chapter IV, p 77, footnote 41.

[41] USSBS, *Employment of Forces Under the Southwest Pacific Command*, p 43.

[42] *Ibid.*

[43] MS, *History of the Fifth Air Force;* chapter 5, "Air Defense of Leyte."

[44] *Kamikaze* was the Japanese Navy's term; the Army called its suiciders *Tokko Tai.*

Japanese in World War II.[45] "Macabre, effective, supremely practical under the circumstances, supported and stimulated by a powerful propaganda campaign, the special attack became virtually the sole method used in opposing the United States striking and amphibious forces, and these ships the sole objective."[46]

The idea of self-immolation as a deterrent to American warships apparently had its origins in June 1944, during the Philippine Sea battle, but it was not put into deliberate effect until 15 October, just prior to the Leyte landings, when Vice Admiral Masabumi Arima flew his plane into an American aircraft carrier "lest the traditional spirit of the Japanese Navy be spoiled."[47] The overwhelming superiority of American planes, pilots and fighter-director techniques had forced the Japanese to the last, most desperate measure. The writer, who witnessed several successful *kamikaze* attacks on the fast carriers and the amphibious forces, was as transfixed as any other American at this bizarre spectacle of men destroying themselves. He was forced to agree with Commander John Thach, who philosophized one day at the great Ulithi carrier base:

> Every time one country gets something, another soon has it. One country gets radar, but soon all have it. One gets a new type of engine or plane, then another gets it. But the Japs have got the *kamikaze* boys, and nobody else is going to get that, because nobody else is built that way.[48]

During the height of the *kamikaze* attacks Radio Tokyo used to intone the names of Japanese "hero gods" who had been promoted two or three ranks (posthumously, of course) instead of the single-rank promotion awarded men killed in the ordinary course of battle. Perhaps more macabre than the attacks themselves were Radio Tokyo's quoted interviews with little boys whose ambition it was to grow up and become *kamikaze* pilots.

Only at war's end did we learn how effective the *kamikaze* had been: 26.8 per cent of them found their shipping targets during the Philippines campaign (174 hits or damaging near misses out of 650 attempts); at Okinawa the percentage was slightly lower, 14.7 per cent, but the number of ships hit was higher (279 in 1,900 attempts). The suicide planes in ten months accounted for 48.1 per cent of all U.S. warships damaged and 21.3 per cent of the ships sunk during the 44-month war.[49]

---

[45] USSBS, *Japanese Air Power*, p 60.

[46] USSBS, *Campaigns*, p 286.

[47] USSBS, *Campaigns*, p 286. I have cited this version in my book *On to Westward*, p 290, as I heard it in January 1945 from Radio Tokyo. Arima must have missed, since no carriers were hit between 14–18 October. *Houston* and *Canberra* were torpedoed in orthodox attacks. At other times the Japanese gave other versions of the origin of *kamikaze*.

[48] Sherrod, *On to Westward*, p 245. The writer reserves judgment on the Russian companies marching in good order through German minefields to explode them.

[49] USSBS, *Japanese Air Power*, pp 23, 74. This survey has an excellent appendix (pp 60–74) on *kamikaze*.

While his own men were inclined to smile at Admiral Halsey's assurances that only one *kamikaze* in a hundred found its mark, few of them realized that they were 26 times as effective as the Admiral said. In fairness to Admiral Halsey it should be pointed out that we thought *all* Japanese pilots had turned *kamikaze*. Actually, the best pilots usually were withheld from the nonreturnable missions, and tactical units continued to fly orthodox cover, reconnaissance, bombing and torpedo missions; suicide pilots came usually from operational-training units.[50]

The near-panic caused within the U.S. Navy by Japan's suicide pilots was not generally known at the time,[51] and is not fully realized even yet.

Although the Japanese claimed that their suicide attacks began on 15 October the Americans took their first alarmed note of deliberate crashes ten days later in the midst of the Battle for Leyte Gulf. Accurate AA fire shot down planes diving for the CVE's *Petrof Bay* and *Sangamon,* but *Suwannee* was hit with heavy casualties. At 1050 eight planes began making suicide dives on other CVE's supporting the Leyte landing. *Kalinin Bay* was hit, and three others received minor damage from near misses. Then a *kamikaze* went through the flight deck of *St. Lô,* causing heavy explosions and fires which sank her.[52] Obviously, the Japanese had found something new and deadly.

On 29 October *Intrepid* became the first ship of the fast-carrier task force to become victim of the *kamikazes,* although her damage was slight and personnel casualties few. Next day the ill-fated *Franklin* was hit for the first time, and had to retire to the U.S. with a 40-foot hole in her flight deck. Another suicider sent CVL *Belleau Wood* to the same destination. Two days later a destroyer was sunk and three others damaged by the "green hornets" (as the sailors began to call these unearthly little men of unprecedented bravery).

Lexington got hers on 5 November, when a suicide bomber crashed the signal bridge, causing 182 casualties. On 25 November *Hancock, Intrepid* (again) and *Cabot* were damaged seriously and *Essex* superficially. On these four carriers casualties totaled 60 dead, 68 wounded.

From 24 October until 29 November, no less than 40 ships were "body-crashed" by flyers of the "Divine Wind"—5 sunk, 23 badly damaged, 12 slightly damaged.[53]

Therefore, Admiral Kinkaid of the Seventh Fleet was unhappy, and Admiral Halsey of the Third Fleet was doubly disappointed—he had wanted so much to make the first scheduled attack on Tokyo. General MacArthur was particularly dissatisfied with Leyte's air defense at early light and late light.

---

[50] *Ibid.,* p 67.

[51] Admiral Nimitz withheld public release until 13 April 1945 (ELD), and because President Roosevelt died a few hours later, the full effect of the *kamikaze* story was lost.

[52] Buchanan, *The Navy's Air War,* p 251.

[53] Figures from Naval Aviation Historical Unit, courtesy Mr. Adrian O. Van Wyen. The 40 included 16 carriers—6 CV's, 2 CVL's, 8 CVE's.

Marines Move to Leyte

MacArthur and Halsey moved at about the same time to bolster the land-based air defense of Leyte. The General proposed on 26 November to trade night-fighter squadrons with Nimitz:

> Japs operating Oscars as night bombers which are too fast for P-61's. In Palau enemy employing bombers which P-61 can effectively cope with. Would appreciate your considering a temporary swap of night fighter squadrons, the Marine squadron at Palau to operate from Leyte and P-61's to go to Peleliu.[54]

Admiral Halsey took up the battle which General Mitchell had initiated six months earlier: to get Marine aviators out of the "milk run" area into "any projected operations to the westward." As Halsey relates his role:

> I had had under my command in the South Pacific a Marine Air Group which had proved its versatility in everything from fighting to blasting enemy vessels. I knew that this group was now under Mac-Arthur's command, and I knew, too, without understanding why, that when Kenney was not keeping it idle, he was assigning it to missions far below its capacity. Kinkaid's complaint of insufficient air cover prompted me to take a step which was more than a liberty; to a man of meaner spirit than MacArthur's, it would have seemed an impertinence. I called these Marines to his attention.[55]

The upshot was that Lieut. Colonel Peter D. Lambrecht's VMF(N)-541 left Palau—where it had flown 287 night-bombing strikes and 461 night patrol missions and shot down one plane—on 3 December, and flew its 12 F6F's the 602 miles to Tacloban. When the remainder of the air echelon was flown in by the R5C's of VMR-952, the Squadron's strength on Leyte added up to 23 pilots, 8 ground officers, 118 enlisted men. They used the facilities of the Army's 421st Night Fighter Squadron, which moved to 541's old quarters on Peleliu.

The first fighters of MAG-12[56] arrived on Leyte a few hours later—66 F4U's which had flown 1,957 miles from Emirau via Hollandia and Peleliu, escorted by PBJ's of MAG-61. Nine more of the Corsairs arrived the following day.

---

[54] CinCSoWesPac to CinCPOA, 26 November 1944.

[55] *Admiral Halsey's Story*, p 231. Another persuasive agent might have been the naval liaison officer attached to Fifth Air Force. He pointed out to General Whitehead that the Marine Group's planes had folding wings, and would save space on crowded Tacloban. Alas! he did not know that the Group had received FG's, the Goodyear-manufactured version of the F4U, which had no folding wings. (Comment by Colonel V. J. McCaul, 14 August 1949.)

[56] VMF's 115, 211, 218, 313.

Colonel William A. Willis's MAG-12 pilots were veterans who averaged about ten months overseas on their current tour (many had also seen service in the Solomons on previous tours). Since it was necessary to bring in experienced ground crews as quickly as possible, Willis received the support of 12 C-47's from the Fifth Air Force to supplement MAG-25's transports in moving the entire group.

Tacloban strip was now the none-too-happy base of 87 Marine planes. Although the invasion had taken place six weeks before the first Marine flyers got there, work on the airfield had progressed but little. Severe storms lashed the east coast of Leyte during the October-January northeast monsoon, and stories about the mud at Tacloban are still legendary—General Kenney noted that three hours were required to haul his WAC detachment six miles through mud that lapped over the trucks' running boards.

The fighting on the ground at Leyte had been facilitated by the Japanese retreat into the interior. But there was still plenty of action at Tacloban. On the night of 26 November—just after MacArthur requested VMF(N)-541—three Japanese planes tried an unsuccessful airborne landing. On the 27th, when rain squalls hindered AAF interception, *kamikazes* crashed into a battleship and two cruisers, causing extensive damage.

This was the situation as the first five Marine squadrons got ready for their first combat in the Philippines, in early December 1944.

CHAPTER NINETEEN

Corsairs on Leyte

MARINE AIR OPERATIONS on Leyte began within a few hours after the first planes arrived. A two-plane section of VMF(N)-541 provided last-light cover for PT boats in Surigao Strait, a four-plane division over the Ormoc Bay area.

Weather grounded all planes on the 4th, but on the 5th four Hellcats were assigned to a predawn patrol covering a convoy south of Leyte. When a Japanese Oscar approached, it was shot down by Lieut. Rodney E. Montgomery Jr.

MAG-12 pilots flew 24 patrols during the day, of four planes each. Only one of the patrols made contact with the enemy—two Zekes which attacked a convoy east of Leyte. Lieut. Johnny D. Lindley of VMF-115, an ex-NAP veteran of the early Guadalcanal fighting, caught one of the Zekes as it finished a run on a ship; he sent it smoking into the sea. Two Corsairs were lost in operational accidents on the 70-foot-wide Tacloban strip and the pilot of one of them, Lieut. Jerome G. Bohland, was killed. During that night Japanese bombers destroyed three more of the F4U's in a bombing raid on the strip.[1]

Attacks on Japanese Shipping, 7 December

December 6 was spent in uneventful patrolling, but the following day brought the most action any Marine aviators had seen since the big tangles over Rabaul early in the year.

The cause of this melee was the tenth Japanese attempt to reinforce their garrison near Ormoc, across the island from Tacloban, on the same day that the 77th Infantry Division was making a counterlanding a few miles to the south of Ormoc.

A night fighter flown by Tech. Sergeant John W. Andre fired 1,060 rounds into a Lily over Ormoc Bay at 0150 on 7 December—one of the three GCI-vectored kills credited to VMF(N)-541 during that squadron's stay on Leyte, and one of four kills Andre scored. Four other night-fighter pilots teamed up to bag another enemy plane at 0610.

But the big show began later in the morning, when 12 F4U's of VMF-211

---

[1] MAG-12 war diary, December 1944.

set out to attack "3 enemy destroyers and 4 cargo ships" which Intelligence said were headed for Ormoc Bay. When the Marine planes found them the cargo ships had already anchored at San Isidro Harbor at the northwest end of the island, 30 miles short of Ormoc, and the destroyers were headed out to sea. The VMF-211 pilots flew through several protecting Zekes to place some near misses alongside one of the destroyers and start oil leaks. While the rest of the planes took on the Zekes, four Corsairs made six strafing runs that left the ship "burning from stem to stern and barely under way."[2] It was discovered later, beached on Semirara Island, south of Mindoro. Enemy AA winged two Marine planes, however, and a Zeke shot down another. All three pilots bailed out, but Lieut. Louis W. Reisner was never recovered, and Lieut. Jacques Allen, who suffered a fractured skull, died two months later. The third pilot, Major Stanislaus Witomski, CO of VMF-211, was rescued.

After this experience, when Army fighters failed to show up and furnish cover as scheduled, the Marines took care always to assign an escort of their own.[3]

The afternoon of the 7th saw MAG-12 and Army fighters attacking the rest of the convoy at San Isidro. VMF-211 furnished 7 Corsairs, VMF-218 4, and VMF-313 10.[4] Lieuts. Slaton and Rutherford sank one cargo ship with their half-ton bombs; Lieuts. Forbes, Catlin and Knight together with Army P-40's sank another. All four planes of VMF-218 claimed direct hits which broke a troop transport in half, "the stern sank immediately and the bow was burning and sinking with flames, smoke and steam rising from it."[5] VMF-313 claimed an AK (by Major McGlothlin and Lieuts. Jarrett and Garrotto) plus a destroyer and another AK which was shared with VMF-211.

Credit for this day's work is difficult to assess. Marine records claim four cargo ships and a high-speed transport sunk, plus two destroyers seriously damaged. JANAC identifies four ships totaling 16,000 tons as sunk on 7 December, crediting them jointly to the Marines and the AAF. *Transport No. 11* (1,500 tons) is credited to the Army flyers alone. General MacArthur's communiqué claim of 13 ships sunk out of 13—repeated by General Kenney in his book—is plainly an exaggeration.

While the Japanese ships were being attacked near San Isidro, the U.S. invasion force off Ormoc was suffering "the greatest *kamikaze* effort yet"[6]— nearly ten hours of sporadic attacks by more than 100 planes. DD *Mahan* and APD *Ward* went down, *LSM 318* was hit while stuck on the beach and had to be abandoned, DD *Lamson* and *LST 737* were damaged and so was APD

---

[2] *Ibid.*

[3] Boggs, *Marine Aviation in the Philippines,* p 33.

[4] Other MAG-12 planes were assigned to patrol over shipping approaching the east coast of Leyte and took no part.

[5] MAG-12 war diary, December 1944.

[6] Captain Walter Karig, Lieut. Commander Russell L. Harris, and Lieut. Commander Frank A. Manson, *Battle Report;* Volume V: *Victory in the Pacific* (cited hereinafter as *Battle Report,* V), p 80.

PHILIPPINES BASES USED BY MARINES

Liddle, which had almost all her personnel in the bridge area killed, including the captain, executive officer, gunnery, medical and communications officers. Coverage of the invasion force was the assignment of the Army P-38's, which claimed 56 enemy planes.[7] The only two planes claimed by marines this date were the two early-morning kills by night fighters.

[7] *General Kenney Reports,* p 488.

The 7 December battle proved the worthiness of the fighter-bomber as a weapon against enemy ships. Already suicide planes were forcing the U.S. Navy to change carrier complements to accommodate more fighters, and ten squadrons of Marine F4U's were in the process of being assigned to help fill the breach.[8] The fighter which could also bomb proved a godsend during the *kamikaze* crisis.

This day's action also proved that the Marines had not lost their sharp-shooters' aim, though 11 months had passed since they sank a ship.[9]

Action of 11 December

MAG-12's fighter-bombers had another chance to prove themselves on 11 December, when the Japanese made their eleventh and last attempt to reinforce their troops on Leyte.

When word came early in the morning that six cargo ships and transports and four destroyers and destroyer escorts were heading for Leyte, 27 F4U's intercepted 40 miles east of Panay Island. Hits were claimed on a transport and an AK; eight Japanese fighters were sent flaming into the sea and one was seen to crash on Panay.

In the afternoon 30 more Marine fighter-bombers and 16 Army P-40's went after the same convoy, which by then was within five miles of Palompon on Leyte's west coast. VMF-313 scored three hits on a "large troop transport" which was seen to sink within four minutes. VMF-211 claimed two destroyers and a transport, VMF-115 a large AK. VMF-218 made hits on a destroyer escort and a transport. During this action another Zeke was shot down. The P-40's, less accustomed to low-level attacks, dived from about 10,000 feet to 5,000 feet, released bombs and "accomplished nothing except to make interesting splashes in the water and wake up the Japs."[10] The Army planes did manage to divert the Japanese AA gunners until the Corsairs, flying fast and low, got through the screening destroyers.

As usual in such cases, there was some duplication of claims. JANAC lists only two cargo ships—totaling 8,700 tons—sunk off Leyte on 11 December, and gives joint credit to Army and Marine planes. Next day 35 MAG-12 Corsairs and 8 P-40's hit the cripples 15 miles off Panay and sank DD *Uzuki* and *Transport No. 159.* Two PT boats caught DD *Yuzuki* being unloaded by barges off San Isidro and sank her, too.[11]

Four F4U's of VMF-313 had the duty of defending the first resupply convoy headed for the 77th Infantry Division beachhead near Ormoc. As the

---

[8] See Chapter Twenty-two.

[9] Possible exception: an "AK" credited to Major Hunter Reinburg of VMF-122 near Yap on 24 October. JANAC allows a special submarine chaser to Marine aviation in the same area, but on the next day.

[10] Boggs, *Marine Aviation in the Philippines,* p 35, quoting Captain Rolfe F. Blanchard, the strike leader.

[11] Karig, Harris and Manson, *Battle Report,* V, p 82.

convoy threaded Surigao Strait at 1715, it was attacked by 16 Zekes carrying a 500-pound bomb under each wing. The suicide planes concentrated on destroyer *Reid,* which managed to shoot down two of them. But they kept coming. One of the *kamikaze*-bent planes crashed 500 yards off the starboard beam, a second hooked its wing on the starboard whaleboat, then swung into the side of the ship; a gunner was knocked down by the upper half of the Zeke pilot's body as it was hurtled through the air. A third plane grazed the bow, then crashed off to port. A fourth crashed to starboard but the fifth came in from dead astern and exploded *Reid's* magazines, sinking her in 15 seconds.[12]

The four F4U's flew through the task force's "friendly" fire which caused them "considerable" damage, too late to save *Reid,* whose attackers were not spotted until they were 2,000 yards away. But the marines shot down five of the attackers to bring their total for the day to 19; Lieut. Clyde R. Jarrett was credited with two of them, the other three pilots with one apiece.[13]

The successes of 11 December were not without cost. Six Corsairs were shot down by AA fire or enemy fighters and three pilots—Lieuts. Stanley Picak, Harry O'Hara and Richard E. Eacobacci—failed to survive. Seven or eight more badly damaged F4U's had to be surveyed.[14]

Lieut. Michael Gudor of VMF-115 was attacked by two Zekes at 10,000 feet. He shot down one of them, dropped his bomb on an AK, then collided with the other Zeke. Part of his F4U's tail section was severed; he bailed out and was picked up by Dumbo the next afternoon. Lieut. William Rainalter of the same squadron collided with an Oscar, returned after five days on Sambuluan Island, where he parachuted.

The sixth pilot, Lieut. Walter D. Bean, was listed as missing, but he showed up nine days later.

After being shot down by a Hamp, Bean landed in the sea. Neither his Mae West nor raft would inflate, but fortunately he found a coconut log and clung to it all night. The current pulled him toward two enemy destroyers and an oil tanker, but about a half mile from the Japanese ships, Bean saw ten small fishing boats. One of these fought the wind to come alongside him. The natives (whose information on the course of the war was a bit rusty) asked him if he were German or American, then picked him up just before he lost consciousness. After he was given artificial respiration, Bean slept until late on the 13th.

On the 14th he was taken to Madredijas on Bantayan Island, northwest of Cebu—the first American the natives had seen since the Japanese occupation. He was showered with luxuries, including chocolate bars whose wrappers bore the historic prophecy, "I shall return." On his journey home, Bean was taken south by ox cart to the town of Bantayan. There the natives brought in two Japanese prisoners from a dive bomber which had crashed on the shore.

---

[12] *Ibid.*

[13] MAG-12 war diary mistakenly places this action on 12 December, as the Squadron documents and naval sources show.

[14] Captain Blanchard's comment on a first draft of this manuscript.

This unfortunate pair was marched into town and down the street under the blows of bolo knives which caused the pilot to cry out, but the gunner took it more courageously (one indication that not all came out of the same mold). The natives told the Japanese if they could make it to the woods they could go free, but as the enemy prisoners took off, the Filipinos shot them down in cold blood. Bean also noticed several Japanese bodies lying on the beaches where the tide had left them. All had been badly mutilated. Bean left the island convinced that the Japanese Co-Prosperity Sphere had failed on Bantayan.

Busy Days for the Night Fighters

Soon after its arrival VMF(N)-541 found that it wasn't going to be used very much as it had been taught under Marine Corps doctrine. Although Colonel Lambrecht suggested patrolling all night—16 three-hour sorties per night—as had been his squadron's custom on Peleliu, the CO of the 308th Bomb Wing said "OK," but what he was most interested in was patrols during the vulnerable dawn and dusk. This was essentially work for day-fighter squadrons, since it did not require radar direction. But the commander told Lambrecht that his Army day fighters were not trained for predawn take-offs and after-dark landings, and the marines would have to do the last-light and early-light missions. "To say the least," Lambrecht reported, "reference (c) was slightly misleading."[15]

The worst of several handicaps was the absence of the Squadron's own well-trained GCI-controllers. On those occasions when the pilots were sent out on true night missions, they were likely to find themselves in the position of Lieut. O. K. Houston, who was chasing two bogeys at 0430 on 10 December when Army GCI vectored him in the wrong direction and caused him to lose not only the enemy planes, but also himself. "Listeners on the ground heard some violent expostulations from 'O. K.' when he discovered he was lost—but then, it isn't a very nice feeling."[16]

During the first three nights the field lights on Tacloban worked about ten per cent of the time, and were never available when needed. Returning planes had to orbit for 15 minutes to an hour, until enough jeeps had been rounded up alongside the runway to show the night fighters home. Lambrecht sent to Peleliu for his own PAM-3 set and its field-lighting crew, and this particular problem was solved.[17]

The Army GCI sets were sited with little understanding of night-fighter operations. The station ("Blue Eyes") south of Tacloban field looked to the east and had a 75° coverage to the northwest for only 40 miles between Leyte

---

[15] VMF(N)-541 report of Leyte operations, 3 December 1944 to 11 January 1945. "Reference (c)" was MacArthur's request for the Squadron's services.

[16] Lieut. A. R. Pilotte's diary, which was distributed to the Squadron in mimeograph 17 May 1946, p 48.

[17] VMF(N)-541 report of Leyte operations, *loc. cit.*

and Samar—and this coverage was partially blanked by 4,000-foot mountains. Its chief value was in assisting instrument approaches. The GCI station at Baybay, on the west side of Leyte, covered about 75° to the northwest over Ormoc Bay. The Army controllers and the two Marine controllers attached to Lambrecht's "Bat Eyes" protested this ridiculously limited scope, and the site was moved—but not to the spot recommended. The new site was next to native huts with metal roofs which absorbed two-thirds of the radar energy. The radar was thereby weakened so that no bogeys could be picked up below 10,000 feet at distances greater than 20 miles. This could have been remedied by moving the site 200 yards to the one recommended, but all pleas fell on deaf Army ears.

The Bat Eyes flew their dawn and dusk patrols in routine fashion, without much excitement, until 12 December. At 0615 a four-plane patrol took off to cover the return of part of the Ormoc invasion force. One plane was late and had to return, but the other three, led by Captain David W. Thomson, proceeded toward the convoy. A four-plane mission under Lieut. Fletcher D. Miller Jr., was airborne at 0650 to cover some PT boats in Carigara Bay, north of Leyte.

Thomson's threesome was notified by GCI that a big Japanese formation was heading for the convoy. When the marines neared Ponson Island they sighted five large groups of bogeys totaling 33. Despite the 11-to-1 odds, the Hellcats sailed in, destroying five enemy planes and breaking up the flight. In answer to Thomson's call for help, Lieut. Miller's quartet rushed up in the best horse-opera tradition and in a furious attack shot down six planes. It was observed that the Japanese showed poor air discipline and evaded combat when possible. The convoy, which cheerfully checked its AA fire upon the marines' arrival, suffered no damage, and when it was over, radioed: "Nice show, boys, thanks a million."[18] There were no night-fighter aspects to this one-sided victory, which began at 0720, but it saved a convoy and gave the Squadron a big lift. The only Marine casualty of the day was an F6F which, upon returning to Tacloban, had its wing clipped by a rampaging P-47.

Mindoro Invaded

MacArthur's next step in the reconquest of the Philippines was extremely daring—a hop to the island of Mindoro, immediately south of Luzon, nearly 200 miles northwest of Leyte. Purpose of the invasion was to secure better ground for airfields—through a quirk in the Philippine weather, Mindoro on the west side of the Archipelago is dry when Leyte is covered by slogging mud. It was known that the island was lightly defended, but it was also certain that the *kamikazes*, flying from Mindanao during the approach and from Luzon during the landing, could crash into the decks of many a ship.

As anti-*kamikaze* measures, Halsey's Third Fleet would blanket Luzon

---

[18] Lieut. Pilotte's diary, p 49; VMF(N)-541 war diary, December 1944.

day and night and the Fifth Air Force would provide coverage down the east coast of Leyte and through the Mindanao Sea. Six escort carriers furnished the cover after the sea had been crossed.

December 13 found the invasion force steaming through the Mindanao Sea. It also found MAG-12 plagued by accidents. Major Theodore Olsen of VMF-313, leader of the first flight to cover the force, took off in a patched-up plane which had been holed 300 times on 11 December; he had to bail out, and when his body was recovered by PT boats it was surmised he had been struck by the vertical stabilizer. Another Corsair crashed while taking off from Tacloban in poor visibility on the same mission. The plane smashed into a jeep, killing the pilot and seriously injuring the two Marine officers in the jeep. Then the plane hit an ambulance and a crash truck, killing four others.

Thirty-five Corsairs helped cover the Mindoro-bound force on this day. They didn't have the duty when a suicide plane flew in low and fast over Negros Island and smacked flagship *Nashville*, spreading gasoline over a third of the ship and setting off AA ammunition. Among the 135 dead lay the chiefs of staffs of the naval force commander and the ground forces commander, the CO of the 310th Bombardment Wing and 28 of the 41 marines in the ship's complement.

On the 14th MAG-12's Corsairs were diverted to bombing airfields on Masbate and Luzon, but on the 15th day fighter squadrons and VMF(N)-541 were back to providing coverage for the Mindoro landing.[19]

Over the beachhead at 0630 four VMF-211 Corsairs intercepted five Zekes intent upon diving into the ships. All were shot down, two of them by Lieut. Frederic Rockefeller. Three F6F's from VMF(N)-541 also got through to the beachhead, ran into several enemy planes between 0805 and 0840 and shot down four of them.[20] Army planes shot down several others, but at least three suiciders got through, destroying two LST's.

In the afternoon 17 Corsairs of VMF-313 were assigned to cover the Mindoro beachhead, but were recalled when the weather worsened. Troops of the 503d Parachute Infantry Regiment—who had been scheduled to jump but it turned out that the Air Force couldn't furnish troop lift from crowded Tacloban—found no opposition ashore on Mindoro, and engineers set to work before dark scraping away the dust for two airstrips.

---

[19] The force made a feint at Palawan Island, and deceived the Japanese into thinking the landing would be made there. But the consequences were gruesome: 150 American prisoners of war were herded into air-raid tunnels, drenched with gasoline and set afire. Only four escaped, by jumping off a cliff, and one of these was killed in the fall.

[20] Captain Harlan Morrison shot down two of these planes, but he "gave" one of them to a pilot who had yielded his share of the plane shot down at 0545 on 6 December. "That deal was worked out in a truly sportsmanlike manner!!!" says Lieut. Pilotte in his diary. Well, maybe. But to his astonishment the writer found that Morrison's pal accepted an Air Medal for a kill that he did not make on a mission that he did not fly.

For their performance from 2 to 15 December MAG-12's four fighter squadrons were commended by Sixth Army:

—the gallantry and fighting spirit of the Marine pilots and the skill and tireless fidelity to duty of the ground personnel, who so well carried out their arduous task of maintaining and servicing the aircraft under the worst possible conditions, constituted a major contribution to the success of the Leyte operations—[21]

Night Hellcats Finish Their Mission

The few days following Uncle-day on Mindoro were relatively quiet. Even "P—— Call Charlie," Tacloban's nightly visitor, seemed to have lost his courage. The only news around the VMF(N)-541 camp was an outbreak of dengue fever. MAG-12 was assigned more and more missions supporting ground troops on the west side of Leyte—not ground-controlled close support, such as they had been trained for, but missions against bivouacs and supply dumps far ahead of the lines which were usually briefed the night before the attack. Daha, Cananga and several other Filipino towns were blown up or burnt up on these missions.

On the night of 22 December Sergeant Andre squeezed his 6-foot-4-inch frame into his Hellcat and set out on the routine dusk mission, hoping to catch the aforementioned Charlie. Over the northern end of Leyte he was vectored toward three Japanese planes. One of them turned east, but Andre followed the other two north, toward Luzon. Over the southeastern end of Luzon he lost the bogeys, and headed home from what seemed a long and futile mission. But when he was over Bulan airfield he noticed four smudge pots, then he spotted two planes circling to land. Andre joined the circle. When a white light went up from the field, signaling the planes to land, the NAP[22] closed in, shot down the rear plane, then put a long burst into the forward plane as its wheels touched the ground. While the two burning planes lighted up the strip, Andre made four strafing runs down each side of it, setting afire two fuel trucks and possibly three aircraft parked alongside.[23]

These two planes brought the Bat Eyes' score on Leyte to 20. During the rest of the Squadron's tour most of the time was spent in unrewarding dawn and dusk hops, poor radar vectoring and missions to cover convoys that never seemed to be where Intelligence had said they would be. On 3 January there was enough excitement, however, to last a month. Two four-plane divi-

---

[21] General Orders No. 123, War Department, 18 October 1946, quoted from Boggs, *Marine Aviation in the Philippines*, p 45. This commendation was superseded 30 March 1949 by a Presidential Unit Citation for the Group, including headquarters and service squadrons.

[22] At this time there were 86 enlisted pilots in the Marine Corps, two of them in VMF(N)-541.

[23] VMF(N)-541 war diary, December 1944; Lieut. Pilotte's diary, p 55.

sions of VMF(N)-541 were just taking off on dawn patrol when a Japanese plane hopped the Tacloban strip and strafed along the edges. He set afire approximately 9 TBF's and 9 PV-1's, caused unimaginable confusion and un-counted explosions. After that, V Fighter Command canceled dawn and dusk missions and called for continuous night patrol.[24]

Captain Morrison's flight reached the convoy north of Mindanao which he was assigned to cover. At a ship controller's direction, two of the planes took off on a search for bogeys that never materialized, but Lieuts. Harold T. Hayes and William J. Cook remained with the ships. Hayes dived from 9,000 feet and caught a Zeke as he was pulling away from the convoy, low on the water. For three miles Hayes pumped bullets continuously into the plane, and it finally nosed over and sank. The two planes climbed to 6,000 feet. Hayes caught a Nick in the port engine, set it afire and watched it explode as it hit the water.

On 11 January VMF(N)-541 returned to Peleliu. Its record during five weeks in the Philippines, flying from an overcrowded strip in generally murky weather, was highly commendable: 924 combat hours flown, 22 planes shot down,[25] 5 more destroyed on the ground. In releasing the Squadron, General MacArthur messaged to Admiral Nimitz: "Your night fighter squadron has per-formed magnificently repeat magnificently during its temporary duty in this area."[26]

The Army's Distinguished Unit Citation was awarded VMF(N)-541, the only Marine aviation outfit so honored during World War II.

Later Leyte Fighter Missions

During the last half of December MAG-12 joined up with two Army fighter groups (348 and 475) and two A-20 and B-25 groups, also stationed at Tacloban, to bomb and strafe enemy concentrations at Palompon on Leyte's west coast (which was invaded Christmas Day by a battalion of the 77th Infantry Division). Most of the Group's work consisted of bombing Luzon villages—Cananga, Daha, San Pablo, Santa Cruz, Hondagua and Los Baños. The F4U's roamed up and down the railway from Legaspi to Laguna de Bay, strafed barges near Batangas, the water tower at Pipa and the railway bridge at Naga.

Shooting up nonmaneuverable trains was considered great sport by all services from the Southwest and South Pacific, whose pilots were used to primitive jungles and pillboxes and well-concealed gun emplacements. By mid-January in the Philippines 79 locomotives and 456 railway cars had been destroyed out of a prewar total of 158 and 1,824, respectively.[27] During the

---

[24] VMF(N)-541 report of Leyte operations.

[25] The Squadron already had one plane to its credit at Peleliu (see p 257), making a total of 23 for World War II.

[26] GHQ SWPA to CinCPOA, 1 January 1945.

[27] Buchanan, The Navy's Air War, p 263.

last days of 1944 MAG-12 flyers, strafing a 200-mile sector from Legaspi to the environs of Manila, destroyed at least 20 locomotives.

Late in December MAG-12 pilots moved from the sardine-can environs of Tacloban strip seven miles south to a piece of the beach at Tanauan, where some Marston mat had been laid over the sand.

"Everytime you landed," one pilot recalled, "there was so much noise you wondered whether or not you had put your wheels down." The marines drew the swampy area; dysentery and dengue fever brought down many of the Group's personnel. Another annoyance was a sniper who chose first light to begin firing from his hillside position some 400 yards away[28] (he never hit anybody).

But the marines soon found natives who were willing to build thatched huts in exchange for cigarettes. These, covered with tent tops, made fair living quarters. The natives also introduced the marines to cock fighting. VMF-211 acquired five fighting cocks, but they usually lost—they had been fed too well, it was finally pointed out to the novices.

MAG-14 Joins Up

On 8 December the Green Island group, Colonel Zebulon C. Hopkins's MAG-14, was put on a 48-hour alert for its move to the Philippines. Some of its pilots were still in Australia on leave when the word came. They needn't have hurried back; the Group had to wait for an airfield to be built on the mud of Samar, the island next north from Leyte.

First of the squadrons to arrive was VMO-251[29] on 2 January, which found the new 7,000-foot coral strip at Guiuan nearly completed. This squadron lived well for the next few days, thanks to the 97th Seabees, but when the rest of the Group began to arrive it had to move across the strip to a virgin camp area. VMO-251's Corsairs flew their first mission the day after arrival: six divisions on combat patrol, including 20 of its 22 planes.

The forward echelon of headquarters and service squadrons began moving from Green 8 January, flying in C-46's and C-47's. VMF-212 began arriving that day in a movement by air of 238 officers and men and 85,000 pounds of cargo—2,350 miles from Piva to Samar. Within the next few days VMF-222 and VMF-223 were at least partially installed, and by 24 January the Group's entire forward echelon had reached the new base in a remarkable—for World War II—airborne achievement. "Needless to say, their expectation of welcome by beautiful Filipina damsels was quickly dispelled."[30]

With the rear echelons of all squadrons it was a different story. They sailed in Liberty ship *Richard Harding Davis* on 16 January, lay over in Hollandia, then in Leyte Gulf. Then they were shunted to Mindoro, remained there (on board ship) for 14 days when it seemed that 1st MAW headquarters might

---

[28] Information from Major Phillip B. May, 20 July 1949.
[29] Redesignated VMF-251 31 January 1945.
[30] VMF-222 war diary, January 1945.

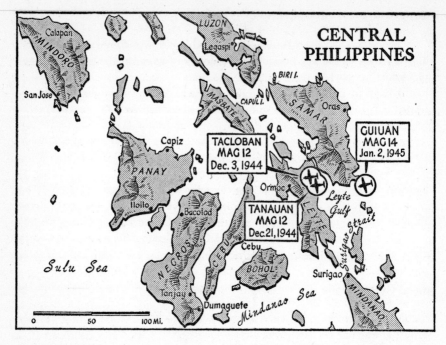

be established there. When that plan fell through, they returned to Samar and unloaded there 24 February.

Operational problems at Guiuan were scarcely less than at Tacloban or at Tanauan, 45 miles to the west, where MAG-12 was now established. The Seabees, laboring in the mud and sheet-like rain, had managed to cut a strip through the coconut trees and surface it with live coral. But there was no room for dispersal, no taxiways, no field-lighting system. B-24 heavy bombers made a washboard of the strip, which the hard-working Seabees had to wet down and regrade every night. As a consequence, MAG-14 lost 19 planes in operational accidents during January.

The worst accident at Samar—and one of the worst the Marines experienced during the war—occurred 24 January. At 0940, while taking off, Lieut. Karl Oerth of VMF-222 hit a lump in the runway, blew a tire and his Corsair careened wildly into his own squadron's revetment area, which was shared with VMF-212. Completely wiped out were the tents housing intelligence, oxygen, parachute and matériel departments. Many men of the Squadron rushed over to rescue the pilot. While they were making this brave effort the plane exploded and set off all its .50-caliber ammunition. Sergeant William H. Rowan and Pfc. Carl Hero of VMF-222 were killed in trying to make the rescue. In addition to these two and the pilot himself, at least 11 others from the two squadrons were killed or died of burns, and more than 50 were injured, many seriously.[31]

---

[31] VMF-212 and VMF-222 war diaries, January, Feburary 1945.

Supporting Luzon Operations

Before the Lingayen landing on 9 January Fifth Air Force was particularly anxious to knock out key bridges at Plaridel and Calumpit, about 25 miles north of Manila, as part of the scheme to dissipate whatever chances the Japanese might have to repel the landing force. It was a long flight for the F4U's—nearly 350 miles each way—and some of them had to land at Mindoro for fuel on the return trip.

On 6 January—three days before S-day at Lingayen—Fifth Air Force sent 23 A-20's and 15 F4U's of MAG-12 against the Calumpit bridges, and a total of 59 A-20's, B-25's and P-38's against the Plaridel bridges, destroying the highway bridge and badly damaging the railway bridge. Next day 40 AAF and 7 MAG-12 planes destroyed the highway and railway bridges at both Plaridel and Calumpit, but failed to destroy the Calumpit dual-purpose bridge.

Thirty-two F4U's further damaged the bridge on 8 January, and so did eight B-25's from Mindoro next day. But its complete destruction was not accomplished until that afternoon of S-day by 31 F4U's and 8 P-38's.[32]

During January MAG-12 flew 306 missions, mostly in support of the Lingayen operation; MAG-14 flew 1,590 sorties.[33] Rolling stock, motor transport, harbor installations and enemy airfields were the fighter and fighter-bombers' principal targets. The two groups shot down only 2 planes and destroyed 12 on the ground during the month. Fifteen pilots were lost. An unusual case involved Captain Louis W. Rancourt, shot down while strafing some Japanese trucks on southern Luzon 22 January with Major May. His was one of the few authenticated instances in the Pacific war of a plane being brought down by rifle fire.[34]

In February the fighter groups threw their weight against the Visayas, having left the Marines' representation on Luzon to the dive bombers. During the month MAG-14 flew a total of 5,562 hours in 1,944 sorties, destroying 12 planes on the ground plus 90 buildings, 20 vehicles, an undetermined number of gun emplacements and ammunition dumps. MAG-12 began flying as far south as the extreme tip of Mindanao, 320 miles from its Tanauan base, in addition to the more familiar runs on Negros and Cebu. The Group's February total was 1,838 sorties for a total of 4,180 hours, about 85 per cent classed as combat.[35]

---

[32] Kenny, Luzon monograph, with Marine Corps figures adjusted from MAG-12 war diary, January 1945.

[33] This probably means MAG-14 flew about 150 missions in its half-month, but the two groups had diffierent bookkeeping systems and nobody can tell.

[34] Information from Major May.

[35] Figures from USMC Division of Aviation analysis, "Marine Fighter Squadrons in the Philippines," June 1945.

CHAPTER TWENTY

Dive Bombers on Luzon

IN MARINE AVIATION annals the Luzon campaign provides one of the notable milestones. Here, for the first time, Marine planes furnished true close support for Army troops. Here the Marines set out to perform a distinct mission and they trained for just that specialty—the assistance of ground troops in advancing against the enemy.

Most important, the Luzon campaign marked a long stride toward the formulation of Marine aviation's postwar mission. The lessons learned on the paddy fields of Luzon paid off five and six years later on the paddy fields of Korea.[1]

Let us review the history of close air support briefly.

Between wars Marine aviators—the reader will recall they were the only American flyers in combat between 1918 and 1941—flew missions for the Marines in Haiti, the Dominican Republic and Nicaragua. In 1940–41 Marine squadrons took part in the Guantánamo, Louisiana and North Carolina maneuvers, mostly with Army troops, and came out with some blunt conclusions:

(1) Adequate and reliable radio communication from air to ground was essential. One-channel radios were entirely inadequate and the later two-channel installations were not much better.

---

[1] To peek into the future and choose one example: on 10 January 1951 Brig. General Homer W. Kiefer, commanding 7th Infantry Division Artillery, wrote the Commandant of the Marine Corps: "During the period 19 September to 20 December 1950 close air support of this division was furnished almost exclusively by the 1st Marine Air Wing . . . in 57 days of combat 1,024 sorties were flown by Marine aircraft (largely Corsairs) in close support of the division without a single casualty among our own troops due to friendly air action. This record I attribute to the fact that adequate control was available with front line units. In many instances Marine planes were bombing and strafing within 200 yards of our front lines. . . . Allow me to reemphasize my appreciation for the outstanding air support received by this division. The Marine system of control, in my estimation, approaches the ideal and I firmly believe that a similar system should be adopted as standard for Army divisions." In his endorsement Major General Edward M. Almond, X Corps commander, declared he wished to "emphasize" Kiefer's final statement regarding the Marine system of Tactical Air Control, which "has proved itself on every occasion." General MacArthur added that "this correspondence again illustrates the outstanding support that Marine air is providing ground forces in the Korean operations." (Fourth endorsement.)

(2) Panels and pyrotechnics were inferior to radio communication but often had to be resorted to because of poor radio equipment and radio discipline. Their use required thorough air-ground coordination.

(3) An airborne coordinator was required for liaison between scout bombers in the air and infantry assault units on the ground.

Valuable as these lessons were, not much was done to exploit them. Not even the Stuka, demonstrating its terrifying power in 1940 as a member of the plane-tank-infantry team, forced the U.S. to adopt a co-ordinated doctrine for close-support aviation. Sure, planes were desirable for knocking out enemy troops, but nobody had drawn up a plan when war came in 1941. Nor had the aircraft radio been developed which could maintain adequate control of supporting aircraft.

Essentially there were—and are—three arguments against aviation being employed immediately in front of ground troops: (1) not effective, (2) too dangerous, (3) too expensive.

Before the war the Army Air Corps, struggling to stretch its scanty funds far enough to buy a few four-engined bombers, naturally reacted against performing missions "to supplement and increase the firepower of ground arms."[2] When The Adjutant General of the Army said experimentation and development for fiscal 1939–40 would be restricted to planes "designed for the close-in support of ground troops," the Army airmen, who were just beginning to get strategic aviation started, naturally fought back.[3]

It is easy now to criticize the Army airmen for their lack of foresight, but their reactions must be placed in time and context. Striving for their independence, they recoiled from too-close ties to the ground forces—the idea was separation, not closer amalgamation. Even the term "air support" was anathema to them. "Support" implies a secondary role—and throughout the war the preferred terms for tactical missions in direct support of ground troops were "air-ground cooperation" or "air-ground coordination." The airmen considered control by infantry officers "an attempt to shackle the air to the ground, and therefore a failure to realize the full capabilities of air attack."[4]

In July 1943, when the war had been on for a year and a half, the Army aviators (in FM 100-20) still insisted: "In the zone of contact, missions against hostile units are most difficult to control, are most expensive, and are, in general, least effective. Targets are small, well-dispersed, and difficult to locate. In addition, there is always a considerable chance of striking friendly forces. . . . Only at critical times are contact zone missions profitable."[5] No more concise—and challenging—criticism was ever written about close air support.

On the other hand, infantry officers in all theaters distrusted close-support

---

[2] AAC Tactical School, Langley Field, Va., "Attack Aviation," January 1938.

[3] Arnold, *Global Mission*, pp 167–168.

[4] Eisenhower, *Crusade in Europe*, p 47.

[5] War Department FM 100–20: *Command and Employment of Air Power*, July 1943, p 12, par 16.

planes' accuracy. The Pacific was replete with cases of men being killed by "friendly" planes. A TBF killed three soldiers on New Georgia and on Bougainville another dropped a bomb on troops of the 3d MarDiv.[6] On Tarawa a carrier pilot killed a marine.[7] An AAF strike killed and wounded some soldiers on Los Negros.[8] A carrier pilot fired three rockets into the 2d MarDiv lines on Saipan which caused 27 casualties.[9] Navy planes dropped several bombs on marines at Guam.[10] Marine aviators would cause some U.S. casualties in the Philippines.[11]

The first close support by American planes in World War II was furnished by Navy carrier planes in the landing phase at Guadalcanal, using F4F's and SBD's. An Air Control Center aboard the flagship of the attack force commander controlled and co-ordinated air support by maintaining radio contact with aircraft on station as well as with the carrier task force. However, there was no direct communication between the landing force and the aircraft on station. Later, support was rendered to the ground troops by Army and Marine pilots but again communication facilities were limited, necessitating front-line messages to be relayed from ground force commander to division command post to Henderson Field, thence back to the supporting planes. These flyers were either briefed on the ground or sometimes they walked up to the front lines and took a look at the targets. Air liaison parties (ALP's) were improvised and trained on the island for future operations.

On New Georgia, pilots were briefed a day ahead for air support missions; even then, the blessing was mixed.[12] Bougainville showed some improvement, and Peleliu more.

Meanwhile, "Naval aviation took the air support ball away from us and carried it until the closing year of the war."[13] Kelly Turner, never a man to miss a trick or neglect a lesson, left the Solomons and took command of the Central Pacific thrust. At Tarawa he had an elaborate organization of ship-based air support control units, working with trained air-liaison parties who were attached to the 2d Division marines, finally using multiple-circuit plane radios. At Tarawa 650 support sorties were flown, some of which might be classed as close support.

In the Marshalls the Navy introduced the command ship (AGC) with its intricate and excellent communications network. At Kwajalein and Roi–Namur a Joint Assault Signal Company (JASCO) was used, including 13

[6] See p 151 and pp 190–191.

[7] Sherrod, *Tarawa*, p 98.

[8] Craven and Cate, *The AAF in WW II*, Vol IV, p 566.

[9] CG 2d MarDiv report, sec 6, p 17; letter ComFifthFleet to ComPhibPacFor, 29 July 1944.

[10] Isely and Crowl, *The U.S. Marines and Amphibious War*, p 385.

[11] See p 321.

[12] See p 151.

[13] Brig. General Vernon E. Megee "Control of Supporting Aircraft," *Marine Corps Gazette,* January 1948, p 9.

air-liaison parties, each consisting of 1 officer and 3 to 7 enlisted technicians.[14] These ALP's acted in a capacity similar to artillery forward observers. The officer, schooled in intelligence and in aviation procedure, stayed with the unit commander of the division, regiment or battalion. It was his duty to relay requests for support missions back to the Commander Air Support Control Unit (CASCU) on board ship, specifying the nature of the target, its location, time for being on station for the attack and location of friendly troops.

Close air support in the Marshalls was the most successful the Pacific war had known up to that time. Just how effectively the Navy carried the air-support ball was determined by the AAF's own Evaluation Board:

> The Seventh Division had, at Attu, experience in working with Army Air Force support (P-38's). At Kwajalein it had experience in working with Naval air support. Hence, it is believed that this division is better qualified than any other to judge the effectiveness of each system.
>
> Personnel of this division were unanimous in the following comments:
>
> (1) Close Air support of infantry—"close" means within 200 yards of front line troops—is very effective and desirable as executed by Naval air.
>
> (2) Support as rendered by Army Air Force is not effective in assisting the advance of the infantry and may be detrimental.
>
> The reasons advanced for the above statements were:
>
> (1) Naval air was a workable system whereby air strikes can be directed effectively at targets within close range of friendly troops without danger to them.
>
> (2) Naval air units practice and rehearse with ground force units so each becomes familiar with the methods to be employed, and ground forces gain confidence in the air units.
>
> (3) Army Air Force units have no system and hence cannot be sufficiently controlled to permit close support of ground forces.
>
> (4) Army Air Force units do not practice or rehearse with ground force units. They do not know how ground force units operate; hence, if brought in close they are quite apt to bomb and strafe our own troops by mistake.[15]

Regarding the Army's FM 100-20 and its conclusions about "contact zone missions," the Evaluation Board declared sharply: "The above doctrine is in error." AAF Headquarters responded by demoting the senior member of the Board.

As we have seen, Marine aviators missed out on the amphibious phases

---

[14] A JASCO included an air liaison, a naval gunfire, and a shore party communications section. The company was attached to the signal battalion of each Marine division.

[15] AAF Evaluation Board "POA Report No. 3," p 15.

of the Gilberts, Marshalls and Marianas because they didn't get their planes on carriers in time.

Training for Luzon

On 10 October 1944 Colonel Lyle H. Meyer told his MAG-24 on Bougainville that the Group had finally been given a mission: to furnish close support to Army troops in the Philippines. All the doctrines and procedures of close air support were assembled and studied under the direction of Lieut. Colonel Keith B. McCutcheon, MAG-24 operations officer and head professor. Written material indicated that "the subject was far from standardized," so the Marines had to do considerable improvising. Three days later MAG-24 started learning in earnest, and for the next two months an intensive course of 40 lectures was presented on subjects ranging from "Introduction to Close Support Aviation" to "Air Liaison Party Duties" to "The People, Flora, Fauna and Culture of the Philippines." Instructors included veteran ALP officers from the Central Pacific,[16] Army ground officers from the 37th and Americal Divisions (also scheduled to leave Bougainville for the Philippines), and Seventh Fleet intelligence officers.

The four squadrons of MAG-24[17] were joined in the classes by officers of the newly constituted MAG-32, made up of VMSB-142 and 243 (shifted from MAG-12) and 224 (from MAG-14)—MAG-32's headquarters and service squadrons were on the way from Ewa under command of the acting CO, Lieut. Colonel John L. Smith. Pupils were rounded up from other AirNorSols bases. VMSB's 341 and 244 were still located at Green Island. VMSB-241 was at Munda until December; 142 and 243 were at Emirau. But lectures were repeated until about 500 officers and gunners of the dive-bomber squadrons had learned all the professors taught about close air support.[18] Pupils who learned on Bougainville went back as teachers to their own squadrons on other islands.

Special courses of 12 lectures were crammed in at the last minute for personnel who had missed parts of the full course, 17 lectures for the tail-end Charlies of MAG-32, and a special course of 10 lectures for group operations officers.

Most important, the Marine aviators adopted a principle which both Army and Navy had been reluctant to concede: "close support aviation is only an additional weapon to be employed at the discretion of the ground commander."[19]

---

[16] Captains John Pratt, Stanley Ford, Franklin McCarthy, Francis R. B. Godolphin, and Samuel H. McAloney, who had served with the 4th Marine Division in the Marshalls and Marianas, but not with Marine aviation. Captain Pratt went to Leyte with MAG-12 and was seriously injured in a plane-jeep accident 13 December.

[17] VMSB's 133, 236, 241, 341.

[18] MAG-24 memo, "Air-Ground Support Training Program," 8 December 1944.

[19] Lieut. Colonel Keith B. McCutcheon, "Close Support Aviation," report in CMC files, from which much of this chapter is written.

Here there was no quibbling about who would control the planes. They were there for the ground commander to use as he saw fit—"against targets that cannot be reached by his other weapons or in conjunction with the ground weapons in a coordinated attack. Close support should be immediately available and should be carried out deliberately, accurately and in coordination with the other assigned units."[20]

This concession was not as difficult for Marine aviators to make as Army and Navy officers had found it. Before the war nearly all Marine aviators had served as company officers. The senior flyers knew the problems of the men on foot, and they were therefore more likely to have a sympathetic understanding of the man who had to assault a pillbox or a hillside cave. Due to the exigencies of wartime expansion, most of the younger flyers had not received the ground soldiers' training,[21] but they were still marines first, aviators second. This conditioned their attitude toward the troops on the ground, and it is of secondary importance that the troops in the Philippines happened to be soldiers rather than marines.

The Fifth Air Force customarily furnished its own support air parties, which were stationed at headquarters of divisions or larger units. ALP's and their equipment were furnished by JASCO's or by the ground forces' own units. Requests for close air support were relayed from the ALP's through battalion, regiment and division to the support air party.

In the Bougainville curriculum the aviators proposed to furnish their own ALP's, though there was nothing in their tables of organization making such a provision. Furthermore, they proposed that the front-line ALP would control planes on his front by direct communication with the planes overhead.

This plan was not altogether new. On occasion both the Army and the Navy had released control of aircraft to the front-line ALP's.[22] But as a deliberate policy front-line control was, to say the least, unorthodox. For the small-scale, limited-front warfare in the Philippines the policy turned out to be ideal.

Next to the effectiveness of close support and its danger to friendly troops, infantry commanders complained of its slowness. A mission set up a day in advance might be worthless by the time it was executed. There might be a delay of several hours between a request and its clearance with a support air controller back at division or corps CP.

To fit the Philippines situation—a limited front, a jungle hide-out, a hillside cave—the Marine planners on Bougainville held to a belief that "front-

---

[20] Ibid.

[21] It is worth noting, however, that between 7 December 1941 and 31 December 1944, 137 ground officers transferred to aviation and became pilots. (Information from USMC Records and Statistics.) Because many of these were captains and majors when they became pilots, their influence was greater than their number indicates.

[22] AAF planes had been controlled by front-line parties in the Admiralties in March 1944. (Craven and Cate, The AAF in WW II, Vol IV, p 569.) Unfortunate experiences in the Marianas had caused Admiral Turner to doubt the feasibility of ALP control. (Isely and Crowl, The U.S. Marines and Amphibious War, p 510.)

line ALPmen could and should talk planes onto a target by direct communication; this, they felt, was far more efficient than relaying the information through intervening echelons and a far-distant controller."[23]

It should be emphasized that the seven dive-bomber squadrons were able to devote all their training time to a very specialized mission. They had no air-defense problems; no long-range missions to worry about. There was three months' time for the experienced aviators to practice their specialization.

The success of the operation depended primarily on good communications. Four nets were to be used:

(1) *Support Aircraft Request* (SAR), which linked the ALP with the Support Aircraft Commander (SAC) and the airborne air coordinator.

(2) *Support Aircraft Direction* (SAD)—a two-way channel linking the SAC, air coordinator and supporting aircraft.

(3) *Support Aircraft Direction Emergency* (SADE)—an emergency channel linking the ALP's with the supporting aircraft.

(4) *Support Aircraft Observation* (SAO), a two-way channel linking the SAO with the airborne observers.

The dive bombermen had an extra card up their sleeves. By this time the SBD's had four very-high-frequency (VHF) channels and two medium-high-frequency (MHF) channels. They equipped their ALP jeeps likewise. On Luzon this was to serve them in good stead when the VHF channels became as jammed as Main Street on Saturday night. They simply switched to medium frequencies and cut out Army planes' traffic altogether.

The plane they used was becoming obsolete, and by the time the Philippines campaign ended it would be discarded altogether. The SBD had served long and faithfully in World War II, but on 21 July 1944 the last SBD (No. 5,936) rolled off the Douglas Aircraft Company's assembly line. The Army (which designated the plane A-24) had given up on dive bombers in 1942, in favor of fighter bombers and the skip-bombing of the faster planes like the A-20 and B-25.[24] The Navy in 1944 turned to the heavier armed and faster SB2C, which it augmented with fighter bombers in large numbers.

The flyers worked out a training schedule with the 37th Infantry Division soldiers. While the infantrymen simulated an attack on a Bougainville pillbox the ALPmen in their jeeps tuned up their radios, the dive bombers simulated attacks ahead of the troops (but dropped no live bombs). If the training did nothing else, it made for friendly relations and mutual confidence between the flyers and the foot soldiers—which, the flyers were soon to learn, is the prerequisite for successful close support, anyway.

General Mitchell's chief of staff, Colonel Clayton C. Jerome, was designated CO of MAG-32 on 7 November, with John Smith as his exec. As senior

---

[23] Boggs, *Marine Aviation in the Philippines*, p 60.

[24] *Ibid.*, p 68, which quotes General Kenney as saying SBD's were too short-ranged and "too slow to argue with the Zeros." The SBD had a combat radius of about 450 miles, a maximum cruising range of 1,230 miles.

Marine officer on Luzon, Colonel Jerome would be over-all commander of both groups (seven squadrons) whenever they operated together.

The Lingayen Landing

The invasion armada which began heading through the Sulu Sea on 3 January 1945, with General MacArthur present on board cruiser *Boise*, counted more than 800[25] ships—biggest to that date and second biggest (after Okinawa) of the war against Japan. Simultaneously, the fast-carrier task force began two days of strikes to the north against Okinawa and other Ryukyus and Formosa, to dam the stream of Japanese aerial reinforcements which up to then had been pouring south. More than 100 aircraft were claimed destroyed, mostly on the ground.

On the 4th the Japanese began to spend as *kamikaze* the hoarded remnants of their Philippines air strength. That day the escort carrier *Ommaney Bay* was sunk. Next day another escort carrier, two cruisers and a destroyer were damaged. It became obvious that all the 52 Japanese airstrips on Luzon could not without help be kept inoperative simultaneously.

General MacArthur requested that the fast carriers come south and hit the 9 fields and 14 strips of the Clark Field Air Center.[26] On 6 and 7 January over 100 more planes were claimed, and this blow, combined with efforts of escort carriers and of land-based strikes "reduced the estimated enemy sorties from some 130 aircraft on the 6th to less than half that number on the 7th and to purely token efforts thereafter."[27]

Nonetheless 6 January was a horrible day for the Seventh Fleet carrying the invasion forces. Sixteen ships were hit by suicide attackers, ten of them incurring serious damage. Among them was *New Mexico*, embarking headquarters of the 308th Bombardment Wing (H) for the Philippines. Twenty-seven were killed on the old BB, including the captain and the communications officer. Dead also were Lieut. General Herbert Lumsden, British Army, and an RAF officer (aboard as observers), 20 Navy enlisted men and 2 of the ship's marines, but Colonel Jerome escaped harm. Lieut. Colonel McCutcheon was as lucky on 9 January when a *kamikaze* crashed into his ship, *Mississippi*.

But the attrition since September had disorganized and demoralized the aerial defenders of Luzon. After the landings pressure on U.S. forces eased. One prisoner said the utter state of confusion, rather than the lack of planes, pilots or supplies, had caused the collapse in intelligent employment of aircraft. Repair shops, storage dumps, and maintenance units were dispersed over a

---

[25] *ONI Weekly*, 10 January 1945, p 117.

[26] See "Clark Field Air Center," *ONI Weekly*, 31 January 1945, p 382.

[27] USSBS, *Campaigns*, p 289. This General Kenney hotly denies. His estimates ("The Luzon Campaign") are 532 Japanese planes on Luzon 4 January, 448 on the 5th, and on succeeding days, 460, 460, 480, 291, 256, 249, 170. His contention: there were 20 suicide attacks before the Third Fleet strikes, 30 on the two days of the strikes and 33 on the following days.

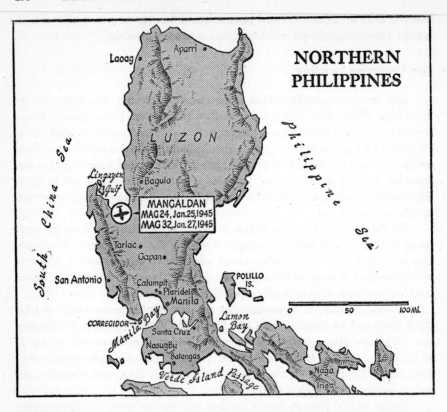

NORTHERN
PHILIPPINES

MANGALDAN
MAG 24, Jan. 25, 1945
MAG 32, Jan. 27, 1945

wide area; some 200 new engines, mostly uncrated, were found in Mabalacat underneath houses, in old rice mills, even on alley sidewalks. Some planes needed only a carburetor or a tire, but the needed items were far away.[28]

The ground defense was also confused. The U.S. assault infantrymen—I Corps (6th and 43d Infantry Divisions) on the left, XIV Corps (37th and 40th Infantry Divisions) on the right—walked ashore with hardly a shot fired. The reserves—25th Infantry Division 158th RCT, 13th Armored Group, 6th Ranger Battalion—followed. The beachhead was rapidly expanded as road junctions and river crossings were taken.

No airstrip had been assigned the Marines, and they had to settle for what acreage they could get, improve it and get an airstrip built. Colonel Jerome got ashore on 11 January (S-day plus 2), but the 308th Wing was already working on an airstrip at Lingayen, and it was overcrowded. The Colonel packed his jeep and with McCutcheon and Corporal Ladislaus Blasko drove across a river on a railroad trestle. They stopped at a spot on the shoreline 15 miles east of Lingayen, where V Fighter Command had selected another airfield site. Here the ground was too soft.

The three marines moved on, five miles south to a spot near Mangaldan.

---

[28] Kenney, "The Luzon Campaign," Annex A.

There, on a rice paddy, was laid out the airstrip which was to serve Marine Air Groups, Dagupan (MAGSDAGUPAN)—MAG's 24 and 32—for the next three months.[29]

Meantime, Colonel Meyer with 14 officers and 283 enlisted men arrived at Lingayen 11 January on board *President Polk* and demonstrated their versatility by helping the soldiers unload and lay steel matting on the Lingayen strip before moving on to Mangaldan. "Although having no previous experience in work of this nature, the men performed their duties enthusiastically and efficiently."[30]

The Mangaldan strip was only a rice paddy. But if the hills of a rice paddy are knocked down without tearing out the roots they make a fine, flat surface which, when oiled, will serve as an airstrip about 12 inches above the water level. Rains would eventually raise the level of the muck but Colonel Jerome, an old Philippines hand from the twenties, figured three dry months were due and that was all he needed at Mangaldan, and recommended that the Army engineers build there.[31]

Headquarters of MAGSDAGUPAN was set up in a bombed-out schoolhouse. As soon as the light bulldozers could turn the rice paddy into an airfield the dive-bomber squadrons began flying up from NorSols via Owi, Peleliu, and Leyte. The first planes arrived 25 January, 46 SBD's of VMSB-133 (Major Lee A. Christoffersen) and VMSB-241 (Major Benjamin B. Manchester III). Meanwhile, ground echelons had continued arriving ever since S-day. By 31 January MAGSDAGUPAN, 7 squadrons, 174 SBD's,[32] 472 officers and 3,047 men, was ready to start functioning from Mangaldan. Headquarters, 308th Bomb Wing, designated Colonel Jerome commander of the base, which came in time to be the home of almost as many more Army planes. Major Sherman Smith, as "strip commander" operating about 300 planes, became one of the busiest airport managers in the Western Pacific.

The First Combat Missions

Following their long indoctrination in close support, the Marines expected to start immediately bombing a path for the advancing infantry. Such was not the case. Neither the AAF nor ground troops were ready to have strikes directed on target from front-line jeeps; the first few days' missions were set up the evening before the attack. The strikes, which began 27 January with raids on San Fernando and Clark Field Air Center, had to clear through a

---

[29] Mangaldan is halfway between San Fabian and Dagupan. Since the latter word makes a better combination the Marines chose MAGSDAGUPAN as their designation, rather than MAGSMANGALDAN or "First Provisional Marine Air Wing," which is what one of their earliest close-support clients, the 6th Infantry Division, called them.

[30] Commendation by Lieut. General Walter Krueger, CG Sixth Army.

[31] Interview Colonel Jerome, 23 May 1949.

[32] SMS's 24 and 32 each had 3 SBD's. MAGSDAGUPAN also had 2 TBF's and 1 R4D.

support air party all the way up to Sixth Army and through 308th Wing. General Krueger's troops were two thirds of the way down from Lingayen to Manila before any close support was wanted or asked for. During the last five days of January five SBD squadrons flew 255 sorties and dropped 104 tons of bombs. One plane was shot down by AA on 28 January and Lieut. Gordon R. Lewis and his gunner, Corporal Samuel P. Melish of VMSB-133, became the first MAGSDAGUPAN marines to die.

Meantime, the 1st Cavalry Division landed on the Lingayen beachhead on 27 January, and started to move to an assembly area 35 miles inland next day. On 30 January General MacArthur visited the area and passed to the 1st's CG, Major General Verne D. Mudge, one of the most passionate orders of the war: "Go to Manila. Go around the Nips, bounce off the Nips, but go to Manila. Free the internees at Santo Tomás. Take Malacañan Palace and the Legislative Building."[33]

On to Manila

At the same time the 37th Infantry Division, partner of the close-support dive-bombermen in the experimentation at Bougainville, was ordered to make a similar dash to Manila on the right (west) flank. XI Corps troops of Eighth Army landed southwest of Manila to drive from the other direction.

No less unusual was the order given to MAGSDAGUPAN: provide an air alert[34] of nine planes from dawn to dusk over the 1st Cavalry Division. The SBD's were ordered, in effect, to guard the flank of the division in its deep, audacious penetration.

Back of this order lay an old school tie, some superior salesmanship and a determination to show the soldiers what Marine flyers, under proper front-line control, could do for them. Captain Francis R. B. Godolphin, already a veteran of the Marshalls and Marianas and one of the principal instructors in the maneuvers with the 37th Division on Bougainville, went over to 1st Cavalry Division headquarters to work out an arrangement. There he found one of his former students at Princeton, Lieut. Colonel R. F. Goheen, G-2 of the division.[35] This made for a sympathetic relationship between the ALPmen and the mechanized cavalrymen. So did a conversation with some of the old-timers of the division, including Brig. General Hugh F. T. Hoffman, who asked: "Godolphin Arabian?" "Yes, sir." Then things were on a sound basis for air.[36]

Next day Captain Samuel Holt McAloney, who had been one of Godolphin's running mates since the first air-liaison parties began training

---

[33] Major B. C. Wright, *The 1st Cavalry Division in World War II*, p 126 (hereinafter cited as Wright, *The 1st CavDiv in WW II*).

[34] "On station" in Navy parlance.

[35] Comment by Godolphin on a first draft of this chapter. After the war Goheen wrote his Ph.D. dissertation under Godolphin's direction.

[36] *Ibid.*

two years earlier, showed up. They went to Sixth Army headquarters for further discussion of the project. As finally planned, Godolphin and McAloney would each be equipped with a radio jeep and a radio-operator-driver. A radio truck with a more powerful transmitter, a crew of communications men and an experienced communications officer would go along with 1st CavDiv headquarters to relay messages back to the airfield when the jeeps got out of its range. A constant watch would be kept at a special radio set at the Mangaldan strip, where Lieut. Colonel McCutcheon would run operations.

The radio truck was put in charge of Captain John A. Titcomb, communications officer of MAG-24, who rounded up emergency repair material, equipped two radio jeeps with both MHF and VHF sets, and supervised the setting up of the receiving station at the airfield.

McAloney was assigned to Brig. General William C. Chase and his 1st Brigade; Godolphin with General Hoffman's 2d Brigade. Chase drew the job of commanding the "flying column" which spearheaded the dash to Manila.

General Chase had no previous information about the project in detail. When he asked what equipment was sent, and found it was just a radio jeep, he merely issued the orders, "Stay beside me and my jeep at all times." Later it was learned that the 308th Bomb Wing had also sent an air liaison party for him, but its equipment of a DUKW (complete with Filipino houseboy), a weapons carrier, a jeep, 27 men and 2 officers was such that it couldn't keep up with the advance or semi-exposed positions. Besides, for air support through that channel, requests would have to be forwarded and approved first by Division, then Corps, then Army and finally by 308th Bomb Wing. The "on station" planes appealed to General Chase.[37]

The outfits started moving out of Guimba at one minute past midnight 1 February and the dash to Manila began at dawn. The nine-plane patrol remained overhead at all times, roaming continuously up and down the valleys, searching every road and trail for signs of enemy movement. When roadblocks were spotted they were reported and, on quickly secured permission from General Chase, were bombed. Because the cavalrymen were in a hurry to free the internees, they sought to avoid a fight. Therefore, the Marine flyers searched the roads and recommended alternates whenever they seemed desirable. The Japanese had been pulling out of the valleys of Luzon into the mountains, and there was always the danger that they would fall upon the slender, three-pronged column.

On 2 February the 2d Squadron, 8th Cavalry, was stopped near Santa Maria by a full Japanese battalion, well dug in on the high ground "in a position capable of withstanding an entire division." Captain Godolphin called the SBD patrol out of the sky, and

---

[37] Comment by McAloney on a first draft of this chapter.

. . . the dive bombers of MAG-32 made several strafing passes at the Japs without firing a shot, due to the proximity of friendly troops, and enabled the squadron to slug its way into the defensive position and rout the occupants.[38]

The same day, as the cavalrymen drove south, SBD's of VMSB's 133, 142 and 241 were diverted from their prearranged assignment to bomb and strafe San Isidro, just ahead of General Chase's troopers. "Target left in shambles" reported the soldiers, who noted that all bombs hit within the assigned area, 200 by 300 yards.[39]

Next day the Marine flyers were able to help save the Novaliches Bridge, when they flew ahead and reported it still intact. The troopers quickly drove ahead to take this Manila gateway before it could be blown. A Navy mine disposal officer, Lieut. (jg) James P. Sutton, ran onto the span through a rain of enemy bullets and cut the fuze to a large mine, which had already been lighted.[40]

The speed of MAGSDAGUPAN communications was well illustrated when Colonel Walter E. Finnegan of the 7th Cavalry Regiment dashed up to Godolphin's radio jeep with a report that a Japanese plane was in the area. Godolphin pointed to the lone enemy plane, still burning on Marikina strip, 2,000 yards away. Staff Sergeant A. A. Byers USMC, in the radio truck, had already relayed the information to two P-51's, vectored them to the plane and watched them shoot it down.[41]

The cavalrymen entered Manila 66 hours after they took off from Central Luzon, quickly rescued the internees at Santo Tomás, then ran into house-to-house resistance from the Japanese which in nearly a month's heavy fighting wrecked one of the more charming cities of the Orient.

By this time the Marine dive-bombermen had sold their services to the 1st Cavalry Division. It might be added that the Marines "bought" this sterling division, too, particularly after Tech. Sergeant Andy Bridgewater USA on 12 February rescued a pilot and a gunner from under the grasp of the enemy. Lieut. Kerwin W. Jacobs and his gunner, Corporal Samuel Scheinfeld, of VMSB-241, crash-landed in no man's land in the Marikina River valley, dazed but not seriously hurt. Bridgewater got to them before the racing Japanese did, kept them with his small group of troopers in enemy territory until they could break out the following day.

General Chase sent word that "I have never seen such able, close and accurate close support as the Marine flyers are giving us" and the division historian also paid generous tribute to the MAGSDAGUPAN pilots:

---

[38] Wright, *The 1st CavDiv in WW II*, p 128.

[39] Boggs, *Marine Aviation in the Philippines*, p 78.

[40] Wright, *The 1st CavDiv in WW II*, p 128. Sutton was elected to Congress from Tennessee in 1948.

[41] Godolphin comment.

Much of the success of the entire movement is credited to the superb air cover, flank protection, and reconnaissance provided by the Marine Air Groups 24 and 32. The 1st Cavalry [Division's] audacious drive down through Central Luzon was the longest such operation ever made in the Southwest Pacific Area using only air cover for flank protection.[42]

But it remained for the 1st Cavalry Division's commanding general to say the final word about the drive to Manila:

I can say without reservation that the Marine divebomber outfits are among the most flexible I have seen in this war. They will try anything, and from my experience with them I have found that anything they try usually pans out. The Marine dive bombers of the First Air Wing have kept the enemy on the run. They have kept him underground and enabled troops to move up with fewer casualties and with greater speed. I cannot say enough in praise of these men of the dive bombers . . . for the job they have done in giving my men close ground support in this operation.[43]

Strikes East of Manila

Twelve miles northeast of Manila lay the Shimbu Line, a system of mutually supporting mountain caves and pillboxes stretching 25 miles north and south from Ipo Dam to Antipolo. Into this line General Yamashita poured an estimated 80,000 Japanese troops who presented a continuous threat to Manila and to its fresh-water supply.[44] Along this line MAGSDAGUPAN would devote a considerable proportion of its dive-bombing efforts for the next several weeks.

The 7th Cavalry Regiment of the 2d Cavalry Brigade captured the Balera water-filter plant on 5 February. The plant was assaulted by Japanese mortar, machine-gun and, finally, rocket fire. Captain Godolphin went to the roof of the plant at midnight with a sextant to determine the azimuth of the rocket-launching position. Six enemy rockets landed within 40 yards of his CP, but he got out alive with enough data to direct the SBD's to the target next morning.[45]

From a water tower Godolphin directed strikes on 8 February against Japanese positions in a nearby ridge which poured heavy machine-gun and mortar fire into the Americans who were seeking to dislodge them. Both General Mudge and his visitor, Major General Edwin D. Patrick, CG of the

---

[42] Wright, *The 1st CavDiv in WW II*, p 127.

[43] Major General Verne D. Mudge USA, interview with Staff Sergeant Bill Allen USMCR, upon entering Manila, quoted from MAG-32 history.

[44] USSBS, *Employment of Forces Under the Southwest Pacific Command*, p 52.

[45] DeChant, *Devilbirds*, p 190.

6th Infantry Division, watched the attack with Godolphin, who had strung a telephone wire to his jeep.

General Patrick had already stated his position when Lieut. Colonel John Smith had paid him a visit, offering the Marine flyers' services: no bombs to be dropped any closer than 1,000 yards from his troops. When Major Manchester, the strike leader, arrived overhead, Godolphin instructed him to hit the Japanese on the reverse side of the slope, lest the Americans on the near side be hit. After the target had been marked by white phosphorus smoke, the first bomb hit near the crest of the ridge, on the Japanese side. The second followed just behind, on target. As seven planes scored, one after another, the cavalrymen cheered like football fans.[46] After the bombs were dropped a patrol of General Mudge's men moved forward over the ridge, against no opposition. They found 8 machine-gun positions and 15 mortar emplacements; 300 enemy dead lay nearby, the others having fallen back across the Marikina River.[47]

The visiting General Patrick asked Godolphin when he could have some close support like that. Mudge said the flyers would have to drop bombs a lot closer than 1,000 yards. Said Patrick: "I don't give a damn how close they hit."[48]

Two days later Godolphin directed a strike of 81 planes[49] under the aerial co-ordination of Manchester, for which unusual preparation had been made. A guerrilla lieutenant, graduate in engineering from the University of the Philippines, had been sent into the target area in civilian clothes. At night he plotted the Japanese positions on a map, and made sketches of them which served as a guide to Manchester and Godolphin. Oil dumps were fired, AA positions hit, at least ten fires started in six towns in a 5,000-yard area in the bend of the Marikina River.[50]

Following his "purchase" of close support, General Patrick decided to try it when his division moved into the line and took up the attack against the Shimbu Line on 24 February. The ALPman directing his first strike was Captain James L. McConaughy Jr., in peacetime a magazine writer. McConaughy was with MAG-32 as an assistant intelligence officer, but he caught the close-support bug and, with other intelligence officers, was given ALPing instruction by Godolphin and McAloney.[51]

McConaughy was assigned to direct support for Patrick's 20th Infantry Regiment. He describes the first effort:

---

[46] Two planes, including Manchester's, had to jettison their bombs in the Gulf.

[47] DeChant, *Devilbirds*, pp 191–192, with adjustments and additions from VMSB-241 ACA Report No. 13, 8 February 1945. One report of the 1st CavDiv put the number of machine guns found at 11 (MAG-32 war diary, 21 February 1945).

[48] DeChant, *Devilbirds*, p 192.

[49] Nine from VMSB-241, 18 each from VMSB's 142, 243, 244, 341. This was the biggest strike of the Luzon campaign.

[50] DeChant, *Devilbirds*, p 190; VMSB-241 ACA Report No 17, 10 February 1945.

[51] McAloney comment.

80. Samoa

81. Nanomea

EARLY CENTRAL PACIFIC BASES

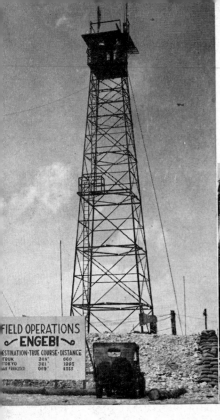

82. Control tower, Engebi

83. MAG-22 lands at Engebi

MARSHALL ISLANDS BASES

84. Dyess Field, Roi

85. Pre-strike servicing

86. En route with half-ton bombs

CORSAIRS IN THE MARSHALLS

87. Wotje

BY-PASSED AND BATTERED MARSHALLS

88. Maloelap

89.   Mille

BY-PASSED AND BATTERED MARSHALLS

90.   Jaluit

91. Refueling on Saipan

GRASSHOPPERS

92. Artillery spotting on Tinian

93. First OY on Iwo

94. Bloody Nose Ridge

95. Napalm delivery, wheels-down

THE PALAUS

96. Nose-thumbing on Babelthuap

97. F6F night fighters

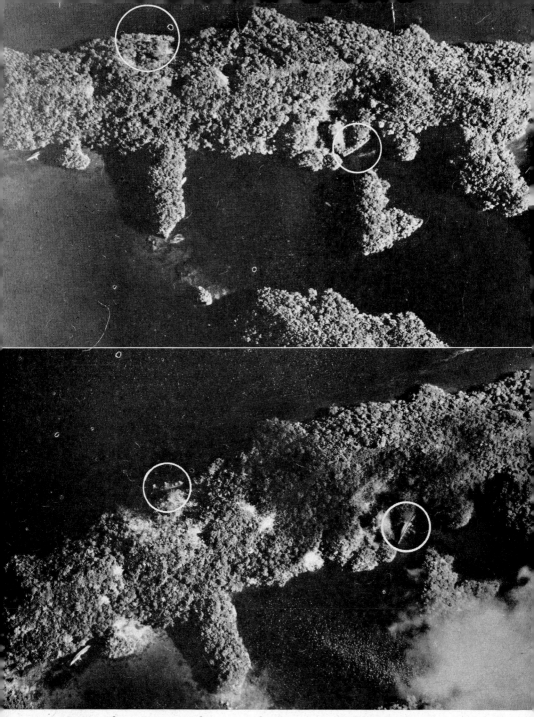

98-99. These Japanese ships were hit in carrier strikes March 1944, then beached and camouflaged. Strikes by VMF-114 in November exposed the camouflage. Another exposed ship may be seen at the left.

CAMOUFLAGE IN THE PALAUS

100.   Runway: 3,514 feet

FALALOP ISLAND, ULITHI

101.   Carrier replacement planes to left; MAG-45 on right; TAG Headquarters
was located in the Quonset hut, top left

102. Roosevelt, MacArthur and Nimitz at Pearl Harbor, July 1944, when decision was made to recapture the Philippines

THE DECISION AND THE PLACE

U.S. Army

103. The initial invasion was at Tacloban, Leyte, where this airstrip was built under great handicaps, including mud and suicidal Japanese

104.   Front-line air liaison team and radio jeep

LUZON

105.   SBD on strike over rice paddies of Central Luzon

MANGALDAN AIRDROME

MAG-32   VSMB 244

A-20's

MAG-24

adio Call—"HONEY"   M.

106.

HOME OF THE LUZON DIVE BOMBERS

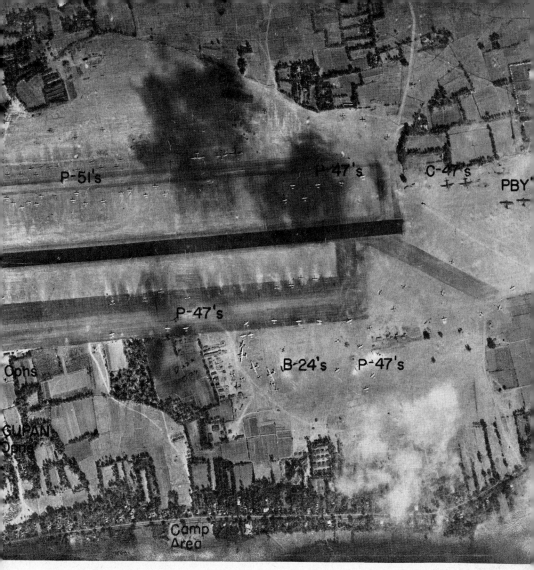

P-51's   P-47's   C-47's   PBY

P-47's

Ophs

B-24's   P-47's

GUPAN
Opps

Camp
Area

Courtesy Major John Dexter

AND PLANES OF OTHER SERVICES

107. Native laborers help enlarge Moret Field

U.S. Army Photo

MINDANAO

108. Humor, Zambo style

109. Guerrillas and PBJ's at Malabang

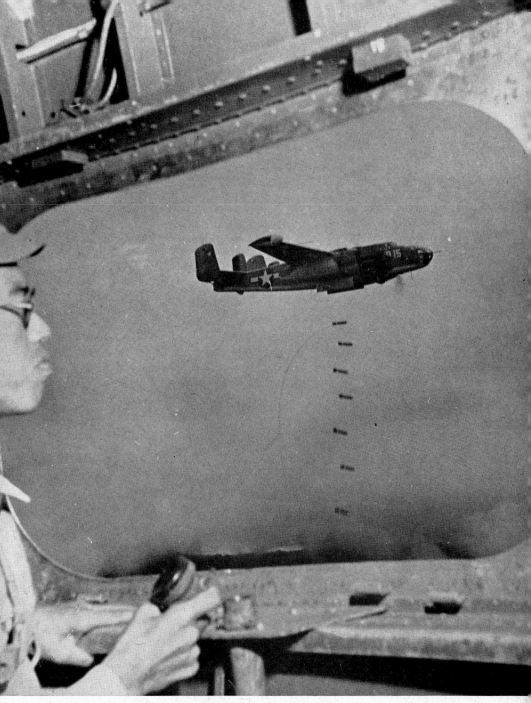

110. Accustomed as they were to Japanese peculiarities, marines of VMB-611 had difficulty understanding why this prisoner of war chose to point out his pals' positions for them to bomb

THE TRAITOR

111. A souvenir from soldiers in appreciation of MAGSZAM's close support

... everything went to perfection—targets initially were 1,000 yards and more away; gradually we worked in to 500 yards and sometimes a bit under. We worked all the tricks, like dummy runs while infantry advanced under them. When the Japs caught on to this, we'd bring in the first section and have them drop, then infantry would advance while the second and third sections (usually nine-plane flights) dove on the target but did not drop.

Then when the Japs caught on to this, we'd bring in the first section and have them drop, followed by the second section which did not drop, followed by the third which did. The pilots—squadron leaders and other senior officers, usually—took to coming over to our forward o.p. When the Japs started fiddling around with rockets they took an especial personal interest in getting good targets and getting on them. I remember an especially able regular Marine officer, Major Frazer,[52] who landed his plane one day and came up forward. When the Japs let some rockets go he hit the dirt hard, like me. While we were loving the dirt a dogface in the same position said: "Hey, were you one of those guys up there this morning?" Frazer grunted uh-huh. "Well," said the soldier, "I'll be damned." It was the first time he'd ever seen a flyer close-up.[53]

On 25 February General Patrick ordered all units of the 6th Division to submit accurate evaluation of strikes, so that "the air forces will continue to give this command an increasing number of support aircraft."[54]

But the other infantry regiments of the division, the 1st and 63d, had shown remarkable sales resistance. Colonel James E. Rees's 1st Infantry had good reason to be leery of airplanes—on 4 February, the day the division captured San José, north of Manila, the regiment had been strafed by AAF planes and had suffered several casualties. But on 28 February "Patrick finally in effect ordered the old boy to try out close support."

He would have tried anything then. A squad or so had been on reconnaissance on the far side of the valley. The lieutenant had fallen into a ravine and busted his leg, and the rest of the men could have got out but they refused to abandon the lieutenant. There were Japs a couple of hundred yards away, though because of the terrain it might take them an hour to reach the stranded party. We said we could help. After a very thorough briefing, all by radio, the regimental commander said the lead plane could drop one wing bomb. It was beautiful to watch. We

---

[52] Major Fred J. Frazer, CO VMSB-236. The policy of alternating pilots in ALP work—to give them "a feel of the ground"—had been planned at Bougainville and was faithfully followed. Similarly, ALPmen and infantrymen often flew missions in the rear seats of the SBD's.

[53] Letter to the writer, 13 May 1948.

[54] Boggs, *Marine Aviation in the Philippines*, p 84.

were on a high cliff on one side of the valley and it was a clear day. The
first drop was dead on. The colonel was impressed and allowed that we
could let the lead plane come in again and drop his belly and other wing
bomb. It took the SBD 20 minutes to climb up again. His second dive
was fantastically accurate, too, and the colonel said he was convinced,
so the other eight planes followed the squadron leader down. The bombing was fantastically successful—the farthest one of 27 bombs being 30
yards off the target. From. then on this colonel couldn't get enough planes
for his regiment. Literally, he asked for nine flights (nine planes each)
as a standing, daily order.[55]

General Patrick contributed a report on close support which marked a
considerable revision of his estimate a few weeks earlier:

> The close air support given this division . . . has been outstanding.
> The advance of our troops over difficult mountainous terrain against a
> well-armed determined enemy is being made possible in no small part
> by such air strikes.
> Particularly noteworthy have been the skillfully coordinated and
> accurate air strikes of the SBD's of the Marine Air Group, Dagupan, based
> at Mangaldan Field. In one strike made on 28 February against Mt.
> Mataba, these Marine pilots dive-bombed a pin-pointed target located
> between two friendly forces with accuracy comparable to that obtained
> by field artillery. The courage, patience, and willingness displayed by
> these men deserve high praise. . . . The work of the close support aircraft
> of the 308th Bombardment Wing has been no less outstanding . . .[56]

Getting Ready for Zamboanga

Plans for future operations were laid when MAGSDAGUPAN had been
functioning barely two weeks. When word came in mid-February that the
Marines would support the Southern Philippines operations, MAG-32 began
pulling up stakes. The Group's headquarters and service squadrons and the
ground echelons of VMSB's 142 (Major Hoyle R. Barr), 236 (Major Fred J.
Frazer), 243 (Major Joseph W. Kean Jr.) and 341 (Major Christopher F.
Irwin Jr.) started packing—the last men to arrive at Mangaldan by sea had
finished unpacking only on the day they were ordered to start getting their

---

[55] McConaughy letter. This strike is claimed by three different squadron CO's
(in comments on first draft of this chapter) and because some documentary evidence
has been lost, I have been unable to determine which is right. All three were flying
in the area on this day. All reported "results unobserved."

[56] Patrick to CO 308th Bombardment Wing and CO Marine Air Group, Dagupan,
1 March 1945. On 14 March a Japanese machine gunner wounded General Patrick
at a frontline OP, and he died three days later in a Manila hospital. Colonel Rees
was killed by the same burst. (The Division Public Relations Section, *The 6th Infantry Division in World War II, 1939–1945*, p 114.)

gear ready to ship again. "Stevedores Union, Local 32," they called themselves.[57]

Two of these squadrons—VMSB's 236 and 341—had been in MAG-24 until the order came to move, when they were transferred into MAG-32. VMSB-244 (Major Vance H. Hudgins) was shifted from MAG-32 to MAG-24. The reason for this switch was not only that Zamboanga required four squadrons; the squadrons with the greatest numbers of old-timers had to be left on Luzon for rotation Stateside.

In all, 90 officers, 1,251 enlisted marines and 41 corpsmen were in the MAG-32 ground echelon which got ready to stage to the new battleground, via Mindoro.[58]

While the gear was stacked on the beach near San Fabian a lone Japanese bomber swooped in low and set afire a stack of oil drums, wounding two men. But no real damage was done, and the troops, commanded again by John Smith, sailed in LST's on 23 February, 15 days before J-day at Zamboanga.

The departure of MAG-32's ground echelon only meant that MAG-24's men would service both groups. The pilots and planes of MAG-32 remained on Luzon nearly a month longer.

In the early hours of 2 March four Japanese bombers raided the Mangaldan beachhead in the only serious aerial attack the Marines experienced on Luzon. An estimated 300 antipersonnel bombs struck the camp area, killing 4 men and wounding 78,[59] including Colonel Meyer. One hundred and ninety-six craters were counted. Supplies were hit heavily, one messhall was set afire and many tents were damaged. One SBD was completely washed out.

Supporting the Guerrillas

Although a big proportion of Marine aviation's work on Luzon was devoted to the Shimbu sector east of Manila, the SBD's were also busy with the other two principal defensive positions: (1) the central Kembu sector, held by 30,000 men defending the area west of Clark Field and Fort Stotsenburg, (2) the Shobu sector held by about 140,000 men in the vast, mountainous area of Northern Luzon.[60]

At various times the Marine flyers supported all ten U.S. divisions on Luzon,[61] although only a few missions were flown for some of the divisions.

About the middle of February the marines were asked to work out some method of supporting another type of fighters, the ragged, ill-equipped Filipino guerrillas. Five "regiments" of these natives roamed the mountains and jungles of Northern Luzon, commanded by Lieut. Colonel Russell W. Volck-

---

[57] Boggs, *Marine Aviation in the Philippines*, p 94.

[58] *Ibid.*

[59] MAG-24 war diary, March 1945 (MAG-32's war diary says 72 were wounded).

[60] USSBS, *Employment of Forces Under the Southwest Pacific Command*, p 51.

[61] Besides the 1st Cavalry and 6th Infantry Divisions, these were the 11th Airborne and 25th, 32d, 33d, 37th, 38th, 40th and 43d Infantry Divisions.

mann USA. They had no transportation except a few captured Japanese trucks. They lacked artillery—and, therefore, happily accepted very close support—had only a few mortars and practically no machine guns.

ALPman McAloney conferred with headquarters 308th Bomb Wing concerning plans to help these primitive warriors with modern close support. On 22 February he, Captain Titcomb the communicator, Lieut. Sydney Taylor, and six enlisted men were landed by LCT at headquarters United States Armed Forces in the Philippines (USAFIP), at Luna, about 50 miles behind the Japanese lines.[62] Their equipment consisted of a radio jeep and a radio truck.

Here the airplane could prove itself as a weapon against enemy troops because there was no confusing it with the field artillery and naval gunfire. If a dead Japanese was found who hadn't been drilled by a .30-caliber bullet, the chances were he owed death to the close-support airplane.

Fifteen miles south of Luna and 40 miles north of Lingayen lay the La Union Province town of San Fernando, dominated by a long, north-to-south ridge named Bacsil. Early in November there had been a plan for a landing at San Fernando by the 158th RCT, to be reinforced later by another RCT from the 25th Infantry Division. This plan was discarded 6 November because the Japanese were found to be strongly entrenched in the area and, in the attempt to get at the enemy at Baguio, another landing was planned farther north on the coast.[63]

Neither landing ever came off because Colonel Volckmann's guerrilla forces captured San Fernando and the 33d Division was able to get there by going overland. Credit for this save was largely due to the work of the Marine and Army aviators, directed by the ALP's.

Many strikes were flown against San Fernando during the early phases of the Luzon campaign, but when McAloney and his ALP party arrived on Washington's Birthday the Japanese still held the dominating positions on Bacsil Ridge and the guerrillas had only a toehold at the northern end.

First, the guerrillas cut a trail from the north up to the top of the ridge. Under cover of darkness they dragged McAloney's radio jeep to the top, concealing it behind a small hill only about 50 yards from the front lines. Remote-control wire was run from the jeep to an OP at the front lines. The radio truck was stationed a few miles to the rear, off the ridge, to act as the master link between the jeep and air-base headquarters, 40 miles to the south.

On the evening before the first strike a liaison plane took a marked aerial photo of the area down to 308th Bomb Wing headquarters. Large N and L panels were laid out just in front of the jeep, and the guerrilla front lines were marked with white sheets as improvised panels.

---

[62] McAloney comment. Also an article by him, "Is Air Support Effective?" in *Marine Corps Gazette,* November 1945, p 38. Captain James I. Best relieved McAloney when he moved to Zamboanga.

[63] Information from Office of Military History, Department of the Army.

The first strike consisted of 12 Army A-20's which reported in to the radio truck. Flying north to south, the flight leader reported: "I see a jeep, then Nan Love panels, then a line of white panels."[64]

The A-20's flew low north to south and dropped 100-pound parafrags to hit less than 200 yards beyond the line of white sheets, covering Japanese positions for 1,000 yards. Three or four live runs were made in dropping these bombs. Then at a prearranged signal the planes flew over again, this time making dry runs as the guerrillas rose from their holes and charged forward. They gained 1,000 yards without a casualty, passing dead Japanese on the way.

No planes were left on station, however, and Japanese began to fire back after the A-20's left. Several hours later MAGSDAGUPAN provided SBD's with 500-pound general-purpose bombs. Japanese positions on the center of the ridge were bombed and again dry runs and strafing runs were employed. One section of planes was "talked" onto houses in the valley where some enemy stragglers had sought refuge. The planes were coached to the houses by instructions to fly down the highway, turn left or right as the case might be, on side runs. Final correction was made by dry runs on specific houses.

During the second phase of the fight for San Fernando the guerrillas attacked Japanese who were well dug in on Reservoir Hill, just north of the town. In this case the Army and Marine planes substituted for artillery—the guerrillas had only two mortars and two .50-caliber machine guns.

A detailed plan was flown back to Mangaldan, and on 26 February the radio jeep was moved down from Bacsil Ridge to the south edge of the small town of Carlatan; the radio truck was located in the center of town to establish contact with the planes as they arrived on station. The flight leader of 18 SBD's of VMSB-142 reconnoitered the Japanese lines and reported the gun positions as he spotted them. After a Filipino officer also pointed out targets, the officer at the radio truck cleared a section of planes to hit the remaining known gun positions. From description via radio the flight leader confirmed locations and led strikes against each target. Guerrilla troops pulled back of a river bank, so that there would be no mistaking of friendly forces, and the 500-pound bombs were placed within 100 yards of these well-emplaced forces without hitting any of them. The radio jeep, which could not dig in as well, was hit by some bomb fragments but survived.

Shortly after the SBD's started striking 15 P-51's reported to the radio truck and were told to orbit until the dive bombers had finished. The Mustangs were brought in, with all eight .50-caliber guns blazing. The Army pilots flew so low that they had to pull up sharply lest they hit the pillbox targets themselves. Then, after repeated strafing runs, mortar shells were fired to signal the guerrilla attack, and subsequent runs were dummy. Farther up the hill planes made live runs to keep the enemy troops down.

The lightly armed guerrillas took the wooded hill, but that night, after the planes had ceased operating the Japanese countered with artillery and sent in soldiers to infiltrate through bamboo thickets to the Filipino positions. The guerrillas had to withdraw. Two days later the SBD's and P-51's did the whole thing over again, and this time the P-51's carried napalm to burn off the bamboo thickets.[65] The guerrillas took the hill for keeps.

There was not a great deal of difference between the San Fernando incident and the one at Ocotal, Nicaragua, 16 July 1927,[66] except that technique, weapons and communications had improved. The tradition of fighting with or against small bands of native troops was strong within the Marine Corps, and nothing that has happened at the turn of the twentieth's half-century has indicated the end of the "small" wars. Even the language was the same at Ocotal and San Fernando.[67]

There were many more San Fernandos, but this one will suffice to show the type of warfare the guerrillas fought with ALPmen's coaching. During the period 5-31 March, 186 missions were flown in support of the guerrillas in Northern Luzon. One of the ALPmen, Captain Titcomb, was killed in the USAFIP front lines on 1 March. A sniper's bullet brought him down "while asking for more planes for a strike, microphone in hand."[68]

Finale on Luzon

Landings at Zamboanga in the Southern Philippines were made 10 March, with some of MAG-32's staff and ground echelon participating. The flight echelon waited until there was room on the Zamboanga airstrip, however, and continued flying missions on Luzon until 24 March.

On 23 March MAG-32's four squadrons flew their regularly assigned missions on Luzon. Three SBD's from VMSB-341 hit enemy troops in bamboo groves three miles north of Nanvacan; six planes from the same squadron and three from VMSB-243 bombed an enemy bivouac area at Canarao, Ilocos Sur. Twenty-seven planes from VMSB's-142 and 243 bombed and strafed enemy positions on a ridge 2,300 yards south of Santa Fé, and 17 more SBD's from VMSB-236 bombed Balete Pass, a target that was bombed frequently by Marine and Army planes in an effort to cut off Japanese supplies and reinforcements.[69]

At 1700 the Group was told that its move to the south would begin on the morrow. Two squadrons took off 24 March for Zamboanga, one on 25 March and the other on the next day. All of the Group's planes reached Zamboanga

---

[65] The dive-bomber squadrons resented being allotted only 583 gallons of napalm on Luzon, out of 6,555 tons FEAF used on the island (Boggs, *Marine Aviation in the Philippines*, p 93).

[66] See p 25.

[67] The account of the San Fernando battle is taken from McAloney's *Marine Corps Gazette* article, supplemented by details from MAGSDAGUPAN squadron war diaries.

[68] McAloney comment.

[69] MAG-32 war diary, March 1945.

except one from VMSB-142, piloted by Lieut. Charles T. Rue, who had Staff Sergeant Robert R. Stanton as his gunner. When their engine failed, they landed on a strip on the island of Panay which had been labeled "in friendly hands" according to preflight intelligence. The strip actually was held by the Japanese, who captured Rue and Stanton, then tortured and beheaded them.[70]

MAG-24's three squadrons continued to support Army and guerrilla forces after the other group had left for Zamboanga. Balete Pass, Solvec Bay and Baguio were the targets most frequently hit, usually by flights of nine carrying 1,000-pound bombs or two 500-pound bombs.

On 2 April MAG-24 received orders to strike camp and begin moving to Mindanao. Despite torrential rains and heavy mud which often made it impossible to move gear to the beach, nearly all the ground personnel were on board LST's or about to go on board, when orders came on 7 April from Sixth Army to resume flying in support of the Army ground troops in the Balete Pass area. The condition of the strip prohibited flying until the 10th, when nine planes dropped 1,000-pound bombs on a ridge near the Balete Pass Rest House. On this day Colonel Meyer and Lieut. Colonel McCutcheon flew down to Mindoro, leaving the Group's flight echelon and a skeleton ground crew in command of Major Manchester, who had become assistant Group operations officer. Ground crews under command of the squadron CO's sailed for Mindanao via Mindoro in the command ship *Wasatch* and four LST's. From the 11th through the 14th MAG-24 flew 221 sorties in support of the 25th and 37th Divisions at Balete Pass.

On the 14th, when it was indicated that rain and mud would completely wash out Mangaldan airdrome's rice-paddy foundation, operations ceased and the flight echelons of the three squadrons began moving south, first to Clark Field, thence on the 20th to Malabang on Mindanao.

On Luzon MAGSDAGUPAN flew a total of 8,842 combat sorties, fired over 1,500,000 .30- and .50-caliber bullets, and dropped 19,167 bombs.[71] For the period 27 January to 14 April the Marines flew an average of 116 sorties per day, or 812 per week.[72]

The startling aspect of this figure is this: it represents 36 per cent of the *average* for all flights of Fifth Air Force (2,240 per week) and 15 per cent of its total flights. In six months Fifth Air Force flew a total of 57,663 support sorties, using a total of 1,294 aircraft in 68 different squadrons; the Marines' contribution for less than half of the time consumed by the Luzon campaign was 8,842 sorties with an average of 180 assigned aircraft in 7 squadrons.[73]

---

[70] This was determined by an investigating party which visited Panay 11 May, after U.S. Army units invaded the island. (VMSB-142 war diary, May 1945.)

[71] Of which 1,912 were 100-pound, 8,484 were 250-pound, 5,586 quarter-ton and 3,185 half-ton.

[72] After organization had been completed on 5 February and for 45 days thereafter (until four of the seven squadrons departed), the Marines averaged 1,113 sorties per week.

[73] Marine Corps statistics from "Record of Ordnance Expenditure 27 January–

The Marines dropped an average of 377 tons of bombs each week (4,145 tons in 11 weeks), which is 21 per cent of the weekly average for Fifth Air Force, though their total is only 9 per cent of the amount the AAF dropped.

MAGSDAGUPAN's excellent record was due in no small measure to the ground crews, whose hard work and technical skill kept the plane availability average at 84 per cent. In other words, out of 180 planes assigned, MAGSDA-GUPAN could count on an average of 151 being ready for action at any given time. Major Vance Hudgins, who personally would fly 89 missions before he left the Philippines, had a squadron average aircraft availability on Luzon of 23 planes out of 24 assigned.[74]

To account for this record Major Hudgins wrote afterward: "Competitive spirit within the squadron was keen. . . . The crews would change an engine at night and run up the required hours before dawn. Early the next morning we gave the plane the necessary flight check and flew it on a strike the same day."[75]

General Krueger, CG of Sixth Army, commended the Marines for their work on Luzon in duplicate citations to MAG's 24 and 32:

> This support was of such high order that I personally take great pleasure in expressing to every officer and enlisted man . . . my appreciation and official commendation for their splendid work.
>
> Commanders have repeatedly expressed their admiration for the pinpoint precision, the willingness and enthusiastic desire of pilots to fly missions from dawn to dusk and the extremely close liaison with the ground forces which characterizes the operations of the Marine fighter [sic] groups. By constant visits of commanders and pilots to front line units in order to observe targets and gain an understanding of the ground soldier's problems, by the care which squadron commanders took to insure maximum hits, and by the continuous devoted work of ground crews in maintaining an unusually high average of operational aircraft the 32d [and 24th] Group exemplified outstanding leadership, initiative, aggressiveness and high courage in keeping with the finest traditions of the Marine Corps.[76]

---

14 April" by MAGSDAGUPAN operations officer. The figure of 57,663 sorties is from USSBS, *Employment of Forces Under the Southwest Pacific Command,* p 55, although USSBS, *The Fifth Air Force in the War Against Japan,* p 37, gives only 47,250 sorties (the former says 38,844 tons of bombs were dropped plus 6,555 tons of napalm; the latter only 38,900 tons of bombs). My total of Marine Corps sorties is slightly higher than Boggs's (*Marine Aviation in the Philippines,* p 106), and include 88 flown by SBD's of MAG-24's headquarters squadron and MAG-32's service squadron.

[74] MAGSDAGUPAN, "Record of Ordnance Expenditure," *loc. cit.*

[75] Comment on a first draft of this chapter.

[76] Krueger to CG 1st MAW, 16 May 1945.

CHAPTER TWENTY-ONE

In the Southern Philippines

MAGSDAGUPAN had been functioning only 15 days when Colonel Jerome was summoned to Leyte for a conference on future operations. He immediately sent a dispatch to General Mitchell on Bougainville, asking for permission to represent him at the conference. No answer had been received by noon, and Jerome had to take off without one.

Arriving at Leyte, he went to MAG-12 headquarters close by the Tanauan airstrip and, to his surprise, found General Mitchell already there. The two officers proceeded to Far East Air Force headquarters.[1]

What the FEAF planners had in mind was bringing Marine aviation into the reconquest of the Southern Philippines—the western Visayas and Mindanao, for which planning had been going on since 31 October.[2] As revised in February these plans for reconquest entailed: (1) Palawan, (2) Panay, (3) Negros, (4) Cebu, (5) Bohol, (6) Zamboanga Province on Mindanao, (7) Sulu Archipelago, (8) further Mindanao landings on the Moro Gulf in the Malabang–Parang area.[3]

All of these operations with the exception of Palawan were supported in varying degrees by Marine aviators operating with Thirteenth Air Force (Major General Paul Wurtsmith USA), furnishing support for troops of General Eichelberger's Eighth Army.

All four Marine groups in the Philippines were involved, and permission was secured to bring in additional units, notably AWS's 3 and 4 from Los Negros and Bougainville, and Lieut. Colonel George A. Sarles's VMB-611 from Ewa.

General Mitchell designated Colonel Jerome of MAG-32 to command the Marine forces of MAG's 12, 24 and 32, which would move to Zamboanga to participate in Mindanao and Sulu Archipelago operations, most important of the actions. MAG-14 would stay on Samar but furnish close support from there

---

[1] Interview Brig. General Clayton C. Jerome, 21 September 1950.

[2] *Ibid.* USSBS, *Employment of Forces Under the Southwest Pacific Command,* p 56. The FEAF planners would have preferred to leave these islands by-passed, but General MacArthur insisted on liberating them (Haugland, *The AAF Against Japan,* p 253).

[3] Other landings by Australian troops in the Netherlands East Indies were also planned, but these are not of immediate concern here, though Marine flyers from CVE's supported the Australians invading Balikpapan, Borneo (see Chapter Twenty-eight, p 416).

for Panay and Cebu as well as the more southerly operations on Mindanao; the Group had already been alerted for movement to Okinawa—a movement that did not begin until 24 May, however.

Jerome requested and received an Army quartermaster truck company to provide his three groups with more mobility on the ground.

While the dive bombers of MAG's 24 and 32 prepared for the move from Luzon to Mindanao, the two fighter groups on Leyte and Samar continued hitting the Central Philippine Islands. Pilots Railsback, Chambers, Collin and Bunce of VMF-115 were credited with exploding a midget submarine on 23 February at Cebu City, skip-bombing 1,000-pound bombs from a height of 25 feet, "probably the first submarine sunk by the Corsair."[4] MAG-14 pilots began working over Mindanao targets long in advance of the landing— which was scheduled for 10 March (J-day)—seeking out hidden planes, keeping airstrips holed, strafing troops and vehicles whenever they were found in daylight. As a preliminary to the Mindanao operation, pilots of the two groups landed frequently during January and February at a small grass strip at Dipolog, on the north coast of Mindanao's Zamboanga Peninsula which was in control of Filipino guerrillas. The Japanese could never call Mindanao theirs; the island was too big, and the guerrillas, commanded by Colonel Wendell W. Fertig USA, were about 25,000 strong—U.S. submarines and planes had supplied them since February 1943.[5] The Marines soon established a mutually profitable, working relationship with the guerrillas, as did also U.S. Army and Navy forces. The first landing on Mindanao took place on 8 March, two days before J-day, at the town of Dipolog, because the Japanese threat against the guerrillas, then holding the town's airstrip, had assumed considerable proportions. Later, on 27 and 28 March, when the U.S. infantry had been withdrawn, MAG-12 flyers were able to repay some of the guerrillas' favors, as Colonel Jerome related:

> The natives were very kind to MAG-12; the guerrillas protected the field, so we couldn't let them down. They got word that the Japs were going to retake Dipolog. The only thing I could spare I sent them, four F4U's which went over just before dark. The pilot of one of the planes contacted a guerrilla leader whom he knew, and said: "Where the hell are the Japs?" The guerrilla said: "They are back in here; I'll show you." And the guerrilla got into the Corsair, the pilot squeezed in and sat on his lap; they flew over where the Japs were, made half a dozen strafing passes and chased them away.[6]

---

[4] VMF-115, ACA 126–129, 23 February 1945.

[5] Eichelberger, *Our Jungle Road to Tokyo*, p 218, estimates that the guerrillas controlled 95 per cent of Mindanao.

[6] Jerome interview. The pilot was Lieut. Winfield S. Sharpe; the guerrilla leader, Major Donald H. Wills USA. Eight planes repeated the strafing next day (VMF-115 war diary, March 1945).

The Landing at "Zambo"

Chief purpose of the Zamboanga landings was to establish air facilities to support future operations,[7] notably the Malabang landings on the main body of Mindanao, across the Moro Gulf from Zamboanga. From Malabang the reconquest of Mindanao would be undertaken.

MAG-32's ground echelon, which left Luzon in six LST's 23 February, stopped at Mindoro, where the convoys for Zamboanga were being assembled. Meanwhile, MAG-12, slated for J-day, had been loaded into LST's at Leyte, in rough weather and rain that made a mess of nearly all items. In addition, Colonel Willis had fallen ill and had been ordered home; his relief was Colonel Verne McCaul, who was on Mindoro at the time, seeking a possible location for 1st MAW headquarters if and when the Wing moved to the Philippines. The Army quartermaster truck company was loaded on board, its trucks filled with bombs.

At Mindoro the MAG-12 LST's were unloaded and the supplies stockpiled, replenished and reloaded, and the forward echelon of HqSq-12, SMS-12 and the operating squadrons embarked for the J-day landing.

Fighter cover for the landing of the 41st Infantry Division's two regiments on Zamboanga on 10 March was furnished by planes of MAG-12, flying from the guerrilla strip at Dipolog. The Marines strafed the beaches ahead of the troops, B-24's, B-25's, and A-20's of Thirteenth Air Force furnished the bombs. There was no aerial opposition.[8]

Neither, at first, was there opposition on land; four dual-purpose 10-cm. coast defense guns were found unmanned. The 8,000 enemy troops which Intelligence had predicted failed to materialize, and so did the suicide boats.[9] But within 30 minutes mortar fire began to fall near the beaches.

Despite this fire, all the gear of the two groups was moved ashore the first day, including the 1,000-gallon gasoline tanks filled with 100-octane, and the truckloads of bombs. Fortunately, none of this vulnerable matériel was hit, and it was moved inland next day.[10]

Objective of the aviators was San Roque airfield, a mile inland. To Jerome, John Smith and McCutcheon, standing at the mud-and-coconut-log strip, it seemed certain that the runway would have to be hard-surfaced before any planes could be brought in. Until that could be completed, however, Colonel Jerome decided that his flyers could operate from a temporary strip which the engineers could scrape and roll, alongside the proposed hard-surface strip. He told Major General Jens A. Doe, CG of the 41st, that he would bring the planes in if mortar fire could be kept off for 24 hours. On J plus 4 Major

---

[7] CominCh, *Operations in POA,* March 1945.

[8] Commander, Amphibious Group Six, Task Group 78.1, "Report on Amphibious Attack on Zamboanga," pp 27–28.

[9] CominCh, *Operations in POA,* March 1945, p 17.

[10] Jerome interview.

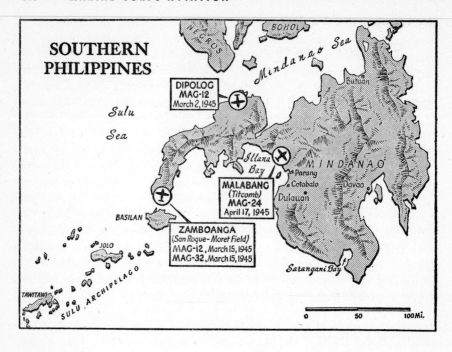

SOUTHERN
PHILIPPINES

Sulu
Sea

DIPOLOG
MAG-12
March 2, 1945

MALABANG
(Titcomb)
MAG-24
April 17, 1945

Illana Bay

MINDANAO

Parang
Cotabato
Dulauan
Davao

BASILAN

ZAMBOANGA
(San Roque - Moret Field)
MAG-12, March 15, 1945
MAG-32, March 15, 1945

JOLO

TAWITAWI

SULU ARCHIPELAGO

Mindanao Sea

BOHOL

NEGROS

Butuan

Sarangani Bay

0   50   100Mi.

Eldon Railsback of VMF-115 landed the first Corsair, and the rest of the
fighters were brought over from Dipolog and Leyte. On J plus 5 the Corsairs
flew their first mission.

The forward echelons of MAG-12 and MAG-32 and AWS-4 followed
the foot soldiers ashore and the rear echelons came in the 17 March convoy.
The SBD's of MAG-32 started arriving on 23 March, as soon as more strip
and parking areas were available. The field was named for Lieut. Colonel Paul
Moret, killed in a transport crash in New Caledonia two years earlier. The
Marine units under Jerome's command were designated MAGSZAM; it was an
all-Marine show (except for detachments of Army P-61 night fighters and Navy
PBY's for rescue) and was thus distinctive among all operations of its size in
World War II. Altogether MAGSZAM eventually included about 293 Marine
planes: 96 F4U's, 151 SBD's, 18 PBJ's, 18 SB2C's, 2 F6F's, 1 FM, 2 TBF's and
5 R4D's.

AWS-4 set up its radio and radar equipment at Moret Field and operated
as 76th Fighter Control Center.

Eighth Army had 52 D-days between Christmas Day 1944, and the surrender of Japan.[11] None of them resembled the bloody landings which marines
came to associate with the term "D-day," and most were unopposed. But for
many of these D-days Marine planes furnished the indispensable close support
which helped to keep the casualties low.

Following the Zamboanga show the more important of these D-days

[11] Eichelberger, *Our Jungle Road to Tokyo*, p 200.

followed in quick succession. After that it was a matter of supporting the soldiers with the aviation they asked for. Panay was invaded by the 40th Infantry Division on 18 March, and with the aid of a highly efficient guerrilla organization had broken organized resistance four days later.[12] For their part the Marines contributed daylight CAP's by MAG-14 Corsairs based on Samar, but the most exciting moment happened when four VMF-251 planes and two Army P-38's caught a freight train on Negros on the return trip; they set its boxcars afire and blew up its engine.[13]

Next Central Philippines target was Cebu, the slender island almost next door to Leyte. "Zeb" Hopkins's MAG-14 planes flew cover for the Americal Division landings on 26 March, destroying an estimated 20 trucks and shooting up an inestimatable number of fleeing troops. Cebu City was estimated by General Eichelberger to have been 95 per cent destroyed. Three days after Cebu, Hopkins's flyers helped support the 40th Division landing on Negros.

During April the Group's principal task was to furnish effective close support to Eighth Army and guerrilla troops on Cebu and Negros—after the war it was learned that there were over 18,000 Japanese troops on Cebu (half of whom were left to surrender after Japan's defeat), 14,000 on Negros.[14]

The Sulu Operations

The first operation covered by the F4U's and SBD's at Moret Field was the 41st Division landing in the Tawitawi group, on the Borneo doorstep, Sanga Sanga and Bongao islands. MAG-12's Colonel McCaul went on board destroyer *Saufley* to serve as Support Air Commander.[15] Captain McAloney, Support Air Controller, went ashore with his radio jeep to take over direction of the strike planes. For these landings MAG-12 furnished air cover and 44 dive bombers of MAG-32 were directed against gun positions, troop concentrations and buildings by the ALP from their radio jeep.

Elements of the 41st Division landed on 9 April on Jolo Island, center of the Sultan of Sulu's domain, 80 miles southwest of Moret Field. This time Lieut. Colonel John Smith acted as the Support Air Commander, Captain McAloney as Support Air Controller on board *Saufley*, and Captain McConaughy was senior of the 5 officers and 11 men who went ashore in two radio jeeps and a radio truck, later augmented by a third jeep. Despite the loss of the

---

[12] USSBS, *Employment of Forces Under the Southwest Pacific Command*, p 57. The natives had written in sand on the Iloilo beach: "Japs have left City," and the guerrilla troops appeared in starched khaki. (Eichelberger, *Our Jungle Road to Tokyo*, pp 208–209.)

[13] VMF-251 war diary, March 1945.

[14] Eichelberger, *Our Jungle Road to Tokyo*, pp 211, 215.

[15] These air support circuits were rigged up on *Saufley*—SAC, Combat Air Patrol, and Air Sea Rescue. To guard all three circuits SAC used a split headset—left ear for SAC, right ear CAP. A small loudspeaker was on ASR. "A mike in each hand and one on a hook under the loudspeaker completed the lash-up." (Boggs, *Marine Aviation in the Philippines*, p 121.)

radio jeep in four feet of salt water—only the truck could be used until replacements arrived and repairs were made—the Jolo operation was a minor classic in close support.

The Support Air Party assumed control of the air four and a half hours after the landing. Between 9 April and 1 May the party ran a total of 70 strikes, 601 sorties; bomb tonnage was 2,881; 4 tanks of napalm dropped, and 32 rockets fired.

About half the total air support was concentrated on 2,247-foot-high Mount Daho, historically a stronghold of the Prophet's Moros—General Leonard Wood had killed a thousand of them at Mount Daho in 1906; General Pershing starved or killed 1,500 more in 1911. The Japanese defenders of Daho were an estimated 400 tough Special Naval Landing Force troops ("Imperial Marines"). These commanded the approaches to Mount Daho with nine dual 20-mm. guns, and heavy and light machine guns.

SBD's from Moret Field hit the Japanese positions heavily for five days. Then on 20 April, 36 of the dive bombers tried to knock out the ravine area and the high ground at the base of Daho. The 1st Battalion, 163d Infantry, advanced, but was repulsed after losing 3 killed, 3 missing, and 29 wounded. The planes were called again.

The air attack had to be postponed a day because Moret Field was weathered in. On 22 April, 33 SBD's[16] and four rocket-firing PBJ's of VMB-611 blasted the strong points, every bomb falling in the target area. This time the infantry occupied Daho easily after killing the handful of enemy who were left.

An inspection later was described in the senior ALP officer's report:

> There was literally not a whole tree in the area, an area about a third of a mile long, and 200 yards deep, with many side alleys. Concussion in there must have been unbearable (one POW said that following each strike he was unable to exercise his faculties for six or seven hours). Dead were everywhere—parts of bodies splattered about. . . . The infantry counted 230 dead, then the figure became meaningless, caves were burnt out with flame throwers and then sealed without inventory. An informed estimate is 400 killed here, probably half by air.[17]

The artillery contributed to the massacre, and the infantry finished the job, of course, but many of the targets, notably in the ravines, were inaccessible to artillery. Credit for the Jolo operation "belongs primarily to the pilots. When they were given targets they were able to see, they hit them, and there was only one really poor strike in the whole 70."[18]

---

[16] Of which 15 were from VMSB-341, 9 from VMSB-142, 9 from VMSB-243.

[17] Captain McConaughy, "Report on Close Support by Marine Air Groups Zamboanga Support Air Party with Jolo Task Force," 5 May 1945. The 41st Division's history (Captain William F. McCartney, *The Jungleers*, p 153) comments: "The combined shelling and bombing was so effective that the doughboys were able to move forward at a rapid pace without a single casualty."

[18] McConaughy report.

Jolo also involved operations with guerrillas. The ALP officer on one occasion describes the informal manner in which air support was rendered for them:

> This particular situation involved taking a road that had a handful of 20 mm's along it, densely wooded. From a hill, the guerrillas could see the artillery liaison officer and myself (when we were damn fools enough to stand up). Directly over them was the L-4. The artillery character was in contact with the L-4. The L-4 was in contact with the battery about 3 miles away. I was at the artillery observer's elbow, and I was in contact with a flight of 9 SBD's a couple of million miles in the sky. The enemy was smart enough to camouflage and not use his guns, knowing that would bring all hell from both air and artillery. So the L-4 plane would spot a target, mark it with WP, and I'd bring in a section of dive bombers. Then the L-4 would see the Japs biting dust, tell his observer on the hillside to tell the gooks to move up. So he and I would stand up and wave a white skivvy shirt two times. The gooks would move up, then the L-4 would see trouble ahead, tell the observer on the hill to tell them to take cover. So he and I would wave that skivvy shirt once. The gooks would take cover, in would come a round of WP to mark the target, then down would come another section of dive bombers. Then a few more rounds from the 105's to rip up a few trees, then a couple of waves of the skivvy shirt. Everything went fine for 15 minutes, until the Japs not unnaturally started rifle fire on that skivvy shirt.[19]

Close Support on Mindanao

The big show in the Southern Philippines was the landing on the Mindanao "mainland," a primitive, brooding world unto itself, 250 by 300 miles, separated by high mountains from the Zamboanga Peninsula (which was, for military planning purposes, not considered part of Mindanao at all).[20] This time X Corps—24th and 31st Divisions—was employed, augmented later by a regimental combat team from the 41st Division and another from the 40th. After landing in the Malabang–Parang area on Moro Gulf, on the west coast of Mindanao, the troops were to drive to the junction of Mindanao's two main highways; from there one prong to drive north to Malaybalay, the other east to Davao Gulf.

At the earliest possible moment after the Malabang landings Colonel Meyer's MAG-24, its mission on Luzon completed, would fly down via Mindoro, to be based at the Malabang Field.

R-day was 17 April. For two weeks before that date Marine planes flew

---

[19] Letter McConaughy to the writer, 13 May 1948.
[20] Eichelberger, *Our Jungle Road to Tokyo*, p 216.

in from Zamboanga and operated from the Malabang field, which was already controlled by guerrillas. Many strikes were flown against enemy troops who were a constant threat to the guerrillas holding the field, and it was estimated that a force of 600–700 trapped nearby were whittled to 300 in ten days of intensive strikes.[21] The role of the Marine aviators was later described by the leader of the Mindanao guerrillas:

> By February, 1945, advance planning by X Corps indicated that the initial landing on the south coast of Mindanao would be made in the vicinity of Parang. With the assistance of MAG Zambo, the guerrillas were able to eliminate the strong Japanese garrisons at both Parang and Malabang. This action presented X Corps with a free beachhead when they landed on 17 April 1945. It would have been impossible for the guerrillas to have completed the elimination of the Japanese garrisons without the assistance of the Marine Air Groups, since the guerrilla troops were not equipped with artillery.[22]

On R-day the first Marine unit ashore at Parang was AWS-3, which set up an SCR-602 radar unit on the beach and initiated communications with the control ship offshore.[23] In the afternoon parts of the ground echelon of MAG-24 got ashore and began the frightful trek to the Malabang airstrip, which they renamed in honor of Captain John A. Titcomb, the ALP officer killed while furnishing air support to the guerrillas on Luzon. MAG-24 air operations began 22 April.

By 27 April AWS-3 had set up six long-range SCR-270 radar stations. SBD's operating from Moret Field and Titcomb Field ranged ahead of the ground forces, which moved rapidly along the highways north and east. Despite extensive Japanese bridge demolitions, the 24th Division reached Digos 27 April, and moved on Davao, first city of Mindanao, which was secured 3 May—145 miles in 15 days.[24] On the northward drive up the central Mindanao Valley the 31st Division, which had landed after the initial assault, ran into some Japanese opposition, which was routed from its Molita River entrenchments by Marine flyers' "close and splendid strike."[25] Valencia fell on 16 May, Malaybalay five days later.

By this time the infantry had come to rely on close air support to an extent rarely matched in operations anywhere in the Pacific. The Marine squadrons neglected to keep precise records, and it is impossible to recapitulate the total effort expended, but one squadron, VMSB-241, recorded 250

---

[21] Boggs, *Marine Aviation in the Philippines*, p 125.

[22] Letter Colonel Wendell W. Fertig USA to Marine Aviation History Board, 25 February 1948.

[23] AWS-3 war diary, April 1945.

[24] USSBS, *Employment of Forces Under the Southwest Pacific Command*, p 58.

[25] Eichelberger, *Our Jungle Road to Tokyo*, p 227.

strikes and missions on Mindanao, compared to 180 on Luzon, although only 1,336 sorties were flown as against 1,518 on Luzon. In the Davao area, where it was estimated there were 30,000 enemy troops, the 24th Division was strung out over 50 miles.[26] In 3,280 sorties in the northwest Davao area, Marine planes dropped 1,450 tons of bombs and 183 tons of napalm. Each day a flight reported in to the 24th Division's Support Air Party every hour on the hour from 0800 to 1600.[27]

One soldier of the 24th, a member of an isolated company, had an intimate view of the SBD's at work:

> I didn't know relief was fighting through to us. . . . I must have fainted . . . my company was gone. I crawled on to the water and drank from the muddy brook. I filled my canteen and pulled myself back into the *kunai*. It was quiet for a long time. Dive bombers woke me up next morning. Plane after plane dove into the Nip positions. They dropped napalm and high explosive bombs all around me. I was covered with dirt and leaves by the explosions and I guess that helped hide me. The Japs were excited and afraid and they ran all around my position. Maybe they thought I was dead. Maybe they were too busy getting out of there to care. Most of them were killed by the bombs or by the bullets when the planes came back and strafed.[28]

One of these missions for the 24th Division ended in tragedy. It happened in this fashion: the air co-ordinator, whose custom it was to land at Libby Field in Davao City, picked up the target information and took off. As usual, he went down and dropped his bomb on the target and signaled the waiting flight leader: "Bomb on my bomb!" On this occasion the flight leader answered: "Okay, I'm a little out of position but I'll bring my planes down right away." After the third or fourth plane dove red smoke began rising from the jungle— the sign that the bombs were falling among friendly troops. Before the strike had been stopped 32 men of the 24th Division lay dead or wounded. Investigation proved that the flight leader had mistaken the bursts of Japanese artillery for the burst of the co-ordinator's signal bomb.

Colonel Jerome went to see Major General Roscoe B. Woodruff, CG of the 24th, to express the Marines' deep sorrow. General Woodruff said it was regrettable, but whenever close support was in order, he would continue to rely on the MAGSZAM flyers.[29]

Before the last mopping-up missions of the Mindanao campaign General Woodruff commended the MAGSZAM flyers as follows:

---

[26] The 24th killed more than 10,000 around Davao, at a cost of 2,700 casualties. (Jan Valtin, *Children of Yesterday*, a book about the 24th Infantry Division, p 387.)

[27] Boggs, *Marine Aviation in the Philippines*, p 130; Eichelberger, *Our Jungle Road to Tokyo*, p 223.

[28] Valtin, *Children of Yesterday*, pp 411–412.

[29] Jerome interview, 21 September 1950.

There have been 1,964 sorties flown by the men of your organization in support of this Division. All of these involved flying over enemy territory in the face of enemy antiaircraft fire, and were flown with determination and courage in spite of losses from enemy fire. Many missions were flown at great risk because of unfavorable weather conditions. The precision of individual attacks on pinpointed targets was greatly admired by front line troops, as was the courage with which they were pressed home at close range. It is believed that no other Division in the Pacific area has had such complete and cooperative air coverage.

The skill of the men in your organization is attested by the confidence which every front line soldier has in your coordinators and pilots. Such confidence and cooperation between two branches of the armed forces can only lead to a rapid and successful conclusion of the war.[30]

The CG of the other X Corps division, Major General Clarence A. Martin of the 31st Division, was equally generous in his praise of the dive-bomber and fighter pilots:

Marine Air Groups 12, 24, and 32 supported the 31st Infantry Division and gave invaluable assistance in the operations on Mindanao, P.I. The efficiency and effectiveness of this air support cannot be overemphasized. At times, because of sudden developments in the situation, the practice of giving advance notice was forgone and it was necessary to request immediate air strikes. The amazing promptness and willingness shown by these air units proved they were constantly on the alert and always ready to be of service. During the period 1 May 1945 to 17 July 1945, these air units flew a total of 221 missions, consisting of 1217 sorties, a majority of which were furnished by Marine Air Group 24.

The terrain with its dense jungles and precipitous mountains, the tops frequently being obscured by clouds, made flying extremely hazardous for the pilots and crews. Some of the targets were located in positions which were surrounded by many steep-sloped, jutting mountain peaks which made dive bombing both difficult and dangerous. Although air units have the prerogative of refusing to fly missions involving unjustified risks to aircraft and personnel, there was never a refusal.[31]

It was the same story with the 41st Division, which presented the Marine flyers with a four-by-six-foot plaque, trimmed with Japanese naval signal flags, mounted by a Japanese light machine gun and bearing the inscription: "IN APPRECIATION—41ST INFANTRY DIVISION." At the presentation Major General Jens A. Doe's message said of the Marine flyers: "Their splendid spirit of cooperation in aiding ground troops has given the division the most effective air support yet received in any of its operations."

[30] Commendation dated 1 July 1945.
[31] Commendation dated 20 July 1945.

General Eichelberger added his tribute:

> I have heard a great number of reports from Major General Franklin Sibert of the X Corps and other unit commanders on the results of Marine-type dive bombing in the Philippines theatre. The value of close support for ground troops as provided by these Marine flyers cannot be measured in words and there is not enough that can be said for their aerial barrages that have cut a path for the infantry. From all quarters, commanders down to the men with the bayonets, I have heard nothing but high tribute.[32]

1st MAW at War's End

The SBD's day was over. On 16 July MAG-24's two "eggbeater" squadrons, VMSB's 133 and 241, were decommissioned, leaving only one dive-bomber squadron, VMSB-244 (which had received SB2C Helldivers late in May). On 1 August the four SBD squadrons of MAG-32 ended their tactical operations and prepared to return to the U.S. two weeks later, though the group designation remained in the Philippines.

Now the 1st MAW, which had been commanded since General Mitchell's departure in June by Louis Woods (one day), Colonel Harold Major (four days) and Lewie Merritt (two months), passed to the command of Major General "Sheriff" Larkin, who was scheduled to take the Wing into the Kyushu invasion.

The Wing's four PBJ squadrons (MAG-61) were ordered to Mindanao, where the fifth squadron (VMB-611) had been operating since 30 March.[33] VMB-611 was ordered to the 4th Wing at Peleliu on 14 August. Five days earlier it had flown a strike on targets pointed out by a captured Japanese lieutenant.

General Larkin never got out of Bougainville until the war ended. On 17 August he arrived at Zamboanga, where Colonel Stanley Ridderhof had been commanding MAGSZAM since Colonel Jerome's departure on 6 July.

The end of the war changed the 1st MAW's plans as drastically as might be expected. On 22 September the Wing began to move to China via Okinawa for occupation duty. At this time its elements included MAG's 12, 24, 25 and 32.

---

[32] Undated message in Marine Corps historical files. In his book, *Our Jungle Road to Tokyo,* p 250, General Eichelberger characterized the MAGSZAM flyers' accomplishments as "superb."

[33] This squadron's CO, Lieut. Colonel George A. Sarles, was killed with two of his crew 30 May in a strike on Kibawe Trail.

CHAPTER TWENTY-TWO

Marines on Carriers

THE WAR WAS ON its last legs—although the participants could not know it—before Marine aviators were flying combat from the decks of carriers. The reasons for this long delay bear investigating.

Almost from the inception of the aircraft carrier after World War I certain high-ranking officers believed that Marine flyers could best support their own ground forces' landings from aircraft carriers, instead of waiting for the establishment of land bases on enemy territory. A Marine Corps recommendation to this effect was made in 1926, and the acute need of a carrier was felt in China the next year.[1]

In 1931–34 two squadrons operated on board *Saratoga* and *Lexington.* The gifted Marine officers who wrote *The Tentative Landing Manual* recognized that naval carrier-based planes would probably have to do the initial support for amphibious operations, but added hopefully—very hopefully for the depression year 1934—"every effort should be made to provide for participation of landing force Marine Corps aircraft in the initial operations. The ideal arrangement involves the assignment of a carrier or carriers solely for the use of these units. . . ."[2]

In June 1934 two squadrons were based on the Navy's original carrier, *Langley,* and during the late 1930's the Corps' tactical squadrons periodically qualified on board *Ranger, Yorktown, Enterprise, Lexington* and *Saratoga* and participated in fleet exercises. In January 1939 the General Board defined the secondary mission of Marine aviation as "replacement squadrons for carrier-based naval aircraft."

We have seen that the Marine planes on Wake, Midway, and Guadalcanal were ferried there on carriers. With a few exceptions, Marine planes kept their tailhooks and folding wings throughout the war against the day when they would return to the carriers.

Once the Marine flyers were thrown into Guadalcanal, they were committed to the limit of their combat strength. "More planes!" was the cry, and fresh squadrons were rushed to the South Pacific as fast as they could be trained and equipped with aircraft. There was no helping the situation. Fast

[1] See p 28.
[2] Isely and Crowl, *The U.S. Marines and Amphibious War,* p 41.

as it grew, Marine aviation couldn't seem to grow fast enough, and the last thing anybody looked for in 1942–43 was additional duty. Missions which normally would have been assigned to the Army Air Forces fell to the Marines; the AAF had no complaints—there was war enough for everybody.

After Guadalcanal there were the Central Solomons, then there was Bougainville. And at the end of the Solomons land bases always stood Rabaul. ComAirPac (Admiral Towers) noted that a third of the pilots being qualified for carrier landings by the Naval Air Operational Training Command were marines. He considered this wasteful and recommended that their carrier-qualification requirement be abandoned. General Rowell agreed, and Admiral Nimitz so ordered it.[3] A new generation of Marine pilots matured without ever knowing the deck of a carrier.

Rabaul's demise as a primary target came with startling swiftness. Until the morning in February 1944 when the Japanese withdrew their remaining planes nobody could predict how much longer the enemy would feed his aircraft into Rabaul. Indeed, it was not until three weeks later that the invasion of Kavieng, which would have been supported by Marine planes,[4] was canceled. After that the sewing up of Rabaul and the rest of the Bismarcks corpse was left to the Marine and AAF sailmakers ensconced on Bougainville, Green and Emirau. The war moved on.

The big push through the Central Pacific had started in November 1943, in the Gilberts. Even if the Marines had not been committed to the land-based warfare of the Solomons, the Navy in 1943 was in no mood to allot carriers to them, and the Central Pacific was made for carriers.

It is not true, however, that the Navy couldn't spare any carriers to the Marine Corps. In addition to 10 CV's and 9 CVL's, the Navy had 35 CVE's.[5] And it would have been a simple matter in late 1943 to turn over one seventh of the smaller flattops for Marine close support.

High-ranking Marine officers—aviators and nonaviators alike—showed a remarkable lack of foresight in failing to insist that their flyers be put on escort carriers at this time. It is easy to say that "Ernie King would never have stood for it," or "Admiral Whoosis doesn't believe in Marine aviation." But it was the job of the Marine Corps to find the right "persuaders."

The truth is that the top Marine aviators didn't pay enough attention to (1) close support, (2) amphibious landings, (3) a combination of the two. They were too deeply interested in shooting enemy planes out of the wild blue yonder, so they lost sight of their primary mission. They stopped being amphibious enough to forget Roy Geiger's blunt statement in 1939: "The primary reason for the Marine Corps' having airplanes is their use in close

---

[3] ComAirPac to CinCPac, serial 0988, 25 June 1943 (Rowell's assent was noted on the routing sheet by his plans officer, Colonel Alexander W. Kreiser); CinCPac to ComAirPac, 30 June.

[4] Operations Plan No. 644, serial 00708, 9 March 1944, mentions only Army and naval aviation, but the latter would have included the Marines.

[5] Secretary of the Navy, *Annual Report,* fiscal 1945.

support of ground troops."[6] This resulted in (1) Marine aviation being laid open to the charge that it was duplicating Army aviation and (2) the Navy grabbing off the mission of supporting troops during amphibious landings.

Playing both ends against the middle didn't work. Nor did the ambition to attain some kind of unattainable autonomy.

The sudden end of the Bismarcks and the neglect of carriers found Marine pilots virtually unemployed during a long stretch in 1944. Pounding the rear areas of the South and Central Pacific was necessary, even if grinding them to powder was excessive. But it was not in keeping with Marine aviation's primary mission or with the ancient "first to fight" spirit of the Corps. For the Marine divisions 1944 was a year of heroism and history. For the aviators it was mostly frustration.

Hindsight tells us that more aggressive representation at CominCh and CinCPac headquarters would have put the Marines on carriers, supporting their own troops with their own type of precision close support, many months earlier. This was the view of Admiral Towers, who had cause to conclude that the Marines "didn't want carriers."[7] Back at Pearl Harbor MAWPac had lapsed into anachronism and complacency. Marine aviation headquarters had virtually no ties to FMFPac; even its connection with CinCPac was remote. MAWPac had no representative attending Nimitz's conferences. Its strength was concentrated far away in the South Pacific, even after CinCPac's eyes were riveted on the new, exciting Central Pacific drive.

Better Late Than Never

Certain Marine officers had seen the handwriting on the wall, even before Rabaul became a dead horse. It was obvious to them that the Marine flyers were going to be without a job. Some efforts were made early in 1944 to have marines assigned to carriers. The Director of Aviation, Brig. General Louis E. Woods, was one of these; Colonel Albert D. Cooley, assistant director at the time, was another. Colonel David R. Nimmer, a nonaviator, did what he could in Washington, as a member of the War Plans Committee of the Joint Staff. Several "Marine-minded" admirals, notably McCain and Fitch, aided and abetted them.

The first public reference to the Marine efforts to get on board carriers occurs in the 12 June 1944 issue of *Time*, which concludes with what might then have been considered undue optimism:

> They [the Marine aviators] only grow indignant when they recall how they are used. The Corps will never be satisfied until its air arm gets assigned to carriers from which it can support its own foot soldiers. Its flyers are browned off on defenses and strategic operations based on

---

[6] Isely and Crowl, *The U.S. Marines and Amphibious War*, p 59.

[7] Conversation with the author, March 1948.

hot atolls. Says General Woods firmly: "The Marine aviator and the Marine foot soldier must be a team." The welcome scuttlebutt this week . . . the Navy was about ready for some all-Marine carriers—was going to give its amphibious outfit what it wanted.

About this time General Vandegrift, the Commandant since 1 January, drove across the Potomac to see the Chief of Naval Operations. Admiral King had been complaining for some time that Marine Corps aviation's expansion had become greater than necessary to carry out its assignment. Considering the decline in missions available, he was right.[8] On 30 June 1944 Marine aviation consisted of 5 wings, 28 groups, 126 aircraft squadrons, total personnel of 112,626, including 10,457 pilots.

General Vandegrift worked out a clever compromise. He proposed that one of the five wings be eliminated.[9] But he also argued that it was unnatural for marines to be committed simply to rear-area duty in the South and Central Pacific, and that therefore the Marine flyers should be assigned to carriers— the only way they could perform their amphibious close-support mission for the rest of the war (which at that time was expected to last about two more years, until the fall of 1946).

King assented to this, with the stipulation that Admiral Nimitz be consulted in advance.[10]

In August 1944, just after Saipan was secured—there was still some fighting on Guam—General Vandegrift flew out to Pearl Harbor with Brig. General Gerald C. Thomas and Brig. General Field Harris, who had recently relieved General Woods as Director. At Pearl Harbor they conferred with Admiral Nimitz, Admiral Towers, Rear Admiral Forrest Sherman, and Major General Rowell. Towers immediately confronted Vandegrift with the argument that "Your own people don't want carriers," but Vandegrift and Harris persuaded Towers that times had changed.

The agreement which came out of that conference was largely the work of Admiral Sherman. It set the course of Marine aviation for the remainder of the war. It provided that

(1) Marine squadrons would be assigned to CVE's;

(2) Control of aircraft directly supporting ground troops in amphibious operations would be taken over by Marine aviation;

(3) In order to "get Marine aviation back into the Marine Corps"—as one of the conferees put it—MAWPac would become Aircraft, Fleet Marine Force, Pacific (AirFMFPac);

---

[8] ". . . Our main trouble at the present time is trying to get our squadrons that have been organized and trained out to the combat zone. . . . we have a backlog of some ten or twelve that have been ready to go for a month or longer that are still sitting around awaiting the request for their services from those who are running the war in the Pacific." (Letter, Woods to Colonel Ivan Miller, 31 May 1944.)

[9] CMC to CominCh AA-213-lfb, 1 October 1944.

[10] Author's conversation with General Vandegrift, September 1949.

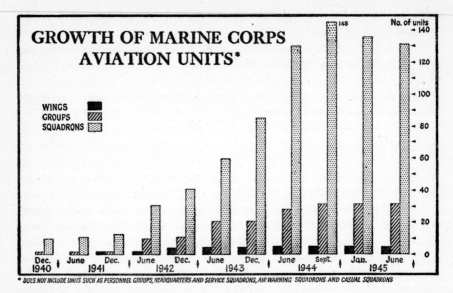

GROWTH OF MARINE CORPS AVIATION UNITS*

WINGS
GROUPS
SQUADRONS

* DOES NOT INCLUDE UNITS SUCH AS PERSONNEL GROUPS, HEADQUARTERS AND SERVICE SQUADRONS, AIR WARNING SQUADRONS AND CASUAL SQUADRONS

(4) A senior Marine aviator would be assigned to the planning staff of CinCPac;[11]

(5) A reorganization would take place, providing that (a) groups be composed of three 24-plane squadrons instead of four 18-plane squadrons, (b) the number of projected Marine Air Warning squadrons be cut from 32 to 24—and perhaps even further—in view of the Army's parallel activity, (c) CinCPac would plan for the following operational Marine aircraft in the Pacific by 15 February 1945:

Type	Total Aircraft
CVE VMF	72
CVE VMTB	48
VMF	720
VMF (Night)	72
VMSB-VMTB-VMBF	384
VMB	96
VMD	36
VMR	120[12]
VMO (Spotting)	72
TOTAL	1,620

The proposal to eliminate one wing got lost in the course of subsequent developments. However, the sensible design for reducing the size of Marine

---

[11] Admiral Towers specified Colonel John C. Munn, but Admiral King wouldn't release "Toby" for the job. (Vandegrift conversation.)

[12] Half two-engined, half four-engined.

Corps aviation was carried out by decommissioning 15 squadrons in October and November (8 VMF, 7 VMSB).

General Vandegrift flew on to Saipan and Guam. Upon returning to Washington he arranged for the relief of Rowell, who had held the top Pacific job since 1941. Upon being relieved at Pearl Harbor on 16 September by Major General Francis P. Mulcahy, General Rowell was assigned as chief of the Naval Air Mission at Lima, Peru.

The CVE Program

Marine Carrier Groups, Aircraft, Fleet Marine Force, Pacific, was established 21 October 1944 as a tactical command with headquarters at Santa Barbara, California, with Colonel Cooley as commanding officer. It comprised two groups—MBDAG-48 at Santa Barbara and MAG-51 at Mojave. Two weeks later they were redesignated Marine Air Support Groups (MASG). An MASG was to be comprised of four carrier air groups (MCVG), each with an 18-plane fighter squadron, designated VMF(CVS), and a 12-plane torpedo-bomber squadron, designated VMTB(CVS). From the standpoint of ship's strength, the composition of an MASG included four Marine CVE's and two Navy CVE's (all ships manned by Navy personnel, naturally). The Navy carriers were to provide antisubmarine patrols, combat air patrols, and so on. Each MCVG was to be assigned to one of the four Marine carriers. The unit of four Marine and two Navy carriers was to be called a carrier division, commanded by a rear admiral. The MASG staff would operate in the flagship as a part of the admiral's staff to direct the operations of the four MCVG's performing support for the ground troops. Therefore, MASG-48 was designated as the first division and MASG-51 was designated as the second division.[13]

For simplicity of administration, all ground crews and administrative personnel were organized into units known as Marine Carrier Aircraft Service Detachments (CASD's), each with its own commanding officer. The CASD's were given consecutive numerical designations to conform with the number of the carrier air group each would serve. Until the CASD became part of the ship's complement when assigned to a CVE, it remained part of the MASG.

During the summer Marine pilots were ordered to start carrier qualification again. Woods found the Corsair "most successful—it is the first time our Marine pilots have engaged in carrier landings with the Corsair."[14] The first landing of a Corsair (Navy-piloted) on board a carrier had taken place almost two years earlier—on 25 September 1942, on board CVE Sangamon. But

---

[13] Three distinctions should be borne in mind: Marine Carrier Groups, Aircraft, FMFPac was the over-all designation for the all-Marine carrier force; Marine Air Support Group (plus its number) was the designation for a six-ship unit called a division; Carrier Air Group (with its number) was the designation of the 30-plane group aboard a single carrier.

[14] Letter to C. J. McCarthy, vice president of United Aircraft Company, 21 July 1944.

many changes in the plane had been made in the meantime to adapt it to carriers. These included raising the pilot's cabin to improve visibility (November 1942), improved aileron action (January 1943), larger bearings in the tail wheels (March 1943), new arresting hook (August 1943), improved stall and landing characteristics (September 1943), extended tail-wheel installation (October 1943), installation of spoiler on right wing to reduce violence of stalls when under acceleration and to provide new stall warning (November 1943), new oleo strut-filling procedure (May 1944). Nonetheless, until the end of the war there would be some objection to the Corsair as a carrier plane.

The Marines would train like Navy CVE units, but with "particular emphasis on training in tactics and techniques employed in close support of amphibious operations."

As skipper of Marine Carrier Groups, Aircraft, FMFPac, Al Cooley set to work to make his flyers the best-trained marines ever to enter combat. About 15 per cent of his pilots had had combat experience, but few of them had ever made a carrier landing. The 85 per cent were fresh out of flight school and had to begin at the bottom.

Separate schools were set up for flight training and ground training. The latter was sandwiched in whenever possible—navigation, communications, flight-deck procedure, recognition, survival and first aid, map reading, ordnance and gunnery, "dunking," and (above all) close air support, along with a dozen other subjects. Flight training included tactics, night flying, field carrier landings, rocket firing, navigation, fixed and free gunnery, and bombing. Air-support problems were worked out with the Navy Amphibious Training Command at Coronado, and with the Army at Camp Cooke, California.

To complete their tour of the California training circuit, the carrier marines went from their home station to El Centro and Mojave for rocket firing. The fighter squadrons of MASG-48's air groups were among the first to fire the 11.75-inch Tiny Tim rocket (at the Naval Air Facility, Inyokern).

During this period of intense training another shortcoming came to light: The Marines had no trained Landing Signal Officers (LSO); however, some were in training at this time. But until they had received proper instruction and some experience, it was necessary to borrow Navy LSO's from FAir-WestCoast.

Landings on board real carriers were made off North Island (San Diego), and the fledgling pilots learned quickly that it takes skill to fly an F4U or TBM on and off the 81-by-502-foot deck of a *Commencement Bay*-class escort carrier. Eight landings were necessary for qualification—which, the pilots were soon to learn, were not enough. At that, the marines could consider themselves lucky—they drew a ship of 24,275 tons that was far more seaworthy than the Kaiser-built carriers of 10,000 tons—and one with 22 more feet of precious flight deck.

By December the training program was in good shape. MASG-48, also under command of Colonel Cooley, was assigned its first carrier, *Block Island*, on 3 February 1945. To it was attached MCVG-1, with squadrons VMF-511, VMTB-233 and CASD-1, under Lieut. Colonel John F. Dobbin. Three other carriers were furnished at intervals of one month. MCVG-2, with VMF-512, VMTB-143 and CASD-2, under Lieut. Colonel William R. Campbell, was attached to *Gilbert Islands.* MCVG-3, with VMF-513, VMTB-234 and CASD-3, under Major Royce W. Coln, was attached to *Vella Gulf.* MCVG-4, with VMF-351, VMTB-132 and CASD-4, under Lieut. Colonel Donald K. Yost, was attached to *Cape Gloucester.* Thus, on 21 May the four Marine CVE's with the addition of the all-Navy *Kula Gulf* and *Siboney* made up Carrier Division 27, under command of Captain Dixwell Ketcham USN. The Marines' goal for OLYMPIC, the invasion of Japan in late 1945, was eight carriers.

Marines to the Rescue

But Cooley's pilots weren't the first marines to fly off carriers. Fate intervened in the form of that eerie symbol of Oriental desperation, the *kamikaze.*

Back at Pearl Harbor the Pacific Fleet high command viewed the *kamikaze* menace with alarm. The problem was to find a defense against the highly successful suicide tactics. A conference on 24–26 November in San Francisco concluded that fighter complements would have to be increased if the *kamikazes* were to be stopped.[15]

Subsequent to this conference, on 27 November, more cries for additional fighters were received from ComThirdFleet, which caused ComAirPac (Vice Admiral George D. Murray) to state that the "critical situation" required "the temporary employment of Marine VF squadrons on the fast carriers."[16] Current complements for CV's were 54 VF, 24 VSB, 18 VTB. Under the new plan 19 additional fighters were allotted to each CV. Dive-bomber and torpedo-bomber squadrons were cut to 15 planes each.

Admiral Mitscher, upon being relieved by McCain as Fast Carrier Task Force commander, took himself back to Washington, and, in the words of Field Harris, "put the Marines on carriers in one day."

It was natural that the Navy should turn to the Marines in its hour of *kamikaze* peril. The naval-aviation pilot program had been cut back, and the Navy did not have enough additional fighter pilots available. Retraining VSB and VTB pilots as fighter jockeys would require some time. The Navy began assiduously making fighter pilots out of its bombermen—TAG hauled scores of them out of Ulithi for retraining in the rear areas—meantime, the Marines filled the gap.

The placing of Marine squadrons aboard the CV's was never regarded as anything but an expedient, to satisfy an urgent need pending availability of an adequate number of trained Navy fighter pilots under the new 73-fighters-per-carrier requirement.[17]

---

[15] ComAirPac to CominCh, 3 December 1944.
[16] *Ibid.*
[17] CominCh to CinCPac, 021256 2 December 1944.

On Board Essex[18]

During the first six months of 1945 ten Marine fighter squadrons served aboard five large carriers. The first of these were VMF-124 (Lieut. Colonel William Millington) and VMF-213 (Major David E. Marshall). Both had been training (land-based) in the Hawaii area, having been ferried in September from the West Coast on board the new carrier *Ticonderoga*. The two squadrons had alternated in the South Pacific during most of 1943, the one relieving the other at intervals in the combat zone. But as they boarded *Essex* in Ulithi harbor three days after Christmas 1944, Millington had only five veteran combat pilots, Marshall only three. By the time the squadrons left Ewa the pilots had been qualified for carrier landings, averaging 12 apiece, on *Saratoga*, *Makassar Strait*, and *Bataan* in the San Diego and Hawaii areas.

On board *Essex* 54 pilots of the two squadrons (with 4 ground officers and 120 enlisted men of VMF-124) operated as one, under the command of Millington. Administrative records, however, continued to be kept separately.

Essex sortied from the vast, necklace-shaped Ulithi lagoon at 0800 on 30 December, part of a total force of 30 carriers and nearly 800 other ships that participated in or covered MacArthur's landings at Lingayen Gulf. This was an auspicious time for the Marine flyers to get back into the "front lines." In the offing was a venture into the South China Sea—the first time the surface ships had dared to carry the war to the very shores of Asia.

From the first day *Essex* marines were in trouble. Lieut. Thomas J. Campion's F4U spun into the sea off the starboard bow after his first takeoff, caught fire as it hit, and he never had a chance to emerge from the 50-foot-high flames. Thus was forever ended his postwar ambition (which he wrote on his squadron information blank)—"Regular Commission—Marine Corps."

Next day was worse. Another F4U spun in, but a destroyer rescued the lucky pilot. Fifteen minutes later Lieut. Barney W. Bennett lost power as he approached the flight deck, and his Corsair flopped into the water on its back. He was not seen again.

On 3 January TF 38 made its first strike in support of the forthcoming landings. The target: Okinawa, which had not been hit since the great strikes of the previous October. The marines escorting VTB-4 claimed their first victim: a Nick (twin-engined fighter) shot down by Millington, one of 27 airborne enemy planes destroyed that day—McCain's pilots claimed a total of 204 on the ground. But one marine didn't come back: 22-year-old Lieut. Robert W. (Moon) Mullins, who was lost at last report and apparently headed out to sea. On 4 January foul Pacific weather claimed another victim: Lieut. Donald R. Anderson failed to return, after climbing 5,000 feet through a solid overcast over the destroyer picket line to obtain a fix.

As MacArthur's forces sailed from Leyte Gulf through Surigao Strait and the Mindanao Sea, northward through the Sulu Sea and Mindoro Strait

---

[18] Principal source for the remainder of this chapter is the author's notes made on board *Essex* in January 1945.

into the South China Sea the *kamikazes* hammered away. Escort carrier *Ommaney Bay* was hit by a suicider and sunk on the 4th. Cruiser *Louisville*, CVE's *Manila Bay* and *Savo Island*, plus a DD and a DE were damaged in the same manner the next day but managed to sail on. CVE's *Kadashan Bay* and *Kitkun Bay* were hit. Three minesweepers were sunk in Lingayen Gulf; 2 battleships, 2 cruisers, 2 destroyers, 1 APA, and another minesweeper incurred serious damage from the more than 50 *kamikazes* which set upon them.

Try as they might, the CVE's could not stop the fanatical Sons of Heaven at the source of their attacks, and land-based Army and Marine planes at Leyte had not only the weather to master but also excessive range. Therefore, McCain and his 13 flattops of the Fast Carrier Task Force set out to do the best they could in the north. The attacks of 6–7 January struck hard at the Northern Philippines, down as far as Lingayen Gulf itself. In two days the flyers off the big carriers encountered only 18 enemy planes in the air, but claimed 207 on the ground.

The weather in the *Essex* pilots' area was worse than ever—zero-zero almost everywhere along the line. Three lieutenants—Kochut, Dorsett and Mortag—all aged 22, went into this weather in the Northern Philippines, somewhere near Aparri, and never came out. Four other F4U's were lost, in water landings or deck crashes, but their pilots lived.

At the end of the first nine days the *Essex* marines took stock: 7 pilots dead, for whom no human enemy could be held responsible, and 13 F4U's lost. One major shook his head: "We just can't learn navigation and carrier operations in a week as well as the Navy does it in six months." Five of the 13 Corsairs had been lost at sea, under instrument-flight conditions; four more would be lost before the month's cruise was ended. (During the period no Navy F6F's were similarly lost from *Essex*.) The record was not good.

But better times and better weather awaited the marines as TF 38 headed into the South China Sea following the successful Lingayen landings.

To the Shores of Asia

By any accounting 12 January 1945 must be regarded as one of the great days of the U.S. Navy. The venture into the South China Sea was as audacious as it was unlikely. Who ever heard of taking all your ships into a pond surrounded by *kamikazes* on four sides? If the enemy had a fanatical bone in his body, now was his chance to throw himself at his tormentor. If he was looking for targets, here they were—11 carriers, 6 battleships, 13 cruisers and 48 destroyers, plus a night-carrier group (2 carriers), and, of all things, a fragile tanker force whose sinking would leave the whole fleet helpless. Plan GRATITUDE might well have gratified the other side.

To get into this "aerial trap," as the fast carriers' commander called it,[19]

---

[19] John Sidney McCain, "So We Hit Them in the Belly," *The Saturday Evening Post*, 7 and 14 July 1945.

the Force had to steam through the narrow Luzon Strait, between Luzon and Formosa. Small islands separate the two narrower channels, Bashi on the north and Balintang to the south. Halsey chose Bashi Channel, at the bottom tip of Formosa, only 80 miles from the Japanese airfield at Koshun and only 53 miles from enemy radar presumably stationed on Batan Island.

What Admiral Halsey was looking for was the rest of the Japanese Fleet that got away from him at Leyte Gulf in October—a fleet, Intelligence said, that still included 2 carriers, 2 "flightdeck battleships" (*Ise* and *Hyuga*), 2 light carriers, 2 escort carriers, 4 battleships, 8 cruisers and 30 destroyers. "A number" of these were presumably located in Camranh Bay.[20] What a fine revenge for Bull Halsey if he could polish off the rest of the Nip Navy! Particularly if he could catch that Navy trying to dash across the South China Sea and interfere with MacArthur's landings on Luzon (as it had almost succeeded in doing at Leyte)!

The fleet fueled on 8 January. Next day, as MacArthur's soldiers went ashore at Lingayen Gulf, Halsey threw all his planes at Formosa. Very few enemy planes were up in the foul weather, but Halsey claimed 15 enemy ships sunk.[21] Admiral Bogan, commanding TG 38.2, suggested another try at Okinawa but got a turndown.

On board *Essex* there was more excitement than the marines had known since they left the U.S. The ship's executive officer, Commander David McDonald, went on the bullhorn at 1700: "We are now heading in a westerly direction, and tomorrow morning we will have breakfast in the China Sea. From there we go south to Camranh Bay and then we swing north to Hong Kong. We hope for better weather and more Japs." To which a sailor in Air Plot muttered: "Better weather but no Japs."

That night TF 38 streaked through narrow Bashi Channel at 24 knots. "Even now," Halsey wrote in 1947, "it is hard for me to realize that we slipped past the Japs."[22] But slip past he did: no enemy detected the Fleet's long single file; the three planes which showed up were splashed by the night fighters. The code experts said these three planes were transports evacuating the operations section of the Philippine Air Command.

News dispatches on the morning of the 10th said that MacArthur's landing went well—68,500 already ashore at Lingayen. In the squadron ready rooms there were recognition lectures. The big prize in Camranh Bay might well be *Yamato*, whose main battery guns Intelligence estimated at 17.5 inches.[23]

"So far as I know," said Lieut. Charles Hughes USN of Intelligence, "there are no carriers in the South China Sea."

---

[20] Sherman, *Combat Command*, p 326; King, *U.S. Navy at War*, p 127.

[21] King, *U.S. Navy at War*, p 127. JANAC, which lists all naval vessels but only merchant ships of 500 tons or more, shows 2 cargo ships, 2 tankers, 2 sub chasers, and a frigate sunk off Formosa that day.

[22] *Admiral Halsey's Story*, p 243.

[23] Only after the war did we learn Japan's big secret: they were 18.1 inches.

Said a Navy TBM pilot: "No Navy Crosses this time."

"What if you hit the *Yamato?*" asked his neighbor.

"Might be," said the pilot, "but posthumously."

The final instructions in this particular ready room session: hit the big ones; leave those little 10,000-ton merchant ships alone.

The 3,000 souls on board *Essex* viewed the South China Sea with immense curiosity. After all, it had been three years since any American surface ships ventured into these waters. A VMF-124 sergeant sniffed the air: "Smell the chop suey."

Not even Admiral Sherman in Flag Plot was immune to the contagion. Said he: "Well, the water doesn't look yellow."

The great armada ploughed through a sea that was moderate to rough, with a 15- to 25-knot wind from the northeast, moderate to bright sunshine, broken cloud cover. To the fledgling carrier flyers of VMF-124 and VMF-213, who had lost so much to the weather in the Philippine Sea, this seemed wonderful for flying.

The marines had a final briefing in Ready Room 4 at 1945 of the 11th. Maps of Indochina were distributed. Lieut. Leo B. Pambrun, the ACIO, talked for an hour and a half about the country and its people; Supply Officer Bennett handed out currency for pilots to use in case they were shot down. (It is a commentary on our knowledge at the time that the currency was not Indochina piasters but Chinese yuan; the "pointee-talkee" chart given to each pilot was printed not in Annamese but in Chinese.)

The *Essex* air group's own primary target was the airfields, from Camranh Bay to Cap St. Jacques to Saigon. Next in priority were ships of the Japanese Navy; last, transports. On the teletype screen was flashed a message from the Bull himself: WE MAY HAVE A GOLDEN OPPORTUNITY TOMORROW TO COMPLETELY ANNIHILATE AN IMPORTANT ENEMY FORCE. YOU ALL KNOW THAT IS WHAT I EXPECT OF YOU. GIVE THEM HELL. GOD BLESS YOU ALL. HALSEY.

The ominous bong-bong-bong of General Quarters sounded on board *Essex* at 0655. Admiral Gardner's night planes from *Enterprise* and *Independence* had already flown off in search of Japanese shipping from Tourane south to Saigon. At 0707 TG 34.5—2 battleships, 5 cruisers and 12 destroyers—was formed for the rush-in to shoot up Japanese warships which might try to break out of Camranh Bay.

During the first three hours after daylight there was nothing to report except disappointment. No enemy warships in Camranh Bay—surface fire accounted for a "sailing vessel" (sampan) offshore. Otherwise, there was nothing big enough to waste a plane's rocket on, let alone a battleship's shell.

"I'm afraid they got the word," said a commander on Ted Sherman's staff.

"Like going rabbit-hunting with a couple of machine guns," said another.

But by midmorning the reports began telling of other game. *Ticonderoga's* strike found and sank a convoy composed of 2 large oilers, 2 medium oilers, 3 destroyer escorts. *Essex's* own torpedo squadron commander came back with stories of finding convoys disappearing up and down the coast of Indo-china as the American planes rammed home their "fish" and their bombs.

During the morning the marines had been assigned to combat air patrol guarding the task force, which turned out to be rather dull, inasmuch as enemy planes never approached the ships all day. But soon after noon the Corsairs warmed up to escort the TBM's on the big strike against Saigon and its nearby airfields—places named Trang Bang, Bien Hoa and Than Son Nhut. The French Underground in Saigon—code-name "Jacques"—radioed there was plenty of shipping in the Saigon River, including a cruiser; also there were docks and oil-storage tanks.

By 1355 the planes were off the deck and headed westward through a fine haze, over a slate-gray ocean. Within half an hour the torpedo planes and Corsairs were within sight of the coast of Asia, majestic green and purple mountains that resembled Hawaii, so far to the rear. The droning planes swung south along the coast.

There was evidence aplenty of the morning strike's effectiveness—a three-mile oil slick left by a ship already on the bottom of the South China Sea, three ships burning a few miles farther south, then another with black smoke billowing up as high as 5,000 feet. In the shallow waters of the Saigon River the flyers could spot another ship lying on her side, broken like a discarded toy.

Along the river the marines and sailors saw the sun—yes, the sun—mirrored in countless rice paddies, the great pattern of irregular checkerboard that means food for the billion bellies of Asia. Little villages along the river fascinated these tourists who were having their first glimpse of Asia—gray-thatched huts, occasionally a red-tiled roof. It had taken a long time to fight our way all the way across the world's greatest ocean, but here, after 37 months of war, we were up against another continent.

Over the red-roofed city of Saigon—the Paris of the mysterious East—the Japanese threw up an occasional puff of heavy AA fire. But the air was ours. Down low the machine-gun fire was more intense. The *Essex* marines, along with fighter pilots of half a dozen other carriers, dived into it.

Scraps of their radio conversation, as penciled in a notebook in a TBM at the time, tell fragments of the story:

"There are three or four planes burning under the camouflage."

"I got one that time."

"You go down there and drop your bomb; I'll stay up here and keep radio contact."

"Seventy-six, did you report a bogey?"

"You make another run and wait for me to rendezvous."

"Watch out over around the hangar. They're firing."

"Yeah, looks like machine guns."

"Roger."

"I'm getting ready to start another run. Have you started yours yet?"

"This is 1 Rebel to 99 Dodger. I would like to hit the docks and wharves at Saigon, or the oil-storage tanks."

"Is that a CL smoking down there?"

"This is 99 Dodger to 1 Rebel. I would like you to escort our VT's back—we want to sweep the airfields."

"I dropped a bomb 1,200 feet, 300 knots."

"There are four huge storage tanks."

"Three AK's down there in the river, south of the bend."

"My belly tank is out and I'm having to use 2,400 r.p.m."

"I'm making my run from east to west—fairly low."

"That was a direct hit—whoever dropped that last one [chuckle]."

"Two miles now to the big smoke, the big smoke! This is 99 Dodger. Bogey right behind you and trying to make a getaway—I'll follow—he's in the clouds."

"There are eight or ten ships here in the harbor at Saigon."

The raid on Saigon that January afternoon was witnessed by hundreds of French and Annamese on the city's rooftops. What they saw was as fine a demonstration of precision bombing as was furnished during World War II. The 500-odd U.S. planes neatly picked off four cargo ships (including one hit by the fighter-bomber of Major Fay V. Domke of VMF-213), a couple of oilers and the French cruiser *Lamotte-Picquet*, which might have been in Japanese hands, for all we knew.[24]

Those which were not burning up planes on the airfields or sinking ships in the river were bombing and strafing the great oil-storage tanks of Caltex and Shell along the river front. These furnished two great gushers of black smoke which merged at about 5,000 feet. "Very accurate bombing—too accurate," said the Caltex manager in 1947, who was still trying to repair his tanks and machinery.

The marines furnished only about three per cent of the total aircraft involved in the great raid of 12 January. But they had done their part in the Navy's greatest day of the war, in terms of ships sunk: 14 warships, 33 merchant ships.[25]

VMF-124's and VMF-213's own claims for 12 January—including a fighter

---

[24] In 1947 the author noted in Saigon that (1) the French resented the sinking of *Lamotte-Picquet;* (2) more than two years later there was still plenty of evidence of the 12 January 1945 raid—four ships upended on the river bottom; (3) the only mention of the 12 January raid in French newspapers of that period consisted of the obituary notice of a lieutenant killed on board *Lamotte-Picquet;* (4) the French admired the accurate bombing of the Navy planes (in contrast to the high-level B-24's and B-29's which, following the Navy raid, blew up the wing of a hospital, the British consulate and many hundreds of civilians). Many Frenchmen thought the Americans should pay for the big bombers' damage. The Navy could have heard in Saigon eloquent testimony to confirm its graphs which showed that 300 tons of dive-bombing do as much damage to a specific target—in this case, oil tanks—as 3,000 tons of bombs released from high altitude (Sherman, *Combat Command,* p 334).

[25] The total tonnage, 157,285, takes second place, however, to the Truk raid, 17 February 1944, which sank 37 ships of more than 200,000 tons. It should be noted that Admiral Halsey claimed sinking only 41 ships of 127,000 tons on 12 January—6 ships and 30,000 tons less than he actually got.

sweep later in the day—amounted to 10 to 12 planes destroyed on the ground near Saigon.

TF 38 as a whole lost 16 planes, all to AA, while shooting down 15 and claiming to burn 97 on the ground, including 50 reinforcing planes which arrived from Singapore at dusk, only to be caught and incinerated by the force's night fighters.

Life and Death in Indochina

Among the losses was the fifteenth *Essex* Marine plane—and the first to enemy fire. During a strafing run the Corsair of Lieut. Joseph O. Lynch caught a burst of AA automatic fire and he crash-landed it in a rice paddy 50 yards from the Japanese landing strip at Trang Bang. Lynch climbed out of his cockpit and the last his pals saw of him he waved his hand in salute, "a lone, straight figure in an alien land."[26]

But even in this alien land Lynch found friends. He was picked up by a native policeman who smuggled him to a French colonial outpost. At French Army headquarters in Saigon he met three Navy pilots from other carriers who also had been shot down during the day. All were fed and clothed, then stowed away in a women's prison, where they stayed six weeks, unbeknownst to the Japanese. On one occasion an SB2C pilot whose French was fluent saved the Americans by convincing the Japanese "nobody here but us Frenchmen."

The pilots were transferred north to Hanoi for internment. Early in March the Japanese declared war on the French and twice the Foreign Legionnaires who were in charge of the Americans (by now a party of five Navy pilots, an Army B-24 pilot, and Lynch) engaged in sharp clashes, during which half the Legionnaires were killed. Through the efforts of an *adjudant-chef* named Gunther (a German) the Americans escaped from the fighting. At the village of Din Ben there was a U.S. Army Intelligence lieutenant named Carpenter waiting to meet them. On 31 March a C-47 from Kunming landed on the airstrip and took the grateful pilots to China.[27]

Not so lucky as Lynch was another *Essex* pilot. Among the planes shot down near Saigon was the TBM of Lieut. (jg) Donald A. Henry, whose radioman, ARM2c Ellsworth Shirley, was killed in the crash. Henry escaped, as Lynch had, and after several weeks joined up with six crew members of a PBM which had made a crash landing 26 January at Quong Ngai.[28]

The adventures of Henry and the six PBM crewmen can not be recon-

---

[26] Report of a combat correspondent, Lieut. Hal Goodwin USMCR, who watched the strike from a TBM. Lieut. Goodwin kindly loaned his file of dispatches recording the doings of the *Essex* marines.

[27] Interview Lieut. Lynch, 17 August 1948; his survival report of 23 April 1945.

[28] Of the 11 members of the PBM, 2 were taken prisoner and liberated after the war, 1 was rescued by a submarine, 2 were captured at Hue and driven by the Japanese in a truck going to Saigon, and were never heard of again.

structed precisely. But somehow they found their way to the primitive Moi village of Pletanang, in the mountains north of Saigon. There, on the morning of 12 March 1945, two months to the day after Lieut. Henry was shot down, they met their fate at the hands of a cruel and remorseless enemy. According to the natives' story, the seven Americans were caught by the Japanese after a 100-mile pursuit. During a fire fight the biggest of the Americans, "Brooklyn" by name, was killed, and the other six surrendered. After accepting their surrender the Japanese commander ordered them to kneel, tied their wrists together, shot them in turn, then kicked each backward into a shallow grave.[29]

The Tragedy of the B-24

Intertheater liaison left much to be desired and a tragedy in its wake. Late in the afternoon of 12 January three Marine pilots on CAP, led by Captain Edmond P. Hartsock, spotted a four-engined plane which had no identifying insignia painted on it. At first they took it to be an Emily flying boat. Above the 7,500-foot overcast along the coast near Phan Rang the three planes closed on the bomber, whereupon they received heavy fire from its waist guns.

Although all hands had been warned that the Japanese were suspected of flying captured American planes in the area,[30] the three fighter pilots withheld their fire. They flew alongside the strange plane to make certain that it had no markings. Captain Hartsock waggled his wings, pressed his "C"-channel button and made every friendly signal in the book. These gestures brought no answer except more fire. Convinced that the plane was enemy, Hartsock determined to attack it as it headed for the overcast.

Hartsock and his wingman made overhead passes from starboard which seemed to cause smoke. The third pilot, who had been flying abeam the plane on the other side, came around from above and behind in a high side attack, concentrated a long burst on the port inboard engine, flamed and exploded the bomber, which fell into the overcast.

The three pilots reported the incident as soon as they landed on board *Essex*. They doubted that the plane was a B-24, although they admitted they had considered such a possibility when they withheld their fire for some time after they were fired upon. Gun-camera films from Hartsock's plane definitely identified the stranger as a B-24, but also bore out the marines' contention that

---

[29] On board *Essex* all hands had hoped Henry and Shirley were safe, particularly after the French Underground reported several pilots in safe hands. The writer again became interested in the case of the Navy flyers during a trip to Saigon in 1947, when he heard the story of the fantastic difficulties the American Graves Registration team of Captain Samuel J. Loyd USA had in recovering the remains of the seven Americans from the mountains in October 1946. Details obtained in February 1950 through courtesy of U.S. Army Chief of Staff's office in Washington, include report No. 314.6 dated 8 February 1947, from Graves Registration Service, India–Burma Zone, and extracts from Captain Loyd's diary, seen in Saigon.

[30] Author's notes taken in ready-room briefing.

the plane bore no markings, not even the standard white star of all American aircraft.[31]

Assertions that the plane was a B-24 were not long in coming from the China-based Fourteenth Air Force.

At least nine B-24's were sighted in the target area by *Essex* planes between 0845 and 1850 that day.[32] Just why one of them should have opened fire on the carrier planes is, of course, unknown. It is possible that, although the B-24 crew expected carrier-based planes, they did not expect nor recognize F4U's, which were newcomers to the fast carriers.[33]

On board the carrier there was deep regret that the marines had been responsible for the deaths of other American flyers. But nobody blamed the three pilots. One major remarked: "I'd have done the same thing. If anybody shoots at me, I'm going to shoot back. I expect the other fellow to know his recognition as well as I do. There are ten lives in a B-24, but it can cause a thousand deaths aboard ship if there are Japs in it."

China Coast and Out

Next day TF 38 prepared to refuel in the middle of the South China Sea; morale was sky-high. From the cockpit of every plane it was obvious that Japan had been dealt a stunning blow. The riches of the "Greater East Asia Co-Prosperity Sphere" were no longer within Japan's reach. The establishment of bases on Luzon, coupled with the U.S. Fleet's ability to move at will, meant that the Japanese were now on their own. The 12 January raid was, in the fleet commander's words, "a strongly worded notice that control of the South China Sea had changed hands."[34]

High, choppy seas made fueling difficult on the 13th, and only about half the ships succeeded in getting a drink. Next day the fueling from Captain Acuff's valiant tanker force was completed and the fast ships moved northward to serve further dispossess notice on the Japanese.

On the way north the carrier planes took another poke at Formosa on 15 January. The weather was foul, but the marines found that the Japanese knew they were there. Plenty of AA, which, for some reason, was technicolored, Captain Mickey Finn swore. Several planes came back with holes in their wings. One pilot, Lieut. Charles J. Chop, also swore a destroyer blew up in his face in Takao Harbor, but he didn't know whether his bomb or those of the dive bombers got it.[35]

---

[31] VMF-124 war diary, January 1945, which contains the pictures.

[32] *Essex* action report, 3–22 January 1945, 050 8 February 1945, pp 8–12.

[33] Major General Claire Lee Chennault, *The Way of a Fighter,* p 333, reports, however, that the last word received from his plane was: "Being attacked by U.S. Navy planes."

[34] *Admiral Halsey's Story,* p 245.

[35] Goodwin's report; JANAC cites 2 destroyers, 1 transport, 1 tanker as sunk at Takao that day.

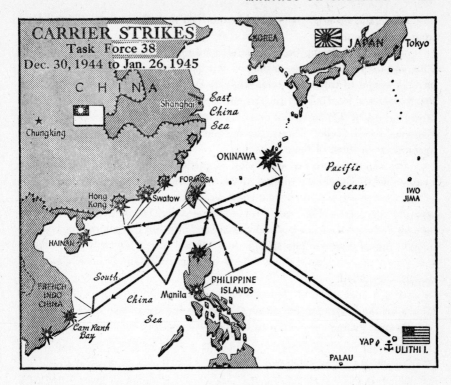

CARRIER STRIKES
Task Force 38
Dec. 30, 1944 to Jan. 26, 1945

Lieut. Colonel Millington became *Essex* air group commander upon the death of Commander Otto Klinsman, who was hit by AA, made a landing alongside a destroyer, but disappeared before he could be rescued.

On the 16th McCain spread his planes like a bridge hand, from Formosa to Amoy to Swatow to Hong Kong to Hainan Island—the carriers' first blows against China. The *Essex* pilots drew the long hop to Hainan Island. Over Hainan Lieut. George R. Strimbeck's belly tank was seen to explode after it was hit by AA; he parachuted but was seen no more.

Portuguese Macao was bombed by mistake by one of the missions, which raised a violent protest from the Portuguese Government. Some TF 38 pilots thought it was a mistake to bomb Hong Kong, too. There they found the AA "from intense to unbelievable." It was hot enough that Halsey lost more planes than he claimed to destroy: 30 lost in combat, 31 in operations, as against 26 enemy planes shot down and 21 destroyed on the ground.[36] Not a good day.

Now that Halsey was ready to leave the South China Sea, how was he going to get out of the bottle? For the three ensuing days the weather was foul and refueling was from difficult to impossible. It was finally accomplished 19 January 160 miles west of Manila. Admiral Halsey wanted to head south, past Luzon and through Surigao Strait. But Admiral Nimitz finally directed him to

---

[36] Sherman, *Combat Command*, p 329.

go north again, through Balintang Channel (on the other side of Batan Island from Bashi Channel).

Admiral Halsey approached the channel uneasily on the afternoon of the 20th, and the radar screen soon showed that his fears were justified. The marines on CAP began to catch snoopers—Helens, Dinahs, Sallys and Bettys—making the suicide try for Halsey's fat targets. During the next two hours they shot down 8 (out of TF 38's total of 15). It took a cowboy from Nevada, Lieut. William McGill (called "Noisy" because he never talked), just three minutes to shoot down three of them.

The marines were fast qualifying as carrier pilots. "Three cheers for the Leathernecks!" CLIPPER (Admiral McCain) messaged.

The force was not so fortunate next day when a final strike against Formosa was mounted from the "safe"—or eastern—side. *Ticonderoga*, steaming a thousand yards on *Essex's* port bow, was *kamikazed* in the sunlight of midday, in full view of *Essex* sailors and marines. About 125 of *Ticonderoga's* officers and men were left dead. Many others, including Captain Dixie Kiefer, were seriously wounded.

After a final strike at Okinawa on 22 January, primarily to obtain photographs for the forthcoming invasion, TF 38 headed back to Ulithi.

Postwar evaluation delineates the Japanese position clearly:

> The Philippines had been lost, true, but much more important was what had been lost with them. The Southern Resources Area, the prize for which the war had been fought, was gone and American fleets sailed with impunity to the shores of eastern Asia. All hope of future resistance had depended upon oil and now the tankers were sunk and the oil cut off. . . . Japan was defeated: it remained only necessary to persuade her of the fact.[37]

The marines totted up their first month's carrier record: 10 enemy planes destroyed in the air, 16 on the ground; 658 sorties, of which 625 were combat; 1,973 hours flown, of which 525 were opposed by enemy planes or AA. Reports credited them with damaging 11 ships, but did not attempt to evaluate damage to enemy ground installations. The marines' own losses were undeniably heavy: 1 pilot and 2 planes lost in combat, 7 pilots and 15 planes lost operationally.

Of the 7 pilots lost in noncombat operations, 5 could be directly charged to deficiencies in instrument flight training. "A bitter lesson," the senior Marine pilot called it, in recommending that instrument flying "would be far better learned in home training areas than left to be learned in enemy territory under combat conditions." Nonetheless, he contended that the Marines, in spite of consistently poor weather, had done "a remarkably good job in carrying out their missions."[38]

Next time out there would be more marines on more carriers.

---

[37] USSBS, *Campaigns,* pp 289–290.
[38] CAG-4 report in *Essex* action report of 3–22 January 1945, 050 8 February 1945.

CHAPTER TWENTY-THREE

Iwo Jima

DUE TO the *kamikazes*, the Pacific war early in 1945 had begun to slip behind the timetable which had been so ambitiously arranged a few months earlier. Admiral Halsey had to stick around the Philippines and didn't get to make the first carrier raid on Tokyo. The invasion of Iwo Jima, which was necessary before the B-29's could gain real effectiveness in the raids on Japan, was postponed from its originally scheduled date, 20 January.

The invasion of Iwo had to await supporting strikes on Tokyo. Those strikes, in turn, were delayed until more fighter planes were available to the fleet. More fighter planes could not be had until more marines were aboard the big carriers.

Admiral Halsey got back to Ulithi on 26 January and turned the Third Fleet over to Admiral Spruance, which meant its designation was changed to the Fifth Fleet, and Task Force 38 under McCain became Task Force 58 under Mitscher. Ships were refueled, rearmed, and resupplied by Commodore Worrall Carter's Service Squadron 10. Officers and men—15,000 at a clip—went ashore at Mog-Mog, one of the islands of the Ulithi atoll, for a touch of land and a swig of beer. By 4 February TF 58 was ready to set out on the mission which had been anticipated for three long years. This time the target finally was Tokyo, 1,560 miles due north of Ulithi.

Three other large carriers joined *Essex*, each with two Marine squadrons on board. *Bennington* had VMF-112 (Major Herman Hansen Jr.) and VMF-123 (Major Everett V. Alward). On 3 February *Wasp* took on board VMF-216 (Major George E. Dooley) and VMF-217 (Major Jack R. Amende). *Bunker Hill* had VMF-221 (Major Edwin S. Roberts Jr.) and VMF-451 (Major Henry A. Ellis). Now, with eight Marine squadrons on board, the fleet had a total of 144 Marine Corsairs and about 216 Marine pilots—16 per cent of the fighter strength of the Fast Carrier Task Force. All had received intensive navigational training at Ulithi and would get more en route to Japan "in weather not previously considered suitable for CV operations."[1]

The 122 ships[2] of the task force weighed anchor on 10 February. Soon

---

[1] Letter Colonel Frank G. Dailey, 2 June 1950. Dailey went on board *Bunker Hill* as Mitscher's Marine Air Officer.

[2] Eleven CV's, 5 CVL's (total planes 1,200), 8 BB's, 1 CB, 5 CA's, 11 CL's, 81 DD's.

afterward the word was passed to all hands that the target was Tokyo, and that Iwo Jima was about to be invaded by the Marines. On D-day and for several days thereafter, the Marine pilots would help furnish air support for the 3d, 4th and 5th MarDivs. This was good news to the pilots, who had long been anxious to qualify in their primary mission of supporting the landings of their comrades on the ground. The schedule did not encompass full-scale air support by marines but at least they were getting a foot in the door.

First came the strikes on Japan, which were planned as supporting missions for the invasion of Iwo, 800 miles to the south. Lieut. Colonel Millington led the first strike from the deck of *Essex*, strafing Tenryu airfield. Major Dave Marshall led an escort for torpedo and photo planes over the Tokyo area. Major Hansen with 11 VMF-112 planes led *Bennington's* first sweep over the Japanese mainland. Major Roberts led the first fighter sweep from Admiral Mitscher's flagship, *Bunker Hill. Wasp* pilots led by Major Dooley stabbed the murky weather for a strike on the Yokosuka and Tateyama airfields. At 25,000 feet over Japan in February, a thermometer showed 55° below zero.

Some snatches from the squadron war diaries give an idea what it was like on this first day over Japan: four planes of VMF-112 on board *Bennington* led by Major David Andre were launched off the wet slippery deck at 0635 to fly CAP. They intercepted a Betty 35 miles off the Japanese coast. All pilots scored hits but Andre and Lieut. Carroll King actually destroyed it. Major Hansen's first strike strafed O Shima, Mobara and Katori airfields, claiming the destruction of 20 planes on the ground. Lieut. George J. Murray accounted for a two-engined Nick fighter. The belly tank of the Corsair flown by Lieut. James M. Hamilton was hit by AA; he was forced to make a water landing but was rescued by destroyer *Blue*.

Another division of the same squadron was thwarted by weather on the Tokyo run, and in a hunt for targets of opportunity, destroyed ten Bettys on Konoike airfield near the eastern coast of Nojima-Zaki Peninsula. One Tojo was shot down by Lieut. Robert B. Hamilton. Captain Donald C. Owen's and Lieut. Randolph Smith's divisions moved to Hokoda airfield and left three hangars flaming from their rocket attacks.

At 0855 12 Corsairs of VMF-123 from the same carrier joined fighters from *Hornet* and *Wasp* and made a sweep over Hamamatsu and Mikatagahara, southwest of Tokyo. One 4,000-ton tanker was strafed and left burning and eight twin-engined aircraft were damaged on the ground. Five Zekes were sighted overhead and the Corsairs climbed to make contact. Despite a large hole in his own wing Major Alward sent a Zeke flaming into the sea. Lieut. Robert M. Cies joined up after the strafing but disappeared and was listed as MIA. The planes of Lieuts. Wallace R. Hathcox and Harry J. Bearlund were badly damaged by flak and enemy gunfire and had to make water landings for lack of fuel. Hathcox escaped from the plane but the billowing chute pulled him under and he was drowned before *Longshaw* could reach him. Bearlund was rescued uninjured.

At 1420, 14 Corsairs of VMF-123 joined fighters from *Wasp* and *Hornet* to escort a bomber-torpedo plane strike over the same targets. Nine twin-engined planes were assessed damaged on the ground and one "P-38-type" plane destroyed on the ground by Major Alward. On returning to the ships the Hellcats and Corsairs strafed a large picket boat and a DE. The DE was left smoking and the picket boat was listed as probably sunk.

Wasp pilots had rough going: Major Amende of VMF-217 with four planes attacked Hamamatsu airfield with flights from *Bennington* and *Hornet* and destroyed at least 6 planes out of 60 observed, but during the rendezvous a Zeke attacked Amende's plane, which began to smoke and drop off into a shallow gliding turn. He was not seen again. Lieut. Vernon H. Salisbury caught the Zeke and shot it down.

Eight other planes from *Wasp* were assigned a sweep over Yokosuka and Tateyama airfields but on take-off Lieut. Roland V. Vaughn Jr. crashed into the sea. The area was searched thoroughly but he was not found. Lieut. Spencer B. Weills did not survive a water landing made while retiring from a strafing run. Twenty miles south of Honshu Lieut. Daniel V. Hayes began to lose altitude until he made a water landing; the plane sank immediately. He was not observed getting out of it.

Captain William N. Snider and Lieut. Donald G. MacFarlane of VMF-221, from *Bunker Hill*, shared the destruction of one Betty while on a fighter sweep in the Tokyo area which also burned three planes and damaged another on the ground and started oil fires in the hangar area.

Lieut. William M. Pemble of VMF-221 was shot down by a Tojo over enemy territory on an escort mission en route to the Nakajima Airframe Plant at Ota.

Lieut. Forrest P. Brown Jr. of VMF-451 was hit by AA from a DE and forced to make a water landing in enemy territory. He was seen to survive the landing in Sagami Wan and rescue operations were commenced immediately, but post-war reports include no record of his being a POW. His squadron had attacked the enemy convoy of three AK's escorted by two DE's. Numerous hits were scored and serious damage claimed on three coastal AK's, one of which was left smoking. One Jake was shot down by Lieuts. Philip S. Wilmot and James Anderson of VMF-451.

Corsairs from *Essex* flew fighter sweep in the Tokyo area, returning with claims of 4 shootdowns, 12 destroyed and 5 probably destroyed on the ground at Tenryu airfield.

Next day, the 17th, the weather was worse and the raids had to be cut short before operations were completed.[3]

But a few missions were flown. Eight VMF-112 Corsairs took off from *Bennington* to bomb Tokyo airstrips. On this particular mission Major Hansen shot down an Oscar. *Hornet* and *Wasp* fighters also fired rockets and released 500-pound bombs on 15 parked planes at Haramachida airfield.

Two Japanese aircraft were splashed by pilots of VMF-217 based on *Wasp*

[3] *ONI Weekly*, 21 February 1945, p 556.

during a bombing attack on Haneda airfield, outside Tokyo. Lieut. James O. Seay accounted for an Oscar, Lieut. William T. Stratton a Zeke.

Carrying four 5-inch instantaneous-fuzed rockets, 8 VMF-123 *Bennington* Corsairs together with 20 fighters from *Hornet* and *Wasp*, attacked Atsugi and Tateyama airfields in the Tokyo area. Major Alward shot down a Tojo over Tokyo Bay and Lieut. Archie J. Clapp accounted for a Zeke. Many excellent opportunities for kills were thwarted by gun-jamming caused by rain water collecting and freezing in the gun mechanisms. The flight fired rockets into a military warehouse and one locomotive was strafed and rocketed. Alward flew so low that his windshield was mud-spattered. Lieut. Edward H. Rohricht had his rudder torn off and bailed out but did not return.

In the estimate of most of the marines the first Tokyo strikes were disappointing, mainly because there was far less air opposition than had been expected. Many of the targets were socked in. The admirals took a more optimistic view. Aircraft plants and airfield installations were heavily bombed. A total of 332 enemy planes, they said, was shot down and 177 more destroyed on the ground.[4] Of these, 21 shootdowns and 60 planes destroyed on the ground were credited to the marines.

With the cancellation of the final operations of the 17th, TF 58 headed southward for D-day at Iwo Jima.

Air Support for the Iwo Marines

Delayed though it was, Iwo Jima came too early for the Marines to furnish close air support from their escort carriers, for which they had been training back in California. Iwo provided the prime example in the Central Pacific war in which finely trained close-support pilots might have excelled. But the escort carriers—11 of them—were all manned by Navy pilots. The Marines were still training aboard escort carriers and their own ground troops suffered for it.

Nowhere else in the Pacific war did preliminary bombing and naval gunfire get such a black eye as at Iwo Jima. The island had been bombed 72 straight days before the landing, mostly by the Seventh Air Force. During the murderous assault itself and for 20 days thereafter, the Navy escort planes—and later, the Army P-51's—did the best they could in the way of close support. But the men on the ground could only shake their heads and plunge forward with their rifles and flamethrowers. The air age was still too young to prevent the death of 5,563 marines on Iwo. But those marines did not die in vain; before the war ended

---

[4] *Ibid.* Karig, Harris and Manson, *Battle Report*, V, p 333, using preliminary reports, say 416 and 354. Japanese records indicate total losses of 166 planes on these two days, 87 in the air and 79 on the ground; 126 Navy, 40 Army. (ATIS 61017, USSBS, *Interrogations*, Vol I, p 120). These records may be incomplete, and the figure of 40 for Japanese Army-plane losses is solely from Major Toga's memory. USSBS, *Campaigns*, pp 322–323, says the Japanese lost 337 planes in combat and 395 operationally during the Iwo Jima campaign.

2,251 B-29's and over 24,700 crewmen were saved by emergency landings on Iwo.[5]

The eight Marine squadrons on board the four *Essex*-class carriers had a taste of supporting the assault, however. The carrier task force launched planes about 100 miles west and northwest of Iwo on the morning of D-day, 19 February 1945.

Colonel Millington led a flight of 24 F4U's and 24 Navy F6F's at 0642 to attack the flanks and high ground along the landing beaches. From H minus 45 to H minus 35, the planes dropped napalm, fired their rockets and strafed. The attacks were delivered from a double-column approach with the divisions of planes breaking to port and starboard, dropping napalm on the first run, pulling out to seaward and repeating attacks with rockets and .50-caliber bullets until the time limit expired. The 48-plane flight then rendezvoused for an H minus 5 strafing attack along the landing beach. These attacks were delivered from south to north in steep dives, all planes pulling out sharply to the right to rejoin the tail element for repeated runs. The attack was moved inland gradually as the landing craft approached the beach so that the bullet-impact area remained 200 yards ahead of the troops. As the troops hit the beach, the bullet-impact area was shifted 500 yards inland to smother the fire from that area against the shore line. Because of naval gunfire in the same area, pull-outs were ordered at 600 feet. Commander Support Aircraft (CSA) gave the group a "Very Well Done". The flight was ready to stand by for close-support missions but none was immediately assigned.[6]

The plan for this low-level attack had been worked out by Millington with Colonel Vernon E. Megee USMC, Commander of the Landing Force Air Support Control Unit and Deputy Commander, Aircraft, Landing Force, who became Senior Air Commander ashore and controlled all aircraft operating over Iwo Jima. "Go in and scrape your bellies on the beach," said Megee to Millington. Although Colonel Megee controlled the land-based squadrons when they finally got ashore, he had only Army planes for support except a forward echelon of tireless VMTB-242, which arrived from Tinian on 8 and 9 March via TBM's, R5C's and R4D's.

On D-day, including pre-H-hour strikes, 26 missions were flown, and although assessment was difficult, they were in general considered very effective. A total of 606 planes—354 VF's, 67 VB's, 170 VT's, and 15 B-24's (only 4 of which attacked because of late arrival)—flew 765 sorties, dropping 1,558 bombs (248 500's, 130 250's, and 1,180 100's) which weighed 274,500 pounds. In addition, 104 napalm tanks, of which it is estimated only 50 per cent detonated, and 2,254 rockets were used.[7]

It is impossible to assess the credit for the invasion strikes of 19 February,

---

[5] Haugland, *The AAF Against Japan*, p 260.

[6] CAG-4 *Essex* ACA report, 19 February 1945.

[7] Captain Clifford P. Morehouse, *The Iwo Jima Operation*, p 113, published monograph prepared for Historical Division, Headquarters U.S. Marine Corps.

or to divide the credit between naval gunfire and carrier aviation (land-based Army air from the Marianas made slight contribution)—but the fact that the Marines got a toehold ashore during the first two hours may indicate that the preparation helped—it was only after H plus 2 that the Japanese cut loose all the hell they could muster on the beaches.

On the afternoon of the 19th, aircraft from *Bunker Hill* made strikes at points of resistance inland from the beaches, strafing and dropping napalm. Next day *Bennington* marines flew two strikes on ground support, eight Corsairs each. On 21 February both *Bunker Hill* squadrons flew on a support mission hampered by light haze and smoke. Eight of *Bennington's* Corsairs with torpedo and dive bombers flew a special strike, using both bombs and rockets, and 12 VMF-216 and VMF-217 planes from *Wasp* participated in a 43-plane strike ordered by Commander Support Aircraft.

The *Wasp* group was ordered to attack an area 400 yards ahead of the 4th MarDiv's front lines on the east side of the island. After planes from *Hornet* had attacked (and caused great confusion at the pushover point, where there were several near collisions) *Wasp* planes went into a 30° glide from south to north, the Hellcats hitting first, followed by the torpedo bombers and the dozen Corsairs. "Great devastation" was caused in the target area which elicited a "Well Done" from CSA.

On the 22d, eight *Wasp* Corsairs also flew in a 23-plane ground-support mission at 1010. *Bunker Hill* squadrons took off for a support mission at 1250 but the weather closed in, so the planes jettisoned their napalm bombs and rockets and returned to base.

That was all the Marine flyers contributed to the support of ground operations on Iwo and little of this could be designated true close air support. Next day the task force moved up to Chichi Jima which had been bombed and rocketed sporadically during the preceding days.

Iwo's Grasshoppers

Like other marines on Iwo, the VMO squadrons had to prove they could take it. The little planes and their pilots and ground crews were subjected to everything from *kamikazes* to artillery fire to faulty launching gear, and all of these took their toll.

VMO-4 and VMO-5, assigned to support the Marine divisions of their respective numbers, were alerted in Hawaii in late December 1944. Half of each squadron sailed for Guam early the next month, these halves to be distributed among eight CVE's. The other halves were checked out in Brodie Gear, an invention of the Army which was installed on LST's for the launching of Grasshopper planes.[8] Three planes were lost in the LST-Brodie experiments, chiefly due to the roll of the ship, but not before five pilots had gone through the hair-raising qualification tests.

---

[8] Brodie Gear consisted of two projecting beams, a cable, arresting gear and a loop. The planes were fitted with hooks which were meant to sling them into the air.

The CVE's and Brodie-equipped *LST 776* stood offshore during the first few days after D-day at Iwo, waiting until a landing strip could be secured. *Kamikazes* which sank escort carrier *Bismarck Sea* on 21 February caused the loss of Lieut. David S. Kincanon and two OY's. Lieut. John F. Sutkus was rescued.

On 26 February two OY's of VMO-4 were landed from CVE *Wake Island*, though the first strip was still under mortar and artillery fire. One plane of VMO-5 landed next day, and by 28 February all planes were ashore from the CVE's and all from *LST 776* except one dunked by the Brodie Gear.

One of the more familiar sights on Iwo was the continuous, frantic effort to patch up the little planes, which were hit often as they sat on the airstrip. Six of VMO-4's seven planes were so badly damaged they were surveyed after the battle.

VMO-4 did artillery spotting for 19 days for the 3d and 4th MarDivs, flying 204 missions in 366.4 flying hours. VMO-5 supported the 3d and 5th Divisions with 379 missions. One VMO-5 pilot, Lieut. Leon W. Ellsworth, was shot down behind the Japanese lines. VMO-1 had been scheduled to spot for the 3d Division, but only one pilot and four enlisted men got ashore to help out the other two overworked squadrons. The 3d MarDiv artillery, without its OY's, was permitted only one plane on station at a time, hence search and firing could not be done simultaneously.[9]

Air Transport at Iwo

The air-transport operation of the invasion of Iwo Jima was TAG's mission and, as part of TAG, VMR's 253, 353, 952, and the Army's 9th Troop Carrier Squadron participated in outstanding supply and evacuation operations. As early as 28 February the 9th TCS had dropped supplies to the ground forces.

Next day, VMR-952, in five passes over the airstrip dropped critically needed mortar shells, machine-gun parts and blood, plus one of the earliest deliveries of mail troops had ever had on a very hot beachhead.[10]

The first Marine transport to land on Iwo was an R5C, brought in 3 March by Lieut. Colonel Malcolm S. Mackay, CO of VMR-952, who flew from Guam via Saipan with 5,500 pounds of mortar shells and ammunition. At this time the runway was barely 3,000 feet long, and the danger from enemy fire was still considerable; one of the Squadron's planes was hit six days later by a sniper's bullet.

On 4 March the first of many hundreds of crippled B-29's made an emergency landing on Iwo's airfield. On the same day VMR-952 and the Army squadron dropped more than 50 tons of the critical mortar ammo. Two days later the field was ready for operations, and TAG planes flew in the gear and personnel of two Army fighter squadrons, whose P-51's and P-61's they escorted

---

[9] Morehouse, *The Iwo Jima Operation*, p 48.

[10] Unfortunately, all the mail was for 3d MarDiv troops—which did raise the hackles of the 4th and 5th Divisions. (Author's observation.)

from Saipan. On 8 and 9 March TAG brought in the forward echelon of VMTB-242 from Tinian which began to fly ASP around the island day and night.

Each supply flight took out wounded on the return trip. VMR-353, which flew its first planes into Iwo Jima on 8 March, made eight flights during the month, and VMR-952 made 79 trips to Iwo, evacuating 625 wounded (281 of them litter cases). VMR-253, which had started evacuating wounded long ago on Guadalcanal, was mostly occupied elsewhere in the Central Pacific, but made 20 flights which included 100 litter and sitter patients.

The first plane to land on Iwo airfield No. 2 was a transport of VMR-952 which on 21 March flew out a flight crew which had been rescued after its B-29 ditched north of Iwo after bombing Japan. Another passenger on this transport was a Japanese prisoner.

VMB-612 on Iwo

Iwo had been secured only two weeks when Lieut. Colonel Jack Cram began moving his 650-man squadron up from Saipan. By basing the outfit at Iwo, Cram could run his night-prowling antishipping strikes all the way up to the coast of Japan.

From its arrival on Iwo 10 April and until its departure for Okinawa 28 July, VMB-612 flew 251 sorties. In 83 of those, targets were located; 53 vessels were claimed damaged, 5 of them probably sunk. The Iwo attacks accounted for half of those made by the Squadron during the war,[11] and undoubtedly sank many small vessels not listed in postwar enemy records.

During its Iwo operations VMB-612 lost 7 PBJ's, 3 in combat. Among them was one piloted by Lieut. John F. Jarrell, which took off in the late afternoon of 2 May on a night search mission. Passing Haha Jima, 120 miles north of Iwo during waning daylight, Jarrell noted a tanker at anchor in Higashi Minato and went after it from an altitude of 700 feet. The tanker's AA shot away the port vertical stabilizer and part of the port horizontal stabilizer. Pilot and co-pilot managed, with the help of the automatic pilot, to hold the controls and keep the plane in the air. All ships off Iwo were notified that the plane would turn on its landing lights and the crew would bail out close to shore, but the plane went in five miles southwest of the island. All managed to parachute except Jarrell, who stayed at the controls and went down with his ship, but only the co-pilot, Lieut. Harold E. Darling, and Staff Sergeant Leon Sutton were recovered.[12]

A Study in Depravity[13]

During the carrier raid of 23 February one Marine pilot was shot down by AA over Chichi Jima. The pilot parachuted from 500 feet into the water

---

[11] VMB-612 summary, 13 November 1944 to 14 August 1945.
[12] VMB-612 ACA report, 2 May 1945.
[13] Principal sources: Record of Proceedings of a Military Commission Convened

and when last seen was swimming ashore. Nothing more was known of his fate until 1946.

The story, as revealed by months of painstaking research, added up to a crime which staggers the twentieth century imagination.

Chichi Jima is 150 miles north of Iwo Jima. During the war it was a subordinate command of Iwo's able and tenacious General Kuribayashi. The senior officer in tactical command at Chichi was Vice Admiral Kunizo Mori. His duty was to repulse the expected American invasion—although he was subordinate administratively to the Army commander, Lieut. General Yosio Tachibana, who had become CG of the 109th Division on Chichi in June 1944. An agreement had been entered into by the Army and Navy early in 1944 which gave the Army supervision of any prisoners who might be taken on the island.

The first American raid on Chichi Jima occurred 15 June 1944, D-day on Saipan, when *Essex, Hornet* and *Yorktown* planes of Rear Admiral "Jocko" Clark's task group flew through a gale to bomb and strafe the island. On 4 July three more carriers returned with a heavy attack. Chichi and Iwo and Haha were hit on three successive days later in that month and during three days late in August.[14]

That was all for Chichi until 19 February 1945, D-day on Iwo, except for sporadic raids by B-24's, B-25's and B-29's.

In addition to the marine shot down on 23 February 1945, several Navy airmen were lost in the vicinity of Chichi Jima, but planes were shot down and pilots lost every day, and the flyers only went down in the books as MIA. Telegrams to next of kin were dispatched from the Navy Department, and the task forces moved on.

In September 1945 General Tachibana, accompanied by nine aides, went on board destroyer *Dunlap* and surrendered Chichi Jima to Commodore John H. Magruder Jr.

On the afternoon of 6 October Colonel Presley M. Rixey, artillerist of the 2d MarDiv, veteran of Tarawa and Saipan, arrived off Chichi on board destroyer *Wilson* as commander of the Bonins Occupation Force. Rixey sent for the chief of staff to Tachibana, who brought along several other officers, including an interpreter, Cadet Oyama, who had lived in Hawaii as a boy, and a lieutenant commander who had once visited Annapolis on board a Japanese warship.

Colonel Rixey discussed plans for evacuating the 25,000 Japanese troops from the Bonins to Japan. After a while the Marine colonel asked: "And what became of the American flyers captured on these islands?"

Rixey's report tells the answer:

To my utter surprise, he answered without hesitation: "Yes, we cap-

---

at U.S. Pacific Fleet ComMarianas, Guam—*Case of Tachibana Yosio et al, No. 154578;* "Japanese Camouflage," a monograph by Colonel Presley M. Rixey USMC; action reports of carriers; squadron war diaries. The names of some Japanese and Korean informants have been altered.

[14] *The Navy's Air War,* pp 206, 214, 215, 219.

tured six. All Navy, I think. They received very kind treatment. Two were sent to Japan by submarine. The last four unfortunately were killed by your own bombs in an air-raid against these islands during the capture of Iwo Jima in 1945. They were blown up by a direct hit. Nothing remains. I am so sorry this happened. I was very beloved of them and wished them no harm. We buried what remained of the bodies after cremation. This is Japanese custom."

This was the first intimation that flyers shot down in the vicinity had not gone into the sea. Rixey said nothing more but decided to investigate further whenever his troops arrived.

He asked for the officer who had had custody of the prisoners. Major Sueo Matoba, a cold-eyed, bull-necked battalion commander, was brought on board the destroyer. Major Matoba was very sorry his troops had neglected to protect the American flyers from air raids. In reply to a question, the chief of staff said the Americans had been honored by the erection of a cross over their grave.

On 8 October Colonel Rixey went ashore with a handful of marines—the first Americans to set foot on Chichi Jima since the surrender. Sure enough, there was a cross planted in the old civilian cemetery overlooking Futami Ko Harbor. But it was made of new wood; it showed no signs of weather during the eight months since its alleged planting!

Rixey bided his time. During the next two months repatriation of Japanese from the Bonins went on. Finally, on 13 December LST's brought in a reduced battalion of 500 marines. They moved ashore to a camp which had been erected for them by the Japanese under Rixey's staff's supervision. The American flag-raising at noon was attended by the marines, lined up on one side, and by 800 picked Japanese enlisted men and all their officers on the other.

One clear day a Japanese Coast Guard cutter entered the harbor bearing Frederick Arthur Savory and his three uncles, all descendants of Nathaniel Savory, a Massachusetts whaler who had settled in the Bonins in 1830. The Japanese had sent the American-Chamorro-Hawaiian Savorys to the main islands after Saipan had fallen.

Fred Savory had heard rumors in Japan, spread by soldiers repatriated from Chichi. "These stories are not nice ones," he said.

Not only had American prisoners on Chichi been tied to stakes and bayonetted, but on one occasion, Savory said, a Japanese major had ordered his medical officer to remove an American aviator's liver, which was served at a *sake* party.

Colonel Rixey's reaction, as recorded in his report:

We were flabbergasted at first. We had expected beheadings, of course. But never cannibalism! What manner of men were these? Polite and cooperative—obedient soldiers, brave and fearless—but beneath this veneer—barbarians and worse—

The first Japanese naval officer Colonel Rixey sought to question had already been repatriated. When SCAP Headquarters in Tokyo attempted to apprehend him, he committed suicide.

On 15 December a Captain Moto inadvertently gave the Americans a tip. He said the disaffected Korean laborers had asked to be allowed to present their case for liberation (which they understood President Roosevelt had promised them). This Colonel Rixey permitted. One of the leaders of the Koreans, Ahn by name, had become very friendly because the treatment afforded them by the Americans was much kinder than that to which they had been accustomed.

One night Ahn came to Rixey and told a story in great excitement:

> I have heard of an execution of an American flyer in July 1944. It is said that Colonel Ito supervised the beheading and that there were about 100 Japanese troops at the scene. The American was very brave. He refused a blindfold. He was smoking a cigarette while they tied his feet. I believe he was an officer but I never heard his name. Other Koreans have heard of other executions. One at the wireless station, high in the mountains, supervised by Commander Yoshii, who was sent to Japan seriously wounded in 1945 and another killed by the Torpedo Boat squadron near Ogiura. I have heard that in Major Matoba's area, he ordered his doctor to cut out the liver of an American aviator after the beheading. This liver was cut into small pieces after drying and Matoba's adjutant placed the pieces in the soup eaten by the enlisted men. I am sure that Matoba has eaten human flesh. He made Navy officers eat some flesh taken from the thigh of the body. He served it as a substitute for goat meat at the Admiral's mess. Many of the Navy officers vomited when told of its true character. Rumor says that the Major bragged about this trick on the Navy. His men hate him. He kicks and hits them with his fist. They are afraid and will not talk.

Rixey's marines were scheduled to "button up" Chichi Jima and go back to Guam, but he asked for an extension, which was granted. He began to work on Moto, who was an intelligent, increasingly co-operative officer, and asked him in for long private talks over a can of beer in his quarters. Rixey flattered Moto by allowing him to lecture to "visiting firemen" from Guam and Iwo.

On New Year's Eve, 1945, Rixey invited Moto for a horseback ride with three other officers and his orderly, Mahaffey. Following the ride the group stopped at the beach house where, by prearrangement, Mahaffey would produce a bottle of bourbon and some ginger ale. Like most Japanese, Moto was a poor drinker of hard liquor, and after a few heavy slugs the Japanese was given the flattery treatment. Said Colonel Rixey:

> Captain Moto, I consider you the only true soldier among the Japanese I have seen on Chichi. You probably are the only officer who knows

anything about International Law and the Rules of Land Warfare as set forth in the Geneva Convention. . . . As a military man, I appreciate what you did for your Emperor and your country. I consider you my friend and I need your aid. You might not know it but I have much information about what went on in these islands before Americans arrived. I know of executions and other acts that followed these killings. I know also that you are not involved. My investigations have convinced me that you apparently tried to befriend captured aviators. . . .

Moto sat motionless as Colonel Rixey continued:

. . . I must have the facts and I shall not rest until I know the full truth. Those guilty must be punished. I will protect you because I know you are innocent of any wrong-doing. . . . Now I appeal to your friendship and your honor . . . to correct your misrepresentation by telling me the whole truth.

Slowly and deliberately, Moto replied:

Yes, Colonel, I have known that you must know all things soon. Cadet Oyama warned me. The Savorys and the Koreans must have told you something. Now you are my friend and I believe as you do. I am not a war criminal. I was beloved of your aviators. They were brave men. I tried to save them but the devil was in my General. He ordered all executions in retaliation for Japanese troops killed in your bombings. There were 11 total. . . .

Next morning a platoon of heavily armed marines under Major Shaffer arrested the Japanese division staff officers. A special squad fetched Matoba, still in his pink bathrobe, from beside his phonograph.

With the arrest of the senior officers, the chief of staff inherited the command of all Japanese Army troops. Rixey ordered him to summon other Japanese who had been named in an anonymous letter. Colonel Rixey spoke to them through Fred Savory:

Do not be afraid to talk. These officers have no more control over you. . . . Now, tell me which of you wrote this letter?

To Rixey's astonishment, the entire group of enlisted men arose. Their sergeant spoke:

Yes, we wrote the letter. We wish to return to Japan and our families. We regret our falsehoods to the Americans and because of your kind treatment, we will now tell the truth. We were told that we would be slaves. Now we know this is wrong. We believe in democracy and wish to be free civilians. We will each give full facts and rumors concerning deaths of American flyers.

One of the Japanese officers accused in the anonymous letter wrote a confession in which he admitted beating one of the Americans to death. Major Matoba (now called "The Tiger of Chichi"), Colonel Ito and Captain Yoshii and several others eventually confessed, but General Tachibana denied his guilt to the end. Matoba even wrote out his recollection of the order regarding the rationing of the flesh of one American.

Full details of the sordid goings-on at Chichi Jima do not bear repetition here. As told in war-crimes trials at Guam, here briefly is what happened to a marine and seven sailors.

On 4 July 1944, a naval aviator who parachuted during the second carrier raid on Chichi was captured. He was interrogated at intervals for more than a month. On 7 August Tachibana ordered this prisoner and another, captured during a later raid, bayoneted to death.

Chichi Jima was not "tainted" again by American prisoners until February of 1945 when an ensign and his radioman were captured while swimming for shore. During the same month two other Americans, an aviation ordnance man and a radioman, also parachuted and were captured. On 23 February, in addition to the Marine pilot, two more flyers were taken on an adjacent island, where they had bailed out, and were brought to Chichi Jima.

All these flyers were executed, most of them beheaded, but at least one of them was bayoneted to death and another beaten to death.

Even greater indignities were suffered by four of the prisoners, including the marine, who was "very brave" at his execution.[15] Major Matoba had served in China where, he said, it had been determined that the eating of prisoners was a stimulant to morale and human liver was a cure for stomach ulcers. He also had ordered the first victim's body dug up—it had been in the ground only one day—and the liver removed for eating. Another pilot, beheaded on 26 May 1945, had his liver and a 6-pound chunk from his thigh removed and delivered to the galley of Matoba, who gave a party at which the "delicacy" (as he designated it) was served. Some of the meat was sent to Admiral Mori who, however, had no knowledge of what he had eaten until he was told the following day.

War-crimes trials of 21 Chichi Jima officers and men were held on Guam during the fall of 1946. These proceedings entailed more than 1,000 pages of testimony and exhibits; 66 witnesses were called. One of the anomalies of the trial was this: there is nothing in International Law providing punishment for cannibalism and the Japanese cannibals could only be charged with "preventing honorable burial," with murder, and with failure to control persons under their command.

---

[15] In a gesture of defiance he insisted on rolling down his own collar for the execution, which was performed on 5 March before an audience of more than 100. Under questioning he never revealed the name of his ship.

Of the 21, one Japanese lieutenant was acquitted who had only been a cannibal inadvertently, with no knowledge of what was taking place.

General Tachibana, Captain Yoshii, Colonel Ito, Major Matoba and Captain Nakajima were sentenced to death by hanging. They were executed at Guam on 24 September 1947 by marines under the direction of Lieut. Colonel G. R. Newton USMC, Officer in Charge of Execution. Although he alone among the major criminals never confessed, Tachibana "seemed rather happy about the occasion as though he were glad to know it would be over soon." The Navy Captain Yoshii, a little man weighing only 125 pounds, before his death conferred with a Navy Christian chaplain in addition to a Buddhist priest, Bunyu Nakajami, who was flown down from Tokyo for the occasion. Major Matoba, the five-foot-ten "Tiger," more blackly guilty than any other, asked only for a cigarette before the noose was placed over his head at sunset.

Admiral Mori and an Army captain named Sato were given life imprisonment. The other defendants were sentenced to prison for 5 to 20 years. The two surgeons, who under protest had removed parts of the slain Americans, were among those receiving the lighter sentences.

In extenuation of the Japanese as a race, it may be added that no word of any atrocity ever reached the people, who were continuously treated to photographs of Japanese soldiers giving candy to children in the occupied areas, or opening schools for them.[16] On the other hand, even if the Japanese people had known of their soldiers' atrocities, they probably couldn't or wouldn't have done anything about it.

---

[16] Kato, *The Lost War*, p 144.

CHAPTER TWENTY-FOUR

The CV Mission Completed

FOLLOWING THE IWO and Chichi Jima strikes, Spruance took the Fast Carrier Task Force back to Japan for another go at the Imperial City. Planes were launched at 0800 on 25 February for an attack co-ordinated with more than 200 B-29's from the Marianas. This time the weather was worse, if anything, than it had been on the 16th and 17th, but the CinCPac communiqué reported that at least 158 planes were destroyed, including 37 in air combat.

Five small enemy vessels were sunk, ground installations and two trains were destroyed in the Tokyo area and radar installations and hangars at the airfields were smashed; the Nakajima airplane plant at Ota, 50 miles north of Tokyo, was heavily bombed by TBF's and SB2C's, as was the Koizumi airplane assembly plant five miles away.[1] Corsairs from *Bunker Hill* helped provide fighter cover for this successful raid.

U.S. losses were 9 planes[2] but only 4 of their pilots. Two of the pilots were marines—Major Alward, skipper of VMF-123, who was shot down by a Zeke over Tokyo Bay, and Lieut. Vincent A. Jacobs, also from *Bennington*.

Lieut. Claude O. Barnhill of *Bennington* shot down one George, and *Essex* pilots Millington, Knight and Finn each was credited with one. But, in most places it was another day of miserable weather, with guns freezing in the midwinter air over Japan. One pilot summed up the marines' cynical attitude: "There below was Tokyo. I spent three hours over the place. What have I got to show for it? Frostbite!"

Not all the Fast Carrier marines suffered such unspeakable fate as the one who parachuted on Chichi Jima. One whose fortune was better was Lieut. Donald Carlson, an *Essex* pilot who trimmed his hair so short he was called "Baldy." During this raid over Tokyo Carlson's Corsair caught a burst of AA and he went down, making a hard landing in a plowed field. "Good luck to you guys; say 'Howdy' to my wife," he said calmly into his throat mike, "I'll be seeing you at Mike's."[3] Carlson made good his promise: six months later

---

[1] *ONI Weekly*, 28 February 1945, p 659; USSBS, *Nakajima Aircraft Company, Ltd.*, pp 1–2. Three buildings of the Kaizumi plant were completely destroyed; the Japanese Navy admitted 25 planes were lost in the air and 30 others on the ground, plus 27 "heavily damaged" (ATIS 61017). I have seen no records of Japanese Army interception this date.

[2] For once, the Japanese claim—six planes—was low.

[3] A Los Angeles bar.

he was liberated, alive and as well as a man could expect who had lost his teeth during frequent beatings, had been starved and put in solitary confinement for 40 days.[4]

On the way south to Ulithi, the planes took a crack at Okinawa. This time the weather was much improved and the planes "accomplished the usual pattern of devastation, which now was almost routine."[5]

Many small craft were destroyed, a few planes were burned on the ground and photographs were secured which would prove helpful in the invasion of Okinawa a month later.

During the 1 March strike Lieut. Albert C. Simkunas, a *Bunker Hill* pilot, was hit by AA and had to set his plane down only five miles off the shore of Okinawa. A life raft was dropped by a squadron mate—Simkunas's own was lost in the crash. Two SOC's from *South Dakota,* covered by two fighters from *Essex,* were sent out immediately to snatch Simkunas to safety. The seaplanes sat down beside the marine's raft, picked him up and returned him to his carrier.[6]

Following the return to Ulithi, VMF-124 and VMF-213 were detached on 10 March from *Essex* and sent back to the United States on board escort carrier *Long Island.* During their two months of combat the two squadrons had shot down 23 planes, destroyed 64 on the ground and accomplished damage to land targets which for want of more details was listed in the records as "excessive." Nine pilots were lost—16 per cent of those who had come on board in late December; plane losses were 24.

On 13 March Carrier Air Group 81, including its two Marine squadrons, was relieved on board *Wasp* by an all-Navy group. VMF's 216 and 217 had spent 38 days on board, had flown 316 combat sorties between 16 February and 1 March. The two squadrons were credited with destroying 4 planes in the air, 15 on the ground. They also listed 1 destroyer and 5 smaller craft as their victims. Five of their own pilots did not survive; plane losses were nine.

"Ground" crewmen of both *Essex* and *Wasp* stayed on board those ships, where they were urgently needed to service the Corsairs (Navy crewmen were generally unfamiliar with the plane). Of the 3 officers and 120 Marine maintenance men on board *Essex,* Lieut. Alex Gagyi and 46 men volunteered to stay and maintain the Corsairs for the Navy. Furthermore, they remained until early June, completing more than five months' service dodging the *kamikazes.*

Similarly, Captain William C. Lewis and 28 enlisted men (8 from VMF-216, 20 from VMF-217) stayed on board *Wasp* to service the 36 F4U's left there. The *kamikazes* saw to it that their sojourn was brief.

---

[4] *Essex* action report; Lieut. Goodwin's dispatch; casualty report dated 4 September 1945; ComThirdFleet liberation report.

[5] Sherman, *Combat Command,* p 342.

[6] *Ibid.*

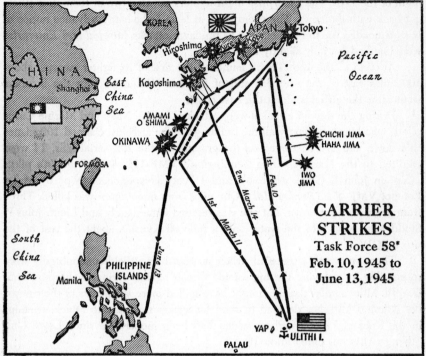

CARRIER
STRIKES
Task Force 58*
Feb. 10, 1945 to
June 13, 1945

* TASK FORCE 58 BECAME TASK FORCE 38 ON MAY 28

Triumph Over Adversity

On 14 March TF 58 weighed anchor in Ulithi Lagoon for a mission of great moment: the "softening" of airfields on the homeland island of Kyushu in preparation for the great invasion of Okinawa two weeks later.

Two of the 16 carriers had had their four Marine squadrons subtracted, but a new arrival brought two more squadrons. Following its repair on the West Coast, CV *Franklin* sailed westward across the Pacific in February with VMF-214 and VMF-452 on board. The latter squadron, under command of Major Charles P. Weiland, had been organized a year earlier and was going into combat for the first time. VMF-214 (the old "Black Sheep") had spent many months in the Solomons, the most notable portion under command of "Pappy" Boyington, now languishing in a prison camp at Yokohama. But now VMF-214 was full of new sheep, barely sooty. Only the squadron commander, Major Stanley R. Bailey, remained of the Boyington crew.

In the previous swipes in the Kyushu–Okinawa area TF 58 had hit and run away. This time the force was going to stay and it would be followed by the mightiest invasion force of the war against Japan.

After refueling at sea on 16 March Spruance began a high-speed run for Kyushu. The Japanese sent snooper planes toward the task force during the night of the 17th. The *Enterprise* night fighters downed two of them, but others got back with the news. The enemy had at least eight hours' advance notice of visitors headed for the homeland.[7] In predawn attacks *Intrepid* and *Enterprise* were bombed but only slightly damaged.

At 0545 of the 18th TF 58 launched the first of its fighter sweeps, about 100 miles east of the southern end of Kyushu. Within an hour the bombers went after the airfields along the east coast.

During the day 45 airfields were attacked by the Navy and Marine Corps pilots, who burnt up nearly all the buildings at the airfields, claimed 102 planes shot down and 275 destroyed on the ground. Of the 102 aerial kills, 14 were credited to the Marines—9 to *Bennington's* VMF-112, 4 to *Franklin's* pilots (Captain John R. Stack got two), and 1 "very inexperienced Nip" by Major Long of VMF-451 (*Bunker Hill*). One pilot from *Bennington* was killed. Three from *Franklin* went down, but one was rescued immediately and Lieut. John P. Stodd, who went into the water only a mile off Kyushu, spent the rest of the war a POW.

These eminently successful strikes on Kyushu's airfields undoubtedly were responsible for delaying the big suicide thrusts against Okinawa shipping until 6 April. More similar damage might have nailed more *kamikazes* in their nests, but Admiral Mitscher decided to send his strikes next day to attack warships in the Kure and Kobe harbors which had been inoperative since Leyte Gulf (though Mitscher didn't know it).[8]

The first CAP went off *Bunker Hill* at 0540, only 65 miles southeast of southern Shikoku. Only one plane was encountered by this CAP, a Zeke which Lieut. James A. Turner exploded at such short range his own plane was blasted out of control. No trace was seen of Turner or his F4U.

Inferno on Board CV 13

On board *Franklin* there were recurrent alarms during the night of 18–19 March. At 0708 on 19 March, 1 hour and 23 minutes after two thirds of the carrier's planes had been launched, an enemy plane dove out of the 2,000-foot clouds and dropped two 250-kilo bombs. On deck at the time were 5 bombers, 14 torpedo planes and 12 fighters, all tuning up, and loaded with general-purpose bombs and Tiny Tim rockets—one of the first times these 11.75-inch rockets had been designated for use against the enemy.[9]

The Japanese bombs set off the bombs and rockets on the 31 aircraft on the deck, creating an inferno unparalleled in the Pacific carrier war. When the ship was first hit, the officers and men of the crew reacted promptly and creditably, but the loss of all interior communications began to create great confusion, particularly on the fo'c'sle and the forward end of the flight deck. Some junior officers, in a mistaken gesture of generosity, passed out officers' clothing

[7] Karig, Harris and Manson, *Battle Report*, V, p 356.
[8] Sherman, *Combat Command*, p 353.
[9] *Franklin* action report, serial 00212, 11 April 1945.

to the enlisted men. The appearance of these pseudo officers, some of whom were abandoning ship without orders, created greater confusion and many other men, seeing their "officers" leave the ship, began to jump overboard also, or to swing over to cruiser *Santa Fe* which had come alongside.[10] About 103 officers and 600 men remained on the ship to fight the flames and explosions.

One witness describes the holocaust as follows:

> There was a tremendous explosion. Instantly a great ball of flame shot along the hangar and flight decks. Great clouds of smoke billowed as the carrier turned out of the wind. Then there were heavy explosions on the flight deck. In a few minutes, the entire ship was engulfed in smoke, broken only by the glare of explosions. Debris was landing in the water 500 yards from the carrier. . . . At the edge of the deck, I found two Marine pilots helping each other; one had a broken ankle. A large section of the flight deck exploded a few feet away. . . . A terrific explosion lashed out when the planes still on deck disappeared as a bomb exploded. . . . Their rockets fired and flashed behind in great orange streaks over our heads. . . . The carrier shuddered as though in an earthquake . . . it seemed impossible that the carrier could remain afloat.[11]

For nearly four hours *Franklin* lay dead in the water, burning, exploding, listing heavily—only 55 miles from the coast of Japan. Despite many attempts, the ship was not hit again. During the next 48 hours cruiser *Pittsburgh* towed *Franklin*, until she could work up to 18 knots. Three destroyers escorted her back to Ulithi where she arrived 24 March to meet the unbelieving stares of thousands of sailors and marines who were preparing to depart for Okinawa.

Among many heroes aboard the ship was a civilian, Mr. Donald Russell, Chance Vought aircraft representative attached to the Marine squadrons, who voluntarily remained on board to help organize fire-fighting crews.[12]

Among the *Franklin's* 772 dead were 65 Marine aviation personnel—1 officer and 32 men of VMF-452 and 6 officers and 26 men of VMF-214. Some pilots of the two squadrons who landed on board *Hancock* and *Bennington* flew combat for several days from those carriers.

With their ship gutted, VMF-214 and VMF-452 were out of the war after only two days' carrier combat. Only the four squadrons on board *Bunker Hill* and *Bennington* were left as Marine Corps units on CV's. They saw a lot of war, however, before they retired from the *kamikaze* arena.

Franklin was the worst casualty of the 19th, but *Wasp*, operating south of Honshu, caught a bomb through her flight deck which went all the way down to the third deck before exploding. There were 302 casualties and *Wasp*

---

[10] *Ibid.*

[11] Lieut. Jim Hardin, Marine radio correspondent, quoted in DeChant, *Devilbirds*, p 212.

[12] He was one of the few civilians in World War II to be awarded the Silver Star by the Navy.

went back to remain under repair until only three weeks of the war remained. Two of the volunteer Marine ground crewmen were wounded.

As *Franklin* battled for her life, Major Herman Hansen led 16 Corsairs of VMF-112 on a strike at Kanoya East Field. Twenty Zeke fighters intercepted them at 19,000 feet. The marines knocked down nine of the Zekes in a brief action and continued on their sweep over the air base. All 16 VMF-112 Corsairs returned. Fifteen planes from the other *Bennington* squadron stirred up a hornets' nest at Hiroshima and Kure fields. When Major Thomas E. Mobley Jr. (who had succeeded Alward as VMF-123's skipper) changed direction to answer a call for help, his Corsairs were hit from behind and above by about 30 enemy planes. In contrast to the previous day's clumsy birds, these Japanese proved to be expert pilots.

They shot down Lieuts. Gordon K. Wooster and Ralph A. Russell immediately but the marines fought back and within the next 30 furious minutes shot nine Japanese planes out of the air. Major Mobley got one of them, but his own instrument panel and compass were smashed by 20-mm. shells and he turned over the lead to Captain William Cantrel, who had himself accounted for two of the enemy planes and had been shot through the foot. The flight back to *Bennington* was highly precarious. Eight of the F4U's had been damaged so badly that they barely made it, and three of them had to be jettisoned upon landing. Another, flown by Lieut. Claude O. Barnhill, didn't get back; the pilot had to bail out over the picket line.[13]

On the same date Commander George M. Ottinger[14] led one of the big strikes against port installations and fuel and warehouse dumps in the vicinity of the great Japanese base at Kure. Twelve VSB's and 14 VTB's from *Bunker Hill* were escorted by 15 Corsairs of VMF-451 and 4 Navy Corsairs.

The strike leader was about three miles ahead of the group as it approached Kure. Within a few miles of the target he radioed the news Mitscher wanted to hear: many ships appeared to be in the harbor. Ottinger ordered half the strike group to attack shipping instead of assigned targets. As Ottinger approached even closer he radioed that the "shipping" was actually a big segment of what remained of the Japanese Fleet—3 carriers, 1 or 2 battleships, several cruisers and destroyers and fleet auxiliaries.[15]

Mitscher's planes fell upon the remnants of the Japanese Fleet—many of the ships crippled at Leyte Gulf—with great enthusiasm. All the battleships and all the carriers were hit at least once, as were two or more cruisers. Few of them were any good at all after this 19 March strike, and what was left was sunk or maimed further in other carrier strikes on 28–29 July.

Ottinger's 41 planes concentrated on the carriers. *Katsuragi* (27,000 tons) had a hole after it was skip-bombed. *Amagi*, a sister ship, had an elevator knocked out. But *Ryuho* caught particular hell. Three bombs hit, one of them

---

[13] VMF-123 war diary, March 1945.

[14] Killed a week later off Okinawa.

[15] Remarkably concise; actually there were 3 CV's, 3 BB's, 7 CL's, though the Commander could hardly see them all.

knocking a 33-foot hole in her flight deck, another blew the No. 3 elevator completely out of the elevator well. Major Herbert H. Long's Corsairs' own contribution was a rocket hit that made five two-foot holes in *Ryuho's* upper hangar deck and a bulkhead in the entrance to the No. 1 boiler room, another which made six one-and-a-half-foot holes in the plates of the middle deck plus seven rockets which hit but did not explode. Twenty Japanese were killed, 30 wounded. After this punishment *Ryuho* was heavily camouflaged and never spotted again by the Americans nor sailed again by the Japanese.[16]

Admiral Mitscher claimed 97 planes shot down during the day and 225 destroyed on the ground.

Covering Okinawa Landings

On 23 March, in continuing the softening up of Okinawa for the 1 April invasion, VMF-112 and VMF-123, together with VF-82, destroyed 26 suicide boats and damaged military installations in the area. On 28 March, during another strike on Kyushu's Kanoya East Field, Lieut. Roy Koons of VMF-112 was hit by AA and rescued by destroyer *McKee*. *Bennington* pilots shot down 2 Japanese planes and destroyed 6 on the field.

Following their final preinvasion operation, the fast carriers moved northward to serve as sentries and to intercept the suicide planes which were bound to come after the invasion force as it lay immobile off Okinawa, only 325 miles south of Japan.

On Love-day at Okinawa[17] VMF-221 and VMF-451 flew 24 Corsairs off *Bunker Hill* for the napalm bombing and strafing of a considerable section of the vacated landing beaches. The VMF-451 marines lost two pilots during launching operations at dawn—a relatively high percentage of that day's weirdly minor casualty roll. *Bennington* Marine pilots also flew in the pre-H-hour napalm and strafing attack on the beach area, and later in the day hit gun positions, bivouac areas, and supply dumps behind the lines.

The next day was relatively quiet also, but on 3 April the carrier marines were in a fight which began that day and lasted many weeks. Flying with 16 Hellcats, a dozen Corsairs from *Bunker Hill* during an attack mission over Amami O Shima and Kikai Jima, ran into a flock of Zekes and shot down 11 of them (three by Lieut. William Peek)—the Navy pilots got the rest of this weird outfit, whose mission apparently was to ram the Corsairs.

Fifteen Corsairs from *Bennington* joined up with Hellcats from *Hornet* and *Belleau Wood* in strikes in the Okinawa area. Lieut. H. J. Steele Jr. was hit by AA over Hirara field on Miyako Jima and he set his plane down eight miles off shore. A Kingfisher rescued him but Captain Harry J. (Dusty) Deal, who had helped in the rescue, was killed as he prepared to land—his engine failed

---

[16] USSBS, *Campaigns*, pp 345, 357.

[17] See next chapter. There is some overlapping between this account henceforward and the Okinawa story, but since the missions of the carrier marines and the land-based Tactical Air Force differed considerably, I have kept the accounts separated.

and he sank with his Corsair. Another captain, William E. Roques, was killed after his plane was hit by AA over Ishigaki. He headed to sea for a water landing, but could not jettison the hood. The engine quit, the plane nosed over and broke in half at the cockpit and he sank with it, much the same as "Dusty" Deal, whose canopy slammed shut when he hit the water.

April 6 was the beginning of the great *kamikaze* attack. In keeping with the spirit of the thing, the great battleship *Yamato* sortied the same day from Tokuyama, in the Inland Sea, on a suicide mission of her own. She weighed anchor intent upon reaching the Okinawa beachhead 8 April to knock off the rest of the United States surface forces before going down herself.

Suicide Rampant

As a prelude to *Yamato's* venture 355 *kamikazes* were launched on 6–7 April, nearly all of them on the 6th. No less than 233 of them were shot down by TF 58, another 55 by the escort carrier planes covering Okinawa close-in and 39 by ships' AA. The other 22 got through and completed their mission by smashing into 22 ships, of which three were sunk and many others grievously wounded.

Marines from *Bunker Hill* destroyed 12 of the suiciders (Lieut. George R. Johns getting three). *Bennington* Corsairs were on CAP and encountered only five; they shot down all of them. The quality of Japanese planes and pilots had deteriorated to a point where four pilots in a single Navy division on board *Yorktown* were able to claim 50.

Yamato came on, accompanied by light cruiser *Yahagi* and eight destroyers, through Bungo Channel (where she was spotted by U.S. submarines), Osumi Channel, past the southern tip of Kyushu. Shortly after noon a whirlwind of planes from the Fast Carrier Task Force pounced upon the Japanese. "Five planes—over 10—over 30!" shouted a lookout on board the great battleship. "Over one hundred hostile planes are heading for us!" yelled the navigator.[18]

At 1423 *Yamato* blew up, holed by five bombs and ten torpedoes.[19] *Yahagi* and four destroyers also went down; the four survivors limped back to Sasebo.[20]

During the search for *Yamato* by 23 F4U's from *Bunker Hill* a flight of three encountered Rex fighters and shot down five of them (two each by Major Roberts and Lieut. Clay D. Haggard, one by Lieut. Eugene D. Cameron). Mostly the marines flew CAP all day.

The lone exception was *Bennington's* Lieut. Kenneth E. Huntington, whose

---

[18] Article by a survivor, Mitsuru Yoshida, published in Japan. Courtesy of Lieut. Pineau.

[19] The other two ships laid down as the same class were already in Davy Jones's locker: *Musashi*, sunk in the Leyte Gulf battle; *Shinano*, converted to an aircraft carrier, became the biggest ship ever sunk by a submarine—*Archerfish* sent her down after she sailed from Yokosuka for the Inland Sea on her maiden voyage, 29 November 1944.

[20] USSBS, *Campaigns*, p 325.

plane was the only Corsair on deck when the ship's strike was hastily launched. (Seven other marines assigned to the strike were left sitting in their planes on the hangar deck.) Huntington went along with 11 SB2C's, 10 TBM's and 7 F4F's. To these 29 planes fell the honor of initiating the attack. They were greeted by a "red, blue, black, white and yellow" flak barrage. The lone marine "didn't actually throw the switch that snuffed out" the Japanese force, but he did race through the technicolored AA, plant his bomb on the forward turret and silence those guns.[21] One marine. One bomb. One Navy Cross.

April 12 was the *kamikazes'* second biggest day, but also the carrier marines' biggest day—26 planes shot down by *Bennington's* flying Leathernecks, 25 by *Bunker Hill's* (as well as 16 by the Okinawa-based marines). For "Hap" Hansen, CO of VMF-112, it was a day truly worth celebrating: he became 25 years old, shot down three suiciders to make himself a five-plane ace, and won the Navy Cross. Another Hanson, Lieut. Bert, from "Hap's" squadron, shot down an Oscar and a Zeke. But the Irish got in it, too—Lieut. John M. Callahan splashed three enemy fighters in five minutes.

The other *Bennington* squadron's exec, Major Donald P. Frame, despite a faulty engine, flew through heavy AA from the American ships to bring down a *kamikaze* bent on exploding himself on one of them.[22]

Of *Bunker Hill's* 25 planes, Major Archie Donahue accounted for one-fifth on TCAP over Izena Shima, which brought his total score to 14. Three others, Lieuts. Raymond H. Swalley, John E. Peterson and John R. Webb of VMF-451, shot down two apiece.

Next day was Friday the 13th. It was unfortunate for the marines; Captain George C. DeFabio's luck ran out. AA over Kikai set his plane afire; he parachuted but was unable to extricate himself from his chute after enemy shore guns blazed away at him. Lieuts. Victor K. Rusling and Franklin R. Kurchinski, also VMF-123 pilots, were hit by AA about the same time; they sank with their planes.

During the rest of April TF 58 spent most of the time dodging *kamikazes* and trying to nail them before they reached the ships off Okinawa. *Enterprise, Intrepid* and several other ships of the Task Force were damaged, but *Bunker Hill* and *Bennington* seemed to lead charmed lives. At least five enemy planes dived for the latter flattop, and three missed by the narrowest of margins. On 16 April one darted out of the sunset and missed *Bunker Hill* by the skin of her bow. Between 13 April and the end of the month the *Bennington* marines claimed 10 planes, *Bunker Hill's* 20.

Bunker Hill got hers on the morning of 11 May. Four smaller ships of TF 58 had already been hit when an undetected Zeke plunged out of low clouds on the starboard quarter and crashed on the flight deck aft of No. 3 elevator. An instant later a Judy smacked the flight deck alongside the island, although it had been hit at least once by 5-inch AA and several times by automatic-

---

[21] VMF-112 and VMF-123 war diaries, April 1945.

[22] Six years later (lacking eight days) Major Frame died while being evacuated from the Korea rice paddy into which he had parachuted.

weapons fire. The first plane released its delayed action bomb as it hit, then skidded across the flight deck to set afire parked aircraft. The bomb went through the deck and pierced the ship's skin at gallery-deck level, but exploded in midair before striking the water, riddling the sponsons and sending large fragments into the ship's side. The Judy pilot released his bomb just before body-crashing. The bomb went through the flight deck and exploded on the gallery deck. The plane penetrated the flight deck at the base of the island and poured gasoline into the gallery and hangar decks, which soon were billowing flame and smoke at all three levels.

Within an hour and a half the fire on the battered flight deck was under control. Alongside, three destroyers and cruiser *Wilkes-Barre* strove mightily to douse the hangar deck fire with their hoses. Fires broke out in the magazine, and *Bunker Hill* began to list slowly to starboard. Two engines were cut out and speed dropped to ten knots. At 1430, after four hours of hell, *Bunker Hill's* fires were under control. At 1630 Admiral Mitscher went on board destroyer *English* which transferred him, his staff and his flag from *Bunker Hill* to *Enterprise*.[23] When "Big E" was hit three days later the harassed Admiral shifted again (to *Randolph*).

When the casualties were counted 389 *Bunker Hill* men were dead or missing, 264 wounded. Among the dead were one Marine pilot and 28 enlisted men, including two master sergeants and two technical sergeants. Of eight ACIO's (6 Navy, 2 Marine) aboard 4 were killed, 2 were badly burned. Lieut. Leo B. Pambrun of VMF-221 went over the side but Lieut. John E. Nayman of VMF-451 was left uninjured on board.

Fifteen of the pilots of the two squadrons were in the air and shot down four planes[24] while the ship was undergoing her agony. They landed on board *Enterprise*.

For VMF-221 and VMF-451 the war was over. During three months' action they shot down 84 enemy planes, lost 13 pilots (9 in combat, 4 operationally).[25]

Bennington Sees it Through

Following *Bunker Hill's* withdrawal, VMF-112 and VMF-123 remained on board *Bennington* with the Fast Carrier Task Force another month, serving with both Spruance and Halsey (who took the fleet command again on 28 May).

June 8 was a memorable day for the last two Marine squadrons on the CV's. Eleven of the Corsairs with a host of Navy aircraft were launched a good 300 miles from their target, Kanoya field on southern Kyushu—"outside the probable range of retaliatory *kamikaze* attack." This time the Navy planes carried a surprise: 500-pound bombs equipped with VT fuzes which were set to explode 10 to 45 feet above the ground. This operation was designed to catch the

---

[23] *Bunker Hill* action report, 5 June 1945.
[24] One by Captain James Swett of Solomons fame.
[25] *Bunker Hill* records were burned, hence statistics are incomplete.

kamikazes in their revetments, riddling the planes with bomb particles. To arm the VT fuzes it was necessary to dive from 16,000 feet to 5,500 feet before releasing.

The air co-ordinator estimated that 80 per cent of the bombs burst at the calculated altitude. Bomb damage could not be assessed.

Upon returning to *Bennington,* the Marine squadrons were called to the ready room. An ACI officer mounted a chair and said: "That was the last mission, fellows, we're going home." The squadrons' war diarist noted: "The cheers shook the room." At 1807 *Bennington,* accompanied by a destroyer squadron, turned to the southwest and sailed for Leyte Gulf.[26]

In combat almost continuously from 16 February to 8 June, the two squadrons had compiled an exceptional record:

Combat sorties	2,554
Total hours flown	12,047
Enemy planes destroyed (air)	82
Enemy planes destroyed (ground)	149
Tons of bombs dropped	102.7
Rockets fired	4,097
Rounds of .50-caliber ammo fired	933,991
Gallons of napalm dropped	8,250

The two squadrons lost 31 planes in combat, 17 others in operational crashes. Forty-one damaged planes were transferred and 54 replacements were received.

Eighteen pilots—one in three of those who came on board—gave up their lives. Fifteen others were rescued after being shot down or forced down.

Marines on Other CV's

At least 13 Marine pilots served in Navy squadrons. Eight of these found themselves on board *Intrepid,* as follows: When the *Wasp* air group arrived at Guam in late March, four flyers of VMF-216 and VMF-217, led by Lieut. George A. Krumm, were detached and assigned to a floating replacement pool in escort carrier *Windham Bay* along with four more Marine aviators. After a few days Krumm's unit was transferred to CVE *Attu* where they heard that *Intrepid* wanted some Marine replacements in its VMF squadrons. Krumm and his three pilots "with a piece of paper in hand" boarded a destroyer to go on board *Intrepid.* It turned out that Navy Air Group 10 was there, had no Marine pilots, but could use some if they could fly Corsairs. Krumm's foursome joined up.

About a week later the other Marine team, led by Lieut. William A. Nickerson, came on board with orders that were slightly more regular. That made eight.

---

[26] VMF-112 and VMF-123 war diaries, June 1945.

One of Nickerson's pilots, Lieut. Carl R. Miller, was killed 5 April by AA fire over Miyara airfield on Ishigaki, an island of the Sakishima group. The remaining seven participated in the great event of 7 April, the sinking of *Yamato,* into which *Intrepid* sent 16 fighters, 12 dive bombers and 12 torpedo bombers and claimed one torpedo hit, six 1,000-pound bomb hits on that big ship, as well as two planes shot down and six destroyed on the ground during a sweep on Tokuno.[27]

During their service on board *Intrepid*—which lasted only until the carrier was *kamikazed* 16 April—Krumm and Nickerson were credited with three planes apiece, Lieuts. Harry O. Taylor and Hugh F. Newell two each.

Under similar circumstances five other wandering pilots wound up in CAG-99 on board CV *Shangri-La.* Lieut. Morris W. Hitson and Lieut. Joseph Januszewski were detached from VMF-512 of MCVG-2 at Santa Barbara and flown by Pan American Clipper to Oahu. They proved their carrier qualification at Ewa and went on to Guam. There they flew several days with VMF-215 before shifting to Saipan.

At the Marpi Point airfield, on Saipan, the two were assigned to Navy Bomber Fighter Squadron 99. Three other Marine pilots joined them to make up a four-plane flight plus one replacement. They requalified as carrier pilots. On 28 May they were ordered to *Bougainville* (CVE 100), which transported them out to the fleet off Okinawa. They managed to get in the middle of the typhoon of 5 June which destroyed several of the CVE's planes.

Put on board a destroyer, the five marines were transferred to *Shangri-La* on 6 June. After his first landing next day Hitson observed that the CV "looked like a runway" compared to the little ships he was used to. After about two weeks' operation against *kamikaze*-bearing airfields, the Fast Carrier Task Force finished nearly three months at sea and headed for Leyte Gulf for replenishment and replacements. At Leyte the five marines saw MCVG-2's carrier, *Gilbert Islands.* Colonel Campbell agreed to get them back into VMF-512. "Glad to be back with the Marine Corps again," they sailed away for Borneo to support the Balikpapan landing, convinced they had seen something of the world in the best Navy tradition.[28]

---

[27] Available records do not indicate what part these marines played, if any, in *Yamato's* sinking.

[28] See p 416. Letter Lieut. Morris W. Hitson to Marine Aviation History Board, 17 September 1950; another from Captain George A. Krumm, 29 July 1949; a third from Tech. Sergeant Hugh F. Newell, 21 July 1949; *Intrepid* action report (Appendix G, casualties); Karig, Harris and Manson, *Battle Report, V,* p 398. After investigating reports that "at least 50" Marine pilots served with Navy groups late in the war, I believe the *Intrepid* and *Shangri-La* cases are the only ones of their kind.

112. Three types of carriers; also battleships, cruisers, destroyers

113. "Murderers' Row" is what they called these big carriers

TWO VIEWS OF ULITHI LAGOON, EARLY 1945

Japanese Paintings from U.S. Army colle

114-115. *"Kamikaze* units leaving a base on the Home Islands"

116. *Franklin*

117. *Bunker Hill*

IN THE WAKE OF THE *KAMIKAZES*

118. *Bunker Hill*

119.   A CVE missed

KAMIKAZES AT WORK

120.   Two ships at Okinawa hit

U.S. Coast Guard Photo

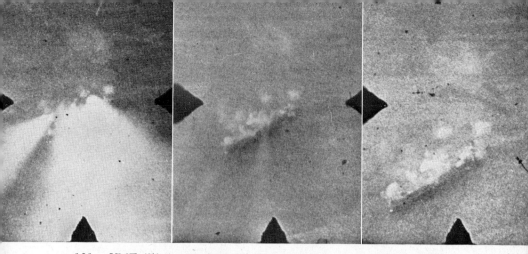

121.   VMF-451 pumps Corsair bullets and rockets into carrier *Ryuho*

and leaves it blazing, Kure, 19 March 1945

GUN CAMERA FILM FROM VMF-112 AND VMF-451

122.   A VMF-112 Corsair sets a Betty afire, same date

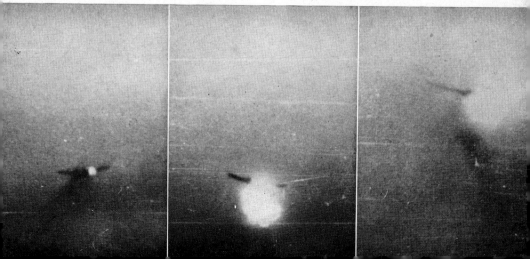

123. Navy PBM settles besides pilot in life raft (arrow)

124. With Lieut. McInnis aboard, the PBM takes off

RESCUE THREE MILES OFF KYUSHU

125. R5C delivers mail to Iwo

126. TBM drops ammo to Okinawa

ESSENTIALS DELIVERED BY PARACHUTE

127. Okinawa—note keystone-shaped native tom

ere Japanese troops frequently employed guns

By LIFE photographer W. Eugene Smith © TIME, INC.

128. Artillery spotting

THE VERSATILE GRASSHOPPER

129. Evacuation of wounded

130. Any old road will do

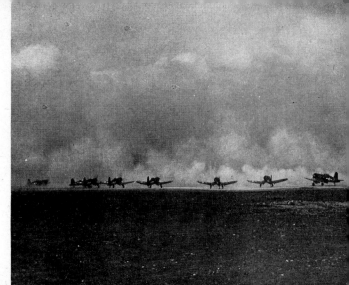

131.   Yontan Ballet, 7 April 1945

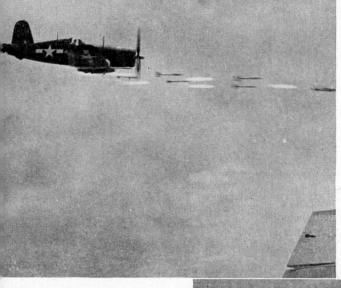

F4U'S AT OKINAWA

132.   Rockets (profile)

133.   Rockets (rear)

134.   TBM close support mission, Okinawa

135.   Air controllers called them
       in by radio from front lines

136.   View of Kadena Field, Okinawa   U.S. Army Photo

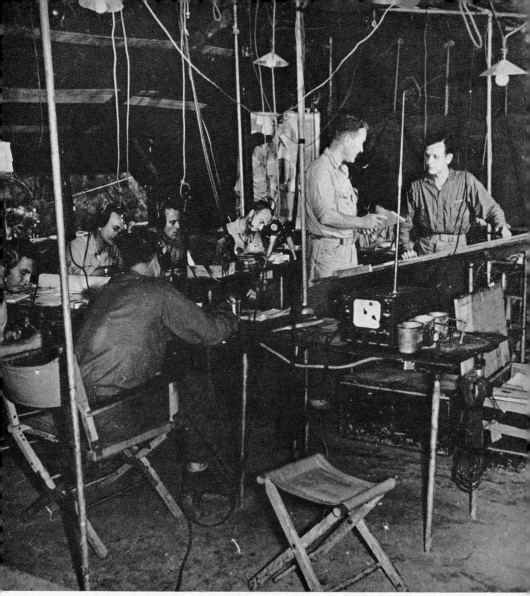

137.   LFASCU No. 3 coordinating requests for close support on Okinawa

138. AA fire during air raid

ENEMY ATTACKS
ON OKINAWA

139.   Humor, Okinawa style

140.   A Japanese plane which crash landed during the *Giretsu* of 24 May

141.   Photo-flash by VMB-612 shows Tiny Tim rocket explosion

142. Generals Mitchell and Woods

143. Lieut. Klingman after chewing up enemy plane at 38,000 feet near Okinawa

144. MAG-31 Corsairs over Fuji, September 1945

Okinawa Invaded

FOLLOWING THE DECISION in the summer of 1944 to invade Luzon after Leyte—thereby canceling Formosa and, ultimately, the China coast—the JCS on 3 October simultaneously ordered the Luzon invasion and directed Admiral Nimitz to seize one or more positions in the Ryukyu Islands (Operation ICEBERG). Target date was originally 1 March 1945, but delays in the Luzon operation plus the prospect of unfavorable weather during March forced post-ponement to 1 April (L-day).[1]

The Ryukyu Islands stretch almost 800 miles from southern Japan to Formosa. The largest of these islands, Okinawa, lies about 325 miles south of Kyushu, the southernmost big island of Japan. It was against this island, 60 miles long and from 2 to 18 miles wide, that Admiral Nimitz planned his main assault, which turned out to be his biggest and costliest single operation of World War II.

Historical Background

The ancient name of Okinawa was "Great Lew Chew," or Liuchu, and it is probable that "Ryukyu" stemmed from the Japanese inability to pronounce the letter L. When Commodore Matthew Calbraith Perry sailed his ships the second time into Naha Harbor in 1854 he extracted a treaty from the Regent. The opening sentence read: "Hereafter, whenever citizens of the United States come to Lew Chew, they shall be treated with great courtesy and friendship"[2]—a treaty which was to be observed in the breach 91 years later.

Japan annexed Okinawa and the other Ryukyus in 1879, and thereafter treated the destitute, stunted natives—of whom there were 436,000 by 1940 —with contempt. The northern two thirds of Okinawa are rugged and moun-tainous. The lower third is rolling and hilly and intensely cultivated, but even here ravines and terraces are frequently encountered, with many caves and tombs dug into the limestone hillsides.

Admiral Spruance of the Fifth Fleet was designated Central Pacific Task

---

[1] Roy E. Appleman, James M. Burns, Russell A. Gugeler and John Stevens, *Okinawa: The Last Battle* (hereinafter cited as *Okinawa*) p 28; Tenth Army, Action Report Ryukyus, Vol I.

[2] Arthur Walworth, *Black Ships Off Japan*, p 260.

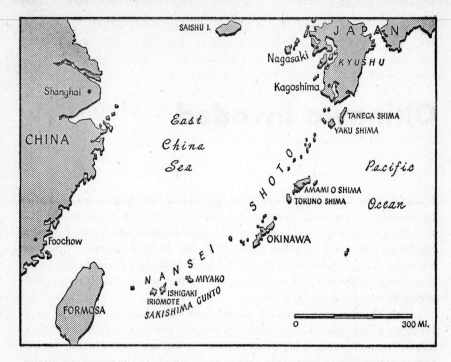

Forces commander. The amphibious forces were again placed under Vice Admiral Richmond K. Turner, who would be in immediate command of the forces in and around the target area. To Lieut. General Simon B. Buckner Jr. USA was assigned command of the new Tenth Army, which would furnish the ground forces consisting of XXIV Corps (Major General John R. Hodge USA) and III Amphibious Corps (Major General Roy S. Geiger USMC)—two divisions each—plus three other divisions, the 2d MarDiv (demonstration landing force), 77th Infantry Division (Western Islands landing force) and 27th Infantry Division (floating reserve). Buckner's combat divisions totaled 154,000 and other units brought his assault forces alone up to 183,000. About 548,000 men of all services took part in the Okinawa battle; the number of ships participating was 1,457;[3] the number of planes was in the thousands.

For Marine Corps aviation, as for other units, Okinawa was the culmination of all that had been learned in the Pacific War. By 1 April 1945 that war was well into its fourth year; the commanders and their forces were well seasoned; their doctrines—naval, air and ground—had been thoroughly tested. Now, on the doorstep of the enemy homeland, came the biggest test of all.

Tactical Air Force

Planning for Okinawa carefully separated strategic and tactical aviation. Strategic aviation was naturally allotted to the AAF: the Twentieth Air Force—

---

[3] King, *U.S. Navy at War*, p 176. Of these, 106 ships were in TF 58 (919 planes) and 22 ships in British TF 57 (244 planes).

principally the B-29's based in the Marianas—operated directly under the JCS, with the Commanding General, AAF (General H. H. Arnold) the executive agent; Admiral Nimitz had his own Pacific Ocean Areas Strategic Air Force with Major General Willis H. Hale USA as commanding general.

Carrier-based tactical aviation, furnished by Rear Admiral Calvin T. Durgin's 18 escort carriers, came under the intricate command set-up of Kelly Turner, and when Mitscher sent TF 58 planes to help out they too became Turner's weapons. Land-based tactical aviation was a direct subordinate task group under General Buckner (who in turn reported to Turner "until the amphibious phase of the operation ended"—not until 17 May, the date tactical command was assumed ashore).[4]

It was determined early that the Tenth Army's Tactical Air Force (TAF) should be commanded by a Marine flyer. When he learned this, Major General Mulcahy asked Rear Admiral Forrest Sherman (Nimitz's plans officer): "How about me?"[5] He got the job.

Mulcahy remained CG AirFMFPac until he could be relieved by Major General James T. Moore, who had come from Peleliu after handing over Air Command, Western Carolines. This relief did not take place until 23 February 1945, five weeks before L-day. Meanwhile, the headquarters squadron of 2d MAW which had moved from Peleliu to Ewa on 15 December (at which time the Wing's tactical units were transferred to the 4th MAW) formed the nucleus of TAF. Certain officers of the Army and Navy were also assigned to TAF by CinCPac and CinCPOA, and final pre-embarkation strength of TAF headquarters was 112 officers (60 USMC, 24 USA, 28 USN) and 398 enlisted men (378 USMC, 20 USN hospital corpsmen). About half the officers and a fourth of the enlisted men were embarked for the assault phase; the rear echelon under Colonel Hayne D. Boyden would reach Okinawa a month after L-day.

Primary missions of the TAF, as outlined in the operations plan, were: (1) establishment of headquarters and tactical units ashore as soon as practicable after L-day; (2) air support missions as assigned; (3) air defense in conjunction with fleet aircraft. Among the tasks of TAF were emergency assistance to carrier aircraft forced to land ashore, control of AA and searchlights, aerial photography and first-phase photo interpretation.

To accomplish these things Pat Mulcahy had handicaps to overcome. As CG of the 2d MAW, he wore another Okinawa hat. But this wing had no tactical units, and only one was assigned by the time Mulcahy and his staff departed for the target area and that one (Colonel Ward Dickey's MAG-33) was at Espíritu Santo, 3,020 miles southwest of Oahu. Although organization was started in December, "the outfits which were supposed to furnish personnel seemed reluctant to give up those requested. As a result . . . nearly every member of the staff reported late in the planning stage, and the burden fell on the

---

[4] "Air Support of Pacific Amphibious Operations," prepared for USSBS (Pacific) by Commander, Air Support Control Units Amphibious Forces, U.S. Pacific Fleet, pp 21, 23.

[5] Interview Lieut. General F. P. Mulcahy USMC (Ret), 9 April 1948.

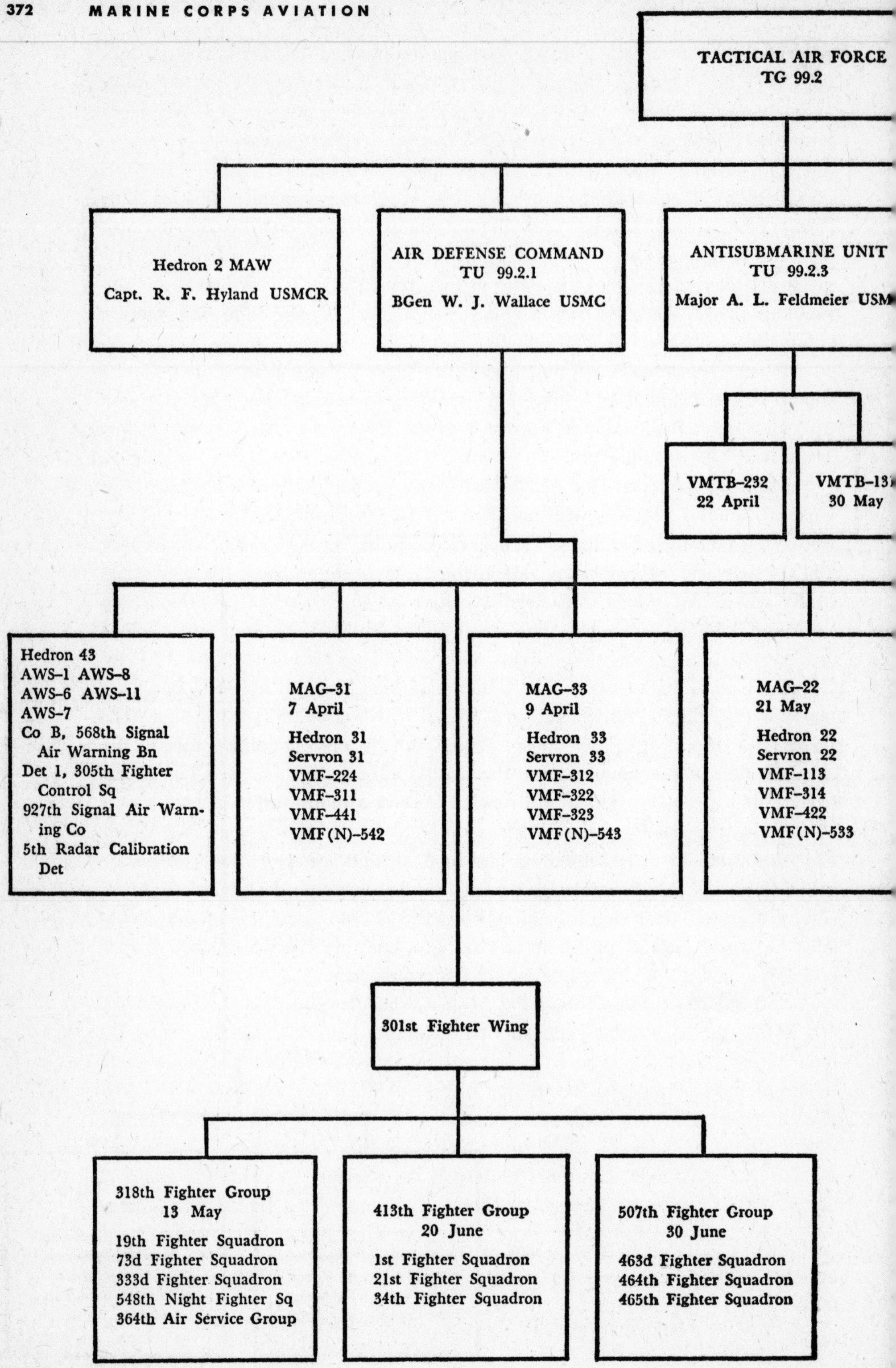

TACTICAL AIR FORCE
TG 99.2

Hedron 2 MAW

Capt. R. F. Hyland USMCR

AIR DEFENSE COMMAND
TU 99.2.1

BGen W. J. Wallace USMC

ANTISUBMARINE UNIT
TU 99.2.3

Major A. L. Feldmeier USM

VMTB-232
22 April

VMTB-13*
30 May

Hedron 43
AWS-1 AWS-8
AWS-6 AWS-11
AWS-7
Co B, 568th Signal
   Air Warning Bn
Det 1, 305th Fighter
   Control Sq
927th Signal Air War-
   ing Co
5th Radar Calibration
   Det

MAG-31
7 April

Hedron 31
Servron 31
VMF-224
VMF-311
VMF-441
VMF(N)-542

MAG-33
9 April

Hedron 33
Servron 33
VMF-312
VMF-322
VMF-323
VMF(N)-543

MAG-22
21 May

Hedron 22
Servron 22
VMF-113
VMF-314
VMF-422
VMF(N)-533

301st Fighter Wing

318th Fighter Group
13 May

19th Fighter Squadron
73d Fighter Squadron
333d Fighter Squadron
548th Night Fighter Sq
364th Air Service Group

413th Fighter Group
20 June

1st Fighter Squadron
21st Fighter Squadron
34th Fighter Squadron

507th Fighter Group
30 June

463d Fighter Squadron
464th Fighter Squadron
465th Fighter Squadron

Dates indicate time of arrival in Okinawa.

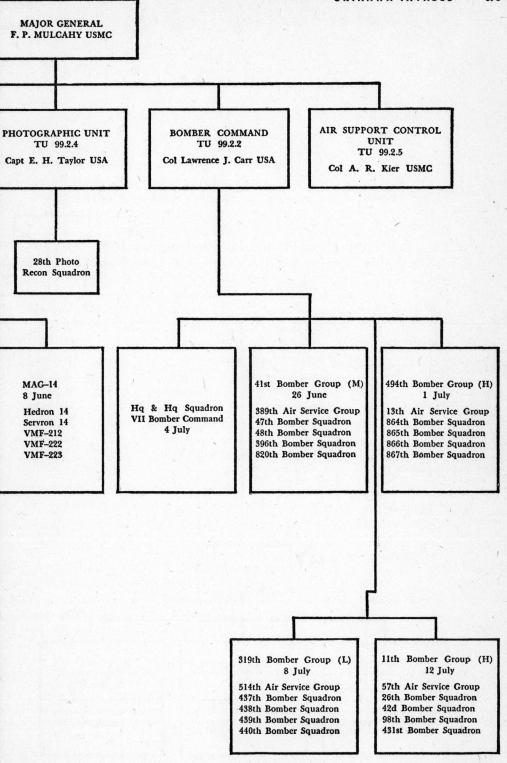

MAJOR GENERAL
F. P. MULCAHY USMC

PHOTOGRAPHIC UNIT
TU 99.2.4

Capt E. H. Taylor USA

BOMBER COMMAND
TU 99.2.2

Col Lawrence J. Carr USA

AIR SUPPORT CONTROL
UNIT
TU 99.2.5

Col A. R. Kier USMC

28th Photo
Recon Squadron

MAG–14
8 June

Hedron 14
Servron 14
VMF–212
VMF–222
VMF–223

Hq & Hq Squadron
VII Bomber Command
4 July

41st Bomber Group (M)
26 June

389th Air Service Group
47th Bomber Squadron
48th Bomber Squadron
396th Bomber Squadron
820th Bomber Squadron

494th Bomber Group (H)
1 July

13th Air Service Group
864th Bomber Squadron
865th Bomber Squadron
866th Bomber Squadron
867th Bomber Squadron

319th Bomber Group (L)
8 July

514th Air Service Group
437th Bomber Squadron
438th Bomber Squadron
439th Bomber Squadron
440th Bomber Squadron

11th Bomber Group (H)
12 July

57th Air Service Group
26th Bomber Squadron
42d Bomber Squadron
98th Bomber Squadron
431st Bomber Squadron

few officers available."[6] Some did not report until the assault echelon sailed for Leyte on board transport *Allendale* on 27 February.

TAF's original task could be foreseen: since Okinawa is in easy range of Japan's main islands, the enemy might be expected to throw everything within reach at the American invaders; increasingly heavy *kamikaze* attacks on ships off the Philippines did nothing to dispel this impression. Therefore, Mulcahy selected an Air Defense Commander 24 December—his AirFMFPac chief of staff, Brig. General William J. Wallace.

The Air Defense Command (ADC) was essentially the old Fighter Command brought up to date. Its duties included the furnishing of air-warning squadrons to assist (and later supplant) ship-based radar units, escort aircraft, fighter aircraft for offensive missions, direction of AA and searchlights. Primarily, ADC had to think about stopping the *kamikazes,* and it was to this task that General Wallace devoted full attention from the beginning.[7]

For ADC's administrative purposes the headquarters squadron of MAG-43 was brought out to Ewa from California, and Lieut. Colonel Robert O. Bisson, the radar expert, was made its commanding officer. On 1 February AWS's 6, 7 and 8—each consisting of about 20 officers and 275 men—joined the Group. AWS-1 on Engebi Island joined on 1 April and arrived at Ie Shima three weeks after L-day, and AWS-11 disembarked at Kume Shima six weeks before the war ended.

On 11 March a second tactical group was formally assigned to the 2d MAW: MAG-31, which had been suffering coral blindness and boredom in the Marshalls for 13 months. Colonel John C. Munn had arrived from Washington five days earlier to take command of the Group.

This was the complement with which TAF started operating on Okinawa: two tactical groups, plus an administrative group with three air-warning squadrons assigned. Before it was over TAF would be joined by 7 more Marine fighter squadrons, 10 Army fighter squadrons, 2 Marine TBF squadrons, 16 Army bomber squadrons, 1 Army photo squadron, 2 Army signal air warning companies, 1 fighter control squadron detachment, and a radar calibration detachment.

The Landing Force Air Support Control Units

Outside the command chain of the TAF were the Landing Force Air Support Control Units (LFASCU), which reported to the Commander, Air Support Control Units, PhibsPac (Captain Richard F. Whitehead, later Rear Admiral Alfred M. Pride), with headquarters on board Turner's flagship, *Eldorado.*

In the original planning for Okinawa, as for Iwo Jima, the CO LFASCU's was scheduled to take over all air support control whenever the amphibious

---

[6] TAF action report, chapter 3.

[7] Interview Major General W. J. Wallace, July 1950.

phase ended and the battle became primarily a land-based affair. It was natural for such control to be vested initially in a shipboard officer, since his was the primary responsibility—before any planes could be land-based—and all planes as well as all radar had to be ship-based at first.

Events at Okinawa made it virtually impossible to shift command ashore (although complete control of close support air strikes was LFASCU's). The amphibious phase could not end while the *kamikazes* endangered the whole operation. Until after Okinawa had been declared secure the responsibility of air defense control remained with the Navy on board ship although some control was ashore. LFASCU's had immediate direction of most of the close support which made Okinawa the only "completely modern" operation of the war. CO LFASCU's, Colonel Vernon E. Megee, had additional duty as chief of staff to ComASCU, PhibsPac from 2 May until he left Okinawa 24 May, and thus alternated between *Eldorado* and his command post ashore with LFASCU 3.

During the early weeks of the operation TAF was so busy with suicide planes that the escort and fast carriers had to furnish LFASCU with most of its planes. Nonetheless, the land-based marines flew 600 support missions between 7 and 30 April.[8] As the *kamikaze* threat diminished, the F4U's were able to support ground troops with increasing quantities of rockets, bombs and napalm. LFASCU requests were co-ordinated by the Tenth Army unit, LFASCU 3, then transmitted to the ASCU aboard the flagship for general allotment of aircraft. As the operation progressed this procedure became a formality—in actual daily operations, requirements were discussed directly with TAF.

Two TBF squadrons, 232 and 131, had originally been designated for antisubmarine warfare. Because Navy patrol squadrons based at Kerama Retto were found able to handle day and night antisubmarine patrol, and because the Marine squadron had no sonobuoy gear, VMTB-232 from its arrival 22 April performed strike missions, made parachute drops (sometimes in zero-zero weather, by radar), heckled the enemy at night, made radar countermeasure flights and such odd jobs as dropping propaganda leaflets. When VMTB-131 joined at the end of May it took up day antisubmarine patrol in addition to the numerous other duties allotted to the torpedo bombers (which did almost everything except haul torpedoes). Late in the Okinawa campaign all antisubmarine patrolling was taken over by TAF.[9]

Other Units

Two escort carriers with Marine air groups on board arrived during the Okinawa campaign: *Block Island* with MCVG-1 (VMTB-233 and VMF-511), *Gilbert Islands* with MCVG-2 (VMTB-143 and VMF-512). Two other Marine carriers, *Cape Gloucester* and *Vella Gulf*, did not come into Okinawan waters

---

[8] See p 408.
[9] TAF Operational Report, Section III, Chapter 6.

until just before the surrender of Japan. Another squadron, Cram's VMB-612, arrived from Iwo on 29 July and flew a few missions toward the end which resulted in some spectacular night photography.

Four VMO squadrons flying artillery-spotting planes participated in the campaign. Numbers 2, 3 and 6 were attached, respectively, to the 2d, 1st and 6th MarDivs, VMO-7 to the III Amphibious Corps artillery.

Army Air Forces fighters operated under TAF, beginning on 13 May with the arrival of the 318th Fighter Group (three day-fighter squadrons and one night-fighter squadron). The 413th Fighter Group began operations 20 June and the 507th on 30 June. The first AAF unit to be attached to TAF, however, was the 28th Photo Reconnaissance Squadron, which arrived on 22 April with 12 F5A's (P-38 photo planes) and furnished the Force's photographs and strike evaluation throughout the battle.

Under the original operation plan the Bomber Command of TAF was to consist of the 41st (Medium) and 319th (Light) AAF Bomber Groups, under command of Colonel Lawrence J. Carr USA. These did not begin operations until 26 June and 8 July, however, and two heavy bomber groups (B-24's) had been added by that time—the 494th on 1 July and the 11th on 12 July. Shortly after these bomber units arrived TAF was dissolved (13 July), the Army units reverted to Army command and all Marine units became elements of the 2d MAW. These details will be recounted in time.

Leaving aside the Army units which served under TAF command, the Okinawa campaign meant service for Marine aviation squadrons as follows: 12 land-based day fighter, 3 land-based night fighter, 2 land-based torpedo bomber, 2 escort-carrier-based fighter, 2 escort-carrier-based torpedo bomber, 6 fast-carrier-based fighter, 1 medium-bomber, 5 air-warning, 4 observation, 5 headquarters, 4 service, and the 3 LFASCU's.[10]

Marine aviation eventually contributed to the Okinawa operation about one-tenth of its own total personnel strength, which on 31 March stood at 15,711 officers and 108,347 enlisted.[11] The plane complements of Marine units assigned to Okinawa totaled about 700. Some of these participated only a short while, but about 450 were in combat during half or more of the campaign.

The Landing

On 24 March the TAF operation plan went into effect, while General Wallace and other members of the ADC were still 1,100 miles south of Okinawa, on board USS *Allendale,* riding at anchor in Leyte Gulf. General Mulcahy and his TAF operations officer, Colonel Perry O. Parmelee, were nearby in *Eldorado,* flagship of Admiral Turner. L-day was still eight days away.

But the greatest amphibious attack in history began that same day, when

---

[10] Four transport squadrons assigned to TAG supported the campaign but were not based on Okinawa.

[11] Of whom 341 officers and 7,261 enlisted were women.

minesweepers began clearing areas south of Kerama Retto, 15 miles west of Okinawa, in preparation for the 77th Infantry Division's landings. Underwater demolition teams began working over the approaches to the Keramas next day. On the morning of the 26th four battalion landing teams of the 77th Division began going ashore on the small, rugged islands. Resistance was light and sporadic; 530 Japanese were killed and 121 captured, at a cost of 31 U.S. soldiers killed and 81 wounded. One group of 300 Japanese soldiers on one of the islands refused to surrender, but promised to leave the Americans alone—their commander broke his isolation only after the Emperor issued his Imperial Rescript of surrender in August. More important, 350 suicide boats were captured, each complete with two depth charges. The Kerama islands furnished a naval base throughout the Okinawa battle, a seaplane anchorage, a place to refuel and rearm ships and a haven for ships broken by the *kamikazes*.

As the Kerama Islands were being invaded the FMF Amphibious Reconnaissance Battalion attached to the 77th Division landed on Keise Shima— four small coral islets about eight miles west of Naha, the capital of Okinawa. Attached was Captain Prescott A. Tolman with 5 officers and 46 men of AWS-8 who set up radar equipment on Nagannu Shima.

While the small islands were being captured the big island was being hammered by the guns of Admiral Blandy's TF 52 and the planes of Admiral Mitscher's 58. During the seven days preceding L-day 13,000 tons of shells were lobbed into Okinawa, and planes from the fast carriers and escort carriers flew a total of 3,095 sorties in this area alone.[12] Meantime, planes of the British carrier force flew 345 sorties against the Sakishima Islands, 150 miles southwest of Okinawa, from which suicide sorties could be expected.

Mitscher's planes struck at airfields on Kyushu, but the suicide planes had already started taking off. *Nevada* had her No. 3 turret knocked out (11 killed, 49 wounded); destroyers *Dorsey, Kimberly, O'Brien* and *Porterfield,* cruiser *Indianapolis* and six other U.S. ships were hit by the *kamikazes* before a single soldier touched an Okinawa beach.

Ironically, on L-day the division which wasn't even scheduled to land took the heaviest casualties: the 2d MarDiv feinting a landing on the south beaches. Transport *Hinsdale* and two LST's—all carrying personnel of the 3d Battalion, 2d Marines—were hit by the suicide bombers.[13]

Nor was that all that was ironical on that Easter Sunday. Resistance to the landing—III Amphibious Corps on the left, XXIV Corps on the right—had been anticipated as "most fanatical." Who could expect anything else? But the Japanese let the Americans get ashore. Before dark 50,000 of them were firmly installed on Okinawa on a beachhead 4,000 to 5,000 yards deep.[14]

---

[12] *Okinawa*, p 64. According to CinCPac, Analysis of Air Operations (Okinawa), p 10, the total fast-carrier sorties in all areas from 23–29 March amounted to 7,166.

[13] Richard W. Johnston, *Follow Me!* (2d MarDiv history), p 263.

[14] King, *U.S. Navy at War*, p 179.

TAF Sets Up

Yontan and Kadena airfields, which were the immediate objectives of the landing forces, were in American hands by 1230 of L-day. They had fallen, not after the hard battle that was anticipated, but with barely a shot fired in their defense. To the soldiers and marines who captured the airfields it seemed that the Japanese had gone mad, for was it not true that the U.S. Army and Navy were invincible once they had secured bases from which to ply their overwhelming aerial might? Who should know this better than the Japanese, with the war nine-tenths over?

Engineers started immediately to work on the fields, which had not been damaged badly by any preinvasion barrage. On 2 April the first Marine planes, OY "grasshoppers" of VMO-2, which needed only 500 feet of runway, flew off the CVE's and soon these artillery spotters had set up shop in force on Yontan, having been joined by VMO-3 and VMO-6. By 3 April all three squadrons were operating, and within eight days VMO-3 alone was working for 11 Marine and Army artillery battalions.[15] VMO-7 arrived in May, having sailed part of the way (from San Diego to Pearl) in the British CVE HMS *Ranee*. VMO-7 began operations on Okinawa 1 June under III PhibCorps control, and evacuated 369 wounded. It flew 300 combat flights without losing any pilots and had only one plane holed by AA.

Having been handed an operating base on a platter, General Mulcahy went ashore on 2 April with his chief of staff, Colonel Bernard A. Bridget USA, and other staff officers. They set up a CP between Yontan and Kadena, which are three miles apart. From *Allendale* General Wallace and his ADC staff went ashore and started digging in nearby.

General quarters sounded three times during this Love plus 1 day. One of the Marine squadrons (VMF(N)-543), standing offshore in AKA *Achernar*, took its first casualties when a *kamikaze* crashed into its ship and wounded five men. Twenty officers and men of the Squadron received commendations for helping put out the fire. Next day *LST 599*, with 30 officers and 169 enlisted men of VMF-322 on board, was smacked by another suicide plane and nothing was saved—lost were 424 tons of vehicles and cargo and all the gear of the marines; seven men were wounded.[16] On 6 April 75 men of MAG-43 also lost *their* gear when their landing boat was rammed by another craft.

While Kadena and Yontan were being made serviceable, all Marine aviation personnel were heavily engaged in camp construction, which was stopped only during bombing and strafing attacks. These attacks proved to be less dangerous than intense AA fire from our ships offshore—on 6 April at least 4 soldiers were killed by it and 34 wounded; several marines were also hit, including Colonel Raymond Scollin, prospective commander of Kadena airfield, whose thigh was penetrated by a 20-mm. shell that didn't explode.

The airfields were not quite ready when the Japanese launched their

---

[15] All three squadrons claimed to be the first to land "on Japanese soil."

[16] VMF-322 war diary, April 1945; CNO, *Capture of Okinawa*, pp 7–27.

suicide mission of 355 planes on 6–7 April, and the Marines' share of that great slaughter was claimed by the four squadrons on board the fast carriers *Bennington* and *Bunker Hill*.[17]

On the afternoon of 7 April, about the time TF 58 planes were sinking the giant *Yamato* 260 miles to the north and the two-day assault was petering out, a lone *kamikaze* charged toward the ships offshore. It happened at this moment that the Corsairs of Colonel Munn's MAG-31 were being catapulted from the CVE's *Sitkoh Bay* and *Breton* for the first landings on Yontan. The Lily was spotted ten miles out, flying at 500 feet straight for the carriers. Two CAP divisions of four planes each, covering the launching of the planes, started charging for the vandal. Five Corsair pilots of VMF-311 caught up and started stitching 20-mm. shells into both engines, nose and fuselage. It was the first time these guns were fired in combat from the F4U-4C. The enemy plane caught fire, but its pilot unwaveringly held his collision course on the fragile little *Sitkoh Bay*, whose hour seemed to have struck. Only 50 yards from its target the Lily's right wing fell off and there was a great splash, and all on board *Sitkoh Bay* heaved a sigh of relief that could be heard back in Guam.

The squadrons of MAG-31 (VMF's 224, 311, 441 and VMF(N)-542) proceeded with the landing and started operating from Yontan immediately with 80 planes available of the 109 assigned. A 12-plane CAP was maintained from 1750 until dark.

On the same day the Air Defense Control Center ("Handyman") went on the air, operating from three amphibian tractors (amtracs) specially equipped with power and communications gear and even a plotting room. This expedient lasted until more commodious quarters were ready 19 April.

Next day (8 April) six Corsairs of VMF-224 caught three would-be suicide planes 40 miles northwest of Yontan which were attacking destroyers on the radar-warning picket line. This time the pickets, which had taken a terrible beating in the first big suicide attack (and would take many another), were spared. The marines splashed all three *kamikazes*.[18]

The 9 April operations resulted in one of the heaviest day's losses of the campaign. Early in the evening ships offshore generated heavy smoke which densely covered Yontan. Three planes of a returning CAP crashed in attempting to land, resulting in one pilot fatality. A fourth plane made a water landing and the pilot was picked up. Four more planes were lost in weather.

Kadena airfield was adjudged ready for its first planes on 9 April, and Colonel Dickey's MAG-33 began tactical operations immediately—VMF-312, VMF-322, VMF-323, and VMF(N)-543.

Hard luck dogged TAF constantly before operations could get well under way. One plane failed to return from CAP on 10 April, and next day a dawn-

---

[17] See p 364.

[18] There were ten organized suicide attacks—of 45 to 355 planes, total 1,465—but additional missions were flown almost every day, such as this one of 8 April. Altogether 185 such additional sorties were flown from Kyushu, 250 from Formosa. (USSBS, *Japanese Air Power*, p 23.)

patrol Corsair hit a soft spot in the Kadena runway and smashed into a parked plane, destroying both aircraft and damaging three others while killing 2 officers and 1 enlisted man. That afternoon a C-47 of the Army's 9th Troop Carrier Squadron, spraying DDT, struck a telegraph pole and crashed in the TAF area, killing Lieut. Commander Thomas T. Flaherty (MC) USN, the 2d MAW senior medical officer who had served with Marine aviation since the Solomons, 4 Army Air Forces officers and 1 enlisted man.[19]

The Second and Third Kamikaze Attacks

The first *kamikaze* attack, 6–7 April, was the biggest. But the second, 12–13 April, was heavy enough—125 navy planes and 60 army, of which 17 managed to get through and hit American craft, most of them the radar picket ships which had to stand out from 20–100 miles in front of Okinawa and take it. DD *Mannert L. Abele* and *LCS 33* were sunk—the former by a double hit: a conventional plane and a *baka* bomb.[20]

Most of the suicide planes again were shot down by the Fast Carrier Task Force, including 51 by marines on *Bennington* and *Bunker Hill*.[21] But the land-based planes also began to pay off. The Japanese recognized the threat of the land-based planes and started working over Kadena airfield early, one plane dropping two bombs at 0356; a third plane dropped two more bombs soon thereafter. Enemy artillery lobbed a few shells toward Yontan, less effectively. Five Corsairs were damaged by bombing and strafing; ten gasoline drums were set afire by 40-mm. fire from ships offshore to add to the diversified excitement. At 0530 31 Corsairs were scrambled.

On this day the Kadena-based planes, still struggling with mud, accounted for 16 enemy planes between 0530 and 1915, half of them on a CAP interception at 1430 by VMF-312 (in its first combat), led by Captain Dan H. Johnson who personally was credited with three Zekes.

Reports "do not tend to indicate that the flyers were top-flight fighter pilots," Fighter Command noted with pleasure.[22] The suicide pilots didn't even attempt evasive action—if they had ever learned it.

But Friday the 13th brought tragedy to the Okinawa flyers, as to the *Bennington* pilots.[23] A pilot of VMF-323, taking off on the dawn CAP from Kadena, veered and crashed into four other F4U's. When the planes caught

---

[19] 9th TCS unit historical summary, April 1945, p 2.

[20] *Baka* is the Americans' derisive term, meaning "foolish" in Japanese; the Japanese called this bomb *Sakura* ("cherry blossom"). It was a rocket-driven projectile, manned by a suicide pilot, which was carried under the belly of a twin-engined bomber—Betty or Lily—until launched within sight of the target. Very few were successful. Invented about August 1944 and named by a Navy petty officer, it was unknown to the Americans until several were captured at Yontan. (USSBS, *Interrogations,* Vol I, p 62.)

[21] See p 365.

[22] Fighter Command Intelligence Section Analysis, 12 April 1945, p 2.

[23] See p 365.

fire .50-caliber ammunition began to explode. Before it was over two lieutenants and a master sergeant of VMF-222 and a corpsman of 323 were dead or mortally wounded. Eight planes were damaged, five of them beyond repair.[24]

Two days after the big suicide mission of 12–13 April the *kamikazes* were back again in force. This time there were not quite so many (165 as against 185) but again it was a very desperate slugging match: planes and ships' AA against enemies determined to blast themselves to Japanese heaven and the Americans out of the Western Pacific. The suiciders began seeping through on the 15th; late in the afternoon a nine-plane CAP from VMF-323 ran into several singles and doubles among the *kamikazes* and shot down six of them. Lieut. Frederick F. Zehring destroyed one of these by chasing it into a hillside, but he went so low to get it during his pull-out that he flew into the same terrain and was also killed.

By this time the Kerama Retto anchorage was filled with broken and slashed ships, mostly the little ships that acted as vital radar pickets to give warning of the suiciders' approaching from the north. Kerama Retto is graphically described by a destroyer communications officer:

> There was *Lindsey,* a destroyer minelayer, with her bow blown back across her bridge. . . . There was *Jeffers* in one berth, her decks all twisted and burned; there was *Zellers* in another. . . . On her fantail a burial crew prepared yesterday's shipmates for the trip to the cemetery . . . she had a hole the size of a garage where her wardroom used to be. . . . There was *Sterrett* with her starboard side caved in and her fuel tanks ruptured; *Gregory,* with her starboard side amidships burned out; *Stanly,* with her bow knocked out of alignment from a Baka bomb near miss; *Riddle, Whitehurst, Rall,* all with gaps in their top hamper. There were *Gladiator, Manlove, Hudson, Porterfield,* and *W. C. Wann,* each torn open by glancing blows from suicide planes.[25]

And so forth.

April 16 dawned bright and clear and full of *kamikazes.* All day Yontan and Kadena airfields were under intermittent artillery fire from a Japanese 150-mm. howitzer which killed 1 man and wounded 3 in the bivouac area at Kadena. But both MAG's flew CAP continuously all day, mostly over the radar picket ships, keeping watch while the 77th Division landed on the offshore island of Ie Shima. During the early morning four F4U's of VMF-311 shot down three Vals as they were making runs on the pickets. At 0900 six Corsairs of VMF-312 heard some DD radio cries: "Bogeys!" They got on station just in time to see the smoking fantail of a destroyer, but they managed to destroy the enemy plane—this one an orthodox bomber—along with one of its com-

---

[24] MAG-33 war diary, April 1945.
[25] Lieut. Commander Frank Manson in Karig, Harris and Manson, *Battle Report,* V, pp 404–405.

panions. The same CAP caught a Betty and a Val farther to the north and shot them down.

About the same time seven F4U's of VMF-323 caught two Hamps and two Jacks 60 miles northwest of Ie Shima. Both Hamps were shot down with the help of a Navy F6F but the Jacks (newest and fastest of the Japanese fighters) got away. The same patrol caught a Lily just after it bombed a destroyer—not all the Japanese were suicide planes, it only seemed that way—and shot it down on its second bombing run. Half an hour later this patrol downed a Kate only four miles west of Point Bolo (Zampa Misaki), well past the picket line. Lieut. Dewey Durnford of VMF-323 got the surprise of his life when the Helen he was shooting spawned a *baka* bomb. "It was carrying a papoose!" he yelled into his throat mike.[26]

The biggest haul of the day fell to VMF-441. At about 1000 a dozen of its planes responded to a distress call by a fighter-director ship 15 miles west of Point Uncle (Izena Shima). There they found 25 Bettys, Vals and Zekes, scattered from sea level to 6,000 feet.

"Marines to the rescue. Just like Hollywood," wrote Lieut. Commander Manson, on board *Laffey*, which had already been hit by five suiciders. A suicide plane knocked off one of *Laffey's* yardarms, and a Corsair, right behind him, took off one of the radars of the DD. Both planes crashed; the Corsair pilot[27] was rescued. The other Corsairs busily mixed it up with the suiciders. When it was over the VMF-441 pilots had shot down 17 planes, 4 of them by Lieut. William W. Eldridge, 3 apiece by Captain Floyd C. Kirkpatrick and Lieut. Selva E. McGinty. One Marine flyer was killed.

It was that way all day. In the evening both night-fighter squadrons, which had set up at their respective fields, claimed their first planes of the Okinawa campaign. Lieuts. Arthur J. Arceneaux and William W. Campbell of VMF(N)-542 each splashed a bogey 45 miles west of Point Bolo. Captain James A. Etheridge of VMF(N)-543 shot down a plane over Kadena as it prepared to bomb or strafe the field—though friendly AA put six holes into his plane while also shooting up another so badly it had to be struck off.[28]

The big shoot of 16 April credited the land-based marines with 38 planes, the *Bennington* and *Bunker Hill* Marine pilots with ten others. Navy pilots and AA brought the total to 270.[29] But not even the most expert shooting could stop all the *kamikazes*: DD *Pringle* was sunk and 11 other ships, including *Intrepid*, were hit.

---

[26] DeChant, *Devilbirds,* p 226.

[27] Apparently Lieut. Marion I. Ryan of VMF-441, but his Corsair's tail was severed by a plane from VMF-311, not by radar.

[28] On the following afternoon Lieut. Charles A. Engman survived through fantastic luck: he shot down a Sally at close range near the water; Engman's propeller hit the water and stopped, but the marine had enough momentum to pull up 50 feet and make a full-stall landing in the water from which an LCI rescued him after four hours.

[29] *The Navy's Air War,* p 288.

The *kamikazes* up to this point had sunk 14 U.S. ships and damaged several times that many.[30] Admiral Turner decided to double and quadruple the small ships on radar picket (to increase their firepower). Admiral Nimitz tried to borrow additional destroyers from General MacArthur, but got a turndown.[31]

Before L-day General Arnold had ordered General LeMay to "volunteer the tactical services of the Twentieth Air Force"[32] to knock out the Kyushu fields, and early in April LeMay had informed Nimitz that the mission had been accomplished, and he wanted to return to strategic bombing. But the B-29's were called back to hitting the *kamikaze* nests, and during the last two weeks of April LeMay's XXI Bomber Command continued to allot a high percentage of his sorties to Kyushu.[33] Altogether the B-29's flew 97 tactical missions and claimed to destroy 489 Japanese planes.[34]

Many more fighter planes—Marine and Army—were ordered up. After 16 April the worst of the *kamikaze* attacks was over, but there were plenty of bad days ahead.

---

[30] The Japanese Combined Fleet claimed 216 U.S. warships sunk or damaged by this date, including 21 carriers, 19 battleships, 16 battleships or heavy cruisers, 55 cruisers, etc., etc., and placed the cost to Japan at 1,000 suicide planes.

[31] Karig, Harris and Manson, *Battle Report*, V, p 412.

[32] Haugland, *The AAF Against Japan,* p 457.

[33] USSBS, *Campaigns,* p 365; *ONI Weekly,* p 1365.

[34] Haugland, *The AAF Against Japan,* p 458.

CHAPTER TWENTY SIX

Slugging It Out

THE UNCONTESTED LANDING didn't mean, as some optimists dared hope, that the Japanese troops wouldn't fight for Okinawa as savagely as they had fought all the way across the Pacific. Lieut. General Mitsuri Ushijima, who had arrived to command 32d Army at the time of the fall of the Marianas in summer 1944, guessed where the Americans would land on the island and approximately when they would land. He decided to concentrate his main defenses in the southernmost ten miles of Okinawa's 60, around Shuri Castle, palace of the ancient Okinawan kings, and let the invaders help themselves to a beachhead that included Yontan and Kadena airfields.

It didn't make much sense at first—if Ushijima had sacrificed a battalion of his 77,199 troops in the beach escarpments and tombs (which were hardly touched by preliminary naval gunfire),[1] he probably could have caused terrific casualties among the Americans; the beachhead would have been thrown into awesome confusion. This confusion certainly would have helped the *kamikazes,* which Ushijima depended on to weaken the attackers and cut off their supplies. He assumed from the beginning that he would lose the battle, anyway, and could only hope to inflict the maximum number of casualties.[2]

For Ushijima it must be said that he inflicted very grave casualties: 22,182 soldiers, 16,507 marines,[3] and 9,731 sailors. He did this by holing up in the strongly fortified positions around Shuri, which were exceeded in devilish shrewdness only by Kuribayashi's cave structures on Iwo Jima. Ushijima built into the hills: his caves, escarpments, blockhouses and pillboxes were connected by elaborate underground tunnels, artillery and mortars in the strongpoints

---

[1] Personal observation; the writer found only two damaged tombs in the entire 6th MarDiv beach area.

[2] *Okinawa,* p 93.

[3] These are figures for the Marine divisions and do not include Marine aviation casualties, which were 86 pilots and 11 crewmen killed in combat flights, plus casualties on the ground amounting to approximately 3 officers and 21 enlisted men killed and 8 officers and 148 enlisted men wounded. They include personnel hit by bombing and shelling, in the airborne landing on Yontan 24 May, and in the ambush of AWS men near the northern tip of Okinawa. The figure of 13 killed, 27 missing and 99 wounded in the whole TAF, as given in *Okinawa,* is only about half the total suffered by TAF marines alone. Marine casualties on board CV's and CVE's during the Okinawa period are not included in this compilation.

were cleverly integrated and mutually supporting.[4] The reverse slopes, as well as the forward, were fortified.

Initial Close Support

The nature of Okinawa's defenses—caves, reverse slopes, clever camouflage —provided targets for far more close air support than any other island in the Pacific. During the early fighting, which began in earnest as the XXIV Corps banged against the Shuri defenses 9 April, most close support was flown from the carriers—from 21 March to 30 April TF 58 attacked targets on Okinawa every day except 7 April, when the *Yamato* force caught all the attention; of the fast carriers' 24,393 sorties during this period, 10,711 were classed as "sweep and strike" against Okinawa and other islands to the north. Likewise, the 18 CVE's offshore flew in the same period 9,361 "sweep and strike" sorties, most of them against targets on Okinawa, out of its total of 18,133.[5] Only about one fifth of the sweeping and striking was "called" missions in direct support of front-line troops.

As soon as the LFASCU's could be established ashore they were directed by ComASCU to take over from shipboard units the control of all planes rendering support of ground troops. LFASCU 1 (Colonel Kenneth H. Weir) was set up near Geiger's III PhibCorps CP to support the marines of that corps, and all its nets were manned by 9 April by the unit's 22 officers and 65 men.[6] LFASCU 2 (Lieut. Colonel Kenneth D. Kerby) began operations with the soldiers of the XXIV Corps on 8 April, and controlled 108 aircraft on the first afternoon. LFASCU 3 (Colonel Avery R. Kier) was the co-ordinating agency attached to Tenth Army for all close-support aircraft activity and was in effect the forward headquarters of Colonel Megee, boss of all the LFASCU's, who reported direct to Admiral Pride on board *Eldorado*.[7]

Because of their later arrival, their devotion to the *kamikaze* menace, and the relatively small number of planes engaged, the Marine land-based flyers flew only 704 ground-support sorties between 7 April and 3 May (of their total of 4,841). Of these support sorties, Major Allan L. Feldmeier's VMTB-232, which arrived 22 April and began operating from Kadena three days later, flew 132.

The first TAF planes in support of ground troops were fighter bombers which flew two missions on 13 April totaling 36 sorties. They worked over Japanese artillery using bombs and rockets with "highly satisfactory results." Next day, when six missions of 95 sorties were flown against a bridge, fortified

---

[4] *Okinawa*, p 95.

[5] ComAirPac, Analysis of Air Operations, Okinawa Carrier Opns, March-June 1945, pp 5–6, 11–12, 26.

[6] All the enlisted men were marines; the officers included three Navy nonflyers. Of the 19 Marine officers, 11 were aviators.

[7] Admirals Turner and Pride departed Okinawa 17 May to plan the invasion of Japan. Colonel Megee, succeeded by Colonel Weir, followed them within the week, after indoctrinating Vice Admiral Hill's ComASCU.

buildings, and gun positions, ground observers described results as "excellent." On the 15th it was reported that "the ground troops like the results our Corsairs are giving and call for more and more."[8] They got more with 91 sorties hitting gun positions, a CP, bivouac area, and vehicles. Only one strike mission of seven sorties was flown on 16 April, when the marines had their hands full of the *kamikazes* over the picket ships, but the XXIV Corps reported that it destroyed a blockhouse.

On 18 April the Corsairs treated the Japanese to the first dose of napalm they had dropped—before Okinawa was secured the Marines alone seared its landscape with 152,000 gallons of the jellied gasoline.[9] Greatest virtue of napalm was its ability to burn off the ingenious Japanese camouflage so that concealed gun positions and fortifications were exposed to attack by other planes, by naval gunfire and artillery.

On 19 April, in a mighty effort to crack the Shuri Line, General Buckner employed 27 battalions of artillery (324 guns), naval gunfire from 6 BB's, 6 CA's and CL's, and 6 DD's and a total of 650 Navy and Marine planes (139 in a single mission). All this weight of metal preceded the three Army divisions' attack; 19,000 artillery shells were fired in 40 minutes. The fact that the attack failed—neither the 7th, 27th nor 96th Divisions managed to break through—was viewed as a gloomy harbinger. Those last ten miles were going to be slow and costly.

Marine aviation's contribution this day consisted almost entirely of direction rather than participation; Lieut. Colonel Kerby's LFASCU 2 controlled the 650 sorties; during one hour it directed 376 planes to strike seven targets simultaneously.[10] Only six close-support sorties were flown by land-based marines all day. The rest of the time the two MAG's flew combat air patrol, on which they saw no enemy. One group commander said that it seemed strange for planes off the carriers to come in for close-support missions, passing Marine planes flying out for CAP duty, when it was the Marines who were supposed to be the close-support experts. The only way he could figure it was that Admiral Turner must have thought the Marines were better shots; those *kamikazes* had the Admiral awfully worried.[11]

TAG on Okinawa

ATC and NATS transport planes began evacuating wounded from Okinawa to hospitals in the Marianas on 8 April. On the same day the AAF's 9th Troop

---

[8] TAF Periodic Report No 2, 20 April 1945.

[9] "Historical Summary of the ADC on Okinawa," p 21. Courtesy of Lieut. Colonel Radford C. West, ADC operations officer, who loaned us this document several months before he was killed in a crash in Korea, 8 February 1951.

[10] LFASCU 2 war diary, April 1945.

[11] The allocation of planes—land-based and carrier—was made each evening for the next day's missions—a certain number for defense, a certain number for attack. This allocation was made by Admiral Turner and his ASCU, and was based on Intelligence reports, chiefly radio intercepts.

Carrier Squadron of Colonel Ben Z. Redfield's TAG began operations when it was assigned for the DDT spraying of Okinawa and Ie Shima. Marines' first mission to Okinawa was ten days later when R5C's of VMR-252 made the first landings. Regular hauls were instituted on that date. VMR-353 made its first trip on 19 April, VMR-253 on 21 April.

On 22 April three planes of VMR-952 flew in from Ulithi via Guam and Iwo, escorting 24 Avengers of VMTB-232 on the 1,810-mile flight. Throughout the battle TAG planes continued to support the operation, bringing in high-priority cargo, mail and passengers; the return flights usually carried out wounded.[12]

TAG Station No. 23 began operations on Okinawa 1 May with 2 officers and 8 enlisted marines.[13] It was set up in a Japanese hangar on Yontan, an old concrete building which housed only one plane. During the battle the transports escorted more than 400 fighter planes on the 1,450-mile flight from Guam via Iwo, carrying in addition the equipment and ground personnel of these units.[14]

At the end of the Okinawa battle TAG could view its wartime record with justifiable pride. No complete figures are available for TAG's last five months of operation, but during the 16 months between 15 November 1943 and 15 March 1945 the airline hauled 115,592 passengers and 29,085 tons of freight and mail. Considering that a high proportion of the flights were from airfields recently captured from the enemy—and many landings and take-offs were actually made under fire—it is more than remarkable that TAG was able to fly over 200,000,000 passenger miles in 21 months without the loss or injury of a single passenger.

Again the Kamikazes

For a few days it seemed that the vicious air attacks were dwindling; on 17 April one Japanese plane was shot down, and next day only two, and on the 19th none whatsoever. The enemy planes were more active at night: on the 20th they deposited a few small bombs in the TAF area, killing 1 officer and 7 men, wounding 3 officers and 13 men,[15] including nearly all of the cooks and messmen in 2d MAW headquarters. Enemy planes were over Yontan next evening from 2100 to 2300, but only one dropped bombs, which wounded one pilot in addition to three enlisted men of an AA battery.

---

[12] On at least one occasion (29 May) VMR-953 flew into Okinawa, carrying five plane-loads of high-priority radio and radar gear. The Squadron, stationed at Ewa, was not a part of TAG.

[13] As the war rolled forward TAG stations in the rear areas were taken over by NATS. By the time of the Okinawa invasion TAG was operating stations only at Saipan, Tinian, Guam, Ulithi, Peleliu and Iwo. Those at Guam, Peleliu and Ulithi were manned by marines, the rest by soldiers.

[14] Letter Captain Robert H. Pease USMCR to Marine Corps Aviation History Board, 1 August 1949.

[15] TAF Periodic Report No 3. Recapitulation of figures in 2d MAW war diary and those in historical summary of ADC totals 27.

April 22 was a good day for the Marine aviators, although no big, organized *kamikaze* attack took place.[16] That day CAP was increased to 32 planes, and 12 additional Corsairs were held on ground alert. Nothing happened all day, but the dusk CAP was vectored at about 1800 to the radar picket line, where 80 Japanese planes were giving the little ships hell. During the half-hour battle which ensued the marines shot down 33¾ enemy planes (the fraction occurs because some planes were shared with Navy pilots, who got the remainder of the 54 splashed). Major Jefferson D. Dorroh, executive officer of VMF-323, burned 5 planes and exploded a sixth, all within 20 minutes. Major George C. Axtell Jr., the Squadron's skipper, shot down 5 planes within 15 minutes. Twenty-one-year-old Lieut. Jerry J. O'Keefe also shot down 5 planes, one of which tried to ram him after it caught fire. The Val swerved off and plunged into the sea when he was only 50 feet from O'Keefe.[17] Pilots of VMF's 224 and 441 destroyed 5 and 3 of the enemy, respectively.

Minesweeper *Swallow* and one LCS were sunk and three other ships were damaged. General Buckner sent a warm message of congratulations to 2d MAW for its pilots' part in saving many other ships.

There was a five-day lull. Then the *kamikaze* attack of 27–28 April brought 115 suicide planes against the shipping at Okinawa, escorted by an undetermined number of orthodox aircraft. Beginning at 1430 on the 27th and continuing for 11 hours, 74 were claimed destroyed by Navy carrier planes, 30 more by ships' AA, mostly at night; the Marines' share was only a Kate and a Tony northwest of the base. The 28th was another day of vicious, slashing attack by the determined suiciders. At 1600 the airborne CAP plus 36 other Corsairs were vectored 40 miles northwest of Okinawa to intercept the oncoming Japanese.

The fight lasted until dark. When it was over the fighters from Yontan and Kadena had been credited with destroying 35½ planes. Of the five squadrons participating, Axtell's VMF-323 again scored highest with 14½. VMF-311 was credited with 13. The Fast Carrier Task Force also intercepted some of the enemy raiders, and 14 of the 33 claimed by that force were credited to VMF-221 on board *Bunker Hill*. More than a third of the 137 enemy planes claimed on the 28th were to the Marines' credit. General Buckner sent his thanks to Mulcahy for "decontaminating the atmosphere and turning 35 more Jap aviators over to the tender mercies of the attraction of gravity." The CG of TAF in turn messaged General Wallace: "Not only brilliant work by fighter pilots but excellent command control and most efficient reservicing by ground personnel were admiration and inspiration to all."

---

[16] Besides the ten big suicide attacks (total 1,465 sorties), others were flown sporadically which amounted to 185 sorties from the north and 250 from Formosa bases. This total of 1,900 suicide attacks marked the majority of the 3,000-plus planes the Japanese lost in combat during the Okinawa campaign. During the period, total Japanese losses were 7,000 planes, including operational crashes. The 1,900 suicide planes hit 279 ships (14.7 per cent effective), as compared to 174 out of 650 in the Philippines (26.8 per cent). (USSBS, *Japanese Air Power*, pp 23–24, 34.)

[17] DeChant, *Devilbirds*, p 227.

At the end of April the two Marine groups could count 142 enemy aircraft shot down. Day CAP sorties amounted to 3,300, night fighter 221 (8 kills). Close-support sorties amounted to only 609. Four Marine pilots had been killed in action, 9 others were missing. Six were killed in operational accidents.

Aircraft losses from all causes amounted to 48, about a fifth of the original complement. At the urging of Captain Clyde W. Smith USN, the naval air base matériel officer, the pipeline flow of replacement planes was increased by one third. This was one factor in keeping all squadrons operating more planes than their authorized complement called for; another factor was the willingness of the overworked ground crews of both groups.

During April the Yontan–Kadena area was bombed and shelled almost every night, and it was remarkable that only 3 marines were killed and 26 wounded. Three Corsairs and TBM's were destroyed and five others damaged. Sometimes these attacks consisted of a single Zeke buzzing around killing sleep. At other times the attacks were more than annoying—on 28 April enemy planes dropped 18 bombs on Yontan and strafed both airfields intermittently from midnight to 0400; the next night a Japanese heavy artillery piece fired 28 shells at Kadena at 0015. In the two attacks one man was slightly wounded and three planes were damaged lightly.[18]

Mad May Begins

Japanese spokesmen in Tokyo tried to minimize the importance of Germany's collapse in the first week of May and Premier Suzuki (who had succeeded Koiso the week of the Okinawa landings) insisted that he was "determined to fight through this war with all I have." This in spite of the fact that America and Britain could now transfer the might of their No. 1 war to wipe up the tattered remnants of the No. 2 war; and in spite of the Soviet Union's ominous declaration in April that her neutrality agreement with Japan had "lost its significance." (Actually, Stalin had already agreed at Yalta in February that the Soviet Union would enter the war against Japan within three months of the collapse of Germany.)

While he was putting up a bold front Baron Suzuki was privately seeking a way to end the war, as the Emperor had discreetly instructed him to do. He ordered his chief cabinet secretary to make a study of Japan's fighting capabilities and whether they were sufficient to continue the war. In May came the report: No. Early that month two topics were before the Inner Cabinet: (1) Japan's inability to fight on, (2) the initiation of talks with the Soviet Union for intercession. But the fanatical Army leaders, despite the Americans on Okinawa, despite the ashes induced in Japan's cities by the B-29's, despite the loss of Japan's navy and merchant marine, insisted on the senseless continuation of the war.[19]

On Okinawa none of these maneuverings was known, and the war con-

---

[18] TAF Periodic Report No 4, 4 May 1945.
[19] USSBS, *Japan's Struggle to End the War*, pp 6–8.

tinued with a vengeance. On 1 May the 1st MarDiv was moved south to relieve the 27th Division and help break the Shuri Line, where even 16-inch naval shells crashing into the concrete and coral "sounded like ping-pong balls to those who were kept deep underground."[20]

The 6th MarDiv had cleaned up the northern two thirds of Okinawa (2,500 Japanese) at a cost of 236 killed, 1,061 wounded and 7 missing.[21] This division also started moving south 2 May and was in the line by 9 May, on which date LFASCU 1 commenced air support direction of III Amphibious Corps in the southern zone. Neither Marine division was employed in an amphibious landing on the shores of the last ten deadly miles; both were used as infantry divisions of the Army. Like the Army divisions, the Marines could only hammer at Ushijima's formidable cave defenses with "blowtorch and corkscrew"—armored flamethrowers and demolitions.[22]

General Buckner decided against a second landing and preferred to buck his way through the Japanese line. Admiral Nimitz concurred.

The second month began on a note of comedy. Three pilots of MAG-33 "proved the ability of the Marines to make a landing anywhere they choose, land or sea."[23] These three became lost while on 30,000-foot patrol on 1 May over northern Okinawa, and wandered several hundred miles to sea. When they were almost without fuel *Yorktown* picked up their distress calls and directed them to land on board, though none had ever made a carrier landing. One of them, after setting his Corsair down perfectly, asked: "What was that man doing waving those paddles back there?" "Brother," he was told, "he's the landing signal officer and he was giving you a wave-off."[24]

The All-Out Counterattack

On the night of 2 May, a hundred feet below Shuri Castle, the top brass among the Japanese defenders of Okinawa held a conference to decide what to do about the situation. Colonel Hiromichi Yahara, operations officer of the 32d Army, was for standing pat. Lieut. General Isamu Cho, chief of staff, argued hotly for an all-out counteroffensive against the relentless Americans. Under the warming influence of *sake* some intense bickering ensued, including invidious comparisons between the 62d and 24th Divisions. General Cho won out. Ushijima ordered a great offensive to take place at dawn 4 May.[25]

The offensive was well planned. Involved were tanks, artillery to the extent of 13,000 shells in preparation, suicide boats and even amphibious landings on both coasts. But the soldiers and marines broke it up, killing about 5,000 of

[20] *Okinawa*, p 255.

[21] Bevan G. Cass (Ed.), *History of the Sixth Marine Division*, p 75.

[22] *Okinawa*, p 256.

[23] Lieut. Robert L. Brandt USNR (Ed.), *Into the Wind* (USS *Yorktown* souvenir book), pp 49–50.

[24] *Ibid.*

[25] *Okinawa*, p 283.

Ushijima's men. Only at one point did the Japanese achieve a breakthrough, and that one didn't last long.

More successful was the *kamikaze* attack from Kyushu which was co-ordinated with the ground offensive. The first waves struck just before sundown of the 3d. Five of them crashed into destroyer *Aaron Ward,* causing 98 casualties. Three hit *Little,* another DD, and sank her. An LSM was also sunk, and four other ships were damaged. Thirty-six enemy planes were shot down by AA and by fighters, three of them by Yontan and Kadena marines.

D-day for Ushijima's big offensive began early. His artillery shelled Kadena at 0225, destroying four tents and wounding one man. At 0345 Captain William P. Mitchell's F6F was vectored 30 miles north of Okinawa, where he picked up a Zeke and, attacking beneath and from the rear, exploded it. At 0815 VMF-224's nine-plane CAP caught and destroyed 12 suiciders. Lieut. Collin H. Rushfeldt got three of them; Lieut. Thomas A. Gribbin II chased a suicide-bent Zeke through very intense AA fire and shot it down 50 feet from a destroyer (he got a Navy Cross for the act).

At least 70 Japanese planes were in this morning attack. VMF-312 found 8 Nates and 2 Vals making runs on ships near Aguni Shima, and shot down five of them.

But the biggest fight was between 36 Japanese planes and a 13-plane CAP from VMF-323. Captain W. G. G. Van Buskirk caught a Val diving on an LCM when it was only 200 feet off the water; after it had been shot down parts of the plane fell on the ship and started a fire on the fantail but failed to sink it. While steaming to the rescue of the stricken destroyer *Luce,* the destroyer-minelayer *Henry A. Wiley* shot down three enemy planes and two buzz bombs, and sent a message of regards for Lieut. Robert F. Muse: "Highest praise is due a Marine Corsair who followed his target into our heavy close-range fire in successfully pressing home his attack on an approaching 'Jill'." The two-plane section of Lieuts. Robert Wade and John W. Ruhsam remained on station and spotted a lone Val 25 miles north of Ie Shima which upon being chased led them to a group of 25 Nates and Vals loaded with bombs of about 500 pounds, milling around at 4,000 feet. These apparently were not suiciders because the Vals had rear-seat gunners. Ruhsam and Wade went to work on the slow planes and with a series of beam runs shot down four apiece. Wade got his last victim by chasing him into the water: neither pilot had more ammunition and both wished they had been more conservative with their bullets.

Lieut. Joseph V. Dillard was also credited with four planes on the same mission. VMF-323's total bag was 24¾, a record at Okinawa for a single squadron in one day. Half an hour later Lieut. Melvin S. Jarvis of VMF-312 had to fly through ack-ack over the area where destroyers *Luce* and *Morrison* had already been sunk and two DE's badly damaged, but he got through and splashed the Judy 200 feet short of a third destroyer. For this Jarvis was awarded a Navy Cross.

VMF-311 destroyed six planes during the same wild morning; at 1905 the same squadron had the dusk CAP which ran into a flock of suiciders. Eight

Tonys and three Dinahs were shot down, four by Lieut. William P. Brown, three by Lieut. Roland T. Hammer.

The Okinawa-based flyers shot down a total of 60¾ planes on 4 May, next to 12 April the highest score the marines made in a single day during the war. But the determination of the fanatical enemy paid off again: Four ships were sunk, the greatest number since the first big attack on 6 April; 14 were damaged, including cruiser *Birmingham* and CVE *Sangamon*. In two days the Navy crews suffered 682 casualties.[26] What the toll might have been but for the willingness of the pilots to take a chance on ack-ack is anybody's guess. General Buckner was comforted by the MAG-31 and -33 pilots' performance, he indicated in a message to Mulcahy: "Your boys do better every time the Japs visit us. Keep 'em falling."

Klingman's Way

No better example of the pilots' eagerness to get at the enemy could be offered than that of Lieut. Robert R. Klingman, a relatively old man of 28 who had served as an enlisted man in both the Navy and Marine Corps. On 10 May he was flying as wingman to Captain Kenneth L. Reusser in a division on the 0800 CAP over Ie Shima. From 10,000 feet they spotted the vapor trails of a Nick two-seater fighter on a photographic mission at 25,000 feet. The four-plane division climbed to investigate; one of the planes dropped out at 32,000 feet, another reached his ceiling at 36,000. Reusser and Klingman fired most of their ammunition to lighten their planes and climb higher. At 38,000, on the Nick's tail, they began closing.

Reusser used up the rest of his .50-caliber bullets to damage the enemy's wing and left engine. Klingman continued the chase, but was exasperated to find, when he was within 50 feet of the Nick, his guns had frozen. But Klingman pressed on and made a pass at the plane with his propeller, almost severing its rudder and sawing into the cockpit containing a rear gunner who was frantically banging his own frozen guns, trying to make them fire. A second pass cut the rudder completely off and damaged the right stabilizer. Klingman didn't believe he had enough gas to get back to Okinawa anyway, so he decided to stay around and finish the job. A third pass cut off the stabilizer and the Japanese plane went into a spin. Reusser and Klingman saw it lose both wings after it had fallen to 15,000 feet.

Klingman made a dead-stick landing at Kadena, with part of the prop missing; his wing, engine and fuselage full of holes from the rear-seat man's guns, and pieces of Nick in his cowling.[27] Flying again two days later, Klingman had some more adventure: his hydraulic system failed and he chose to bail out rather than attempt a crash landing on one wheel. A DE picked him up

---

[26] *Ibid.,* p 296.

[27] ADC daily intelligence summary, 11 May 1945; VMF-312 war diary, May 1945.

and Admiral Turner, who needed some luck, invited him to dinner on board *Eldorado.*

The Kamikaze Attack of 11 May

The Tenth Army had not driven as far south as it had planned before launching a general offensive, but Admiral Turner was growing restive over the heavy losses, particularly to the picket ships. So, General Buckner ordered for 11 May an attack all along the line,[28] which now extended approximately from the Asa River estuary across the island to Yonabaru—smack up against the main line of the Shuri defenses.

The Japanese chose the same day for another big suicide attack—the one that got *Bunker Hill.* This time there were more Army suiciders than Navy, 80 to 70.

The ADCC plotted 19 raids between midnight and 0420, 1 to 9 planes each, which dropped quantities of "window" to confuse the radar screens but withdrew after approaching within about ten miles. At 0530 Lieut. Edgar F. Gaudette Jr. of VMF(N)-543 was directed by GCI to a raider 60 miles northeast of Point Bolo. He picked up the bogey on his five-mile scope and closed to one mile, then to a quarter-mile, where he made visual contact. The F6F approached from beneath and directly astern, gave the Tony a burst which exploded it; the engine appeared to come off entirely.[29]

The Yontan and Kadena marines shot down 19 of the fanatics, most of them as they were attacking destroyers *Hadley* and *Evans.* Each destroyer was hit four times; *Evans* claimed to shoot down 15 of the planes, *Hadley* 23, in what *Evans's* doctor described as "a whirlwind of planes coming at us from every direction."[30]

Hadley's crew paid extraordinary tribute to the Marine aviators who did their best to ward off the *kamikazes* of 11 May. Her skipper, Commander Baron J. Mullaney, said:

> It can be recorded that the aviators who comprised the Combat Air Patrol assigned to the *Hadley* gave battle to the enemy that ranks with the highest tradition of our Navy's history. When the leader was asked to close and assist us, he replied, "I am out of ammunition but I'm sticking with you." He then proceeded to fly his plane at enemy planes attacking in attempts to head them off. Toward the end of the battle I witnessed one Marine pilot attempting to ride off a suicide diving plane. This plane hit us but not vitally. I am willing to take my ship to the shores of Japan if I could have these Marines with me.

---

[28] *Okinawa*, p 311.

[29] ADC daily intelligence summary, 12 May 1945.

[30] Lieut. James M. Smith (MC) USN, in Navy Department press release, 14 July 1945.

Lieut. J. T. Stevenson USN, fighter director on board *Hadley*, reported some additional details:

> Both Ruby 15[31] planes began picking off the stragglers at the begin-
> ning of the action, then opposed raid 4, estimated 20-30. When enemy
> planes closed, these two planes came in with them. One very outstanding
> feat by one of these two planes was that, though out of ammunition, he
> twice forced a suicide plane out of his dive on the ship and the third time
> forced him into such a poor position that the plane crashed through the
> rigging but missed the ship, going into the water close aboard. This was
> done while all guns on the ship were firing at the enemy plane. The high-
> est award for flying skill and cool courage is not too much for this pilot.
> His wingman stayed at masthead height in the flak and assisted in driving
> the planes away from the ship.[32]

---

[31] Call sign for Kadena-based Corsairs.

[32] Probably Lieuts. Edward C. Keeley (Ruby 26-3) and Lawrence N. Crawley (Ruby 26-2) of VMF-323, who shot down four planes apiece at 0830. All eight of their planes were "on the deck" except one Tojo, which would make them logical candidates for the accolade, but if they are the pilots either they or the intelligence officer who took down their story are simply un-American in their understatement: "Friendly AA was encountered. Mission of all enemy aircraft was apparently to attack shipping."

CHAPTER TWENTY-SEVEN

Okinawa Secured

THE ATTACK ON THE Shuri Line which began on 11 May did not break the enemy's back, but it cut off another inch of his tail almost every day. The going was slow—Tenth Army gained an average of 133 yards a day between 8 April and 31 May[1]—but the southward pressure was steady all along the line, 2 Marine divisions on the right, 2 Army divisions on the left (plus 1 in reserve). It was a question of how long it would take to excavate and kill all the Japanese, and how many U.S. casualties would be required before the job was done.

Despite the lack of sensational developments on the ground, 11 May can be considered a milestone in the battle for Okinawa. For the divisions it meant the battle was half over—41 days down, 41 to go—with 40,000 casualties divided in the same ratio. In the period immediately following 11 May many more aircraft (including the Army's) arrived to base on the fields newly completed by the Army engineers and Seabees. The *kamikazes*, while refusing to lie down and knock off their peculiarly Oriental antics, became less of a threat after the arrival of more planes. TAF was able to furnish the ground troops a much greater volume of bombs, rockets and napalm.

On 17 May Kelly Turner left Okinawa in the hands of General Buckner and Vice Admiral Harry W. Hill. Turner got his fourth star and went back to plan the invasion of Kyushu (which was ordered by the JCS on 25 May, target date 1 November). Whenever this explosive, competent admiral went away, it was a good sign; a lot of the trouble was over.

Arrival of the First Marine CVE's

The escort carrier *Block Island*, bearing 8 F4U's, 8 F6F-5N's, 2 F6F-5P's and 12 TBM's of MCVG-1 (Lieut. Colonel John F. Dobbin) weighed anchor at Ulithi late in April and flew its first strike at 0635 on 10 May. This was a close-support job on southern Okinawa by four TBM's which attacked mortar and trench positions. A neutralizing mission to the south in the Sakishima Gunto,

---

[1] U.S. Military Academy, *The War With Japan*, Part 3 (January to August 1945), p 84.

halfway between Okinawa and Formosa, was also made this day when 8 TBM's with 4 F4U's and 4 F6F's were sent against Hirara and Nobara airfields on Miyako Jima—targets of opportunity including revetted planes, repair shops and storage areas. One TBM was lost, presumably to the spotty AA, in its last rocket run on Nobara, with Lieut. Douglas M. Herrin, Sergeant Joseph L. Butehorn and Staff Sergeant Edward T. Gunning aboard. Another TBM caught a medium shell in the landing gear and hydraulic system, and had to ditch alongside destroyer *Butler;* several other planes were damaged less severely by the AA.

This day's strikes were part of the attempt to block off the *kamikazes*—most of the suicide planes came from Kyushu, but others flew up from the south. The U.S. carriers alternated with British TF 57 in trying to seal off this route—British carrier planes hit Miyako and Ishigaka Islands on the 9th, 12th, 13th; the Americans on the 10th, 11th, 14th, 15th, and so on. Between Sakishima missions the *Block Island* planes flew TCAP's and close-support strikes—four or eight planes at a time—on Okinawa targets, including the fearsome caves in the Shuri area.

During their turn on 27 May the Marines lost their fighter squadron commander, Major Robert C. Maze of VMF-511, in a rocket attack on several small craft off the piers at Ishigaki Island. It was believed that the Corsair was hit by AA. It crashed in shallow water but no trace of plane or pilot was found after the war.[2] Two days later another TBM, with Lieut. Jack Marconi and Staff Sergeants Joe Frank Surovy and Ben Davis Cannan on board, had its port wing shot off while attacking barracks in Ishigaki town.

The second Marine CVE, *Gilbert Islands,* sortied from Ulithi 17 May with MCVG-2 (Lieut. Colonel William R. Campbell). On 21 May it joined Task Unit 52.1.1 and began operations against Sakishima Gunto. On 1 June *Gilbert Islands* joined *Block Island* in 32.1.3 and the two Marine carriers were at least in the same five-carrier group.[3]

Gilbert Islands had its first casualty in the combat area on 23 May when Lieut. Edgar T. Miller crashed into the sea ten miles astern of the carrier. On the same day another pilot went over the starboard side of the ship, taking a parked Corsair with him, but he was rescued within five minutes by destroyer *Helm.* The first loss to enemy action was the TBM of Lieut. Robert B. Cromwell, Staff Sergeant William Clay Boyd Jr. and Corporal Robert L. Wood, whose aircraft was hit and set afire on 3 June by the sharpshooting gunners at Ishigaki, during a run on the airfield. The plane got away and did not crash until it was ten miles beyond the target; Cromwell and Wood were rescued by a PBM Dumbo but Sergeant Boyd went down with the plane. *Gilbert Islands* flew 42

---

[2] *Block Island* action report; conversation with Major Maze's stepfather, Admiral Arthur W. Radford USN, 9 February 1951.

[3] On 28 May Admiral Halsey relieved Admiral Spruance, the Fifth Fleet became the Third Fleet and all designations beginning with 5 were changed to 3. The Japanese called Halsey and McCain our "second team." "They'll find out!" predicted MAG-31's intelligence officer.

sorties in close support on Naha and other targets during the last week in May, in company with Navy planes from other CVE's.

Two more carriers with Marine flyers got out to the Pacific at the end: *Cape Gloucester* and *Vella Gulf*. The former with MCVG-4 (Lieut. Colonel Donald Yost) departed Leyte Gulf 1 July and spent a few days covering minesweepers off the southern coast of Okinawa. On 1 August *Cape Gloucester* sortied from Okinawa with three other CVE's (*Fanshaw Bay, Makin Island, Lunga Point*) under the command of Rear Admiral Ernest W. Litch for an adventure off the coast of China, almost all the way up to Shanghai. On 4 August Lieut. Thomas W. Doyle shot down a Tabby over the East China Sea, and next day Don Yost was credited with his eighth and final plane of the war: a Frances 73 miles west of TG 95.8. *Vella Gulf* (MCVG-3, Lieut. Colonel Royce W. Coln) arrived at Guam 20 July, and made two strikes on oft-socked Pagan and Rota during the next week. It arrived off Okinawa 9 August, the day the second atomic bomb was dropped, and proceeded on to Japan for the occupation.

The four Marine carriers were on paper as CarDiv 27 (Rear Admiral Dixwell Ketcham), formed at San Diego 21 May, but they never operated as a unit. The close support of amphibious landings for which the project was intended never functioned, and the CVE's never supported a U.S. landing. (They did have a brief fling at supporting Australian soldiers.)[4]

The CVE's were badly used during their brief taste of the Pacific war. The airfields of Sakishima might better have been left to less-specialized aviators. For only a few days were the CVE marines allowed to do any bombing on Okinawa.[5]

The reason for this switch is not difficult to find. The boss of all the escort carriers at Okinawa, Rear Admiral Calvin T. Durgin, frowned upon the idea of the Marine specialization which had been agreed upon:

> . . . In this connection it must be remembered that CVEG and VC squadrons are similarly specially trained. The advent of Marine Air Groups in CVE's should not be permitted to complicate the support carrier picture any more than is necessary. . . . Marine Air Groups should be and probably are as flexible as Navy squadrons and groups, and should remain so, and should expect no preferential treatment. To assign all Marine squadrons to direct support work would probably work to the detriment of morale of the Navy groups and squadrons and this command sees at the present writing no reason for such assignments and has no intention of allowing it to occur.[6]

The core of this argument is reminiscent of nothing so much as the Army's thesis that "anybody can do amphibious operations." In postwar planning the

---

[4] See p 416.

[5] Eight days for *Block Island,* five for *Gilbert Islands.*

[6] First endorsement of ComCarDiv 22 confidential letter 0215 20 July 1945 to CominCh by ComTG 32.1 (Ex), 27 September 1945.

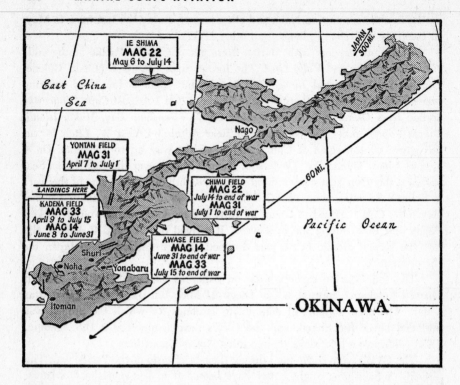

Admiral was overruled, and carrier-based Marine flyers continued to concentrate on close support of Fleet Marine Force troops, with whom they were *en rapport* to an extent never achieved by the Navy flyers who had plenty else to think about.

Planning for the Kyushu invasion (OLYMPIC) contemplated eight Marine CVE's rendering close support. Considering Japanese preparations for repelling the invasion, it is fortunate that the operation became unnecessary. The Marine-CVE theory was a good one, as was proved in Korea in 1950–51, but it was put into practice too late to have much effect in World War II.

MAG-22 and Army Aviators Arrive

TAF grew very rapidly beginning the middle week of May, with the opening of the first two strips on Ie Shima, where the Army engineers had been slowed by mines that caused some casualties.[7] AWS-1 had landed on 21 April and was operating its radars at their permanent sites by the end of the month.

Next to arrive at Ie Shima was the 318th Fighter Group of four squadrons, commanded by Colonel Lewis M. Sanders USA, who had been a second

---

[7] Howard and Whitley, *One Damned Island After Another*, p 359; Bureau of Yards and Docks, *Building the Navy's Bases in World War II*, Vol II, pp 397–411. The latter (p 403) puts the total number of Army and Navy construction troops on Okinawa at 95,000; the plans called for facilities for 4,000 aircraft.

lieutenant on Oahu when the Japanese struck Pearl Harbor. The Group had
spent the war, along with the rest of the Seventh Air Force and the 4th MAW,
in the backwash of the Central Pacific and had claimed to shoot down only 48
planes in 40 months of war.[8] Its three squadrons of P-47 high-altitude fighters
arrived 14–15 May, its P-61 Black Widow night-fighter squadron a month later.

Colonel Daniel W. Torrey Jr.'s MAG-22 ground echelon began arriving
at Ie Shima 6 May; the planes of its three day-fighter squadrons (VMF's 113,
314 and 422) came along from Engebi beginning 21 May.[9] Its night-fighter
squadron, Lieut. Colonel Marion Magruder's VMF(N)-533 arrived at Yontan
10 May and did not join its parent on Ie until 15 June. The Group's torpedo-
bomber squadron, VMTB-131, flew in 29 May (after being weathered in for a
week at Iwo) and began antisubmarine operations.

Like the AAF group, MAG-22 had spent long months in the Pacific doldrums. It remained at Midway nearly two years after the battle—though its
squadrons were rotated—then had over a year at Engebi.

The arrival on Ie of more than 200 planes of these two groups coincided
with the departure of Admiral Turner. Responsibility for Okinawa's air defense
was retained by Vice Admiral Hill, Turner's successor.

The War at Night

May 11 marked the mid-battle point for the infantry but, even if it is
considered to have ended 21 June (the day Okinawa was declared secure), the
flyers weren't half through. From L-day through 11 May TAF planes shot
down 234 enemy planes; from 11 May to 21 June 318 more were added. Moreover, the flyers had to fight on long after no more Japanese opposition remained
on the ground—85 more planes were downed between 21 June and the end
of the war, 15 August.

The land-based planes assumed a greater share of responsibility for defense,
however. The Fast Carrier Task Force departed the Okinawa area for strikes
on Japan and finally (10 June) retired to Leyte for replenishment. Some of the
CVE's, as we have seen, began to devote their efforts to stopping the Formosa-
based *kamikazes* at their Sakishima staging point. Consequently, much greater
land-based effort was devoted to close air support, with the arrival of many
more planes.

Thus, although the Japanese by 11 May had already flown 1,095 of a total
of 1,465 organized suicide sorties from Kyushu, the ADC was charged with the
responsibility of dealing largely alone with the rest of them and with an undetermined proportion of the 435 other suicide planes which either were not in
the big organized drives or which flew from Formosa bases.[10]

---

[8] Howard and Whitley, *One Damned Island After Another*, p 375. This history
of the Seventh Air Force frequently omits all mention of dates, which are supplied
from Fighter Command intelligence reports.

[9] Three F4U's of VMF-314 were lost in flight from Iwo 24 May, due to weather.

[10] USSBS, *Japanese Air Power*, pp 23, 65–69.

On 13 May, for the first time, TAF flew a strike mission off the island—16 F4U's of VMF-441, each carrying one 500-pound bomb and eight 5-inch rockets, struck the airfield and installations at Kikai Jima, almost halfway to Kyushu. These strikes at the islands to the north continued throughout the rest of the Okinawa campaign. They were not unanimously cheered; they caused, in fact, considerable argument between the air support controllers and ADC officers whose thoughts chiefly ran to the shooting down of enemy planes. "The request board at LFASCU 1 would be full of calls for close support," one officer recalled, "but the planes weren't there—they were way up north putting holes in runways."

On the night of 17 May Okinawa-based fighters heckled Japan proper for the first time. Two Army pilots flew their long-ranged P-47's all the way up to Kagoshima, fired rockets, then flew straight down the lit-up streets of Kanoya, strafing as they went. A more bizarre performance took place over Okinawa where another heckler, Lieut. Fred F. Folino of VMTB-232, bombed and strafed for two hours behind the enemy lines. A night-fighter control unit identified an enemy plane in the vicinity and gave Folino permission to attack it—unorthodox procedure for a torpedo bomber, night or day. He got in close enough and fired his remaining .50-caliber and four rockets but missed the bogey. Following it in a dive he let go with three more rockets. Two of them struck the root of the starboard wing of the bogey, causing a slight explosion. The night-fighter control unit confirmed the disappearance of the enemy aircraft. This shooting down of a plane at night with rockets was called by Pat Mulcahy "one of the most unique military achievements of this campaign," which indeed it was.

Such night raids by the Japanese were only a nuisance but, as a nuisance, first class.[11] Night-fighter defense had been disappointing, averaging only two kills per week during the first five weeks. Admiral Spruance, before turning over the fleet command, expressed to Admiral Halsey his dissatisfaction with "several features of the shore establishment . . . especially its radars."[12]

So long as the land-based radars failed to provide the required intercept information, the picket ships—not handicapped by land-mass interference—had to stand out front and bear the brunt of the suicide attacks (16 of the 19 original picket ships were hit). Therefore, Halsey went to Buckner, who, it seems, hadn't heard of the radar trouble,[13] and matters were soon straightened out. The chief trouble lay not in the radar's technical performance, but in the short range for voice communication at night over the land mass and in the siting of the sets—to which the high command had paid too little attention.

Admiral Spruance put his finger on this deficiency:

> It is recommended that in planning all future operations much greater emphasis be placed on securing outlying land areas or islands at the earliest

---

[11] From 6 April to 15 August Okinawa was bombed on 46 nights, in 64 raids (ADC historical summary, p 9).

[12] *Admiral Halsey's Story*, p 251.

[13] *Ibid.*

practicable date and installing adequate land-based radars and fighter director units thereon in order that vulnerable shipping will have to remain on exposed stations no longer than is absolutely necessary.[14]

There was no valid reason why the 77th Infantry Division or the 2d Mar-Div—which had been sent back to Saipan—could not have seized the outlying islands of Iheya and Aguni before 3 June and 9 June, respectively. It turned out that no enemy troops were there, anyway. A long-range early-warning radar set of AWS-1 was sent to Iheya and began operating 9 July; AWS-1 and AWS-8 sent detachments and equipment to Aguni 29 June and 3 July. If Iheya—20 miles north of Ie—had been able to start operating six weeks earlier, when Ie went on the air, it is a safe guess that many picket ships might have been spared loss or heavy damage. It is true that the 2d MarDiv was originally scheduled to capture Kikai Jima in July, but the failure to provide substitutes for the picket ships (which stood just off Iheya at Roger Peter One) was a costly omission.

What gave the night-fighting business a real boost was the arrival on 10 May of VMF(N)-533. Colonel Magruder had trained the Squadron ever since he assumed command in December 1943, and he worked it so hard on Engebi (with AWS-1) that nobody went "rock happy" during 360 days there—no mean achievement, considering that the Squadron never saw an enemy plane. Finally, at Okinawa the training and the flight discipline paid off.

The Squadron's first kill was scored at 0300 on 16 May, by Lieut. Robert M. Wilhide, after he was coached to a Betty at 12,500 feet. The Betty pilot never knew the F6F was after him until its guns opened up. A Frances was damaged by another pilot but got away.

Next night Lieut. Wilhide, whose twenty-third birthday was only five days away, made close contact on two enemy bombers approaching Ie Shima. He was warned that AA fire could be expected, but he refused to turn off. He was not heard from again,[15] and presumably was shot down by U.S. gunners.[16] His brother, Wilfred W. Wilhide, aged 22, of VMF-311, was killed three weeks later when his engine cut out and he crashed at sea while returning from a strike against the home islands of Japan.

The night of 18 May saw two pilots achieve the most spectacular score of the campaign: Between 2230 and 2300 Lieut. Robert Wellwood shot down three Bettys, to which he was coached by Lieut. Hugh Gallarneau (a one-time all-American football player at Stanford) at the fighter-director's radar controls; and Lieut. Edward LeFaivre downed two others under the tutelage of Lieut. Jack Wilson.

---

[14] CNO, Amphibious Operations: Capture of Okinawa, OpNav 84-P-0700, pp 3–24.

[15] "A History of MAG-22 in the Okinawa Campaign," p 3.

[16] Only one other Marine pilot is listed as a victim of friendly AA; another was shot down but survived. Many planes were damaged in this manner. Two Marine planes were shot down during the campaign by other Marine pilots.

Just how a director at a land-based radar guides a night fighter to his target is described by a Marine combat correspondent. Gallarneau notes Wellwood's and LeFaivre's planes on his radar scope. Then, on the top of the scope, another blip appears which shows no IFF. Gallarneau clicks his microphone button and talks to Wellwood:

"Hello, Muscles One Seven. I have a customer for you, starboard three-five-zero."

"One Seven to Poison. Three-five-zero. Roger and out."

"Hello, One Seven. Target range 25 at 11 o'clock and 17,000 feet indicating 160 m.p.h. Firewall, Poison, out!"

"She had altitude on me and was closing fast," Wellwood said. "When Hugh told me to firewall, I jammed the throttle forward and began to climb. We were closing fast . . . 10 miles . . . 7 miles. . . . I charged my guns again, just to make sure."

"Hello One Seven," called Gallarneau. "Target range 3 at 10 o'clock starboard two-two-zero. Target crossing. . . . Punch! [Get him!]"

Wellwood said, "When I went into my turn, I knew this was it. If Hugh had judged his vectors right and if I'd followed him as I should, I'd be coming right in on her tail. If either of us had doped off, there wouldn't be anything out there but empty sky. As I came out of my turn, I flipped my finder and peered at the little orange-colored gauge on my panel. There wasn't a blip (a tiny light on the radar screen) on it. Then I got her signal. It came swimming down from up in the left-hand corner of the screen and I yelled 'Contact' so loud Hugh could have heard me even without his radio.

"I watched the blip getting bigger and bigger and coming nearer and nearer. When I thought I was close enough, I started squinting through the windscreen out into the dark. Then I saw her . . . dead ahead and 300 feet above me . . . a vague black shape in the light of the moon. I nosed up to climb a little and swung to port to get on the dark side of the moon from her, and started closing in. The twin-engine Betty didn't know I was in the sky. At 300 feet I gave the trigger a short quick squeeze. At the wing-root, between the Jap's left engine and the fuselage, I saw the white sparks flickering where the armor-piercing incendiaries were going in . . . little glints of light . . . dancing along the wing . . . like the sparklers the kids play with on the Fourth of July.

"I gave the Betty another squirt . . . the port gas-tank blew up in a red glare . . . and her right wing was gone. She went down in a tight spin. I followed a bit. She hit the water and her bombs blew up."[17]

The improvement of night-fighter techniques was one of the notable achievements on Okinawa. The troublesome altitude vector was finally per-

[17] Lieut. Harold H. Martin, quoted in DeChant, *Devilbirds*, pp 234–235.

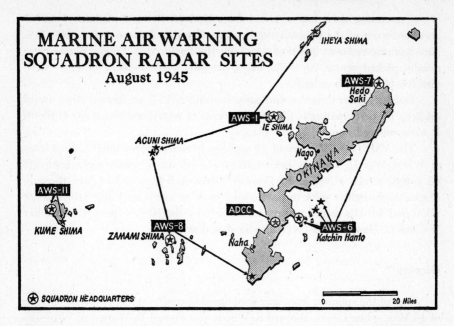

MARINE AIR WARNING
SQUADRON RADAR SITES
August 1945

fected to bring the night fighter within 500 feet of the bogey, from which point the pilot could make visual contact—and had to worry mostly about getting so close as to be splattered by his victim's disintegrating plane. Radar equipment of the AWS's was eventually established at 14 points on Okinawa and the outlying islands, and the fighter directors mastered the technique of leading the night-borne planes to their quarry.

On 30 June Bisson's MAG-43 group personnel amounted to 1,926 officers and men, over 1,500 of them in the AWS's, plus 505 in the attached Army units.[18]

Isolated on the extreme tips of Okinawa and the smaller islands, detachments of these air-warning units had to provide against attack by enemy stragglers. Frequently they were surprised by a few Japanese with rifles or grenades. On 4 June AWS-7 was faced with a task in the north of Okinawa that had little to do with operating radar: repulsing a counterlanding of 21 Japanese who had sailed 60 miles from the north in five small boats. The marines killed 9, captured 2; soldiers of the garrison force disposed of the rest. Two marines, a hospital corpsman and two Army officers of the same squadron were killed 24 June when the truck they were riding in was ambushed. On 30 June Private John F. Lenz killed a Japanese major at 30 paces who was prowling about MAG-43's new camp site on Okinawa's east coast.

Busiest of the squadrons were AWS-1 on Ie Shima, its long-range search detachment on Iheya, 7 on the northern tip of Okinawa and 8, which had

---

[18] As follows: Company B, 568th Air Warning Battalion, 191; Detachment 1, 305th Fighter Control Squadron, 40; 727th Signal Air Warning Company, 258; 5th Radar Calibration Detachment, 16. (MAG-43 war diary, June 1945.)

begun operating even before L-day from Kerama Retto. Squadrons 1 and 7 bore the brunt of the fighter direction; one day they had more than 600 U.S. planes on the radar at one time—tops for the Pacific war. Enemy planes were usually picked up at 70 to 80 miles; friendly planes—night or day—were directed at 50 to 75 miles.[19]

Besides fighter direction and early warning AWS-7 performed other useful missions by participating in 25 air-sea rescues of which one was made at night. It also vectored home 128 lost planes.

The VMF(N)-533 score of 35 apparently was a record for U.S. squadrons in World War II. Captain Robert Baird shot down 6 enemy night intruders (3 Bettys, a Jake, a Nell and a Frances) between 9 June and 14 July, the only Marine night-fighter pilot to be credited with as many as 5 kills (three other pilots had 4). His record was exceeded only by the Navy's Lieut. Commander William L. Henry of VF(N)-79, who shot down 7.

Giretsu[20]

One of the sporadic *kamikaze* flare-ups occurred in the later afternoon haze of 13 May, when Lieuts. Richard S. Wilcox and Forrest B. Warren of VMF-322 intercepted two Vals south of Kerama Retto, evidently on their way up from one of their nests on Formosa. These suiciders' target was destroyer *Bache,* which had already been damaged ten days earlier by one of their fellow desperadoes.

A destroyer shot down one of the Vals. Warren went after the other, following it through 2,000 yards of AA fire. He set it afire, but it spun crazily and hit *Bache* anyway. A 40-mm. shell knocked off Warren's wing-tip and he had to bail out. Five minutes later Wilcox intercepted a Zeke on suicide bent, and knocked it down.

"Admirable and courageous work . . ." messaged the destroyer's skipper, "please convey to these pilots the gratitude of the officers and men of the *Bache.*" Each was awarded a Navy Cross.[21]

Such suicidal stabs at the pickets occurred almost daily, but the Japanese saved up for two weeks before staging their seventh mass attack on 24–25 May. The attacks began shortly after 2000 of the 24th, as two planes of VMR-353 from Ie Shima were in the landing circle, and seven raids were staged in the next four hours. At 2110 an enemy plane dropped six bombs northeast of Yontan. Seven bombs were dropped north and west of MAG-31 headquarters at 2204. Two or three bogeys at a time were reported continuously.

At 2225 a Sally approached Yontan much lower than any others, and was

---

[19] Bisson interview, 1 April 1948.

[20] Rough translation: "act of heroism." Sources: MAG-31 Special Report on Enemy Action of 24–25 May, supplemented by conversation with Colonel Munn, 1 February 1951; *Okinawa,* pp 362–363.

[21] Board of Awards records; ACA report; *Bache* to CTF-51, 21 May; Fighter Command intelligence summary, 14 May 1945.

shot down by the AA protecting the field. About 2230 three more enemy aircraft, which were unmistakably and audaciously trying to land on Yontan, were shot down or crashed near the field—here was no ordinary *kamikaze*, but a *giretsu* which brought on the first airborne attack in the Central Pacific! MAG-31 personnel thought they could hear the Japanese screaming as the flaming aircraft passed over their quarters. At least two of the occupants survived the crash, still others may have been responsible for firing two small gas dumps east of the field. The two were shot near their crashed plane. Another of the enemy planes crashed south of the field, its wing shearing an AA mount so as to bury eight marines, two of whom suffocated.

A fifth plane belly-landed on the NE–SW runway about 250 feet from the tower. An estimated dozen Japanese soldiers survived and gave a practical demonstration of what a few determined men can accomplish.

Almost immediately demolition charges started destroying aircraft parked about the field. Three Corsairs, two Navy Privateers of Fleet Air Wing One and four transports were destroyed (including that of Major General James T. Moore, CG AirFMPac, who had flown in from Pearl on a special mission for Admiral Nimitz). Damaged were 29 other planes: 22 F4U's, 3 F6F's, 2 B-24's and 2 transports. Seventy thousand gallons of gasoline went up in flames.

The confusion which accompanied this weird gambit can hardly be imagined. Indiscriminate rifle and machine-gun fire laced the airfield and vicinity, probably accounting for most of the U.S. casualties—the tower duty officer, Lieut. Maynard C. Kelley of VMF(N)-533, died of wounds. Eighteen were wounded, including two enlisted men of the crash crew of MAG-31 who each had a leg blown off. Japanese hiding in a damaged R5C set off grenades which wounded four others of the 18.

The last Japanese was killed at 1255 on 25 May a quarter mile behind HqSq-31 as he tried to crawl from the road into the underbrush. In all, 69 Japanese bodies were counted and buried by the Seabees; none was taken prisoner. Some had committed suicide.

All in all, the Japanese could count their *giretsu* successful. They had destroyed 9 planes and damaged 29, at a cost of only 5. It can be assumed that not much concern was felt in Tokyo over the loss of 69 more men at this stage of the war.

Mastering the Mud

Shuri Castle finally fell to troops of the 1st MarDiv on 29 May, and two battalions pushed on south of Shuri. Very heavy rains rendered supply routes completely impassable, and it seemed for a time that the marines, critically low on supplies, might be without any food or ammunition.

Heavy clouds obscured the marines' location. But the front-line air liaison parties, plus the old reliable "torpeckers" saved the situation. Coaching the planes as they had so often coached them for air strikes, the ALP's brought the TBM's with packages of food and ammunition over the troops' position. These were dropped by parachute. Torpedo bombers were used because they were more accurate than C-47's.[22]

It was the same throughout the last week in May and the first week in June, when the U.S. troops, particularly the 1st MarDiv and 77th Infantry Division, had to be supplied by air. Major Feldmeier's VMTB-232, the pioneer TBM squadron on Okinawa, made most of the drops, totaling more than 600. Major Douglas A. Bangert's VMTB-131 made 163 drops in June.

Several times the TBM's had to rely on radar to hit their targets but it was estimated that 98 per cent of the packages were recovered by the ground troops, at a time when air drops frequently were the sole means of resupply.

Most of the drops were made between 22 May and 5 June, when 12 inches of rain fell on Okinawa.[23] An analysis of 327 sorties shows that 1,350 parachute loads carried 135 tons. Items: 512,873 rounds of ammunition, 9,034 hand grenades, 3,790 rounds of mortar shells, 22,429 rations, 3,810 gallons of water, 28 miles of telephone wire, a switchboard and field telephones, 325 batteries, and many other items.[24]

But for the air drops the whole momentum of the drive southward toward the Yaeju Dake escarpment, where General Ushijima holed up for the last time, might have been lost.[25]

The packing of parachutes and the packaging of supplies is a technique requiring as much skill as the dropping of the packaged goods through the clouds. This technique was skillfully demonstrated by the III Amphibious Corps Air Delivery Section (Lieut. Richard Sinclair). Total load packed: 334 short tons, 830 planeloads.

Major Feldmeier summarized the lessons in his report: the most important single factor is marking the target, and it is best marked by colored smoke; 200 feet is the best altitude; 110 to 120 knots the best speed; use planes in column, not formation; marker panels should be carried by every squad.

More Kamikazes

While the 24–25 May *giretsu* was going on, 23 enemy planes bombed the airfield at Ie Shima, causing 60 casualties.[26] During the night AA batteries claimed 16 planes over Ie, 11 over Okinawa. Pilots of VMF(N)-533 shot down five Bettys, Jakes and Sallys between 2105 and 2220, three of them by Lieut. Albert F. Dellamano. Lieut. Carl M. Davis of VMF(N)-543, based at Kadena, flew through friendly AA to splash a Betty at 2345.

The assault continued with unabated fury on the morning of the 25th. At 0730 four F4U's of VMF-312 splashed 12 out of 20 enemy planes which ap-

---

[22] *Okinawa*, p 409.

[23] *Ibid.*

[24] OpNav, *Marine Air Intelligence Bulletin*, August-September 1945, p 19.

[25] Headquarters USMC, *An Evaluation of Air Operations Affecting the U.S. Marine Corps in World War II*, p iii–99.

[26] The records do not show that any of those were marines.

peared singularly nonaggressive—the low state of training of *kamikazes* was becoming more and more evident. Fifteen minutes later VMF-422 scored the first kills for MAG-22: 6 of 12 enemy planes near Iheya Shima and Izena Shima.

At 0830 the Japanese planes—*kamikazes* and their escorts—were skimming in from all directions in an attempt to knock out the radar pickets and the ships just offshore. VMF-312 pilots knocked down 16 planes for the loss of 1: Captain Herbert J. Valentine got 5½, Lieut. William Farrell 4½. VMF-322, also from Kadena, shot down 8, of which Lieut. James E. Webster accounted for 3; VMF-323, which held its top scoring position throughout the Okinawa battle, also was credited with 8.

Of the 75 planes shot down by the U.S. fighters that morning, the marines scored 39, but the high-scoring group was the newly arrived AAF's 318th Group, whose long-range P-47's got first crack at the enemy, about 100 miles north of Okinawa. The Group began the morning with 0 and ended with 34, including 5 by Lieut. Richard H. Anderson USA.

Despite the valiant work of the Army and Marine pilots, the 165-plane suicide attack left 11 more U.S. ships sunk or crumpled and smoking—another was damaged in an Occidental manner by torpedo. Transport *Bates* and an LSM were sunk; 2 more transports, 3 DD's, 2 DE's and 2 minesweepers were damaged—all by *kamikazes.*

The next *kamikaze* attack came only two days later, and provided the longest single alert of the Okinawa campaign: 9 hours and 16 minutes. During 25 hours, beginning at 0730 on 27 May, the suiciders stabbed at the Okinawa ships with 56 separate raids of two to four planes each—a total estimated at 150.[27] Marine planes knocked down 32 in the two days; Army P-47's got 17 more. Ten ships were hit, including destroyer *Drexler,* which sank within two minutes. Six of the ships were hit at night, despite seven kills by night fighters. At the end of this period TAF could claim a total of 421 planes shot down.

After these raids there were no more organized *kamikaze* attacks which could mount as many as a hundred planes. Between 3 June and 7 June the total in sporadic suicide raids was 50. During this period the Marines shot down 52½ enemy planes, the Army 33 additional.

The last *kikusui* took place on 21–22 June, when 45 planes managed to sink a suicide-plane decoy and damage four other ships. The postmidnight hours of the 22d saw the Marine night fighters down 6 planes, 2 of them by Captain Baird.

But the most spectacular performance of the day was that of Lieut. John W. Leaper of VMF-314, who shot down two Bettys, one of which was mothering a *baka* bomb. Having finished this chore, and nursing a windshield shattered by a 12.7-mm. bullet, he looked up to find a Zeke diving from above, about ten o'clock. He fired his last ten rounds of ammunition at the Zeke, which took out after Leaper's wingman, Lieut. William L. Milne, who had just destroyed

---

[27] According to Japanese postwar records 110 planes—60 Navy, 50 Army—were in the *kamikaze* table of organization in these raids (USSBS, *Japanese Air Power,* p 23).

two planes in the melee. Leaper unhesitatingly climbed until he was just under the Zeke, and tried to saw off its tail with his propeller. He missed, climbed above the Japanese plane and on the second try ground his blade into the nose, forward of the cockpit. That did it, but almost did Leaper in. His Corsair's right pylon tank exploded, ripping off his right wing. Despite his plane's violent spin, Leaper managed to bail out, but split his parachute, broke two shroud lines and tore the dye marker off his Mae West. As if enough had not happened to him, Leaper saw another Zeke about to make a run on him, with six Corsairs chasing. Leaper collapsed his precarious parachute by yanking on the left shroud lines. He dropped like a bullet for 3,000 or 4,000 feet; then the chute reopened and he descended not too swiftly into the water. After an hour and a half *Cheyenne* picked him up.

The Close-Support Record

Close support was employed more efficiently in the 82-day Okinawa battle than in any other Central Pacific operation. Improved communications, better-trained personnel and more precise techniques enabled the aviators to bring their supporting weapons to bear in a manner that was generally—and often enthusiastically—praised by the ground commanders they were trying to help.

Between 1 April and 21 June a total of 14,244 "support sorties" was flown by carrier-based and land-based planes—4,970 for III PhibCorps' two divisions and 9,274 for the four divisions operating at various times under control of XXIV Corps.[28] A fourth of these came in the first ten days, before Colonel Megee's LFASCU's were set and before tough enemy opposition was met.

Once the LFASCU's were operating, they controlled a total of 10,506 close-support sorties up to and including 30 June—3,287 by LFASCU 1 for III PhibCorps and 7,219 by LFASCU 2.[29]

The weapons used:[30]

	LFASCU 1	*LFASCU 2*	*Total*
Bomb tonnage	1,229	3,496	4,725
Rocket (5-inch)	12,347	25,306	37,653
Napalm (tanks of)	472	644	1,116

Most of the true close support was controlled by Megee's units. A total of 6,908 sorties was directed by ASCU's from *Estes, Panamint, Teton* and *Mt.*

---

[28] III Amphibious Corps Action Report, Ryukyus Operation, Appendix 3 (Summary of Air Support); XXIV Corps Artillery Action Report, Ryukyus Operation, Annex C (Air Support).

[29] LFASCU 1 Action Reports of Okinawa Campaign, 1 April–30 June 1945; LFASCU 2 war diary, June 1945.

The LFASCU 1 score is lower because its corps was not so heavily engaged as XXIV during the early fighting. In the first five weeks (through 16 May) LFASCU 2 directed 5,963 sorties, compared to 879 for LFASCU 1; in the last six weeks the preponderance was the other way—2,409 to 1,256.

[30] OpNav, *Marine Air Intelligence Bulletin*, August-September 1945, pp 25–27.

McKinley before the LFASCU's got started and perhaps half of these might be classed as "close support" rather than simply "support."

But the application of close support was anything but a Marine monopoly. Probably as much as 60 per cent of the direct support on Okinawa was flown from the CV's and CVE's (which included a small proportion of Marine flyers).

Although close support on Okinawa was generally praised—it was "superior throughout," said Major General James L. Bradley, commanding the 96th Infantry Division—there were some criticisms. The most common: (1) planes not available, and (2) bad weather.[31] Sometimes flight groups reported on station with the wrong grid charts or with no charts whatsoever—adequate gridded charts frequently were not available and aerial photographs had to be relied upon. Over-all air co-ordinators of senior rank were not habitually appointed; co-ordination was usually left to flight leaders.

The 6th MarDiv reported bluntly: "The basic difference between air support as carried out in the Okinawa operation and that which is desired by this command is that instead of having the ASCU direct the strike group it is advocated that the ALP's be permitted to contact the airplane directly on the SAD net."

This was the system used so successfully in the Philippines, usually on one- or two-division fronts. It was possible to use it there or in northern Okinawa, where only the 6th MarDiv was involved. But, as explained later by Megee, "to have permitted each battalion air liaison party to control striking aircraft on a corps front of only ten miles, when many simultaneous air strikes were being run, would obviously have led only to pandemonium and grave hazard for all concerned. On the other hand, where conditions approximated those in the Philippines, i.e., battalion or regimental actions in an uncrowded area, actual control of aircraft was frequently delegated to the air liaison party."[32]

A study of 242 missions of the III PhibCorps on Okinawa showed that an average of 55 minutes elapsed from the time of the request for air support and the start of the attack.[33] Another study shows that only 37 per cent of 1,388 missions flown up to 17 May were the result of air liaison party requests.[34]

The great bugaboo of close support was, as always, casualties among friendly troops. Ten instances of faulty drops were recorded by the LFASCU's on Okinawa.[35] Two of these were due to hung bombs which caused two casualties on 17 April and one on 19 May.

---

[31] Of 850 missions requested of LFASCU 1, 370 were denied—109 for lack of aircraft, 104 because of weather. LFASCU 2 received 700 requests, accomplished 371 of them.

[32] Isely and Crowl, *The U.S. Marines and Amphibious War*, p 567.

[33] III Amphibious Corps Action Report, Ryukyus Operation, Appendix 3 (Summary of Air Support).

[34] CNO, Capture of Okinawa, pp 3–28.

[35] Headquarters USMC, *An Evaluation of Air Operations Affecting the U.S. Marine Corps in World War II*, pp iii–96, and DeChant, *Devilbirds*, p 242, erroneously report only three cases.

The others were reported as follows:

(1) On 18 April friendly aircraft rocketed a battalion CP 3,000 yards short of the target. (1 killed, 3 wounded.)

(2) 20 April. Bomb within 400 yards. (7 killed, 15 wounded.)

(3) 30 April. Three unidentified Corsairs killed 7, wounded 18 of our troops behind the lines.

(4) 11 May. Six to eight TBF's dropped bombs on 1st MarDiv troops. (No casualties.)

(5) 18 May. Bombs intended to support XXIV troops fell in 1st MarDiv lines, killing 1, wounding 1.

(6) 26 May. One "dilbert"[36] got out of assigned zone and strafed a plainly marked hospital unit in XXIV area, causing "several" casualties.

(7) LFASCU 1 reported on 29 May that TBM's wounded 10 men when three bombs were dropped and eight to ten rockets fired into friendly areas.

(8) The 1st Marines were hit on 8 June by five planes supporting XXIV Corps; number of casualties not reported.

Like artillery shorts, faulty bomb drops are likely to cause casualties in any battle, and it is remarkable that so few of our own troops were hit by our own bombs during 10,506 sorties controlled by LFASCU's 1 and 2. It is possible that there were other casualties before 17 April which are not in the LFASCU reports. It is known that one day early in April General Geiger was subjected to a strafing on Motobu Peninsula and took cover in a ditch while he said unprintable things about the U.S. plane overhead.

Mostly the troops liked the close support they got on Okinawa, and they asked for about twice as much as could be supplied. It must be admitted at the same time that the division histories are less enthusiastic about certain missions than the people who ran the missions.

A good example is a strike run for the 383d Infantry of the 96th Division. Eight TBM's from *Essex* were flown in to join four TBM's of VMTB-232 on 20 May for a special strike on Charlie Hill, which had already cost the regiment 300 casualties. It was particularly difficult because the bombs would have to be dropped in a reverse-slope pocket within 100 yards of friendly troops by planes flying *toward* the soldiers.

Captain James Nauss of VMTB-232 led the strike, which was made at an unbelievably low altitude—15 feet, according to the 96th Division's history:

He, the squadron leader, came in at a terrific speed. It appeared as though he would never come out of the dive. Observers behind the U.S. lines lost sight of the plane below the 200-foot crest of the hill. Then suddenly the plane came up out of nowhere with a terrific roar, climbing almost straight up. . . . The rest of the squadron dived on the hill, each loosing a bomb. . . . A second bomb run was made. Then the torpedo bombers

---

[36] Zany pilot.

made a second strike while the Corsairs strafed. . . . Not one plane over-shot its mark, which would have been disastrous to the awaiting dough-boys who, once the runs were over, advanced and seized the hill which had held up their progress.[37]

Essex, which furnished the eight visiting TBM's, was equally enthusiastic in its action report: "This strike was reported to have been the most successful in the campaign thus far . . . the closest, most hazardous mission yet attempted. . . . There were two ridges taken by ground troops immediately after comple-tion of the strike, with only two casualties."

In the face of these enthusiastic reports the 96th Division's history com-mented two years later: "Back came the infantry—and it was the same old story. . . . It had been a well-conceived and executed plan, but it just didn't work."[38] It did divert the Japanese troops' attention so that a nearby hill was captured. This story is cited as a warning to aviators that the long-suffering infantrymen are probably the world's premier cynics, rarely given to wishful thinking. It was a realization of this factor which prompted the Marine Corps in 1946 to reinstitute its ancient orders that would-be aviators must first serve two years as infantry officers—a scheme that works very well in peacetime but goes by the board when war forces a great expansion.

Nonetheless, General Hodge's soldiers, unaccustomed to the luxury of close air support, became insatiable in their demands; Megee said they ex-pected aviation to "dig the Japs out of caves and lay them out to be counted!"[39]

New Arrivals

On 11 June General Mulcahy was relieved by Major General Louis E. Woods, who set a record by commanding within a month all three Marine air wings in combat in the Pacific. Relieved on 12 May from the 4th at Kwaja-lein, he arrived 5 June at Bougainville to take over the 1st. After one day there he was ordered by Admiral Nimitz to command the 2d (and TAF) at Okinawa.

Louis Woods arrived in the midst of a period of reinforcement. As early as 26 March, MAG-14, based at Samar, had been alerted for the move to the Ryukyus[40] (to be based on Miyako in the Sakashima Group after its capture by the V Amphibious Corps). But it remained in the Philippines until after Admiral Halsey's visit to Okinawa in May. Halsey wanted to give his weary fast carriers a rest before they hit Japan again. So, he recommended that MAG-14, "which I knew was quite capable of taking over our job," be brought

---

[37] *The Gunto Graphic,* newspaper of XXIV Corps, quoted in VMTB-232 war diary, May 1945. TBM's were not capable of "terrific speed," but that's the way it seemed to the soldiers.

[38] Orlando R. Davidson, J. Carl Willems, and Joseph A. Kahl, *The Deadeyes,* p 154.

[39] Comment on a first draft of this chapter.

[40] ADC historical summary, p 12.

forward.[41] MAG-14 got its new F4U-4's 15 May and Colonel Edward A. Montgomery ordered a fortnight of familiarizing the pilots with the faster plane that had a four-bladed prop. The advance ground echelon was ashore at Kadena early in June, and the first flight of planes arrived 8 June, by way of Clark Field. Next day the Group flew its first CAP, and on 10 June Lieut. Douglas West shot down a Val, VMF-212's first kill since 15 February 1944. No more opposition was encountered until 21 June when VMF-223 pilots shot down four—the first aerial enemy met by this squadron since March 1944.[42]

During the *kamikaze* attack of 22 June three enemy were splashed by VMF-223, one of them by Captain Ken Walsh, his first since 1943 in the Solomons. The Group was credited with nine planes during these closing days of Okinawa.

But the fourth Marine fighter group was only a small part of the whole. Planes of the AAF's 413th Fighter Group began arriving with its P-47's on 14 June, and contributed 9 kills, 7 of them in the *kamikaze* attack of 22 June. On 25 June 657 sorties were flown by ADC planes. The 507th Fighter Group brought in 48 more P-47's on 27 and 28 June and shot down ten enemy aircraft, all of them Navy Willow training planes which attempted to intercept a raid on the Empire on 9 July.

ENEMY AIRCRAFT SHOT DOWN BY PLANES UNDER THE CONTROL OF TAF DURING THE OKINAWA CAMPAIGN

Unit	Type of plane	Enemy aircraft destroyed
MAG-31 (38,187 HOURS)		
VMF-224	F4U	55
VMF-311	F4U	71
VMF-441	F4U	47
VMF(N)-542	F6F	18
TOTAL		191
MAG-33 (36,968 HOURS)		
VMF-312	F4U	59½
VMF-322	F4U	29
VMF-323	F4U	124½
VMF(N)-543	F6F	15
VMTB-232	TBM	1
TOTAL		229

[41] *Admiral Halsey's Story*, p 253.
[42] VMF-223 war diary, June 1945; Fighter Command intelligence summary.

ENEMY AIRCRAFT SHOT DOWN BY PLANES UNDER THE CONTROL OF TAF DURING THE OKINAWA CAMPAIGN

Unit	Type of plane	Enemy aircraft destroyed
MAG-22 (22,912 HOURS)		
VMF-113	F4U	12
VMF-314	F4U	14
VMF-422	F4U	15
VMF(N)-533	F6F	35
VMTB-131	TBM	1
TOTAL		77
MAG-14 (18,551 HOURS)		
VMF-212	F4U	2
VMF-222	F4U	3
VMF-223	F4U	4
TOTAL		9
318TH FIGHTER GROUP (13,683 HOURS)		
19th Fighter Squadron	P-47	60
73d Fighter Squadron	P-47	13
333d Fighter Squadron	P-47	33
548th Night Fighter Squadron	P-61	5
TOTAL		111
413TH FIGHTER GROUP (5,966 HOURS)		
1st Fighter Squadron	P-47	9
21st Fighter Squadron	P-47	1
34th Fighter Squadron	P-47	0
TOTAL		10
507TH FIGHTER GROUP (2,320 HOURS)		
463d Fighter Squadron	P-47	10
464th Fighter Squadron	P-47	0
465th Fighter Squadron	P-47	0
TOTAL		10

	Marine	Army	Total
Day Fighters	436	126	562
Night Fighters	68	5	73
VMTB	2	0	2
GRAND TOTAL	506	131	637

On 16 June the 8th Marines of the 2d MarDiv returned to Okinawa to supply the final punch required to end the long and bloody battle. While standing at a forward observation post of the 8th, General Buckner was killed on 18 June; a Japanese artillery shell exploded against a rock, and a fragment of the coral pierced his chest.

Roy Geiger was appointed CG of Tenth Army, thus becoming not only the only marine, but also the only aviator of any service, ever to command an army. Three days later General Geiger was able to announce that organized resistance had ended. That evening, when U.S. troops were less than ten feet from the entrance of their cave, Generals Ushijima and Cho committed ceremonial *hara-kiri*.[43]

Geiger was relieved on 23 June by General Joseph W. Stilwell, the former CG of the CBI Theater. On 1 July Headquarters, Ryukyus Area, was set up under Stilwell's command, and TAF Tenth Army became TAF Ryukyus.

ADCC, quartered in a farmhouse near Yontan, was assuming more control of air defense as units of the air-warning squadrons were being redeployed on outlying islands gradually to relieve the picket ships. On 29 June land-based units relieved the Navy of control and became responsible for all air defense functions. Three days before the war ended ADCC moved to a permanent site overlooking Buckner Bay (Nakagusuku Wan).

VMO's on Okinawa

Twice as many Marine artillery-spotting planes were used on Okinawa as in any other operation during World War II—a total of four squadrons operating normally 48 planes (8 planes per squadron plus half as many in reserve). Only VMO-3, attached to the 1st MarDiv, and VMO-6, 6th MarDiv, operated throughout the battle. VMO-2 returned to the 2d MarDiv on Saipan 15 April; VMO-7 arrived between 7 and 11 May and was attached to III Amphibious Corps.

The VMO squadrons not only spotted for the artillery, but also flew message pick-ups and drops, laid wire, transported personnel and performed general utility, but performed superbly in the evacuation of wounded with planes modified to carry a stretcher patient. VMO-7, for example, flew out 369 wounded men in an 11-day period, in addition to flying 243 artillery missions, 35 reconnaissance flights and 17 photo-reconnaissance chores. To spare a wounded man a ride over Okinawa's abominable roads was indeed an act of mercy!

Altogether, III PhibCorps OY planes flew 2,214 sorties. Ten planes were lost, 5 of them in combat, and 5 officers and 2 enlisted men were killed.

---

[43] *Okinawa,* pp 470–471.

CHAPTER TWENTY-EIGHT

One War Is Won

DURING LATE JUNE and early July, Army bombers began to pour into Okinawa. The 41st Group, with B-25's, arrived 26 June. Headquarters of the Seventh Air Force's Bomber Command arrived 4 July, three days after the 494th Group (Heavy) came in with four squadrons. On 8 July the 319th Bomb Group (Light) brought four squadrons of A-26's, and on the 12th a second B-24 Group, the 11th, arrived.

The Marines, their close-support mission completed with the securing of Okinawa, and with the *kamikazes* checked, stepped aside for the new arrivals which would have much of the responsibility for trying to bomb Japan out of the war before the Kyushu landings. On 1 July MAG-31 moved from Yontan to the new field at Chimu, and MAG-22's flight echelon joined it from Ie Shima on 16 July. MAG-14 moved from Kadena to Awase Field on 31 June, and MAG-33 followed 16 days later.

For a brief time TAF commanded the whole kaboodle of planes on Okinawa, up to and including four-engined B-24's. On 1 July the Marine Corsairs escorted Army B-25's in the first medium-bomber attack on the Japanese homeland since the Doolittle raid of April 1942. Four days later 102 P-47's escorted 47 B-24's and 25 B-25's on another Kyushu raid.

TAF could list 758 planes in the task organization chart for 30 June: 288 F4U's, 36 F6F(N)'s 144 P-47's, 12 P-81's, 64 B-25's, 64 A-26's, 96 B-24's, 36 TBM's, 16 P-38's, 2 F6F-5P's.[1]

This obviously was a function not contemplated for the Marines, whose history was base defense and tactical aviation. According to plan, TAF Ryukyus was dissolved on 13 July. Marine units stayed in the 2d MAW and Army units became part of the Far East Air Force, including both the Seventh (Central Pacific) and Fifth (Southwest Pacific) Air Forces, which also began to arrive. On 10 July a new plan for the B-29's was announced from Washington: the Eighth Air Force would operate B-29's out of Okinawa as part of the U.S. Strategic Air Force under General Carl Spaatz.[2] The B-29's actually flew one mission from Okinawa the last night of the war.[3]

---

[1] TAF serial 00199, 30 June.
[2] *General Kenney Reports*, p 564.
[3] King, *U.S. Navy at War*, p 191.

One more Marine unit arrived on Okinawa before the war was over: Lieut. Colonel Jack Cram's VMB-612, the experts in firing rockets by radar. On 28 July the Squadron flew its last mission off Iwo, and next day flew its first off Okinawa, an antishipping strike along the northwestern coast of Kyushu. Attached administratively to MAG-31, the Squadron was under the operational control of Fleet Air Wing One, thus maintaining its record of never having operated directly under a Marine command. Between 1 and 15 August VMB-612 flew 31 sorties, and claimed to damage 20 enemy vessels in Tsushima Strait, the Japan Sea, and along the east Korea coast. Following experimental work at Iwo, Cram's crews flew three sorties using the Tiny Tim rocket on 11, 12 and 13 August.[4]

CVE's to Borneo and Formosa

In mid-June *Block Island* and *Gilbert Islands* were pulled out of Okinawa and sent south to Leyte, where they arrived on the 19th. There they were organized with the Navy-manned *Suwannee* into Rear Admiral William Sample's CarDiv 22 and handed the job of furnishing close air support for the Australian 7th Division landing at Balikpapan on the east coast of Borneo.

The Thirteenth Air Force had already pounded the target for three weeks, and a naval task force had been shelling it for a fortnight, so there was almost no opposition on the beaches on D-day, 1 July. Air support became unpopular when a flight of Navy planes from *Suwannee* bombed and rocketed some barracks which had already been captured by the Australians, who had neglected to inform the aviators. Several soldiers were killed; faulty communications and lack of familiarity with the tactical situation on the ground were blamed. Confessed the Navy lieutenant who acted as co-ordinator, "Pilots should not make their attacks during close support unless they have definitely located the target."[5]

After this D-day tragedy the Australians dispensed with close support, and the carrier planes were confined to targets of opportunity farther inland. One of these paid off surprisingly well when 48 planes led by Lieut. Colonel Campbell bombed, rocketed and strafed a big concentration of Japanese supplies, vehicles and a column of troops 30 miles inland ("We shot off everything we had and wished we had more").[6]

The lone Japanese plane that turned up was a Jake floatplane at half an hour past midnight on 3 July. Lieut. Bruce J. Reuter, flying an F6F night fighter off *Block Island,* sent it down in flames.

Following this brief venture into the Netherlands East Indies, the Marine

---

[4] CO VMB-612 to CO 2d MAW, "Airborne Forward Firing Rocket Monthly News Letter," 31 August 1945.

[5] VT-40 and VF-40 action reports, 6 July 1945.

[6] Campbell interview, 12 February 1948; *Gilbert Islands* action report; *ONI Weekly,* p 2105.

carriers pulled out on 4 July and returned to Leyte Gulf where Colonel Cooley reported on board *Block Island* as CO of MASG-48. There they were again split up, *Gilbert Islands* going to Ulithi, *Block Island* to Guam. The former on 4 August joined the logistic support group for TF 58 south of Japan. *Block Island* saw no more war, but transported 600 POW's out of Formosa in September.

Although Colonel Cooley had no opportunity for combat command with the CVE squadrons he had mothered from their infancy—the Navy exercised operational control—he was handed a warm potato at Formosa. Assigned by Admiral Ketcham to supervise the removal of Allied prisoners of war, Cooley decided that he probably would get along better with the Japanese if he took only 5 officers and 10 men ashore (rather than two improvised battalions of marines and sailors). On the morning of 5 September Cooley approached Keelung in destroyer *Gary;* it was ticklish—the Japanese initially refused to answer radio messages and nobody could be certain whether the troops on Formosa would obey the Emperor's Rescript, or whether they had even heard of it.

The American ships got through the minefields all right, and were finally escorted to the dock by the Japanese, who decided to co-operate. With the help of a British colonel, a POW, who had organized the prisoners into companies, Cooley evacuated from Taipeh and Keelung 1,160 prisoners, mostly British, but also including 3 Australians, 12 Netherlanders, 69 Americans (of whom one was a corporal in the old 4th Marines). All prisoners were suffering from malnutrition, and 121 had to be left in hospitals for later evacuation.

What Might Have Been

On Okinawa the *kamikazes* had dwindled to a trickle long before the atomic bombs were dropped on 6 and 9 August, before the Red Army invaded Manchuria on 8 August, or the Emperor read his Imperial Rescript on the 15th.[7] It seemed that the Japanese had either run out of (1) pilots, (2) gasoline, or (3) planes.

Not so. The Japanese were only saving their planes against the day when the homeland would be invaded. By and large, they were not very good planes —chiefly trainers—but there were plenty of them, nearly 11,000, mostly hidden near small grass or sod fields or in underground hangars, and about half of them had already been converted for suicide purposes when the war ended,[8] as shown in the table below the chart on the next page.

---

[7] The last plane shot down by a marine was a Tony splashed by Lieut. William E. Jennings in an F6F night fighter at 0308 on 8 August. Occasional *kamikazes* wandered over Okinawa until after the war ended; one crashed on Ie Shima, 16 August, injuring two men.

[8] USSBS, *Japanese Air Power,* p 24. In addition, there were 7,200 additional planes available but not currently effective (p 70).

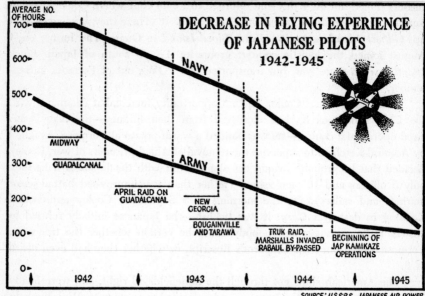

DECREASE IN FLYING EXPERIENCE
OF JAPANESE PILOTS
1942-1945

SOURCE: U.S.S.B.S., JAPANESE AIR POWER

	Army	Navy	Total
Planes assigned to suicide units:			
Combat types	900		900
Advanced trainers	1,750		1,750
Primary trainers		2,700	2,700
TOTAL	2,650	2,700	5,350
Combat types assigned to units not yet designated suicide units	2,150	3,200	5,350
GRAND TOTAL	4,800	5,900	10,700

To fly these planes Japan had 18,600 pilots left.

Two thousand Army pilots had already been trained about 70 hours each for *kamikaze* work, which required little more than the ability to put the plane into a dive. Of the others, 5,000 were in tactical units and had more training; 1,000 were instructors. The Navy had even more pilots, about 10,000 in all. Of these, 2,450 were capable of day and night missions, 1,750 were equipped to perform dawn and dusk missions. The remaining 5,950 were less competent. All training at war's end was aimed at teaching the less experienced pilots how to be *kamikazes*.

The gasoline situation was even more surprising. There was a shortage, which severely limited the amount of training that could be given pilots.

The Japanese nevertheless would have had ample aviation fuel for sustained suicide attacks on any invasion force if invasion had taken place

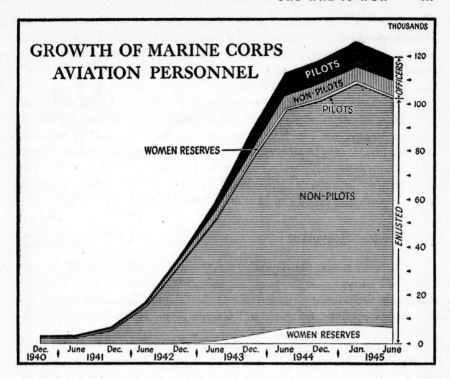

GROWTH OF MARINE CORPS
AVIATION PERSONNEL

THOUSANDS

PILOTS

NON-PILOTS

PILOTS

WOMEN RESERVES

NON-PILOTS

OFFICERS

ENLISTED

120
100
80
60
40
20
0

WOMEN RESERVES

Dec. 1940 | June 1941 | Dec. | June 1942 | Dec. | June 1943 | Dec. | June 1944 | Dec. | Jan. 1945 | June

in November 1945. Ten thousand suicide sorties, each of five hours' duration, would consume a maximum of about 50,000 barrels of fuel. At the end of the war Japanese possessed stocks of more than 1,000,000 barrels of fuel.[9]

Whenever the Allied invasion force appeared off the coast of Kyushu—which the Japanese expected in October or November—the plan was to fly a wave of 300 to 400 *kamikazes* against the ships every hour. The Japanese expected that the shorter distance would enable them to make a greater success of *kamikaze* than they had made at Okinawa.

If the Japanese had been able to maintain their Okinawa rate (1.8 per cent for ship sinkings, 18.6 per cent for hits or damaging near misses), they would have sunk about 90 ships in the Kyushu landing and damaged about 900. It seems likely, however, that U.S. defenses would have improved considerably by 1 November—just as Okinawa showed a better defense, percentagewise, than the Philippines.[10]

Operation OLYMPIC, the invasion of Kyushu on 1 November, would have provided the *kamikazes* plenty of targets: 3,033 ships.[11] It was planned that the Sixth Army would land two corps of 6 divisions on the east coast; V Phib-

[9] *Ibid.*, p 25.
[10] *Ibid.*
[11] *War Reports*, p 685.

Corps of 3 Marine divisions across from Kagoshima on the west coast; 1 infantry division on the Koshiki Retto off the west coast, with one corps in floating reserve.[12] OLYMPIC plans included 3 Marine aircraft wings—1st MAW in Kyushu, 2d MAW to support OLYMPIC from Okinawa, and 3d MAW with 8 carrier groups on board CVE's.[13]

For Operation CORONET, about 1 March 1946, the Eighth and Tenth Armies (9 infantry divisions, 2 armored divisions, 3 Marine divisions) would land on Honshu and march west 40 miles across the Kanto Plain to Tokyo, with the First Army (10 infantry divisions, 1 airborne) redeployed from Europe, in floating reserve. Navy and naval aviation plans for CORONET appear to have been less firm than the Army's—possibly because the Navy was less convinced than Generals MacArthur and Marshall of the necessity of the invasion.

Postwar Redeployment

On 7 September, five days after the war was ended officially by the signing of the surrender on *Missouri*, Major Paul T. Johnston, CO of VMF-441, landed the first Marine plane in Japan at the Yokosuka naval base airfield. The rest of his squadron followed, and Colonel Munn set up headquarters the same day.

On 15 September operational control of MAG-31's squadrons—all of which had arrived by the 11th—passed from Third Fleet to the Far East Air Force. The Group's mission was surveillance and reconnaissance over the Tokyo Bay area. MAG-31 returned to the U.S. 4 July 1946 under the command of Lieut. Colonel John P. Condon.

MAG-22 began flying out of Okinawa on 20 September in the transports of VMR-353 and VMR-952 and the PBJ's of VMB-612, which landed the Group at its new base, Omura on Kyushu. The entire move, 600 miles, was made by air and with 275 tons of gear was completed in 14 days without injury to personnel or loss or damage to equipment. After a few weeks of wretched living conditions—their gear was delayed by a typhoon and they subsisted on K rations the first week—the Group was shifted to Sasebo, where Colonel Elliott Bard embarked it for the U.S. On 5 December 1945 MAG-22 saw the U.S. for the first time. Since its organization on Midway in 1942 it had served on one Pacific island after another.

Headquarters of 2d MAW remained on Okinawa, along with MAG-14 and MAG-33. All departed for the U.S. in February 1946.

As a preliminary in the planning for the Kyushu invasion, 1st MAW headquarters was scheduled to move from Bougainville to join its three groups at Zamboanga. This movement had begun before the war ended, and on 15 August

---

[12] U.S. Military Academy, *The War with Japan*, Part 3 (January to August 1945), map 18.

[13] CinCPac-CinCPOA Joint Staff Study, serial 0005082, 18 June 1945.

elements of the Wing started arriving in the Philippines. On 21 September MAG's 12, 24, 25 and 32, along with Wing headquarters and other units, began moving north from Mindanao. Attached to III PhibCorps, they spent two weeks on Okinawa, moved thence to Tientsin, Peiping and Tsingtao. On 1 November Louis Woods took command from "Sheriff" Larkin, who had relieved Ralph Mitchell on 10 August.

MAG-32's tactical squadrons arrived at Tsingtao 16 October, five days after the Corps. MAG-24 sent two night-fighter squadrons and two air-warning squadrons to Peiping; MAG-12's flight echelon joined up 25 October. Two squadrons of MAG-25 furnished the only kind of reliable transport in China, where the war against Japan had long since given way to the civil war between Nationalists and Communists.

The 1st MAW planes began flying show-of-strength patrols on 1 November, and they were frequently fired upon from the ground. There were no casualties until 8 December, when 6 of a 12-plane flight of SB2C-5's of VMSB-343 were lost in a snowstorm near Communist-controlled Laichow. Only 2 of the 12 flyers survived and only 8 bodies were recovered. Villagers provided 48 ceremonial bearers to carry the coffins of the dead flyers to trucks and jeeps which got through; this was in the days when Chinese Communists still wrote touching mottoes about their friends, the Americans. "May the friendship of America and China increase!" was inscribed on a ceremonial arch in the village square; a reward of 3,000,000 yuan paid for recovery of the bodies was returned.[14]

MAG-12 was transferred to Marine Air West Coast in April 1946, MAG-32 followed a month later, and all dive bombers were transferred to Guam.

This left only fighters, transports and observation planes in China. The last elements of MAG-24 and headquarters of the Wing remained in China until 1 May 1947, when they too were transferred to Guam. On the same date AirFMFWesPac was activated (by changing the name of Marine Wing Service Squadron 1). It remained in Tsingtao, though its parent administrative organization, MAW-1, was on Guam.

On 1 October 1947 1st MAW headquarters went to El Toro, leaving MAG-24 (reinforced) on Guam, where it stayed until early 1949, when it, too, was withdrawn to the States. The last elements of AirFMFWesPac were brought out of Tsingtao in January 1949. These included the headquarters squadron, VMF-211, VMR-153 and Marine Ground Control Intercept Squadron 7 (formerly AWS-7). VMF-211 qualified for carrier duty on 20 January 1949 and went on board CVE *Rendova*, which continued to operate in the western Pacific until mid-April.

It wasn't much more than a year before the Marines—including 1st MAW —were on their way back to the western Pacific to fight another Oriental enemy.

The end of the war witnessed a great cutback in the strength of Marine aviation, as follows:

---

[14] MAG-32 war diary, December 1945.

	Total Personnel	Pilots	Tactical Squadrons
31 August 1945	116,628	10,049	103
30 June 1946	36,144	3,343	27
30 June 1947	19,334	2,484	21
30 June 1948	14,163	2,271	21 (2 jets)
30 June 1949	17,084	2,190	21 (2 jets)
30 June 1950	14,406	2,139	16 (4 jets)
31 December 1950	25,306	2,788	18 (5 jets)
31 March 1951	27,717	3,191	21 (5 jets)
31 August 1951	29,073	3,488	21 (5 jets)
31 December 1951	31,933	4,018	21 (5 jets)

These figures include only squadrons with planes that fire guns or drop bombs, and do not include such nontactical aircraft squadrons as VMR and VMO. There were 25 of these at the end of the war.

On 30 December 1949 orders had been issued cutting Marine aviation to 12 tactical squadrons. These were modified before the Korean war began in June 1950 to allow the maintenance of 16 squadrons.

The above table does not include units of the Organized Reserve, which comprised 21 squadrons on 30 June 1946 and 30 squadrons when the Korean war began in June 1950. Two of these were called up as units 18 September 1950; three more were added 1 March 1951. By the beginning of 1952 the personnel of all 30 had been mobilized and absorbed into various units. In addition, all 12 of the nontactical Ground Control Intercept (formerly AWS) squadrons had been called up.

The story of the Korean war is left for later telling. All published reports during the first 18 months indicated that a strong nucleus of Marine aviators had been able to prove the theory and practice of close-support aviation whose lessons had been so hard-won from the jungles of Nicaragua to the rice paddies of Okinawa.

Appendixes

I. Medal of Honor

Name[1]	Squadron	Place	Dates of Action
Bauer, Harold W, LtCol	VMF-212	Guadalcanal	28Sep; 3,16Oct43
Boyington, Gregory, Maj	VMF-214	Solomons–Rabaul	12Sep43–3Jan44
DeBlanc, Jefferson J, Lt	VMF-112	Solomons	31Jan43
Elrod, Henry T, Capt	VMF-211	Wake	8–23Dec41
Fleming, Richard E, Capt	VMSB-241	Midway	4–5Jun42
Foss, Joseph J, Capt	VMF-121	Guadalcanal	9Oct42–25Jan43
Galer, Robert E, Maj	VMF-224	Guadalcanal	Aug–Sep42
Hanson, Robert M, Lt	VMF-215	Rabaul	1Nov43,24Jan44
Smith, John L, Maj	VMF-223	Guadalcanal	21Aug–15Sep42
Swett, James E, Lt	VMF-221	Guadalcanal	7Apr43
Walsh, Kenneth A, Lt	VMF-124	Solomons	15,30Aug43

[1] Names in *italics* indicate posthumous awards.

II. Awards to Marine Aviation Units

> PUC = *Presidential Unit Citation*
> NUC = *Navy Unit Citation*
> DUC = *Distinguished Unit Citation (Army)*

Headquarters Squadrons

Unit	Unit Cited	Citation	Campaign	Dates
1stMAW	1stMarDiv(R)	PUC	Guadalcanal–Tulagi	7Aug–9Dec42
2dMAW	2dMAW	PUC	Okinawa–Ryukyus	4Apr–14Jul45
MAG-11	1stMarDiv(R)	PUC	Guadalcanal–Tulagi	7Aug–9Dec42
MAG-11	MAG-11	NUC	Peleliu–Western Carolines	15Sep44–31Jan45
MAG-12	MAG-12	PUC	Philippine Islands	3Dec44–9Mar45
MAG-12	MAGSZAM	NUC	Southern Philippines	10Mar–30Jun45
MAG-14	1stMarDiv(R)	PUC	Guadalcanal–Tulagi	7Aug–9Dec42
MAG-14	2dMAW	PUC	Okinawa–Ryukyus	28May–14Jul45
MAG-22	MAG-22	PUC	Midway Island	Jun42
MAG-22	2dMAW	PUC	Okinawa–Ryukyus	12May–14Jul45
MAG-23	1stMarDiv(R)	PUC	Guadalcanal–Tulagi	7Aug–9Dec42
MAG-24	MAG-24	NUC	Lingayen Gulf–Manila Area	23Jan–10Apr45
MAG-24	MAGSZAM	NUC	Southern Philippines	11Apr–30Jun45
MAG-25	1stMarDiv(R)	PUC	Guadalcanal–Tulagi	7Aug–9Dec42
MAG-25	SCAT	NUC	South Pacific	11Dec42–15Jul44

Unit	Unit Cited	Citation	Campaign	Dates
MAG-31	2dMAW	PUC	Okinawa–Ryukyus	10Apr–14Jul45
MAG-32	MAG-32	NUC	Lingayen Gulf–Manila Area	23Jan–15Mar45
MAG-32	MAGSZAM	NUC	Southern Philippines	16Mar–30Jun45
MAG-33	2dMAW	PUC	Okinawa–Ryukyus	7Apr–14Jul45
MAG-43	2dMAW	PUC	Okinawa–Ryukyus	4Apr–14Jul45

Service Squadrons

Unit	Unit Cited	Citation	Campaign	Dates
MAG-11	MAG-11	NUC	Peleliu–Western Carolines	15Sep44–31Jan45
MAG-12	MAG-12	PUC	Philippine Islands	3Dec44–9Mar45
MAG-12	MAGSZAM	NUC	Southern Philippines	10Mar–30Jun45
MAG-14	1stMarDiv(R)	PUC	Guadalcanal–Tulagi	7Aug–9Dec42
MAG-14	2dMAW	PUC	Okinawa–Ryukyus	28May–14Jul45
MAG-22	MAG-22	PUC	Midway	Jun42
MAG-22	2dMAW	PUC	Okinawa–Ryukyus	12May–14Jul45
MAG-23	1stMarDiv(R)	PUC	Guadalcanal–Tulagi	7Aug–9Dec42
MAG-24	MAG-24	NUC	Lingayen Gulf–Manila Area	23Jan–10Apr45
MAG-24	MAGSZAM	NUC	Southern Philippines	11Apr–30Jun45
MAG-25	1stMarDiv(R)	PUC	Guadalcanal–Tulagi	7Aug–9Dec42
MAG-25	SCAT	NUC	South Pacific	11Dec42–15Jul44
MAG-31	2dMAW	PUC	Okinawa–Ryukyus	12Apr–14Jul45
MAG-32	MAG-32	NUC	Lingayen Gulf–Manila Area	23Jan–15Mar45
MAG-32	MAGSZAM	NUC	Southern Philippines	16Mar–30Jun45
MAG-33	2dMAW	PUC	Okinawa–Ryukyus	7Apr–14Jul45

Fighter Squadrons

Unit	Unit Cited	Citation	Campaign	Dates
VMF-112	1stMarDiv(R)	PUC	Guadalcanal–Tulagi	7Aug–9Dec42
VMF-113	2dMAW	PUC	Okinawa–Ryukyus	25May–14Jul45
VMF-114	MAG-11	NUC	Peleliu–Western Carolines	15Sep44–31Jan45
VMF-115	MAG-12	PUC	Philippine Islands	3Dec44–9Mar45
VMF-115	MAGSZAM	NUC	Southern Philippines	10Mar–30Jun45
VMF-121	1stMarDiv(R)	PUC	Guadalcanal–Tulagi	7Aug–9Dec42
VMF-121	MAG-11	NUC	Peleliu–Western Carolines	15Sep44–31Jan45
VMF-122	1stMarDiv(R)	PUC	Guadalcanal–Tulagi	7Aug–9Dec42
VMF-122	MAG-11	NUC	Peleliu–Western Carolines	15Sep44–31Jan45
VMF-124	CV *Essex*	PUC	Philippines–China Sea	3–22Jan45
			Japan–Bonins	16Feb–1Mar45

Unit	Unit Cited	Citation	Campaign	Dates
VMF-211	VMF-211	PUC	Wake Island	8–22Dec41
VMF-211	MAG-12	PUC	Philippine Islands	3Dec44–9Mar45
VMF-211	MAGSZAM	NUC	Southern Philippines	10Mar–30Jun45
VMF-212	1stMarDiv(R)	PUC	Guadalcanal–Tulagi	7Aug–9Dec42
VMF-212	2dMAW	PUC	Okinawa–Ryukyus	7Jun–14Jul45
VMF-213	CV *Essex*	PUC	Philippines–China Sea	3–22Jan45
			Japan–Bonins	16Feb–1Mar45
VMF-214	VMF-214	PUC	Guadalcanal	7Apr43
			Munda	17Jul–30Aug43
			Northern Solomons	16Sep–19Oct43
			Vella Lavella–Torokina	17Dec43–6Jan44
VMF-215	VMF-215	NUC	Solomons–Bismarcks	24Jul43–15Feb44
VMF-216	CV *Wasp*	NUC	Japan–Bonins–Ryukyus	16Feb–1Mar45
VMF-217	CV *Wasp*	NUC	Japan–Bonins–Ryukyus	16Feb–1Mar45
VMF-218	MAG-12	NUC	Philippine Islands	3Dec44–9Mar45
VMF-218	MAGSZAM	NUC	Southern Philippines	10Mar–30Jun45
VMF-221	MAG-22	PUC	Midway Island	Jun42
VMF-221	CV *Bunker Hill*	PUC	Japan–Bonins–Ryukyus	16Feb–11May45
VMF-221	VMF-221	NUC	Guadalcanal–Solomons	17Mar–17Nov43
VMF-222	2dMAW	PUC	Okinawa–Ryukyus	11Jun–14Jul45
VMF-223	1stMarDiv(R)	PUC	Guadalcanal–Tulagi	7Aug–9Dec42
VMF-223	2dMAW	PUC	Okinawa–Ryukyus	11Jun–14Jul45
VMF-224	1stMarDiv(R)	PUC	Guadalcanal–Tulagi	7Aug–9Dec42
VMF-224	2dMAW	PUC	Okinawa–Ryukyus	7Apr–14Jul45
VMO-251	1stMarDiv(R)	PUC	Guadalcanal–Tulagi	7Aug–9Dec42
VMF-311	2dMAW	PUC	Okinawa–Ryukyus	7Apr–14Jul45
VMF-312	2dMAW	PUC	Okinawa–Ryukyus	9Apr–14Jul45
VMF-313	MAG-12	PUC	Philippine Islands	3Dec44–9Mar45
VMF-313	MAGSZAM	NUC	Southern Philippines	10Mar–30Jun45
VMF-314	2dMAW	PUC	Okinawa–Ryukyus	25May–14Jul45
VMF-322	2dMAW	PUC	Okinawa–Ryukyus	9Apr–14Jul45
VMF-323	2dMAW	PUC	Okinawa–Ryukyus	9Apr–14Jul45
VMF-422	2dMAW	PUC	Okinawa–Ryukyus	24May–14Jul45
VMF-441	2dMAW	PUC	Okinawa–Ryukyus	7Apr–14Jul45
VMF-451	CV *Bunker Hill*	PUC	Japan–Bonins–Ryukyus	16Feb–11May45
VMF(N)-533	2dMAW	PUC	Okinawa–Ryukyus	12May–14Jul45
VMF(N)-541	MAG-11	NUC	Lingayen Gulf–Manila	
			Carolines	15Sep44–31Jan45
VMF(N)-541	VMF(N)-541	DUC	Philippine Islands	3–15Dec44
VMF(N)-542	2dMAW	PUC	Okinawa–Ryukyus	7Apr–14Jul45
VMF(N)-543	2dMAW	PUC	Okinawa–Ryukyus	9Apr–14Jul45

Scout-Bomber and Torpedo-Bomber Squadrons

VMSB-131	1stMarDiv(R)	PUC	Guadalcanal–Tulagi	7Aug–9Dec42

Unit	Unit Cited	Citation	Campaign	Dates
VMTB-131	2dMAW	PUC	Okinawa–Ryukyus	29May–14Jul45
VMSB-132	1stMarDiv(R)	PUC	Guadalcanal–Tulagi	7Aug–9Dec42
VMSB-133	MAG-24	NUC	Lingayen Gulf–Manila Area	23Jan–10Apr45
VMSB-133	MAGSZAM	NUC	Southern Philippines	11Apr–30Jun45
VMTB-134	MAG-11	NUC	Peleliu–Western Carolines	15Sep44–31Jan45
VMSB-141	1stMarDiv(R)	PUC	Guadalcanal–Tulagi	7Aug–9Dec42
VMSB-142	1stMarDiv(R)	PUC	Guadalcanal–Tulagi	7Aug–9Dec42
VMSB-142	MAG-32	NUC	Lingayen Gulf–Manila Area	23Jan–15Mar45
VMSB-142	MAGSZAM	NUC	Southern Philippines	16Mar–30Jun45
VMSB-231	1stMarDiv(R)	PUC	Guadalcanal–Tulagi	7Aug–9Dec42
VMSB-232	1stMarDiv(R)	PUC	Guadalcanal–Tulagi	7Aug–9Dec42
VMTB-232	2dMAW	PUC	Okinawa–Ryukyus	22Apr–14Jul45
VMSB-236	MAG-32	NUC	Lingayen Gulf–Manila Area	23Jan–15Mar45
VMSB-236	MAGSZAM	NUC	Southern Philippines	16Mar–30Jun45
VMSB-241	MAG-22	PUC	Midway Island	Jun42
VMSB-241	MAG-24	NUC	Lingayen Gulf–Manila Area	23Jan–10Apr45
VMSB-241	MAGSZAM	NUC	Southern Philippines	11Apr–30Jun45
VMSB-243	MAG-32	NUC	Lingayen Gulf–Manila Area	23Jan–15Mar45
VMSB-243	MAGSZAM	NUC	Southern Philippines	16Mar–30Jun45
VMSB-244	MAG-24	NUC	Lingayen Gulf–Manila Area	23Jan–10Apr45
VMSB-244	MAGSZAM	NUC	Southern Philippines	11Apr–30Jun45
VMSB-341	MAG-32	NUC	Lingayen Gulf–Manila Area	23Jan–15Mar45
VMSB-341	MAGSZAM	NUC	Southern Philippines	16Mar–30Jun45

Medium-Bomber Squadrons

Unit	Unit Cited	Citation	Campaign	Dates
VMB-611	MAGSZAM	NUC	Southern Philippines	16Mar–30Jun45
VMB-612	VMB-612	NUC	Central Pacific	1Nov44–31May45

Transport and Photographic Squadrons

Unit	Unit Cited	Citation	Campaign	Dates
VMJ-152	1stMarDiv(R)	PUC	Guadalcanal–Tulagi	7Aug–9Dec42
VMJ-152	SCAT	NUC	South Pacific	11Dec42–15Jul44
VMJ-153	SCAT	NUC	South Pacific	11Dec42–15Jul44
VMD-154	1stMarDiv(R)	PUC	Guadalcanal–Tulagi	7Aug–9Dec42
VMJ-253	1stMarDiv(R)	PUC	Guadalcanal–Tulagi	7Aug–9Dec42
VMJ-253	SCAT	NUC	South Pacific	11Dec42–15Jul44

Unit	Unit Cited	Citation	Campaign	Dates

Observation Squadrons

Unit	Unit Cited	Citation	Campaign	Dates
VMO-1 (P&AO)*	VAC Assault Troops	PUC	Iwo Jima	19–28Feb45
VMO-1 (less det)	VAC Support Troops	NUC	Iwo Jima	19–28Feb45
VMO-3	VMO-3	PUC	Okinawa	2Apr–21Jun45
VMO-4	4thMarDiv(R)	PUC	Saipan–Tinian	15Jun–1Aug44
VMO-4 (P&AO)*	VAC Assault Troops	PUC	Iwo Jima	19–28Feb45
VMO-4 (less det)	VAC Support Troops	NUC	Iwo Jima	19–28Feb45
VMO-5 (P&AO)*	VAC Assault Troops	PUC	Iwo Jima	19–28Feb45
VMO-5 (less det)	VAC Support Troops	NUC	Iwo Jima	19–28Feb45
VMO-6	6thMarDiv(R)	PUC	Okinawa	1Apr–21Jun45

Air Warning Squadrons

Unit	Unit Cited	Citation	Campaign	Dates
AWS-1	2dMAW	PUC	Okinawa–Ryukyus	24Apr–14Jul45
AWS-5(det)	4thMarDiv(R)	PUC	Saipan–Tinian	15Jun–1Aug44
AWS-6	2dMAW	PUC	Okinawa–Ryukyus	17Apr–14Jul45
AWS-7	2dMAW	PUC	Okinawa–Ryukyus	12Apr–14Jul45
AWS-8	2dMAW	PUC	Okinawa–Ryukyus	6Apr–14Jul45
AWS-11	2dMAW	PUC	Okinawa–Ryukyus	23Apr–14Jul45

Air Support Control Units

Unit	Unit Cited	Citation	Campaign	Dates
LFASCU-1	VAC Support Troops	NUC	Iwo Jima	19–28Feb45

Separate Commands

Unit	Unit Cited	Citation	Campaign	Dates
ADC-2	2dMAW	NUC	Okinawa–Ryukyus	4Apr–14Jul45

* Pilots and air observers only.

III. Marine Corps Aviation Casualties

7 December 1941 Through 2 September 1945

		OFFICERS			ENLISTED		
	Pilots	Ground	Women	Pilots	Ground	Women	Total
1. Killed in combat action	355	16	0	12	411	0	794
2. Killed in U.S. (plane crash)	607	11	0	9	187	1	815
3. Killed overseas (operational)	321	10	0	4	225	0	560
4. Missing in action	196	1	0	2	120	0	319
5. Wounded in action	306	71	0	1	758	0	1,136
6. Missing (not in action)	22	1	0	0	2	0	25
TOTALS	1,807	110	0	28	1,703	1	3,649[1]
Dead and missing	1,501	39	0	27	945	1	2,513

[1] Does not include 423 who died of routine causes (253 in U.S., 170 overseas).

IV. Enemy Aircraft Shot Down

Squadron	Aircraft	Squadron	Aircraft
VMF-121	208	VMF-451	34
VMF-221	185	VMF-322	29
VMF-112	140	VMF-216	26 1/3
VMF-215	137	VMF(N)-541	23
VMF-212	132 1/2	VMF-113	20
VMF-223	132 1/2	VMF-217	19
VMF-214	127	VMF-218	18
VMF-323	124 1/2	VMF(N)-542	18
VMF-213	117	VMF-422	15
VMF-224	115 1/2	VMF(N)-543	15
VMF-211	91	VMF(N)-531	12
VMF-124	78	VMF-314	11
VMF-311	71	VMTB-132	9
VMF-312	59 1/2	VMF-251	9
VMF-123	56	VMF-313	9
VMF-222	53	VMTB-144	8
VMF-441	49	VMTB-232	8
VMF-321	39	VMTB-233	8
VMF-122	35	VMTB-143	7 1/2
VMF(N)-533	35	VMSB-231	7

Squadron	Aircraft	Squadron	Aircraft
VMF-115	6 1/2	VMD-154	2
VMSB-241	6	VMSB-341	2
VMSB-142	5	VMF(N)-532	2
VMTB-131	5	VMTB-134	1
VMF-452	4	VMF-225	1
VMSB-236	4	VMF-511	1
VMTB-141	3	VMF-512	1
VMTB-234	3	VMF(N)-534	1
VMSB-244	3		
VMF-351	3	TOTAL	2,344 5/6[1]

[1] Ten planes not included in this total were shot down by Marine pilots while attached to Navy carrier squadrons.

V. Marine Corps Aces in World War II

No.	Name	Number of Planes Shot Down	No.	Name	Number of Planes Shot Down
1.	Boyington, Gregory	28[1]	26.	Magee, Christopher L	9
2.	Foss, Joseph J	26	27.	Mann, Thomas H Jr	9
3.	Hanson, Robert M	25	28.	Overend, Edmund F	9[1]
4.	Walsh, Kenneth A	21	29.	Thomas, Franklin C Jr	9
5.	Aldrich, Donald N	20	30.	Loesch, Gregory K	8 1/2
6.	Smith, John L	19	31.	Morgan, John L Jr	8 1/2
7.	Carl, Marion E	18 1/2	32.	Snider, William N	8 1/2
8.	Thomas, Wilbur J	18 1/2	33.	Case, William N	8
9.	Swett, James E	15 1/2	34.	Dobbin, John F	8
10.	Spears, Harold L	15	35.	Gutt, Fred E	8
11.	Donahue, Archie G	14	36.	Hernan, Edwin J Jr	8
12.	Cupp, James N	13	37.	Hollowell, George L	8
13.	Galer, Robert E	13	38.	Kunz, Charles M	8
14.	Marontate, William P	13	39.	Narr, Joseph L	8
15.	Shaw, Edward O	13	40.	Post, Nathan T	8
16.	Frazier, Kenneth D	12 1/2	41.	Warner, Arthur T	8
17.	Everton, Loren D	12	42.	Yost, Donald K	8
18.	Segal, Harold E	12	43.	Baker, Robert M	7
19.	Trowbridge, Eugene A	12	44.	Brown, William P	7
20.	DeLong, Philip C	11 1/6	45.	Caswell, Dean	7
21.	Bauer, Harold W	11	46.	Crowe, William E	7
22.	Sapp, Donald H	11	47.	Haberman, Roger A	7
23.	Conger, Jack E	10 1/2	48.	Hamilton, Henry B	7
24.	Long, Herbert H	10	49.	Jensen, Alvin J	7
25.	DeBlanc, Jefferson J	9	50.	McClurg, Robert W	7

[1] Includes 6 planes shot down with the Flying Tigers in China.

No.	Name	Number of Planes Shot Down	No.	Name	Number of Planes Shot Down
51.	O'Keefe, Jeremiah J	7	87.	Kirkpatrick, Floyd C	5 1/2
52.	Owens, Robert G Jr	7	88.	Lundin, William M	5 1/2
53.	Pittman, Jack Jr	7	89.	Payne, Frederick R Jr	5 1/2
54.	Reinburg, Joseph H	7	90.	Sigler, Wallace E	5 1/3
55.	Ruhsam, John W	7	91.	Alley, Stuart C Jr	5
56.	Wade, Robert	7	92.	Baldwin, Frank B	5
57.	Williams, Gerard M H	7	93.	Braun, Richard L	5
58.	Mullen, Paul A	6 1/2	94.	Carlton, William A	5
59.	Durnford, Dewey F	6 1/3	95.	Davis, Leonard K	5
60.	Dillard, Joseph V	6 1/3	96.	Dawkins, George E Jr	5
61.	Axtell, George C Jr	6	97.	Doyle, Cecil J	5
62.	Baird, Robert	6	98.	Drake, Charles W	5
63.	Bolt, John F Jr	6	99.	Elwood, Hugh McJ	5
64.	Chandler, Creighton	6	100.	Farrell, William	5
65.	Conant, Roger W	6	101.	Finn, Howard J	5
66.	Dillow, Eugene	6	102.	Fontana, Paul J	5
67.	Dorroh, Jefferson D	6	103.	Ford, Kenneth M	5
68.	Drury, Frank C	6	104.	Hacking, Albert C	5
69.	Fisher, Don H	6	105.	Kendrick, Charles	5
70.	Fraser, Robert B	6	106.	Laird, Wayne W	5
71.	Freeman, William B	6	107.	McCartney, Henry A Jr	5
72.	Hall, Sheldon O	6	108.	McGinty, Selva E	5
73.	Hundley, John C	6	109.	Olander, Edwin L	5
74.	Jones, Charles D	6	110.	Phillips, Hyde	5
75.	McManus, John	6	111.	Poske, George H	5
76.	Percy, Gilbert	6	112.	Powell, Ernest A	5
77.	Pierce, Francis E Jr	6	113.	Ramlo, Orvin H	5
78.	Pond, Zenneth A	6	114.	Scarborough, Hartwell V Jr	5
79.	Presley, Frank H	6	115.	Scherer, Raymond	5
80.	Shuman, Perry L	6	116.	See, Robert B	5
81.	Stout, Robert F	6	117.	Synar, Stanley	5
82.	Terrill, Francis A	6	118.	Weissenberger, Gregory J	5
83.	Valentine, Herbert J	6	119.	Wells, Albert P	5
84.	Vedder, Milton N	6	120.	Yunck, Michael R	5
85.	Hansen, Herman	5 1/2			
86.	Hood, William L	5 1/2			

TOTAL   976 1/6

VI. Directors of Marine Corps Aviation[1]

Cunningham, Alfred A, Maj	17Nov19–12Dec20
Turner, Thomas C, LtCol	13Dec20–2Mar25
Brainard, Edward H, Maj	3Mar25–9May29
Turner, Thomas C, Col	10May29–28Oct31
Geiger, Roy S, Maj	6Nov31–29May35
Rowell, Ross E, Col	30May35–10Mar39
Mitchell, Ralph J, BrigGen	11Mar39–29Mar43[2]
Geiger, Roy S, MajGen	13May43–15Oct43
Woods, Louis E, BrigGen	15Oct43–17Jul44
Harris, Field, MajGen	18Jul44–24Feb48
Wallace, William J, MajGen	24Feb48–1Sep50
Jerome, Clayton C, BrigGen	1Sep50—

[1] On 1 Apr 36 the title of the senior aviator attached to Headquarters, Marine Corps, was changed from Officer-in-Charge, Aviation, to Director of Aviation.

[2] Colonel Clayton C Jerome was acting Director 30Mar–12May43.

VII. Squadron Commanders Killed During World War II

Name	Squadron	Date	Base
Parks, Floyd B, Maj	VMF-221	4Jun42	Midway Island
Henderson, Lofton R, Maj	VMSB-241	4Jun42	Midway Island
Norris, Benjamin W, Maj	VMSB-241	4Jun42	Midway Island
Iden, Ruben, Capt	VMSB-231	20Sep42	Guadalcanal
Bell, Gordon A, Maj	VMSB-141	14Oct42	Guadalcanal
Ashcroft, Wortham S, Lt	VMSB-141	8Nov42	Guadalcanal
Bauer, Harold W, LtCol	VMF-212	14Nov42	Guadalcanal
Sailer, Joseph Jr, Maj	VMSB-132	7Dec42	Guadalcanal
Britt, Wade H Jr, Maj	VMF-213	13Apr43	Guadalcanal
Gise, William E	VMF-124	13May43	Guadalcanal
Bowker, Howard F, Maj	VMSB-233	9Jun43	Espíritu Santo
Pace, William H, Maj	VMF-214	7Aug43	Russell Islands
O'Neill, William J, Maj	VMSB-233	4Sep43	Guadalcanal
MacLaughlin, John S, Maj	VMF-422	25Jan44	Ellice Islands
Pollock, Ernest E, LtCol	VMD-354	19May44	Cherry Point
Carlson, Claude J Jr, Maj	VMF(N)-543	2Jul44	Cherry Point
Vaupell, Robert W, Maj	VMSB-233	14Feb45	Santa Barbara
Amende, Jack R Jr, Maj	VMF-217	16Feb45	CV *Wasp*
Alward, Everett V, Maj	VMF-123	25Feb45	CV *Bennington*
Stout, Robert F	VMF-114	4Mar45	Peleliu
Nelson, Quintus B, Maj	VMF-122	16Apr45	Peleliu

Day, Richard M, Maj	VMF-312	14May45	Okinawa
Maze, Robert C, Maj	VMF-511	27May45	CVE *Block Island*
Sarles, George A, LtCol	VMB-611	30May45	Philippine Islands
Fraser, Robert B, Maj	MCVG-7	18Jun45	Santa Barbara

VIII. Growth of Marine Corps Aviation

Units

	Wings	Aircraft Groups	Aircraft Squadrons
1939			
31 Aug	0	2	9
1940			
31 Dec	0	2	10
1941			
30 Jun	0	2	11
31 Dec	2	2	13
1942			
30 Jun	2	10	31
31 Dec	4	10	41
1943			
30 Jun	4	20	60
31 Dec	4	21	88
1944			
30 Jun	5	28	130
30 Sep	5	31	145[1]
1945			
31 Jan	5	32	135
30 Jun	5	32	131
31 Aug	5	29	132

[1] Peak.

Personnel

	OFFICERS					ENLISTED					GRAND TOTAL
	Student Pilots	Pilots	Ground	Women	TOTAL	Student Pilots	Pilots	Ground	Women	TOTAL	
1939											
31 Aug	185	20	16		221	47	4	1,111	0	1,162	1,383
1940											
30 Jun	200	11	17	0	228	45	6	1,581	0	1,632	1,860
31 Dec	385	22	20	0	427	40	17	2,573	0	2,630	3,057
1941											
30 Jun	453	0	27	0	480	52	1	3,050	0	3,103	3,583
31 Dec	610	28	41	0	679	49	67	5,672	0	5,788	6,467
1942											
30 Jun	1,284	63	282	0	1,629	85	98	15,140	0	15,323	16,952
31 Dec	2,240	52	1,191	0	3,483	131	135	33,515	0	33,781	37,264
1943											
30 Jun	4,898	91	2,322	10	7,321	132	135	51,857	86	52,210	59,531
31 Dec	8,266	56	3,356	169	11,847	93	53	72,706	2,885	75,737	87,584
1944											
30 Jun	10,416	67	4,339	318	15,140	41	248	90,998	6,199	97,486	112,626
31 Dec	10,355	78	5,036	345	15,814	86	92	94,598	7,440	102,216	118,030
1945											
31 Jan	10,349	88	5,059	345	15,841	63	88	101,805	7,365	109,321	125,162[1]
30 Jun	9,998	107	4,970	328	15,403	43	94	96,116	7,065	103,318	118,721
31 Aug	10,005	104	5,055	334	15,498	44	116	93,858	7,112	101,130	116,628

[1] Peak.

IX. Unit Sketches

Glossary of terms herein which are not generally found elsewhere

AAF	Auxiliary Air Facility		**MASCU**	Marine Air Support Control Unit
AAWS	Assault Air Warning Squadron		**MB**	Marine Barracks
ABG	Air Base Group		**MCA**	Marine Corps Activity
AES	Aircraft Engineering Squadron		**MCAB**	Marine Corps Air Base
ARS	Air Regulating Squadron		**MCAF**	Marine Corps Air Facility
ASD	Artillery Spotting Division		**MCAAF**	Marine Corps Auxiliary Air Facility
ATG	Air Transport Group		**MLG**	Marine Glider Group
AWG	Air Warning Group		**MOG**	Marine Observation Group
AWRG	Aviation Women's Reserve Group		**MOTS**	Marine Operational Training Squadron
AWRS	Aviation Women's Reserve Squadron		**MWSS**	Marine Wing Service Squadron
BAD	Base Air Detachment		**NAB**	Naval Air Base
CNAOPTr	Chief of Naval Air Operational Training Command		**NBG**	Northern Bombing Group (WWI)
CP	Cherry Point, N. C.		**ND**	Naval District
DofA	Director of Aviation		**Pers Grp**	Personnel Group
DCNO(A)	Deputy Chief of Naval Operations for Air		**ProvASC**	Provisional Air Support Command
FSU	Ferry Service Unit		**Prov Mar CASU**	Provisional Marine Carrier Aircraft Service Unit
MABS	Marine Air Base Squadron		**Ser Grp**	Service Group
MACS	Marine Air Casual Squadron		**TCG**	Troop Carrier Group
MADC	Marine Air Defense Command		**VML**	Marine Glider Squadron
MADS	Marine Air Depot Squadron		**USNS**	U.S. Naval Station
MAR&S	Marine Aircraft Repair and Salvage Squadron		**VMTD**	Marine Towing Detachment

[These records were compiled from war diaries, unit histories and muster rolls. In a few cases slight discrepancies existed among these records. Such differences were resolved according to the best judgment of the researchers.]

Div of Avn. Estab 1Apr36 and OinC of MarAvnSec became first DofA. From its inception as Div until 1940 4 officers and 3 civilians were attached. The officers included the DofA, then a colonel, and an OinC of each of the three sections: Regular, Reserve and Material. On 7Dec41 Div consisted of four sections, Records Sec having been added; personnel strength then 11 off, 1 enl and 15 civilians. In Aug45 a majgen was DofA, a col was Asst DofA and 117 other offs (30 WR's) were attached, in addition to 164 enl (150 WR's) and 51 civilians. Meanwhile war and expansion had wrought many changes in the Div. On 20May43 DofA also became Asst Comdt (Air). Previous to 1943 the Div was attached to BuAer but after DCNO(A) was estab 18Aug43 DivofAvn transf and reported to DCNO(A) 15Sep43. DofA inherited multiple duties, among which were liaison with DCNO(A), planning, organizing, equipping, training and deployment, promotions and distribution of personnel, and budgetary matters for MarCor aviation. (For Directors, see Appendix VII.)

AirFMFPac. Org 15Aug42 at San Diego as MAWPac. Responsible for organization, administration and distribution of personnel and supplies of 1st and 2dMAW's and 4thMBDAW. It comprised a HqSq and a SerGrp. On 29Sep42 HqSq departed in *Lurline* and arrived at Ewa 5 days later. SerGrp remained on West Coast to distribute personnel and material, but rapid expansion necessitated a larger unit; hence, 21Jan43 MarFAirWest was comm. SerGrp redesig PersGrp 1Jul43, cleared all personnel returning from combat. On 16Sep44 MAWPac was redesig AirFMFPac. Two new commands were added to AirFMFPac 21Oct44 when the Prov Air Support Command and MCVG's were organized. As parent organization of all Marine aircraft in the Pacific, it administered, organized, deployed and supplied every Marine aviation unit that fought the Japanese from Guadalcanal to Okinawa. CG's: MajGen Ross E Rowell 15Aug42 to 15Sep44; MajGen Francis P Mulcahy 16Sep44 to 22Feb45; MajGen James T Moore 23Feb45 to date of surrender.

MASP. Estab 21Apr43 under command CG 1st MAW pending approval for it as a separate entity. Conceived as parent organization to handle the more detailed logistical and administrative functions of 1st and 2dMAW's in SoPac and to obviate duplication of effort in obtaining supplies and services. Functioned under CG 1stMAW until 9Dec43 when CMC authorized activation of Hq and HqSq MASP and directed CG 1st MAW to assume command of MASP; then to assign a general officer under his command as CG MASP. On 1Feb44 Hq and HqSq MASP activated and existed as separate organization until 31Jul44 when abolished. MABS-1 assumed MASP's logistical responsibility for 1st MAW and SMS-11 that for 2dMAW. CG's: MajGen Ralph J Mitchell 21Apr43 to 14Jun44; BrigGen Claude A Larkin 15Jun44 to 31Jul44.

MarFAirWest. Comm 21Jan43 at San Diego. Its mission was the administration, operation, training and equipping of all FMF aviation units and personnel on the West Coast, and supplying of personnel and material to Marine Aircraft Wings, Pacific. As of 1May44 MarFAirWest controlled MBDAG's 41 and 46 at El Toro, 42 and 45 at Santa Barbara, 43 at El Centro, 44 at Mojave, MAG-35 at Corvallis, Ore, and AWG-2 and Personnel Group at Miramar. MBDAG-48 comm at Santa Barbara 3Aug44. Estab MCVG, AirFMFPac on 21Oct44. Carrying out its administrative function when hostilities ceased. CO's: Col Lewie G Merritt 21Jan to 29Sep43; Col William J Wallace 30Sep43 to 13May44; MajGen Francis P Mulcahy 14May to 11Sep44; Col L H M Sanderson 12Sep44 to 19Mar45; BrigGen Claude A Larkin 20Mar to 23Jul45; BrigGen Ivan W Miller 24Jul to 14Aug45; BrigGen William J Wallace 15Aug45 to date of surrender.

MAHA. Estab 1Sep43 at Ewa to administer all Marine aviation units in Hawaiian area, less HqSq MAWPac. Upon arrival 3dMAW in Hawaiian area MAHA was disbanded 8May44 and Wing Hq assumed its responsibilities. CO's: Col Lawrence T Burke 1Sep to 3Dec43; Col Walter G Farrell 3Dec43 to 8May44.

1st MAW. Had as antecedents NBG units which served in France in WWI. Org 7Jul41 at Quantico comprising HqSq and 1stMAG. On 10Dec41 departed for San Diego; arrived 21st. Fighter sq's placed under 1st Interceptor Command, bombing sqs with Naval Scouting Force. Reorg into 5 groups in Mar42. On 20Aug42 forward ech of 1stMAW landed at Guadalcanal to support 1stMarDiv(R). MAG-21, transf from 2d to 1stMAW, moved into Russells 13Mar43 and became first aviation to operate there. Wing units participated in New Georgia, Vella Lavella, Treasury and Bougainville landings. Forward ech became AirNorSols for Bougainville operation. After almost a year of "milk runs" against by-passed bases in Bismarcks area, 1stMAW sq's moved into Leyte 6 weeks after landings, providing close air support for Army troops until war ended. SCAT, part of 1stMAW, performed initial large-scale evacuation of wounded in SoPac and provided first extensive delivery of supplies by air. CO's: LtCol Louis E Woods 7Jul to 19Aug41; Col Roy S Geiger 20Aug41 to 20Apr43; MajGen Ralph J Mitchell 21Apr43 to 31Jan44; BrigGen James T Moore 1Feb to 14Jun44; MajGen Ralph J Mitchell 15Jun44 to 4Jun45; MajGen Louis E Woods 5Jun45; Col Harold C Major 6Jun to 10Jun45; BrigGen Lewie G Merritt 11Jun to 10Aug45; MajGen Claude A Larkin 11Aug45 to date of surrender.

2d MAW. Org 10Jul41, comm 19Jul41 at San Diego, comprising HqSq and 2dMAG, subsequently redesig MAG-21. Hq of Wing remained on West Coast until end of 1942, but some Wing units were first Marine aviation to engage Japanese. One of its units fought at Wake. Most of its planes at Ewa were destroyed during enemy's 7Dec41 attack. Two sq's participated in Battle of Midway Jun42. 2dMAW sq's transf to 1stMAW and formed van of Marine aviation in SoPac, although Wing's own sq's did not arrive Guadalcanal until Feb43. As ComAirNewGeorgia, Gen Mulcahy, CG 2dMAW, moved to Munda airfield shortly after capture. When AirNewGeorgia was disbanded 20Oct43, 2dMAW went back to Efate and set up camp for flight ech's which rotated between combat areas and Efate. The 2dMAW functioned largely as a training command until Jun44 when preparations for move to Palaus began. Ground personnel of 2dMAW landed on Peleliu 15Sep44 with 1stMarDiv. Wing furnished air defense and air support for Peleliu troops, and neutralized enemy bases in Western Carolines. By mid-Dec44 2dMAW sq's transf to 4thMAW except HqSq-2, which went to Ewa to prepare for invasion of Okinawa. HqSq-2 augmented by Army and Navy personnel became hq for TAF Tenth Army on Okinawa. CO's: Col Francis P Mulcahy 10Jul to 14Sep41; BrigGen Ross E Rowell 15Sep41 to 6Aug42; Col Francis P Mulcahy 7Aug42 to 16Mar44; BrigGen Harold D Campbell 17Mar to 6Jul44; MajGen James T Moore 7Jul44 to 22Feb45; MajGen Francis P Mulcahy 23Feb to 10Jun45, MajGen Louis E Woods 11Jun45 to date of surrender.

3d MAW. Comm 10Nov42 at Cherry Point. By 1Feb43 had 5 HqSqs, 4 Serons, and 4 tactical sq's in commission but personnel far under authorized strength. By mid-Jul43 although eight MAG's had been commissioned, there were only that many sq's in existence. Despite plane shortages and other obstacles MAG-31 departed 1Sep43 for San Diego. The numerous operational crashes due to insufficiently trained pilots resulted in activation of HqSq-3 into a flight section, as a pool and training school for inexperienced pilots. The first PBJ sq departed for combat 3Dec43; a second sq (night fighter) was detached two weeks later. Three AWS's had been organized, equipped and detached by 6Dec43. Wing grew from 13 offs 25 men in Nov42 to 15,470 personnel by 24Mar44, and its plane strength increased from one trainer on 17Nov42 to 465 of all types. The 3dMAW began departing CP 5Apr44 for NAS, San Diego. On 21Apr44 ordered to Ewa and sailed on board three CVE's. Arrived 8May44 and assumed functions of MAHA which was thereupon disbanded. Now comprised of only HqSq-3, its mission was chiefly administrative but included training MAWPac sq's and pilots in specialized tactics such as night fighting, air warning and radar bombing. CO's: LtCol Calvin R Freeman 10Nov42 to 21Jan43; BrigGen Claude A Larkin 22Jan43 to 7May44; BrigGen Walter G Farrell 8May to 16Nov44; Col Byron F Johnson 17Nov to 31Dec44; Col Ford O Rogers 1–7Jan45; Col Byron F Johnson 8Jan to 11Aug45; BrigGen Lewie G Merritt 12Aug45 to date of surrender.

4th MAW. Comm 22Aug42 at Ewa as 4thMBDAW and charged with providing air defense for bases, search and patrol, air-sea rescue, and shipping escorts. At its inception one each of its MAG's was at Midway, Ewa, and Samoa. Wing hq remained at Ewa until 19Aug43, then transf to Tutuila, then to Funafuti, and on 25Dec43 to Tarawa. By Mar44 forward ech moved to Kwajalein, the rear to

Majuro. Because its mission had changed from defensive to offensive, 4thMBDAW was redesignated 4thMAW 10Nov44. Remained in CenPac until after surrender, neutralizing by-passed Japanese mandated bases. When war ended 4thMAW units were based at Majuro, Kwajalein, Engebi, Guam, Tinian, Iwo Jima, Ulithi, Peleliu. CO's: LtCol Ward E Dickey 22–30Aug42; Col Claude A Larkin 31Aug to 2Dec42; LtCol Thomas J Walker Jr 3–18Dec42; BrigGen James T Moore 19Dec42 to 7May43; Col Thomas J Walker Jr 8–11May43; Col William L McKittrick 12May to 7Jul43; BrigGen Harold D Campbell 7Jul to 4Oct43; BrigGen Lewie G Merritt 5Oct43 to 15May44; BrigGen Thomas J Cushman 15May to 20Aug44; MajGen Louis E Woods 21Aug44 to 11May45; BrigGen Lawson H M Sanderson 12May45 to date of surrender.

9th MAW. Comm 1Apr44 with HqSq-9 at Cherry point. Succeeded 3dMAW to train, equip and prepare Marine aviation units for combat. Its subordinate commands, in addition to HqSq-9, were auxiliary air facilities at Atlantic, Bogue, New River, Oak Grove, Kinston and Congaree, and outlying fields at New Bern and Greenville. Later MCAS, Edenton, was assigned to 9thMAW. CO's: Col Christian F Schilt 1Apr to 16Jun44; BrigGen Lewie G Merritt 17Jun44 to 16Jan45; BrigGen Christian F Schilt 17Jan to 15Feb45; Col Lawrence T Burke 16Feb to 22Apr45; BrigGen Harold D Campbell 23Apr45 to date of surrender.

MCAB's, Cherry Point. Estab 21Sep44 to administer all facilities and outlying fields in CP area, including MCAS, CP which previously was parent org. In addition to MCAS's and MCAAF's, MCAB's included AES's 41, 42, 43, 44, 45 and 46, a guard det, AWRG-1, AWRS 15, 17, 18, 19 and 20 at time of its inception. CG 9thMAW was also CG MCAB's. Peak personnel strength reached 30,446 in Mar45 and was 26,454 at war's end. CO's: BrigGen Lewie G Merritt 21Sep44 to 16Jan45; BrigGen Christian F Schilt 17Jan to 15Feb45; Col Lawrence T Burke 16Feb to 3May45; BrigGen Harold D Campbell 3May to 4Aug45; MajGen Ralph J Mitchell 4Aug45 to date of surrender.

MCA, 11thND. Org 15Sep44 at MCAS, El Toro to direct and administer coordination of Marine aviation activities which formed part of NAB. HqSq comm 4Jun45 to carry on its rolls personnel of DepCom's staff and ultimately comprised 28 offs (2 WR) and 53 enl (34 WR's). MCA, 11thND was aviation liaison between CMC and ComNAB's on public works and development of technical aviation matters to expedite services and supplies for fleet aviation units. DepCom also had cognizance over MCAS's at El Toro, Santa Barbara, Mojave and El Centro; MCAD, Miramar; HqSq, MCA, NAB, 11thND; MCAAF, Gillespie; Marine Chino Field at Ontario, and Ryan Field, Hemet, Calif, outlying fields of El Toro. CO's: Col William J Fox 15Sep44 to 9Jan45; BrigGen Walter G Farrell 9Jan45 to date of surrender.

MCAS, Cherry Point. Org 18Aug41 at New Bern, NC, as Air Facilities under Development at Cherry Point. Adm offices estab in Post Office Bldg at New Bern; 3Sep41 moved from New Bern to construction camp site CP; next day designation changed to Air Facilities under Development at Cunningham Field. On 1Dec41 desig MCAS and comm as such 20May42. Flight opns commenced 18Mar42. On 22Apr42 command reorg into HqSq and AES-41. Same day Navy Sq VS-201 arrived for ASW duty, followed a month later by Army Observation Sq's 105 and 121. First Marine sq to operate at CP comm 16Nov42 but by end 1942 only one Marine aircraft available. On 6Aug42 four more AES's formed. Third MAW comm 10Nov42 and remained until 6Apr44. In Jan43 AES-46 added to serve as utility sq of station and to ferry all TE planes from eastern US factories to MarCor activities. In eight months 506 planes were ferried without damage or loss. First WR's reported 29May43 and AWRG-1 comm at CP 15Apr44. Eleven outlying fields were part of MCAS, CP. Six became MCAAF's (auxiliary air stations). Between 22Mar42 and 31Dec44 there were based at CP or its outlying fields 2 MAW's, 18 Army and Navy sq's, more than 60 Marine tactical sq's, 20 AWS's, 4 MOTS's and 6 AWRS's. On 1Dec41 total personnel strength was 5; a year later 4,167, and by Dec44 25,139. CO's: LtCol Thomas J Cushman 18Aug41 to 22Aug43; LtCol Raymond W Conroy 23Aug to 10Sep43; Col Christian F Schilt 11Sep43 to 31Mar44; Col Pierson E Conradt 1Apr44 to 29May45; BrigGen Thomas J Cushman 30May45 to date of surrender.

MCAS, Edenton. Desig Marine Corps Glider Base 14Jul42 under 5th ND. Site selected 14May42 and construction commenced 10Aug42; first marine on board

5Oct42. At end of Dec42 Marine complement totaled 6 off, 30 enl. Desig MCAS 13Jul43 and two months later cognizance transf from 5th ND to Chief of Naval Air Operational Training Command. First sq's to base Edenton, VMB's 413 and 423, arrived Oct43 for final training before going overseas. First WR's arrived 4Aug43 and their numbers expanded sufficiently to form a sq comprised entirely of enl WR's (AWRS-13) which later included all off and enl women on the station, Navy, Marine and Coast Guard. Some of MOTG-81 arrived in Dec43 followed in Jan44 by remainder of Group, necessitating org AWRS-12 as adm unit for WR personnel assigned to six sq's under MOTG-81. Emporia, an outlying field comm by ComAirLant 25Mar44 and provided service, limited repairs and maintenance for Edenton's aircraft. MCAS, Edenton, ordered transf 1Dec44 from CNAOpTr to Comdr MCAB, CP. Personnel moved to CP by 25Feb45; next day MCAS reestab and redesig NAS, Edenton. CO's: LtCol Zebulon C Hopkins 14Jul42 to 6Feb44; LtCol Chester J Peters 7Feb to 4Oct44; LtCol Wilfred J Huffman 5–9Oct44; LtCol Henry C Lane 10Oct44 to date of disbandment.

MCAS, Parris Island.   Org as Air Det, Marine Barracks, Parris Island, 5Oct40 as an outlying field of 1st MAG at Quantico. Redesig MCAS on 1Dec41. Although Page Field used as early as 1928 by Navy to moor dirigibles, no Marine sq stationed there until 23Sep38, when VMS-1 reported. Expansion commenced in 1941 and from Jan to Nov41 Marine Glider Group 71 stationed there, as well as Army 35th Air Base Sq. On 1Feb42 Air Det, Page Field changed to HqSq, MCAS, PI. Several Navy sq's were first to train at PI. Ten Marine sq's trained there between Apr43 and May45. First WR's arrived in Nov43 and AWRS-11 was formed (178 WR's) at PI on 15Apr44. Airport at Georgetown, SC, assigned as an outlying field of MCAS, PI, 27Apr44 for gunnery staging field for two Marine tactical sqs. When war ended 34 offs (9 WR's) and 429 enl (169 WR's) and a VMF attached. CO's: Maj John S E Young prewar to 21Aug42; LtCol Harold I Larson 22Aug to 30Nov42; Maj Ben F Prewitt 1Dec42 to 15Jun43; Col Thomas C Green 16Jun to 20Dec43; LtCol Ferry Reynolds 21Dec43 to 31Aug44; LtCol William K Lanman Jr 1Sep44 to date of surrender.

MCAS, Quantico.   Desig from BAD-1, MB, Quantico, 1Dec41. Although MCAS comprised Brown and Turner Fields which were dedicated in 1922 and 1936, respectively, it had ceased operational activities and was charged with overhaul, repair and salvage of aircraft, and maintenance of fixed installations. Subordinate units were HqSq and AES's 11, 12, 13 and 14. MCAS also served as receiving station for aviation-duty recruits. Between 1May41 and 30Apr42, 3,710 were classified to determine their fitness for aviation trade schools. Brown Field housed the A&R hangar which, during fiscal year 1943–44 alone, processed 556 aircraft. Quantico was responsible for specialized training of all VMO personnel in line org and tactics, arty techniques, and procedures of air spotting. Eight VMO sqs were org at Quantico. AWRS-21 org 1Apr44 and comprised nearly one-fourth the complement of 2,236 personnel on board. On 10Mar43 first det of Peruvian airmen arrived for a year's training in photography, radio and aviation mechanics. A det of British aviation personnel reported in 1944 for a two-month course. CO's: Maj Ivan W Miller prewar to 9Dec43; Col Ira L Kimes 10Dec43 to date of surrender.

MCAS, St. Thomas, VI.   Redesig MCAS 1Dec41 from MCAF, Bourne Field, St. Thomas, VI. Facilities included VMS-3 and a BAD which had been redesig from BAD-3 15Mar41. On 1Feb42 BAD became HqSq of MCAS, Bourne Field. On 4Mar43 MCAS became part of NOB, St. Thomas. After VMS-3 was decomm 20May44 station redesig MCAF 1Jul44 and operated as such under USNS at St. Thomas until war ended. CO's: LtCol Ford O Rogers, prewar to 24Jun42; LtCol Harold C Major 25Jun42 to 20Jun44; Capt Rogers Humphreys 21Jun44 to date of surrender.

MCAS, Eagle Mountain Lake.   Org 19Sep42 and comm 1Dec42 at Fort Worth, Texas, to function as a glider base. Marine Glider Group 71 and Marine Glider Sq 711 formed first and only units to train in gliders. Glider program abandoned and Eagle Mountain Lake station transf to Navy 30Jun43, but reassigned to MarCor on 1Apr44. Navy Hedron-52 det estab on 6Apr44. On 9Apr44 MAG-33 arrived but left for San Diego 17Aug44. MAG-53 arrived during Dec44. FSU-10 estab 5Jan45 and absorbed Hedron-52. VMF(N)-544 arrived 28Feb45. FSU-10 redesig VRS-1 on 4Aug45 but continued to service seaplanes that used the station as a ferry stop.

Station still functioning as training base when war ended. CO's: LtCol Harold R Lee 19Sep42 to 29Jun43; LtCol Sidney R Williamson 1Apr44 to date of surrender.

MCAS, El Centro.   Org 10Jul42 and comm 23Jul43. Good flying weather enabled sq's that trained there to fly a record number of flight hours. MBDAG-43 arrived 1Jan43. After completion of expansion of base facilities 1Dec44, MAG-35 came on board. MAG-42 arrived 1Jan45. A total of 24 sq's trained at El Centro where a rocket range and rocket ground school were also estab. First contingent of WR's arrived 15Dec43 and became AWRS-3 on 1May44. CO's: LtCol Thomas J McQuade 10Jul42 to 9Dec43; LtCol Karl E Voelter 10Dec43 to 20Nov44; LtCol Hugh C Brewster 21Nov44 to 14Aug45; LtCol Theodore W Sanford Jr 15–27Aug45; Col Thomas J McQuade 28Aug45 to date of surrender.

MCAS, El Toro.   Org 4Nov42 and comm 17Mar43. Construction began 3Aug42; by Dec42 runways, taxiways and warmup platforms completed. Flights started Jan43 when sq's formed for combat in SoPac commenced opns at El Toro. Early in 1944 already largest air station on West Coast, but funds for doubling its size and operations approved. Four WR offs and 96 enl WR's were on board by 14Nov43 to operate Link trainers, gunairstructors, teach recognition and run a plant nursery and landscape El Toro. From a bean field and 30 personnel in Aug42 El Toro grew to a station of 1,248 off 6,831 enl by late 1944. Early in 1945 second auxiliary field, Marine-Chino, was opened 20 miles north of El Toro. CO's: LtCol Theodore B Millard 4Nov42 to 6Jun43; Col William J Fox 7Jun43 to 18Feb45; Col John S E Young 19Feb to 18Jun45; Col Frank H Lamson-Scribner 18Jun45 to date of surrender.

MCAD, Miramar.   Org 1Mar43 as MCAB, Kearney Mesa, San Diego. Redesig MCAD, Miramar, 2Sep43. Base served as the West Coast depot for Marine aviation going to combat. CO's: Col Caleb T Bailey 1Mar to 12Aug43; LtCol Livingston B Stedman Jr 13Aug to 3Sep43; Col Thomas J Walker Jr 4Sep43 to 20Aug44; Col Livingston B Stedman Jr 21Aug to 10Oct44; LtCol Hugh C Brewster 2–23Oct44; Col Francis E Pierce 24Oct44 to 1Apr45; LtCol Joyce E Aldahl 2Apr to 28May45; Col Peter P Schrider 29May to 9Jul45; LtCol Joyce E Aldahl 10Jul to 26Aug45; Col Lyle H Meyer 27Aug45 to date of surrender.

MCAS, Mojave.   Est 24Sep42 and comm 1Jan43 to provide, equip and maintain facilities necessary to train MAG's. A Plans and Training Div was maintained to anticipate and provide for the constant improvement and expansion of station facilities. Early in Jan43 VMSB-236 first sq on board and first WR's arrived 29Nov43. AWRS-1 activated 10Apr44. Mojave selected as training site for carrier-based Marine sqs and MASG-51 arrived in Sep44 to begin training for carrier based operations. MarFAirWest training still in progress on station when war ended. Total of 32 sq's trained at Mojave. CO's: LtCol John S Holmberg 24Sep42 to 1Jun43; LtCol Joseph P Adams 2Jun43 to 30Oct44; LtCol Leonard W Ashwell 31Oct44 to 17Apr45; Col Melvin J Maas 18Apr to 9May45; Col Thomas B White 10May45 to date of surrender.

MCAS, Santa Barbara.   Org 13Aug42, although the first Marine unit, MAG-24, arrived 14Jun42. Santa Barbara Municipal Airport in Goleta, Calif, selected as site for MCAS and by end of 1942 much of construction was completed. Comm formally 4Dec42. Advanced ech MBDAG-42 arrived 11Jan43 and remained throughout war. WR's arrived 13Oct43 and 91 joined station HqSq. MBDAG-45 estab 1Feb44. AWRS-2 formed 1May44. MBDAG-48 org 3Aug44. MBDAG-45 departed overseas 9Sep44. Total of 24 Marine sq's trained at Santa Barbara during war. CO's: LtCol Livingston B Stedman Jr 13Aug42 to 29Jan43; LtCol William A Willis 30Jan to 21Aug43; LtCol Chauncey V Burnett 22Aug43 to 13Jul44; Col Frank D Weir 14Jul to 5Dec44; Col Vernon M Guymon 6Dec44 to date of surrender.

MCAS, Ewa.   Estab as MarCor airfield 3Feb41 when planes of 2dMAG were flown from Ford Island, Oahu, to Ewa Mooring Mast Field. Navy had built Mast for *Shenandoah* in 1925 but she crashed before leaving States; then mast was lowered for *Macon* which also crashed without ever using it. First marines to use Ewa Mooring Mast Field came ashore from Yorktown in 1932. Wake and Midway personnel were trained at Ewa, which was struck heavily during Pearl Harbor attack. In Jan41 Ewa was a field with one small house for a CPO and his family a few sheds, an unused mooring mast and a little-used runway. By 1945 it had 594 buildings, 15 miles of water mains, 18 miles of hard-surfaced roads, 10 miles of electric lines, 12 miles of telephone trunk line, and 921,800 square yards of paved runways and aprons scattered over the 894 acres of the station's land area. Early in 1945 first WR's reported and AWRS-14 was activated. Combat units and personnel of all five MAW's operated from or staged through this great crossroads of Marine aviation. CO's: LtCol Lewie G Merritt 3Feb to 18Nov41; LtCol Claude A Larkin 18Nov41 to 3Oct42; LtCol John S E Young 4Oct42 to 3Oct44; Col Ferry Reynolds 4Oct44 to 4May45; Col Jacob F Plachta 5May45 to date of surrender.

PersGrp.   Org as SerGrp, MAWPac, FMF, at San Diego, 20Aug42. In Jan43 assigned to MarFAirWest and moved to Kearney Mesa. On 1Jul43 redesig PersGrp and comprised HqSq, four ARS's, and a supply sq. Group served as receiving and replacement center for aviation personnel. Personnel classified and reassigned, and those going overseas were equipped, clothed and given further training. Moved to Miramar Jul44. CO's: Col Lewie G Merritt 20Aug42 to 22Feb43; LtCol Francis E Pierce 23Feb to 8Mar43; Col Stanley E Ridderhof 9Mar to 29Sep43; Col Francis E Pierce 30Sep43 to 23Oct44; Col William P Kelly 23Oct44 to date of surrender.

MASCU, PhibsPac.   Org 21Oct44 at MCAS, Ewa, as ProvASC, FMFPac to furnish close air-support control for ground forces in amphibious operations to be comprised of a hq and four teams called LFASCU's 1, 2, 3 and 4. Training schedule inaugurated 24Nov44; hq estab 22Dec44. ProvASC responsible to CO, ASCU, PhibForPac. On 21Apr45 Command disbanded and MASCU, PhibsPac org next day and continued administrative functions at Ewa until war ended. CO: Col Vernon E Megee.

AWG-1.   Comm 1Jul43 at Cherry Point to implement air-warning program recommendations of MarCor Radar Policy Board convened Feb43. Originally planned that air-warning group would function only as a "warning" unit; but by 1Oct43 all controllers, fighter directors and ground-radar personnel were ordered attached to AWS's. AWG-1 org and trained 18 AWS's and served at CP as a training and replacement center until war ended. CO's: LtCol Walter L J Bayler 1Jul43 to 5Apr44; LtCol Ethridge C Best 6Apr to 14Nov44; Maj James E Webb 15Nov44 to 27Aug45; Maj Robert Barry 28Aug45 to date of surrender.

MADC-1.   Org 1Apr44 at Cherry Point as MAG-62; comprised HqSq-62 and SMS-62. Primary mission: to org and train ground and air personnel. Comm VMB's 611, 612, 613, 614 and 621 during Apr44. Comm VMB's 622 and 623 in May and 624 and 453 in Jun44. Comm VMB's 473 in Jul and 483 in Aug44. Advanced ech, HqSq-62, estab at MCAF, Newport, Ark, 18Jul44. MAG-62 arrived Newport 17Feb45. Departed NAS, Port Hueneme, Calif, 5May45 for duty overseas. Arrived Okinawa 2Jul45 to direct air defense there. Effective 1Aug45 MAG-62 redesig MADC-1 and HqSq-62 became HqSq-MADC-1. CO's: Col Byron F Johnson 1Apr to 22Sep44; Col Thomas J Walker Jr 23Sep44 to 1Mar45; LtCol Carl J Fleps 2Mar to 31Aug45; Col William C Lemly 1Sep45 to date of surrender.

MOG-1.   Activated 15May45 at Ewa to assume adm control over all VMO's. Group hqs moved to NAS, Kahului, Maui, 20Jun45. VMO's 1, 4, 5 and 8 joined MOG-1 15Jun45 but were operationally attached to VPhibCorps. Group remained Kahului until 26Aug45 when hqs and subordinate units embarked for occupation duty at Sasebo, Japan. MOG-1 at sea on board APA *Thomas Jefferson* when war ended. CO: Maj John W Ryland.

ABG-2.   Formed by redesig from BAD-2, 14Feb42 at NAS, San Diego, to which it was attached. BAD-2 responsible for adm of Marine recruits attending Navy Trade Schools at San Diego. AES's 21, 22, 23 and 24 att for adm purposes after redesig as ABG-2. Training of pilots and crews, modification and testing of planes were some of Group's functions. Remained at San Diego until 17Jun45 when moved to El Toro. CO's: Maj Alexander W Kreiser Jr prewar to 25Jun42; LtCol Stanley E Ridderhof 26Jun42 to 9Mar43; Maj Desmond E Canavan 9–31Mar43; LtCol Valentine Gephart 1Apr43 to date of surrender.

AWG-2.   Its Hq and SS-2 comm 11Oct43 at MCAD, Miramar, and AWG-2 org 8Jan44. Also comprised AWS's 3 and 4. Mission of AWG-2: to make AWS's available to MAWPac and to store and service air-warning equipment. Also gave final six-week training course to AWS's going to combat. Eleven sq's detached from AWG-2 and sent overseas. Decomm 1Aug45. AWG's superseded by Air Control Groups; ground-control interceptor sqs replaced AWS's. CO's: Capt Ira Brock

11Oct43 to 7Feb44; LtCol Robert O Bisson 8Feb to 26Dec44; Maj Evans Spalding 27Dec44 to 23Jan45; Maj Ira Brock 24Jan to 2Apr45; Maj Frederic Solomon 3Apr to 31Jul45.

MADC-2.   Org 1Jan43 at El Centro, as MABDG-43; two months later redesig MBDAG-43. Became MAG-43 10Dec44. Original mission: training and air defense, but in Jan45 embarked for Ewa to join 2dMAW and became adm unit of ADC. MAG-43 on board USS *Allendale* 22Feb45 en route to Okinawa via Ulithi and Leyte. BrigGen W J Wallace, CG ADC, joined Group with staff 23Mar45. On 2Apr45 Gen Wallace and staff went ashore at Okinawa. On 7Apr45 ADCC went on the air, operating from three LVT's. Nine days later control center operating from an abandoned Japanese farmhouse. During May45 Group provided air-warning facilities for four AWS's and functioned as liaison between TAF, three MAG's and an AAF fighter group. On 1Aug45 MAG-43 became ADC-2. CO's: LtCol Allen C Koonce 1Jan to 18Nov43; LtCol John S Holmberg 20Nov to 15Dec43; LtCol Robert M Haynes 16Dec43 to 31Jan45; LtCol Robert O Bisson 1Feb to 4Aug45; LtCol Robert A Black 5Aug to date of surrender.

MOG-2.   Org 1Jun45 at Quantico on a provisional basis "in preparation for any move which may be forthcoming" (presumably the invasion near Tokyo Mar46). CO's: Lt James B Shaeffer 1–20Jun45; Maj Nelson B Palmer 21Jun45 to date of surrender.

MAG-11.   Org 1Aug41 at Quantico after existing under various designations since 1926. On 7Jul41, while still designated 1st MAG, was highest ech in Marine aviation. When combined with newly formed HqSq-1 became nucleus of 1stMAW. When Japanese raided Pearl Harbor, MAG-11 comprised six tactical sq's, vanguard of which left Quantico for West Coast 9Dec41, becoming air-defense group of San Diego area. First and oldest MAG in Marine aviation provided nuclei for four new MAG's 1Mar42. At Espíritu from Nov42, MAG-11 was spigot from which pilots, gunners, ground crews, and planes flowed into battle zones. Also responsible for air-sea rescues and searches. Units of MAG-11's forward ech landed at Peleliu D-day 15Sep44. Pilots covered landing on Ngesebus and furnished close support on Bloody Nose Ridge. Units also shuttled to Ulithi, neutralizing Babelthuap, Yap and other enemy bases. A night-fighter sq of MAG-11 was first Marine sq to serve in Philippines. Group still in Palaus area when Japanese surrendered. CO's: LtCol Harold D Campbell 1Aug41 to 1Apr42; Maj Frank H Lamson-Scribner 2Apr to 3May42; Col Lewie G Merritt 4May to 6Sep42; LtCol William O Brice 7Sep to 16Dec42; LtCol Samuel S Jack 17–31Dec42; Col Lawson H M Sanderson 1Jan to 7Mar43; Col Christian F Schilt 8–31Mar43; LtCol John C Munn 1Apr to 12Jul43; LtCol Joe A Smoak 13Jul to 11Dec43; Col William G Manley 12Dec43 to 7Jun44; Col John S Holmberg 8Jun to 5Aug44; Col Caleb T Bailey 5Aug to 22Dec44; Col Clarence J Chappell 23Dec44 to 2Aug45; Col Edward L Pugh 3Aug45 to date of surrender.

MAG-12.   Org 1Mar42 at Camp Kearney. Forward ech sailed for Efate 29Dec42; joined by entire Group 28Jan43. Arrived Guadalcanal 4Apr43 for duty until 4Sep43, then sailed for Auckland, NZ. In Nov43 returned Efate and remained until Apr44; moved to Emirau to participate in Bismarcks campaign. Ordered to Leyte to reinforce Fifth AF for invasion of Lingayen area, and began operating from Tacloban 3Dec44. Covered Ormoc landings 7Dec44 and a week later those at Mindoro. Supported Lingayen operation in Jan45. By Feb45 MAG-12 was supporting guerrilla troops and Army landings on Capul and Biri. Covered Zamboango landings 10Mar45. MAG-12 planes covered landings at Masbate, Burias, Basilan, Panay, Cebu, Negros, Sanga Sanga, Bongao and Jolo during Mar and Apr45. Provided close support for Macajalar Bay operation in May and during Jun45 for 24th, 31st and 41stInfDivs in Davao, Malaybalay and Agusan areas. Close air-support missions continued during Jul and Aug45. In Philippines opns MAG-12 planes flew 8,462 combat missions, supported 25 Army landings and destroyed 60 planes at a cost of 18 pilots. CO's: Capt John P Condon 1–5Mar42; Maj Samuel S Jack 6–10Mar42; LtCol William O Brice 11Mar to 7Sep42; LtCol Samuel S Jack 8–28Sep42; LtCol Edward L Pugh 28Sep42 to 28Jan43; LtCol Luther S Moore 29Jan to 5May43; LtCol Edward L Pugh 6May to 24Jul43; Col William G Manley 25Jul to Sep43; Maj Wyatt B Carneal Jr 3Sep to 3Nov43; Col Vernon M Guymon 4Nov43 to 25Sep44; Col William A Willis 26Sep44 to 26Feb45; Col Verne J McCaul 27Feb45 to date of surrender.

MAG-13.   Org 1Mar42 San Diego. Week later forward ech en route Samoa. First Group planes arrived Tutuila 2Apr42 and unit assumed air defense of American Samoa area. By 27May43, part of Group based at Funafuti and one unit moved to Nanomea 15Dec43. Sq's of Group based at Wallis, Nukufetau, Tarawa and Makin. Group hq moved from Funafuti to Majuro and by Apr44 entire Group at Majuro to neutralize by-passed Marshalls, where it remained until war ended. CO's: Col Thomas J Walker Jr 1Mar to 4Oct42; Col Pierson E Conradt 5Oct42 to 14Sep43; Col Lawrence Norman 15Sep43 to 16Dec44; LtCol Chauncey V Burnett 17Dec44 to 10Aug45; LtCol Gordon E Hendricks 11Aug45 to date of surrender.

MAG-14.   Org 1Mar42 at Camp Kearney. On 16Oct42 relieved MAG-23 at Guadalcanal in time to participate in Battle of Santa Cruz 26Oct42. Participated in naval Battle of Guadalcanal in Nov42. Left Guadalcanal 4Apr43 for Auckland, NZ. Returned to Solomons in Aug43 and set up Fighter Command at Munda. Part of Group moved to Ondonga in Oct43. Supported New Georgia and Bougainville operations from Munda, Vella Lavella, and Ondonga. Less than two weeks after landing on 15Feb44, MAG-14 disembarked at Green. Throughout Green campaign all marines on Green att to MAG-14. By 24Jan45 four fighter sqs of MAG-14 operating from Guiuan on Samar. In Philippines Group covered convoys, supported Army and guerrilla troops on Negros, Mindanao, Cebu, and Leyte. Forward ech arrived Kadena airfield, Okinawa, 15May45. Moved to Awase field early in Jul45. CO's: LtCol Albert D Cooley 1Mar42 to 5Apr43; Col William O Brice 6Apr to 31Jan44; LtCol Roger T Carleson 1Feb to 25Sep44; Col Zebulon C Hopkins 26Sep44 to 17May45; Col Edward A Montgomery 18May to 31Jul45; LtCol Carl W Nelson 1–9Aug45; LtCol William M Hudson 9Aug45 to date of surrender.

MAG-15.   Org 1Mar42 at Camp Kearney, where it remained as transport-training group to train pilots and crews for SCAT and CenCATS. HqSq-15 departed San Diego 2Mar44 and arrived Apamama 1Apr44. Until Oct44 MAG-15 operated as part of TAG, supplying planes and personnel. In Oct44 ordered to estab and maintain ATG to furnish air-transport service in Marshalls-Gilberts area. In Nov44 ATG became TCG, Mar-Gils. Redesig TU 96.1 and dissolved 25Mar45; its functions assumed by NATS. Then HqSq-15 transf to Ewa where it was joined by VMR's 953 and 352 and became part of TAG, flying cargo to Gilberts, Marshalls, Marianas, Carolines, Philippines, Iwo Jima and Okinawa. CO's: Maj Thomas J McQuade 1Mar to 30Jun42; Maj Deane C Roberts 1Jul42 to 23Feb44; LtCol Ben Z Redfield 24Feb to 31May44; Col Thomas J McQuade 1Jun to 30Sep44; LtCol Ben Z Redfield 1Oct44 to 19Apr45; LtCol Edward F Knight 20Apr to 18Jun45; LtCol Frederick S Angstadt 19Jun to 19Aug45; Col Warren E Sweetser 20Aug45 to date of surrender.

MAG-21.   Org in 1928 as a Hq Det. In May39 became 2dMAG and went to Ewa in Jan41. On 10Jul41 integrated with newly formed 2dMAW. On 1Aug41 redesig MAG-21. Suffered 17 casualties in attack on Pearl Harbor and all but one of its planes destroyed. Its units participated in actions at Wake, Midway, and early days on Guadalcanal, but Group itself remained at Ewa until Feb43 when ordered to Russells. Forward ech went ashore at Banika 14Mar43 to build airfield and by 16Jun43 began large-scale operations against NorSols. Moved to Efate 18Nov43. Departed Efate in Jun44 and by 4Aug44 Group was united on Orote Field, Guam. Later moved to Agaña Field. CO's: LtCol Lewie G Merritt 1Aug to 17Nov41; LtCol Claude A Larkin 18Nov41 to 21Aug42; LtCol William A Willis 22Aug to 3Oct42; LtCol Raymond E Hopper 4Oct42 to 17May43; LtCol Nathaniel S Clifford 18May to 27Jun43; Col Raymond E Hopper 28Jun43 to 6May44; Col Peter P Schrider 7May to 6Sep44; Col Edward B Carney 7Sep44 to 31Mar45; Col Ernest R West 1Apr to 14Jun45; Col Karl S Day 15Jun45 to date of surrender.

MAG-22.   Org 1Mar42 at Midway where it remained until 8Feb44. Transf to Eniwetok, arriving Engebi 19Feb44. Carried out strikes against by-passed enemy bases on Wotje, Maloelap, Mille and Jaluit. Ground ech arrived Ie Shima 6May45 and joined by flight ech 21May45. Operated from Ie Shima until 16Jul45 when Group moved to Chimu Field on Okinawa. CO's: LtCol William J Wallace 1Mar to 18Apr42; Maj Ira L Kimes 19Apr to 19Aug42; LtCol Charles J Schlapkohl 20Aug to 16Sep42; LtCol Marion L Dawson 17Sep42 to 27Feb43; LtCol William B Steiner 28Feb to 5Mar43; LtCol Marion L Dawson 6Mar to 18Jun43; LtCol William B Steiner 19Jun to 4Jul43; LtCol Lawrence T Burke 5Jul to 30Aug43; LtCol James M Daly 31Aug43 to 9Oct44; Col Daniel W Torrey Jr 10Oct44 to date of surrender.

MAG-23.   Comm 1Mar42 at Ewa. Group formed forward ech of 1stMAW and landed first units on Henderson 20Aug42. Joined ten days later by rear ech. Remained Guadalcanal until 16Oct42. Although MAG-23 comprised only four Marine sqs, personnel and planes of six Navy carrier sqs, AAF's 67th Pursuit Sq, and dets of Marine sq's stationed at various SoPac bases operated with Group. Transf to NAS, San Diego, where it served from 18Nov42 to 9Jan43, then moved to El Toro. Landed at Ewa 19Sep43 and served as part of MAHA until 8May44, thence to Midway where it stayed until war ended. CO's: LtCol Stanley E Ridderhof 1–21Mar42; Maj Raymond C Scollin 22Mar to 30Apr42; LtCol William J Wallace 1May42 to 5Feb43; Maj Frederick R Payne Jr 5Feb to 2Mar43; LtCol Calvin R Freeman 3Mar to 19Aug43; LtCol Samuel F Patterson 20Aug to 19Sep43; Col Lawrence T Burke 20Sep to 12Dec43; LtCol Joslyn R Bailey 13Dec43 to 10Jan44; Col Peter P Schrider 10Jan to 23Apr44; LtCol Joslyn R Bailey 24Apr to 10May44; Col Kenneth H Weir 11May to 1Oct44; LtCol Richard A Beard 1–9Oct44; Col Livingston B Stedman Jr 10Oct44 to date of surrender.

MAG-24.   Org 1Mar42 at Ewa. Two weeks later forward ech departed for Efate to prepare airstrip at Vila. Left Efate 24May42 for duty at Santa Barbara but 20Jan43 departed San Diego to return to Ewa. Although its units served at Midway, Palmyra and Johnston, Group remained at Ewa until Sep43, then went to Efate. Arrived in Russells 17Nov43 and on 21Dec44 was on Bougainville. Forward ech arrived Mangaldan 11Jan45 after staging through Milne Bay, New Guinea. Operated with MAG-32 as MAGSDAGUPAN from Mangaldan during Luzon campaign, as part of AAF's 308th Bomb Wing. By 17Apr45 MAG-24 joined with MAG's 12 and 32 to form MAGSZAM on Mindanao. Operated from Malabang until war ended, supporting 24th and 41stInfDivs. CO's: Maj Ira L Kimes 1Mar to 30Apr42; Capt Lewis H Delano Jr 1May to 2Jun42; LtCol Franklin G Cowie 3Jun to 16Jul42; LtCol William L McKittrick 17Jul42 to 19Feb44; LtCol Lewis H Delano Jr 20Feb to 10Aug44; Col Lyle H Meyer 11Aug44 to 31May45; Col Warren E Sweetser Jr 1Jun to 9Aug45; Col Edward A Montgomery 10Aug45 to date of surrender.

MAG-25.   Org 1Jun42 at Camp Kearney. Forward ech arrived Ewa 24Aug42 and joined by Group in Sep42. HqSq-25 moved to New Caledonia in Sep42 and Group's planes began flights to Guadalcanal. In Nov42 all transport units consolidated as SCAT which operated throughout all SoPac campaigns. In Jul44 HqSq-25 moved to Bougainville and in Oct44 SMS-25 transf to Los Negros. Following dissolution of SCAT in Feb45 MAG-25 planes commenced operations to Mindanao via Morotai and by May45 Davao was included. Hq remained at Bougainville. CO's: LtCol Perry K Smith 1Jun42 to 9Jul43; Col Wyman F Marshall 10Jul to 23Dec43; Col Allen C Koonce 24–30Dec43; Col William A Willis 31Dec43 to 27Jul44; Col Allen C Koonce 28Jul44 to 12Feb45; Col Harold C Major 13Feb to 1Jul45; Col William J Fox 2Jul to 1Sep45; Col Elmore W Seeds 2Sep45.

MAG-31.   Comm 1Feb43 at Cherry Point. Transf to Miramar for embarkation and in late Sep43 sailed for Samoa. By 6Oct43 units had been disembarked and stationed at various Samoan bases. In Jan44 a fighter sq went to Funafuti, and a night-fighter sq left for Tarawa, deploying MAG-31 units from American Samoa to the Gilberts. By 7Feb44 forward ech had moved into Marshalls to base at Roi. By middle of Mar44 neutralization of by-passed Marshalls bases had begun. On 7Apr45 arrived Yontan for Okinawa campaign. MAG-31 operated from 7Apr to 15Aug45 over Kyushu, the China coast, East China Sea area, and over more than a dozen enemy-held islands between Formosa and Kyushu, in addition to furnishing close support on Okinawa. It was located at Chimu, Okinawa, when war ended. CO's: Maj Ralph K Rottet 1Feb to 9Sep43; Col Calvin B Freeman 10Sep43 to 12Sep44; LtCol Ralph K Rottet 13Sep to 13Dec44; LtCol Martin A Severson 13Dec44 to 5Mar45; Col John C Munn 6Mar45 to date of surrender.

MAG-32.   Comm 1Feb43 at Cherry Point; trained there until 2Jan44 when movement to West Coast commenced. HqSq-32 and SMS-32 embarked for Ewa in late Feb44; remained Hawaii until Oct44 then sailed to SoPac. Stationed Emirau by Nov44 but forward ech left for Philippines in Dec44, arriving Mangaldan 27Jan45, where it became part of MAGSDAGUPAN under AAF's 308th Bomb Wing. Supported Sixth Army on Luzon. Some of Group went ashore with assault troops at Zamboanga 10Mar45; opns set up two days later at San Roque field despite enemy mortar and arty fire. MAG-32 became part of MAGSZAM on 13Mar45. First planes arrived 15Mar45 and provided air support for 41st infDiv at Bongao and Jolo in Tawi Tawi. Continued air support for Army and guerrillas and covered Parang-Cotabato, Sibago, Macajalar, and Sarangani landings. When MAGSZAM was dissolved 30Aug45, MAG-32 prepared for occupation duty in China. CO's: Maj Pelham B Withers 1Feb to 31Mar43; Maj John L Smith 1Apr to 29Sep43; Col Frank H Wirsig 30Sep43 to 31Aug44; LtCol John L Smith 1Sep to 17Nov44; Col Clayton C Jerome 18Nov44 to 3Jul45; Col Stanley E Ridderhof 4Jul to 16Aug45; Col Thomas G Ennis 17Aug45 to date of surrender.

MAG-33. Comm 1 Feb43 at Cherry Point. Moved to Bogue Field 27Sep43. On 6Apr44 transf to Eagle Mountain Lake. Went to Miramar in Aug44 and from there departed for Marshalls. Ultimately arrived Espíritu 29Nov44 via Pearl Harbor, Eniwetok, Peleliu, Ulithi, and Manus. Arrived off Okinawa 2Apr45 and camp set up at Kadena. Served throughout Okinawa campaign. CO's: Maj James L Beam 1Feb to 5Nov43; Col Ward E Dickey 6Nov43 to 30Jul45; Col Samuel S Jack 31Jul45 to date of surrender.

MAG-34. Comm 25Jul44 at Cherry Point as MAG-94. Primary mission: admin, training and preparing for combat Group personnel under its jurisdiction. On 1Nov44 MAG's 94 and 34 switched designations. Moved to MCAAF, Oak Grove, NC, 16Mar45 and continued training operations there until war ended. CO's: LtCol John T L D Gabbert 25Jul to 6Dec44; Col James M Daly 7Dec44 to 7Mar45; LtCol John T L D Gabbert 7Mar to 2Jun45; LtCol Joslyn R Bailey 3Jun to 27Aug45; Col Zebulon C Hopkins 28Aug45 to date of surrender.

MAG-35. Comm 1Apr43 at Cherry Point, NC. Units att were HqSq-35, SerSq-35, VMJ-352 and VMO-351. Departed 20Apr44 for Miramar but destination changed en route and Group arrived 27Apr44 at AAF, Corvallis, Ore, which was redesig MCAF. MAG-35 org and trained personnel in all phases of transport aircraft, and furnished replacement aircraft and crews for duty overseas. Due to prevailing poor flying weather, Group moved to El Centro in Oct44. Continued operations at El Centro admin and training group until war ended. CO's: LtCol John Wehle 1Apr to 30Jun43; LtCol Hamilton D South 1Jul to 30Nov43; Col Frank M June 1Dec43 to 16May44; Col Wyman F Marshall 17May to 31Aug44; LtCol John P Coursey 1–7Sep44; LtCol Neil R MacIntyre 8Sep to 26Nov44; LtCol Harry H Bullock 27Nov44 to 31Mar45; Col Allen C Koonce 1Apr45 to date of surrender.

MAG-41. Org 1Jan43 at El Toro as MBDAG-41. On 10Nov44 redesig MAG-41. Created to admin and supervise training and activities of att sqs for combat duty in Pacific, it originally comprised only a HqSq, an SMS, and a fighter sq. By war's end, approximately 20 fighter, dive-bomber and torpedo-bomber sqs had completed the syllabi. In 1944 Group was charged with training carrier sqs with emphasis on close-air support. HqSq-41 with its training section was probably largest hq in Marine aviation history, and at peak strength comprised 2,000 personnel. Total of 19 offs 14 enl killed in operational crashes. CO's: Maj Lyle H Meyer 1Jan to 9Mar43; LtCol Lawrence Norman 10Mar to 9Sep43; LtCol William A Willis 10Sep to 15Dec43; LtCol Luther S Moore 16Dec to 31Dec43; Col Boeker C Batterton 1Jan to 23Jun44; Col Frank M June 23Jun to 25Jul44; LtCol Louis B Robertshaw 26Jul44 to 1Jun45; LtCol Rivers J Morrell Jr 2Jun to 31Aug45; LtCol Gordon H Knott 1Sep45 to date of surrender.

MASG-42. Org 1Jan43 at San Diego as MBDAG-42. Transf to Santa Barbara 22Jan43. Sent its first fighter sq into combat in Sep43. Redesig MAG-42 in Nov44. Group remained in US during war and supplied sqs and flight personnel to combat area. Redesig MASG-42 in Jul45. CO's: Maj Stewart B O'Neill Jr 1Jan to 19Feb43; Maj Ernest R West 20Feb to 24May43; Col Lawson H M Sanderson 24May43 to 22Feb44; LtCol William D Roberson 23Feb to 3Mar44; Col Frank D Weir 4–13Mar44; Col Lawson H M Sanderson 13Mar to 11Sep44; LtCol William D Roberson 12Sep44 to 1Mar45; LtCol Nathan T Post Jr 2–17Mar45; LtCol Owen A Chambers 18Mar to 3Jun45; Col Thomas J McQuade 4Jun to 20Aug45; LtCol Owen A Chambers 21Aug45 to date of surrender.

MAG-43. See **MADC-2.**

MASG-44. Org 1Jan43 at Mojave as MBDAG-44. Comprised HqSq-44, SMS-44, VMF-225 and VMSB-236. VMF-218 and VMO-251 att in Jul and VMD-254 in Aug43. MBDAG-44 formally comm 15Sep43. VMF's 121 and 124 joined in Oct43. VMF's 451 and 452 comm and att in Feb44. MBDAG-44 redesig MAG-44 on 10Nov44. Departed San Diego in Nov44 and arrived Ewa in Dec44, MAG-44 redesig MASG-44 1Mar45. Was performing assigned mission of training units at Ewa when war ended. CO's: Maj Daniel W Torrey Jr 1–11Jan43; LtCol Edward B Carney 11Jan to 26Oct43; LtCol Daniel W Torrey Jr 27Oct to 8Dec43; Col Edward L Pugh 9Dec43 to 4Jan44; LtCol Daniel W Torrey Jr 5–20Jan44; Col Harold R Lee 21Jan to 4Jun44; LtCol Daniel W Torrey Jr 5Jun to 15Sep44; LtCol Milo G Haines 17Sep44 to 31Aug45; Col Luther S Moore 1Sep45 to date of surrender.

MAG-45. Org 1Feb44 at Santa Barbara as MBDAG-45. On 9Sep44 departed US for Ulithi to provide air protection for Fleet. Participated in neutralization of airstrips on Yap and Gagil-Tomil Is. Still at Ulithi when war ended. CO's: Maj Thomas E Mobley Jr 1Feb to 5Mar44; Col Perry O Parmelee 6Mar to 27Jul44; Col Frank M June 28Jul44 to 27Jan45; Col Richard C Mangrum 28Jan45 to date of surrender.

MASG-46. Comm 1Mar44 at El Toro as MBDAG-46. Primary mission: to administer and supervise training and activities of attached sqs for combat duty. Comm SMS-46, VMF's 481 and 482 and VMSB's 474 and 484 in Apr44. VMF's 462 and 471 joined in Oct44. MBDAG-46 redesig MAG-46 on 10Nov44 and VMF-215 joined Group. VMF-461 joined in Jan45. MAG-46 redesig MASG-46 in May45. Remained at El Toro throughout war. CO's: Maj William W Wood 1–19Mar44; Col Frank D Weir 20Mar to 11Jul44; LtCol Edward W Johnston 12Jul44 to 8Mar45; Col John Wehle 9Mar to 11Jun45; Col William G Manley 12Jun45 to date of surrender.

MASG-48. Org 3Aug44 at Santa Barbara as MBDAG-48. Consisted of HqSq, SMS, and 3 tactical sqs. Four MCVG's att to this unit. Primary mission: training and admin of carrier sqs. Redesig MASG-48 on 5Nov44. Remained at Santa Barbara until end of May45 when HqSq reported to Pearl Harbor. By end of Jun45 Group and staff were in Leyte Gulf on board *Block Island* and participated in Balikpapan landings on Borneo 1Jul45. Two days after Japanese surrender, 5 offs 10 enl of MASG-48 landed on Formosa, which had not yet surrendered, to evac more than 1,100 Allied POWs. CO's: Col Perry O Parmelee 3Aug to 17Sep44; LtCol John P Condon 18Sep to 17Oct44; LtCol Alben C Robertson 18Oct44 to 31Jan45; Col Albert D Cooley 1Feb45 to date of surrender.

MASG-51. Comm 1Jan44 at MCAAF, Oak Grove, NC, as MAG-51. Operated there until 5Sep44 when transf to Mojave. On 5Nov44 redesig MASG-51. Group continued training on West Coast until war ended. CO's: LtCol Wilfred J Huffman 1–25Jan44; Col Edward L Pugh 26Jan to 31Aug44; LtCol Donald K Yost 1Sep to 17Oct44; Maj Edward V Finn 18Oct44 to 25Jan45; Maj Bernard G Evans 26–31Jan45; Col Frank D Weir 1Feb45 to date of surrender.

MAG-52. Comm 20Jun44 at Cherry Point as MAG-91 and comprised HqSq-91. Mission: to train and equip att sqs for combat. VMF's 911, 912, 913, VMSB-344 and SMS-91 were comm and att in Jul44. Moved to Kinston, NC, in Aug44 and comm VMF-914. Transf to Congaree, and on 1Nov44 MAG-91 redesig MAG-52 and HqSq-91 became HqSq-52. On 1Dec44 SerGrp-52 comm at Congaree with a HqSq and SMS. On 14Feb45 SerGrp-52 decomm and personnel transf to MAG-52 as SMS-52. CO's: LtCol Samuel F Patterson 20–29Jun44; LtCol Wilfrid H Stiles 30Jun44 to 6Jun45; LtCol John W Stage 7Jul45 to date of surrender.

MAG-53. Comm 1Apr43 at Cherry Point, MarCor's first night-fighter group. In Jun43 its first sq departed for combat. During Mar44 went to Vero Beach, Fla, for training for night operations. Transf to Eagle Mountain Lake in Nov44 and remained there until war ended. Trained total of 8 night-fighter sqs and sent 7 into combat. CO's: LtCol Frank H Schwable 1Apr to 27Jun43; LtCol Edward A Montgomery 28Jun43 to 1Oct44; LtCol Martin A Severson 2Oct to 11Nov44; LtCol Gordon E Hendricks 12Nov to 14Dec44; LtCol John D Harshberger 15Dec44 to date of surrender.

MAG-61. Org 13Jul43 at Cherry Point. Function was admin and maint of PBJ sqs, 8 of which were comm between Dec43 and 1Apr44, when Group left CP for Miramar. Departed West Coast in three echs arriving Espíritu 23 and 30May and 21Jun44. On 12Jul sailed for Emirau, remaining there until war ended. All PBJ sqs in SoPac att to MAG-61 and contributed to neutralization of Bougainville-Bismarcks area. CO's: LtCol Frank H Wirsig 13Jul to 1Oct43; Col Perry K Smith 2Oct43 to 4Jun45; LtCol Stewart W Ralston 5–20Jun45; Col Herbert P Becker 20Jun45 to date of surrender.

MAG-62.   See **MADC-1.**

MLG-71.   Org 10Jan42 at MB, Parris I, and desig Glider Det. Comprised 10 off 17 enl at inception. Redesig MLG-71 24Apr42 when Det disbanded. Consisted of HqSq-71 and VML-711 and att to FMF. Remained PI until 20Nov42 when transf to MCAS, Eagle Mountain Lake, where Group was when glider program was abandoned 24May43. The 36 off 246 enl were dispersed to other aviation units and their 21 gliders allocated to Army and Navy. CO: LtCol Vernon M Guymon.

MOTG-81.   Comm 1Feb43 at Cherry Point as OTS-8. Operated under CNO Training, and was to provide VB-2 operational training for Marine pilots but later received PBJ's instead of PV's. Between Jun and Dec43 trained 141 pilots, 345 air crewmen and 195 ground crewmen. Transf to Edenton 9Dec43. Redesig MOTG-81 on 1Jan44. Returned to CP Jan45 and remained there until war ended. CO's: Maj Sidney R Williamson 1–3Feb43; Maj Harold A Johnson 3Feb to 8Mar43; Col Karl S Day 8Mar43 to 2May44; LtCol Warren E Sweetser Jr 3May to 31Dec44; LtCol John S Carter 1–31Jan45; LtCol Neil R MacIntyre 1Feb to 6Mar45; Col James M Daly 7Mar45 to date of surrender.

MAG-91.   Comm 10Aug44 at Cherry Point as MAG-92 and comprised HqSq-92, SMS-51, VMF's 921, 922, 924, 513 and 514. VMF-923 comm on 15Sep44. Transf to Oak Grove 17Sep44. Moved to CP on 30Oct44 and on 1Nov44 MAG-92 redesig MAG-91. Then comprised HqSq-91, SMS-91, VMF's 911, 912, 913 and 914. SerGrp-91 comprising a HqSq and SMS was comm 1Dec44. SerGrp-91 decomm 14Feb45 and personnel transf to MAG-91 as SMS-91. CO's: Col Raymond E Hopper 10Aug44 to 5Mar45; LtCol Joseph N Renner 6Mar to 11Jun45; LtCol Herbert H Williamson 12Jun45 to date of surrender.

MAG-92.   Comm 15Mar44 at Cherry Point as MAG-52 and comprised HqSq-52. VMF's 521 and 522 and SMS-52 comm 1Apr44. VMF-523 comm and joined 5May44 and VMF-524 on 10May44. Moved to Congaree, SC, 22May44. SMS-51 and VMF's 513 and 514 transf to MAG-92 from MAG-51 on 28Aug44. Began preparations for move to Walnut Ridge, Ark, in Oct44 and on 1Nov44 MAG-52 after arriving Walnut Ridge redesig MAG-92. Decomm 15Mar45. CO's: Maj John C Musselman Jr 15–28Mar44; Maj John S Payne 28Mar to 10Apr44; LtCol Birney B Truitt 10Apr to 2Jul44; Col Verne J McCaul 3Jul to 9Oct44; LtCol Birney B Truitt 10Oct to 4Mar45; LtCol Barnette Robinson 5–15Mar45.

MAG-93.   Comm 1Apr44 at MCAAF, Bogue, with primary mission of organizing and training personnel for combat. VMSB's 931, 333, 334 and 342 joined Group. On 10May44 VMO-351 joined and VMSB-931 transf. Comm VMSB-932 on 15May44 and SMS-93 on 17May44. CO's: Maj James L Fritsche 1–23Apr44; LtCol Roswell B Burchard Jr 24Apr to 11May44; Col Richard C Mangrum 12May to 31Aug44; LtCol Leo R Smith 1Sep to 14Nov44; LtCol Ethridge C Best 15Nov44 to 16Jan45; Col Roger T Carleson 17Jan45 to date of surrender.

MAG-94.   Comm 1Feb43 at Cherry Point as MAG-34. Transf 4Mar44 to MCAAF, Kinston, and in Nov43 went to Newport, Ark. On 1Nov44 redesig MAG-94. Arrived Miramar 26Dec44. Departed West Coast 18Jan45 and after staging through Pearl Harbor and Eniwetok arrived Kwajalein 13Feb45. Advance ech went to Engebi with HqSq-94 and by Apr45 was joined by entire Group to relieve MAG-22. CO's: LtCol Walter L J Bayler 1Feb to 31Mar43; Maj Lee C Merrell 1–13Apr43; Maj Kenneth D Kerby 14Apr to 3Jul43; LtCol Frederick B Winfree 4–11Jul43; Maj Kenneth D Kerby 12Jul to 16Aug43; Maj Norman E Denning 17Aug to 18Oct43; LtCol Raymond C Scollin 19Oct43 to 31Mar44; LtCol Ernest R West 1Apr44 to 18Mar45; Col Thomas J Walker Jr 19Mar to 16May45; LtCol Arthur H Weinberger 17May to 6Jul45; Col Ernest R West 7Jul45 to date of surrender.

MAR&S-1.   Org 25Nov42 as Aircraft Repair and Salvage Sq as part of SerGrp, MAWPacFMF, San Diego. Although similar to an SMS, was equipped to do the more intricate work of aircraft repair. Joined MAG-11 on 17Aug43 at Espíritu, thence in

Jan44 to SCAT, Tontouta. Decomm 27Jul44 when merged with SMS-25. CO's: Lt Roscoe V Thurman 25Nov42 to 25May43; Lt Carson I Simms 26May to 22Jul43; MG Frank J Van 23Jul to 24Aug43; Capt Walter A Johnson 25Aug to 2Dec43; Lt Carlos C Cadwell 3Dec43 to 27Jul44.

PROV MAR CASU I. Org 15Jun45 at Ewa with proposed strength of 16 off 549 enl. Mission: to perform all line services and maintenance of fighter and torpedo-bomber planes for approximately 3 MCVG's at one time during training period. CO's: Capt Walter W Kessler 15Jun to 26Aug45; Maj William A Carlton 27Aug45 to date of surrender.

AWS-1. Comm 1Sep43 at Cherry Point. About two months later proceeded El Toro for further training prior to leaving for Hawaii. After a month at Ewa ordered to Engebi. Arrived 20Feb44 and assumed primary control of all aircraft in area. One man killed, several injured, in air attack 8Mar44. In Apr44 a night controller and crew sent to Eniwetok to take over night-fighter direction and train personnel. In Jul44 controller and crew sent to Roi to provide night-fighter direction. Two officers, 6 enl left for Peleliu to assist in similar mission in Aug44. Sq arrived off Okinawa 19Apr45 and two days later debarked at Ie Shima. By May45 Sq fully operational. On 12May45 two radars and part of day-control unit moved to Tori Shima. From May45 to Aug45 Sq's score was 36-1/2 day-controlled interception kills and 26 night-controlled. CO's: Captain William D Felder Jr 1Sep43 to 20Dec44; Capt Edward R Stainback 21Dec44 to 3Jul45; Capt Lumir F Slezak 4Jul45 to date of surrender.

CASD-1. Org and desig CASD-1 on 1Feb45 at Santa Barbara to maintain and service planes of MCVG-1. Transf to *Block Island* and sailed for Pearl Harbor 20Mar45. From 30Mar to 13Apr45 in and out of Pearl on training operations. Under way for Ulithi 17Apr45; arrived 28Apr45 and two days later left for forward area. In Okinawa area during May and Jun45 and to Balikpapan 1–6Jul45. At Guam when war ended, thence to Formosa to support surrender of that island. CO: Capt Charles B Peterson.

LFASCU 1. Org in Nov44 at Ewa as part of Prov ASC. On 3Jan45 det to report to CG, VPhibCorps, and 1Feb45 embarked for Iwo Jima. Air support controlled from *Auburn* until 1Mar45 when Unit started operations ashore on Iwo Jima. Returned Saipan 12–15Mar45 to prepare for invasion of Okinawa. Personnel and equipment unloaded midnight 4Apr45 south of Yontan. By 9Apr45 control of support planes passed to LFASCU 1, and strikes conducted within 400 yards of front lines. First close-support operations for IIIPhibCorps commenced 9May45 from Futema. By 9Jun45 part of Unit moved to Naha to facilitate communications with Corps which had advanced south. Besides close-support control LFASCU 1 controlled planes dropping supplies to troops in southern Okinawa. Received NUC for service with VPhibCorps at Iwo Jima. Arrived Ewa 23Jul45 where it was when war ended. CO's: Col Vernon E Megee 3Jan to 15Mar45; Col Kenneth H Weir 15Mar to 15May45; Col Avery R Kier 15May to 19Aug45; LtCol Harold J Mitchener 20Aug45 to date of surrender.

MABS-1. Org 1Feb43 at Guadalcanal. Moved to Ondonga, New Georgia, during Nov and Dec43, to Munda 26May44, there assumed complete charge of airstrip and all aircraft operating from it. Departed for Peleliu May45 and shortly took over the maintenance and operation of MCAB, Peleliu. CO's: Maj Hugh C Brewster 1Feb to 18Oct43; Maj William F Hausman 19Oct43 to 19Apr44; Maj Francis H Smyth 20Apr44 to 30Apr45; Capt Norman J Florance 1May to 14Jun45; Maj George B Woodbury 15Jun45 to date of surrender.

MACS-1. Activated 10Feb45 to serve as replacement sq for personnel for overseas duty, formed from personnel of MWSS-1 at Miramar. Remained on West Coast performing its assigned mission until war ended. CO: Capt Province L Pogue.

MADS-1. Redesig 17Dec42 from rear ech 1stMAW. Mission: to handle supplies and replacement personnel for 1stMAW units. Moved to Nouméa Jan44; thence to Espíritu 12Apr44. On 23Aug44 estab forward ech at Guadalcanal. Remainder of Sq arrived Guadalcanal 5Dec44 and 20Dec44 forward ech left for Los Negros where it was joined by rear ech 25Jan45. Forward ech located in Leyte-Samar area from Mar until Aug45. CO's: Capt William M Frash 17Dec42 to 1Feb44; Maj Charles F Hansel 2Feb to 25Jul44; Col Dean C Roberts 26Jul44 to 5Feb45;

Maj Virgil P Schuler 6Feb to 10Mar45; LtCol Carl L Jolly 11Mar45 to date of surrender.

MWSS-1. Org 1Aug42 at San Diego as ARS-1. Mission: to provide replacement unit for personnel and material serving 1stMAW. On 18Aug42 transf to MAG-11, 3Sep42 to MAWPac,FMF, San Diego. Redesig MWSS-1 on 15May44. Org became responsible only for enl replacements. On 10Feb45 MACS-1 formed from personnel of MWSS-1. On 19Aug45 skeleton org of MWSS-1 embarked for Philippines and joined 1stMAW. CO's: Maj Carl L Jolly 1Aug to 25Aug42; Capt Lawrence L Jacobs 26Aug to 2Oct42; Lt Bernard M Rowold 3Oct42 to 29Jan45; Capt Province L Pogue 30Jan to 28Jun45; Capt Alaric W Valentin 28Jun to 19Jul45; Capt Province L Pogue 20Jul to 5Aug45; Lt Hunter C Barker 6Aug45 to date of surrender.

VMJ-1. Org 21Mar45 at Barking Sands, Kauai, TH, as Marine Towing Detachment 1. On 1May45 redesig VMJ-1 and assigned to 3dMAW. CO's: Capt George H Severinghaus 21Mar to 29Jun45; Lt Ivy G McWhorter 30Jun to 14Aug45; Capt Richard A Zigler 16Aug45 to date of surrender.

VMO-1. Org 27Oct43 at Quantico as ASD (VMO-155), first sq of its kind. Arrived San Diego 23Nov43 and participated in 4thMarDiv maneuvers at Camp Pendleton. Redesig VMO-1 on 7Jan44. Sailed 13Jan44 in *Kitty Hawk,* arriving Espíritu 31Jan44, Guadalcanal in Feb44. Part of ground personnel arrived Guam 21Jul44. Air ech flew from four CVE's 30Jul44 and joined ground ech at Orote, Guam. VMO-1 under tactical control of IIIPhibCorps Arty during Guam occupation. In mid-Dec44 remainder of ground ech at Guam. On 10Feb45 forward ech embarked on board *Funston.* First of Mar45 forward ech stationed at Iwo Jima, ground ech at Guam. Week later ech returned to Guam. CO's: Maj Gordon W Heritage 27Oct43 to 21Jan45; Lt Anthony E Barrett Jr 22Jan to 29Aug45; Capt Richard K Morris 30Aug45 to date of surrender.

VMTD-1. See **VMJ-1.**

AWS-2. Activated 1Sep43 and comm 25Sep43 at Cherry Point. Departed CP 15Nov43 for Miramar. Only partially equipped, left San Diego arriving Ewa 9Jan44. On 6May44, 4 offs 64 enl transf to IIIPhibCorps at Guadalcanal to form air-warning assault ech which later participated in Guam landings. Remainder of Sq departed for Guam 1Jun44. Assault ech landed Guam 21Jul44; three days later first Marine radar set operable. Main body arrived 27Jul44. During this period AWS-2 responsible for supplying air warning and fighter direction against air and sea attacks for ADC of Guam and Marianas area. In Mar45 advance party went to Peleliu to relieve Argus 20. By early May45 Sq hqs at Peleliu with one unit on TAD at Ulithi. CO's: Capt George T C Fry 1Sep43 to 15Dec44; Capt Lumir F Slezak 16Dec44 to 17Jun45; Capt Charles K Dyer 17Jun to 5Jul45; Maj Frank B Freese 5Jul45 to date of surrender.

CASD-2. Org 1Feb45 at MCAS, Santa Barbara. Transf 21Feb45 to *Gilbert Islands* and arrived Pearl Harbor 18Mar45. Serviced and maintained planes of MCVG-2 on board the CVE for Okinawa and Balikpapan operations and off Japan coast when war ended. CO: Capt Eldon Fulwood.

LFASCU 2. Org in Jan45 when first personnel reported to ProvASC 13Jan45 for assignment to LFASCU 2; started operational training for Okinawa. Unit arrived there 31Mar45. Moved ashore 4Apr45 and operations with Army XXIV Corps started at Nozato on 6Apr45. Assumed control of planes of Southern Attack Force of this corps 8Apr45. On 10May45 unit moved from Nozato to Unjo. Closed operations 21Jun45 when organized resistance ceased after having controlled total of 7,826 aircraft. Returned to Hawaii in Jul45. CO's: Col Kenneth D Kerby 12Feb to 20May45; LtCol Ethridge C Best 20May45 to date of surrender.

MACS-2. Formed 10Feb45 from personnel of MWSS-2 at Miramar. Mission: to join Marine and Navy enl personnel from schools and other bases to higher echs and units outside US. CO: Maj James G Hopper.

MWSS-2. Org 1Jul42 at NAS, San Diego, as ARS-2, first of its type in Marine aviation. Mission: to provide a replacement unit for both personnel and material serving 2dMAW overseas. Redesig MWSS-2 on 15May44. All but nucleus of personnel transf to MACS-2 on 10Feb45. On 2Jun45 its CO, only member of Sq, sailed in *Laurens* for Okinawa and arrived there 20Jul45. There 8 offs 201 enl joined to process return of all transient personnel to US. CO's: LtCol Francis E Pierce 1Jul to 25Aug42; Capt Kenneth N Hilton 26Aug42 to 8Apr43; Capt Robert A Oakes 9Apr43 to

15Feb44; Capt Joseph R Dolard 16Feb to 20Mar44; Capt James G Hopper 21Mar44 to 1Jun45; Maj William H Boggs 1Jun45 to date of surrender.

VMJ-2. Comm 1Oct44 at MCAS, Ewa, as VMTD-2 to train in towing aerial targets and tracking missions for Marine AA bns. After two months at Maui towing for 5thMarDiv entire det of 117 enl with 6 JM-1's and 6 R5C's of VMR-953 left 24Nov44 for Agaña, Guam. JM-1's of det did towing and radar tracking daily for AAA units on Guam, Saipan and Tinian. Det was redesig VMJ-2 on 1May45. CO's: Capt K K Bigelow 1Oct44 to 6Jul45; Lt Warren E Engle 7Jul45 to date of surrender.

VMTD-2. See **VMJ-2.**

VMO-2. Comm 1Nov43 at Quantico as ASD (VMO-251). Departed for San Diego 27Dec43. Redesig VMO-2 in Jan44. On 7Feb44 left San Diego and after short stay at Ewa joined 2dMarDiv in Hawaii for further training. Arrived Saipan 17Jun44; Sq moved few days later to Aslito airstrip where operations began with 2dMarDiv. Sq participated in Tinian campaign and shortly thereafter moved to East Field, Kagman Point, Saipan. Mar45 found it en route to Okinawa where routine recon and arty spotting missions were performed until middle of Apr45 when ordered back to Saipan. CO's: Maj Robert W Edmondson 1Nov43 to 26Jun44; Capt John A Ambler 27Jun44 to 15May45; Lt Willis B Anderson 16May to 27Aug45; Capt John E Lepke 28Aug45 to date of surrender.

AWS-3. Comm 12Oct43 at Cherry Point. Sq opns moved to air-warning installations at MCAAF, Oak Grove, NC, where crews were formed and trained as operating units. In Nov43 Sq returned to CP for further assignment; 12Dec43 arrived Miramar. Arrived Espíritu between 15–22Mar44. On 23Nov44 at Bougainville and 3Mar45 embarked for Mindoro, arriving 20Mar45. AWS-3 landed on R-day at Mindanao and communication operations set up at Malabang, Cotabato, Fort Pikit, Bubuan, and in Davao Area. Unit operated as 77th Fighter Control Center. On 15Aug45 departed for Ewa. CO's: Capt Harold W Swope 12Oct43 to 1Jul45; Capt Freeman R Cass 2–27Jul45; Capt Edward L Schappert 28Jul to 10Aug45; Capt Edward J Norstrand 11–20Aug45; Maj John W Huey Jr 21Aug45 to date of surrender.

CASD-3. Formed 1Feb45 at Santa Barbara as part of MASG-48. Boarded *Vella Gulf* 4May45 at San Diego to service planes of MCVG-3 during carrier-qualification practice. En route from San Diego to Hawaii 17Jun45. CVE arrived Guam 20Jul45 and air group made strikes on Pagan and Rota. CO: Capt Wesley M Burns Jr.

LFASCU 3. Formed 13Jan45 when personnel reported to ProvASC at Ewa and assigned to LFASCU 3. Trained at Ewa until 12Feb45 when first ech boarded *Procyon*, followed by second in *Cepheus* on 23Feb45. Both ech's ashore Okinawa 5Apr45 and served with Tenth Army as coordinator between IIIPhibCorps and Army XXIV Corps until after Okinawa secured. Arrived Manila 14Aug45; att to IIIPhibCorps to prepare for invasion of Japan. CO's: Col Avery R Kier 13Feb to 17May45; Col Kenneth H Weir 17May to 16Aug45; LtCol John T L D Gabbert 16Aug45 to date of surrender.

MACS-3 and MWSS-3. Org 1Nov42 at NAS, San Diego as ARS-3 to provide an org for off personnel en route to and returning from MAWPac overseas. Later its function modified to include processing of enl personnel joining MarFAirWest from overseas. On 15May44 redesig MWSS-3 but on 10Feb45 Sq placed on inactive status and remained so at war's end. MACS-3 formed to assume its functions, both retaining same CO. CO's: Lt Charles N Butler Jr 1Nov42 to 31Dec42; Lt George O Podemski 1Jan to 2May43; Capt Robert E Farlow 3–5May43; Capt Crusselle D Woodward 6–31May43; Capt Robert E Farlow 1Jun to 14Jul43; Capt Crusselle D Woodward 15Jul to 30Sep43; Capt Robert O Caulkins 1Oct43 to 14Mar44; Capt Dave J Woodward Jr 15Mar44 to 8Jun44; Maj Joseph T Cain 9Jun44 to date of surrender.

VMJ-3. Comm 1Oct44 at MCAS, Ewa, as VMTD-3, to provide towing and tracking for Marine AA bns which had been formerly performed by Navy sq's. Att to 3dMAW and operated in practice beach assaults with 4thMarDiv. Redesig VMJ-3 on 1May45 at Ewa; in Aug45 a det to Midway to tow for Marine def bn. CO's: Capt Thomas B Wood 1Oct to 16Nov44; Capt Richard K Todd 17Nov44 to 3Jul45; Capt Thomas B Wood 4–12Jul45; Capt William H Costello 13Jul45 to date of surrender.

VMO-3. Comm 1Dec43 at Quantico, Va, as ASD(VMO-351). Redesig VMO-3 on 15Jan44. In Feb44 departed San Diego and arrived Espíritu 4Mar44. At Russells in May44 and spent next 3-1/2 months preparing for invasion of Palaus. Forward ech went ashore at Peleliu 17Sep44 and commenced building 500-foot strip. On 28Sep44 VMO-3 supported Ngesebus landing. On 22Oct44 Sq sailed for Russells and ordered to TAD with IIIPhibCorps Arty. On 10Mar45 ordered to Ulithi where personnel boarded CVE's, en route to Okinawa. Operations from Yontan commenced 4Apr45 and next day Sq was serving 11 Army and Marine bns. CO's: Capt Bernard B Shapiro 1–26Dec43; Capt Wallace J Slappey Jr 27Dec43 to 30Jun45; Capt Peter Fritz 1Jul45 to date of surrender.

VMS-3. Redesig from VMO-9 1Jul37 at St. Thomas, VI, where it served from 1934 until decomm 20May44. Performed search, convoy escort and patrol missions. From 11–14May42 participated in alert to circumvent expected escape attempt of French Fleet from Guadaloupe. CO's: Maj Roger T Carleson prewar and on 7Dec41 to 1Jul43; Maj Edward B Carney 2–6Jul42; Maj Martin A Severson 7Jul42 to 9Feb43; Maj Arthur H Weinberger 10Feb to 11Oct43; Maj William H Dooley 12Oct43 to 22Feb44; Maj Christian C Lee 23Feb to 20May44.

VMTD-3. See **VMJ-3.**

AWS-4. Comm 1Nov43 at Cherry Point. Departed for West Coast late Dec43, arrived Miramar 5Jan44. Embarked 29Feb44 in *Hornet* and arrived Ewa 4Mar44 and assigned to MAHA. In mid-Nov44 Sq arrived Los Negros where routine training continued. AWS-4 arrived for landing at Zamboanga 10Mar45 and operated as 76th Fighter Control Center though att operationally to MAGSZAM. CO's: Lt John D Taylor 1–11Nov43; Capt John M von Almen 12Nov43 to 14Nov44; Capt Charles T Porter 15Nov44 to 14Aug45; Lt John C Adams 15–20Aug45; Maj Freeman R Cass 21Aug45 to date of surrender.

CASD-4. Comm 2Feb45 at Santa Barbara as part of MASG-48 to service and maintain planes of MCVG-4. Departed Santa Barbara 29Mar45 and boarded *Cape Gloucester* next day for training. Under way from San Diego, Calif, 23May45 and remained on board for operations in East China Sea area until war ended. CO's: Capt Bernhard K Schaefer 2Feb to 24Aug45; Capt Chauncey W Butler Jr 24Aug45 to date of surrender.

LFASCU 4. Activated Feb45 as a team of ProvASC at Ewa. Trained with AWS-11 in May45. To Maui in Jul45 for training with 5thMarDiv. On board *Thomas Jefferson* with VPhibCorps 26Aug45 for occupation of Japan. CO: Col Robert M Haynes.

VMO-4. Comm 20Dec43 at Quantico as ASD(VMO-951); redesig VMO-4 on 15Jan44. After completing training in OY's, departed for San Diego and overseas. On 28Mar44 assigned duty with VPhibCorps at Ewa. In Apr44 ordered to Maui for duty with 4thMarDiv. Departed Pearl Harbor 29May44 for combat area. Two Sq planes landed Saipan 17Jun44 and commenced opns. By 23Jun44 all Sq personnel and gear ashore and opns shifted from Charan-Kanoa airstrip to Aslito field. Two Sq planes participated in Tinian landing 24Jul44. On 10Aug44 sailed for Pearl. Departed Pearl for Guam Jan45 and received new aircraft which were flown to Saipan and loaded aboard CVE's for Iwo Jima. First aircraft landed on Iwo Jima 26Feb45. Departed Iwo 19Mar45, returning Maui in Apr45. CO's: Capt Nathan D Blaha 20Dec43 to 26Jun44; Lt Thomas Rozga 27Jun44 to 8May45; Lt Robert W McGinness 8May to 23Jul45; Capt John P Garriott Jr 24Jul45 to date of surrender.

MACS-4 and MWSS-4. Comm as ARS-4 at San Diego 1Nov42. Mission: to process transient personnel awaiting transf overseas or to units within US. Redesig MWSS-4 on 15May44 but on 10Feb45 placed on inactive status and MACS-4 org to perform all functions and duties of former org until war ended. Same CO commanded both units. CO's: MG Loyd B Rice 1Nov42 to 1Nov43. Capt Edward M English 2Nov43 to 25Jan44; Capt Dave J Woodward Jr 26Jan to 14Mar44; Capt Robert O Caulkins 15Mar to 9Apr44; Capt Harry C Gibbs 10–30Apr44; Lt Milton B Rogers 1May to 9Nov44; Capt Morris T Nelson 10Nov44 to date of surrender.

AAWS-5. Comm 1Dec43 at Cherry Point as AWS(AT)-5, first air-transportable air-warning sq. Sq divided into three divisions: lightweight search-radar, control center, and ground observer. Assault ech flew to Naval Radar Training School, St Simon's Island, Ga, for special training; returned to CP 18Jan44. Transf to San Diego in Feb44. On 28Mar44 departed San Diego for Ewa, arriving there early in Apr44. On 17Apr44 divided into three dets for operations with VPhibCorps: one assigned to Northern Troops and Landing Force, other two to 2d and 4thMarDivs, for invasion of Marianas. Sq went ashore at Saipan between 17–19Jun44. On 10Jul44 Sq redesig

AAWS-5. Eighteen days later left Saipan for Ewa, and assumed routine duties. Decomm 10Nov44 and personnel transf to other air-warning sqs. CO: Capt Donald D O'Neill.

CASD-5. Comm 1Feb45 at Santa Barbara as part of MASG-48 to service and maintain planes of MCVG-5. Boarded *Salerno Bay* with MCVG-5 on 20Jun45 for shakedown. Serviced MCVG-5 during flight opns off southern Calif in Jun and Jul45. CO's: Lt Robert I Nelson 1–22Feb45; Capt John T Bode 23Feb to 11Mar45; Lt Edward W Blossman 12Mar45 to date of surrender.

MACS-5. Activated 10Feb45 at Miramar to receive, process, equip and clear all transient enl personnel for duty with MarFAirWest and AirFMFPac. CO: Capt Ralph G Hand.

Supply Sq-5. Comm 1Sep42 at NAS, San Diego. Primary mission: to supply critical aviation materials and special services to Marine aviation. Moved to Miramar 1Feb43. Carried out assigned functions until war ended. CO's: Capt Melville M Menefee 1Sep42 to 19Mar43; Capt John C Alexander 20–30Mar43; Maj Joseph N M Berger 31Mar to 9Jul43; Capt John C Alexander 10Jul to 13Sep43; Capt Granville Mitchell 14Sep43 to 10May44; Maj Douglas J Peacher 11May44 to 9Feb45; Maj Homer Sterling 10Feb to 14Apr45; Capt Clem W Fairchild 15Apr45 to date of surrender.

VMO-5. Org 15Feb44 at Quantico. After three months' training in OY's, departed for Camp Pendleton, Calif, and arrived 25Apr44. Began training with 5thMarDiv. Arrived Pearl Harbor 1Sep44, proceeded to Camp Tarawa, Hawaii, for further training. In Jan45 Sq divided into two groups and after staging through Guam and Saipan both ech's standing by on CVE's off Iwo on 19Feb45. All planes ashore 28Feb45. During Mar45 Sq operated in support of 5thMarDiv. Sq left Iwo 27Mar45 and returned to Camp Tarawa. Remained in Hawaiian area until war ended. CO's: Lt Roy G Miller 15Feb44 to 5Jun45; Capt Gordon Walker 6Jun45 to date of surrender.

AWS-6. Comm 1Jan44 at Cherry Point. Early in Mar44 ordered to West Coast. On 3Jan45 Sq departed for Kauai, TH. Arrived Okinawa 17Apr45 and set up installations on Kachin Hanto, Taka Banare, and Ike Banare. Continued opns at Okinawa until war ended. CO: Capt Clarence C Gordon.

CASD-6. Comm 1Feb45 at Mojave as part of MASG-51, to service planes of MCVG-6. Remained at Mojave until MCVG-6 went on board *Matanikau* in May45. On 13Jul45 boarded *Puget Sound* for routine flight opns during Jul and Aug45 off Calif coast. CO's: Lt Alonzo L Taylor 1–15Feb45; Lt Edward L Brown 15–28Feb45; Lt Alonzo L Taylor 1–31Mar45; Maj Bruce H Platt 1Apr45 to date of surrender.

VMO-6. Comm 20Nov44 at Quantico. After short training period in OY's, departed for West Coast and trained with 6thMarDiv until 26Jan45. Staged through Guadalcanal, and arrived Okinawa 2Apr45. Operated from Yontan airfield. On 8Jul45 Sq departed Okinawa for Guam where it served at Agaña airfield until war ended. CO: Capt Donald R Garrett.

AWS-7. Comm 1Feb44 at Cherry Point. In Mar44 ordered to Miramar for additional training. Departed for Kauai, TH, Jan45. Arrived Okinawa 6Apr45 and set up operating units at Zampa Misaki. Eight days later units of Sq moved to Hedo Saki where on 19Jun45 was joined by one platoon of Army air-warning bn. CO's: Capt Geoffrey A Sawyer 1Feb to 8Nov44; Capt Paul E Bardet 9Nov44 to 2Aug45; Capt Thomas Turner 2Aug45 to date of surrender.

CASD-7. Org 15Feb45 at Mojave as part of MASG-51 to operate with MCVG-7 when it would go on board a CVE. Conducted routine operations at Mojave until Jul45 thence to Santa Barbara. Went on board *Puget Sound* 10Jul45. CO's: Lt Alonzo L Taylor 15–28Feb45; Lt Edward L Brown 1–11Mar45; Capt John T Bode 12Mar45 to date of surrender.

VMO-7. Org 15Dec44 at Quantico. After brief training period Sq was transf; arrived Ewa 27Feb45. Training continued under operational control of IIIPhibCorps. Departed Pearl 17Apr45 in two CVE's, and between 7–11May45 arrived Okinawa where it camped at Chatan Cub strip and supported IIIPhibCorps Arty. CO's: Lt Lloyd G Russell 15Dec44 to 4Jan45; Capt William A Seward 5Jan45 to date of surrender.

AWS-8. Org 1Mar44 at Cherry Point. After training at Oak Grove, NC, Miramar and Mojave, Sq arrived Oahu 9Jan45, remaining until Feb45. A det att to FMF Amphibious Reconnais Bn set up radar installations in Keise Group late in Mar45. As part of MAG-43 remainder of Sq arrived off Okinawa 1Apr45 and debarked 6Apr45. Soon it estab a day fighter-direction station at Zamami Shima. By 25Apr45 a control center estab on Ie Shima. In Jun45 a camp was set up near Ama Town, Zamami Shima, where routine duties were carried out until end of war. On 3Jul45 equipment and a crew moved to Aguni Shima. CO's: Capt Frank B Freese 1Mar44 to 30Jun45; Capt Robert O Caulkins 1Jul45 to date of surrender.

CASD-8. Comm 15Feb45 at Mojave as part of MASG-51 to maintain and service planes of MCVG-8 on board a CVE. Conducted operational training with MCVG-8 but did not serve on board a CVE during war. CO's: Lt Russell R Dalzell 15Feb to 13Mar45; Lt Robert S Logan 14Mar to 26Apr45; Maj James T Breen 27Apr45 to date of surrender.

VMO-8. Org 28Dec44 at Quantico. After a short training period in OY's, Sq departed Quantico arrived West Coast 6Mar45; en route overseas 25Mar45 and arrived Guam 13Apr45. Placed under operational control of VPhibCorps but att to MAG-21. Continued operations with VPhibCorps Arty until war ended. CO's: Lt William J Spalding 28Dec44 to 29Jul45; Lt Charles K Barton 30Jul to 31Aug45; Capt Arthur R Laret 1Sep45 to date of surrender.

AWS-9. Comm 1Apr44 at Cherry Point. Trained in CP area and in May44 transf from 9thMAW to Miramar, reporting 10Jun44. After a year's training Sq transf to Ewa and remained there until war ended. CO's: Capt Leon H Connell 1Apr44 to 16Feb45; Capt William A McCluskey Jr 17Feb to 17May45; Capt Charles T Ingersoll 18May to 21Jul45; Capt William A McCluskey Jr 22Jul45 to date of surrender.

CASD-9. Comm 1May45 at Santa Barbara as a unit of MASG-51 to maintain and service planes of MCVG-9 on board a CVE. Conducted routine training at Santa Barbara. CO: Capt Andrew M McBurney.

MWSS-9. Comm 1Mar44 at Cherry Point as ARS-9 to receive and assign personnel and equip 3dMAW units, and to train QM personnel. ARS-9 transf to 9thMAW on 2Apr44; redesig MWSS-9 on 15May44. In addition to regularly assigned duties MWSS-9 operated a combat-training and conditioning camp. CO's: LtCol Elliott E Bard 1Mar to 5Jun44; LtCol Eugene B Diboll 6Jun44 to date of surrender.

AAWS-10. Comm 1Jan44 at Cherry Point as AWS(AT)-10, a light air-transportable air-warning unit. After a month's training transf to Camp Lejeune. In Mar44 transf to Miramar and joined AWG-2 on 7Mar44 for further training. In Aug44 desig changed to AAWS-10. Following revision of air-warning program AAWS-10 decomm 10Nov44 and personnel integrated into other air-warning sqs. CO: Lt Herbert C Storey.

CASD-10. Activated 1Jun45 at Santa Barbara as a unit of MASG-51 to service and maintain planes of MCVG-10 on board a CVE. Conducted routine training with MCVG-10 at Santa Barbara from its inception until the surrender. CO: Capt Oscar J Deavours.

AWS-11. Comm 1Apr44 at Cherry Point; trained at Bogue, until early Jun44 then ordered to West Coast. Training continued at Miramar and Camp Gillespie until 23Mar45 when sent to Hawaii. Remained there until late May45; left for Okinawa where it arrived 4Jul45. Moved to Kume Shima and started operations 17Jul45 providing early warning for south and west of Okinawa. CO: Capt John L Carnegie.

CASD-11. Activated 1Jun45 at El Toro as part of MASG-46 to maintain and service planes of MCVG-11. Carried out routine maintenance and training at El Toro until war's end. CO: Capt Joseph J Dodson Jr.

AWS-12. Comm 1May44 at Cherry Point. Trained on East Coast until Aug44 and transf to Miramar and AWG-2. On 4Oct44 moved to Santa Barbara to operate as a combination replacement and training sq. Although alerted for overseas duty in Feb45 did not leave until Jun45. Arrived at Ewa 22Jun45 and two days later a det ordered to Kwajalein to relieve an Army unit. During Jul45 Sq personnel sent on TAD with Pac Fleet Radar Center, the Navy's Radar Maintenance School, and Army 508th Air Warning Bn. CO: Capt Emil H Heintz.

CASD-12. Activated 1Jul45 at El Toro as part of MASG-46 to service and maintain planes of MCVG-12. Routine maintenance and training carried out from time of inception to surrender. CO: Capt Robert E Bruce.

AWS-13. Org 5May44 at Cherry Point. Moved to Bogue 27May44 but ret to CP 16Jul44. Arrived NAS, Vero Beach, Fla, 11Aug44. Back to CP 8Jun45 and on 28Jun45 left for Miramar. On 1Jul45 Sq divided into four units, one each to be located at El Toro, Mojave, El Centro, and Santa Barbara. Continued routine training at these locations until war ended. CO's: Capt William A McCluskey Jr 5May44 to 31Jan45; Capt John F Trainor 1Feb to 12Jun45; Capt William E Hooper 13Jun to 16Jul45; Capt Lester B Holmes 17Jul45 to date of surrender.

CASD-13. Org 1Jul45 at Mojave as part of MASG-51 to maintain and service aircraft of MCVG-13 at Santa Barbara. CO: Capt Philip H Irwin.

AWS-14. Comm 1Jun44 at Cherry Point. Six weeks later went to Oak Grove and assumed all air-defense opns. Ret to CP in Sep44. In Nov44 transf to Congaree, and took over operation of control center, remaining there until time of surrender. CO's: Capt Edward R Stainback 1Jun to 27Nov44; Capt Robert M McCormick Jr 28Nov44 to 1Mar45; Capt William E Hooper 2–30Mar45; Capt Robert M McCormick Jr 31Mar45 to date of surrender.

CASD-14. Formed 1Aug45 at Santa Barbara as part of MASG-51 to maintain and service planes of MCVG-14. CO: Maj William Alexander.

AAWS-15. Comm 1Feb44 at Cherry Point as AWS(AT)-15. On 27Mar44 left CP for Miramar, where it arrived and reported to AWG-2 on 31Mar44. In Jun44 nearly half of Sq transf to MBDAG-43 at El Centro. Two months later desig changed to AAWS-15. In mid-Oct44 ret from El Centro to Miramar and decomm 10Nov44. CO: Lt Craig W Parris.

CASD-15. Comm 1Aug45 at El Centro as part of MASG-42 to maintain and service aircraft of MCVG-15. CO: Capt George D Helton.

AWS-16. Comm 1Jun44 at Cherry Point. On 16Jul44 transf in two ech's one to Morehead City, second to Atlantic, and estab communications and radar operations. Both ech's ret to CP 24Sep44 and assumed night opns of AWG-1's control center. Remained at CP and operated ADCC until war ended. CO's: Capt Lumir F Slezak 1Jun to 24Nov44; Capt Thomas Turner 25Nov44 to 13Apr45; Capt Frank W Schraedel 14Apr45 to date of surrender.

CASD-16. Org 1Aug45 at El Centro as part of MASG-42 to maintain and service aircraft of MCVG-16. CO: Capt Richard R Mathison.

AWS-17. Comm 10Aug44 at Cherry Point. Moved to Oak Grove in Sep44 and began operation of air-defense system. A det sent to MCAAF, Bogue, for similar duties. Training and opns carried out in CP area until war ended. CO's: Maj Richardson Dilworth 10–15Aug44; Capt Joseph W Huey Jr 16Aug to 24Nov44; Capt Freeman R Cass 25Nov44 to 19Mar45; Capt Thomas R C Hood 20Mar to 13Apr45; Capt Henry L Sobocinski 14Apr45 to date of surrender.

AWS-18. Comm 1Sep44 at Cherry Point. Later moved to MCAAF, Bogue, with one det being sent to MCAAF, Atlantic. Operated as training and replacement sq. Moved to CP 15Aug45 and reorg as general duty sq att to AWG-1. CO's: Maj John V Collins 1Sep to 12Nov44; Capt Henry W Bransom 13–24Nov44; Capt William E Hooper 25Nov44 to 12Jun45; Capt John F Trainor 13Jun to 15Aug45; Capt Leland F Hanley 16Aug45 to date of surrender.

AWS-20. Comm 1Mar44 at Cherry Point as an air-transportable sq equipped with light radar gear. Transf to Miramar 1May44, to Santa Barbara 12Jun44. Redesig assault air-warning sq 1Aug44. Returned to Miramar 30Oct44. Decomm 10Nov44. CO: Lt Lloyd B Hatcher.

VMF-111. Org 1Jul37 at Quantico as VMF-1. Redesig VMF-111 on 1Jul41. On maneuvers at New Bern when war declared, but next day ret to Quantico and thence to San Diego. Arrived Samoa 11Mar42 and remained until Jan44. Ground ech arrived Roi 7Feb44. Flight ech went to Makin 9Mar44; joined by ground ech 15Mar44. In Nov44 Sq operated temporarily at Roi and then moved to Kwajalein. CO's: Maj Thomas J Walker Jr 1Jul41 to 28Feb42; Capt Daniel W Torrey Jr 1Mar to 30Sep42; Maj Harold J Mitchener 1–4Oct42; Maj Donald K Yost 5Oct to 17Dec42; Maj Leonard K Davis 18Dec42 to 19Sep43; Maj J Frank Cole 20Sep43 to 6Apr44; Maj William E Clasen 7Apr to 27Oct44; Maj William T Herring 28Oct44 to 1Mar45;

Maj Robert D Kelley 2Mar to 18Jul45; Maj Thomas A Todd 19Jul45 to date of surrender.

VMF-112. Formed 1Mar42 at San Diego. Departed Camp Kearney 13Oct in *Mumu,* arrived Nouméa 28Oct42. First ech landed Henderson 2Nov42 and Sq remained in Solomons until 13Aug43 when it embarked for States, arriving Miramar 5Sep43. Sq reorg and trained as carried sq. Redesig as such 5Nov44. Forward ech on board *Bennington* 3Dec44 to 17Jun45 making strikes at Tokyo and participating in Iwo and Okinawa campaigns. To El Centro in Jul45. CO's: Maj Wilfred J Huffman 1Mar to 10May42; Maj Paul J Fontana 11May42 to 27Mar43; Capt Robert B Fraser 28Mar to 8Jul43; Maj Herman Hansen Jr 9–25Jul43; Maj Gregory Boyington 26Jul to 11Aug43; Maj Herman Hansen Jr 12Aug43 to 26Aug45; Lt John G Leonard 26Aug45 to date of surrender.

VMF-113. Org 1Jan43 at El Toro and comm 15Sep43. Departed West Coast 28Sep43 for Ewa. In Jan44 ordered to Tarawa thence to Kwajalein and by Feb44 operating at Engebi. Covered Ujeland landings in Apr44 and continued neutralization of Wotje, Maloelap, Mille and Jaluit; ground ech arrived Ie Shima 6May45; joined by flight ech 24May45; Sq moved to Okinawa and operated there from 16Jul45 until war ended. CO's: Capt John H King Jr 1Jan to 4Feb43; Lt Frank C Drury 5–6Feb43; Capt Loren D Everton 7Feb43 to 7Sep44; Maj Charles Kimak 8Sep to 18Dec44; Maj Philip R White 19Dec44 to 20Oct45; Maj Hensley Williams 21Feb45 to date of surrender.

VMF-114. Org 1Jul43 at El Toro. Arrived Ewa 23Oct43 and trained for two months. From 18Dec43 until 27Feb44 Sq flew CAP and escort missions from Midway, then ret to Ewa. To Espíritu in Mar44 whence flight ech went to Green 28Mar44 to carry out strikes against Bismarcks targets until 8May44. Ground ech ashore at Peleliu 17Sep44 followed by flight ech on 26Sep44. Furnished close support for 5th Marines landing on Ngesebus. In Oct44 began strikes against Yap and Babelthuap. A det went to Ulithi on 10Mar45 for CAP duties while remainder of Sq continued routine missions. Ceased opns 1Jun45 and prepared to ret to West Coast, where it was when war ended. CO's: Maj Edmund F Overend 1Jul to 17Sep43; Capt Robert F Stout 18Sept43 to 3Mar45; Maj Robert Tucker 4Mar to 12Apr45; Maj Martin E W Oelrich 13Apr to 1Jun45; WO Alvin J Carmody 2Jun to 1Aug45; Maj Herbert H Long 2Aug45 to date of surrender.

VMF-115. Org 1Jul43 at Santa Barbara. Arrived Epsíritu 4Mar44. Ground ech moved to Guadalcanal but flight ech remained at Espíritu until 18Apr44 when it left for Bougainville. Ground ech arrived Emirau 20Apr44 to be joined by flight each 2May44. Moved to Leyte Dec44 and covered Ormoc landings and supported those at Mindoro. Furnished ground support and flew escort missions in Cebu opns during Feb45. Supported landings on Mindanao during Mar45 and in mid-Mar45 moved to Zamboanga. In Apr45 covered Bongao Sanga Sanga and Jolo landings, supported Dumaguete and Negros invasions. Continued routine sorties against targets on Mindanao for remainder of war. CO's: Maj John S MacLaughlin Jr 1–16Jul43; Maj Joseph J Foss 17Jul43 to 20Sep44; Maj John H King Jr 21 Sep44 to 29May45; Maj John S Payne 30May to 17Aug45; Maj Thomas M Coles 18Aug45 to date of surrender.

VMF-121. Comm 24Jun41 at Quantico. Departed for San Diego 11Dec41. Arrived New Caledonia Aug42. On 25Sep42 forward flight ech landed on Guadalcanal followed by remaining pilots 9Oct42 and ground ech 13Oct42. Completed three tours of combat in Solomons. Located at Mojave in Oct43 where it was re-oufitted and re-trained. In Jul44 sailed on board *Kwajalein* for Espíritu where it arrived 4Aug44. Ground ech arrived Peleliu 15Sep44 and went ashore 16Sep44. Flight ech arrived from Emirau 25Oct44 and began strikes against Yap. Served at Peleliu until 1Sep45 when embarked for US. CO's: Maj Samuel S Jack 24Jun41 to 28Feb42; Capt Leonard K Davis 1Mar to 16Dec42; Lt William F Wilson 17–31Dec42; Maj Donald K Yost 1Jan to 12Mar43; Maj Joseph N Renner 13–26Mar43; Maj Ray L Vroome 27Mar to 14May43; Capt Robert E Bruce 15May to 23Aug43; Lt Henry O DeFries 24Aug to 24Oct43; Capt Quintus B Nelson 25Oct to 30Nov43; Maj Walter J Meyer 1Dec43 to 25May45; Maj Claude H Welch 26May to 12Jun45; Maj Robert Tucker 13Jun to 31Jul45; Lt Richard M Loughery 1Aug45 to date of surrender.

VMF-122. Org 1Mar42 at Camp Kearney. Arrived Epíritu 9Nov42 and four days later some of its pilots reported at Guadalcanal for duty with VMF-121. Ground ech arrived Henderson 17Jan43 and for next six months serviced not only planes of their own sq but also those of four other Marine and two Navy sq's. Flight ech departed for Espíritu 25Apr43 and during Jun and Jul43 participated in New Georgia campaign. On 23Jul43 sq finished its tour in Solomons and departed for US. Arrived Miramar 16Aug43 and reorg and trained at El Centro. Sq departed in Jul44 on board *Hollandia* to ret to Espíritu. In Aug44 ground ech embarked in *Tryon* for Palaus landing and flight ech flew to Emirau. By 1Oct44 flight and ground ech's were reunited and began strikes against Babelthuap, Koror and Yap. Covered Army landings at Pulo Anna in Nov44. Sq remained at Peleliu until war ended. CO's: Capt Elmer E Brackett Jr 1Mar42 to 19Apr43; Maj Gregory Boyington 20Apr to 7Jun43; Maj Herman Hansen Jr 8Jun to 7Jul43; Maj Robert B Fraser 8Jul to 21Aug43; Maj Joseph H Reinburg 22Aug43 to 31Jan45; Maj Francis E Pierce Jr 1Feb to 14Mar45; Maj Quintus B Nelson 15Mar to 15Apr45; Maj Israel E Boniske 16–18Apr45; Maj John R. Bohnet 19Apr to 27May45; Maj Donald H Sapp 28May45 to date of surrender.

VMF-123. Org 7Sep42 at San Diego. Departed for combat zone 8Jan43. Began opns 4Feb43 from Guadalcanal where Sq served two tours. To Munda 14Aug43 but during Sep43 Sq divided and half flight ech operated from Russells. Left Solomons 28Nov43 arriving West Coast 14Dec43. Reorg and trained at Santa Barbara and Mojave during 1944. On board *Bennington* from New Year's Eve 1945 to 16Jun45. Flew strikes against Tokyo, supported Iwo landings and entire Okinawa campaign. Arrived El Centro Jul45. CO's: Capt Richard M Baker 7–21Sep42. Maj Edward W Johnston 22Sep42 to 20Apr43; Maj Richard M Baker 21Apr to 11Sept44; Maj Everett V Alward 12Sep44 to 25Feb45; Maj Thomas E Mobley Jr 25Feb45 to date of surrender.

VMF-124. Formed 7Sep42 at Camp Kearney from remnants of VMF-122. Departed San Diego 8Jan43 in *Lurline;* arrived Guadalcanal 11Feb43. First sq equipped with Corsairs. Remained Solomons until 7Sep43 participating in Russells, New Georgia and Vella Lavella opns. Arrived Miramar 13Oct43; reorg and trained at Mojave until 18Sep44. Departed San Diego in *Ticonderoga* arriving Pearl 24Sep44. On board *Essex* 28Dec44 to 24Mar45 after supporting Lingayen landings, striking Tokyo and covering Iwo in Feb45, and making pre-invasion strikes on Okinawa in Mar45. Except for 1 off and 47 enl who remained in *Essex*, Sq arrived West Coast Apr45. Reorg, trained and embarked in *Tripoli* 1Sep45 for Ewa. CO's: Lt Cecil B Brewer 7–23Sep42; Maj William E Gise 24Sep42 to 12May43; Capt Cecil B Brewer 13May to 25Jun43; Maj William H Pace 26Jun to 13Jul43; Maj William A Millington 14Jul43 to 23Mar45; Maj James M Johnson 24Mar45 to date of surrender.

VMTB-131. In Jul41 redesig VMSB-131 from VMS-1. Ordered to San Diego in Dec41. Sailed from San Francisco on board *Mount Vernon* for Ewa 6Sep42. Became first Marine torpedo-bombing sq and arrived Espíritu and Guadalcanal in Nov42. Pilots and combat crews rotated between Guadalcanal and Espíritu until relieved 18Feb43. Returned to combat in Apr43; in Jun43 sailed for US, redesig VMTB-131 same month. Sailed from San Diego on board *Petrof Bay* 29Mar44, arrived Espíritu 15Apr44. Forward ech departed 12Jun44, arrived Eniwetok Harbor 27Jun44 to await orders to Marianas. Flight ech flew 3,400-mile transoceanic flight via Gilberts and Marshalls to Guam. By 13Aug44 Sq reunited at Guam. There flew ASP eight months. Att to MAG-22 on 27Apr45 and departed for Okinawa. Flight ech arrived Ie Shima 29May45 to commence ASP's, and support missions for ground troops on Okinawa. On 25Jul45 transf to MAG-14 and went to Awase airfield. CO's: Capt Paul Moret 7Jul41 to 28Feb42; Maj Nathaniel S Clifford 1–23Mar42; Maj Paul Moret 24Mar to 20Nov42; Capt Jens C Aggerbeck Jr 21Nov42 to 14Mar43; Capt George E Dooley 15Mar43 to 1Nov44; Maj Douglas A Bangert 2Nov44 to 10Jul45; Maj Thomas A Reese 11Jul to 9Aug45; Maj Wilbert H Fuller Jr 10Aug45 to date of surrender.

VMTB-132. Org 1Jul41 at Quantico as VMSB-132 when redesig from VMB-1. Departed US 15Oct42, arrived Nouméa 28Oct42. Next day went to Guadalcanal. Pilots and gunners evacuated to Epíritu in late Dec42, joined there in Jan43 by ground ech. Flight ech left ground ech at Espíritu and ret to Guadalcanal in Jun43. Sq ret to US 26Oct43. Reorg at El Toro and Santa Barbara. Redesig VMTB-132 on

14Oct44. On board *Cape Gloucester* 21May45 and arrived Leyte 29Jun45. Operated in East China Sea during Jul and Aug45. CO's: Maj Albert D Cooley 1Jul41 to 28Feb42; Capt Joseph Sailer Jr 1 Mar to 7Dec42; Maj Louis B Robertshaw 8Dec42 to 26May43; Maj Russell D Rupp 27May to 26Sep43; Lt William H Cohron 27–30Sep43; Maj Claude J Carlson 1–21Oct43; Maj Otis V Calhoun Jr 22Oct43 to 26Oct44; Capt Henry W Hise 27Oct44 to date of surrender.

VMSB-133. Org 1May43 at El Toro. Arrived Ewa 9Sep43, divided into two ech's and proceeded one to Johnston, second to Palmyra for ASP. After six months returned to Ewa. Departed Oahu 25Jun44, arrived Espíritu 6Jul44. On 19Aug44 forward ech and part of ground ech departed and arrived at Torokina. Carried out strikes against targets in Bougainville and New Britain areas during Oct and Nov44. Sq departed Piva 12Dec44 for Emirau. After staging through New Guinea, ground ech arrived Lingayen Gulf 21Jan45 where it was joined by flight ech. Sq moved to Mindanao 21Apr45 and supported Army 24th and 31st Inf Divs. During Jun and Jul45 continued attacks on Japanese installations in preparation for landing in Sarangani Bay area. Decomm 1Aug45. CO's: Capt Julian F Acers 1May to 30Jun43; Maj Harrison Brent Jr 1Jul43 to 28Apr44; Maj Lee A Christoffersen 29Apr44 to 8Mar45; Maj Floyd Cummings 9Mar to 1Aug45.

VMTB-134. Org 1May43 at Santa Barbara as VMSB-134. Redesig VMTB-134 on 1Jun43. Forward ech departed San Diego 18Oct43 followed by remaining personnel four days later, proceeded to Espíritu. On 25Nov43 flight ech transf to New Georgia and began close-support missions on Bougainville. Flight ech rejoined ground crew at Espíritu 31Dec43. On 17Jan44 ground ech went to Bougainville to prepare camp at Torokina and was joined a month later by flight ech. In Mar44 Sq moved to Green to fly strikes against Rabaul and Kavieng. Flight ech ret to Espíritu in May44; ground ech transf to Emirau. Ground ech joined flight ech at Espíritu in Jul44 and on 29Sep44 arrived Peleliu. After staging through Emirau and Owi, flight ech landed at Peleliu 6Oct44. Sq remained in Palaus flying ASP and strikes against enemy-held islands until war ended. CO's: Lt Alfred Anger 1–7May43; Maj Jens C Aggerbeck Jr 8May to 8Aug43; Maj Alben C Robertson 9Aug43 to 1Jul44; Maj Russell R Riley 2Jul44 to 27Apr45; Maj Walter F Cornnell 28Apr45 to date of surrender.

VMTB-141. Org 1Mar42 at Camp Kearney as VMSB-141. On 30Aug42 departed for New Caledonia. Arrived for def of Guadalcanal 23Sep42. Remnants of flight ech evac 19Nov42 and transf to Samoa, but ground ech remained until 19Jan43 when transf to New Hebrides. Left Efate in May43 and proceeded to Auckland, NZ, where they took over command of a NZ airdrome. Departed SoPac 17Sep43, arrived in US late that month. On 14Oct44 redesig VMBF-141 and equipped with Corsairs. In May45 redesig VMTB-141 and operated with TBM's as a replacement-training sq at El Toro until war ended. CO's: Capt George A Sarles 1Mar to 30Jun42; Maj Gordon A Bell 1Jul to 13Oct42; Lt Wortham S Ashcroft 14Oct to 8Nov42; Lt Robert M Patterson 9–12Nov42; Lt Walter R Bartosh 13–18Nov42; Maj George A Sarles 18Nov to 16Dec42; Capt Claude J Carlson Jr 17Dec42 to 8Mar43; Lt Oscar J Camp Jr 8Mar to 1Apr43; Maj Howard F Bowker Jr 1Apr to 14May43; Capt Middleton P Barrow 15May to 25Aug43; Lt John E Lepke 26Aug to 23Oct43; Capt John H McEniry Jr 24Oct43 to 21Jan44; Maj Wayne M Cargill 21Jan to 15Dec44; Capt Lee J Crook 16Dec44 to 15Mar45; CWO William H Sherman 15Mar to 11May45; Maj Richard E Figley 11May to 25Jun45; Maj Thaddeus Levandowski 26Jun45 to date of surrender.

VMSB-142. Org 1Mar42 at Camp Kearney. Departed West Coast 15Oct42 for Guadalcanal. Flew ASP's in Espíritu area and ret to Guadalcanal by Mar43. Flight ech left Guadalcanal 27Apr43 for Fiji Is, and stayed until Sep43, then moved to Emirau to participate in neutralization of Rabaul. Forward ech departed for Philippines 24Dec44 while rear ech remained at Emirau until 24Jan45. Provided close support for Army in Luzon area until 17Mar45. In Apr45 covered Sanga Sanga and Bongao landings and provided support during May and Jun45 in Davao area. Had returned to West Coast by war's end. CO's: Maj William K Pottinger 1Mar to 6Sep42; Maj Robert H Richard 7Sep42 to 8Jun43; Maj William A Houston Jr 9Jun to 10Jul43; Capt Jack L Brushert 11–17Jul43; Capt Hoyle R Barr 18Jul43 to 8Jun45; Maj James L Fritsche 9Jun45 to date of surrender.

VMTB-143. Org 7Sep42 as VMSB-143 but redesig VMTB-143 on 31May43. Departed San Diego 28Dec42, arrived Efate 16Jan43. Flight ech arrived Guadalcanal 18Feb43; laid aerial mines in Kahili Harbor 21Mar43. Furnished air support for ground troops during New Georgia campaign. Supported Vella Lavella operation in Aug43 and part of Sep43 when Sq returned to Espíritu. In Oct43 flight ech divided into three parts: one at Espíritu, one at Guadalcanal, third at Munda. Participated in Empress Augusta Bay landings 1Nov43. Moved to Bougainville from Munda in Jan44 and made strikes on Rabaul. Ret to US in Jun44 where it was reorg and trained as a carrier sq at Santa Barbara. Departed 12Apr45 in *Gilbert Islands*. Participated in Okinawa campaign from May to Jul45 when participated in support of Balikpapan landings. Off Japanese mainland in Aug45 and at time of surrender. CO's: Maj Graham H Benson 7Sep to 26Nov42; Maj John W Sapp Jr 27Nov42 to 14May43; Maj Warren G Mollenkamp 15May to 11Nov43; Lt William O Cain Jr 12–26Nov43; Capt Henry W Hise 27Nov43 to 31Mar44; Maj Arthur W Little Jr 1Apr to 7May44; Capt Myron Sulzberger Jr 8–26May44; Capt George A Smith 27May to 29Jun44; Maj George B Woodbury 30Jun44 to 1Jan45; Capt John E Worlund 2Jan45 to date of surrender.

VMTB-144. Org 7Sep42 at San Diego as VMSB-144. Flight ech arrived Guadalcanal 5Feb43 after staging through Nouméa and Efate where ground ech remained. Flight ech ret from first combat tour 12Mar43. On 8May43 ground ech transf to Guadalcanal and on 13Jun43 flight ech rejoined ground ech. By 26Jun43 flight ech at Russells and operated until 26Jul43; ret to Henderson, thence to Efate. Flight ech arrived Munda 15Oct43. Between 1–21Nov43 furnished close support to troops on Bougainville. Ret to Efate 22Nov43 and rejoined ground ech. Sq embarked for US 12Jan44. Redesig VMTB-144 on 14Oct44; redesig VMTB(CVS)-144 on 5Nov44. In May45 Sq moved to Mojave and desig reverted to VMTB-144. Based at Santa Barbara during Jul and Aug and on 12Aug44 reported on board *Salerno Bay* where it was when war ended. CO's: Maj John L D Gabbert 7Sep to 22Nov42; Capt Roscoe M Nelson 23Nov42 to 21Apr43; Capt Frank E Hollar 21Apr to 26Nov43; Capt Morris T Nelson 27Nov43 to 11Jan44; Capt Robert H Griffen 12Jan to 2Feb44; MTSgt Robert Edens NCOinC 3Feb to 8Mar44; Capt Archibald M Smith Jr 9–10Mar44; Maj Arthur M Moran 11Mar44 to date of surrender.

VMTB-151. Redesig VMO-151 from VMO-1 1Jul41 at Quantico, and 15Sep42 redesig VMSB-151. Left for San Diego with other 1stMAW units in Dec41 but ret to Quantico 10Jan42. Departed Norfolk 9Apr42, arrived Samoa 9May42 where it remained 13 months. On 10Jun43 arrived Uvéa I, Wallis Group. Departed for Eniwetok 25Feb44, arrived Engebi 29Feb44. Part of Sq remained at Roi for patrol and to cover minor landings. Between 9–12Mar44 covered Marine landings on Wotho, Ujae, and Lae. Made "milk runs" against by-passed Marshalls bases until 31May45. On 9Jun45 embarked in *Silverpeck* for US; assigned to MASG-51 for carrier training and redesig VMTB-151. CO's: Maj Thomas C Green prewar to 11May42; Maj Raymond B Hurst 12May to 2Dec42; Capt John E Bell 3–9Dec42; LtCol George A Sarles 9Dec42 to 2Jun43; Maj Maurice W Fletcher 3Jun43 to 23Feb44; LtCol Gordon H Knott 24Feb to 30Oct44; Maj Randolph C Berkeley Jr 31Oct to 4Dec44; Maj Bruce Prosser 5Dec44 to 25Jan45; Maj Robert J Shelley Jr 26Jan to 26Mar45; Maj John H Stock 27Mar to 5Jun45; WO Robert L Harmon 6–30Jun45; Maj Walter J Carr Jr 1Jul45 to date of surrender.

VMR-152. Redesig from VMJ-1 to VMJ-152 at Quantico 7Jul41. Departed San Diego 10–11Oct42. Joined SCAT for Guadalcanal opns, made supply drops during New Georgia campaign. Redesig VMR-152 on 3Jun44. Remained Bougainville until war ended but Sq's planes moved personnel and equipment from Solomons into Philippines and from there into Okinawa. CO's: Maj Thomas J McQuade 7Jul41 to 28Feb42; Maj Deane C Roberts 1Mar to 9Jul42; Maj Elmore W Seeds 10Jul42 to 13Feb43; Maj Dwight M Guillotte 14Feb to 24Aug43; Maj Carl J Fleps 25Aug to 10Oct43; LtCol Elmore W Seeds 11Oct43 to 14Jan44; LtCol Frederick E Leek 15Jan to 1Jun44; LtCol Albert S Munsch 2Jun to 13Nov44; LtCol John P Coursey 14Nov44 to date of surrender.

VMR-153. Org 1Mar42 at San Diego as VMJ-153. In Mar43 forward ech went to New Caledonia as part of SCAT and in May43 rear ech joined flight ech at Tontouta. Flew cargoes into Russells and Munda and evac wounded. Began opns at Bougainville in Nov43. By Mar44 flights made to Green; by Apr44 to Emirau, and by Jun44 to Los Negros. Redesig VMR-153 on 3Jun44; cargo flights went to Palaus in Dec44 thence to Philippines, and by Jun45 included Okinawa. CO's: Maj Ben Z Redfield 1Mar to 5Aug42; Maj Warren E Sweetser Jr 6Aug42 to 16Mar43; Maj Harry R Van Liew 17Mar to 4Apr43; Maj William K Lanman Jr 5Apr to 31May43; Maj Elmore W Seeds 1Jun to 4Jul43; Maj Robert B Bell 5Jul to 4Nov43; Maj Freeman W Williams 4Nov43 to 22May44; Maj Theodore W Sanford Jr 23May to 29Jul44; LtCol Harold F Brown 30Jul44 to 7Jul45; Maj Frank M Richards 8Jul to 20Aug45; Maj Charles J Prall 21Aug45 to date of surrender.

VMD-154. Org 1Apr42 at San Diego as VMD-2 but redesig VMD-254 15Sep42. In Oct42 Sq was better trained for combat than the one then desig VMD-154, so desig's exchanged. Forward ech departed San Diego 13Oct42 for Espíritu where it was later joined by remainder of Sq. More than 300 photo recon missions flown from Espíritu and Guadalcanal over Japanese bases in Solomons. On 26Jan43 a Sq plane photographed Puluwat Group, becoming first to penetrate Truk area. Departed Espíritu 6Jan44, arrived San Francisco, Calif, 19Jan44, thereupon joined advance ech as part of MAG-15 at Camp Kearney. In Jun45 Sq personnel transf to VMD-954, and VMD-154 placed on inactive status. CO's: Maj Elliott E Bard 1–12May42; LtCol William C Lemly 13May to 16Aug42; LtCol Elliott E Bard 17Aug42 to 31Jan44; Maj William G Thrash 1Feb to 1Jun44; LtCol Michael Sampas 2Jun44 to 12Jan45; Maj William G Thrash 13Jan to 20Feb45; Maj Albert L Jones 21Feb to 29Jun45; Lt John E Ward 30Jun45 to date of surrender.

VMF-155. Comm 1Oct42 at Samoa as VMO-155. On 5Dec42 Sq and part of personnel ret to US and remainder moved to Guadalcanal area. Sq reorg at Camp Kearney 9Jan43. On 17Apr43 a unit of Sq went on board CVE *Nassau* to participate in occupation of Attu. Transf to El Centro in Jun43. In Feb44 Sq departed San Diego for Midway. After four months there Sq ret to Ewa and from there sailed for Marshalls. On 1Nov44 flight ech flew to Roi, thence to Kwajalein where it joined ground ech. Redesig VMF-155 on 31Jan45. Continued strikes on by-passed Marshalls until war ended. CO's: Capt John P Haines Jr 1Oct42 to 13Jan45; Maj John E Reynolds 14Jan to 14Feb45; Maj Wayne M Cargill 15Feb to 30Jun45; Maj John B Maas Jr 1Jul45 to date of surrender.

VMF-211. On 1Jul41 redesig VMF-211 from VMF-2 at Ewa. Forward ech landed at Wake 4Dec41 and participated in its def. By 14Apr42 newly org VMF-211 embarked in *Lexington* for Palmyra and base-defense duty there. Ret to Ewa in May43, departed for Espíritu in Aug43 where it remained until Oct43 when flight ech moved to Russells. Furnished support for Bougainville landings and by Dec43 Sq was operating from Bougainville against Rabaul. In Mar44 part of Sq went to Green where it remained until 25Apr44, then to Emirau to be joined by rear ech in May44. Flight ech went to Leyte Dec44 to cover Ormoc and Mindoro landings. Covered Lingayen landings 9Jan45. Furnished support for Biri and Capul landings during Feb45. Supported Zamboanga operation on 9Mar45 and two days later ground ech and part of flight ech landed at Zamboanga. Supported landings at Bongao, Jolo and Malabang during Apr45. Covered Sarangani Bay landing 12Jul45. CO's: Maj Charles L Fike 1Jul to 16Nov41; Maj Paul A Putnam 17Nov to 23Dec41; Maj Luther S Moore 24Dec41 to 8Feb42; Maj Harold W Bauer 9–28Feb42; Maj Luther S Moore 1Mar to 7Aug42; Maj Radford C West 8Aug to 24Oct42; Maj Charles N Endweiss 25Oct42 to 6Apr43; Maj Harold J Mitchener 7Apr to 15Jul43; Maj Robert A Harvey 16Jul43 to 26Jan44; Maj Thomas V Murto Jr 27Jan to 5May44; Maj Thaddeus P Wojcik 6May to 19Oct44; Maj Stanislaus J Witomski 20Oct44 to 30Jan45; Maj Philip B May 31Jan to 20Mar45; Maj Angus F Davis 21Mar45 to date of surrender.

VMF-212. Comm 1Mar42 at Ewa and on 29Mar42 forward ech arrived Efate. Flight ech arrived Tontouta 11May42 to await completion of field at Efate. During Jun and Jul42 Sq divided between New Hebrides and New Caledonia. Eight pilots went to Guadalcanal in Aug42 to operate with VMF-223. In Sep and Nov42 Sq operated from Henderson. Ret to US 22Nov42 and remained on West Coast until Jun43 then sailed for Midway. After two months there proceeded to Espíritu. By Aug43 Sq was back in Solomons participating in Vella Lavella and Bougainville campaigns. Based at Barakoma 20Oct to 27Nov43 supporting Treasury-Choiseul-

Bougainville opns. Ground ech departed Espíritu for Russells in Nov43 and on 9Dec43 arrived Torokina and remained until 20Jan44 then moved to Piva and stayed there until 20Mar44 when sent to Green. Jan44 found flight ech at Vella Lavella. Remained in Solomons-Bismarcks area, striking Rabaul and supporting Bougainville ground forces until end of 1944. By 8Jan45 Sq was on Samar flying missions to Mindoro, Luzon, Visayas and Mindanao. Flew close-support for Army troops during Mar and Apr45. By 7Jun45 flight ech was on Okinawa and opns were carried out there until war ended. CO's: Maj Harold W Bauer 1Mar to 14Nov42; Maj Frederick R Payne Jr 14Nov42 to 5Feb43; Capt Robert F Stout 6Feb to 2Apr43; Maj Richard H Hughes 2Apr to 31May43; Maj Stewart B O'Neill Jr 1Jun to 31Dec43; Maj Hugh M Elwood 1Jan to 23Apr44; Maj Wilbur A Free 24Apr to 8May44; Maj Boyd C McElhany Jr 9May to 18Nov44; Maj Quinton R Johns 18Nov44 to 27Apr45; Maj John P McMahon 27Apr45 to date of surrender.

VMF-213. Org 1Jul42 at Ewa. On 21Feb43 left for Espíritu. Arrived 1Mar43 and on 11Mar43 first Corsairs arrived and familiarization commenced. Sq's pilots went to New Caledonia where they catapulted 39 F4U's from CVE *Copahee* for first time and flew to Tontouta. Six Corsairs flown to Espíritu where pilots remained until 4Apr43, then to Guadalcanal. Ground ech remained Espíritu until 30May43, although 60 enl had been ordered from Ewa 22Feb43 to Russells to help build strip at Banika. On 17Jun43 relieved VMF-124 in Russells. While there Sq covered New Georgia landings. Sq went to Guadalcanal 5Sep43 and started strikes against Kahili 11Sep43. Same day part of Sq moved to Munda. Ret to Espíritu and embarked in *Kitty Hawk* 9Dec43 for US, to be re-formed and re-equipped at Mojave. Sq on board *Ticonderoga* 18Sep44. Continued training at Ewa until 13Dec44 when departed for Ulithi in *Hollandia* and arrived Christmas Day 1944. Flight ech boarded *Essex* 28Dec44. Supported Lingayen landings in Jan45 with strikes on Luzon, Formosa and Indochina. Struck Tokyo area in Feb45, Okinawa in Mar45. To Santa Barbara in Mar45 and still there when war ended. CO's: Capt Herbert T Merrill 1Jul to 31Aug42; Maj Charles N Endweiss 1–30Sep42; Maj Wade H Britt Jr 1Oct42 to 13Apr43; Maj Gregory J Weissenberger 13Apr to 21Aug43; Maj James R Anderson 22Aug to 21Oct43; Capt Leonard W McCleary 22Oct to 4Nov43; Maj Stanley R Bailey 5–16Nov43; Capt James R Wallace 17Nov to 10Dec43; Lt Edward O Shaw 11Dec43 to 12Jan44; Maj Sherman A Smith 12–31Jan44; Maj Donald P Frame 1Feb44 to 28Jan45; Maj Louis R Smunk 29Jan to 4Feb45; Maj David E Marshall 5Feb to 9Jul45; Maj Conrad G Winter 10Jul45 to date of surrender.

VMF-214. Comm 1Jul42 at Ewa with nucleus of veterans of Midway. Arrived Espíritu Feb43 in *Wright* and *Nassau*. Flight ech to Guadalcanal 10Mar to 17May43. Trained in F4U's at Efate in Jun and Jul43 and ret to Russells 21Jul43, rejoining ground ech for first time. Following Munda's capture VMF-214 moved there. Sq reorg in Sep43 and operated from Munda in Sep and Oct43, then ret to Espíritu. On 28Nov43 at Vella Lavella and made first fighter sweep against Rabaul 17Dec43. Transf to US in Jan44 and began training for carrier duty. Boarded *Franklin* 4Feb45 and began opns off Japan 18Mar45. Next day *Franklin* bombed with great loss of life after which Sq ret to El Centro, Calif, where it was when war ended. CO's: Capt Charles W Somers 1–20Jul42; Capt George F Britt 21Jul42 to 8Jun43; Maj Henry A Ellis Jr 9Jun to 11Jul43; Maj William H Pace 12Jul to 6Aug43; Capt John R Burnett 7Aug to 6Sep43; Maj Gregory R Boyington 7Sep43 to 3Jan44; Capt Lawrence H Howe 4–28Jan44; (Sq inactive at Santa Barbara, Calif, 29Jan to 8Feb44); Lt Ransom R Tilton 9Feb to 1Mar44; Maj Warren H McPherson 2Mar to 10Apr44; Maj Stanley R Bailey 11Apr44 to 9Jun45; Maj James W Merritt 10–30Jun45; Lt Robert J McDonnell 1–31Jul45; Maj George L Hollowell 1Aug45 to date of surrender.

VMF-215. Org 3Jun42 as VMSB-244, redesig VMSB-242 on 14Sep42, then VMF-215 on 15Sep42. Departed for Pearl Harbor 23Feb43, for Midway 12Apr43. Arrived Espíritu 1Jul43 and 25Jul43 began attacking enemy bases in northern Solomons. Moved to Munda 12Aug43. Second tour spent at Vella Lavella from where it covered Empress Augusta Bay landings 1Nov43. Started opns 27Jan44 from Torokina with fighter sweeps over Rabaul. Sq re-formed with new personnel in Mar44 and Apr44 found newly org flight ech at Bougainville. From Bougainville Sq's planes struck Rabaul, Kavieng and shipping in Bismarcks. On 7May44 Sq was re-formed at Turtle Bay from where flight ech left for Emirau to be joined by ground crew on 5Aug44. On 14Sep44 entire Sq left Emirau for Guadalcanal en route to US where it arrived 20Oct44 and from then until war ended was replacement-training sq. CO's: Capt Robert W Clark 3Jun to 9Jul42; Capt James L Neefus 9Jul42 to 30Sep43; LtCol Herbert H Williamson 1Oct to 5Dec43; Maj Robert G Owens 6Dec43 to 26Feb44; Maj James K Dill 27Feb to 7Jun44; Maj Benjamin S Hargrave Jr 8Jun to 30Aug44; Maj Quinton R Johns 31Aug to 11Sep44; Lt Albert E Ennis 12Sep to 6Nov44; (Sq inactive at El Toro, Calif, 6–21Nov44); Maj William P Boland 21Nov44 to 27Feb45; Maj Eyestein J Nelson 2Mar to 1May45; LtCol William A Millington 2May to 30Jun45; Maj Alan J Armstrong 2Jul45 to date of surrender.

VMF-216.   Org 1Jan43, at El Centro; comm 16Sep43, departed that day for Pearl Harbor in *Long Island*. Arrived Espíritu 6Nov43. Ground ech remained at Efate as flight ech relieved VMF-211 in Russells 23Nov43. Arrived Bougainville 10Dec43. Flight ech moved to Piva 14Feb44. Sq sent to Guam 4Aug44, attacked Rota and Pagan during following months. In Dec44 went to Oahu for carrier training, and flight ech reported on board *Wasp* at Ulithi 5Feb45. Sq supported Iwo landings, and made strikes on Japan and Okinawa. Ret to Pearl Harbor and left for US 26Mar45 on board *Copahee*. Remained at Santa Barbara for rest of war. CO's: Capt William P Addington 1–26Jan43; Capt Max R Read Jr 26Jan to 23Jun43; Maj Rivers J Morrell Jr 23Jun43 to 22Jan44; Maj Benjamin S Hargrave Jr 22Jan to 4May44; Maj John Fitting Jr 5May to 30Oct44; Maj Richard L Blume Jr 31Oct to 7Dec44; Maj George E Dooley 8Dec44 to 18Apr45; Lt George F Kelley 19Apr to 20May45; Maj Robert L Anderson 21May45 to date of surrender.

VMF-217.   Org 1Jul43 at El Centro and trained there until 12Dec43. One week later transf to North Island whence Sq embarked in *Barnes* for combat area. Arrived Espíritu 5Jan44; left for Bougainville 28Jan44. Commenced strikes against Rabaul 30Jan44. Ground ech remained at Espíritu servicing planes of six sq's. Flight ech ret Espíritu 19Mar44 and remained until 1Jun44 when Sq embarked in *Santee, Cetus, Typhoon* and *Young America* for Guam. Flight ech at West Field, Guam, 4Aug44; all personnel ashore by 20Aug44. On 7Aug44 commenced strikes against Rota. Flight ech qualified for carrier duty in Dec44 and boarded *Wasp* 3Feb45; rear ech remained Ewa. Made carrier-based strikes against Japan, Iwo Jima and Okinawa. Flight ech to Ewa 25Mar45; arrived Miramar 2Apr45. Small ech remained on board *Wasp* until 3Apr45; disembarked at Ewa and stayed until 10Apr45 when it embarked in *Lurline* for West Coast, arriving Miramar 16Apr45. On 17May45 Sq moved to El Toro where it continued carrier training until war ended. CO's: Maj Max R Read Jr 1Jul43 to 16Dec44; Maj Jack R Amende Jr 17Dec44 to 16Feb45; Maj George S Buck 17Feb to 19Apr45; Lt William Mackey 20Apr to 8May45; Capt Newell P Weed Jr 9–23May45; Maj Herbert A Peters 23May45 to date of surrender.

VMF-218.   Org 1Jul43 at Mojave, comm 15Sep43. Departed on board *Barnes* in Dec43 and disembarked 5Jan44 at Espíritu. On 20Jan44 ground ech proceeded to Bougainville where it was joined by flight ech 1Feb44. Covered Green landings 15Feb44. By 19Mar44 flight ech again at Espíritu where it remained until 27Apr44, then moved to Green. Departed there in late Nov44 for Leyte and operated in Philippines. During Dec44 made attacks on southern Luzon. During Jan45 Sq united at Tacloban. Engaged in convoy cover, attacks on Iloilo, and ground-support missions in Cebu. On 10Mar45 covered landings at Zamboanga where forward ech landed with Army troops. During rest of Mar45 flew close-support missions at Capisan and made pre-invasion strikes on Bongao and Jolo. In Apr45 covered Jolo landings and later that month covered those at Cotabato-Parang-Malabang. Continued attacks on Mindanao targets until war ended. CO's: Capt Robert R Read 1–15Jul43; Maj Horace A Pehl 16Jul43 to 28Sep44; Maj Robert T Kingsbury III 29Sep44 to 30Jan45; Maj John M Massey 31Jan45 to date of surrender.

VMF-221.   Org 11Jul41 at San Diego. Sailed for Hawaii 8Dec41. Upon arriving at Pearl a det ordered to relief of Wake and boarded *Saratoga* next day. When Wake fell Sq was diverted to Midway where it lost 15 planes in attack of 4Jun42. Following Battle of Midway Sq moved to Ewa where it remained until 11Feb43, then forward ech departed for Guadalcanal. Sq operated there for two tours; third tour spent at

Vella Lavella. Covered Treasury landings on 27Oct43 and supported Bougainville invasion four days later. Moved to Munda 4Nov43 and on 11Nov43 supported carrier strike on Rabaul. Ret to Efate 19Nov43 and 14Dec43 Sq departed for San Francisco. Between 2–9Jan44 Sq was reorg at Miramar and on 10Jan44 went to Santa Barbara for carrier training. Went on board *Bunker Hill* in Dec44. Participated in first naval air missions against Tokyo and covered Iwo landings. During Apr and part of May45 supported Okinawa invasion and opns. On 9Jun45 carrier ech joined rear ech at El Centro where Sq was located when war ended. CO's: Maj William G Manley 11Jul to 5Oct41; Maj Verne J McCaul 6Oct41 to 18Apr42; Capt James L Neefus 19Apr to 17May42; Maj Floyd B Parks 8May to 3Jun42; Capt Kirk Armistead 4Jun to 31Jul42; Capt Robert R Burns 1–7Aug42; LtCol Luther S Moore 8Aug to 5Oct42; Maj Harold J Mitchener 6Oct42 to 18Feb43; Capt Robert R Burns 19Feb to 31May43; Maj Monfurd K Peyton 1Jun to 16Aug43; Capt John S Payne 17–24Aug43; Maj Nathan T Post Jr 25Aug43 to 11Oct44; Maj Edwin S Roberts Jr 12Oct44 to 31Jul45; Capt Frank B Baldwin 1–17Aug45; Lt Harry Pierkowski 18–28Aug45; Lt Franklin T Hovore 29Aug45 to date of surrender.

VMF-222. Comm 1Mar42 at Midway. Transf to Ewa during Apr42 then moved to West Coast Sep42, but ret to Ewa 1Mar43. Flight ech departed for Midway 9May43 where it was joined by ground ech 21May43. Remained at Midway until Jul43, then sailed for Espíritu. Flight ech flew to Guadalcanal 3Sep43, thence to Munda. By mid-Nov43 Sq based at Vella Lavella. On 17Dec43 participated in first fighter sweep over Rabaul. During Jan44 flight ech at Efate, ground ech at Bougainville. Shelling of Piva during Mar44 forced Sq to move to Emirau. Moved to Espíritu from Emirau on 18Jun44. From 5Aug44 to 14Jan45 based at Green. Transf to Samar in Jan45 and participated in liberation of Philippines. Moved to Okinawa 22May45. CO's: Capt Robert M Haynes 1Mar to 5Sep42; Lt Ralph Martin 6–27Sep42; Capt Max J Volcansek Jr 28Sep42 to 4Nov43; Maj Alfred N Gordon 5Nov43 to 5Apr44; Maj Roy T Spurlock 6Apr44 to 27Apr45; Maj Harold A Harwood 28Apr45 to date of surrender.

VMF-223. Org 1May42 at Ewa. Sailed from Pearl Harbor 3Aug42 and was first fighter sq in Solomons. Left Guadalcanal 16Oct42 and arrived San Francisco 1Nov42 thence to El Toro. In Jul43 sent to Midway. In Nov43 ground ech at Efate, pilots at Vella Lavella. In Feb44 went to Piva Yoke but in Mar44 ground ech sent to Green. On 18Jun44 flight ech ret to Espíritu and ground ech departed for Bougainville 24Jun44. Participated in neutralization of Rabaul until moved to Samar Jan45. In Philippines 14Jan45 through May45. In May45 ground ech to Okinawa but flight ech didn't move up from Samar until Jun45. CO's: Capt John L Smith 1May to 31Dec42; Lt Conrad G Winter 1–13Jan43; Capt Howard K Marvin 14–25Jan43; Maj Marion E Carl 26Jan43 to 3Feb44; Maj Robert P Keller 4Feb to 2Jul44; Maj David Drucker 3Jul to 13Oct44; Maj Robert F Flaherty 14Oct44 to 24Mar45; Maj Robert W Teller 25Mar to 16Apr45; Maj Howard E King 17Apr to 23Jul45; Maj Julius W Ireland 24Jul45 to date of surrender.

VMF-224. Comm 1May42 at Ewa. Trained at Barbers Point until 14Aug42. Arrived Henderson 30Aug42. Flight ech evac from Guadalcanal 16Oct42. On 2Nov42 remaining Sq personnel departed for Nouméa. In Dec42 Sq at San Diego and 1Jan43 transf to El Toro. On 30Jul43 advance ech departed San Diego, arrived Pearl Harbor 5Aug43. Rear ech arrived ten days later. By 22Sep43 Sq at Pago Pago. Went to Funafuti in Oct43. Left Funafuti Jan44 and forward ech arrived Roi in Feb44 to begin strikes against Marshalls. On 7Apr45 arrived at Yontan airfield. Began opns from Chimu airfield in early Jul45. CO's: Maj Robert E Galer 1May to 4Dec42; Maj Darrell D Irwin 5Dec42 to 24Aug44; Maj Howard A York 25Aug to 31Dec44; Maj James W Poindexter 31Dec44 to 30May45; Maj Robert C Hammond Jr 31May to 14Jun45; Maj Allen T Barnum 15Jun45 to date of surrender.

VMF-225. Comm 1Jan43 at Mojave. Departed from San Diego 24Oct43 and arrived at Ewa six days later. Left Pearl Harbor 5Mar44 and arrived Espíritu later that month. On 1Jun44 departed for Eniwetok in two ech's. Ground ech arrived on Guam one week after D-day and flight ech arrived 4Aug44 to assume air defense of Guam. Ordered to Mojave for carrier training 12May45. There when war ended. CO's: Capt Jack R Amende Jr 1Jan to 25Aug43; Maj James A Embry Jr 26Aug43 to

2Sep44; Maj Jack R Amende Jr 3Sep to 7Dec44; Maj John C Musselman Jr 8Dec44 to 16Apr45; Maj Joseph H Reinburg 17Apr to 16May45; Maj John A Reeder 17May to 30Jun45; Maj John R Stack 1Jul45 to date of surrender.

VMTB-231. Redesig VMSB-231 from VMS-2 on 1Jul41 at Ewa. En route to Midway in *Lexington* 7Dec41. Ret to Ewa 10Dec41 and one week later 17 SB2U's flew to Midway where it remained until 1Mar42 then part of personnel ret to Ewa. Bulk of Sq remained at Midway to become VMSB-241 and as such fought Battle of Midway. On 30Jun42 most of those who had fought as VMSB-241 ret to Ewa and rejoined 231. Reorg 231 arrived Guadalcanal 30Aug42. Stayed until 2Nov42. Arrived San Diego 19Nov42 and moved to El Toro in Jan43. Advance ech left West Coast 18Jul43 and arrived Midway 15Aug43. Departed Midway in Jan44 for Majuro. Arrived there 4Feb44. Began opns against by-passed Marshalls. Equipped with Corsairs in Oct44 and redesig VMBF-231, but on 30Dec44 redesig VMSB-231 and remained in Marshalls until Aug45 when ret to US for carrier duty and redesig VMTB-231. CO's: Maj Clarence J Chappell Jr 1Jul41 to 28Feb42; Maj Raymond C Scollin 1–10Mar42; Maj Charles J Schlapkohl 11Mar to 20Jun42; Maj Leo R Smith 21Jun to 18Sep42; Capt Ruben Iden 19–20Sep42; Maj Elmer G Glidden Jr 20Sep42 to 30Sep43; Capt Homer V Cook 1–31Oct43; Maj Elmer G Glidden Jr 1Nov43 to 4Sep44; Maj William E Abblitt 5Sep44 to 3Feb45; Maj Joseph W White Jr 3Feb to 8Aug45; Capt John G McAllister 9Aug45 to date of surrender.

VMTB-232. Redesig VMSB-232 from VMB-2 on 1Jul41 at Ewa. Suffered heavy damage to aircraft when Japanese struck Pearl Harbor. Sent a det of enl with VMF-211 to Wake. All killed or captured there. Sq arrived Guadalcanal 20Aug42 as first dive-bomber sq to operate in Solomons. Remained in SoPac until 12Oct42 then left for El Toro to be reorg and trained. At Espíritu in Jul43 but in early Sep43 left for Guadalcanal and thence to Munda and supported Bougainville landings in Nov43. Joined in strikes against Rabaul in Dec43 and transf to Piva in Mar44. In May44 flight ech operating from Green and later in month from Emirau. Ground ech remained Espíritu. Moved to Ulithi in Oct44 where Sq remained until Okinawa invasion. Flight ech landed Kadena airfield 22Apr45 and began close-support missions three days later. Began strikes against Japanese home islands from Awase airfield in Jul45. CO's: Maj Ira L Kimes 1Jul41 to 6Jun42; Maj Richard C Mangrum 7Jan42 to 15Jan43; Lt Henry W Hise 16Jan to 5Feb43; Capt Rolland F Smith 6Feb43 to 25Apr44; Maj Menard Doswell III 26Apr44 to 19Jan45; Maj Allan A Feldmeier 20Jan45 to date of surrender.

VMTB-233. Org 1May42 at Ewa as VMSB-233. Arrived Espíritu 12Dec42 and on 24Dec42 flight ech flew to Guadalcanal followed by ground ech 18Jan43. Flight ech ret to Espíritu in Feb43 but by 12Mar43 was back on Guadalcanal. Flight ech ret to Espíritu 22Apr43 and on 12May43 ground ech arrived. On 22May43 reorg as torpedo-bombing sq. Sent to Guadalcanal in early Aug43 and on 29Oct43 at Munda. During Jan44 elements of Sq operated at Munda, Piva, and Torokina. Ret to US in Mar44 for reoutfitting at Santa Barbara. Redesig VMTB-233 in Oct44 and began training for carrier opns. On board *Block Island* in Mar45. Flew close-support missions on Okinawa and made strikes in other Ryukyus areas during May and Jun45. During Jul45 participated in support of Balikpapan campaign. Was off Korea when war ended. CO's: Maj Benjamin W Norris 1–21May42; Maj Clyde T Mattison 22May42 to 19Jan43; Capt Elmer L Gilbert Jr 20Jan to 30Apr43; Maj Claude J Carlson Jr 1–25May43; Maj Howard F Bowker Jr 25May to 8Jun43; Maj Robert H Richard 9–30Jun43; Maj William J O'Neill 1Jul to 3Sep43; Maj Royce W Coln 4Sep43 to 20Mar44; Capt Russell R Riley 21Mar to 16May44; Maj Royce W Coln 17May to 4Jul44; Capt Edward J Montagne Jr 5Jul to 3Aug44; Maj Robert W Vaupell 4Aug44 to 14Feb45; Capt Edmund W Berry 15Feb45 to date of surrender.

VMTB-234. Comm 1May42 at Ewa as VMSB-234. Departed for Espíritu 1Dec42. Began its first combat tour at Guadalcanal 28Jan43. Second combat tour began Guadalcanal 15Apr43. Flight ech went to Fiji Is for patrol duty but ret to Henderson in time to furnish air support on New Georgia. Operating from Munda, Sq began its third tour in Oct43 with strikes in Bougainville area. In Nov43 Sq was at Efate whence it ret to US. Began reorg and training at Miramar in Feb44. Redesig VMTB-234 on 24Oct44 and 1Nov44 began training as carrier sq and again redesig as VMTB-(CVS)-234. On board *Vella Gulf* 10May45, and 23Jul45 began strikes against Pagan and Rota. CO's: Maj Avery R Kier 1May to 6Sep42; Maj William D Roberson 7Sep42 to 4Apr43; Capt Otis V Calhoun Jr 5Apr to 30Sep43; Maj Harold B Penne 1Oct43 to 26Oct44; Capt Edward J Montagne Jr 27Oct44 to date of surrender.

VMSB-235. Comm 1Jan43 at El Centro. On 28Mar43 sailed from San Diego, arriving 4Apr43 at Pearl Harbor, but by 31Aug43 located at Efate. Began opns from Guadalcanal in Sep43; by 31Oct43 ground ech stationed at Munda and flight ech at Efate. In Jan44 ground ech moved to Bougainville. By Apr44 entire Sq on Bougainville. Flew strikes against Bismarcks and Bougainville targets. Its third tour ended in May44 and part of Sq's personnel ret to US. Began fourth combat tour on Bougainville in Jun44. Transf 24Jun44 to Green and continued opns against Rabaul and New Britain. Discontinued opns 13Sep44 and arrived San Francisco 18Oct44 and proceeded to Miramar. Decomm 10Nov44. CO's: Capt Everett E Munn 1Jan43 to 10Feb44; Maj Glenn L Todd 11Feb to 17May44; Capt Edward C Willard 18May to 16Aug44; Maj James A Feeley Jr 17Aug to 13Sep44; Capt Lawrence A Morgan 14–26Sep44; Capt William C Tassos 26Sep to 24Oct44; Lt Ralph W Dorius 25Oct to 2Nov44; Capt Reginald S Ward 3–10Nov44.

VMSB-236. Activated 1Jan43 at Mojave. Located Ewa in Apr43. On 4Sep43 part of flight ech arrived Guadalcanal to relieve VMSB-234. Participated in first dive-bombing attack on Bougainville 23Sep43. Ground ech at Munda by 22Oct43. Forward ech arrived Munda 25Nov43. Forward ech moved to Torokina 25Jan44. From 24Apr to 20May44 flight ech at Ocean Field on Green, then ret to Torokina. Meanwhile ground ech had been at Efate since Feb44. Sq reunited at Munda in Jun44. Back to Torokina from Aug44 to Jan45 when it went to Luzon. Ground-support missions flown throughout Luzon and Mindanao campaigns. Decomm 1Aug45. CO's: Capt William A Cloman Jr 1Jan to 10Mar43; Capt Robert L Knight 11Mar to 15Apr43; Maj Floyd E Beard Jr 16Apr to 10Nov43; Maj William A Cloman Jr 11Nov43 to 13Jun44; Maj Edward R Polgrean 14Jun to 14Oct44; Maj Glen H Schluckebier 15–31Oct44; Maj James A Feeley Jr 1Nov to 8Dec44; Maj Fred J Frazer 9Dec44 to 24Jul45; CWO Herman E Rasmussen 25Jul to 1Aug45.

VMSB-241. Comm 1Mar42 at Midway and participated in that battle. Sq reorg with new personnel and remained at Midway until Mar43. Departed Midway and joined MAG-24 at Ewa. Arrived Tutuila 24Apr43 and remained eight months. Moved to Efate 16Dec43. Left there 2Feb44 and was operating from Piva by 7Feb44. Ret to Efate 18Mar44. Flight ech arrived Emirau 13May44 to continue bombing of Rabaul. Ground crews arrived Munda 18Jun44; flight ech ret to Efate but rejoined ground ech 8Jul44. Arrived Luzon in Jan45. Ground ech sailed for Mindanao 10Apr45, followed five days later by flight ech. Decomm 1Aug45. CO's: Capt Lewis H Delano Jr 1Mar to 10Apr42; Capt Leo R Smith 11–16Apr42; Maj Lofton R Henderson 17Apr to 3Jun42; Capt Marshall A Tyler 4Jun to 3Sep42; Capt William E Clasen 4Sep to 14Oct42; Maj Joseph P Fuchs 15Oct42 to 14Apr43; Maj Wayne M Cargill 15Apr to 11Oct43; Capt William W Wood 12Oct to 15Nov43; Maj James A Feeley 16Nov43 to 11Aug44; Maj James C Lindsay 11Aug to 31Oct44; Maj Jack L Brushert 1Nov to 9Dec44; Maj Benjamin B Manchester III 10Dec44 to 19Feb45; Maj Jack L Brushert 20Feb to 22Jul45; Capt Armon Christopherson 23Jul to 1Aug45.

VMTB-242. Comm 1Jul43 at El Centro. Departed on board CVE *Kitkun Bay* 28Jan44 for Espíritu, where it arrived 15Feb44. Flight ech flew to Bougainville from 9–27Apr44. Strikes made against Rabaul and enemy positions at Buka Passage. Ground ech departed 12Jun44 on board *Cape Mears* and *Crater* and arrived Eniwetok 21Jun44. Flight ech departed Espíritu for Tinian 13Aug44 on 3,400-mile flight and assumed garrison duty. In Mar45 forward ech moved to Iwo and rear ech remained at Tinian. Operated as separate units on Iwo and Tinian until war ended. CO's: Maj William W Dean 1Jul43 to 30Apr45; Maj John J Conrad 1May to 7Jun45; Maj Thomas J O'Connor 8Jun45 to date of surrender.

VMSB-243. Comm 3Jun42 at Santa Barbara. On 18Jan43 departed San Diego for Ewa. Split into two ech's 12Mar43, one to Johnston, other to Palmyra. In late Sep43 both ech's ret to Ewa and remained there until 26Oct43 when Sq left for SoPac. Flight ech arrived Munda 20Nov44 while ground ech remained Efate. Made attacks in Nov and Dec43 on Ballale, Kahili and Kara in Bougainville invasion. Flight ech rejoined ground unit at Efate in Dec43. In Mar44 flight ech sent to Green. From

Apr to Jun44 flight ech at Efate, but rejoined ground crews at Emirau in Jun44. On 25Dec44 ground ech and on 27Jan45 flight ech departed for Philippines. Fought throughout Luzon and southern Philippines campaigns. Arrived San Diego in Sep45. CO's: Capt James A Booth Jr 3Jun to 22Nov42; Maj William M Hudson 23Nov42 to 22Jul43; Capt James L Fritsche 23–27Jul43; Maj Thomas J Ahern 28Jul43 to 12Oct44; Maj Joseph W Kean Jr 13Oct44 to 9Aug45; Capt Elton D Boone Jr 10–14Aug45; Capt Donald E Coyle 15Aug45 to date of surrender.

VMSB-244. Org 1Mar42 at Midway as VMSB-242. Transf to Ewa 11Apr42; on 20May42 departed Ewa for Santa Barbara. Redesig VMSB-244 on 14Sep42. Left San Diego 7Jan43 for Midway via Ewa and arrived Midway 20Mar43. Split into two ech's 18Aug43 and proceeded to Hawaii area. Both ech's arrived Espíritu in Oct43. First flight ech moved to Guadalcanal 16Oct43, thence to Munda. First flight ech joined ground ech at Efate 30Nov43 while second flight ech remained at Munda. Sq arrived Piva 10Feb44 while ground ech moved to Torokina. Between 22–25Mar44 flight ech ret to Efate, while ground ech remained at Bougainville. On 13May44 flight ech flew to Green and operated until 21May44 when moved to Emirau. Departed Emirau 24Jun44 and flew to Munda. Transf to Green 18Sep44 and operated there until Dec44 when it went to Philippines where it operated until the surrender. CO's: Capt Clyde T Mattison 1Mar to 10Apr42; Capt Lewis H Delano Jr 11–30Apr42; Maj Edward E Authier 1May42 to 17Jan43; Maj Robert J Johnson 18Jan43 to 24Jan44; Maj Harry W Reed 25Jan to 30Apr44; Capt Richard Belyea 1May to 1Jul44; Maj Frank R Porter Jr 2Jul to 17Dec44; Maj John L Dexter 17–19Dec44; Maj Vance H Hudgins 20Dec44 to date of surrender.

VMSB-245. Formed 1Jul43 at El Toro. Transf to Ewa 31Dec43. Went to Midway 5Jan44 but ret to Ewa 1Apr44. Went on board *Copahee* 5May44 and arrived Majuro 13May44. Transf to Makin late in May44. Between 1Jun and 29Oct44 made strikes against by-passed Marshalls. Moved from Makin to Majuro in Oct44 and continued strike schedule. On 15Mar45 began opns at Ulithi. CO's: Maj Richard L Blain 1Jul to 24Aug43; Maj Julian F Acers 25Aug43 to 23Sep44; Maj Robert F Halladay 24Sep44 to 30Jun45; Maj John E Bell 1Jul45 to date of surrender.

VMF-251. Comm 1Dec41 at San Diego as VMO-251. Ordered to New Zealand in May42 but orders changed and Sq went to Espíritu. Mission changed from observation to fighter sq. Sq photographers flew regularly with Army B-17's from Tontouta and Espíritu until 30Oct42. VMO-251 operated field at Espíritu, maintained and serviced Army, Navy and Marine planes. Entire Sq moved to Guadalcanal 17Jan43 although many pilots had served at Henderson previously. By Jul43 Sq was in US but 29Feb44 departed West Coast and arrived at Espíritu 9Mar44. Moved to Green, then to Bougainville where from Jun to Dec44 participated in neutralization of Bismarcks area. On 2Jan45 arrived at Samar. Redesig VMF-251 on 31Jan45. Operated in Phillippines until 12May45. Decomm 1Jun45. CO's: Capt Elliott E Bard 1–11Dec41; Maj John N Hart 12Dec41 to 29Oct42; LtCol Charles H Hayes 30Oct to 30Nov42; Capt Ralph R Yeaman 1–7Dec42; Maj William R Campbell 8–10Dec42; Maj Joseph N Renner 11Dec42 to 8Mar43; Lt Walter W Pardee 9–31Mar43; Capt Claude H Welch 1Apr to 14May43; Capt Michael R Yunck 15May to 3Jun43; Maj Carl M Longley 4 Jun to 31Oct43; Capt Robert W Teller 1–5Nov43; Maj William C Humberd 6Nov43 to 9Feb45; Maj William L Bacheler 10Feb to 14Apr45; Maj Thomas W Furlow 15Apr to 20May45; Lt Glen F Keithley 21May to 1Jun45.

VMR-252. Redesig VMJ-252 from VMJ-2 on 1Jul41 at Ewa. By May42 had initiated first air-transport service to Midway and other outlying Pac bases. Became unit of TAG. Redesig VMR-252 on 13Jun44. Supply and evac missions flown from Marshalls, Saipan, Tinian, Guam and Iwo invasions. Moved to Kwajalein in Mar45 and following month was operating in and out of Okinawa. CO's: Maj Perry K Smith 1Jul41 to 21Feb42; Maj William A Willis 22Feb to 20Apr42; Capt John S Carter 21Apr to 29May42; Maj William A Willis 30May to 30June42; Capt John S Carter 1Jul to 24Dec42; Maj Harry H Bullock 25Dec42 to 21Jan43; LtCol James M Daly 22Jan to 25Jun43; Maj Harry H Bullock 26Jun to 31Dec43; Maj Neil R MacIntyre 1Jan to 3Mar44; Maj Robert B Meyersburg 4 Mar to 31May44; LtCol Neil R MacIntyre 1Jun to 20Jul44; Maj Robert B Meyersburg 21Jul to 1Aug44; LtCol John V Kipp 2Aug to 26Oct44; Maj Ernest C Fusan 27Oct to 8Nov44; LtCol Russell A Bowen 9Nov44 to 7Apr45; Maj Nicholas A Sisak 8Apr45 to date of surrender.

VMR-253. Org 11Mar42 at Ewa as VMJ-253. Arrived New Caledonia 1Sep42 and two days later landed its first plane at Guadalcanal. Became unit of SCAT, then of TAG. Redesig VMR-253 on 30Jul44. First flight ech landed on Guam 18Aug44 and next day second flight ech arrived Tinian. Due to inadequate facilities on Guam, Sq returned to Apamama. Moved to Tarawa 4Sep44. Reunited with ground ech at Guam 10Oct44. Evac wounded from Iwo Jima during Feb and Mar45 and began flights to Okinawa in Apr45. CO's: LtCol Perry K Smith 11Mar to 31May42; Maj Harold A Johnson 1Jun to 11Oct42; Maj Henry C Lane 12Oct42 to 14Oct43; Maj Freeman H Williams 15Oct to 3Nov43; Maj Douglas E Keeler 4Nov43 to 23Jan44; Maj James F Moran 24Jan to 12Oct44; Maj William P Addington 13Oct to 2Nov44; LtCol John V Kipp 3Nov44 to 9Mar45; Maj Jack F McCollum 10Mar to 2Apr45; LtCol Desmond E Canavan 3Apr45 to date of surrender.

VMD-254. Comm 25Sep44 as VMD-954 at Cherry Point as replacement-training sq. Moved to Greenville outlying field 1Nov44. Redesig VMD-254 on 28Mar45. Remained Greenville until 22Jul45 when first ech departed for Miramar. First ech on board *Appling* at time of surrender. Remainder of Sq awaiting transportation overseas. CO: Maj Vernon O Ullman. (See also VMD-954.)

VMF-311. Org 1Dec42 at Cherry Point. Moved to Parris I 18Apr43. Departed for Miramar 31Aug43 and in Sep43 left San Diego for Pago Pago. Flight ech flew 8Oct43 to Wallis I and was joined there 11 days later by ground ech. Arrived Roi 6Feb44. Ground ech proceeded to Kwajalein 24Feb44, joined five days later by flight ech. Late in Mar44 Sq ret to Roi. From May44 to Jan45 flew missions against Marshalls. On 7Apr45 flight ech landed Yontan airfield. Continued opns from Okinawa until war ended. CO's: Maj Ralph K Rottet 1Dec42 to 31Jan43; Lt Harry B Woodman 1–5Feb43; Lt Roy A Neuendorf 5–15Feb43; Lt Michael J Curran Jr 16–26Feb43; Capt Jack D Kane 27Feb to 31May43; Maj Harry B Hooper Jr 1Jun to 5Jul43; Maj Jack D Kane 6Jul to 31Aug43; Maj Robert L Anderson 1–13Sep43; Maj Harry B Hooper Jr 13Sep43 to 23Oct44; Maj Charles M Kunz 24Oct44 to 10Feb45; Maj Perry L Shuman 11Feb to 15June45; Maj Michael R Yunck 15Jun45 to date of surrender.

VMF-312. Formed 1Jun43 at Parris I. Arrived Miramar in Jan44 and on 28Feb44 embarked for Ewa. After three months' training Sq departed for Espíritu Santo. Ground ech arrived Ulithi 10Oct44, remained until 20Nov44, then left for Espíritu. Flight ech arrived 12Oct44 at Ponam I in Admiralties and 15Nov44 flew to Guadalcanal and Espíritu. Ground ech landed Okinawa 6Apr45 followed by flight ech three days later. Supported Iheya Shima landing and flew strikes against Japan. CO's: Maj Richard M Day 1Jun43 to 13May45; Maj Hugh I Russell 14–24May45; Maj J Frank Cole 25May45 to date of surrender.

VMF-313. Comm 1Oct43 at El Centro. Arrived Ewa 22Mar44. Went to Midway 13Apr44 and remained until Jun44 then ret to Ewa. Transf to Emirau in Sep44 and began opns against Kavieng. Stationed on Leyte by 3Dec44 and covered Mindoro operation on 18Dec44. Ground ech embarked for Mindoro in Feb45 to participate in Zamboanga landings. Flight ech remained on Leyte to furnish air support for guerrillas on Cebu but left for Zamboanga 16Mar45. By 17Mar45 entire Sq reunited at Moret Field, Zamboanga. Decomm 1Jun45. CO's: Maj Hugh I Russell 1Oct to 9Nov43; Maj Philip R White 10Nov43 to 23Feb44; Maj Joe H McGlothin Jr 24Feb44 to 26Apr45; Capt Jay E McDonald 27–29Apr45; Lt John M Lomac 30Apr to 1Jun45.

VMF-314. Comm 1Oct43 at Cherry Point. Embarked 18Jun44 for Ewa thence to Midway. Ret Ewa in Dec44 and remained until Apr45. Part of Sq remained at Guam and ground ech went to Ie Shima 6May45. Flight ech arrived Okinawa in May45. Moved to Chimu airfield 18Jul45 where it was joined three days later by rear ech and operated from there until war ended. CO's: Capt Theodore E Olsen 1Oct to 1Nov43; Capt Raymond A Rogers Jr 2–10Nov43; Capt Frederick G Steckelberg 11–19Nov43; Capt Robert E Schneider 20–28Nov43; Maj Robert E Cameron 29Nov43 to 1Aug45; Maj Christian C Lee 2Aug45 to date of surrender.

VMF-321. Comm 1Feb43 at Cherry Point. Moved to MCAAF, Oak Grove, 19May43 for training, left for SoPac via Samoa. On 20Nov43 Sq was at Efate. Flight ech to Barakoma 24Dec43 and on 1Jan44 operated from Bougainville. Operating from Green Is Mar and Apr44. In Aug44 went to Guam for strikes against

Rota and Pagan. On 17Dec44 departed for Miramar. Transf to Mojave and Santa Barbara for carrier and close-support training. On board *Puget Sound* in Jul and Aug45. CO's: Maj Gordon H Knott 1Feb to 30Sep43; Maj Edmund F Overend 1Oct43 to 28Oct44; Maj Justin M Miller Jr 28Oct44 to 22Mar45; Maj William P Boland Jr 22Mar45 to date of surrender.

VMF-322. Comm 1Jul43 at Cherry Point but transf to Parris I for training. In Jan44 departed for West Coast and Ewa. Arrived Emirau 18Sep44. Flight ech to Espíritu in Oct44, joined by rear ech in Nov44. Flight ech departed Espíritu Mar45 and reached Okinawa 9Apr45. Ground ech arrived Okinawa 1May45. Supported 2dMarDiv landing on Iheya Shima in Jun45. Moved to Awase airfield 15Jul45 and continued opns there until war ended. CO's: Maj Frederick M Rauschenbach 1Jul43 to 30May45; Maj Walter E Lischeid 31May45 to date of surrender.

VMF-323. Comm 1 Aug43 at Cherry Point and trained at MCAAF, Oak Grove until 12Jan44 then moved to El Centro. Departed San Diego 21Jul44 and arrived Ford I a week later. Flight ech arrived Emirau 18Sep44. Ground ech stayed at Ewa. Flight ech ordered to Espíritu 24Oct44 and by 29Nov44 both ech's there. Moved to Manus I in Mar45 and later in month left for Okinawa via Ulithi. Forward ech arrived Okinawa 2Apr45 and by 9Apr45 entire Sq operating from Kadena airfield. Began strikes against Japan in Jun45. Moved to Awase airfield 15Jul45 where it continued opns until war ended. CO's: Maj George C Axtell Jr 1Aug43 to 14Jun45; Maj Martin E W Oelrich 15Jun45 to date of surrender.

VMF-324. Comm 1Oct43 at Cherry Point. Moved to MCAAF, Oak Grove. One month later moved to Simmons-Knott Field, New Bern. Departed for Miramar 15Jul44. Forward ech det 4Aug44 to Mojave for instruction in rockets and heavy bombs. Sailed from San Diego 30Aug44. After staging through Ewa arrived Midway 16Sep44 and remained there until transf to Ewa late Aug45. CO's: Maj Philip R White 1Oct to 9Nov43; Capt Robert W Van Horn 10–11Nov43; Capt George W Wilcox 12–14Nov43; Maj Carl M Longley 15Nov43 to 28Jul45; Maj Robert C Hammond Jr 29Jul to 3Aug45; Maj James W Merritt 4Aug45 to date of surrender.

VMSB-331. Org 1Jan43 at Cherry Point. Transf to Bogue in Jun43; transf to San Diego in Sep43, staged through Tutuila and Wallis I and arrived Nukufetau 15Nov43. Operated there under Ellice Defense and Utility Group during Gilbert Is invasions. On 30Nov43 forward ech sent to Tarawa to aid in patrol opns until 26Dec43; then ret to Nukufetau. Flight ech arrived Majuro 25Feb44; ground ech on 2Mar44. Redesig VMBF-331 in Oct44 but reverted to original desig 30Dec44. Continued attacks on enemy-held islands in Marshalls until war ended. CO's: Capt Robert B Cox 1–26Jan43; Maj James L Beam 26–31Jan43; Capt James A Feeley 1Feb to 15Apr43; Maj Paul R Byrum Jr 16Apr43 to 9May44; Maj James C Otis 10May to 17Dec44; Maj John H McEniry 18Dec44 to 2Feb45; Maj Winston E Jewson 3Feb45 to date of surrender.

VMTB-332. Comm 1Jun43 at Cherry Point as VMSB-332. Transf to Bogue 27Aug43. Departed for West Coast in early Jan44 and continued training at Mojave. On 7Feb44 departed San Diego in *Gambier Bay* and arrived Ewa 13Feb44. Transf to Midway 5Apr44 then back to Ewa 9Jul44 and received SB2C dive bombers. Redesig VMTB-332 on 1Mar45 and operated with TBM's until end of war. CO's: Maj Richard A Beard Jr 1Jun43 to 1Jul44; Maj Robert J Hoey 2Jul to 31Dec44; Maj Miles A Towner 1Jan to 21Mar45; Capt Jonathan L Adams 22–31Mar45; LtCol Jens C Aggerbeck Jr 1 Apr to 31May45; Capt Andrew J Voyles 1–12 June45; Maj Warren G Mollenkamp 13Jun45 to date of surrender.

VMSB-333. Org 1Aug43 at Cherry Point. On 6Sept43 moved to MCAAF, Bogue. Portion of Sq sent to Boca Chica, Fla, in Apr44 for antisubmarine training. Departed for West Coast 1Jun44. On 18Jun44 sailed from San Diego arriving Ewa late that month. In early Jul44 transf to Midway. On 14Oct44 redesig VMBF-333 and transf to Ewa where it received F4U-1D's. Redesig VMSB-333 eff 30Dec44 and reverted to dive-bomber functions. Continued at Ewa until war ended. CO's: Capt Robert F Halladay 1Aug to 30Sep43; Maj Robert J Hoey 1–20Oct43; Maj Leon M Williamson 21Oct43 to 23Aug45; Maj Jack Cosley 24–30Aug45; Maj Perry H Aliff 31Aug45 to date of surrender.

VMSB-334. Comm 1Aug43 at Cherry Point. In Apr44 trans to MCAAF, Atlantic, and in Jul44 ordered to Newport, Ark, for further training. Decomm 10Oct44.

CO's: Maj Bruce Prosser 1Aug43 to 11Aug44; Lt Paul J Gatterdam 12–21Aug44; Capt Henry A Brostek 22Aug44; Maj William A Cloman Jr 23Aug to 10Oct44.

VMSB-341. Comm 1Feb43 at Cherry Point. Moved to MCAAF, Atlantic, 31May43 but ret to CP 1Aug43. Flight ech arrived Pago Pago 6Oct43. Ground ech departed San Diego 30Sep43 and joined flight ech at Upolu 27Oct43. On 17Dec43 ground ech to Efate, united with air ech 23Dec43. From Efate flight ech to Munda as part of Strike Command and alternately served at Munda, Bougainville and Efate until Mar44. Ground ech remained Efate but by Apr44 entire Sq based at Green for opns against Rabaul. Ground ech operating from Emirau by end of May44, while flight ech at Efate. On 24Jun44 Sq was united again at Emirau. To Green in Jul44. In Jan45 ground ech on Luzon, att to MAGSDAGUPAN. Flight ech remained Green until 22Dec44, then flew to Emirau and thence to Luzon 26Jan45. Flew close support throughout Luzon and southern Philippines campaigns. En route to US when war ended. CO's: Capt William E Clasen 1Feb to 30Sep43; Maj George J Waldie Jr 1–7Oct43; Maj William E Clasen 8–30Oct43; Maj George J Waldie Jr 31Oct43 to 23Jan44; Maj James T McDaniel 24Jan to 19May44; Maj Walter D Persons 20May to 14Aug44; Maj Christopher F Irwin Jr 15Aug44 to 3May45; Maj Robert J Bear 4May to 14Aug45; Lt Robert L Morrissey 15Aug45 to date of surrender.

VMSB-342. Comm 1Jul43 at Cherry Point. In Apr44 ordered to MCAAF, Atlantic, and following month some pilots trained at Boca Chica, Fla. In Aug44 transf to Newport, Ark, where Sq remained until decomm 10Oct44. CO's: Maj Joseph W Kean Jr 1Jul43 to 12 Aug44; Lt Richard B Fielder 13–22Aug44; Capt James R LePhew 23–24Aug44; Maj Paul L Andre Jr 25Aug to 10Oct44.

VMSB-343. Comm 1Aug43 at MCAAF, Atlantic. Transf to Greenville in Dec43 and trained there until 15Jul44, when Sq was alerted for overseas duty. Sailed from Miramar 31Aug44 for Ewa. An 1,100-mile overwater hop to Midway made 27Oct44. Operated at Eastern I as part of Hawaiian Sea Frontier. Transf to Sand I in Apr45 where it was when war ended. CO's: Maj Walter E Gregory 1Aug43 to 2Aug45; Maj Harold G Schlendering 3–17Aug45; Maj Perry H Aliff 18–30Aug45; Maj Jack Cosley 31Aug45 to date of surrender.

VMSB-344. Comm 1Jan44 at Cherry Point. Transf to Greenville for training and 20Aug44 ordered to Newport, Ark. Decomm 10Oct44. CO's: Maj Norman E Denning 1Jan to 31Aug44; Maj Kenneth R Chamberlain 1Sep to 10Oct44.

VMF-351. Comm 1Mar43 at Cherry Point as VMO-351. Original mission changed from observation sq to fighter sq. Based at MCAAF, Bogue 11May to 5Sep44 training for European mission (Project DANNY) that never came off. Arrived Mojave 19Sep44. Reported on board *Ranger* early in Dec44 for carrier qualification and redesig VMO(CVS)-351. After short stay at Santa Barbara redesig VMF-351 and assigned to *Commencement Bay* Feb45. Transf to *Cape Gloucester* in Apr45. Arrived Leyte 29Jun45. In Jul45 provided support for minesweeping and strikes in East China Sea. In Okinawa area when war ended. CO's: Maj Hamilton D South 1–31Mar43; Capt Douglas B Lenardson 1Apr to 30Jun43; Maj Robert B Cox 1Jul to 16Aug43; Maj Thomas O Bales 17Aug to 31Oct43; Maj John J Canney Jr 1Nov43 to 29Feb44; Maj Armond H Delalio 1Mar44 to 4Jun45; Maj Charles E McLean Jr 5Jun45 to date of surrender.

VMR-352. Comm 1Apr43 at Cherry Point as VMJ-352. Carried out training with infantry bns at Camp Lejeune. Redesig VMR-352 on 10Jun44. Furnished air transportation for CP area until 1Dec44 when departed for El Centro. On 1Feb45 part of Sq det and transf to Ewa. In late Jul45 remainder of Sq to Ewa and was operating there when war ended. CO's: Maj Hamilton D South 1Apr to 30Jun43; Maj John R Walcott 1Jul43 to 5Mar44; LtCol Robert B Bell 6Mar to 14Nov44; Maj John L Whitaker Jr 15Nov44 to date of surrender.

VMR-353. Comm 16Mar43 at San Diego as VMJ-353. On 26Sep43 advance ech sent to Samoa. Remainder of Sq arrived 15Oct43. On 1Nov43 began operating as Samoan Combat Air Transport Service (later TAG). Arrived Funafuti 20Dec43. By 29Mar44 Sq was at Apamama Atoll where inter-island transportation was set up. Redesig VMR-353 on 15Jul44. Moved to Kwajalein early Sep44, to Saipan 19Feb45. Sq evac wounded from Iwo and later from Okinawa where one of its planes was destroyed on Yontan by Japanese *Giretsu*. Continued operating from Saipan until war ended. CO's: Capt Edmund L Zonne 16Mar43 to 30Sep44; Maj John R Walcott

1Oct44 to 31May45; LtCol John S Carter 1Jun to 31Aug45; LtCol Charles W Somers Jr 1Sep45 to date of surrender.

VMD-354.   Comm 1Jul43 at Cherry Point. In Apr45 transf to Miramar and following month to Guam. From Jun45 until war ended elements of Sq operated from Peleliu, Ulithi and Okinawa. CO's: Maj Albert S Munsch 1Jul43 to 26Mar44; LtCol Ernest E Pollock 27Mar to 18May44; Maj John L Whitaker Jr 19May to 7Jun44; Maj John W Burkhardt 8Jun to 27Oct44; Maj Douglas B Lenardson 28Oct to 1Dec44; Maj John W Burkhardt 2Dec44 to 11Mar45; Maj Douglas B Lenardson 12Mar45 to date of surrender.

VMB-413.   Comm 1Mar43 at Cherry Point as first medium-bomber sq. Departed for West Coast Dec43. Left North I 3Jan44 for SoPac. Arrived Espíritu 27Jan44; remained until 7Mar44 then sent to Stirling in Treasury Is. Flew heckling missions against Rabaul until May44 then ret to Espíritu. In Jul44 commenced operating from Munda. Continued bombing and strafing of Kahili-Choiseul area until 18Oct44 when moved to Emirau and operated against New Ireland and New Britain until war ended. CO's: Maj Robert B Cox 1Mar to 30Jun43; LtCol Ronald D Salmon 1Jul43 to 5Feb44; LtCol Andrew B Galatian Jr 6Feb to 13Aug44; LtCol Stewart W Ralston 13Aug to 7Nov44; LtCol Roswell B Burchard Jr 7Nov to 31Dec44; LtCol Robert B Cox 1Jan to 16Aug45; Maj Arthur C Lowell 17Aug45 to date of surrender.

VMF-422.   Org 1Jan43 at San Deigo; moved to Santa Barbara 27Jan43. Embarked in *Bunker Hill* for Pearl Harbor, arriving 12Oct43. Transf to Midway and served as fighter-defense unit there until 24Dec43. On 17Jan44 embarked at Pearl in *Kalinin Bay* for Tarawa and from there took off on flight to Funafuti. Only one of 23 planes reached destination through weather; 16 pilots recovered. Remainder of Sq arrived Engebi 19Feb44 where Sq was joined by survivors and some replacement pilots 24Mar44. On 27May44 part of flight ech went to Roi to stage attacks against by-passed Marshalls. On 16Oct44 strike ech ret to Engebi and flew attacks against Ponape. Departed for Okinawa 26Apr45. Ground ech arrived Ie Shima 7May45, flight ech three weeks later and commenced opns in Ryukyus. Moved to Chimu field 16Jun45 where it was when war ended. CO's: Capt James K Dill 1Jan to 1Apr43; Capt Edwin C Fry 2Apr to 16Jul43; Maj John S MacLaughlin Jr 7Jul43 to 24Jan44; Maj Edwin C Fry 25Jan to 1Feb44; Maj Elmer A Wrenn 2Feb to 31Dec44; Maj Elkin S Dew 1Jan45 to date of surrender.

VMB-423.   Comm 15Sep43 at Cherry Point. In Oct43 transf to Edenton. Departed for El Centro in Dec43 and arrived 3Jan44. Ground ech landed Espíritu 11Mar44 and joined by flight ech a month later. By middle of May44 flight ech operating from Stirling I but departed 21Jun44 for Green Is to join ground ech which arrived from Espíritu. Carried out attacks on New Britain and New Ireland targets for the next year. Furnished close support for Australian troops on Bougainville. By middle of Jun45 Sq was operating from Emirau where it remained until 10Aug45. Arrived in Philippines 16Aug45 just as war ended. CO's: LtCol John L Winston 15Sep43 to 18Jul44; LtCol Norman J Anderson 19Jul44 to 15Aug45; LtCol Louis L Frank 16Aug45 to date of surrender.

VMB-433.   Comm 15Sep43 at Cherry Point. Received training at CP and Camp Lejeune. Joined MarFAirWest 27Jan44 and continued training at El Centro. By 26May44 ground ech under way for NorSols. Next day flight ech departed. Arrived Ewa by 1Jun44. After staging through Palmyra, Canton, Funafuti and Espíritu arrived Green Is 14Jul44 for temporary duty with MAG-14. Month later both ech's operating at Emirau with MAG-61. Stayed there until war ended. CO's: Maj John G Adams 15Sep43 to 22Apr45; LtCol Winton H Miller 23Apr to 23May45; Maj Boyd O Whitney 24May to 16Jul45; Maj Andrew G Smith Jr 17Jul45 to date of surrender.

VMF-441.   Org 1Oct42 at Samoa. Advance ech sent to Funafuti in Mar43 and by end of May43 entire Sq there. On 28Sep43 moved to Nanomea. By Dec43 Sq ret to Tutuila for training in F4U's. Advance ech to Roi 11Feb44. Joined by remainder of Sq in Mar44 to carry out opns against Wotje and Maloelap. On 21Aug44 flight ech to Majuro to carry out raids against Mille and Jaluit. Arrived at Yontan 7Apr45 for Okinawa campaign and remained there until war ended. CO's: Maj Daniel W Torrey Jr 1Oct to 2Dec42; Capt Walter J Meyer 3Dec42 to 30Sep43; Maj James B Moore 1Oct43 to 4Apr44; Maj Grant W Metzger 5Apr44 to 20Jan45; Maj Robert O White 21Jan to 13Jun45; Maj Paul T Johnston 14Jun45 to date of surrender.

VMB-443. Comm 15Sep43 at Cherry Point. Transf to Peters Point Field 20Oct43 for training; mid-Jan44 flight personnel and some of ground ech went to Boca Chica, Fla, for torpedo training and tactics. Stationed at El Centro Feb to Apr44. On 18May44 ground ech sailed from San Diego and arrived Espíritu in mid-Jun44. One month later at Emirau. Flight ech arrived Emirau 13Aug44. Participated in Bismarcks neutralization. Transf to Philippines Aug45. CO's: Lt Robert C McConnell 15Sep43; Maj Alton D Gould 16Sep to 13Oct43; LtCol Dwight M Guillotte 13Oct43 to 21Mar45; LtCol Alton D Gould 21Mar to 16Aug45; Maj Earl E Anderson 16Aug45 to date of surrender.

VMF-451. Comm 15Feb44 at Mojave. On 24Jan45 flight ech reported for duty on board *Bunker Hill.* Ground ech remained at Mojave. After strikes on Tokyo targets, supported Iwo landing. During Mar45 made pre-invasion strikes in Ryukyus area. After *Bunker Hill* was *kamikazed* 11May45 Sq ret to US and joined ground ech at El Centro. Stayed there until war ended. CO's: Maj Henry A Ellis Jr 15Feb44 to 17Jul45; Maj Archie G Donahue 18Jul to 16Aug45; Lt Martin C Allesandro 17Aug45 to date of surrender.

VMF-452. Org 15Feb44 as VMF(CVS)-452 at Mojave and commenced training in carrier opns. Went to Army airfield at Bishop, Calif, in Aug44 and remained until 15Sep44 practicing field carrier landings. After rocket training VMF-452 transf to Santa Barbara and in Dec44 operated with CAG-5 at NAS, Santa Rosa. Pilots checked out in carrier landings on board *Ranger* Jan45 and forward ech went on board *Franklin* 8Feb45; rear ech remained at El Centro. Began opns against Japan 18Mar45 but next day *Franklin* was *kamikazed.* VMF-452 ret to El Centro 16Apr45 where it stayed until war ended. CO's: Maj Charles P Weiland 15Feb44 to 21Jun45; Lt Peter L Schaefer 21Jun to 26Jul45; Lt Carl S Detmering 27–31Jul45; Maj Edwin S Roberts Jr 1Aug45 to date of surrender.

VMB-453. Comm 25Jun44 at Cherry Point. Decomm 20Feb45. CO's: Maj John W Stevens II 25Jun to 30Jul44; LtCol Joseph R Little Jr 31Jul to 14Nov44; Maj Donald G H Jaeckels 15Nov44 to 20Feb45.

VMTB-453. Comm 1Jul45 at El Toro where it was training for carrier duty when war ended. CO: Maj George D Wolverton.

VMTB-454. Org 1Mar44 at El Toro as VMSB-454. On 14Oct44 desig changed to VMTB-454 but redesig VMTB(CVS)-454 on 5Nov44. Transf to Mojave in Jan45 and in Jun45 went to Santa Barbara. On 17Jul45 boarded *Puget Sound* for requalification. Ret to Santa Barbara early in Aug45. CO: Maj James H Clark.

VMF-461. Comm 15Mar44 at El Centro. On 10Oct44 absorbed personnel, equipment and aircraft of VMF-462 (CO and desig transf to El Toro) and VMF-472 which had been decomm. For tactical and identification purposes VMF-461 divided into three ech's: Sugar (VMF-461), Uncle (VMF-462) and X-ray (VMF-472). On 16Nov44 assumed status of replacement-training unit and continued operating as such at El Toro until war ended though it was redesig VMF-461 on 1Jul45. CO's: Maj William R Lear 19Mar to 14Aug44; Maj Jack C Scott 15–20Aug44; Maj Elkin S Dew 21Aug to 3Nov44; Maj Richard F Harrison 4Nov to 23Dec44; Maj Edmund F Overend 23Dec44 to 31May45; Maj Thaddeus P Wojcik 1Jun45 to date of surrender.

VMF-462. Comm 15Apr44 at El Centro. On 10Oct44 absorbed personnel and equipment of VMF-481 and redesig fighter-pilot replacement-training unit. Transf to El Toro and remained there until war ended. CO's: Maj Perry L Shuman 15Apr to 9Oct44; Maj William P Boland Jr 10–22Oct44; Maj Hamilton Lawrence 23Oct44 to 29Apr45; Maj Honore G Dalton 30Apr to 27Aug45; Maj William M Watkins Jr 28Aug45 to date of surrender.

VMB-463. Comm 20Jul44 at Cherry Point. Decomm 28Feb45. CO's: LtCol Freeman W Williams 20Jul to 31Aug44; Maj Andrew G Smith Jr 1Sep to 16Nov44; Maj David Horne 17Nov44 to 28Feb45.

VMTB-463. Activated 15Jul45 at Santa Barbara with primary mission of training personnel for carrier duty. CO's: Capt Hollis H Keiter 16Jul to 6Aug45; Maj Bernard McShane 6Aug45 to date of surrender.

VMTB-464. Org 15Apr44 at El Toro as VMSB-464 to train personnel. On 16Oct44 status changed to that of replacement-training sq. Redesig VMTB-464 on 1Jun45. CO's: Capt Kenneth P Storey 19Apr44; Maj Alfred H Mathieson Jr 20Apr to 15May44; Maj Earl P Paris Jr 16May44 to date of surrender.

VMF-471.   Org 15May44 at El Centro to train replacement pilots and crews. Sent a det to Camp Pendleton 23Jul44. In Oct44 Sq joined personnel and material of VMF-482, which was decomm. Opns continued at El Toro until war ended. CO's: Lt Harold G Sandbach 15–21May44; Capt Warren J Turner 22May to 8Jun44; Maj Robert B Fraser 9Jun to 30Nov44; Maj Horace A Pehl 1Dec44 to 20May45; Maj Arthur T Warner 21May to 15Jul45; Maj John R Spooner 16Jun to 5Jul45; Maj Robert J Holm 6–23Jul45; Maj Hugh I Russell 24Jul45 to date of surrender.

VMF-472.   Comm 1Jun44 at El Centro. After four months' training decomm 10Oct44 and Sq's personnel, material and aircraft transf to VMF-461. On 1Mar45 another VMF-472 comm at Mojave. In May45 Sq commenced carrier opns training and for short period desig VMF(CVS)-472 but Sq assumed original desig 1Jun45. CO's: Lt Charles M Jackson 1Jun44; Capt George C Hays 2–12Jun44; Maj John A Reeder 13–25Jun44; Maj Richard F Harrison 26Jun to 6Jul44; Maj Hamilton Lawrence 7Jul to 10Oct44; Maj Robert L Bryson 1Mar45 to date of surrender.

VMB-473.   Comm 25Jul44 at Cherry Point. Moved to MCAAF, Kinston, 15Dec44. Decomm 15Mar45. CO: Maj William M Frash.

VMTB-473.   Org 1Aug45 at El Centro to train personnel for carrier-based duty. CO: Capt Charlton A Main.

VMSB-474.   On 10Apr44 Bomber-Training Unit, MBDAG-46, El Toro, disbanded and VMSB's 474 and 484 comm from remnants. Primarily org to train and supply replacements for dive-bomber sqs. CO's: Maj Richard L Blain 10Apr to 12Jul44; Maj Glenn L Todd 12Jul44 to 31Mar45; Maj Walter J Carr Jr 1Apr to 29Jun45; Capt Henry D Noetzel 30Jun to 6Aug45; Capt John F Adams Jr 7Aug45 to date of surrender.

VMF-481.   Org 5Apr44 at El Toro to train fighter-pilot replacements. Decomm 10Oct44, personnel and equipment, less aircraft, transf to VMF-462. Another VMF-481 activated 1Aug45 at Santa Barbara to train pilots and crews for carrier duty. CO's: Maj William P Boland Jr 5–26Apr44; Maj Robert G Owens Jr 26Apr to 1Jul44; Maj William P Boland Jr 1Jul to 10Oct44; Maj Ian A McNab 1Aug45 to date of surrender.

VMF-482.   Comm 7Apr44 at El Toro to train replacement pilots and crews. Decomm 10Oct44. CO: Maj Kenneth J Kirk Jr.

VMB-483.   Comm 26Aug44 at Cherry Point. Moved to MCAAF, Kinston, Dec44. Decomm 15Mar45. CO's: Maj Louis L Frank 26Aug44 to 4Jan45; Maj Duncan E Slade 5Jan to 15Mar45.

VMSB-484.   On 10Apr44 Bomber Training Unit, MBDAG-46, MCAS, El Toro, disbanded and VMSB's 484 and 474 comm from that unit to train and supply dive-bomber sq replacements. CO's: Maj William W Wood 15Apr44 to 19Mar45; Maj George E Koutelas 20Mar to 25Apr45; Maj George D Wolverton 26Apr to 30Jun45; Capt Robert Floeck 1–23Jul45; Capt Carl F Eakin Jr 24Jul45 to date of surrender.

VMF-511.   Comm 1Jan44 at MCAAF, Oak Grove. Transf 13Apr44 to Simmons-Knott Field. During Jul44 pilots ordered to NAS, Boca Chica, NAAF, Manteo, and NAS, Quonset Point, for rocket training in preparation for European mission (Project DANNY). Resumed routine training when project was cancelled. Arrived Mojave 10Sep44. Redesig VMF(CVS)-511 on 28Oct44. Departed 20Mar45 for Pearl Harbor on board *Block Island*. During May and Jun45 flew support missions for Okinawa opns. Supported Balikpapan invasion. Still on board to support surrender of Formosa when war ended. CO's: Capt Howard L Seiss 1–2Jan44; Maj Cecil B Brewer 3–9Jan44; Maj Robert C Maze 10Jan44 to 26May45; Capt James L Secrest 27May45 to date of surrender.

VMF-512.   Comm 15Feb44 at MCAAF, Oak Grove. After Project DANNY cancelled Sq was transf with MAG-51 to Mojave 5Sep44. On 5Nov44 redesig VMF(CVS)-512. On 8Dec44 transf to Santa Barbara where trained until boarding *Gilbert Islands* in Mar45 with VMTB-143 to form MCVG-2. Group flew support missions on Okinawa in May45. Daily sorties flown against enemy bases on Sakishima Retto during Jun45 until CVE departed for Leyte, thence to Balikpapan, to support invasion. Still carrier-based when war ended. CO's: Maj Edward V Finn 15Feb to 17Mar44; Maj Blaine H Baesler 17Mar44 to date of surrender.

VMF-513.   Comm 15Feb44 at MCAAF, Oak Grove. After cancellation of Project DANNY transf to MCAF, Walnut Ridge, Ark, 14Sep44. On 4Dec44 to Mojave and redesig VMF(CVS)-513. On 17Jun45 departed San Diego on board *Vella Gulf* with VMTB-234. Arrived Pearl Harbor 25Jun45 and moved to Ewa. In early Jul45 departed in *Vella Gulf* and arrived Saipan late that month. In Aug45 departed for Okinawa. Ship remained two days in Ryukyus area and ret to Guam 15Aug45. CO: Maj Thomas O Bales.

VMF-514. Comm 20Feb44 at Cherry Point. Moved to nearby Pollocksville 1Apr44 to train for Project DANNY. On 28Aug44 transf to MCAAF, Oak Grove. Ordered 21Sep44 to Walnut Ridge, Ark. Desig changed to VMF(CVS)-514 6Dec44 and sent to Mojave. In May45 reassumed original desig of VMF-514. Went on board *Salerno Bay* late in Jun45 for carrier qualification but ret to Mojave 13Jul45. En route to Hawaii in *Salerno Bay* when war ended. CO's: Maj James W Merritt 20Feb44 to 1Apr45; Maj Darrell D Irwin 2Apr to 27Jul45; Maj William V Brooks 28Jul45 to date of surrender.

VMF-521. Comm 1Apr44 at Cherry Point. Transf to MCAAF, Congaree 18May44. On 16Oct44 became replacement-training sq and remained such until war ended. CO's: Capt Ralph G McCormick 1–18Apr44; Maj Robert D Kelley 19Apr to 10Sep44; Capt William L Beerman 11–15Sep44; Capt Donald J Van Oeveren 16Sep to 13Nov44; Maj Otto H Brueggeman Jr 14Nov44 to 9Jan45; Capt Donald J Van Oeveren 10–17Jan45; Maj Paul T Johnston 18Jan to 15Feb45; Capt Donald J Van Oeveren 16–26Feb45; Maj James K Dill 27Feb to 7Jun45; Maj Stanislaus J Witomski 8Jun45 to date of surrender.

VMF-522. Comm 1Apr44 at Cherry Point. In May44 moved to MCAAF, Congaree. On 16Oct44 became replacement-training sq and continued as such until war ended. CO's: Capt Eugene Dillow 1–4Apr44; Capt David W Rankin 5–19Apr44; Maj John S Payne 19Apr to 22Aug44; Capt Vincent W Carpenter 23Aug to 5Sep44; Maj Lewis S Butler Jr 6Sep to 26Oct44; Capt Gerard M Schuchter 27Oct to 5Nov44; Maj Burnette A Kempson Jr 6Nov44 to 1Jun45; Capt Willard F Letts Jr 2–13Jun45; Maj Fay V Domke 14Jun45 to date of surrender.

VMF-523. Comm 5May44 at Cherry Point. A week later moved to MCAAF, Congaree. Was replacement-training sq from 16Oct44 until war ended. CO's: Maj Stanley S Nicolay 5May to 15Oct44; Capt Selden P Spencer III 16Oct to 19Dec44; Maj Edward J McGee 20Dec44 to 31Jul45; Maj Warren H McPherson 1Aug45 to date of surrender.

VMF-524. Comm 10May44 at Cherry Point. Late that month moved to MCAAF, Congaree. Assumed status of replacement-training sq 16Oct44. On duty at Page Field, Parris I, 23Jan to 8Feb45, when Sq returned to Congaree. Late in Mar45 ret to Parris I where it remained until war ended. CO's: Capt James J Powell 10–17May44; Capt Lewis S Butler Jr 17–31May44; Maj Donald H Sapp 1Jun44 to 12Mar45; Maj Harlan Rogers 13Mar to 8Apr45; Maj Edward R Dyer Jr 9–27Apr45; Maj Donald S Bush 28Apr45 to date of surrender.

VMF(N)-531. Comm 16Nov42 at Cherry Point. Transf to El Centro and embarked 31Jul42 in *Long Island* at San Diego for Hawaii where PV's were prepared for flight. Sq left 19Aug43 for Espíritu, arriving six days later. Pilots arrived Russells 11Sep43, joined there 23Sep43 by ground ech. VMF(N)-531 was first naval-aviation night-fighter sq in SoPac. Operated from Russells, Vella Lavella and Bougainville. Ret to CP Aug44, disbanded 3Sep44 and re-formed 9Oct44 as part of 9thMAW. Transf to Eagle Mountain Lake 29Nov44, stayed there until war ended. CO's: LtCol Frank H Schwable 16Nov42 to 31Mar43; Maj John D Harshberger 1Apr to 16Jun43; LtCol Frank H Schwable 17Jun43 to 17Feb44; LtCol John D Harshberger 18Feb to 12May44; Capt James H Wehmer 13May to 31Aug44; Capt Ralph J Garza 1–3Sep44; LtCol Radford C West 13Oct to 10Nov44; Maj Edward V Mendenhall Jr 11–16Nov44; Capt Robert R Finch 17Nov44 to 15Mar45; Maj Alfred N Gordon 16Mar to 10Jun45; Capt James H Wehmer 11Jun45 to date of surrender.

VMF(N)-532. Comm 1Apr43 at Cherry Point. Sq arrived West Coast 24Dec43 and departed San Diego 26Dec43 for Ewa. Arrived Tarawa 13Jan44 and began NCAP's. Flew to Roi via Makin 15Feb44. On 27Feb44 flight ech sent to Engebi I to provide night cover until 11Jun44, then rejoined Sq at Roi. In Jun44 began night raids against Wotje. Transf to Saipan in Jul44 and began NCAP's in that area and later over Guam. Arrived Miramar 25Oct44. In early Dec44 transf to Eagle Mountain Lake where it continued routine training until war ended. CO's: Capt Ross S Mickey

1Apr to 23May43; Maj Everett H Vaughan 24May43 to 23Sep44; Capt Warren S Adams II 24Sep to 14Nov44; Capt John B Colby 15Nov44 to 4Jan45; Capt Nathan Bedell 5Jan to 6May45; Maj Jack C Scott 7May45 to date of surrender.

VMF(N)-533.   Comm 1Oct43 at Cherry Point. Arrived West Coast in early Apr44 and on 16Apr44 embarked on board *Long Island.* Arrived Eniwetok via Hawaii 6May44. On 11Jun44 relieved VMF(N)-532 and assumed night defense of area. Moved to Engebi 30Nov44 and continued opns. Flew to Yontan airfield 14May45 and ground ech arrived Ie Shima 20May45. On 15Jun45 flight ech joined remainder of Sq at Ie. On 14Jul45 moved to Chimu and remained on Okinawa until war ended. CO's: Maj Marion M Magruder 1Oct43 to 7Jul45; Maj Samuel B Folsom Jr 8Jul to 17Aug45; Maj Robert P Keller 17Aug to date of surrender.

VMF(N)-534.   Comm 1Oct43 at Cherry Point. Departed San Diego 19Apr44 in *Breton.* Arrived Espíritu 4May44. Departed for CenPac Jun44. Arrived Guam 4Aug44. Flew first night CAP 7Aug44. In May45 part of Sq based at Kobler airfield on Saipan to provide night air defense of Saipan-Tinian areas, and another sec sent to Eniwetok to assume night air defense of Gilberts–Marshalls areas. Continued to operate at Guam, Eniwetok, Saipan until war ended. CO's: Maj Peter D Lambrecht 1Oct43 to 14Feb44; Maj Ross S Mickey 15Feb44 to 23May45; Maj James B Maguire Jr 24May to 15Jun45; Maj Clair C Chamberlain 21Jun45 to date of surrender.

VMF(N)-541.   Comm 15Feb44 at Cherry Point. Sailed from North I 9Aug44 on board *Long Island,* arrived Espíritu 24Aug44. On 8Sep44 ground ech sailed for Palaus, arriving 15Sep44. Flight ech flew to Emirau and remained until 24Sep44 when first planes were flown into Peleliu. Flight ech transf to Leyte 3Dec44 at request of Gen MacArthur. Ret to Peleliu 11Jan45. Elements of flight ech based at Ulithi until 28Aug45. CO's: LtCol Peter D Lambrecht 15Feb44 to 20Jun45; Maj Norman L Mitchell 21Jun to 7Jul45; Maj Reynolds A Moody 8Jul45 to date of surrender.

VMF(N)-542.   Comm 6Mar44 at Cherry Point. Flight ech transf to San Diego and departed 29Aug44 on board *Kitty Hawk.* Ground ech departed West Coast 9Sep44 in *Dashing Wave.* Flight ech arrived Manus in Admiralties 18Sep44; on 26Sep44 moved to Pityilu. Ground ech arrived Ulithi 9–12Oct44 to be joined by flight ech 29Oct44. Assault ech departed 15Feb45 for Leyte; landed 8Apr45 on Okinawa. Flight ech departed Ulithi and arrived Yontan airfield 7Apr45. Ground ech arrived 1May45. Sq moved to Chimu airfield 1Jul45 and continued strikes in Ryukyus area. CO's: Maj William C Kellum 6Mar44 to 22May45; Maj Robert B Porter 23May to 31Aug45; Maj William C Kellum 1Sep45 to date of surrender.

VMF(N)-543.   Comm 15Apr44 at Cherry Point. Transf to El Centro 30Sep44 whence it departed for Ewa 4Jan45. Sq divided into three echelons. Assault ech departed for Pearl 18–21Feb45 on board *Achernar* and *Meriwether;* arrived Okinawa 7Apr45 where it was joined two days later by flight ech. Rear ech arrived 1May45. Moved to Awase airfield 15Jul45. CO's: Maj Claude J Carlson Jr 15Apr to 2Jul44; Maj Clair C Chamberlain 3Jul44 to 17Jun45; Maj James B Maguire Jr 18Jun45 to date of surrender.

VMF(N)-544.   Comm 1May44 at Cherry Point. Departed late Oct44 for West Coast. Flight ech arrived El Centro 3Nov44, joined week later by ground ech. During next two months some pilots det from Sq and assigned carrier duty. Remainder of Sq transf to Eagle Mountain Lake for duty late in Feb45 where training continued until war ended. CO's: Maj James B Maguire Jr 1May44 to 15Apr45; Maj Reynolds A Moody 15May to 14Jun45; Capt Robert R Finch 15Jun to 22Jul45; Maj Ross S Mickey 23Jul45 to date of surrender.

VMB-611.   Org 1Oct43 at Cherry Point. Flight ech sailed from San Diego 24Aug44 and arrived Ewa following week. On 23Sep44 rear ech left Miramar, reached Pearl Harbor 2Oct44, departed week later for Emirau. By Dec44 entire Sq reunited at Emirau, from where night heckling missions and strikes were flown against Vanakanau and Tobera. Ground ech arrived 17Mar45 at Zamboanga. Joined by flight ech 30Mar45. Operated in southern Philippines until war ended. CO's: Capt Prescott D Fagan 1Oct to 15Nov43; LtCol George A Sarles 16Nov43 to 30May45; Maj Robert R Davis 1Jun to 19Jun45; Maj David Horne 20Jun45 to date of surrender.

VMB-612.   Org 1Oct43 at Cherry Point. Directed in Jan44 to experiment in night-radar opns. From Jan until Aug44 alternated between Boca Chica, Fla, and

New River for tactical training. In Aug44 departed for Saipan via Ewa, Majuro and Eniwetok, arriving late Oct44. From Nov44 to Feb45 flew strikes against shipping in Bonin and Volcano Is areas. Transf to Iwo Apr45. To Okinawa Jul45 and operated from Chimu airfield until war ended. CO's: Capt James W Cunningham 1Oct to 16Nov43; LtCol Jack R Cram 16Nov43 to 14Feb45; Maj Lawrence F Fox 15Feb to 1May45; LtCol Jack R Cram 2May to 31Aug45; LtCol Lawrence F Fox 1Sep45 to date of surrender.

VMB-613. Org 1Oct43 at Cherry Point. Transf to Boca Chica late in Feb44. Ret to CP 22Mar44, remained there until Aug44 when moved to Newport, Ark. Flight ech departed 21Oct44 for San Diego and embarked in *Tulagi* for Ewa, arriving 4Nov44. Ground ech joined flight ech 3Dec44 but week later sailed for Kwajalein. Flight ech flew to Kwajalein and was joined by ground ech 23Dec44. Began opns against Marshalls Jan45. Forward ech moved to Eniwetok for ASP 11Jan45 but by 13Mar45 had rejoined Sq at Kwajalein. CO's: Capt Robert C Woten 1Oct to 16Nov43; Maj Harry F Baker Jr 17Nov43 to 25Feb44; Maj George W Nevils 26Feb44 to date of surrender.

VMB-614. Comm 1Oct43 at Cherry Point. Sq trained there and at Boca Chica, Fla, and Newport, Ark. Flight ech departed Alameda 25Jul45 and arrived Ewa 1Aug45. Ground ech left San Diego in early Aug45 and by 31Aug45 both ech's were operating at Midway. CO's: Capt Roger M Bowman 1Oct to 16Nov43; Maj John G Walsh Jr 17Nov43 to 9Nov44; Maj Harold L Lantz 9-28Nov44; Maj George F Mackey 29Nov44 to date of surrender.

VMTB-621. Comm 10Apr44 at Cherry Point as VMB-621. Redesig VMTB-621 on 31Jan45. Arrived Santa Barbara 15Feb45. Sailed for San Diego on board *Card*, arriving Pearl Harbor 27Aug45. Training at Ewa when war ended. CO's: Maj Robert J Klitgaard 10Apr to 23May44; LtCol Donald E Huey 24May to 19Nov44; Maj George F Mackey 20-28Nov44; Maj Robert J Klitgaard 29Nov44 to 1Feb45; Lt Joseph F King 2-25Feb45; Lt Thomas L Kizer Jr 26Feb to 25Mar45; Maj Allan H Ringblom 26Mar45 to date of surrender.

VMTB-622. Comm 10May44 at Cherry Point as VMB-622. Moved to MCAF, Newport, Ark, 10Sep44 and continued operational training until 14Feb45 and Sq moved to Mojave. Redesig VMTB-622 on 15May45 and outfitted with TBM's to start training for carrier duty. Training in Jul45 at Antisubmarine Warfare School, and Torpedo Training Unit, San Diego. Pilots and planes on board *Wake Island* for carrier qualification when war ended. CO's: Maj Russell A Bowen 10May to 18Oct44; Maj Pat W Densman 19Oct to 3Nov44; Maj David C Wolfe 4-16Nov44; Maj Finley T Clarke Jr 17Nov44 to 6Feb45; Lt Edward L Ogden 7-23Feb45; Lt Robert N Jackson 24Feb to 24Mar45; Maj William W Wood 25Mar45 to date of surrender.

VMTB-623. Comm 15May44 at Cherry Point as VMB-623. Proceeded with training until 10Feb45 when desig changed to VMTB-623. By May45 Sq located at Santa Barbara and was training for carrier duty when war ended. CO's: Maj Lawrence F Fox 15May to 11Jun44; Maj Carl J Fleps 12Jun to 17Dec44; Maj Henry N Carrier Jr 18Dec44 to 9Feb45; Lt Sam H Boren Jr 10-23Feb45; Lt James R Stone Jr 24Feb to 12Mar45; Maj Eric D Schwarz 13Mar45 to date of surrender.

VMTB-624. Comm 20Jun44 at Cherry Point as VMB-624. Redesig VMTB-624 on 15Feb45 and transf to Mojave for carrier training. In Jun45 moved to Santa Barbara and remained there until war ended. CO's: Maj Harry W Taylor 20-25Jun44; Maj Winton H Miller 26Jun to 16Nov44; Maj Harry W Taylor 17Nov to 16Dec44; Maj Edward J Doyle 19Dec44 to 13Feb45; Lt Frank Onischuk 15Feb to 12Mar45; Maj Dayton Swickard 13Mar to 31Aug45; Capt J B Shirley 1Sep45 to date of surrender.

VML-711. Org 1May42 at MB, Parris I, as subordinate unit of MLG-71 to implement glider program. Arrived Eagle Mountain Lake 23Nov42. Decomm when glider program was abandoned 24May43. CO's: Maj Eschol M Mallory 1May42 to 7Feb43; Capt Barnette Robinson 8Feb to 24May43.

MOTS-811. Comm 1Jan44 at Edenton as MTS-811. Mission: training pilots in SNB and PBJ aircraft. Redesig MOTS-811 on 1Feb45 and transf to Cherry Point 23Feb45. CO's: Maj Norman L Gidden 1Jan to 18Jul44; Capt James A Leckie 19Jul to 3Sep44; Maj Frank H Collins 4Sep to 12Oct44; Maj Norman L Gidden 13Oct44 to 19Jan45; Maj Charles S Manning 20Jan to 22Jul45; Maj George H Dole 23Jul45 to date of surrender.

MOTS-812.   Comm 1Jan44 at Edenton as MTS-812. Mission: training pilots in PBJ's. Redesig MOTS-812 on 1Feb45 and transf to Cherry Point 20Feb45. CO's: Maj Winton H Miller 1Jan to 13Apr44; Maj James W Long 14Apr to 13Oct44; Maj Frederick L Woodlock Jr 14Oct44 to 19Feb45; Maj Donald G H Jaeckels 20Feb to 6Mar45; Maj James F Moran 7Mar to 5Aug45; Maj Karl H Schmidt 6Aug45 to date of surrender.

MOTS-813.   Comm 1Jan44 at Edenton as MTS-813, to train pilots, air and ground crews in operation, maintenance and upkeep of multi-engined aircraft. Redesig MOTS-813 on 1Feb45 and transf to Cherry Point 19Feb45. CO's: Maj Sidney R Williamson 1Jan to 5Apr44; Maj Donald E Huey 6–12Apr44; Maj Edward V Mendenhall Jr 13Apr to 12Oct44; Maj Frank H Collins 13Oct44 to 26Jan45; Maj Samuel M Graves Jr 27Jan to 28Feb45; Capt Jerome H Gordon 1–14Mar45; LtCol William M Frash 15Mar to 4Jun45; Maj Hal R Kolp 5Jun45 to date of surrender.

MOTS-814.   Comm 1Jan44 at Edenton as MTS-814 to train pilots, air and ground crews in VMB operations. Redesig MOTS-814 on 1Feb45 and transf to Cherry Point 17Feb45. CO's: LtCol Stanley W Trachta 1Jan to 13Apr44; Maj Donald E Huey 14Apr to 19May44; Maj David Horne 20May to 29Aug44; Maj Robert F Thompson 30Aug44 to 12Jul45; Maj Frederick L Woodlock Jr 13Jul45 to date of surrender.

VMF-911.   Org 25Jun44 at MCAAF, Kinston. Moved to Cherry Point and on 16Oct44 became replacement-training sq. Continued as such until war ended. CO's: Maj James B Moore 25Jun to 5Nov44; Maj Henry S Miller 6Nov44 to 21Jun45; Capt Jack B Gifford 22Jun to 10Aug45; Maj Robert T Kingsbury III 11Aug45 to date of surrender.

VMF-912.   Comm 10Jul44 at Cherry Point. Moved to MCAAF, Kinston, in Aug44. Became replacement-training sq 16Oct44. Ret 3Nov44 to CP and in Jan45 started familiarization flights in F7F. Continued as training sq until war ended. CO's: Maj J Frank Cole 10Jul44 to 12Feb45; Maj Thomas M Coles 13Feb to 11Apr45; Maj David M Williams 12Apr to 10Aug45; Maj Roy T Spurlock 11Aug45 to date of surrender.

VMF-913.   Comm 15Jul44 at Greenville, NC. Moved to Cherry Point and on 16Oct44 became replacement-training sq. Continued as such until war ended. CO's: Maj Julius W Ireland 15Jul44 to 9Apr45; Capt Jack B Gifford 10–23Apr45; Maj John E Reynolds 24Apr45 to date of surrender.

VMF-914.   Comm 14Aug44 at Greenville, NC. Became replacement-training sq 16Oct44. Continued as such until war ended. CO's: Maj William A Carlton 14Aug to 6Nov44; Maj Joseph F Quilty Jr 6–27Nov44; Maj William A Carlton 28Nov44 to 4Apr45; Maj William H Whitaker 5Apr to 1May45; Maj Frank S Hoffecker Jr 1May45 to date of surrender.

VMF-921.   Comm 21Aug44 at Cherry Point. Moved to MCAAF, Oak Grove, in Sep44. Decomm 10Oct44. CO: Maj Henry S Miller.

VMF-922.   Comm 21Aug44 at Cherry Point. Moved to MCAAF, Oak Grove, in Sep44. Decomm 10Oct44. CO: Maj Joseph F Quilty Jr.

VMF-923.   Comm 15Sep44 at Parris I. Decomm 10Oct44. CO: Maj John M Massey.

VMF-924.   Comm 10Apr44 at Cherry Point. Moved to Parris I in Sep44. Decomm 10Oct44 and Sq's personnel transf to HqSq-92. CO: Maj John C Musselman Jr.

VMSB-931.   Comm 15Apr44 at Cherry Point. On 10May44 transf to Eagle Mountain Lake. In Oct44 redesig VMBF-931 and transf to MCAAF, Oak Grove, 18Nov44. On 30Dec44 redesig VMSB-931 and remained at Oak Grove until war ended. CO's: Capt James E Campbell 15Apr to 1May44; Maj John L Dexter 1May to 9Nov44; Lt Roy E Rigsby 10–17Nov44; Maj James T McDaniel 18Nov44 to 10May45; Capt Robert W Johannesen 11May45 to date of surrender.

VMSB-932.   Comm 15May44 at Cherry Point. On 19Jun44 ordered to Eagle Mountain Lake. Redesig VMBF-932 on 16Oct44 but reverted to VMSB-932 on 30Dec44. Departed 20Nov44 for MCAAF, Oak Grove, and operated there until war ended. CO's: Maj Fred J Frazer 15May to 15Nov44; Capt Albert L Clark 16–21Nov44; Maj Jack W Morrison 22Nov44 to 15Jan45; Capt George T Lumpkin 16Jan to 11Mar45; Capt Edward C Willard 12Mar45 to date of surrender.

VMSB-933. Comm 20Jun44 at Eagle Mountain Lake. Transf to MCAAF, Atlantic, NC, 1Oct44. Moved to MCAAF, Bogue, 15Nov44. Conducting routine training when war ended. CO's: Maj Robert J Bear 20Jun to 18Oct44; Maj Ernest R Hemingway 19Oct44 to date of surrender.

VMSB-934. Comm 25Jul44 at MCAAF, Bogue. Moved to MCAAF, Atlantic, 21Aug44. Ret to Bogue and continued routine training until war ended. CO's: Maj Floyd Cummings 25Jul to 15Nov44; Maj William A Houston Jr 16Nov to 25Dec44; Maj Edward R Polgrean 26Dec44 to date of surrender.

VMSB-941. Comm 15Jul44 at MCAAF, Bogue. Decomm 10Oct44. CO's: Maj Walton L Turner 15Jul to 24Sep44; Maj James L Fritsche 25Sep to 10Oct44.

VMSB-942. Comm 24Aug44 at MCAAF, Bogue. Decomm 10Oct44. CO: Maj Ernest R Hemingway.

VMTB-943. Activated 1Jul44 at Santa Barbara as VMSB-943. Transf to El Toro 27Oct44 and redesig VMTB-943 on 20Nov44. Became replacement-training sq. Continued as such at El Toro until war ended. CO's: Capt W H Fuller 1Jul to 23Aug44; Capt Henry W Hise 23Aug to 24Oct44; Capt Floyd G Phillips 25–26Oct44; Maj Harold B Penne 27Oct to 28Nov44; Capt Floyd G Phillips 29–30Nov44; Maj Allan H Ringblom 1Dec44 to 2Mar45; Maj Otis V Calhoun Jr 2Mar to 3May45; Maj William M Ritchey 4May to 26Jul45; Maj Russell R Riley 27Jul45 to date of surrender.

VMSB-944. Org 10Apr44 at Cherry Point. Moved to MCAAF, Camp Lejeune, 15Jun44. Decomm 10Oct44. CO's: Maj Paul L Andre Jr 10Apr to 31May44; Maj Richard M Caldwell 1Jun to 10Oct44.

VMO-951. Comm 20Sep44 at Cherry Point. Decomm 10Oct44. CO: Maj Russell D Rupp.

VMR-952. Org 15Jun43 at Camp Kearney as VMJ-952. Redesig VMR-952 on 4Jul44. Flight ech departed for Ewa 5Feb44, followed by ground ech 29Feb44. Flew inter-Hawaiian Is and outlying bases transport. Moved to Emirau 29Aug44. Escorted tactical planes to and evac wounded from Peleliu. By Nov44 transport missions encompassed Tarawa, Ulithi, Saipan, Tinian and Guam. Sq transf to Guam and by 24Dec44 had estab opns there. CO's: Maj Harry F Baker 15Jun to 1Jul43; Maj Malcolm S Mackay 2Jul43 to 4Apr45; Maj John J Canney Jr 5Apr to 30May45; LtCol Stanley W Trachta 31May45 to date of surrender.

VMR-953. Org 1Feb44 at Camp Kearney as VMJ-953. Transf to Corvallis, Ore, 2May44. Redesig VMR-953 on 17Jul44. Ground ech arrived Ewa 18Aug44. Flight ech joined 30Sep44 and opns started with flights extending into Pac combat areas including Leyte in Dec44 and Okinawa in May45. CO's: LtCol Elliott E Bard 1–10Feb44; Col Wyman F Marshall 11Feb to 16May44; LtCol Frederick S Angstadt 17–30May44; Maj John R Walcott 31May to 15Jun44; LtCol John V Kipp 16–30Jun44; Maj Miles A Towner 1Jul to 26Aug44; LtCol Frederick S Angstadt 27Aug44 to 18Jun45; LtCol Robert W Gallaway 19Jun to 26Aug45; Maj David Ahee 27Aug45 to date of surrender.

VMD-954. Comm 1Apr42 at San Diego as VMD-1. On 15Sep42 redesig VMD-154 and moved to Camp Kearney. Redesig VMD-254 in Oct42 and VMD-254 became VMD-154. To Espíritu in Nov43. Sq conducted photo recon flights from New Hebrides and Solomons. Gradually moved farther north in Pac as war advanced. On 4Feb44 two Sq planes executed first photo recon of Truk Atoll. On 30Mar44 Sq hqs moved to Guadalcanal. By 1Jul44, 260 combat photo missions flown to Yap, Woleai, Guam, Truk, New Hanover, New Ireland, New Britain, Green, Emirau, Ulithi, Solomons, and New Hebrides. Moved to Emirau 10Jul44. Ret to US and in Mar45 redesig VMD-954 at Kinston, where unit operated until war ended. CO's: Capt Edwin P Pennebaker Jr 1–19Apr42; Maj Ernest E Pollock 20Apr to 19Aug42; Maj Edwin P Pennebaker Jr 20Aug42 to 2Mar45; LtCol James R Christensen 3Mar45 to date of surrender. (See also VMD-154 and VMD-254)

Index

(Names of U.S. vessels are in SMALL CAPITALS, foreign vessels in *italics*)